GOLD WARRIORS

GOLD WARRIORS

America's Secret Recovery of Yamashita's Gold

NEW EDITION

———————◆———————

STERLING & PEGGY SEAGRAVE

VERSO

London • New York

First published by Verso 2003
This new edition published by Verso 2005
© 2003, 2005 Sterling and Peggy Seagrave

5 7 9 10 8 6 4

Verso
UK: 6 Meard Street, London W1F 0EG
USA: 20 Jay Street, Suite 1010, Brooklyn, NY 11201
www.versobooks.com

Verso is the imprint of New Left Books

ISBN 1-84467-531-9 (pbk)
ISBN 1-85984-542-8 (hbk)

British Library Cataloguing in Publication Data
A catalogue record for this book is available from the British Library

Library of Congress Cataloging-in-Publication Data
A catalog record for this book is available from the Library of Congress

Typeset in Garamond by Sumberssive Studios
Printed and bound by CPI Group (UK) Ltd, Croydon, CR0 4YY

To Robert & Yolanda Curtis

And all the other victims
Who had no voice.

Also by Sterling Seagrave
YELLOW RAIN
SOLDIERS OF FORTUNE
BUSH PILOTS
THE SOONG DYNASTY
THE MARCOS DYNASTY

with Peggy Seagrave
DRAGON LADY
LORDS OF THE RIM
THE YAMATO DYNASTY

CONTENTS

CAST OF MAIN CHARACTERS

ACKERMAN, Robert A. – Washington lawyer, explained how ex-CIA officials tried to regain control of black gold accounts in New York banks.

ANDERSON, Robert B. – Toured treasure sites with MacArthur, set up Black Eagle Trust with Japanese war loot, member of Eisenhower cabinet.

ANGLETON, James Jesus – Top CIA official, used Nazi and Japanese war loot to rig post-war elections in Italy and Greece.

ASAKA Yasuhiko, Prince – Commanded rape and looting of Nanking.

BARANGAN, General Santiago – His memos to Marcos describe secret talks with top Japanese officials for joint recovery of war loot in Manila.

BELLI, Melvin – San Francisco lawyer, sued Citibank for misappropriating war gold from Santa Romana accounts.

BUSH, George H. W. President – Wrote personal note to head of Japan's LDP that enabled Alexander Haig to negotiate a billion-dollar IOU.

CANNON, Colonel Jack – Used war-gold to finance death squads in occupied Japan, to eliminate leftists and labor organizers.

CASEY, William – CIA director; involved with Lansdale gold recoveries and Black Eagle Trust; later removed Marcos from power.

CATHCART, Daniel – California lawyer whose successful suit against Marcos for theft of the Gold Buddha won a $43-billion judgment.

CHICHIBU, Prince – Brother of Emperor Hirohito; headed Golden Lily campaign to loot all of East & Southeast Asia, then hid the treasure.

CLINE, Ray – CIA deputy director; used Japanese war loot to manipulate foreign governments; fought for control of Santa Romana gold at Citibank.

CURTIS, Robert – Mining expert brought in by Marcos to launder gold; engineered major recoveries, photographed 173 original Golden Lily maps.

DOIHARA, General – Japan's senior secret agent, one of five top men in Golden Lily, masterminded the looting of Manchuria and China.

DULLES, Allen – CIA director, brother of J.F. Dulles, oversaw the Black Eagle Trust and setting up scores of slush funds around the world.

DULLES, John Foster – Arch-conservative Secretary of State, contrived false 1951 peace treaty to shield Japan's elite from reparations.

FORINGER, Alan – CIA agent in Nippon Star and Phoenix Exploration; explained how war-gold would finance private American gestapo.

HIROHITO, Emperor – Received and never returned the finest cultural treasures stolen from 12 countries; kept secret Swiss gold accounts.

JONSSON, Olof – Swedish psychic brought in by Marcos to pinpoint treasure vaults and sunken ships, saw warehouses filled with stolen gold.

KISHI Nobosuke, Prime Minister – Headed looting of Manchuria, served in Tojo's war cabinet; Nixon gave him control of the M-Fund.

KODAMA Yoshio – Japan's top gangster; aided Golden Lily by looting China's underworld; used proceeds to set up Japan's ruling LDP.

KOJIMA Kashii – Chauffeur of General Yamashita, tortured by Lansdale and Santa Romana to reveal a dozen vaults where treasure was hidden.

LANSDALE, Edward G. – Became America's most famous Cold Warrior thanks to torture of Kojima and recovery of Japanese gold.

LAUSIER, Edmond C. –Banking expert whose file of Japanese documents proved that notorious "57" debt instruments were *not* forgeries.

MACARTHUR, General Douglas –Used war loot to create a trust fund for Hirohito at Sanwa Bank; also set up the secret M-Fund to back the LDP.

MARCOS, Imelda – Former Philippine first lady, accused of hiding gold in banks around the world; bribed witnesses to lie about Gold Buddha.

MARCOS, Ferdinand – Philippine dictator, recovered Japanese treasure in the 1970s, shared the gold with CIA and White House until his downfall.

MCCLOY, John J. – Original planner of global Black Eagle Trust based on Nazi and Japanese war loot; became head of the World Bank.

MCMICKING, Joseph – MacArthur protégé who presided over torture of Major Kojima; used some of the war gold to become a global financier.

MIYAZAWA, Kiichi – Finance Minister and one of three Japanese who negotiated rigged 1951 peace treaty; still chief controller of the M-Fund.

ROXAS, Roger – Found solid gold Buddha looted from Burma; after President Marcos stole it, Roxas was tortured and murdered to silence him.

SANTA ROMANA, Severino – Tortured Yamashita's driver, recovered 12 treasure vaults; became CIA 'gatekeeper' of the Black Eagle Trust.

SCHLEI, Norbert – Former deputy U.S. attorney general, falsely convicted for trying to negotiate a "57" IOU; ruined financially and professionally.

SCHWEITZER, General Robert – Advisor to President Reagan; begged Robert Curtis to help White House recover more war loot.

SINGLAUB, General John – Schweitzer's partner in gold recoveries, he spent millions in the Philippines digging holes in the wrong places.

TAKEDA Tsuneyoshi, Prince – Cousin of Hirohito, grandson of Meiji; took charge of hiding war treasure at 175 vaults in the Philippines.

VALMORES, Ben – Philippine rice farmer; as a boy he was valet to Prince Takeda, visiting all 175 treasure vaults; was given a copy of Takeda's maps.

WHITNEY, General Courtney – MacArthur's lawyer and intelligence chief, set up M-Fund to influence Japanese elections with massive bribes.

WILLOUGHBY, General Charles – MacArthur's G-2 chief, paid war criminals to rewrite history and manipulate Japan's government.

YAMASHITA, General Tomoyuki – Japan's top general, conqueror of Singapore; wrongly linked to plunder by the misnomer Yamashita's Gold.

SLAYING THE MESSENGER

Many people told us this book was historically important and must be published – then warned us that if it were published, we would be murdered. An Australian economist who read it said, "I hope they let you live." He did not have to explain who 'they' were.

Japan's looting of Asia, and the hiding of this war-gold in American banks, is closely linked to the issue of Holocaust gold hidden in Swiss banks. Revealing the secrets of either is a dangerous business. Jean Ziegler, a Swiss professor and parliamentarian, did much to expose five decades of official amnesia in his book *The Swiss, the Gold and the Dead*. After publishing it and testifying in 1998 before the U.S. Senate Banking Committee about Jewish assets in Swiss banks, he was charged with 'treason' by Swiss Federal Prosecutor Carla del Ponte. The charge was brought by twenty-one financiers, commercial lawyers, and politicians of the far right, many of them major stockholders in large Swiss banks. They accused Ziegler of being an accomplice of Jewish organizations who 'extorted' vast sums of money from Switzerland.

Ziegler is only one of many who have been persecuted for putting ethics before greed. Christophe Meili, a Union Banque Suisse (UBS) security guard, was threatened with murder and the kidnapping of his wife and children after he testified before a U.S. Senate committee about documents he rescued from UBS shredders. He and his family were given asylum in America.

We have been threatened with murder before. When we published *The Soong Dynasty* we were warned by a senior CIA official that a hit team was being assembled in Taiwan to come murder us. He said, "I would take this very seriously, if I were you." We vanished for a year to an island off the coast of British Columbia. While we were gone, a Taiwan hit team arrived in San Francisco and shot dead the Chinese-American journalist Henry Liu.

When we published *The Marcos Dynasty* we expected trouble from the Marcos family and its cronies, but instead we were harassed by Washington. Others had investigated Marcos, but we were the first to show how the U.S. Government was secretly involved with Marcos gold deals. We came under attack from the U.S. Treasury Department and its Internal Revenue Service, whose agents made threatening midnight phone calls to our elderly parents. Arriving in New York for an author tour, one of us was intercepted at JFK airport, passport seized, and held incommunicado for three hours. Eventually the passport was returned, without a word of explanation. When we ran Freedom of Information queries to see what was behind it, we were grudgingly sent a copy of a telex message on which every word was blacked out, including the date. The justification given for this censorship was the need to protect government sources, which are above the law.

During one harassing phone call from a U.S. Treasury agent, he said he was sitting in his office watching an interview we had done for a Japanese TV network – an interview broadcast only in Japanese, which we had never seen.

After publishing *The Yamato Dynasty*, which briefly mentioned the discovery that is the basis for *Gold Warriors*, our phones and email were tapped. We know this because when one of us was in a European clinic briefly for a medical procedure, the head nurse reported that 'someone posing as your American doctor' had been on the phone asking questions.

When a brief extract of this book was published in the *South China Morning Post* in August 2001, several phone calls from the editors were cut off suddenly. Emails from the newspaper took 72 hours to reach us, while copies sent to an associate nearby arrived instantly.

In recent months, we began to receive veiled death threats.

What have we done to provoke murder? To borrow a phrase from Jean Ziegler, we are 'combating official amnesia'.

We live in dangerous times, like Germany in the 1930s, when anyone who makes inconvenient disclosures about hidden assets can be branded a 'terrorist' or a 'traitor'. A few months ago, three ex-ambassadors to Japan declared that former American POWs and civilian slave laborers, suing giant Japanese corporations for compensation, were tantamount to terrorists. Now a CIA official says that leaks of classified information must be stopped, even if it is necessary to "send SWAT teams into journalists' homes".

Everybody's national security is a serious matter. We have no argument with that. But national security can be invoked to hide official corruption, and conflict of interest. It's called tyranny. The only cure is openness and sunlight.

In this book, we do not question whether President Truman did the right thing in keeping these war-gold recoveries secret. That is for others to debate. What we point out is that total secrecy enabled corrupt people to abuse the resulting slush funds, and these abuses have multiplied like a cancer, ever since. A global network of corruption has grown around the slush funds. Bureaucrats, politicians, spooks, and generals, have become addicted to black money. There are indications that a lot of this war-gold has been siphoned off by America's far right, under the guise of patriotism. The unintended consequences of Truman's decision have become a poisonous part of the world financial system, putting innocent people at hazard. Those people and institutions benefiting from this corruption will do everything possible to hide it, including murder.

The only way to get rid of an illness is first to recognize what it is. But when the emperor goes crazy from syphilis of the brain, the first person to be tortured and burned at the stake is the doctor who made the diagnosis – slaying the messenger.

Despite the best efforts of the American and Japanese governments to destroy, withhold, or lose documentation related to Golden Lily, we have accumulated thousands of documents, conducted thousands of hours of interviews, and we make all of these available to readers of this book on two Compact Disks, available from our website *www.bowstring.net* so they can make up their own minds. We encourage others with knowledge of these events to come forward. When the top is corrupt, the truth will not come from the top. It will emerge in bits and pieces from people like Jean Ziegler and Christophe Meili, who decided they had to 'do something'.

As a precaution, should anything odd happen, we have arranged for this book and all its documentation to be put up on the Internet at a number of sites.

If we *are* murdered, readers will have no difficulty figuring out who 'they' are.

Readers will find exhaustive annotations at the back of this book. Those wishing to see additional documentation, maps, images, and photographs in both black-and-white and color, may obtain two compact discs containing more than 900 megabytes of data from the authors' website at <www.bowstring.net>.

"Money is the sinew of war."
– *Cicero*

"The first casualty, when war comes, is truth."
– *Senator Hiram Johnson, 1918*

"The study of money, above all other fields in economics,
is one in which complexity is used to disguise truth
or to evade truth, not to reveal it."
– *John Kenneth Galbraith*

BURIED ALIVE

In the closing months of World War II in the Philippines, while General Yamashita Tomoyuki fought a delaying action in the rugged mountains of Luzon, several of Japan's highest-ranking imperial princes were preparing for the future. They were busy hiding tons of looted gold bullion and other stolen treasure in nearby caves and tunnels, to be recovered later. This was the property of twelve Asian countries, accumulated over thousands of years. Expert teams accompanying Japan's armed forces had systematically emptied treasuries, banks, factories, private homes, pawn shops, art galleries, and stripped ordinary people, while Japan's top gangsters looted Asia's underworld and black economy. In this, the Japanese were far more thorough than the Nazis. It was as if a giant vacuum cleaner passed across East and Southeast Asia. Much of the plunder reached Japan overland through Korea. The rest, moving by sea, got no farther than the Philippines as the U.S. submarine blockade became complete in early 1943. Hiding the treasure there was crucial, so that if Japan lost the war militarily, it would not lose financially. In whatever settlement concluded the war, Japan always expected to keep the Philippines. Overseen by the princes, 175 'imperial' treasure vaults were constructed throughout the islands. Early in June 1945, when U.S. tanks were less than twenty miles from Bambang, the 175 chief engineers of those vaults were given a farewell party 220 feet underground in a complex known as Tunnel-8, stacked wall-to-wall with row after row of gold bars. As the evening progressed, they drank great quantities of sake, sang patriotic songs and shouted Banzai ('long life') over and over. At midnight, General Yamashita and the princes slipped out, and dynamite charges were set off in the access tunnels, entombing the engineers. They were buried alive. Those who did not kill themselves ritually would gradually suffocate, surrounded by gold bars. The vaults would remain secret. In subsequent days, the princes escaped to Japan by submarine, and three months later General Yamashita surrendered to American troops.

For half a century, this grisly live burial remained unknown. The hidden treasure was brushed off as 'the legend of Yamashita's Gold'. But an eyewitness to the entombment has taken us to Tunnel-8 and given us his personal account. During the war, Ben Valmores was the young Filipino valet of an exceptional Japanese prince, who was in charge of building, inventorying and sealing all imperial treasure sites in the Philippines. Highly educated and sometimes sentimental, the prince spared Ben's life at the last moment and led him out of Tunnel-8, just before the dynamite was detonated. Ben, in poor health in his mid-seventies when we interviewed him, told us over many months what he saw and experienced in the company of his prince, from 1943 to 1945. He provided us with essential clues that eventually enabled us to identify his prince, and most of the other princes involved.

Japan's looting of Asia was overseen by Emperor Hirohito's charming and cultivated brother, Prince Chichibu. His organization was code-named *kin no yuri* (Golden Lily), the title of one of the emperor's poems. Lesser princes headed different branches of Golden Lily across the conquered territories. Japanese sources now have confirmed that Ben's wartime master was Prince Takeda Tsuneyoshi, first cousin of Emperor Hirohito and a grandson of Emperor Meiji. To corroborate this, in 1998 we gave Ben a 'blind test' with obscure 1930s photographs of many princes; photos that we obtained from the British Library Oriental Collection. These were photos of the princes in army uniform, as they looked on the eve of Pearl Harbor. Although we removed the names from each photo, and mingled photographs of ordinary soldiers, Ben instantly identified Prince Takeda, Hirohito's two brothers Prince Chichibu and Prince Mikasa, and the elder Prince Asaka who had commanded Japanese armies at the Rape of Nanking. Ben said he had spent time with each of them, bringing them food, tea and cigarettes while they inventoried and closed treasure sites. Ben Valmores was a rural rice farmer who never left the Philippines, and never went beyond grade school, so his instant correct identification of the princes was persuasive. When he came upon our photo of Prince Takeda, Ben froze, then began crooning the Japanese folk song *Sakura, Sakura* ('Cherry Blossoms'), which he said Takeda often sang to himself.

The discovery of Prince Takeda's identity provided us with a piece missing from a much larger puzzle. While we were writing a biography of Japan's imperial family, *The Yamato Dynasty*, we were told that in October 1945, American intelligence agents learned the location of some Japanese treasure vaults in the Philippines, and secretly recovered billions of dollars worth of gold, platinum, cultural artifacts, and loose gems. This information, if true, revealed the existence of an extraordinary state secret that the U.S. Government had kept hidden for over half a century. So serious were the implications that we decided they merited separate investigation. Here is some of what we have learned:

On September 2, 1945, after receiving official notice of Japan's surrender, General Yamashita and his staff emerged from their mountain stronghold in the Kiangan Pocket and presented their swords to a group of U.S. Army officers led by Military Police Major A.S. 'Jack' Kenworthy, who took them to New Bilibad Prison outside Manila. Because of gruesome atrocities committed earlier by Admiral Iwabuchi Kanji's sailors and marines in the city of Manila (after Yamashita had ordered them to leave the city unharmed), the general was charged with war crimes. During his trial there was no mention of war loot. But there was a hidden agenda.

Because it was not possible to torture General Yamashita physically without this becoming evident to his defense attorneys, members of his staff were tortured instead. His driver, Major Kojima Kashii, was given special attention. Since Yamashita had arrived from Manchuria in October 1944 to take over the defense of the Philippines, Kojima had driven him everywhere. In charge of Kojima's torture was a Filipino-American intelligence officer named Severino Garcia Diaz Santa Romana, a man of many names and personalities, whose friends called him 'Santy'. He wanted Major Kojima to reveal each place to which he had taken Yamashita, where bullion and other treasure were hidden.

Supervising Santy, we learned, was Captain Edward G. Lansdale, later one of America's best-known Cold Warriors. In September 1945, Lansdale was 37 years old and utterly insignificant, only an advertising agency copywriter who had spent the war in San Francisco writing propaganda for the OSS. In September 1945, chance entered Lansdale's life in a big way when President Truman ordered the OSS to close down. To preserve America's intelligence assets, and his own personal network, OSS chief General William Donovan moved personnel to other government or military posts. Captain Lansdale was one of fifty office staff given a chance to transfer to U.S. Army G-2 in the Philippines. There, Lansdale heard about Santy torturing General Yamashita's driver, and joined the torture sessions as an observer and participant.

Early that October, Major Kojima broke down and led Lansdale and Santy to more than a dozen Golden Lily treasure vaults in the mountains north of Manila, including two that were easily opened.

What lay inside astounded everyone.

While Santy and his teams set to opening the rest of these vaults, Captain Lansdale flew to Tokyo to brief General MacArthur, then on to Washington to brief President Truman. After discussions with his cabinet, Truman decided to proceed with the recovery, but to keep it a state secret.

The treasure – gold, platinum, and barrels of loose gems – was combined with Axis loot recovered in Europe to create a worldwide covert political action fund to fight communism. This 'black gold' gave the Truman Administration access to virtually limitless unvouchered funds for covert operations. It also provided an asset base that was used by Washington to reinforce the treasuries of its allies, to bribe political leaders, and to manipulate elections in foreign countries. In the late 1940s, this agenda was seen as entirely justified, because the Soviet Union was aggressively supporting communist and socialist movements all over the world, putting the survival of the capitalist world in peril.

Most readers will be as surprised as we were by this information. Some may be deeply troubled by Truman's strategic decision, which others may heartily endorse. It is not within the scope of this book to examine that decision, or to explore whether it was right or wrong. It might have been a wise decision at the time, which had tragic consequences in the longer term. Ours is only a preliminary report, and in what follows we try to remain politically neutral. The only purpose of this book is to lift the veil of secrecy, and to bring forward and examine the unforeseen consequences, which are many, and troubling.

It was not Truman's decision alone. The idea for a global political action fund based on war loot actually originated during the Roosevelt administration, with Secretary of War Henry L. Stimson. During the war, Stimson had a braintrust thinking hard about Axis plunder and how it should be handled when peace came. As the tide turned against the Axis, it was only a matter of time before treasure began to be recovered. Much of this war prize was in the form of gold looted by the Nazis from conquered countries and civilian victims. To eliminate any trace of original ownership, the Nazis had melted it down, and recast it as ingots hallmarked with the swastika and black eagle of the Reichsbank. There were other reasons why the gold was difficult to trace. Many of the original owners had died, and pre-war governments had ceased to exist. Eastern Europe was falling under the control of the Soviet Union, so returning gold looted there was out of the question.

Stimson's special assistants on this topic were his deputies John J. McCloy and Robert Lovett, and consultant Robert B. Anderson, all clever men with outstanding careers in public service and banking. McCloy later became head of the World Bank, Lovett secretary of Defense, Anderson secretary of the Treasury. Their solution was to set up what is informally called the Black Eagle Trust. The idea was first discussed with America's allies in secret during July 1944, when forty-four nations met at Bretton Woods, New Hampshire, to plan the postwar world economy. (This was confirmed, in documents we obtained, by a number of high-level sources, including a CIA officer based in Manila, and former CIA Deputy Director Ray Cline, who knew of Santy's recoveries in 1945. As recently as the 1990s, Cline continued to be involved in attempts to control Japanese war-gold still in the vaults of Citibank.)

After briefing President Truman and others in Washington, including McCloy, Lovett, and Stimson, Captain Lansdale returned to Tokyo in November 1945 with Robert B. Anderson. General MacArthur then accompanied Anderson and Lansdale on a covert flight to Manila, where they set out for a tour of the vaults Santy already had opened. In them, we were told, Anderson and MacArthur strolled down "row after row of gold bars stacked two meters tall". From what they saw, it was evident that over a period of years Japan had looted many billions of dollars in treasure from all over Asia. What was seen by Anderson and MacArthur was only the gold that had *not* reached Japan. Far from being bankrupted by the war, Japan had been greatly enriched.

According to Ray Cline and others, between 1945 and 1947 the gold bullion recovered by Santy and Lansdale was discreetly moved by ship to 176 accounts at banks in 42 countries. Secrecy was vital. If the recovery of a huge mass of stolen gold became known, thousands of people would come forward to claim it, many of them fraudulently, and governments would be bogged down resolving ownership. Truman also was told that the very existence of so much black gold, if it became public knowledge, would cause the fixed price of $35 an ounce to collapse. So many countries had linked their currencies to the U.S. dollar, and the dollar linked to gold, that currency values throughout the world would plummet, causing financial disaster. This argument may have been greatly exaggerated by those who stood to benefit from the Black Eagle strategy, but nobody could be certain what the consequences would be. If the gold was kept secret, prices could be kept at $35 an ounce, the dollar would remain strong, and currencies pegged to gold would be stable. Meanwhile, the black gold would serve as a reserve asset, bolstering the prime banks of Allied countries, strengthening the governments of those nations. As a safeguard, the bullion placed in those banks was carefully controlled; strict limits were placed on the use that could be made of the gold (a process called earmarking). This enabled Washington to bring pressure, from time to time, on those governments, central banks and prime banks. Put simply, so long as a country and its leaders cooperated, and remained allied to the United States in the Cold War, derivatives of the sleeping bullion could be used for patronage through political slush funds.

Documents do show that between 1945 and 1947 very large quantities of gold and platinum were deposited in the world's biggest banks, including Union Banque Suisse and other Swiss banks, which became major repositories of the Black Eagle Trust. Swiss banks played a pivotal role because Switzerland had remained neutral during the war and its banks had not been looted, damaged, or depleted. Documents signed by senior Swiss banking officials show that very large loans backed by this asset base were then extended to the British government, the Egyptian government, the Chinese Nationalist regime, and other governments struggling to recover from the war.

What went wrong in the longer term is that the cloak of national security created a situation ripe for abuse. What protects national secrets also protects government officials and their collaborators in the private sector. In later chapters we see numerous documented instances when these underground funds surfaced as huge bribes, or were used to buy elections in Italy, Greece, Japan, and elsewhere. Beneficial trusts were set up in behalf of influential people throughout the world. Gold bearer certificates were given as inducements. In the hands of clever men, the possibilities were endless.

Over a period of decades, some of the world's biggest banks became addicted to playing with the black gold in their vaults. Now they will do whatever is necessary to keep the gold, even if it means defrauding account holders or their heirs, as happened with Holocaust gold in Swiss banks.

In retrospect, recovering Golden Lily treasure vaults and setting up the Black Eagle Trust were the easy parts, done for patriotic reasons and a noble cause. Making intelligent use of so much underground money during the Cold War was not so easy, when national security made peer review impossible. Who is to supervise clandestine funds, except those who benefit by using them?

There were other abuses as well. To hide the existence of this treasure, and to secure America's position against the tide of communism sweeping across Asia in the late 1940s, Washington told a number of major diplomatic lies. Especially lies about Japan, which had stolen most of the gold.

Japan's ruling elite were traditional hard-core conservatives, greatly alarmed by communism. America wanted Japan to be its anti-communist bastion in Asia, so the source of Tokyo's hidden wealth must never be acknowledged. The most ardent anti-communists in Tokyo happened to be indicted war criminals. So while America introduced democratic reforms and a new constitution, it put Japan back under the control of men who were devoutly undemocratic, and kept them in power with huge infusions of black money.

Washington insisted, starting in 1945, that Japan never stole anything, and was flat broke and bankrupt when the war ended. Here was the beginning of many great distortions, which would become terrible secrets.

Because the treasure amassed by Golden Lily and recovered by Washington had to be kept secret, citizens of Japan and America were grossly deceived. The 1951 peace treaty with Japan was skewed by these deceits, so thousands of POWs and civilians (who were forced to perform slave labor for Japanese corporations) received no compensation for their suffering. To shield Japan from demands for war reparations, John Foster Dulles met privately with three Japanese to work out the treaty terms in secret. One of the three, Miyazawa Kiichi, later served as Japan's prime minister and repeatedly as its minister of finance. According to Article 14 of the treaty, "It is recognized that Japan should pay reparations to the Allied Powers for the damage and suffering caused by it during the war. Nevertheless it is also recognized that the resources of Japan are not presently sufficient."

To reinforce the claim that Japan was broke, Article 14 stated, "the Allied Powers waive all reparations claims of the Allied Powers *and their nationals* arising out of any actions taken by Japan". (Our italics.) By signing the treaty, Allied countries concurred that Japan's plunder had vanished down a rabbit hole, and all Japan's victims were out of luck.

In return for going along with the treaty, we document that Washington sent secret shipments of black gold recovered by Santa Romana, to beef up the Allies' exhausted central banks.

Because the Black Eagle Trust and the political action funds it spawned remained off the books, some of these slush funds fell into the wrong hands, where they remain to this day, bigger than ever. According to reliable sources in Washington and Tokyo, in 1960 Vice President Nixon gave one of the biggest of these funds, the M-Fund, to the leaders of Japan's Liberal Democratic Party in return for their promise of kickbacks to Nixon's campaign for the American presidency. This in itself is deeply disturbing. But the M-Fund, then worth $35-billion and now said to be worth upwards of $500-billion, has been controlled ever since by LDP kingmakers who use it to buy elections, to keep Japan a one-party dictatorship, and to block any meaningful reforms. Similar abuses with other secret funds are to be found all over the world. Secrecy is power. Power corrupts. Secret power corrupts secretly.

As Japan expert Chalmers Johnson nicely put it, "The Cold War is over. Whatever the United States may have believed was necessary to prosecute the Cold War, the Cold War itself can no longer be used to justify ignorance about its costs and unintended consequences. The issue today is not whether Japan might veer toward socialism or neutralism but why the government that evolved from its long period of dependence on the United States is so corrupt, inept, and weak."

•

Where did all this treasure come from? Until now, Japan's looting of Asia has been brushed off as a few random acts of theft and violence committed by drunken soldiers. This is disinformation.

Looting as an extension of war is nothing new. In 1860 British and French armies on a punitive expedition to North China got drunk, ran wild and looted the magnificent Summer Palace outside Peking, smashing, breaking, or burning everything they could not carry, and finished by torching all but one of the palaces and pavilions. Unable to believe the gold they found was real, these uneducated soldiers threw most of it away, or traded it for alcohol. (The commander of this joint force was Lord Elgin, whose father had removed most of the sculpture from the Parthenon in Athens.) In 1900, Western armies again marched into Peking, this time to lift the so-called Boxer Siege of the Legations, then went on a drunken rampage looting and smashing treasures inside the Forbidden City.

What Japan did between 1895 and 1945 was qualitatively different. This was not drunken looting and smashing. The Japanese were serious, sober, and deliberate, giving special attention to the theft of valuable books and manuscripts that would have been ignored by common thieves or footsoldiers. They devoted special attention to looting the Asian underworld – triads, sects, racketeers. Japan also flooded China with narcotics, giving gangsters drugs in exchange for gold, which brought treasure out of every hiding place. On a personal level, extortion was used to terrorize wealthy individuals, including tycoons, clan elders, bankers and businessmen.

Among the most valuable articles taken back to Japan were artworks and historic artifacts. It is a matter of record that to this day only a tiny bit of this patrimony has been returned to the countries or individuals from whom it was stolen. Some major artifacts, including solid gold Buddhas, have been seen recently in underground hiding places in the Philippines. But most of the art and artifacts are still in private vaults in Japan, or in the imperial collections in Tokyo. Why was Japan allowed to keep it?

Officially, we are told that Japan's wartime elite – the imperial family, the *zaibatsu*, the *yakuza*, and the 'good' bureaucrats – ended the war as impoverished victims of a handful of 'bad' military zealots. As readers will see, this is not true. Many of Japan's elite, including Emperor Hirohito, ended the war far richer than when it began, and some made billions just before and after the surrender.

We are told that Japan was badly damaged and barely able to feed itself at war's end. In fact, surprisingly few factories and mansions were destroyed or even seriously damaged, and there was little damage to infrastructure. Most of the damage that has been so widely publicized was to the matchbox homes of millions of ordinary Japanese, whose suffering did not count in the view of their own overlords.

Obsessed by the urgent need to make Japan a bulwark against communism, Washington excused its wartime leaders, imperial family and financial elite, from any responsibility for the destruction and destitution of twelve Asian countries. Only a handful of Japan's wartime leaders were executed as scapegoats. Several were coerced or framed into taking the blame for the rest of the leadership. At the end of the postwar occupation, all Japan's indicted war criminals were set free, including gangsters and godfathers who had directed the world's largest drug trafficking system across East Asia during the 1930s and 1940s. Washington saw to it that

Japan's government was put back in the hands of the same men who had started the war. This was equivalent to reinstating the Nazi party in postwar Berlin. There was little protest in Japan, because all opposition was silenced by a campaign of witch-hunting far more severe than the McCarthy witch-hunts in America. As we demonstrate, the rebirth of Japan's far right was financed with war loot, and corporate profits wrung out of Asia during the war by Japan's *zaibatsu*.

It is an inescapable fact that from the beginning of the U.S. occupation, General MacArthur, President Truman, John Foster Dulles, and a handful of others, knew all about the plunder, and the continuing extraordinary wealth of the Japanese elite. In an official report on the occupation prepared by MacArthur's headquarters and published in 1950, there is a startling admission: "One of the spectacular tasks of the occupation dealt with collecting and putting under guard the great hoards of gold, silver, precious stones, foreign postage stamps, engraving plates, and all currency not legal in Japan. Even though the bulk of this wealth was collected and placed under United States military custody by Japanese officials, undeclared caches of these treasures were known to exist." MacArthur's staff knew, for example, of $2-billion in gold bullion that had been sunk in Tokyo Bay, later recovered.

Another great fortune discovered by U.S. intelligence services in 1946 was $13-billion in war loot amassed by underworld godfather Kodama Yoshio who, as a 'rear admiral' in the Imperial Navy working with Golden Lily in China and Southeast Asia, was in charge of plundering the Asian underworld and racketeers. He was also in charge of Japan's wartime drug trade throughout Asia. After the war, to get out of Sugamo Prison and avoid prosecution for war crimes, Kodama gave $100-million to the CIA, which was added to the M-Fund's coffers. Kodama then personally financed the creation of the two political parties that merged into Japan's ruling Liberal Democratic Party (LDP), strongly backed to this day by Washington.

•

Hard evidence of Santy's secret recovery of Japanese war-gold comes from straightforward legal actions in America. Such simple things as the probating of his will, the verification of his tax records in the state of New York at Albany, and legal evidence of his fortune deposited in the United States, Switzerland, Hong Kong and elsewhere, provide hard evidence that the world is awash with clandestine bank accounts growing out of Golden Lily.

As we shall see, when Santa Romana died in 1974, some of his biggest black gold accounts were quickly transferred to the name of Major General Edward G. Lansdale, the man who participated with Santy in the torture of Major Kojima thirty years earlier, in 1945. By 1974, Lansdale had been retired from the CIA for over a decade, raising puzzling questions that are only answered by recognizing the role of Lansdale and other former spooks and generals in America's new network of private military and intelligence firms.

There are many other famous names tied to this curious story. Long-time Citibank CEO John Reed was named in some of these lawsuits as a key figure in the movement of Santa Romana black gold. Among those instrumental in the lawsuits was San Francisco attorney Melvin Belli. Writing to the editor of *The Las Vegas*

Sun, Belli said, "I'm now convinced that some very important banks around the world did have deposits of money [for Santa Romana]." Belli's suit read in part: "Defendant John Reed, the Chairman and Chief Executive Officer of defendant Citibank, has spearheaded Citibank's conversion of the gold bullion which was owned by [Santa Romana]. ...Reed and Citibank have systematically sold and are selling said gold bullion to buyers and converting the sales proceeds to their own use."

Other lawsuits prove that Golden Lily war loot was indeed hidden in the Philippines. Rogelio Roxas, a Filipino locksmith, found a one-ton solid gold Buddha and thousands of small gold bars hidden in a tunnel behind a hospital in the mountain resort of Baguio, which had served as a headquarters for General Yamashita. The moment he heard what Roxas had found, President Marcos sent thugs to confiscate the Gold Buddha. When Roxas protested, he was arrested, tortured and ultimately poisoned. In 1996, a U.S. court in the state of Hawaii awarded his heirs a judgment of $43-billion against the Marcos estate, the largest civil award in history.

Documents discovered in Malacanang Palace show that in 1968, President Marcos sent a team of army officers to Japan to make a deal for joint recoveries. According to a member of the team, they met with a prince, "a high-ranking Japanese officer... a cousin of Emperor Hirohito", who told them that Japan had hidden over $100-billion worth of treasure in the Philippines and it would take "more than a century" to recover it all.

A related legal battle was that of former U.S. Deputy Attorney General Norbert Schlei, who had to fight for his survival after being stung by the U.S. Treasury Department for asking too many questions about Japan's secret M-Fund. While Schlei was indicted, prosecuted, bankrupted, and professionally ruined for trying to negotiate a financial certificate based on the M-Fund, former Secretary of State Alexander Haig – according to eyewitnesses – went to Japan and negotiated a similar certificate successfully, with the help of a personal letter from President George H.W. Bush. Why one man succeeded while the other was destroyed is a chilling story of financial collusion between Washington and Tokyo.

•

We have been deeply skeptical about the huge dollar values cited about Golden Lily. Officially, there are said to be only about 130,000 metric tons of processed gold in the world including bullion, coinage and jewellery. Official records maintain that Asia, with more than 75 per cent of the world's population, holds less than 5 per cent of the total world supply of gold, a statistic that is ridiculous on the face of it. But in the West at least, the law of gold is drummed into us like the law of gravity. In fact, nobody really knows how much gold there is. We do not know how much was looted by Spain from the New World, because once it reached Europe most of it was passed on to the great European banking families, the Fuggers and Welsers, who had financed the conquest of Mexico and Peru. Whatever the Fuggers and the Welsers did with that gold they kept very secret. We also have no way of knowing the actual wealth of families like the Krupps, Rothschilds, Oppenheimers,

Warburgs, or Rockefellers, except that they have been very rich for a very long time and their wealth is dispersed in a multitude of clever ways. A trillion dollars sounds like a lot, but economists tell us that today there is some $23-trillion in the hands of the well-heeled, much of it sleeping in offshore private accounts where banking secrecy and local laws keep these assets hidden from the tax-man, spouses, and clients. We know even less about the gold holdings of the great Asian and Middle Eastern dynastic families, trading networks, and underworld syndicates. Western tycoons may own banks and oil companies, and influence or control governments, but wealthy Asians never trusted governments or banks, preferring to keep their wealth in small gold or platinum bars, and gems. In China this absolute distrust goes back thousands of years. We can be sure that what was tucked under the rug in Asia over 2,000 years is far more than what has been deposited in U.S. and European banks since Western banking (and the gold market as we know it) came into existence barely three centuries ago. The U.S. Government refuses to disclose how much gold it holds, and the last public audit of Ft. Knox was in the early 1950s. In short, gold is one of the world's biggest secrets. There are good reasons for this.

The point of our book is not to guess how much was stolen, how much was hidden, how much was secretly recovered, or how much is still waiting to be found. Because of all the lying and deception, the full details may never be known.

In this book, in its annotations, and in our two archival CDs containing over 900 megabytes of documents, photographs, maps and other images, we provide hard evidence that huge quantities of war-gold remain today in the coffers of international banks such as Citibank, Chase, Hongkong & Shanghai Banking Corporation (HSBC), Union Banque Suisse, and others. We provide photocopies of letters, contracts, waybills, state government tax records, insurance covers, and interviews with brokers who carried out Black Eagle deals.

We document how a secret trust was set up at Japan's Sanwa Bank, jointly held by General MacArthur and his old adversary Emperor Hirohito. This account, known as the Showa Trust after Hirohito's reign title, was so big that by 1982 it was paying nearly $1-billion interest per year. We also have identified one of the three trustees of the Showa Trust. And we show how President Marcos discovered the existence of this account and used it to blackmail the government of Japan.

We include documents and color photos of major postwar gold recovery operations while they were under way, on land and sea. Santa Romana and Lansdale only recovered a portion of the treasure from 1945 to 1947. A decade passed before other significant recoveries occurred, as Japanese began coming back to the Philippines, alone or in groups, to reclaim parts of the hoard.

We were given exclusive access to an archive of some 60,000 documents, and hundreds of hours of audio and videotapes made or collected over 25 years by American mining expert and metallurgical chemist Robert Curtis, who actually recovered $8-billion in gold bars for President Marcos from Teresa-2. After nearly being murdered by Marcos, and fleeing the Philippines, Curtis became absorbed by the historical importance of documenting the treasure. In the course of engineering five major Golden Lily recoveries for Marcos, Curtis was able to study many of the sites personally, in and around the city of Manila, giving him an unrivaled understanding of the techniques employed by Golden Lily engineers.

During the months that Curtis worked with President Marcos, he photographed 172 of the 175 original treasure maps. We reproduce several of the maps on our CDs.

We also tell the epic saga of Japan's recovery of the *Op ten Noort*, a captured Dutch passenger liner used by Golden Lily to carry treasure safely to Japan under guise of being a hospital ship. After returning to Japan in 1945, she was scuttled by Japanese navy officers near the Maizuru Naval Base with tons of gold and platinum aboard. Her treasure was recovered in the early 1990s. The names of the Japanese recovery ships, and the Australian recovery ship and submersible, all are clearly visible in the photographs we reproduce, taken by one of the participants.

Included here are handwritten letters and diagrams showing how a group of senior U.S. Government officials and Pentagon generals hoped to use Golden Lily treasure to create a new private FBI and a military-industrial complex controlled by them, in partnership with the John Birch Society, the Moonies, and far-right tycoons. This is confirmed by tape recordings of a 1987 conference in Hong Kong that included retired U.S. Army General John Singlaub and General Robert Schweitzer of the National Security Council under President Reagan. As a measure of their common sense, we show readers how their group dug a hole 400 feet deep beneath a kitchen near Manila, in the misguided belief that the Japanese had dug a similar hole in 1942 to hide gold bullion. More than 300 feet of this hole was under water, so the generals and colonels brought in U.S. Navy deep-sea divers and decompression chambers to carry out the recovery. After many months of toil, and over $1-million in costs, they found nothing and gave up.

We recount a number of equally bizarre misadventures that show why peer review and full disclosure are urgently needed. National security not only shields bureaucrats and hides corruption, it also hides folly.

•

It has taken Holocaust victims nearly six decades to recover assets hidden by Swiss banks, to win compensation for slave labor at German corporations like Volkswagen, and to regain possession of art stolen from their homes and offices. Their success, along with the 50th anniversary of the surrender of Japan, encouraged other victims to come forth with valid demands for compensation. This led to unprecedented cooperation among the victims.

This last battle of the Pacific War was being waged in California state courts, where surviving POWs, slave laborers, comfort women, and civilian victims filed billion-dollar lawsuits to win compensation so mysteriously denied them after the war. In 1995, it was estimated that 700,000 victims of the Pacific War still had received no compensation. Their numbers are dwindling rapidly because of age and illness. Backing them is an extraordinary coalition of activists and law firms. Britain tried to sidestep this tide of legal discovery by making one-time pay-offs to victims, to shut them up.

Washington took a different approach by moving the California lawsuits to federal courts, where they were blocked by political pressure and intervention by government agencies. The Department of State and Department of Justice are using Article 14 of the 1951 peace treaty to prevent POWs and other victims from suing immensely rich Japanese corporations such as Mitsubishi, Mitsui and Sumitomo. At U.S. Senate hearings in June 2000, chairman Orrin Hatch of Utah challenged State and Justice attorneys about the legitimacy of their claim that the 1951 Peace Treaty canceled all rights of victims. "You mean our federal government can just say, 'To hell with you, Bataan Death Marchers, and you people who were mistreated, we're just going to waive all your rights...' Constitutionally, can our government take away the rights of individual citizens just because they put it in a treaty...? We're not asking the Japanese government to pay. We're asking the companies that did the acts to pay, some of these companies are multi-billion-dollar companies today."

Despite such impassioned appeals, on September 21, 2000, U.S. District Court Judge Vaughn Walker ruled against American POWs and other slave laborers. Walker dismissed their suits, saying it was dangerous to upset the diplomatic alliance that existed between America and Japan since the end of the war.

Three former U.S. ambassadors to Japan then published a letter in *The Washington Post* making the astounding assertion that these American ex-POWs and their attorneys were virtual terrorists.

The real issue is conflict of interest. During the Clinton Administration, U.S. Ambassador to Japan Thomas Foley was adamant in rejecting compensation for POWs and other slave laborers, insisting that "The peace treaty put aside all claims against Japan." His Deputy Chief of Mission, Christopher J. Lafleur, echoed this dogma at every opportunity.

It was a matter of some interest to victims that Foley's wife was a well-paid consultant to Sumitomo, one of Japan's biggest *zaibatsu* conglomerates, heavily involved in wartime slave labor and a target of the lawsuits. The moment Foley ended his tenure as ambassador and returned to America, he signed on as a paid advisor and lobbyist to another huge conglomerate – Mitsubishi – one of the biggest wartime users of slave labor.

Of greater significance, perhaps, is that Lafleur is married to the daughter of former prime minister and finance minister Miyazawa, one of the three Japanese who secretly negotiated the 1951 treaty with John Foster Dulles. (Miyazawa also is considered by Professor Lausier and others to be the financial overseer of the M-Fund.) Conflict of interest does not seem to be an obstacle in diplomatic appointments to Tokyo.

Today, there is enough evidence of financial collusion between Tokyo and Washington to merit Congressional hearings and a General Accounting Office investigation. After half a century of diplomatic lies, corruption, and cover-up, it is time to strip off the fig leaf of national security, which is an insidious form of tyranny. To Congress, to the American people, and to the principles of democracy itself, Washington owes a full and guileless accounting.

●

Just down the coast from Manila in Batangas Province is a dramatic treasure site that someday could be turned into a Golden Lily theme park. It has been the target of several Japanese recovery efforts in recent years. Overlooking the South China Sea, it is a big headland with so many tunnels and gun emplacements that it earned the nickname 'Guns of Navarone'. (We were asked not to identify the location precisely.) This underground complex was started by the Japanese in the early 1920s, as part of their long-term strategy for the conquest of the Philippines. It was filled with treasure in 1944. Three of its tunnels have since been opened by Japanese groups, who found trucks loaded with gold bars. They were so happy with what they found in these outer reaches of the tunnels that they went no farther. Deeper passages appear undisturbed. Where did all this treasure come from? It all began with Korea.

CHAPTER ONE

BEHIND THE MASK

During the night of October 7, 1895, thirty Japanese assassins forced their way into Korea's royal palace in Seoul. Bursting into the queen's private quarters, they cut down two ladies-in-waiting and cornered Queen Min. When the Minister of the Royal Household tried to shield her, a swordsman slashed off both his hands. The defenseless queen was stabbed and slashed repeatedly, and carried wailing out to the palace garden where she was thrown onto a pile of firewood, drenched with kerosene, and set aflame. An American military advisor, General William Dye, was one of several foreigners who heard and saw the killers milling around in the palace compound with drawn swords while the queen was burned alive. Japan declared that the murders were committed by "Koreans dressed as Japanese in European clothes" – a gloss greeted with ridicule by the diplomatic community. According to the British minister in Tokyo, Sir Ernest Satow, First Secretary Sugimura of the Japanese legation in Korea led the assassins.

The grisly murder of Queen Min was a turning point in Japan's effort to gain control of Korea. Her husband King Kojong was a weakling, controlled by the queen's faction, who were allied with China against Japan. Once the queen was dead, the Japanese could easily control the king, and put an end to Chinese interference.

The coup was planned by Miura Goro, agent of Japan's aggressive Yamagata clique. At first, the killing was to be done by Japanese-trained Korean soldiers, so it could be passed off as an internal matter. But to make sure nothing went wrong, Miura called for help from the Japanese terrorist organization Black Ocean. Many of its members were in Korea posing as business agents of Japanese companies, including the oldest *zaibatsu*, Mitsui. Black Ocean and another secret society called Black Dragon functioned as Japan's paramilitaries on the Asian mainland, carrying out dirty work that could be denied by Tokyo. They were in position throughout Korea and China, running brothels, pharmacies, pawnshops, and building networks of influence by supplying local men with money, sexual favors, alcohol, drugs, pornography, and Spanish Fly. While Black Ocean was obsessed with Korea, Black Dragon (named for the Amur or Black Dragon River separating Manchuria from Siberia) was dedicated to blocking Russian encroachment, and seizing China for Japan. Black Ocean provided Miura with the professional assassins he needed, and the rest of the killers were security men from Japan's consulate. Whether they intended to kill the queen in full view of foreign observers is another matter. Japanese conspiracies often began quietly, then went out of control.

Many Japanese leaders like statesman Ito Hirobumi were enlightened and reasonable men who would have vetoed the murder, had they known. But there was a deep contradiction inside Japan following the Meiji Restoration in the nineteenth century. Two cliques competed ruthlessly for power behind the throne, and for influence over the Meiji Emperor. Those associated with Ito were more cosmopolitan, emulating the role of Bismarck in guiding Kaiser Wilhelm, or Disraeli in guiding Queen Victoria. Those allied with General Yamagata were throwbacks to medieval Japan, where power worked in the shadows with assassins, surprise attacks, and treachery. While Yamagata built a modern conscript army to replace Japan's traditional samurai forces, he also built a network of spies, secret police, *yakuza* gangsters and superpatriots. These were key elements of the police state Yamagata was creating in Japan. Underworld godfathers were a vital component of Japan's ruling structure. Members of the imperial family, and the financial elite that controls Japan, had intimate ties to top gangsters. When Yamagata's armies invaded Korea and Manchuria, gangsters were the cutting edge. Thereafter, Japan's underworld played a major role in looting Asia over fifty years, 1895-1945.

Queen Min's murder marks the beginning of this half-century of extreme Japanese brutality and industrial scale plunder. Her killing shows how easily the mask of Japan's good intentions could slip, to reveal hideous reality.

Other Japanese strategies also began quietly, then got out of hand. For example, it is unlikely that Japan intended all along to have its army stage the Rape of Nanking in 1937, butchering some 300,000 defenseless people in full view of foreign observers with cameras. Had the Rape happened only once, it might have been a grotesque accident. But variations of Nanking occurred many times during Japan's lightning conquest of East and Southeast Asia. By the time they overran Singapore in 1942, the atrocities committed against Overseas Chinese civilians there – the *Sook Ching* massacres – were happening all over Southeast Asia, and not only to Chinese. That this occurred so often suggests there was more to Japan's aggression than a purely military operation. Why, after successfully conquering a neighboring country, did Japan torment the Chinese and others who had money or property? The explanation lies in the shadows behind the army. Few history books take into account the role of the underworld, because scholars rarely study outlaws. With Japan, we must always consider the underworld because it permeates the power structure, as darkly satirized by the films of Itami Juzo.

The conquest of Korea was Japan's first experiment in foreign plunder on an industrial scale, so there was plenty for the underworld to do. Westerners know so little about Korea that it is surprising how much there was to steal. Today, North and South Korea are only vestiges of a distinguished past. Historian Bruce Cumings points out that "Korea's influence on Japan was far greater than Japan's influence on Korea". In ancient times Japan was raided by marauders from the Korean peninsula, and raided Korea in return, but these were bands of swordsmen and archers, not armored regiments. Such raids caused a mutual loathing of Koreans and Japanese that has its parallel in the Catholic and Protestant troubles of Northern Ireland. A quick thumbnail history explains this hatred, and shows how Japan's aggression began.

•

When they first started feuding two thousand years ago, there was no Korea or Japan, as we know them today. In different parts of the Korean peninsula were city-states with highly developed economies supporting magnificent religious, literary and artistic cultures. Their porcelain is among the most prized in the world today, along with elegant paintings, sculpture, and gold filigree. The elite lived in palaces on great estates, with thousands of slaves. Taking no interest in commerce or warfare, they developed astronomy, mathematics, wood block printing, and invented movable type long before anyone else. Until the sixteenth century, Korea had one of the world's most advanced civilizations.

Meanwhile, in the secluded islands of Japan, immigrants from China and Korea were linked in a loose confederation ruled by Shinto priests and priestesses. For a thousand years, these rival domains feuded among themselves, before finally submitting to the central military dictatorship of the shoguns. Chronic conspiracy produced what one historian calls Japan's 'paranoid style' in foreign relations. If Japanese treated each other ruthlessly, why treat foreigners otherwise?

Koreans regarded Japanese as 'uncouth dwarfs'. Chinese were more cultivated, so Korea willingly accepted a tributary role with China. In return, China protected Korea from Japan.

In the sixteenth century, after Japan was unified by Toyotomi Hideyoshi, he launched an invasion of Korea with 158,000 men. His plan was to crush Korea and erase its culture from the face of the earth. He nearly succeeded. After several years of cruel occupation, Korea was rescued by Admiral Yi Sun-shin's famous Turtle Ship, the world's first ironclad – 65-feet long, firing cannon balls filled with nails. Admiral Yi cut Japan's supply routes and destroyed its ships. Humiliated, Hideyoshi died soon afterward.

Despite this failure, the invaders profited richly by looting Korea. Their army included monks and scholars assigned to steal Korea's finest manuscripts. Samurai kidnapped masters of ceramics such as the great Ri Sam-pyong, and made them slaves in Japan. A Korean scholar said the Japanese were "wild animals that only crave material goods and are totally ignorant of human morality". Centuries later, when Japan invaded Korea again, its armies once more included teams of monks and scholars to find and loot the finest artworks.

Korea never recovered. In the nineteenth century, it was the weakest, least commercial country in East Asia, ripe for picking. China's Manchu government, on the verge of collapse, was in no shape to defend Korea.

Following the Meiji Restoration, Japan made a convulsive effort to modernize, becoming the first Asian nation able to compete militarily with the West. As her army and navy developed, she was in a position to launch a campaign of mechanized conquest on the mainland, to acquire a colonial empire of her own. Her first target was Korea. Politicians and army officers argued that if Japan did not grab Korea, Manchuria, and Taiwan, they would be grabbed by Russia, France or England. General Yamagata and Black Ocean boss Toyama Mitsuru needed an incident that would give them an excuse to invade, while putting the blame on Korea. Yamagata told Toyama to "start a conflagration" – then it would be the army's duty to go "extinguish the fire".

Starting a fire in Korea was easy. Black Ocean terrorists attacked a rural religious sect called Tonghak. The Tonghaks struck back, causing some Japanese casualties. With this excuse, Tokyo rushed in troops to 'protect' its citizens in Korea. When news came that China was sending 1,500 soldiers aboard a chartered British ship, the S.S. *Kowshing*, a Japanese squadron intercepted the vessel and sank her with all aboard. This surprise attack set a precedent, followed many times by Japan in later decades.

China's tottering Manchu government foolishly declared war on Japan. In September 1894, in the mouth of Korea's Yalu River, the Japanese destroyed half of China's navy in a single afternoon. Japan then captured Manchuria's 'impregnable' Port Arthur, and the fortified harbor at Weihaiwei in Shantung province, sinking all Chinese ships in the harbor. China sued for peace. By the end of February 1895, Japan controlled the whole of Korea and also Manchuria's strategic Liaotung peninsula. China also gave Japan control of Taiwan, which became Tokyo's first colony. When South Manchuria and Port Arthur also were turned over to Japan, France, Germany and Russia pressured Tokyo to return them.

It was at this point that Queen Min refused to cave in to Japanese bullying, and was murdered. The stage was now set for the unprecedented cruelties of the twentieth century.

•

Having humiliated Manchu China, Japan felt ready to take on Tsarist Russia, which was building railroads into Manchuria. On February 8, 1904, Japan launched two more surprise attacks, one on the Russian naval base at Vladivostok, another on two Russian warships in the mouth of Korea's Inchon harbor. In reply, the Tsar sent his Baltic fleet half way around the world, only to see it destroyed by Japan's navy in the battle of Tsushima, in May 1905. As China had done, Russia sued for peace, giving Japan the lower half of Sakhalin Island, transferring to Japan its lease on South Manchuria, and giving Japan control over the southern section of its Manchurian Railway, between Port Arthur and Changchun.

Now feeling invincible, Japan formally declared Korea a colony. Nobody asked Koreans what they thought. Western governments did not protest. Great numbers of Japanese arrived in the peninsula to make their fortunes. With them came legions of agents for the great *zaibatsu* conglomerates, seizing every commercial opportunity, every natural resource. Japan took control of law and order, creating new police and secret police networks. No longer making any pretense of chivalry,

Japanese abused Korean sovereignty at every turn, crushing all resistance. A newspaper editor was arrested when he wrote: "Ah, how wretched it is. Our twenty million countrymen have become the slaves of another country!"

Not all Japanese were predators. Some earnestly believed that they were in Korea to help, not to plunder. Ito Hirobumi told Korean officials, "Your country does not have the power to defend itself... I am not insisting that your country commit suicide... I expect that if you thrust forward boldly, the day will come when you will advance to a position of equality with us and we will cooperate with one another."

The appointment of Ito as the first Japanese viceroy of Korea gave the country some hope of rational government. But General Yamagata saw to it that Ito's staff included Black Dragon boss Uchida Ryohei. Secretly financed from army funds, Uchida's thugs went on a rampage, murdering 18,000 Koreans during Ito's time as viceroy. Disgusted by the bloody meddling, Ito resigned in 1909 only to be shot dead by paid assassins. His murder was used as a pretext to demand full annexation of Korea. On August 22, 1910, Korea ceased to be a mere colony and was fully incorporated into Japanese territory. Japan's army now had its own domain on the Asian mainland, free of interference from Tokyo politicians. One of Yamagata's most rabid followers, General Terauchi Masatake, was appointed first governor-general of Korea. Terauchi, who had lost his right hand during a great samurai rebellion in the 1870s, had been army minister during the Russo-Japanese War. He now supervised the looting and plunder of Korea.

Although some Japanese Army officers were chivalrous, showed mercy, or refused to indulge in wanton killing, Terauchi was extraordinarily brutal, setting a precedent for Japanese behavior in all the countries it would occupy over coming decades. Determined to crush all resistance, he told Koreans, "I will whip you with scorpions!" He set up a sadistic police force of Korean *yakuza*, ordering it to use torture as a matter of course, for "no Oriental can be expected to tell the truth except under torture". These police were closely supervised by Japan's gestapo, the *kempeitai*.

Most *kempeitai* agents wore civilian clothes, identified only by a chrysanthemum crest on the underside of a lapel. Eventually Japan spawned a network of these spies, informants, and terrorists throughout Asia. At the height of World War II, 35,000 official *kempeitai* were deployed throughout the Japanese Empire. The unofficial number was far greater, because of close integration with Black Dragon, Black Ocean, and other fanatical sects, working together 'like teeth and lips'. Black Ocean boss Uchida reviewed all appointments of *kempeitai* officers sent to Korea.

Korean resistance was intense, but futile. In 1912, some 50,000 Koreans were arrested; by 1918 the number arrested annually rose to 140,000. During Korea's first ten years of Japanese rule even Japanese schoolteachers wore uniforms and carried swords. Japan's army stood guard while *kempeitai* and Black Ocean thugs pillaged the peninsula. Japanese police controlled rice production from paddy field to storehouse, so the majority could be shipped to Japan. *Yakuza* were expert at extortion. In Japan, they used intimidation, extortion, kidnapping and murder, restrained only by prudence in selecting the victims. On the mainland there was no need for such restraint. Because Terauchi's style was so brutal, Japanese bankers and businessmen made a public display of showing contempt for mercy. Eventually, the Terauchi style spread across Asia, remaining in place till 1945.

To be sure, Japan did modernize Korean industry, to some extent, but at terrible cost. Korean workers were paid one-fourth the wages of Japanese counterparts in the same factories. Terauchi forced Koreans to eat millet, while their rice was sent to Japan.

In this merciless way, the peninsula was stripped of everything from artworks to root vegetables. As Korea now belonged to Japan, the transfer of cultural property – looting – was not theft. How can you steal something that already belongs to you?

First on the wish-list was Korea's famous celadon porcelain, which many thought surpassed China's Tang porcelain. Korean stoneware was distinctive for its translucent blue-green glaze, with floral designs incised in the clay and filled with color before glazing. A Western expert called it "the most gracious and unaffected pottery ever made". Although Japan had kidnapped Korea's celadon masters in the sixteenth century, and these experts had discovered sources of fine clay in Kyushu, the porcelain they made in Japan was not the same spiritually. Japanese valued Korean celadon above all others for ritual purposes and tea ceremony. Coveted also were examples of Korea's *punch'ong* stoneware, and Choson white porcelain.

Some of this plunder was put on display at Tokyo's Ueno Museum. Most ended up in private Japanese collections where it was never on public view, and rarely was seen even in private. Japanese collectors keep their treasures in vaults, taking single pieces out for personal viewing. So, most of Korea's stolen antiquities remain lost from sight to this day.

When all Korea's private collections were confiscated, experts studying court records and ancient manuscripts determined that the finest celadons still slept in the tombs of kings. To disguise the looting of these tombs, Terauchi introduced laws for the 'preservation' of historic sites. By preservation, he meant that the tombs would be looted and the valuable contents preserved in Japan. He then opened some two thousand tombs, including a royal tomb in Kaesong, which were emptied of their ancient celadons, Buddhist images, crowns, necklaces, earrings, bronze mirrors, and other ornamental treasures. Along the Taedong River near Pyongyang, some 1,400 tombs were opened and looted.

This wholesale theft was overseen by General Terauchi, personally. One of his first acts was to destroy the 4,000-room Kyungbok-goong Palace to make way for the construction of a residence for himself. To decorate his personal quarters, he chose 600 artworks from thousands being prepared for shipment to Japan.

Japanese private collectors and antique dealers carried off not only artworks, but classic literary texts and important national archives – all in the name of academic research at Japanese museums and universities. Tens of thousands of the finest books listed as Korean national treasures, including all 1,800 volumes of the Ri dynasty archives, were shipped to Japan. Scholars say some 200,000 volumes of ancient books of lesser distinction were then burned, as part of a deliberate program to erase Korea's distinctive culture. They list more than 42,000 cultural relics, including ancient manuscripts, taken to Japan for 'study', and never returned. For good measure, the Japanese used dynamite to blow up a monument to King Taejo

(1396-1398), and a monument to Sam-yong, the militant Buddhist priest who led the resistance to Japan's samurai invasion in 1592.

"Japan's aim," said Korean historian Yi Kibeck, "was to eradicate consciousness of Korean national identity, roots and all, and thus to obliterate the very existence of the Korean people from the face of the earth."

Once stripped of their heritage and identity, Koreans were to be made-over into second-class Japanese. Divested of their inherited land, they had their names changed to Japanese names, and were forced to adopt Shinto in place of their own Buddhist, Confucian or Christian beliefs. Japan's emperor would be their only god, and any Korean who refused to acknowledge his divinity was arrested. Temples were looted of bronze bells and Buddhist statuary. Even ordinary religious metalwork was removed and melted down for weapons as 'spiritual cooperation behind the guns'. Koreans were to speak only Japanese; Korean-language newspapers were closed, political parties disbanded; Korean writers could only publish in Japanese, and all schools taught only in Japanese. At home, Koreans were expected to speak Japanese to each other.

In 1907, Tokyo forced King Kojong to abdicate in favor of his retarded ten-year-old son. They styled the boy 'Crown Prince Imperial Yi Un' and sent him off to Tokyo, claiming he would be educated side-by-side with Meiji's grandsons – Princes Hirohito, Chichibu and Takamatsu. In truth, the boy was a hostage, whose survival depended on continued cooperation by Korea's royal family. For some reason, Emperor Meiji found the boy sympathetic, and lavished attention and gifts on him, the sort of affection he never demonstrated toward his own grandsons. The boy was easily persuaded to sign away his claim to the Korean throne.

In subsequent decades, thousands of other Korean cultural artifacts were forcibly removed by Japan and never returned, despite promises. When people are so thoroughly terrorized, it is impossible to come forward later with a precise list of what was stolen, or a stack of receipts. In 1965, the South Korean government demanded the return of 4,479 items that it was able to identify individually. Of those, Japan grudgingly returned only 1,432, taking another thirty years to do so. The great mass of Korean cultural treasure remains in Japan to this day, in private collections, museums, and the vaults of the Imperial Family. Much of this patrimony is beyond price. Here alone is evidence that Japan was far from bankrupt at the end of World War II.

There always are collaborators. Over forty years, a Japanese antique dealer named Nakada amassed a fortune looting and exporting ancient Koryo celadons. His partner was a former high official of the Ri dynasty, who also became a millionaire.

Most Korean landowners were stripped of their estates and agricultural properties, which were snapped up by Japanese developers. One developer acquired over 300,000 acres in Korea, where he intended to settle Japanese immigrants. As tenant farmers lost their land, they and the urban poor were rounded up and shipped off as slave labor to work in mines and construction brigades in Japan, or in the desolate Kurile Islands. Sixty thousand Koreans were forced to toil as slave labor in coal mines and military factories in the Sakhalin peninsula of Siberia. Of these, 43,000 were still in Sakhalin at the end of World War II, when they came under Soviet control, and had great difficulty getting home.

Before 1945, it is believed that over six million Korean men were forced into slave labor battalions. Of these, nearly one million were sent to Japan. Others were sent to the Philippines or to the Dutch East Indies, to do construction work for the Japanese Army and navy, and to dig tunnels and bunkers for war loot, where they were worked to death or buried alive to hide the locations. On August 24, 1945, a group of 5,000 Korean slave laborers who had spent the war digging a major underground complex for war loot in Japan's Aomori Prefecture, were put aboard the warship *Ukishima Maru* to be 'taken home to Korea'. The ship sailed first to Maizuru Naval Base on the west coast of Japan. There the Koreans were sealed in the cargo holds, and the ship was taken offshore and scuttled, by blowing a hole in the hull with dynamite. Out of 5,000 Koreans aboard, only 80 survived. Tokyo claimed that the Koreans locked in the hold had scuttled the ship themselves. Fifty-seven years later, 15 of these survivors, and relatives of others, at last won a lawsuit against the Japanese government, for compensation. A court in Kyoto ruled in August 2001 that the Japanese government must pay 3-million yen (less than $30,000) to each of the plaintiffs. But the court also ruled that there was no need for the government of Japan to apologize for the 'incident'.

Aside from the six million Korean men dragooned as slave labor, tens of thousands of young Koreans were conscripted into the Japanese Army, to serve as cannon-fodder in campaigns far to the south, many ending up in Burma or New Guinea.

Saddest of all were thousands of Korean girls duped into going to Japan for employment, instead ending up in brothels. It was in Korea that the *kempeitai* set up its first official army brothels in 1904. These were filled with kidnapped women and girls, forerunners of hundreds of thousands of Korean women later forced to serve as Comfort Women in army brothels all over Asia. Koreans were targeted because it was believed that if Japanese women and girls were forced into prostitution for the army, soldiers might mutiny. The Japanese Army took pains to characterize Korean women and girls as mere livestock. Mercy was in short supply.

Bruce Cumings sums up their predicament: "Millions of people used and abused by the Japanese cannot get records on what they know to have happened to them, and thousands of Koreans who worked with the Japanese have simply erased that history as if it had never happened."

Korea's tragedy can only be appreciated fully by contrast to the mellow experience of Taiwan, Japan's other new colony. Neglected by China, Taiwan had never become an independent nation, although an attempt was made in 1661 when a half-Chinese, half-Japanese merchant warlord called Coxinga chased away Dutch traders and set up his own domain there. Unluckily, Coxinga built his headquarters beside a mosquito-infested swamp and died a year later of cerebral malaria, his rebel kingdom collapsing. A play based on his romantic legend became popular in Japan, so many Japanese had an idealized image of Taiwan as an unspoiled paradise, where they could do what they pleased. There was little resistance by native Taiwanese. Unlike Koreans, they had no ancient loathing of Japan, and no experience of war. Most important, they had nothing to steal – no rich cultural patrimony built up over thousands of years, no magnificent artistic heritage, and few big tombs to loot.

In Japan's eagerness to turn what they renamed Formosa into a money-making venture, they made life on the island better than ever before. They rationalized its agriculture, established an efficient government, and imposed strict public order. As always, along with the army, police, and colonial administrators came *yakuza*, carpetbaggers and businessmen looking for local partners. Their chief enterprise was to set up morphine and heroin laboratories, to pour drugs into China's mainland across the strait. By the 1930s, Taiwan also became Japan's most important staging base for the conquest of South China, and Southeast Asia. Huge sums were invested to create a permanent military platform on the island. The First Air Fleet made its headquarters in an underground complex at Kookayama Mountain, with quarters for 1,000 men. From bases on Taiwan, Japanese bombers took off to destroy America's air force on the ground at Clark Field in the Philippines. Conscript labor was not required of Taiwanese until the 1940s, when thousands were sent off to the Philippines as slave labor. But Taiwan's bland experience was an exception. Korea's terrible subjugation and plunder were the norm, as millions of people in China were about to discover.

CHAPTER TWO

ROGUE SAMURAI

Racing through the streets of Tokyo with drawn swords in September 1905, mobs led by Black Dragon thugs burned Christian churches, streetcars, police boxes, and ransacked a pro-government newspaper – all symbols of foreign influence. Riot police charged them with batons and swords, leaving 17 dead and 500 wounded before calm was restored. The riots were staged to intimidate American railway magnate E. H. Harriman, and to discourage Japan's government from selling him the South Manchurian Railway, a war prize from Japan's victory over Tsarist Russia earlier that year.

Harriman watched the smoke and flames from the secure vantage of the Mitsui Club, a mansion near the Imperial Palace. He was not alarmed but amused. The club, staffed with European-trained stewards, interpreters, and hostesses, boasted all the facilities of the finest men's clubs in New York or London. His host, Baron Mitsui, had arranged for Harriman to be entertained by a demonstration of the martial arts. It was performed by Black Dragon boss Uchida, the same man who had arranged the riots. Harriman wanted to buy the South Manchurian Railway to complete a round-the-world transportation network under his exclusive control – a plan that Uchida and Baron Mitsui intended to block. The riots alarmed Japan's government, which decided not to sell Harriman the railway.

While Black Dragon knew all about Harriman, he knew little about them, or their plans for Manchuria. To Japan's superpatriots, Manchuria would be the test bed of empire, and a base from which to invade China. However, Manchuria posed unexpected problems.

Korea had been a poorly guarded warehouse, filled with the wealth of two thousand years. Once Korean resistance was beaten down, it was only a matter of confiscating everything and shipping it to Japan. This was too easy, and the Japanese became complacent, thinking all of Asia would be as facile.

The challenge of Manchuria was different. Though twice as big as Texas, and many times the size of Korea, it was not a packed warehouse but a great wilderness.

Its only conspicuous wealth was in the industrialized cities of the Kwantung Peninsula in the south. The Treaty of Portsmouth, which concluded the Russo-Japanese War, gave Japan all of Russia's interests in South Manchuria, including the commercial port of Dalian, the naval base at Port Arthur, and the southern spur of the Russian-built railway running from Port Arthur north to Changchun. (Eventually, this railroad would open the way for Japan to seize the whole of North China.) Many Russian firms had invested in South Manchuria, so thousands of Russian families there immediately fell prey to Japanese soldiers, *kempeitai*, bureaucrats, and gangsters. But the rest of China's great northeastern province was a vast expanse of desolate mountains and windswept plains, extending north into Siberia and west into Mongolia, inhabited only by poor farmers growing sorghum and other crops that, like the farmers themselves, could somehow endure poor soil, hard summers, and brutal winters. Manchuria's real wealth, like that of Alaska or British Columbia, was in land, forests, and mineral deposits. So Russia and Japan were drawn to Manchuria not by art, antiquities, and gold bullion, but by its strategic position, and fine harbors that controlled naval access to the commercial centers of North China. Railway links would someday bind this region into a hive of prosperity. Till then there was little to steal except land. If Japan were going to squeeze blood out of this stone, it would take determination and ingenuity. Meanwhile, many utopian plans would be abandoned, and the dreamers would turn Manchuria over to the rogues.

Japan's rogues, called *tairiku ronin*, were carpetbaggers, spies, secret policemen, financial conspirators, fanatical gangsters, drug dealers, and eccentric army officers. Together they did what the dreamers could not do. They turned Manchuria into Asia's biggest center for hard drugs, and a black money machine. In the process, they committed Japan to conquer China next.

Manchuria's economy was managed by Japan's South Manchurian Railway Company (Mantetsu). Half of Mantetsu's stock was owned by the Japanese government, with Emperor Hirohito as the largest private shareholder, followed by the Mitsui and Mitsubishi industrial and banking conglomerates, each with its own spy networks. Mitsui spent $500,000 a year to maintain spies. Its overseas business offices provided cover for secret military operations. Driven by patriotism and greed, Mitsui executives collaborated with Black Dragon in stroking and coddling the Kwantung Army – for only the army could grab the Chinese concessions that Mitsui wanted.

Under cover of research, Mantetsu began building a huge intelligence service of its own. Highly-educated Mantetsu researchers provided the army with inside information needed to hijack Chinese resources in Manchuria "to feed the Japanese war machine and to expand the front farther South". Meticulously, they began itemizing China's agricultural, industrial, cultural and personal wealth, for the day when it all could be confiscated. Mantetsu research bureaus soon had branches in Shanghai, Nanking, Hankow, Canton, Hong Kong, and elsewhere. This brain trust flowered into Japan's most influential center for China studies. In time, its experts would be sent to assist the army in looting, all the way south to Java, and west to Burma.

While Mantetsu managed the economy, the Japanese Army applied strong-arm tactics. In 1911, when China's imperial government collapsed, chaos made all of Manchuria vulnerable to aggression. The army pressed local warlords for more and more mining and timber concessions, and the right to extend Mantetsu rail lines in all directions. Mitsui and Mitsubishi made huge unsecured loans to bribe more cooperative warlords, and groups of Japanese officers were assigned to them as advisors. The most powerful warlord, Chang Tso-lin, had fifty Japanese watching him closely. They supplied him with weapons in return for more concessions. A secret arms-supply agency – ironically called the Taiping (Heavenly Peace) Company – was set up by Mitsui in 1907, with the army keeping all but five percent of the profits. This gave Japan's Kwantung Army so much financial independence, its senior officers grew rich. Freed of Tokyo's economic and political control, they turned Manchuria into a separate power base. Here the Kwantung Army could do as it wished. If Tokyo politicians tried to interfere, they would be murdered, and replaced by generals. The Kwantung Army and *tairiku ronin* had become self-sustaining, a dangerously independent force.

Whoever controlled warlord Chang Tso-lin controlled Manchuria. More than a match for the Japanese at first, he played them off against Russians and Chinese. Tough and wily, he was also remarkably charming. The son of a poor seamstress, as a boy Chang had borrowed a hunting rifle, shot a bandit, took his horse, and organized his own cavalry. During the Russo-Japanese War he rented this cavalry to the Japanese for a small fortune. A patriot nonetheless, he then turned against Japan, allying himself to Dr. Sun Yat-sen's Kuomintang Party, the KMT, to block Japanese expansion in Manchuria. In 1916, the Japanese struck back when an assassin threw a bomb into his horse-drawn carriage, but Chang Tso-lin survived and ruled Manchuria twelve more years, collaborating with the Japanese only when it helped him stay in position. A small, delicate, good-looking man with a thin moustache and tiny hands, he cut a dashing, chain-smoking figure in fur-lined greatcoats, always accompanied by beautiful teenage concubines.

During those turbulent years, it was hard to keep track of the warlords without a dance-card. China's northern capital at Peking changed hands frequently. At the end of 1924, 'Christian' warlord Feng Yu-hsiang (who baptized his men with a fire hose) took control and forced the last Manchu emperor, Pu Yi, to vacate the Forbidden City for more modest quarters in the outskirts. A few weeks later, with Japanese backing, Chang Tso-lin arrived with an elite force and expelled General Feng, installing in his place the hard-eyed Marshal Tuan Chi-jui, as the new military boss of North China. With Marshal Tuan as their puppet in Peking, Japan enjoyed a free hand until 1925, when Dr. Sun Yat-sen died and his KMT political party was taken over by conservatives supporting Generalissimo Chiang Kai-shek. This was one of history's fateful turning points, for in April 1927, Generalissimo Chiang turned on his former allies, the communists, staging a bloody purge that crippled the communist urban center, and led to civil war. Whether right or left, patriotism and nationalism were catching on in China, becoming a nuisance to Japan's plans for conquest. Chinese students demanded the return of political and economic concessions wrested from China earlier. In Manchuria, nationalists boycotted Japanese goods, and staged noisy demonstrations. When warlord Chang Tso-lin allowed the boycotts to go ahead, the Japanese were greatly annoyed. After decades of bribing him, they decided to kill him.

His murder was planned by Colonel Komoto Daisaku, one of many Japanese rogue adventurers who carried out conspiracies with Tokyo's blessing. Such men craved fame, excitement, and a share of the spoils. Whatever they did was cloaked in patriotism, so assured of support. To divert suspicion, the colonel blew up minor railway bridges, calling them 'terrorist attacks'. He then poisoned two Chinese gangsters, planted incriminating documents on them, and put their corpses next to track belonging to Chang Tso-lin's company, and mined the track with Russian explosives.

Whenever he traveled, Chang Tso-lin sent his current teenage mistress ahead in a decoy train, following later in his own luxury express. Accompanying him on the night of June 2, 1928, was a Japanese advisor, Major Giga, who earlier had been based in Manila and Shanghai. While the train clattered north through the night, the two men drank beer and played *mah-jong*. Just shy of Fengtien the major excused himself to pee, hurried to the rear of the train, and braced himself with a tight grip on the steel railing. A huge explosion lifted the train and flung it aside, killing Chang Tso-lin and everyone else but Major Giga, who suffered only a few cuts and bruises.

Colonel Komoto expected China to retaliate, giving Tokyo a pretext to send more troops, and seize all of Manchuria. To his dismay, Japan's cabinet refused to send more troops, so the conspiracy fizzled. But the warlord's murder was not in vain. According to the diaries of his own military aides, Emperor Hirohito showed no anger when he heard that officers acting on their own had murdered the Manchurian leader. He personally sanctioned a cover-up, indulged this insubordination, and thereby encouraged the army rogues to continue in the same manner. The emperor's message was clear: Ronin were free to conspire all they wanted, so long as they enlarged Japan's domain.

The dead warlord's son, 'Young Marshal' Chang Hsueh-liang, had a long memory. In 1938, after a lapse of ten years, assassins sent by him tracked Major Giga to the military academy in Tokyo and murdered him.

As killing Chang Tso-lin had not produced the desired results, the Japanese high command next sent its most brilliant and eccentric agent – Lieutenant Colonel Ishihara Kanji. He had served in Berlin, read Nietzsche, and was fascinated by the apocalyptic doctrines of Japan's medieval Buddhist monk Nichiren. This led Ishihara to promote a final, cataclysmic Total War with the West, in which Japan would completely destroy the Soviet Union and America, to become the dominant world power. His suicidal visions excited students at Japan's War College, and contributed to Ishihara's fame as an unorthodox genius.

It was Ishihara's mission to contrive a new incident where Japan would seem the victim, China the bully. Whatever Japan did would then seem defensive and justified. (Historian Louise Young said: "Inverting the roles of victim and aggressor ... transformed a Japanese military conspiracy into a righteous war of self-defense.")

For three years Ishihara waited for the right moment. Then Generalissimo Chiang gave it to him.

In spring 1931, the Generalissimo refused to extend the lease to Manchuria's Kwantung Peninsula, demanding that Japanese forces pull out and relinquish the railway system that was Mantetsu's heart and soul. Tokyo refused, denouncing China's government as anti-Japanese. Tempers rose as native Manchurian farmers attacked Japanese immigrants, and were put down harshly by Japanese police. A minor fracas, it was inflated to war frenzy by the Japanese media. In a separate incident, a Japanese officer carrying surveying instruments and packs of narcotics for bribes was arrested by Chinese soldiers and executed on the spot.

Here was the moment Colonel Ishihara had been waiting for. He blew up a lonely stretch of Mantetsu track and blamed the 'sabotage' on Chinese soldiers. In what was called self-defense, the Kwantung Army swarmed onto a Chinese base at Fengtien, used artillery to flatten crowded barracks, then machine-gunned Chinese soldiers as they scrambled out of the rubble. In the confusion, following Ishihara's game plan, the Kwantung Army waged a series of lightning campaigns that brought four provinces of northeast China under its control, including all 440,000 square miles of Manchuria. To dress up the aggression, Japan announced that Manchuria would now become the 'independent' nation of Manchukuo.

China had so many problems it was unprepared for war. Generalissimo Chiang ordered Chinese soldiers not to resist. But he vigorously protested the seizure of Manchuria, and demanded that the League of Nations intervene. According to Prince Mikasa, Hirohito's youngest brother, the League of Nations delegation sent to Manchuria, headed by the Earl of Lytton, was served fruit laced with cholera germs in an attempt to frustrate their fact-finding mission. Luckily, no one in Lytton's team got sick. They concluded that the Manchurian Incident was phony, the state of Manchukuo was only a Japanese puppet, and Tokyo had committed aggression. When the League of Nations endorsed Lytton's report in spring 1933, Japan's delegation withdrew from the League, committing Japan to a collision with its Western rivals.

War fever was sweeping Japan. Magazines and newsreels gave heavy coverage to army actions, boasting that ten Japanese could defeat a hundred Chinese. All Chinese were engaging in "looting, violence and atrocities". Killing Chinese civilians was justified because "anyone in the street in Manchuria [is] a plainclothes soldier". In one of the more outrageous justifications of rape and murder, a Japanese soldier told readers, "Everybody thinks that only men are plainclothes soldiers. But there are women, kids... all kinds. Once a young woman of twenty-two...came up to me looking very friendly... But then I had a bad feeling...and I shouted out a warning. ...I strip-searched the girl...she couldn't understand me so I gestured with my hands ... Underneath her clothes she was wearing two pairs of panties. Hidden inside, sure enough, there was a pistol. I did not want to kill her but she tried to hit me with the gun and that was why she died... I was provoked."

Glorification and public hysteria drove government and business leaders to give the army all it wanted, to carry out its Manchurian Experiment.

Manchukuo became a Japanese Army dictatorship fronted by the figurehead Pu Yi, the last Manchu emperor of China, rescued from 'evil warlords' in Peking. Spirited out of Peking by Colonel Doihara Kenji, Pu Yi was kept temporarily in luxurious quarters at the Japanese concession in the port of Tientsin. Doihara was one of Japan's top secret agents. He posed as mayor of Mukden in Manchuria, but was actually director of military intelligence for the whole region. He read widely, including the works of T.E. Lawrence, so he was called the Lawrence of Manchuria. Unlike Lawrence, Doihara was overweight and deceptively mild-looking. He knew where all the bodies were buried, having put many there himself. When he first offered to make Pu Yi an emperor again, the young man hesitated. With plenty of money and amusement, why should Pu Yi involve himself in tedious ritual and protocol? Doihara insisted. To make his point, he sent Pu Yi a basket of fruit containing an unexploded bomb.

Once in the palace at Changchun, Pu Yi and Empress Elizabeth were supplied with heroin by Doihara and watched over by his sidekick Major Tanaka Takayoshi. Here was another old China hand, a great bull of a man who had spent two decades running covert operations in Shanghai. Tanaka saw to it that Empress Elizabeth was sexually exhausted by the attentions of a 24-year-old Manchu princess called Eastern Jewel – a daughter of Prince Su – who had served the Rising Sun with both men and women since her late teens. Rounding out the group was Colonel Itagaki Seishiro, a bon vivant who later became Japan's war minister. Their counterpart as chief of the military secret police in Manchukuo was Colonel Tojo Hideki, later to be Japan's wartime prime minister. From 1932 to 1936, this quartet of Doihara, Tanaka, Itagaki, and Tojo ran all black operations in Manchukuo, including kidnapping, extortion, and murder.

On his enthronement, Pu Yi was congratulated by Hirohito, who sent his brother Prince Chichibu to the coronation. (Congratulations also came from Chang Yuching, one of Shanghai's underworld bosses.) In June 1935, Pu Yi flew to Tokyo, where Hirohito held a banquet in his honor. Pu Yi responded by helping Japan plunder northeast China. Before he was kicked out of the Forbidden City, Pu Yi had removed a hoard of imperial treasure. He later admitted to taking "the most valuable pictures, calligraphy and antiques in the imperial collections out of the palace by pretending that I was giving them to [my brother] Pu Chieh…" These included imperial seals of the Emperor Chien-lung, and thousands of manuscripts, scrolls and paintings. He said, "Pu Chieh [also] used to take a large bundle home after school every day for over six months, and the things we took were the very finest treasures in the collections. As it happened, the heads of the Household Department and my tutors were checking through the pictures and the calligraphy at the time, so all we had to do was to take the items they selected as being of the very highest grade. In addition to paintings and calligraphy we also took many valuable ancient editions of books. We must have removed over a thousand hand scrolls, more than two hundred hanging scrolls and pages from albums, and about two hundred rare Sung Dynasty printed books." These were moved to Manchuria and stored on the palace compound in a small white building behind the Hall of Harmony and Virtue. Later, Pu Yi said, "when it was becoming increasingly obvious that Japan was losing the war… I spontaneously gave a lot of gold, silver and jewelry to the Kwantung Army. …I presented them with the carpets from the palace floors and hundreds of items of clothing. All these actions of mine were widely publicized and made the task of looting easier for the Japanese officials…" When the puppet kingdom of Manchukuo collapsed in August 1945, all these treasures had vanished, shipped to Japan long in advance of the surrender.

Once Pu Yi was enthroned, the Kwantung Army launched its hugely expensive attempt to industrialize Manchuria overnight as a model of central-controlled state capitalism. To justify the cost, Manchuria was promoted as the solution to all Japan's problems. Its agricultural potential, mineral wealth, industry, and cheap Chinese labor, would boom overnight, providing Japan with a broad range of industrial and consumer goods. Bright young economic planners rushed to Manchuria to perform magic, foremost among them Kishi Nobosuke. He put Mantetsu under the control of one relative, and put Manchuria's economy in the hands of another, who headed the Nissan *zaibatsu*. Kishi's circle was called the *Ni-ki-san-suke* clique (the 'two ki, three suke' clique). The two 'ki' were men whose names ended in 'ki': General Tojo Hideki, now the Kwantung Army chief of staff, and the opium monopoly boss Hoshino Naoki, who later became Emperor Hirohito's chief cabinet secretary. The three others were economist Kishi Nobusuke, Mantetsu president Matsuoka Yosuke, and Nissan boss Aikawa Gisuke, whose names ended in 'suke'. They controlled everything in Manchuria through a mega-corporation called Manchurian Heavy Industries. Nissan provided the brains. Tojo supplied the muscle.

They spent recklessly. Between 1932 and 1938, forty-eight Manchurian cities were laid out with running water, sewer systems, flush toilets, electricity, gas, telegraph, roads, railway, and military facilities. Japanese government funds poured in. Financiers in Osaka and Tokyo had serious doubts, but they feared being murdered if they did not support the army. What was not borrowed from banks was stolen.

The Kwantung Army had deep pockets because it looted all the banks in Manchuria. The day after Colonel Ishihara staged his bogus Manchurian Incident, in September 1931, the Kwantung Army advanced into Mukden and seized all the assets of the Frontier Bank, and the Bank of the Three Eastern Provinces, and their administrative records. While soldiers sealed the borders, Tojo's *kempeitai* stormed all branches of the Kirin Provincial Bank, and the Heilungkiang Provincial Bank. All these banks were Chinese owned and operated. The assets were used to set up the Central Bank of Manchukuo, which printed its own occupation scrip, posing as the new national currency. Everyone was ordered to exchange Chinese money for this scrip. The Choson Bank of Korea (a Japanese bank based in Korea) established twenty branches in Manchuria to help carry out this vandalism; its New York office hustled American loans for the development of Manchuria, which were never repaid.

Another source of easy money was extortion. Simon Kaspe, son of a Jewish hotel and theater owner in Harbin, was kidnapped in 1933. When a ransom note arrived demanding $100,000 his father refused to pay. Although Japanese police 'cooperated' in searching for the boy, many in the Jewish community suspected that the *kempeitai* was involved in the kidnapping. On December 3, Simon Kaspe's body was found; he had been beaten, starved, tortured, mutilated, and kept in an underground pit, before he was finally shot. The extreme brutality was taken as evidence that it was done by Tojo's *kempeitai* or its Black Dragon or Black Ocean allies. At his funeral, mourners shouted "Down with the *kempeitai*!", "Down with the Imperial Japanese Army!" Police arrested some alleged kidnappers. They were tried, then released. Outraged but frightened, the Jewish community in Manchuria began crossing the border to settle in what they hoped would be more peaceful circumstances in China.

Bank robberies, currency fraud, and extortion could be done only once or twice before the victims were exhausted. Steadier cash flow came from narcotics, which became Manchukuo's chief product. Accounts of the Manchurian Experiment avoid this dark side. In fact, Japan as a whole became deeply involved in Manchurian opium, heroin and morphine production. In 1911, the region had produced less than 2,500 kilos of opium. Fifteen years later annual production on Mantetsu territory, and huge farms taken over by the Japanese underworld, rose to 36,000 kilos. After Japan seized all of Manchuria in 1932, tens of thousands of hectares were put under poppy production, and dozens of laboratories were built to convert opium tar into various grades of morphine and heroin. Under protection of the Kwantung Army, drug traffickers in Manchuria spread their distribution across the Great Wall, down into North and Central China. The Central Bank of Manchukuo built up major reserves from profits generated by the army drug monopoly. Pharmaceutical factories flooded China with heroin tablets, to soften it up for invasion.

The Opium Monopoly was directed by Hoshino Naoki, one of the ruling *Ni-ki-san-suke* clique, a former tax official who managed all Manchukuo's financial affairs. Thus the economy of Japanese Manchuria was inextricably bound to hard drugs. Later, when Naoki was promoted to become Emperor Hirohito's chief cabinet secretary, a direct link was established between the emperor and Japan's massive drug trade. Given this link, it would be hard to believe that Hirohito was ignorant of Japan's profiteering in narcotics. In 1934, the Opium Advisory Commission in Geneva accused Japan of operating the world's largest single venture in illicit drugs. Japan gave farmers in Manchuria cash-incentives to take up poppy cultivation. It was Mitsui itself, Japan's oldest *zaibatsu* (today one of the world's richest conglomerates), that processed the opium into morphine and heroin. The Opium Monopoly actively encouraged addiction, hooking new users by distributing free medicines spiked with morphine, and free cigarettes trademarked Golden Bat, laced with heroin. This drug-trade grew quickly into a major source of income for the Kwantung Army, estimated to have been as much as $300-million a year ($3-billion a year in today's values). Hoshino was able to use heroin futures as collateral for bank loans. Both the *kempeitai* and Special Section 8 of the Imperial Intelligence Division operated narcotics dens. By 1937, ninety percent of the world's illicit opium and morphine were of Japanese origin. The Manchurian Experiment had changed from a fantasy to a pipedream.

Manchuria also became the main proving ground for Japan's biological warfare program, called simply Unit 731. Headquartered at Ping Fan, outside Harbin, it was headed by Colonel Ishii Shiro, a 1920 graduate of Kyoto University, who persuaded the high command to let him develop chemical and biological weapons, and test them on Chinese in Manchuria. Pu Yi said he learned that his subjects were being enslaved by the Japanese to build these installations, then were poisoned to keep the locations secret. Later, during the Pacific War, other labs were set up in Peking, Canton, and Singapore, experimenting on Allied POWs and civilian prisoners. Emperor Hirohito was briefed about it in detail during at least one recorded meeting with Colonel Ishii. The emperor's brothers toured Ping Fan to observe experiments. Prince Mikasa, Hirohito's youngest brother, revealed after the war that he had seen films in which "large numbers of Chinese prisoners of war...were made to march on the Manchurian plain for poison gas experiments on live subjects". Others, he said, were "tied to posts in a wide field [and] gassed and shot. It was a horrible scene that could only be termed a massacre."

Narcotics aside, by 1936 Manchuria's boom was acknowledged to be an expensive failure. Its products were inferior, consumer goods were in short supply; not enough coal or other material was available to supply the needs of its private industry. The system of economic controls invented by Kishi was a botch, dragging down Japan's home economy as well. The child was cannibalizing its parent. Even so, fortunes were made in sweetheart deals cooked by Kishi, who arranged unsecured loans at zero interest. In exchange for these loans, kickbacks were paid to Kishi, other members of his clique, and the Kwantung Army brass.

There are many ways to plunder a country. What happened in Manchuria was different from what had happened in Korea, but the end result was the same. Like any binge, it did not last long. From the seizure of all of Manchuria in 1932, to recognition of the army's failure in 1936, only four years passed. For the victims, time passed differently.

The Kwantung Army was stoned on its success with narcotics. Some officers recognized that the wealth generated by drugs, and by the looting of Korea and Manchuria, was artificial, the result of armed robbery. But that's what they did for a living. While there was more to be stolen, why stop? Planners said the Manchurian Experiment could yet be made to work, if the army seized control of China, putting Japan in monopoly control of that vast consumer market. If utopia did not work in Manchuria, it would work in China. And if it did not work in China, well, there was still Southeast Asia, India, and Australia.

The army was impatient. With so many careers at stake, and so many young officers moving up the ranks hoping to share the glory, stopping was out of the question. Everyone looked longingly at the 'unopened treasure house' just across the Great Wall to the south.

CHAPTER THREE

THE RAPE OF CHINA

In the rest of China, Japan's violent seizure of Manchuria provoked rage and apprehension. Many believed the Japanese would continue to bite off parts of China in the years ahead, until they swallowed the entire country. A Mantetsu researcher said: "We need to think more about why it was that our good intentions…did not communicate to the Chinese masses." In Shanghai, portraits of Hirohito were paraded with paper daggers piercing his heart. Chinese newspapers reported a failed attempt by a Korean patriot to assassinate Hirohito, the bullet hitting another carriage. Ten days later, on January 18, 1932, five young Japanese dressed as Buddhist monks paraded down a crowded Shanghai street, singing songs celebrating Japan's victories. Outraged Chinese lynched one of them on the spot. The monks were expendable agents sent by Special Services Major Tanaka Ryuchi. The provocation was staged to give Japan an excuse to intervene, to protect its citizens. The Imperial Navy had ships stationed in Shanghai's Whangpoo River, to guard its commercial interests. Japanese marines poured ashore. Hundreds of *yakuza* and Black Dragon thugs joined the fray, armed with Mauser pistols, rifles, swords, and baseball bats. The fight was joined by the Chinese 19th Route Army camped outside the city. With Hirohito's approval, 90,000 additional Japanese troops were rushed in. Parts of the city were flattened by field artillery and naval guns, while Japanese aircraft strafed and bombed the crowded streets; some 18,000 civilians were killed, and 240,000 Chinese lost their homes. Amazed Westerners watched from the relative safety of rooftops in the International Settlement and French Concession. During Japan's takeover of Korea and Manchuria, only a handful of Western observers were present, mostly diplomats. In Shanghai, thousands of foreigners were eyewitnesses to Japan's overkill. Among journalists caught in the crossfire, Ernest Hauser reported that "dogs and rats were celebrating a holiday of their own: there were places where one could no longer distinguish the corpses beneath the ravenous packs". In London, Japan's ambassador Yoshida Shigeru said the assault on Shanghai had been a "grave miscalculation". Thomas Lamont of the House of Morgan lamented that Tokyo's action would make it "impossible to arrange any [further] credit [for Japan], either through investment or banking circles". On March 2, after thirty-four days of fighting, the 19th Route Army began a general retreat. Next day, Japan declared a unilateral truce, followed by an official armistice. The Japanese Army would return five years later, in the summer of 1937, to finish the job.

At the time, the image of China was as the sick man of Asia, a country of unparalleled corruption and vice, on the verge of collapse. Many Westerners thought China was so decadent it had been bled of its wealth long ago. Nothing could be further from the truth. The wealth that changed hands from one warlord to another did not evaporate, and was minor compared to what remained deeply hidden. The repeated plunder of Peking took away quantities of imperial treasure, to be sure, but did not disturb bullion, artworks, and patrimony belonging to the aristocracy, to merchant families, or to racketeers and gangsters. Because they had good reason not to trust anyone outside the family or clan, Chinese did not put their liquid assets in banks; they kept quantities of gems and small gold bars called biscuits, ingeniously hidden. For three thousand years, the Chinese had been a society of antiquarians, art critics, and collectors. They acquired ancient bronzes, porcelains, jades, books, scrolls, paintings, and other fine decorative arts. Shang bronzes in particular were coveted. These collections were catalogued, and the catalogs themselves became precious records shared by collectors and purveyors of antiquities. Copies of these catalogs were purchased by Japanese collectors; there was no great mystery about who in China owned what. At the beginning of the twentieth century, China's imperial collections alone included over 100,000 pieces of priceless jade, varying in size from several inches to several feet, carved by artists over many centuries, plus over 1.2-million books and manuscripts, and porcelains in the millions.

For the Japanese, the only challenge was how to find the gold, platinum, jade and gems laid down in private hoards, because wealthy Chinese were obsessively secret. In *Lords of the Rim*, we traced China's evolving merchant class from ancient times to present global networks of super-rich Overseas Chinese, who are thought to control over $3-trillion in assets worldwide. Because emperors always had a monopoly on trade disguised as tribute, all other commerce was illegal in China, punishable by death. Merchants were targets of repression, and were imprisoned or exiled with their families to 'barbarian' lands beyond the frontiers. So in China all business traditionally was done covertly, as an illicit underworld, bribing magistrates to look the other way. By necessity, the bulk of China's wealth remained out of sight, carefully hidden. Only toward the end of the nineteenth century did the crumbling Manchu regime permit merchants to come above ground, partly as a grudging concession to Western influence, but mostly for tax revenues. Western banks in the treaty ports were off-limits to Chinese, but native banking networks existed to serve particular merchant clans, and pawnshops provided loans to farmers. A parallel situation existed in Japan, historically, because rulers and samurai alike regarded merchants as vermin. So the Japanese understood that China's treasure would not be lying around waiting to be confiscated. Seizing this hidden wealth became a glorious obsession for Japan's financiers. The *zaibatsu* vigorously backed army conquest, hoping to gain control of China's well-developed mineral resources, industrial base, and immense consumer market, but the heads of these corporations had their own personal collections to enlarge.

When we think of looting in the West, we think of banks, museums, palaces, cathedrals and mansions, and overlook black money sources. In China, all money was black. It could not be stolen without the use of extortion and terror.

Japan's rogue samurai had gained practical experience in extortion and terror in Korea and Manchuria. They left to the *kempeitai* obvious targets like banks, museums and mansions, and turned their own attention to finding personal fortunes, and great pools of wealth from drugs, alcohol, prostitution, gambling, smuggling and other rackets. To make it easy, they reached temporary partnerships with Chinese racketeers, hard men who felt no remorse about victimizing their own countrymen. It was this unholy alliance of rogues and racketeers that caused China in the 1930s and 1940s to hemorrhage treasure like never before.

Haphazard collaboration between the Japanese underworld and the Chinese underworld had been going on for centuries. For example, Chinese trading networks based in coastal Fukien province had oceangoing junks voyaging as far west as Africa and Arabia. Each syndicate had its own private navy and marines, with treasuries of gold biscuits stashed in strongholds along the coast and offshore in island strongholds. Since their common enemy was China's imperial government, the natural allies of these pirate syndicates were the Japanese. Traders from Fukien often sought refuge in Japan's Goto Islands, on the southwest coast of Kyushu, where they were protected by the domain lord. His samurai often joined the pirates to pillage the south bank of the Yangtze, where there were many wealthy estates. So, in the twentieth century, it was natural for Japanese and Chinese gangsters to renew this profitable random collaboration.

If there was a single genius behind the underworld alliance, it was General Doihara, the mastermind of the Manchurian drug trade, whose personal circle included Japan's top gangsters. He was also on first-name terms with leaders of China's Green Gang, based in Shanghai. Above ground, Shanghai was administered by three governments. Biggest was the Chinese municipality, run by the KMT regime of Generalissimo Chiang Kai-shek. Next were two prosperous foreign enclaves, concessions squeezed from the Manchu throne in the nineteenth century. The smaller was the French Concession with a population of around 500,000. To say it was French is an exaggeration as there were only about 2,400 French civilians and 300 French gendarmes. The rest were 14,000 Europeans of various nationalities including White Russians, and Chinese who preferred French rule to Chinese tyranny. The French Concession was home to China's most powerful godfather, Tu Yueh-sheng, boss of the Green Gang. He enjoyed French protection in return for generous contributions from rackets in drugs, brothels and gambling.

Beyond the French Concession was the International Settlement, dominated by Britain and, to a lesser extent, America. Its foreign population was less than 40,000. In China as a whole, Britain's influence was pre-eminent, and her government and citizens had nearly $1-billion dollars invested there, most of it in Shanghai. By the 1920s, however, the largest single foreign community in Shanghai was Japanese, mostly businessmen, bankers, hoteliers, gangsters and secret agents. Hostile toward Westerners and Chinese, the Japanese inhabited a district called Little Tokyo in the suburb of Hongkew. Many of them were advance agents of invasion. Japan had been preparing feverishly, using industrial cover. All over East and Southeast Asia, military projects were under way, including airfields, port facilities, and coastal surveys. Right in the heart of Shanghai's riverfront, Japanese companies bought three large wharves and dug a tunnel from those warehouses to a reinforced-concrete Japanese Army headquarters and arsenal on Jiangwan Road.

Little was done in Shanghai without the knowledge of Boss Tu, who took a bite of every pastry. Businessmen who refused to pay off Tu risked being kidnapped or shot, or having their houses bombed. Once Tu abducted May-ling Soong, bride of Chiang Kai-shek, to remind the generalissimo who really was in charge. By 1932, 44-year-old Boss Tu already had a great fortune. He was a self-made man with a vengeance, born in desperate poverty across the river in Putung, in a squalid slum called Kaochiao, his father a coolie in a grain shop. In his teens, Tu became a runner for the drug-lord of the French Concession, a chief detective known as Pockmarked Huang. At the time there were three gangs – Red, Green and Blue – competing for control of the drug trade. Tu showed Pockmarked Huang how they could work together as a cartel. Eventually, the Red and Blue gangs withered, leaving Tu's Green Gang in charge of all rackets far up the Yangtze River into China's interior.

By the 1930s, gambling was on a greater scale in Shanghai than anywhere else on earth, with proceeds of more than $1-million a week. Tu's three-storey Fushen Casino on Avenue Foch provided customers with chauffeured limousines. There was dog racing at Tu's Canidrome. Over 100,000 prostitutes worked in brothels, cabarets and dance halls like Farren's and Del Monte's where White Russian women danced and more with paying clients.

Once they understood each other, Tu became one of Chiang Kai-shek's chief backers. He shared drug profits directly with the generalissimo, and in return was licensed by the KMT government. This allowed Chiang to pretend that he was pursuing an aggressive campaign of opium suppression. But only Tu's rivals were suppressed. The Opium Suppression Bureau turned over confiscated opium to the Green Gang, for conversion to heroin and morphine. The generalissimo received his cut through the Farmers Bank of China, owned by Tu and referred to sarcastically as the Opium Farmers Bank. Chiang used his cut to upgrade his army, which annoyed Tokyo.

During the initial Japanese assault on Shanghai in 1932, Boss Tu sent Green Gang toughs to fight the invaders. Chiang praised him for this gallant display of patriotism, but it was only turf warfare. Tu was not prepared to let the Japanese undermine his control of gambling, prostitution and narcotics. General Doihara worked out a compromise by which the Green Gang, the KMT regime, and the Japanese, secretly divided the spoils, much as the Red, Blue and Green Gangs had done earlier. The deal was implemented by the Ku brothers, one of whom was the Green Gang boss of the Shanghai waterfront, while the other was a KMT general.

This enabled the *kempeitai* to open its first Shanghai brothel in 1932, while

Japanese investors started cotton mills, ironworks, railways, paper mills, power plants and banks. Where once British shipping dominated, Japanese steamships linked Yangtze River ports deep into the interior, ready to be converted into troop carriers.

In violation of the deal, Japan began to subvert the KMT opium monopoly by bringing in larger and larger quantities of drugs. What better way to demoralize China than by flooding it with cheap drugs from Manchuria, including heroin tablets and cigarettes laced with heroin. This caused dismay and consternation in KMT and Green Gang circles. The Japanese were growing opium on an unprecedented scale in Manchuria, supplementing it with opium imported by ship from Iran. The paste was converted into morphine and heroin at factories in Manchuria, Korea and Taiwan, then smuggled directly across the strait on motorized junks, to mainland warehouses owned by Mitsui, Mitsubishi, and other conglomerates. An army factory in Seoul that produced over 2,600 kilos of heroin in 1938-39 was only one of several hundred factories in Manchuria, Korea, Taiwan, and in Japanese concessions in mainland cities like Hankow. At its peak, more than a thousand Japanese firms were manufacturing and selling drugs, including cocaine and amphetamines.

Japan so undercut Green Gang prices that at one point the generalissimo ordered his men to buy narcotics from the Japanese, and sell them at a mark-up in areas controlled exclusively by the KMT.

By the end of 1936, the Manchurian Experiment had failed and Tokyo was ready to seize the whole of China. The first step was to stage an incident outside Peking, as an excuse to overrun the northern capital. On July 8, 1937, a Kwantung Army regimental commander at Fengtai near the Marco Polo Bridge ordered his men to fire on a Chinese barracks in retaliation for an imaginary insult. Emperor Hirohito was reluctant to commit too many troops to China when there was growing Soviet pressure along the Siberian frontier. But advisors reassured him that "war with China ... could be finished within two or three months".

China also miscalculated. The generalissimo's brother-in-law, Finance Minister T.V. Soong, scoffed, "within three months... Japan will be on the verge of bankruptcy and facing revolution". Both predictions were wildly off. The Marco Polo Bridge incident escalated into a China War that bogged down nearly a million Japanese troops for eight years, and then it was China that faced bankruptcy and revolution.

As all northeast China came under Japan's control, President Franklin Roosevelt threatened trade embargoes, to stop the 'epidemic' of Japanese aggression.

To preserve his own KMT army, which was his only means of staying in power, Generalissimo Chiang abandoned all of North China, and crossed to the south bank of the Yangtze River. This shifted the focus of confrontation, exposing Shanghai and other big southern cities to attack. On August 7, 1937, Chiang decided to stage a pre-emptive strike on the Japanese at Shanghai, hoping to draw America and Britain into the conflict, to protect their own investments. Three KMT divisions attacked the small Japanese garrison of 5,000 men in Hongkew. Both sides quickly threw in additional forces. But indecision and wrong moves by

Chiang Kai-shek squandered his numeric advantage, as the Japanese countered with superior tactics, training and equipment. There was incredible bungling. On August 14, Chinese air force planes intending to sink the Japanese flagship *Izumo* in the Whangpoo River dropped their bombs prematurely into crowded city streets, with gruesome consequences. In one month of fighting, nearly a quarter million Chinese were killed, many of them women and children. During the confusion (to Tokyo's dismay), all Chinese banks, industries, and financiers loaded their wealth onto convoys of trucks, and hurried into the French Concession or the International Settlement, where they were protected by the warships of the Western Powers.

The Chinese army fought bravely until early November, when Chiang suddenly and inexplicably moved his armies and his headquarters 180 miles west along the Yangtze to Nanking. Pursuing the generalissimo westward, the Imperial Army ravaged the beautiful ancient city of Soochow, giving a foretaste of what was to come. As the Japanese began to circle Nanking, the generalissimo decided once more to abandon his civilian population without a fight. First he withdrew upriver to Wuhan, then five hundred miles farther up the Yangtze to Chungking in the mountains of Szechuan Province, safe from all but the most determined conqueror. There, he set up his wartime government, and told the world he still ruled China.

Chiang took with him hundreds of big wood crates filled with art treasures. Anticipating the worst, he had ordered his secret police chief, General Tai Li, to crate up the contents of the national museum in Peking, and as many art treasures as could be assembled from other museums. Ultimately, these crates were sent deep into the western mountains, to Chengtu. But there were limits to what could be crated and shipped.

Just before the Japanese began their assault on Nanking, Emperor Hirohito sent his uncle, Prince Asaka Yasuhiko, to take over command from General Matsui Iwane, who was suffering from tuberculosis. In any aristocracy there are always extreme nationalists and racists with a narrow education, and Japan was no exception. Men like Prince Asaka regarded themselves as demigods, and felt only contempt for Chinese, Koreans, and other Asians. In addition, he was an alcoholic, given to wild bouts of drunken rage. On taking command outside Nanking, he told his aides that it was time to "teach our Chinese brothers a lesson they will never forget".

In the Rape of Nanking that followed, some 300,000 defenseless civilians were slain by Japanese troops, between 20,000 and 80,000 women of all ages were raped repeatedly, including children, adolescent girls, and grandmothers, many of them disemboweled in the process. Men, women and children were subjected to acts of such barbarism that the world recoiled in horror. Thousands of men were roped together and machine-gunned, or doused with gasoline and set afire. Others were used for bayonet practice, or to practice beheading, in a sporting competition to see which officer could behead the greatest number that day. Weeks passed while atrocities continued, streets and alleys piled high with corpses. Unlike previous mass atrocities, done out of sight, these were witnessed by hundreds of Westerners including diplomats, doctors and missionaries, some of whom smuggled out photographic evidence.

It was at this bitter moment that Golden Lily came into existence.

When the Japanese Army swarmed down the China Coast in 1937, crossed the Yangtze, and moved westward to Nanking, so many units were involved across such a broad front that there was danger of Japan's ruling elite losing control of the financial side of conquest, as rival commanders competed for spoils. How could you keep army or navy officers from side-tracking gold bullion and priceless art works, not to mention smaller scale theft by soldiers? At the same time, groups of *yakuza* were moving through newly occupied areas, conducting their own reign of terror. To keep everything under strict control at the highest level, the Imperial General Headquarters created Golden Lily (*kin no yuri*), named after one of Hirohito's poems. This was to be a palace organization of Japan's top financial minds and specialists in all forms of treasure including cultural and religious antiquities, supported by accountants, bookkeepers, shipping experts, and units of the army and navy, all overseen by princes of the blood. When China was milked by Golden Lily, the army would hold the cow, while princes skimmed the cream. This organization was put directly under the command of the emperor's brother, Prince Chichibu. We know the date because the Imperial General Headquarters itself was only set up in the imperial palace in Tokyo in November 1937, just as the Rape of Nanking was commencing. The purpose of the Imperial Headquarters was to keep control of the war in the hands of the emperor and his senior advisors, to avoid repeating what happened in Manchuria, where the Kwantung Army grew recklessly independent in all respects. The Imperial Army already had a number of Special Service Units, among them intelligence teams specializing in different kinds of cultural and financial espionage, and secret service agents like General Doihara, outside the ordinary command structure. These were reassigned to Golden Lily, giving it the resources needed to find treasure of all kinds, from the sublime to the most prosaic.

In Nanking, the first wave of Golden Lily helpers were *kempeitai*. Special *kempeitai* units moved through the city seizing all government assets, blowing open bank vaults, breaking into and emptying homes of wealthy families of whatever gold, gemstones, jewelry, artworks, and currency could be found. Nanking had been rich for over a thousand years. Many wealthy and prominent Chinese had mansions in town, and estates in the surrounding countryside. This was not the only time Nanking was ransacked by conquerors, but it was by far the most deliberate, meticulous, and systematic. At least 6,000 metric tons of gold are reported to have been amassed by the *kempeitai* during this first pass. Historical research into looting shows that what is officially reported typically is only a tiny fraction of what is actually stolen. Also looted were many of the small biscuit bars that individual Chinese prefer to hoard, along with small platinum ingots, diamonds, rubies and sapphires, small works of art, and antiquities. These were taken from private homes and from tombs vandalized by the army in the countryside. Remorselessly thorough, the Japanese hammered the teeth out of corpses to extract gold fillings.

While the *kempeitai* removed even the furniture, mirrors and rugs for crating and shipment to Japan, Golden Lily's Special Service Units – the elite of the secret service – focused on individual Chinese who owned banks, headed guilds, ran pawn shop networks, or were the elders of clan associations. Particular attention was paid to heads of triads, and racketeers. Although some escaped from the city, relatives were tracked down, taken into custody, and used for leverage. In this methodical fashion, Japan went far beyond the wild pillaging of Mongol hordes, or the drunken rampaging of British and French troops at the Summer Palace in Peking.

Golden Lily was driven by greed but also by necessity. In 1937 Japan's gold reserves had shrunk by half, paying for the military machine. Princes of the first tier personally compiled inventories of everything stolen, then shipped it to Shanghai in railway carriages and freight cars guarded by special army units. Military commanders thought twice before offending the princes.

Prince Chichibu was well chosen as Golden Lily's overseer. Unlike Hirohito, whose education as crown prince had been narrow and tightly controlled, Chichibu had been permitted a cosmopolitan education with foreign travel, part of a year at Oxford University, holidays climbing in the Swiss Alps, and diplomatic assignments including dinner with Adolf Hitler. Of Hirohito's three brothers, he had the most evident sense of humor, and indulged in the least likely amusements: roller skating with his young wife in the upstairs hallways of their Tokyo palace. When we first learned from Japanese sources that Chichibu headed Golden Lily, we were puzzled, because his independent spirit seemed ill-suited for extremes of brutality. However, what was at stake was the national treasury, on which depended the survival of the dynasty. Because of the breadth of his education and foreign experience, Chichibu was the best choice. His relatively broad mind enabled him to grasp readily the spectrum of possibilities for plunder put to him by his advisors.

Extraordinary pains were taken by Prince Chichibu to see that only princes carried out final inventories, or sealed the containers of treasure being sent home. From Shanghai, the plunder was shipped by sea directly to the Home Islands, or was carried by freight train or truck convoy to Manchuria, where precious metals were graded, jewelry and irregular pieces were melted and recast in uniform ingots, before onward shipment through Korea to Japan.

A number of other princes joined Golden Lily at this stage, spending the war enriching Japan, rather than participating in less glamorous and dangerous combat assignments. Aside from Prince Asaka, we know Prince Chichibu and Prince Takeda were at Nanking because both later confided to friends that they had horrific nightmares from witnessing atrocities. Some sources insist that Hirohito's youngest brother, Prince Mikasa, also was physically present at Nanking; this has not been confirmed, although he was positively identified later at Golden Lily sites in the Philippines.

A prime example of Japan's extraordinary attention to detail was a handpicked Special Service Unit of antiquarians with special knowledge of rare books and manuscripts. Some were militant monks from the Nichiren sect. Their job was to pick through the contents of China's libraries, museums and private collections, or the libraries of Buddhist orders, and send these treasures back to Tokyo. Before the campaign began, they traveled widely in China, befriending private collectors, compiling lists of the most valuable items.

In spring 1938, after the rape, more than a thousand of these experts arrived in

Nanking to begin picking through collections of rare books and manuscripts. While much of the city was in ruins, buildings housing these collections had been put under tight security. The Imperial Palace Library would have first choice of this plunder, and the very best items were set aside for the emperor's personal review. Each item was carefully numbered, wrapped and placed in a waterproof crate. Multiple copies of inventories were made to ensure that nothing vanished on the way home. Some 2,300 Chinese conscript laborers did the physical toil of packing, watched closely by 400 soldiers. Over 300 trucks were needed to move the crates to Shanghai, for loading on ships.

In Tokyo, some of these stolen books were used to set up the Institute of East Asian Studies, Institute of Oriental Culture, Institute of East Asian Economy, Institute of Endemic Disease in East Asia, Great East Asia Library, and others.

After the war, Chinese scholars began demanding the return of these treasures. America was aware of the theft, having conducted a survey that identified seventeen locations in Japan where looted books were kept, among them the Imperial Palace, the Imperial Household Ministry, Yasukuni Shrine, Tokyo Science Museum, Tokyo Art College, Waseda University, Tokyo Imperial University, and Keio University. U.S. occupation authorities concluded that Japan was holding nearly 3-million precious books and manuscripts taken from Chinese libraries. Today, scholars call Japan's libraries the finest in Asia, because Japan has returned very little of what she stole. China recovered fewer than 160,000 volumes, less than six percent.

While Golden Lily teams were hard at work plundering China, so were Japanese tycoons like Sumitomo Kichizaemon, head of Japan's immense Sumitomo conglomerate. He specialized in looting Shang bronzes. Sumitomo began his collection with trophies stolen during the 1900 Siege of the Legations in Peking, and continued during the takeover of Manchuria and North China. But it was only during the eight year China Incident from 1937-1945, that he amassed the bulk of his collection, which ranks with that of Avery Brundage as one of the world's finest. How he acquired it would make interesting reading.

•

Six months before the rape of Nanking, General Doihara called in the one man who could take full charge of looting China's underworld – Kodama Yoshio, Japan's top gangster. Normally based in Tokyo, Kodama moved to Shanghai, where he became Doihara's chief liaison with Boss Tu and the Green Gang. Before the war ended, Kodama was Golden Lily's most effective negotiator with gangsters in Indochina, Siam, Malaya, Burma, the Philippines and Indonesia, holding their feet to the fire or, when necessary, shooting them.

Kodama was short, burly, squat, and had the meaty face of a professional fighter, with thick lips and heavy scar tissue. His fingers were knobby from karate, and could crush a larynx. The son of a failed businessman in Nihonmatsu, at age nine he was sent off to his aunt in Korea, where he worked in a steel mill. At twelve he fled back to Japan, where he was adopted by *yakuza* who put him to work beating up labor organizers. By 1931 he was a favorite of Black Dragon boss Toyama, implicated in the attempted murder of cabinet ministers. Sentenced to prison, Kodama wrote a memoir that became a handbook for fanatics. After his release, Toyama sent him to Manchuria to do wet work for General Doihara. In Tokyo a few months later, he was jailed for plotting to bomb imperial advisors, staying in jail until 1937.

He was sprung from jail by Doihara in April 1937, on the condition that he devoted his violent energies to looting China's underworld. This epiphany, the transformation of Kodama from thug to super-patriot, was suggested by Black Dragon's Toyama, whose own stature as a patriot was affirmed in 1924 when he was a guest at Emperor Hirohito's wedding.

In November 1937, after six months of briefings in the Foreign Ministry, Kodama arrived in Shanghai to deal with the problem of carelessness. In a postwar memoir, he denounced "the wanton spending of secret funds, on wine, women and debauchery… in every city under Japanese occupation". And the careless destruction of valuable objects: "…in every temple and shrine…in the occupied areas, I found the heads of Buddhas…broken or cut off". If soldiers, mostly uneducated farm boys, were too stupid to steal the whole Buddha, they must be shot. While Kodama's lieutenants put these orders into effect, he spent his days taking control of alcohol, drugs, and other prime commodities. All proceeds were diverted from Chinese racketeers to Golden Lily, minus a handling charge for Kodama himself. Ultimately, Kodama was responsible to Prince Chichibu, and to the throne.

Princes were not equipped to deal with gangsters. Kodama saved them from soiling their hands. He converted narcotics into bullion by the simple method of trading heroin to gangsters for gold ingots. How brokers got the ingots was not his concern. He closed a deal with waterfront boss Ku Tsu-chuan to swap heroin for gold throughout the Yangtze Valley. Thanks to Ku's brother, KMT senior general Ku Chu-tung, Japan also gained access to U.S. Lend-Lease supplies reaching western China by way of the Burma Road, or on aircraft flying over the Hump from India. Once in warehouses in Kunming or Chungking, the Lend-Lease was re-sold to the Japanese Army, with Kodama as purchasing agent.

One of Kodama's most important converts was drug broker Ye Ching-ho. At the end of 1937, Ye dropped all pretense of patriotism and transferred his loyalty to Kodama and Japan, in return for honorary Japanese citizenship under the name Nakamura Taro, and his own drug domain on the island of Taiwan, where he enjoyed the prerogatives of a warlord, and was kept supplied with Japanese mistresses. From Taiwan, Ye shipped narcotics directly across the strait to China's mainland.

When he was not otherwise busy, Kodama and his flying squad of *yakuza* thugs roved the Yangtze Valley, stopping in every town and village. Summoning local notables, Kodama immediately shot the mayor or headman in the face. This ensured immediate cooperation in donating all valuables to Emperor Hirohito. Kodama was careful to turn over to Golden Lily all artworks, gold bullion, and general treasure, but set aside the platinum, which fascinated him. The story is told that he once loaded so much platinum on a military aircraft bound for Japan that the landing gear collapsed. Thereafter, he kept only the biggest and best rubies, sapphires, and diamonds, which could be shipped home unobtrusively.

Officially, Kodama was in Shanghai as a buyer for the Imperial Navy Air Force, under the rubric of the Kodama Kikan, or Kodama Agency. (Special Service Units were named after the officer in charge and then called an agency.) On paper, his mission was to locate and acquire supplies of copper, cobalt, nickel and mica. In most cases he bought these directly from KMT secret police chief General Tai Li, who was paid in heroin. According to U.S. intelligence, the Kodama Agency took over the salt monopoly, molybdenum mines, farms, fisheries and munitions plants. He also ran a huge shoe factory. Drugs paid for the construction of Kodama's splendid new home and garden in Tokyo. He was generous, sent gifts to the right people, and was a favorite of Hirohito's aging uncle, Prince Higashikuni. His personal circle included Vice Admiral Onishi, General Ishihara, Lieutenant Colonel Tsuji, and Hirohito's cousin Prince Takeda, a key figure in Golden Lily's movement of treasure.

Just before Pearl Harbor and the Strike South, Kodama accompanied Prince Takeda to Japan's southern military headquarters in Saigon to confer with Field Marshal Terauchi, son of the general who had looted and brutalized Korea. Because the Strike South would involve Japan's navy, and the navy would administer the Malay Archipelago through which treasure ships must pass, Kodama was transferred overnight from the army to the navy, and given the rank of rear admiral. This was like making Al Capone a U.S. Navy admiral. Kodama's rank enabled him to commandeer ships, and gave him leverage with Chinese smugglers who roved the archipelago. As Jonathan Marshall explains, "because the Japanese lacked a coastal navy, they granted Chinese 'pirates' a monopoly on smuggling in return for information...The Japanese sold them narcotics for $1,600 an ounce, which the pirates in turn could sell along the coast for $6,000."

Kodama returned to Shanghai just in time for Pearl Harbor. The attack made little difference to millions of Asians who had been under Japanese assault for years, but it altered circumstances for Westerners. Immediately, Japan seized all their business assets, and emptied Western banks. In the countryside, how you were treated depended on the local commander. Myra and Fred Scovel were relatively fortunate. They were American missionaries running a hospital at Tsining, in Shantung province. The day Pearl Harbor was attacked, Japanese soldiers arrested them and an officer said: "You are not to leave the house. Everything you formerly owned is now the property of the Imperial Japanese Government...You are to make lists in triplicate of everything in the house. Your money is to be counted, the house searched in the presence of this officer." The Scovels were interned in prison camps before being repatriated. Each time they were moved, their meager possessions were searched for American money. "Hems of dresses were felt carefully, shoulder pads ripped open, shoe soles torn off, and long hair thoroughly combed out." Returning to China after the war, they found their hospital stripped even of the window frames, doors, and plumbing. A box of silverware buried under their back porch was gone.

A few weeks before Pearl Harbor, paleontologists in Peking devised a plan to rescue one of the world's great anthropological treasures, the 500,000-year-old bones and teeth of Peking Man. They had been discovered in the Dragon Bone Hills about 30 miles from Peking in the 1920s. The staff at Peking Union Medical

College, where the bones were stored, decided to move them to the Smithsonian Institution in America, to be returned after the war. They were padded and wrapped, and placed inside nine steel ammunition boxes. These were turned over to U.S. Navy Lieutenant William T. Foley, a legation doctor now headed home with his assistant, Navy Pharmacist's Mate Herman Davis. With luck, they and their baggage would be protected by diplomatic immunity. But when Pearl Harbor occurred before they left Peking, they became prisoners of war. Two and a half weeks later, Foley, Davis, their boxes, and eleven U.S. Marines from the legation were taken to a railhead outside Peking and put in a boxcar, bound for prison camps in Japan. After a two-week journey, the train reached an industrial harbor. A squad of Japanese soldiers led by a gruff officer put Foley and his group in a shed and searched their baggage outside. A Marine who had served in Japan and spoke some Japanese, heard the officer say: "Here they are." When Foley and the others were taken out of the shed later, the nine steel crates were gone. The men were taken by sea to Hokkaido where they spent three and a half years as slave labor in Mitsubishi mines.

In 1986, after hearing Dr. Foley tell this story many times in New York City, journalist Joseph Coggins flew to Tokyo to talk with a Japanese cardiologist who had studied under Foley. Over supper at a restaurant facing the Imperial Palace, the cardiologist told Coggins some fossils associated with Peking Man had been reported in Tokyo after the war. He gestured toward the palace and added, "Peking Man probably ended up not far from where we are sitting." Dr. Foley had always told Coggins: "I would swear on a stack of Bibles that those bones are in the basement of the Imperial Palace."

CHAPTER FOUR

STORMING THE INDIES

It was failure in Manchuria that caused the Japanese to invade China, and failure in China that caused them to invade Southeast Asia. In each instance they thought expanding the war zone would solve their problems. How can victory mean failure? The answer is surprisingly simple. Great quantities of treasure came from each victory, but quickly vanished into the usual hiding places, so Japan's ruling elite became very much richer. Meanwhile, the public treasury was exhausted by military expenditures, and ordinary Japanese were squeezed to make up the deficit. In short, the underlying problem of a corrupt ruling elite was only aggravated by infusions of stolen treasure. Disaster lay ahead, but in a culture where conspicuous patriotism is the bottom line, few dared to speak out. Getting bogged down in China removed all restraints on military spending, so both the army and navy gambled on advancing farther south. Tokyo was counting on a sequence of surprise attacks, followed by a quick negotiated settlement, which would allow her to keep Taiwan, Korea, and Manchuria, while gaining at least the Philippines and Indonesia. Few Japanese officials believed they could win a protracted war with the West. However, in the Autumn of 1941, Hirohito was persuaded that Japan had the advantage of surprise, and if he delayed, the opportunity would be lost. Weeks before Pearl Harbor, he was in contact with Pope Pius XII, hoping the Pope would negotiate a peace settlement at the right moment. To sweeten his bid for the Pope's favor, Hirohito had his financial advisors move $45-million into the Vatican bank in Rome, and to Vatican-controlled banks in Portugal and Spain.

When it was launched, the Strike South moved with stunning speed. The day after Pearl Harbor, Shanghai's international settlement was overrun. Japanese troops landed in Siam, the government in Bangkok surrendered and obligingly declared war on the Allies. Two days later, sailing from Singapore to block a landing on the Malay Peninsula, Britain's *Prince of Wales* and *Repulse* were sunk by Japanese planes. Japanese troops on folding bicycles moved swiftly down the Malay Peninsula, as others invaded Burma and Sumatra. By the end of December, Hong

Kong, Guam and Wake had fallen, and Japan was invading the Philippines. On March 9, 1942, resistance collapsed in Java. Bataan surrendered on April 9, Corregidor on May 6. Five months after Pearl Harbor, Japan controlled East and Southeast Asia.

Seen as armed robbery, the twelve months of 1942 were pure hell. Japan was in a hurry, and used terror to force submission. Loot amassed for Golden Lily by the *kempeitai* and Special Service Units was funneled into Penang or Singapore, then carried by sea through the spice islands to Manila, to be sorted and inventoried by the princes before the next leg north to Japan.

Tokyo's policy on looting was set by Hirohito at an Imperial Headquarters Liaison Conference, in a document titled *Principles for the Implementation of Military Administration in the Occupied Southern Area*. He directed the military to enforce "the acquisition of strategic materials, the establishment of the self-sufficiency of the occupying army, and the restoration of law and order". In plain language, acquisition meant armed robbery, self-sufficiency meant forcing local populations to bear the full burden of paying for the occupation, and restoration of law-and-order meant using terror to suppress all opposition. These orders gave a free hand. At a meeting of the Imperial Liaison Conference in March 1942, Hoshino Naoki, head of the narcotics trade and now Hirohito's top aide, said: "There are no restrictions on us. These were enemy possessions. We can take them, do anything we want."

One part of World War II that receives little attention is the financial treachery – coercion, terror, extortion, and secret betrayal. Little is written about it because prominent citizens chose to betray their own nation, their own families, rather than forfeit personal wealth. Financial collusion with Japan remains one of the world's most closely guarded secrets even today. While many books have been published about Nazi looting and economic conspiracy, records of Japan's looting and economic conspiracy have been removed from Western archives and databases, remain under secret classification, and will not be made public for another half-century. There must be a reason for this. Recent efforts in the U.S. Congress led to passage of Public Law 106-567 to assure public access for the first time to classified documents about Japan's conduct of the war. At the last moment, a loophole was added permitting the CIA director to decide which documents are 'relevant' and to withhold for reasons of 'national security' any that might reveal what the CIA was doing half a century ago. This permits the CIA to filter out all documents that might reveal unsavory American collusion with Japan in the period immediately following the war. Until those archives are fully opened, we can only see a partial picture. Even that is devastating, as we will see in later chapters.

As Japan struck south, mundane materials qualified as plunder: copper wire, oil, coal, iron, rice, dried fish, preserved meats, and salt. In Malaya, the Philippines and Dutch East Indies, every kind of real estate was confiscated, from private homes and hotels to granaries, petroleum tank farms, and fish farms.

Failure to arrange a quick truce through the Pope left no alternative but more robbery. Despite initial victories, by mid-1942 it was obvious to Prince Chichibu, his brother Prince Takamatsu, and to many others, that the war would be lost militarily. So it was more important than ever not to lose financially.

After the fall of Singapore, Chichibu established a regional headquarters of Golden Lily there, staffed with clerks, bookkeepers and accountants. He flew north to the banking hub of Kuala Lumpur and the island of Penang, major centers for collection and transshipment of loot. In Ipoh he made deals with Overseas Chinese tin mining factories to melt down and recast confiscated gold jewelry. Ingots in many shapes from Laos, Cambodia, Siam, and Burma were being shipped by rail to Ipoh, or by freighter to Penang or Singapore. Wu Chye-sin was a Hokkien businessman in Ipoh who made a fortune taking a small percentage of precious metals he recast for Golden Lily, stolen from Burma and Siam. Because he spoke Chinese and English, the bars he cast were hallmarked in those languages, using English spelling for Cambodia instead of that country's Khmer or French names. This added to the variety of hallmarks that Golden Lily dealt with. Half a century later, hundreds of the bars cast at Wu's factory in Ipoh were found deep in a cavern on Luzon by Igorot tribesmen, who showed them to a camera crew from Asahi Television. The amazed TV crew videotaped the gold bars, and drilled core samples. When these were analyzed in Tokyo, metallurgical 'fingerprints' established where the gold originated. (See Chapter 13.)

Ingots from Burma were in pyramid shapes, 15.5 x 5.5 x 3.8 centimeters, each 20 karats and weighing 6.2 kilos. Gold Buddhas also arrived. Rich Burmans prepared for reincarnation by endowing pagodas, or had solid gold Buddhas cast. Some Buddhist sects accumulated hoards of gold and cast Buddha images weighing up to eight tons. These were disguised by encasing them in plaster, painted white and decorated with painted faces. Only senior members of a sect knew that inside the plaster was solid gold. The first thing Japanese officers did at pagodas was to fracture the plaster Buddhas to see if they were gold inside.

In July 1942 a gold Buddha over 15 feet tall arrived at Manila's Pier 15. It weighed so many tons the only solution was to cut it up. But that might cause bad karma. Instead, the Buddha was lowered onto a barge and taken up the Marikina River to an airstrip called Marikina Field. There, two bulldozers pushed and dragged the statue into a pit, covering it with soil to dig up after the war. When those officers were transferred, it was forgotten. Decades later this gold Buddha was rediscovered by accident, when a housing development was built on Marikina Field. (Chapter 13.)

In Kuala Lumpur, Golden Lily found vaults at Bank Negara packed with 23.97 karat bars of 6.250 kilos each, measuring 1 x 2 x 5.75 inches. Other gold was seized from Hokkien, Hakka and Teochiu communities, rich from tin mining and rubber plantations. More was extorted from rajahs and *datos* in each Malay state. Tons came by rail from Cambodia, in bars measuring 15.5 x 5 x 3.7 centimeters, rated 92.3 percent pure.

Through 1942, 1943 and 1944, Prince Chichibu and his staff spent the dry season in the Philippines, then moved to the relative comfort of Singapore when typhoons began battering Manila. Chichibu had contracted tuberculosis in Manchuria in the late 1930s, and had to avoid the rainy season in the Philippines. TB also provided cover for his disappearance from Japan. There it was announced that the prince had left the army for medical reasons, and was recuperating on an estate at the foot of Mount Fuji, nursed by his wife. In a memoir published long after her husband's death, Princess Chichibu said he spent the war years in such total isolation that he was seen by his own brothers only on two or three occasions. In between, nobody could say where he was. A number of Japanese and Filipinos have attested to the prince being in Manila, adding that they saw him spitting blood into his handkerchief, a telling detail because his tuberculosis was not widely known.

Despite many warnings, the Japanese assault took governments, bankers and citizens by surprise. Before Japan invaded the Philippines, anxious Americans asked the State Department about sending home wives and children. State refused to give frank advice. Later, it defended this lamely before Congress, saying it did not want to prejudice on-going peace negotiations by sending the wrong message, evacuating women and children. So, many mothers and children spent the next four years in concentration camps. Dutch colonials were especially anxious. By the summer of 1940, they could no longer go home as the Netherlands were occupied by the Nazis. There was safe-haven in Australia, where many British colonials already had fled. But the Dutch government in exile in London declared that Dutch colonials must stay put. In Java and Sumatra, thousands of Dutch men and women were called for military duty or civilian defense throughout the archipelago, whose islands sprawl over 780,000 square miles. They were forbidden to send money out. Yet, in the final months of 1941, the Dutch colonial government covertly moved its remaining official gold reserves (worth 120-million guilders) from Java to Australia, America and South Africa, aboard chartered merchant ships such as the *Java* and the *Phrontis*. (Some 250-million guilders' worth of gold were moved earlier to the U.S. to clear payments for American weapons and aircraft.) These transfers were kept secret to instill false confidence.

Many colonial government officials were caught napping. Philippine President Manuel Quezon, an intimate friend of General Douglas MacArthur, was vacationing at the mountain resort of Baguio when he received a phone call on December 8 informing him that the Pacific War had started. MacArthur himself was caught with his military aircraft parked in the open at Clark Field, where nearly all were destroyed by Japanese bombers from Taiwan. On December 22, the Japanese landed in Lingayen Gulf. The next day, MacArthur declared Manila an open city and withdrew U.S. and Filipino forces to Bataan and Corregidor. Boats carried munitions, food and medicines to the island. MacArthur ordered his G-2, Colonel Charles Willoughby, also to move the contents of the Philippine National Treasury, the Philippine Central Bank, and private deposits from National City Bank. (Twenty-three big Mosler safes that Willoughby's teams emptied, were later used by Golden Lily to hide gold bars in ventilation shafts at Fort Santiago, for recovery after the war.)

The Philippine National Treasury consisted of over 51 metric tons of gold, 32 metric tons of silver bullion, 140 tons of silver coins, and $27-million in U.S. Treasury notes, plus an undisclosed amount in bonds, precious gems, and Treasury certificates.

The gold alone was worth $40-million at the time. National City Bank held private deposits of two metric tons of gold, along with gems, currency and precious metals in safe deposit boxes. It took four days to move all this from Manila to Corregidor using Navy tugboats and small pleasure yachts. The job was completed on December 27, 1941. Willoughby's wife helped with the inventory, and was surprised that gold did not glitter. "It was dull and not recognizably gold at all; most of it was dark brown with some chunks of dirty yellow. Some of the variously sized bars were wrapped, some were without wrapping; some had tickets attached, others had figures and weights stamped into them... I had to use both hands to lift a bar about the size of a pound of butter." (A cube of gold 12 x 12 x 12 inches, weighs 2,000 pounds.)

This treasure was stored in Corregidor's tunnel complex. Exactly 1,430 tons of silver pesos were placed in the Malinta Tunnels. Two tons of private gold were stored inside the Stockade. The 51 tons of government gold (2,542 ingots of 20 kilos each), along with government securities, were placed in laterals of the Navy Tunnel, on the south side of the Malinta tunnels. At the end of April, 115 tons of silver coins were dumped into San Jose Bay, where they were dispersed by tides.

On February 3, 1942, the USS *Trout*, an American Tambor class submarine, arrived at Corregidor with a cargo of anti-aircraft rounds, food and medical supplies. After unloading, the skipper said he needed ballast to replace the cargo. MacArthur decided to put treasure aboard. Two trucks were sent to the Stockade to bring the private gold. Then 16 tons of silver pesos were loaded, along with currency, stocks, bonds, and Treasury certificates. The *Trout* continued its patrol, sinking two Japanese vessels before heading home to Pearl Harbor, where the gold was turned over to the San Francisco mint. When Corregidor fell, the Japanese navy recovered the remaining treasure and shipped it to Tokyo. It never occurred to the defenders to wall up this treasure in a side passage, to hide it.

As each country was overrun, tens of thousands of colonials were trapped. They were ordered to take only two small suitcases and go to collection points, for transfer to internment camps. *Kempeitai* units immediately seized all property. Except for residences chosen for high-ranking officers or civil administrators, special squads arrived in vans to strip these homes bare. Pianos, paintings, light fixtures, kitchen appliances, flush toilets, sinks, clothing, and food-stocks were taken to warehouses. Copper wiring and lead plumbing were ripped from walls. Jewelry, candlesticks, tableware and picture frames were placed in oil drums and taken to sorting centers for melting down. Hardwood floors and doors were torn out.

In the Philippines, Carlos Romulo (later ambassador to the UN) told how this was done on the island of Leyte: "Their army trucks came to every door, and soldiers entered the houses taking everything that might be of use, and throwing all else out of the windows, or firing it there. All their loot was taken on ships to Japan, leaving the Philippines stripped."

In Manila, Japanese soldiers moved through upper class and middle class neighborhoods, kidnapping pretty wives and daughters who were taken to hotels set aside for higher-ranking army and navy officers. Over several weeks mothers and daughters were raped repeatedly until many were in a stupor, servicing up to fifty men a day. The *kempeitai* offered to return kidnapped family members in exchange for hidden treasure or securities, or information about neighbors and relatives. At hospitals, nurses were sought as mistresses for Japanese officers. In poor families with no assets, wives and daughters were herded into brothels for non-commissioned officers and ordinary soldiers.

On the eve of the invasion, many Dutch colonials hastily sold homes and emptied bank accounts, buying gold biscuits, or gems that could be tucked in a cheek. Some buried valuables in their gardens. Watchful servants retrieved them, only to have them taken by the Japanese, who paid repeated visits for this very reason. Other Dutch brought tiny hoards to freighters, passenger ships, inter-island ferries, and private yachts, hoping to escape to Australia. Although some vessels reached safety, most were captured or sunk. Few saw their valuables again.

Like British in Malaya or Burma, some Dutch had holiday homes in mountain towns of Java or Sumatra, where they could escape the heat. Here they fled, hoping to be overlooked. But *kempeitai* came to the smallest kampong, locking these cottages. To be so methodical over such a vast region required a very large organization and considerable forethought.

Panic hit bankers and private citizens alike as they sought ways to hide wealth. Banks called in bearer bonds, listed numbers, sent the lists to the home country and destroyed the bonds. Serial numbers of high-denomination banknotes were recorded and the bills burned. When time ran out, smaller denominations were burned without listing the numbers. In Malaya, $104-million in bonds were processed this way. In Singapore, $4-million in privately-owned jewels and small valuables were received by government agents and shipped to Australia. After noting serial numbers, Singapore banks burned $75-million in currency, and shipped another $39-million to India. When the Japanese marched in they brought a phalanx of officials from Yokohama Specie Bank and Bank of Taiwan (a Japanese government bank) who were to sequester all bank operations. Those from Yokohama Specie Bank worked in territories under army control, those from Bank of Taiwan in areas under navy control. Taiwanese bankers, who could speak Mandarin, Cantonese, Hokkien, Hakka, or Teochiu, were assigned to monitor Chinese owned banks and pawnshops.

Earnest officials made desperate efforts to hide or destroy government tax ledgers, property ledgers, and internal banking records, but the Japanese tortured or frightened bureaucrats and bank managers to reveal secret account information and business practices, to open safes and vaults, or to turn over hidden safe-deposit keys. Collaborators were discovered among native clerks, disgruntled targets of racist abuse by their colonial masters. They provided tax-rolls and ledgers, and identified wealthy local residents for fleecing.

In Singapore, all foreign bank holdings were confiscated. On March 8, 1942, managing directors of all commercial banks in the Dutch East Indies were forced to hand over the contents of their vaults. In this first sweep, the Japanese took 52-million guilders in cash from banks in Java alone. Another 12-million guilders were seized from import-export firms in Java and the neighboring island of Madoera. They even sealed pawnshops and small native banks. This was done by staff from the Bank of Japan, Bank of Taiwan, Mitsui Bank and Kanan Bank, led by Yamamoto Hiroshi, a senior Bank of Japan officer who served as controller of the Office of Alien Property. Everything was turned over to Prince Chichibu's Golden Lily organization for inventory, and shipment to Japan.

Across Southeast Asia, mid-level bank employees were herded into internment camps, and escorted to work each day. Fearing for their lives, they soon handed over the remaining secrets. Those who refused to cooperate, or were thought to have deceived the Japanese, were turned over to the *kempeitai* for special treatment. Journalist Jos Hagers of the Dutch newspaper *De Telegraaf*, who was born in a Japanese prison camp in Sumatra, has investigated many accounts of Japan's looting in Indonesia, including that of eyewitness Willemsz Geeroms. As a boy of fifteen, Geeroms watched while a Japanese, said to be a brother of Emperor Hirohito, visited his internment camp. While the prince was there, the father of Geeroms' best-friend, a director of the Palembang branch of Java Bank, was taken to the commandant's office for interrogation. Informers had told the Japanese that he had burned a large quantity of guilders and hidden a lot of bullion to prevent its confiscation. When he refused to answer questions, he was brutally beaten in full view of internees including young Geeroms, and later died of his injuries.

The Japanese recovered far more gold than they thought possible. It became evident that there was more gold and platinum in private hands across Southeast Asia than anyone knew existed. Some had been hoarded for many generations, but some was new. During the 1930s, the Great Depression made people everywhere shy away from paper currency. By the late 1930s, anxiety about the intentions of Germany and Japan made gold a vital asset. Governments hoarded gold against the likelihood of war. Increased demand made it profitable to open new mines, including the Tjikotok mine on Java where gold was extracted by tunneling as deep as 3,000-feet, approaching the depth of the deepest mines in South Africa. In the Philippines also, 1939 was a record year for gold production from Benguet mines northeast of Manila.

The Japanese quickly reactivated these mines with slave labor. With a limitless supply of slaves, they did not have to worry about cost or risk. When the Japanese 25th Army took control of mines on Benkalis island, off Sumatra, gold production jumped ten-fold to over 400-kilos per year. Similar increases were recorded in all other mines during the occupation.

Not all Southeast Asia's wealth was acquired at gunpoint. Wherever possible, it was simpler to purchase it with scrip. By the end of the war, the amount of currency in circulation was seven times normal. First, the army and navy distributed their own scrip in each country, valued at ¥1 to one Straits dollar (doubling the value overnight). Because the scrip was poor quality, with no serial numbers, it was easy to counterfeit. Such large quantities were distributed that it lost more value from over-supply. In an orgy of false sincerity, the Japanese rushed in to fix the unfixable. New scrip was issued by the Southern Development Bank, to replace the military scrip. So, victims were defrauded twice. Each note bore the printed notice 'Face Value Guaranteed' and 'backed by a giant reserve'.

As Hong Kong was occupied, homes, hotels, businesses, real estate, artworks and antiques were confiscated from wealthy Chinese families, given military scrip or bank scrip in exchange. Half a century later, these families still are pursuing legal action in an attempt to force Japan to redeem millions of dollars' worth of scrip. Farcically, the Japanese claim the scrip was issued by a former government, so the current government has no responsibility to honor it. Many of Hong Kong's finest art collections remain in private Japanese hands, paid for with 'Monopoly money'.

Ricksha pullers also were paid in scrip. If they did not express gratitude, they were beheaded. POWs (when paid at all), were paid in scrip, then had monthly withholding taken out that would be returned 'when they were sent home'. There was even a luxury tax. Car owners had to pay the equivalent of US$300 a month for the privilege of having tires on their cars.

Joseph Grew, the U.S. ambassador in Tokyo from 1932 until he was repatriated in 1942, said: "Even the Japanese militarists could not continue indefinitely a program of outright larcenies and burglaries. The robbery is reduced to a system. They have made that system resemble finance. Like our finance, it deals with money. Like ours it uses the familiar terms of cash, credit, loans, stock companies, government subsidies, traffic, taxes and so on. ...There the resemblance ceases...Once new territory was acquired, the Japanese invaders...built up a currency system that rested on the fiat of the Japanese Army and issued bank notes payable only in death to anyone who did not honor them. With this currency, the Japanese military manipulated exchange so as to conduct trade on a ruthlessly unfair basis. They supplemented this with outright confiscation, or capital levies, or simply with the murder of the property owners and the enslavement of the workers. Japanese-run monopolies fixed prices on what they wanted at ridiculously low levels, and Japanese military patrols 'bought' at these prices. On this basis, Japan was able to develop a flourishing flow into Japan of goods, until the occupied area was pumped dry. Then some concessions would be made, in an attempt to prime the pump and sink it deeper into the well."

To squeeze more, Japan set up lotteries and gambling houses where players had to spend hard currency. Winners took home their jackpots in scrip.

Periodically, Japanese sold rationed goods like rice, cigarettes, sugar and salt at very high prices. Instead of making these goods available openly, they were channeled to local gangsters and black marketeers, who collaborated in return for narcotics. Ordinary people wanting to buy food, tobacco, salt and medicine on the black market had to dig into secret caches of colonial hard currency, gold, or jewelry.

When treasure was sorted by Golden Lily, the gold, platinum, gemstones and artworks were crated for shipment first to Manila. Confiscated stocks, bonds, gold bearer certificates, were channeled to Yokohama Specie Bank or Bank of Taiwan, for transfer to Japanese accounts at foreign banks in neutral countries. The single biggest shareholder in the Yokohama Specie Bank was Emperor Hirohito, owning 22 percent. Consequently, the Imperial Household Agency controlled the bank's shareholder meetings. By the end of the war, it has been established that Hirohito had over $100-million ($1-billion in today's terms) hidden in gold and foreign currency accounts in Switzerland, South America, Portugal, Spain and the Vatican.

Near the end of the war, Yokohama Specie Bank discovered that it had not correctly balanced its books, and owed a significant sum to banks in the conquered territories. The overdraft was cleared by paying those banks in worthless scrip. (As the emperor continued to be the biggest shareholder after the war, the argument that management of the bank had changed is particularly absurd.)

Nazi Germany typically laundered looted gold and non-monetary gold by re-smelting it and casting it into bars that were hallmarked with black eagle swastikas, numbered in keeping with standard practice of the Reichsbank. This gold was moved to banks in Switzerland, Sweden, Portugal, or Argentina. Japan used the same techniques, moving gold through Swiss banks in Tokyo, Portuguese banks in Macao, and banks in Chile and Argentina. When gold was physically moved to those countries it was carried by large cargo submarines.

As a center of the world's unofficial gold trade, Macao was enriched. When the Allies got together at the Bretton Woods Conference in 1944 to put a stop to the laundering of Nazi and Japanese war loot through neutral countries, Portugal somehow forgot to include Macao on the list, and nobody drew attention to the oversight. As historian Bertil Lintner noted: "Macao merchants were soon buying gold abroad at $35 an ounce from banks, shipping it back to the enclave and selling it at a premium to whoever wanted to buy it. The syndicate was led by Ho Yin, an Overseas Chinese who had fled from Guangdong to sit out the war." Macao was a wartime haven for rich Overseas Chinese who enlarged their fortunes by precious metal trading. The only significant source of gold at the time was Japanese plunder. In the China Seas, only Japanese banks were open for business. Macao pawnshops, brokers, and private citizens made fortunes turning hard currencies into gold for the Japanese. At war's end, when colonial authorities returned, Macao millionaires were able to use the colonial currency they had acquired to buy the most desirable land, buildings, and factories at knock-down prices.

Some of Hirohito's personal wealth was laundered through Macao, the rest through Swiss banks in Tokyo. Journalist Paul Manning, who had a chance to review some of Hirohito's financial records at the end of the war, when they were in the custody of U.S. Occupation authorities, saw that the emperor's personal assets began to be moved abroad to neutral havens at the end of 1943, preparing for the inevitable defeat. Privy Seal Kido called a meeting of Japan's leading bankers who were also the emperor's financial advisor. On their recommendation, funds were transferred from Tokyo to Switzerland, virtually emptying Hirohito's cash reserves in Tokyo. Nazi gold, which had been moved to the Swiss accounts of Yokohama Specie Bank to pay for purchases from Japan, also were transferred to Hirohito's accounts in Switzerland. At the same time, Kido moved other imperial gold reserves to Argentina by sub, and to Macao where it was sold for hard currencies, and this money was then moved to Switzerland by bank transfer. Historian James Mackay separately concluded that Hirohito had U.S. $20-million in Swiss accounts, U.S. $35-million in South American banks, and U.S. $45-million in Portugal, Spain and the Vatican.

Because most of the stolen treasure reaching Japan made its way into private vaults and the vaults of the Imperial Family, Tokyo's strategy for the economic exploitation of Southeast Asia was a failure. It was also sabotaged by Overseas Chinese, who controlled the region's raw materials, industries, agriculture, smuggling, and rackets. While they despised the Japanese for the rape of China, they hated them in particular for bombing Amoy, Swatow, and other harbors along the China coast that were the ancestral homes of their dialect groups. In the past, Western companies had been successful in Southeast Asia only when they found ways to work with the Overseas Chinese. As Japan took over and tried to set up equivalent monopolies of oil, sugar, rice, salt, and other commodities, whole sectors of local economies collapsed. Prices shot up, the supply of goods came to a halt, and there was massive unemployment, famine, inflation and hoarding.

In retaliation, Overseas Chinese became special targets. Experts in terror were sent to punish them. Colonel Watanabe Wataru spent ten years in North China developing techniques, such as kidnapping members of prosperous Chinese families, amputating body parts starting with ears, noses, and fingers, then continuing to breasts and testicles. He was especially effective when he threatened to castrate eldest sons. In this manner, Watanabe was credited with bringing in great quantities of gold, gemstones and artworks. In China, he had headed one of the Special Service Agencies (*Tokumu Kikan*) whose duties were espionage, counter-espionage, propaganda, and fifth column subversion. Watanabe was then given the job of terrorizing Malaya's Overseas Chinese. His techniques are well known from speeches he made and papers he drafted: "The Chinese ... are prone to maintain a false obedience, and they are as crafty as anything, and hard to control. They ought to be dealt with unsparingly." To help, he enlisted cronies from his days in Manchuria. One was his old friend Colonel Tsuji Masanobu, a flamboyant leader of the Total War cult, who had helped plan the Strike South and the Malaya campaign of General Yamashita. Another was Takase Toru, who had served in China as an intelligence officer with Special Service Section Eight, and was an expert in 'the Chinese problem'. Watanabe described Takase as 'a complicated character, conceited, quarrelsome, aggressive', but his ruthlessness was exactly what was needed.

Colonel Tsuji was Japan's most ruthless Special Service agent, combining traits that made Goebbels, Heydrich, and Skorzeny uniquely feared in the Nazi Party. Prior to the Strike South, Imperial General Headquarters issued to officers a handbook written by Tsuji, which makes repeated references to plundering the wealth of the 'treasure-house of the Far East'. The methods he recommended were based on terror. Compassion and sympathy were to be avoided. No longer could the Overseas Chinese "indulge themselves in a hedonistic and wasteful way of life..." Japan would force them "to account for their past mistakes and to make them ready to give up their lives and property". Tsuji got everyone's attention with a horrific atrocity. By noon on February 21, 1942, all male Chinese on the island of Singapore between age eighteen and fifty were assembled in five locations. Each walked past a row of hooded informers. When a hood nodded, that Chinese was condemned to death, his skin stamped with a triangular ink chop. Others were stamped with squares and released. A total of 70,699 Singapore Chinese were taken off for torture and killing. Mass executions lasted many days, with Tsuji watching closely. Most were shot, bayoneted or beheaded, but 20,000 were roped together on barges and taken into the sealanes off Singapore, where they were forced over-board. Those who did not drown quickly were machine-gunned. This nightmare was called *Sook Ching* or ethnic cleansing. Tsuji then extended *Sook Ching* to the whole Malay Peninsula, where another 40,000 were slain, including women, school children, and babies. Similar mass executions of Chinese happened elsewhere.

Colonel Watanabe declared that Singapore Chinese must atone to Emperor Hirohito to the sum of 50-million yen, as a gift on the emperor's birthday in April. This was equal to one fourth of the total currency in circulation in Malaya at the time. Takase was to collect the contributions. Since nobody could produce that much cash on short notice, Takase arranged a loan of 22-million yen from the Yokohama Specie Bank so the birthday present did not fall short. Chinese were required to repay the loan (and interest) with gold bullion, hard foreign currency, or other tangible assets.

While Sumatra had its Royal Dutch Shell oilfields, Malaya was the greatest rub-ber-producing region in the world. Using scrip, Watanabe bought up all rubber stocks for shipment to Japan. He then ordered all rubber estates and processing facilities sold to Japan's *zaibatsu* conglomerates, again for scrip.

The shock of this anti-Chinese reign of terror brought results for a few weeks, but ultimately backfired as the flow of rice, salt, and other commodities dwindled fur-ther. Watanabe offered special discounts and rebates to quislings and collaborators. A few mavericks wanted an abundant supply of narcotics, so Japan's major collab-orators were drug dealers and gangsters.

Only with slave labor was Japan not frustrated. There were three groups of vic-tims: local people, Overseas Chinese, and Westerners. Each was treated differently. By mid-1942 the Japanese held some 140,000 Allied POWs, about half-a-million Western civilians, and more than a million Overseas Chinese internees. Though camp conditions for Western civilians were Spartan in the extreme, POWs were treated with barbaric cruelty. Many Allied servicemen were really civilians hastily drafted at the last moment. The father of Dutch journalist Jos Hagers was put to work, with thousands of others, building the Pakan Baroe railway in Sumatra. Although he survived the war, his health was broken and he eventually died in the Netherlands of his injuries. Others toiled a thousand feet below ground, working naked in coalmines belonging to Mitsui and Mitsubishi.

Local populations were treated as garbage. After the war, the government of Indonesia said 4-million of her people were pressed into slave labor battalions, car-ried away on slave ships and worked to death in distant lands. Some 225,000 of them worked on the Kwai River Death Railway between Siam and Burma. When they died, their bodies were used as fill for railway embankments. In Malaya, by 1944, all males between 15 and 40 not employed in vital jobs, were dragooned into slave labor battalions. Korea maintained she lost 6-million as slave labor, many sent to Southeast Asia on slave ships. The number of Chinese slaves was bigger yet. Each year, Japan dragooned about one million Chinese and one million Koreans as slaves. Some were shipped to Japan. Because all Japanese miners had been drafted for military service, Kishi Nobusuke, former head of Manchuria and now Tojo's minister of Mines and Industry, imported 750,000 slaves from Korea, and 50,000 from China. Historian Stephen Roberts explains that as subjects of the Japanese empire, Koreans were given 'preferential handling' as slaves, while the Chinese, with no rights at all, were "treated worse than draft animals". Another 50,000 from China, and an unknown number from Taiwan, were taken by slave ships to the Philippines, where most died. Eyewitnesses told us that thousands of Chinese and Taiwanese dug tunnels and treasure vaults for Golden Lily, then were buried alive when the vaults were sealed. As they were only fed rice gruel or seaweed soup, many starved to death on the job.

Japan's biggest corporations used slaves to work mines, to build roads, railways, airfields and harbors. The biggest single employer of slaves was Mitsui, and many of the slave ships were Mitsui vessels. But records show that POWs also slaved for Kawasaki Heavy Industries, Mitsubishi, Nippon Steel, Showa Denko, and other corporations. Mitsubishi's market position at the war's end in 1945 was described by a Western economist as being equivalent to the merger of U.S. Steel, General Motors, Standard Oil, Alcoa, Douglas Aircraft, Dupont, Westinghouse, AT&T, National City Bank, Woolworth Stores and Hilton Hotels. As for Mitsui, it boasted 1.8-million workers at home and abroad, and owned at least 356 major companies. Today, these conglomerates deny any obligation to compensate those who survived, on the argument that their management changed at the end of the war, so today's corporations are not the same. Strangely, their corporate banks escaped any punishment during the U.S. occupation.

The death rate for Allied POWs held by the Japanese was nearly 30 percent, compared to 4 percent for those held by the Nazis. It would take thousands of pages to recount the brutalities they suffered. Japanese camp administrators and medical staff deliberately allowed POWs to suffer horrible deaths from beriberi, a disease resulting from deficiency of vitamin B1. Author Gavin Daws makes clear that camp doctors knew these men were dying because their diet of polished white rice was deficient in B1. Unpolished brown rice contains B1, but the vitamin is removed in the polishing process. Simply feeding prisoners cheaper brown unpolished rice would have cured the problem. At a POW camp on Hainan Island, Captain Kikuchi Ichiro, withheld Vitamin B tablets while calculating absolute minimum food needed to keep POWs barely alive. The men developed puffy chests, distended bellies, testicles like balloons. Fluid filled their lungs and they suffocated. Everyone knew the choking sound of men gagging to death from beriberi.

Thousands of POWs were taken to Japan on Hell Ships, sealed in cargo holds. Conditions were so grim that of 1500 prisoners, 100 to 200 were dead when they reached Japan. Ships carrying POWs were supposed to be marked a certain way, to avoid being attacked. Japan did not mark its Hell Ships, so when they were attacked by Allied subs or aircraft the ships went down with all prisoners sealed in the holds. Albert Kelder's research shows that submarines unwittingly torpedoed 16 Hell Ships crowded with British, Australian, American and Dutch POWs, plus thousands of Indonesian coolies called Romushas. Kelder told us that a total of 17,036 men died when these16 iron coffins went down. Most were mistankenly sunk by U.S. subs; three (*Pampanito*, *Paddle* and *Sea Lion II*) unintentionally set the awful record with 2,776 drowned POWs.

Chinese shipping lines were forced to lease ships to Japan for scrip, so kidnapped Comfort Women and slaves could be sent to Japan or to Southeast Asia. Investigators have found records establishing beyond question that the Hell Ships, slave ships, and fake hospital ships were operated by top Japanese corporations, including three of the world's biggest shipping lines, their predecessors, or companies that merged with them during or after the war. Among them is NYK Line (Nippon Yusen Kabushiki), the successor to Tokyo Yusen Kabushiki, which acquired one of the slave ship operators, Chosen Yusen Kabushiki. Another is KKK Line (Kisen Kabushiki Kaisha), part of the Kokusai Kereitsu, parent of Hitachi Corporation and owner of some of Japan's biggest banks. Another is Mitsui's OSK Line (Osaka Shosen Kabushiki). Their biggest shareholders include global giants Mitsubishi and Sumitomo. These corporations never were obliged to pay a penny to redeem the scrip they passed around, or to compensate their slaves. All efforts to bring them to trial have been blocked by Tokyo or by Washington, in a perverse collusion we examine later in this book.

Many POWs who reached Japan were used as slaves by Nippon Steel or Mitsui Mines, working ten-hour days, seven days a week. Malnutrition led to dysentery, jaundice, beriberi, scurvy and pellagra. Guards beat them with pick handles or shovels. Few survived. Those who did bore scars inside and out. Frank Bigelow's experience was harrowing but typical. A 20-year-old seaman second class from North Dakota, he was taken to Japan in a Hell Ship belonging to Mitsui, and worked as a slave in a Mitsui coalmine. At six foot four, he weighed only 95 pounds, living on seaweed soup. He ate charcoal to stay alive. As he worked at a coalface deep in the mine one night, a large rock fell on his leg and snapped the brittle bones.

"There was another American POW, Dr. Thomas Hewlett," he recalled. "He improvised with two sharpened bicycle spokes, one to my knee and one to my ankle. It didn't work. Eventually I got gangrene. ...Since we had no medical supplies, much less surgical supplies, we had to do what was called a guillotine operation. He had a hacksaw blade and a razor blade, some knives and four guys holding me. He resorted to a primitive method to battle the growing infection. He put maggots inside the bandage and when he took them out and pulled out the infection, that man saved my life and my leg. The rest of my leg, I should say."

When the war ended, Bigelow and other POWs were taken to Guam, where they were harangued and browbeaten by U.S. military intelligence officers and forced to sign papers promising not to tell anyone about their terrible experiences. "We were told to read and sign and keep our mouths shut," Bigelow said, "and I'm just putting that politely." For some reason both Washington and Tokyo wanted total silence on the abuse of POWs.

Worst of Japan's slave programs was that of the Comfort Women. Young girls, many not even 13 years old, were shanghaied into sexual slavery. After the war, Tokyo insisted all Comfort Women were merely prostitutes who volunteered, and that the entire operation was run by private enterprise. Both statements are demonstrably false. Beginning in 1904 in Korea, the *kempeitai* took full charge of organized prostitution for the Japanese armed forces. One reason was the possibility that military secrets might be passed along in bed, so its agents could ferret out careless soldiers or spies. At first, the brothels were subcontracted. By 1932, the *kempeitai* resumed full control. A typical military brothel had ten barracks, each divided into ten rooms, plus a supervisor's hut, all enclosed in barbed wire to keep the women inside. Rural brothels were tents, while railway cars were fitted out as mobile brothels. Korean and Japanese *yakuza* provided brutal security. Fees were based on a woman's ethnic origin. Japanese girls were top-rated, followed by Koreans, Okinawans, Chinese, Southeast Asians. Later, Caucasian internees were added. Commissioned officers paid ¥3, non-commissioned ¥2.50, privates ¥2. Bookkeeping was thorough, with forms for each woman listing daily earnings and number of clients. Up to 200,000 young women and adolescent girls were forced into this sexual slavery, to serve more than 3.5-million Japanese soldiers. Each was expected to have fifteen partners a day. Theoretically, they received ¥800 a month, minus cost of food, clothing, medical care, soap and water. As many girls were illiterate, they were easily cheated. Most made zero, and were destitute at the end of the war.

Because of the extreme secrecy to this day surrounding Japan's treatment of POWs, civilian slaves, and Comfort Women, we are prevented from knowing important details. However, among files captured by Britain's Royal Marines in 1945 is a revealing document, written by the commander of a camp for POWs at Taihoku, in Taiwan. The commander had just received instructions dated August 1, 1944, from the chief of staff, 11th Unit of Formosa POW Security No. 10 (*kempeitai*). In any emergency, he is instructed to deal with his prisoners in the following way: "Whether they are destroyed individually or in groups, or however it is done, with mass bombing, poisonous smoke, drowning, decapitation, or what…it is the aim not to allow the escape of a single one, to annihilate them all and not to leave any traces."

CHAPTER FIVE

HIDING THE PLUNDER

By May 1942, cargoes of plunder were piling up at Pier 15 in Manila. All treasure from Southeast Asia had to move by sea, because the Japanese did not control a ground route from Southeast Asia through China until late in 1944. Manila was the logical place to bring it together for final sorting and inventory before sending it on to Japan aboard returning freighters or damaged warships limping home for repairs. It was still Japan's hope that it could hold on to the Philippines and Indonesia, whatever negotiated settlement brought the war to an end. But these expectations collapsed a month later in June 1942, six months after Pearl Harbor and three months after the fall of Singapore, when Japan lost the Battle of Midway and never regained the upper hand. The sea route to Japan remained open, because U.S. submarines were armed with defective torpedoes that went astray or bounced off Japanese hulls. This was not corrected until early 1943. To protect the precious cargoes from being attacked by Allied planes, Emperor Hirohito provided Prince Chichibu initially with four 10,000-ton fast passenger ships, painted white with huge green crosses to indicate that they were hospital ships (Japan refused to use the international red cross). Each ship's identity was hidden with false superstructure and extra funnels. To confuse sightings further, each was given the name of a legitimate Japanese hospital ship. The phony hospital ships took on cargoes of treasure at Singapore or Batavia, and also boarded hundreds of VIP passengers. Japanese diplomats or senior officers and their families felt safer traveling aboard hospital ships protected from attack by international law. As many people can personally attest, the Japanese never hesitated to bomb and strafe hospitals or hospital ships, later excusing this action by saying they had never consented to the Geneva conventions on warfare. But they were certain that Allied planes and subs would not intentionally attack a Japanese hospital ship. Setting sail, the fake hospital ships avoided main sealanes, steamed east through the Java Sea to the Celebes, followed the coast of Borneo north to Mindanao, then threaded their way through the Philippine islands to Manila Bay.

Other ships were added when suitable foreign vessels were captured. A prime example was the Dutch passenger liner *Op ten Noort*, named after a famous pioneer of the age of steamships. Her capture off Java in February 1942 began an extraordinary odyssey. She made many voyages carrying treasure to the Philippines and Japan, then at war's end was filled with gold bullion and scuttled off Maizuru Naval Base, to be recovered by the Japanese in 1990. Our photos of her recovery, obtained from one of the participants, reveal the continuing involvement of senior government officials and major Japanese corporations in profiteering from Golden Lily plunder half a century after the end of the Pacific War. (See CDs.)

Built in Amsterdam in 1927, the *Op ten Noort* entered service as a passenger liner for the Royal Packet Navigation Company in the East Indies. Based in Java, she plied a regular course known as the Great Express Service between Surabaya, Semarang, Batavia, Belawan-Deli, and Singapore. She was a pretty ship with a plumb bow, single tall funnel and graceful cruiser stern, very popular with Dutch in the archipelago. Just over 6,000 tons, her Lentz steam engine gave her a cruising speed of 15 knots, and she could accommodate two hundred passengers in first and second classes, carrying another 1,200 native deck passengers. With the outbreak of the Pacific War she was refitted as a hospital ship for the Dutch Navy, with Red Cross hull numbers clearly displayed. Through diplomatic channels Japan was notified, and Tokyo sent a reply officially recognizing her as a hospital ship. Nevertheless, on February 21, 1942, when the *Op ten Noort* was in the western entrance to Surabaya, being degaussed to protect her from magnetic mines, she was attacked by two Japanese aircraft. Their bombs damaged the ship and killed one doctor and two nurses. Captain G. Tuizinga took her slowly into Surabaya harbor for repairs. Six days later the Battle of the Java Sea began. It was less a battle than a massacre. The Japanese fleet was armed with new torpedoes that had an astounding range of 30,000 yards, with an oxygen propulsion system that left no revealing trail of bubbles. The British cruiser *Exeter* was damaged by one of these, the Dutch cruisers *De Ruyter* and *Java* were sunk along with three destroyers, gutting the Allied fleet.

Hurrying out of the repair yard in Surabaya to look for survivors, the *Op ten Noort* came upon the battle scene and was immediately intercepted by two Japanese destroyers, whose boarding parties crippled her radio room. She was forbidden to assist any wounded, and told to remain where she was. At noon the next day, Captain Tuizinga decided to make a run for Australia, and headed down the Java coast at top speed. Three hours later they were intercepted by a Japanese plane that dropped bombs and ordered them to turn back. Following orders, they proceeded to Bandjarmasin, where they took aboard 970 Allied POWs for transport under guard to Makassar, including 800 survivors from the cruiser *Exeter*, many of them naked. There the ship remained for eight months as a hospital facility for the POW camps. When he tried to stop a Japanese guard from contaminating sterilized surgical instruments, one of the medical staff, S. J. Wiemans, was badly beaten in front of the entire ship's complement. On November 23, 1942, the *Op ten Noort* sailed for Yokohama, wearing a Japanese flag. Arriving on December 5, 1942, Captain Tuizinga asked to speak to the Swiss representative of the International Red Cross but was refused. Instead, the full ship's crew and medical staff – 29 men and 15 nurses – were put in a prison camp at a former American missionary school in Myoshi, 75 kilometers from Hiroshima where, as members of the Red Cross, they were treated better than POWs.

At Yokohama, meanwhile, the *Op ten Noort* was fitted out with a false profile, a second funnel, painted white with huge green crosses, and given the name *Tenno Maru*. Three months later, in March 1943, she was again renamed, this time posing as the *Hikawa Maru*, a much bigger 11,000-ton Japanese fast liner built for the NYK line in 1929, and officially registered as a hospital ship. The real *Hikawa Maru* remained berthed in Yokohama, serving as a hotel and tourist attraction. The disguised *Op ten Noort* then sailed for Singapore carrying armaments and VIP families. For the remainder of the war she sailed between Singapore and Manila, carrying treasure for Golden Lily. On October 7, 1944, she was sighted in the Java Sea by the Dutch submarine *Zwaardvisch* (Swordfish), but the sub's skipper let her pass because he thought she was a legitimate Japanese hospital ship. On November 1 of that year, her name was changed back to *Tenno Maru*. Just weeks before the war ended, she reached Yokohama again loaded with treasure. Instead of offloading, she was taken to Maizuru Naval Base on the west coast of Japan, where more gold and platinum bars were put aboard, along with large quantities of diamonds and rubies. Two days before Japan's surrender was announced, she was taken out into Maizuru Bay late at night, her Japanese captain and small crew were shot dead, and the ship was scuttled by opening her Kingston valve. The Japanese government informed the Dutch government that what had once been the *Op ten Noort* had been sunk by a mine during the war. (When it was recovered in 1990, Japanese sources valued the cargo at three trillion yen, or US$30-billion; we return to the story of her recovery in Chapter 14.)

The *Op ten Noort* was just one of Japan's many fake hospital ships. What became of all the treasure moved around on them is a fascinating and complex riddle that has remained secret to this day. Pieces of the puzzle lie scattered around the Pacific Rim, only requiring patience to assemble. Here is what we have pieced together:

Once plunder reached Japan, strategic materials like bauxite and tungsten went to war production or were concealed in underground bunkers on military installations, from which they surfaced years later. There were many such bunkers around Maizuru Naval Base, for example.

As for hard currencies, Japan was confronted by a logistical problem coping with coinage stolen from so many countries. Gold and silver coins were kept intact, while brass, bronze and copper coins were melted down for war industries. In the Dutch East Indies, Japan later admitted seizing over 196-million guilders worth of coins. Many of these had just been minted in the United States. When Holland was overrun by the Nazis in 1940, the Dutch colonial government in Java was unable to obtain coinage from home and had to have new coins made at mints in San Francisco, Denver and Washington, D.C. These coins had just been distributed throughout the islands when Japan invaded and seized them. In 1946, American sources told the Dutch military mission that 110 cases of these coins were known to have been transferred from Yokosuka Naval Base to the Bank of Japan.

Lieutenant General Schilling of the Dutch military mission reported to his government in September 1947 that thirty tons of Dutch silver (5,637 ingots), had been recovered from Tokyo Bay. This had been confiscated by the Japanese 16th Army on Java and shipped aboard fake hospital ships to the Osaka Mint. Other Dutch ingots were recovered from Etchugina Bay. Thanks to postwar detective work by Dutch Navy Lieutenant A. A. Looijen, 187 tons of stolen Dutch silver bullion from Java, traced to the Bank of Japan, was later returned to the Netherlands mint. Lt. Looijen, who spent the war in Japan as a POW slave laborer, said Dutch, Indian, British, Filipino, Chinese and Indo-Chinese coinage was brought in oil drums to a company named Kokusho, housed in the former Standard Oil refinery at Asundori, just south of Tokyo between Kawasaki and Yokohama. The manager of the facility was army Captain Yamasaki. One of the Dutch POWs there, C. H. L. Broekhuizen, helped sort the coins. His Japanese foreman told him it was the government's intention to conceal the gold and silver coins until after the war, then melt down and re-cast the metal as ingots, to launder it. Other POWs saw re-smelting of copper coins at a factory in Hitachi, a hundred miles north of Tokyo.

American POW Ed Jackfert, interned at Tokyo Area POW Camp #2 in Kawasaki, told us, "I had the occasion of working on a slave labor detail known to us as Kokusho. It was an oil refinery that was owned prior to WWII by the Standard Oil Co – we saw Standard Oil signs everywhere on the property. They had huge warehouses there. On many occasions we were assigned duties of working in these warehouses. Much to our surprise, we discovered that much of the loot brought by Japanese ships from Southeast Asia was stored in these warehouses. We examined hundreds of bags of silver coins of almost every Southeast Asian nation. There had to be tons of these coins warehoused there. There were other types of stolen booty there to which we paid little attention."

Among these were great quantities of loose diamonds, also kept in oil drums. Ultimately, the diamonds and colored gems were sorted and graded, the finest set aside, while the smallest were consigned to industrial use. The rest were poured back into the barrels for storage in warehouses and private vaults of the elite.

Admiral Kodama and other Japanese officers and gangsters in Southeast Asia kept the biggest and best diamonds, sapphires and rubies. Kodama was able to ship his back to Japan aboard military aircraft, but most officers hid their collections of jewels in officer stashes, to be recovered and sold after the war. In our CDs we reproduce documents describing several very large stones recovered from officer stashes in the Philippines and offered for private sale.

Gold and platinum ingots reaching Japan overland from China or by sea were placed either in private vaults or in tunnels and underground bunkers in the Japan Alps, massively built to withstand bombs and earthquakes. All indications are that relatively little of the treasure was put directly into Japanese banks because the ruling elite had no intention of sharing this treasure with the lower orders. It was for this very reason that Golden Lily had been created in the first place, to secure the bulk of the treasure for the imperial family, Japan's most powerful clique, and the tycoons who were its most important supporters.

The biggest underground bunker complex is at Matsushiro, in the mountains near Nagano, site of the 1998 Winter Olympics. The Matsushiro bunker is a hon-eycomb of reinforced concrete tunnels 10-kilometers long, with more than 60,000 cubic feet of underground space originally intended to house the imperial family, leading members of the aristocracy, and all government agencies, if Japan was invaded by the Allies. Japanese sources told us some of its branch tunnels were used to house enough gold and platinum bars to underwrite Japan's postwar recovery. Matsushiro was dug by 10,000 Korean slave laborers, most of whom never were seen again, said to have been buried alive when the branch tunnels were sealed.

Tragically, this was not a rare occurrence. After the war, Allied investigators learned that 387 American, British, Australian and Dutch POWs had suffered a sim-ilar fate on the Japanese island called Sado, off the northwest coast of Honshu. This beautiful but remote island was traditionally used as a place of exile for deposed emperors, aristocrats, poets, priests, and convicted criminals. It had a gold mine, owned and operated by Mitsubishi, notorious for brutal treatment of slave labor-ers. These Allied POWs were working in one of the shafts of the mine, near the island town of Aikawa. Normally, fifty men worked on the surface, transferring coal from wheeled ore bins into hoppers. But, on August 2, 1945, just before Japan's sur-render, all the prisoners were herded into the deepest part of the mine, 400 feet below the surface, where they were put to work hewing out a seam of gold. Guards discreetly withdrew to the surface, where they were ordered to push all the wheeled ore bins into the mineshaft. The night before, Japanese demolition experts had concealed explosive charges in the mineshaft at depths of 200 and 300 feet. At 9:10 a.m., while all the Allied slave laborers were deep below, orders were given to blow the mine. Lieutenant Tsuda Yoshiro, second in command of the forced labor camp, described the event to war crime investigators: "I was watching from a distance of 100 yards and witnessed a rush of smoke and dust from the mine's entrance. While waiting for the smoke and dust to clear, every available guard was set to work dis-mantling the narrow-gauge steel track and then carrying portions of it into the mine entrance. By 10:30 a.m. ...all traces of the steel track had been removed. [Then] the demolition detail entered the mine to set more explosive charges just inside the entrance. It was while returning to the prison camp that I heard a loud explosion. Looking back, I saw an avalanche of rock and earth completely cover where the mine entrance had been." Tsuda did not mention seeing treasure put into the mine before it was blown, but what other reason would there have been for so com-pletely removing all traces of track and obscuring the entrance? If Mitsubishi had nothing to hide, the 387 Allied POWs on Sado could have been repatriated with-out complications, like many others.

More than a thousand Korean slave laborers working another Mitsubishi gold mine on Sado Island also vanished without a trace at war's end. Their existence only became known in 1991 when official records were released of Mitsubishi Corporation's distribution of cigarette rations to its wartime slave laborers. It is per-verse to be remembered as a victim of mass murder only by a tally of cigarette butts.

It is a matter of public record that American forces reported finding immense hoards of war loot in Japan before all information of this type was obliterated from archives in the United States. (The document is titled, *Reports of General MacArthur:*

MacArthur in Japan: The Occupation Military Phase, Volume 1 Supplement, prepared by his General Staff, Library of Congress Catalog Card Number 66-60006, Facsimile Reprint, 1994, Center for Military History, Pub 13-4.) Here are troves of "Japanese-owned gold and silver"…"property that was acquired by Japan under duress, wrongful acts of confiscation, dispossession or spoliation"…"property found in Japan and identified as having been located in an Allied country [China] and removed to Japan by fraud or coercion by the Japanese or their agents"…"great hoards of gold, silver, precious stones, foreign postage stamps, engraving plates"…"precious metals and diamond stockpiles owned or controlled by the Japanese"; 30,000 carats of diamonds in one stash, and a single find of "52.5 pounds of hoarded platinum" with a value at the time of 54-million yen (over US$13-million in 1945 values). The document says, "One of the spectacular tasks of the Occupation dealt with collecting and putting under guard the great hoards of gold, silver, precious stones, foreign postage stamps, engraving plates, and all currency not legal in Japan."…"Eighth Army was directed to seize and maintain custody of precious metals and diamond stockpiles, owned or controlled by the Japanese or Axis governments in Japan during the war. Eighth Army agencies were also authorized to confiscate and deposit precious metals and gems in United States vaults in Tokyo or Osaka whenever such items were …found."

From this it is abundantly clear that America knew Japan looted treasure from countries it occupied. What happened to the treasure thereafter remains a state secret to this day.

In 1947, General MacArthur brought a number of American gemologists to Tokyo. One of these was Edward P. Henderson. According to an oral history interview conducted by the Smithsonian Institution, MacArthur invited Henderson to Japan to appraise some $50-million in gems that the U.S. Army had recovered in Tokyo. Some were found in the ashes of buildings that had burned to the ground. Henderson recalled: "We got buckets full of sand and gravel with a lot of diamonds in it. So one of our big problems was getting the dirt and smoke and stuff off… We were working in the Bank of Japan, down in their vaults where they keep all their gold." According to journalist Robert Whiting, some 800,000 karats of diamonds were later transferred from the Bank of Japan to the custody of MacArthur's command, and these diamonds were never seen again. All attempts to trace any documentary record of them in U.S. archives have failed. It would be interesting to know how 800,000 karats of diamonds, looted by Japan during World War II, now qualify in Washington as "top secret for reasons of national security". Whose national security?

Five tons of silver bullion found in a Mitsui warehouse, illustrate the problem Japan had keeping war loot from falling into Allied hands. Because warehouses were insecure, caves, tunnels and mine shafts were a far better solution. Even Admiral Kodama, Japan's top gangster, was stymied when he ran out of hiding places for his personal loot, and had to avail himself of a privileged hiding place: the vaults of the Imperial Palace. According to the *Tokyo Journal,* "Kodama had a good portion of these valuables transported to the vault of the Imperial Family in the Imperial Palace. Eventually the Minister of the Imperial Household told him to remove them before they were discovered by the Occupation authorities. The rumor was that the official's action was at the direct request of the Emperor."

What about all the treasure still in the Philippines?

•

By early 1943, America had solved its torpedo problems, and the submarine blockade just north of the Philippines became nearly impenetrable. Thereafter, much of the plunder would have to remain in the Philippines. This posed a new challenge to Prince Chichibu and his advisors. The solution was obvious, for gold is a curious commodity. It does not have to change hands. Once you take physical possession of gold bullion, you can put it in any secure place and leave it there for decades or centuries, providing no one else can remove it. Golden Lily could hide all the gold and platinum in deep vaults in the Philippines or Indonesia. It could remain asleep there as secure as if it were in the Matsushiro bunker. Even if Japan were invaded and occupied by the enemy, the location of this bullion would remain secret. When the world lost interest, individual vaults could be recovered discreetly. This was the argument put forth by Prince Chichibu's advisors, including Japan's best financial brains at the time, known as the Four Heavenly Kings.

Engineering deep vaults was not a problem. In Japan, tunneling had been done for a thousand years. Every domain lord had earthworks, tunnels, and bunkers. In the late nineteenth century, railway tunnels had been dug, and mining for coal and other minerals had become a major industry in Japan, so the *zaibatsu* had employed tens of thousands of Japanese men and women as miners. They were now in the army, so Japanese soldiers were inveterate tunnelers. Give them a gun and they dug a hole. America developed flame-throwers primarily to burn them out of these holes, which often continued for miles. No better example exists than the island of Okinawa, where tunnels dug during the war connected natural caverns to blockhouses and gun emplacements. Chinese tombs dotting Okinawa were transformed into pillboxes connected by side tunnels to this underground defensive labyrinth.

The geology of the Philippines provided many natural caverns, and Manila was full of hiding places. During four centuries of Spanish colonial rule, elaborate tunnels had been dug under the city by prisoners, and under American rule these were expanded and reinforced by the U.S. Army. The tunnels were linked, in some cases, to churches, cathedrals and monasteries with catacombs, or to Spanish forts with elaborate dungeons. In 1571, the Spaniards had moved their headquarters to Manila from Cebu, taking over the fortress of the local Moslem ruler, Dato Suliman. Renaming it Fort Santiago, the Spaniards enclosed it in a massive wall of earthworks, encompassing sixty hectares of adjoining land. They called the whole complex Intramuros ('Within the Walls'), and soon added two great cathedrals and numerous government buildings. At the time, Intramuros lay on the south bank of the Pasig River estuary where the river flowed into Manila Bay, so they dug a broad moat around the walls and turned Intramuros into a man-made island. Since then, the water's edge had withdrawn, and the moat became a park. Spanish soldiers, traders, and priests all lived inside the walls of Intramuros with their Filipino servants. Slaves and prisoners alike were put to work digging tunnels beneath

Intramuros to store wine, brandy, manchego cheese, chorizo, serrano ham, olives, grain, silver, gold, and gunpowder. Churches and monastic orders dug catacombs for storage, or for burial crypts.

This underground maze offered Prince Chichibu a ready-made hiding place for war loot. The *kempeitai* had made Ft. Santiago their headquarters, so security in Intramuros was tight. It would be a simple matter to wall off an existing tunnel, or to dig side tunnels, which could be sealed and cleverly camouflaged so nobody would ever guess treasure was hidden inside. The most pressing problem facing Chichibu was how to move the treasure discreetly to Intramuros from bayfront warehouses. Convoys of army trucks would arouse local curiosity. Manila was crowded with homeless refugees, peddlers, prostitutes, street urchins, gangsters, hustlers, and riffraff. There was too big an audience.

The solution was to dig a new tunnel directly from Pier 15 to Fort Santiago, where it could join the existing Spanish-era tunnels under Intramuros. Work began in early May 1942. Great quantities of excavated rock and soil were dumped into Manila Bay as landfill in the Ermita district just south of Pier 15. The digging was done by thousands of POWs, plus slave labor from Korea, China, and the Philippines. Mel Gutierrez was only eight years old when he was taken there to dig, with all other able-bodied males from a barrio in Batangas City. Little Mel was forced to work twelve hours a day, seven days a week, for two years. *Kempeitai* officers in plain clothes made sure he filled his daily quota. On slim rations, many diggers keeled over dead. By May 1943, 35 miles of primary tunnels were completed, wide enough for two army trucks to pass in opposite directions, all of it lined with steel-reinforced concrete.

One end of the tunnel was at Santa Lucia Gate in the Spanish wall around Intramuros, ten miles as the crow flies from General MacArthur's pre-war headquarters at Fort McKinley. Most of the tunnel was relatively shallow, dug in the clay immediately beneath Intramuros, remaining just above the water table and basaltic bedrock. But Chichibu's engineers made an exception at the Pasig River, where they dug down through the bedrock, creating a watertight tunnel under the river. All in all, this was an exceptional feat of engineering, unknown to the outside world. In 1975, it was still possible to drive from one end of the 35-mile-long tunnel network to the other, as Robert Curtis learned when he discovered the tunnel, while reverse-engineering Japanese treasure-site maps. But today its existence is unknown to most Filipinos. All but two of the entrances have been blocked by more recent construction.

Through the summer of 1942, while the tunnel was being dug, Chichibu and other princes toured potential treasure vault sites around Manila. They traveled in a convoy of heavy six-wheeled Model 93 staff cars accompanied by motorcycle outriders. These limousines drew a lot of attention. Developed originally from a pre-war Studebaker or Hudson chassis, they were open touring cars, with canvas tops folding back behind the rear seat. They had two rear axles providing two rear wheels on each side. The white sidewall tires were mounted on chromed spoke wheels. Behind each front wheel the fender dipped to nestle a spare tire. On the right front fender was a stubby flagstaff with a red 14-petal chrysanthemum on a white field, the crest of first-tier imperial princes (the crest of the emperor has 16-petals). The Model 93 came in gasoline and diesel versions, rated respectively at 68 and 70 horsepower, but given its 7,500 pound weight, the beast could only do a top speed of 60 mph.

Behind the princes came Chichibu's military staff and engineers in six ordinary Nissan sedans, which looked like all the ugly black sedans made everywhere in the world in the 1930s. Following them were three truckloads of heavily armed Imperial Guards.

The princes were especially interested in Manila Cathedral, San Augustin Church, Ft. Santiago, Ft. McKinley and Santo Tomas University. They hoped to find a way to create a treasure vault at each of these historic monuments, and to do this invisibly by connecting the vault with a branch shaft to the new main tunnel. Chichibu's engineers had prepared a large-scale map of Manila on which every potential site was marked. The map showed the route of the main tunnel and indicated where it would be necessary to construct smaller access tunnels to each future vault.

A main consideration was to avoid having vaults discovered accidentally, by a direct hit from artillery or aerial bomb, or by future construction on the same site. As the Geneva Convention forbade the bombing of hospitals, schools, prisoner of war camps, churches, and historic monuments, creating treasure vaults in those places provided the best insurance. As a further precaution, each vault would be built at a depth of around 90 feet – too deep for a bomb to penetrate. These vaults might be discovered during future construction, involving excavation, pile-driving, or drilling for water. So they chose sites under historic monuments that would be off limits to future building projects, and other sites near existing water supplies, figuring no one drills a well next to another well. Some choices seem oddly poetic, such as those near large acacia trees. Chichibu's brother, Prince Mikasa, was the family expert on Middle Eastern affairs. Acacia wood was said to have been used to build the Ark of the Covenant, and was mentioned in the Bible as a sign of Messianic resurgence. In practical terms, acacias have deep roots, and thus are unlikely to be killed by drought or uprooted by typhoon.

One of the first sites the princes visited was General MacArthur's headquarters at Ft. McKinley. A close inspection was made of MacArthur's air raid shelter, sixty feet below a grass-covered quadrangle in front of the headquarters building. Two flights of concrete steps led down to three large reinforced concrete rooms. The Officers' Club at Ft. McKinley was built on one end of a gently sloping ridge where you could enjoy cooling breezes from the distant sea. On one side of this ridge were tennis courts, on the other side a parade ground. It was decided to dig Golden Lily's main tunnel beneath the parade ground, then into the hill below the Officers' Club. At the bottom of the concrete stairs leading down to MacArthur's bomb shelter, the new tunnel would take a jog to the left for 100 feet, to a point directly under the Officers' Club swimming pool. There, at a depth of ninety feet below the pool, Chichibu ordered excavation of a small treasure room. Because the hill was solid rock, there was no need for shoring.

Inside Intramuros, it was decided to place several treasure vaults at San Augustin

Church and the monastery next door. Both were built in the sixteenth century during the reign of King Philip II, who had sent the ill-fated Spanish Armada to
Elizabethan England. The church was built of cut stone, quarried east of Manila.
Beneath the church were catacombs holding remains of priests, nobles, and wealthy
commoners. In the courtyard of the cloister, a garden of tropical plants surrounded a fountain shaped like a huge stone flower. In arched passageways on each side,
the walls were hung with twenty-six large oil paintings, six feet wide and eight feet
tall, portraying priests tending their Filipino flock.

Beside the church was the monastery. When the princes visited it in 1942 the
monastery was crowded with religious relics, statues of saints, and displays of ornate
priestly vestments. Its Recibidor, or main reception room, was 150 feet long by 50
wide, with a grand staircase at the far end. In one wall, a narrow staircase led down
to the catacombs.

Chichibu's plan for San Augustin quickly took shape. The stone fountain in the
cloister of the Church was four hundred meters from the Santa Lucia Gate, where
the main Golden Lily tunnel began. It was decided to dig a branch tunnel from the
gate to a treasure chamber directly beneath this fountain. The vault would be only
thirty feet square, packed tight with gold and artworks. Like the vault under
MacArthur's swimming pool, this under the fountain at San Augustin would be
secure long into the future.

From under the fountain, another spur tunnel would be dug under the church
catacombs, directly below the crypt of Padre Juan de Macias. A vault would be created there, measuring twenty feet by thirty, lined with reinforced concrete. When
these two vaults were filled with treasure, the entrances to their access tunnels
would be sealed with a super-hard ceramic-concrete compound, and made invisible. Golden Lily employed Japanese ceramics experts who were able to produce
concrete of extraordinary hardness. By molding a cement plug to resemble a normal section of tunnel wall, tinting the composite with pigments and local soil, the
entrances blended perfectly with their surroundings. Nobody would ever guess that
an entrance to a branch tunnel existed. Robert Curtis found them because he had
the original maps.

The Recibidor in the monastery adjoining San Augustin Church also became a
treasure repository. When Spaniards first built the huge room, to support the ceiling and the weight of additional floors and roof above, their masons installed a
massive cut-stone arch two-thirds of the way back. Chichibu found a pile of the
same pale grey cut-stones in the grounds behind the Church. Using these stones,
and a similar mortar, Golden Lily masons filled in the arch so that it became a solid
wall. This closed off one-third of the Recibidor, creating a treasure room measuring
twenty feet by fifty feet. The Recibidor was not a public space; it was meant only
for inhabitants of the monastery. As such, not many people knew what it looked
like. However, current occupants of the monastery would notice that the room had
been changed, so the *kempeitai* was given the job of killing all the priests and church
laborers who were familiar with the Recibidor. Meanwhile, church archives and
records were searched for all related documents and drawings. These were burned,
and the archivists stabbed to death. (When American forces retook Manila, forty-

five bodies dressed in clerical garb were found in shallow graves in the basement of the monastery; most had their hands tied behind their backs and had been killed with bayonets to avoid attracting attention with gunshots.)

In a flash of good humor, Chichibu led the other princes out to the cloister passage hung with huge oil paintings, stopping before one titled, *Saint Augustin Blessing a Native*. The saint had his right hand raised, as if he was gesturing in the direction of the new Recibidor treasure vault. Chichibu ordered his aides to have an extra finger painted on the hand, pointing directly at the disguised entrance. The engineer who prepared the construction drawing for this site used the saint's sixth finger as the fulcrum point. (This became known as the 'Six-Finger Site'.)

Next, the princes turned their attention to nearby Manila Cathedral, where they selected two sites. One vault was dug beneath a huge acacia tree in front of the cathedral, a second directly beneath the altar. The princes were certain that in the future nobody would excavate beneath the altar. Both vaults were excavated by way of a branch tunnel coming from under the stone fountain at San Augustin Church.

At Santo Tomas University on Rizal Avenue, they found a large basement room and decided to close off one end to make a substantial treasure chamber. This building was safe from bombs, for it was an internment camp for American civilians including women and children. The Red Cross notified the U.S. military, so the university was off limits to bombers.

In subsequent days, the princes toured all the buildings and grounds comprising Ft. Santiago. As *kempeitai* headquarters, work could be done anywhere. Several hiding places were chosen. One would be under the big fountain in Ft. Santiago's front park. It would be approached by a branch tunnel from the acacia tree vault at Manila Cathedral. (In the 1980s, when treasure hunters drilled an exploratory 3-inch hole beneath this fountain, the gas of decomposed corpses sickened them. Allied POWs had been buried alive in that end of the 35-mile tunnel in 1943. Ft. Santiago had to be closed for a week while the smell dissipated.)

The second hiding place at Ft. Santiago was under an acacia tree in the Spanish officers' courtyard, beside a monument to the martyred nineteenth century poet and novelist Jose Rizal, wrongly executed by the Spaniards for sedition. (This vault was recovered in 1985 by a military unit loyal to Imelda Marcos.) A spur led to a third vault beneath the Bastion de San Miguel.

Back in 1942, more than four thousand American and Filipino prisoners were confined in the dungeons of Ft. Santiago, where they were interrogated before being put to death. The smell of thousands of unwashed prisoners and moldering corpses gave the fort its characteristic aroma. A mass grave by the Pasig River was already full in 1942, so the *kempeitai* trucked most bodies to the bay front, loaded them on a barge, and dumped them in Manila Bay. Tides carried the corpses past Corregidor and into the South China Sea. The main structure of the fort had three dungeons, each on a lower level. The deepest, Basement Three, was below the surface of the Pasig River. Each day two hundred men at a time were herded into this dungeon, and valves opened to let water in. It was a terrible way to die, starving men drowning in panic, but it saved ammunition. When they were dead, other prisoners using old bilge pumps cleared the water.

Basement Two on the north side was much larger – 60 feet by 120 feet – and known as the Execution Chamber. Most prisoners at Ft. Santiago were murdered individually by the *kempeitai* here, in the course of interrogation. Imperial war loot had priority, so Prince Chichibu ordered the dungeon emptied and hosed down to remove the smell. When this was done he returned for an inspection. Here, Chichibu ordered a pit made below water level. While the pit was dug, it took several hundred POWs to maintain a wall of sandbags and to operate hand-pumps against the influx of river water. The bottom of the pit then was covered with old railway ties, and slabs of a red-hued marble laid on top of the wood. Wood crates were placed on the marble slabs, and the crates were filled with gold bars. The POWs who had dug the pit were then murdered, the dirt they had removed was piled over their bodies, and a concrete slab was poured, filling it to the usual level of the basement floor.

Basement Three was next. When Dato Suliman's fort was first modified, the Spaniards had created four airshafts. The largest led down to the deepest dungeon. It was now enlarged by Golden Lily engineers, and reinforced. This became the resting place for Mosler safes taken from various Manila banks and the Intendencia, the pre-war central bank of the Philippines, the same safes emptied by Colonel Willoughby in early 1942 when government and private gold was taken to Corregidor. While still empty, twenty-two of these big safes were lowered down the biggest airshaft to its dirt floor. There the safes were filled with rough gold chunks cut off 75-kilo bars. The safes were then locked. As in Basement Two, a one-foot-thick slab of concrete was poured over the whole assembly. POWs began filling in the vent with loose rock and dirt when another Mosler safe was delivered. Hurriedly, this one was lowered onto the backfill, more dirt and rocks were added, and another slab of concrete was poured. On the flat roof of the fort, the top of the biggest airshaft was rebuilt and sealed with some of the original stones quarried in the Spanish era, so nobody would guess it was there. (In the late 1970s these Mosler safes were recovered for President Marcos by a team headed by his protégé, Dr. Gil Gadi.)

One of the remaining small airshafts had boxes of gold bars lowered into it, followed by oil drums of gold and silver coins. This shaft was then filled with superfine sand, packed down hard, and the shaft capped just below roof-level with a five-foot-thick slab of reinforced concrete. If anybody dug his way into the airshaft from the sides, the superfine sand would cave in and bury him alive. Small glass bottles of cyanide, easily broken, were mixed into the sand.

Two other stashes completed the Ft. Santiago hiding places. One was in an underground room that once had been used to store provisions for the Spanish garrison. Another was a rainwater cistern, in the foundations of Suliman's palace.

All this planning by Prince Chichibu and his engineers took many weeks to evolve into 'blue series' engineering drawings for the construction phase. Eventually, coded recovery maps were drawn by Japanese cartographers. At some future date, these 'red series' recovery maps would guide Japanese teams back to each site, give them the fulcrum point by which to judge depths, and other data essential to avoid booby-traps and make a recovery. Stylistically, these red series maps were uniquely Japanese, done in a form of caricature familiar to anyone who had served in Japan's armed forces. Terrain features such as mountains, rivers, trees and roads were represented as if they were drawn on a chalkboard. Each map was marked prominently with what appeared to be the overall value of the treasure contained in that particular vault; for example ¥111-billion, ¥777-billion, or ¥888-billion (always with the yen mark). In fact, like all the other map markings, this is only a code. To know how much actually was hidden there, you had to have the key. For example, it might be necessary to remove six zeros. All other signs and symbols in the maps are similarly confusing. All you could assume was that a 777 site was bigger than a 111 site. These maps bore notes written in different scripts including Kana (syllabic alphabet) and Kanji (Chinese ideograms). Some also bore English inscriptions, written by Japanese engineers trained at universities in Britain and the United States. One encryption key was a flag flying to the left or right, indicating whether the map needed to be looked at straight on, or reversed in a mirror; a clock face indicating depths and bearings, and a fulcrum point indicating where all measurements for that site began. Without one of these maps showing the fulcrum point, you would never know where to dig. (Thirty years later, for example, President Marcos assigned 2,000 soldiers to search the 35 miles of tunnels under Manila for over two years before giving up empty-handed, except for one 75-kilo gold bar found in the back of an army truck abandoned in a tunnel; Marcos never understood the maps.)

Such technical details obscure the tragic human cost. Allied POWs working under the grimmest conditions dug these tunnels and vaults. For special jobs, Korean and Chinese slave laborers were used, because they could not communicate directly with Allied POWs working in the same place. Without exception, eyewitnesses told us that each time a treasure vault was filled and sealed, the POWs and slave laborers were buried alive inside, to guarantee their silence. Shinto priests gave each site their blessing, waving wands of tree branches, making sure the spirits of the dead would guard the site. The real purpose of this mass murder was tight security. Thousands of Dutch, British, Australian, Canadian, New Zealand and American POWs vanished below ground in Manila, never again to see the light of day. At one site alone, in Teresa, southeast of Manila, eyewitnesses attest to 1,200 Allied POWs being buried alive (see Chapter 11). When Teresa was opened by Robert Curtis in October 1975, his efforts to collect hundreds of dog-tags among human remains in the tunnel, to identify the victims, were thwarted by security men who forced him at gunpoint to leave the site.

By August 1942, the rains had come and Chichibu had been in Manila for six months, living in the Manila Hotel penthouse of General MacArthur. Many of the general's personal belongings remained in place, including his books. The windows overlooked Pier 15, and the splendid sunsets over Bataan across the great bay. But Chichibu fled to Singapore, where he was less bothered by his tuberculosis.

One measure of Japan's total plunder is that all these treasure vaults being created in Manila, plus the tunnels at Corregidor, were not enough. Other vaults were being dug in Mindanao, in Mindoro, and other islands in the archipelago. And in the mountains north of Manila, another imperial prince was hard at work enlarging natural caverns to create the biggest treasure vaults of the war outside Japan.

CHAPTER SIX

THE EYEWITNESS

In the highlands far to the north of Manila was another world, where rugged mountains hid quiet villages in cool green valleys, remote from the war. Climbing by smoke-belching bus out of the lowlands of Luzon, zigzagging up a pockmarked road into the 3,000-foot Caraballo Mountains to the town of Santa Fe, you entered Nueva Viscaya, a region named after Spain's Basque country on the Bay of Biscay. Once over this initial mountain range, you descended into the fertile Cagayan Valley around the town of Bambang. The Cagayan, dotted here and there with what look like mini-volcanoes, was a well-watered region with rice paddy fields, plowed by carabao water buffaloes guided by little boys. To the west was the Cordillera range, to the east the taller Sierra Madre. You were completely surrounded by impenetrable mountains covered with rainforest, populated by hill-tribes wearing only G-strings. From Bambang the Cagayan Valley opened out to the north, widening as it descended to the northern tip of Luzon, the coastal town of Aparri, and a big offshore island called Camiguin.

This tranquil upland setting around Bambang became a primary base of Golden Lily operations from 1942 to 1945, because the region had many natural caverns. Some held Stone-Age tools and charcoal drawings. Although the underlying basement rock was very hard, upper layers of sandstone and limestone or sediment were washed away by torrential rains and subterranean springs, creating natural passages and vaults. Much of this crust was easy to tunnel, often without shoring. The Japanese appreciated the advantages this offered for military purposes and for safe storage of treasure. From the Cagayan, aircraft could fly easily to Formosa and then to Japan, refueling at Okinawa. As early as the 1920s, Japanese strategists planned to take over the Philippines and absorb it into their new empire.

So in the early 1920s thousands of Japanese began to trickle into Luzon as settlers, businessmen, or geologists, while Japanese fishing boats appeared along the coast in increasing numbers. These were scouts and intelligence agents. They settled near the South China Sea coast and in the mountains around Bambang, Baguio and Aparri.

They learned to speak Tagalog and Ilocano, took notes about who was prosperous and influential, and gathered details about local infrastructure, roads, and utilities. Harbors were charted, coastline mapped. In the mountains, Japanese hikers were a common sight. With help from farmers, caves were found and explored.

At the time, Bambang had less than two thousand inhabitants. Rural Filipinos live close to their land in barrios or villages separated by a kilometer or two. One of the tiny barrios outside Bambang was called Dulao. Its headman was Lino Valmores, who worked in the rice fields with his teenage nephew Ben, a handsome boy who had about him an air of innocence and sincerity.

Ben had been born in March 1925, when his parents were still living in the steamy lowlands of Pangasinan, north of Manila, where his father found work as a day laborer. But Ben spent much of his childhood at his uncle's home in Dulao, attending the Catholic church school in Bambang. He remained in school there through the sixth grade, taught by Father Disney to read and write, and to speak some English, but the rest of his days were spent working in the paddies with his uncle, plowing in the Spring behind a grunting carabao, in the Autumn cutting clumps of rice stalks with a sickle. Being Ilocano set them apart, for while most Filipinos speak Tagalog, they spoke the Ilocano dialect of the parched Ilocos region along the northwest coast of Luzon. There are pockets of Ilocanos everywhere, in Bambang, in the resort of Baguio, and especially in Manila, where they have their own political organizations and their own underworld gangs.

Ben was turning seventeen when the Japanese invaded the Philippines. His family was in Pangasinan at the time, directly in the path of the invaders. His father, Esteban, was blind in one eye from a shooting accident as a U.S. Army recruit. Because most people are right-handed, rifles are made to eject spent cartridges to the right, away from the eyes. On the shooting range for the first time, being left-handed, Esteban put the rifle up to his left shoulder to fire it. The cartridge ejected directly into his left eye, blinding it. When the American forces surrendered, he ended up in a prison camp with thousands of other POWs. Unlike the Americans, the Filipino troops were interrogated and, after a short time, sent home.

In Esteban's absence, looters torched their house in Pangasinan and the family fled into the mountains, hoping to reach Dulao safely. As the eldest child, Ben led the way on foot, followed by his mother and grandmother, brothers and sisters. Like all refugees, each one carried a load of family possessions. Penniless, all they had to eat for weeks was rice with *bagoong*, a fermented fish paste. Japanese soldiers were everywhere, and Ben had to answer a lot of questions. He was afraid, because he saw many Filipino men working as slaves, cruelly beaten by the soldiers. By mid-February they reached San Jose where it took four days to get passes from the Japanese garrison. When they got to Dulao after midnight they were overcome with relief and happiness. Ben's uncle Lino immediately killed and cooked a pig, and stood over them saying, "Go ahead, my children, just keep on eating till you get very full." A few days later Ben's father was released, joining them, and they all hugged and cried again.

Uncle Lino gave Ben's father a parcel of land to farm in Dulao, so he could support his family through the war. Ten months later, in January 1943, they were cutting sugarcane to make sugar, rum, and hard candy for their own use. Ben was told to go cut dry bamboo so they could make a fire to cook the cane juice. He took two buffalo carts and went up a nearby hill where there were stands of giant bamboo. While he was hacking the cane with his bolo, he heard the leaves rustle and was astonished and frightened to see Japanese soldiers appear out of nowhere around him, sprigs of bamboo in their helmets, pointing their guns at him. He froze with fear, expecting to be killed instantly.

A soldier jerked his gun at him, so Ben dropped his bolo and crouched with his back to a cartwheel. An officer, Colonel Adachi, spoke to Ben first in Tagalog, then in Ilocano. What was Ben doing there?

"Cutting firewood."

"Where is the road to San Antonio barrio?" Ben pointed. Adachi insisted that Ben guide them there. Ben said he could not go without his father's permission.

"Then take us to your father," the colonel said. So far Ben had not heard a word from their leader, a young man with a shaved head, dressed all in white, who smiled at Ben in a friendly way. He looked to be only in his mid-twenties, yet Colonel Adachi and other officers in the group treated him with great deference. At his side he had a large samurai sword in a wood and leather sheath, and a short sword opposite. On the left breast pocket of his tunic was a bright red circular emblem, five or six inches across, trimmed in gold thread. Colonel Adachi addressed him respectfully as 'Kimsu'.

When they reached the modest Valmores house in Dulao, Ben's father was impatient for him to get back to work, but his uncle said it was wiser for Ben to guide the Japanese to San Antonio.

On the way to San Antonio, the officers riding in the carabao cart with him, Ben was certain he was going to be killed. Tears began rolling down his cheeks. Colonel Adachi asked why was he crying. He smiled kindly and told Ben not to be afraid; they would not hurt him. They stopped by a coconut palm, and Ben climbed up nimbly to get some nuts, opening them with his bolo. They asked his name. He said "Ben-ha-MEEN", the way the name is pronounced by Tagalog and Ilocano speakers. Kimsu said something in Japanese, and Adachi told Ben they no longer wanted to go to San Antonio but back to San Fernando, which was their main camp, in the opposite direction. Ben said he must ask his father's permission again. This seemed to impress the young man in white, so they returned to Ben's home. Once more his father protested, but the Japanese promised they would 'borrow' Ben for no more than a week. They told Ben to wrap some extra clothes in a banana leaf and bring them.

On their way to San Fernando, a distance of a kilometer and a half, they heard a woman screaming in the undergrowth. Kimsu and Ben jumped down from the cart and hurried to investigate. They found two Japanese soldiers ripping the clothes off a village woman, trying to rape her. Kimsu drew his samurai sword and whacked the two soldiers with the flat of the blade. The two men fell on their faces, pressing their foreheads in the dirt, begging forgiveness. Kimsu turned to his own men and shouted at them. They froze at attention, faces shocked. Each of the officers said only, "Hai!" Kimsu had them arrest the two soldiers. He covered the naked woman with his own tunic, and ordered his men to escort her to her house. Later, when the group reached the army camp in San Fernando, Ben was amazed to see all the Japanese there bow down as they entered. Colonel Adachi called the whole camp together. Kimsu gave the two rapists a severe reprimand, and ordered the soldiers never to have sex with Filipinas on pain of death. Everyone in the camp was absolutely silent, foreheads pressed in the dirt. Later Ben asked Adachi who the man in white was. The colonel just said, "Kimsu".

Kimsu was in charge of a very large team of officers, hundreds of men, including mining engineers, geologists, architects, chemists, specialists in ceramics, electricians, demolitions experts, and a battalion of soldiers. There were well over a thousand men in the San Fernando camp, whose only job was to move and hide war loot. Ben saw thousands of boxes made of bronze, and some of wood, which were extremely heavy. It took four, five, six or even eight men to carry each box, using slings made of webbing. He also saw hundreds of completely naked Korean, Chinese, and Filipino slave laborers moving the boxes, sometimes blindfolded, sometimes not. He knew they were slaves because they had ankle chains, and ropes binding their wrists together, with just enough play to wield a pick or shovel. Trucks arrived continually at the San Fernando camp loaded with these heavy boxes, and after they were unloaded the men in the trucks were sent away. Then the slaves or Kimsu's own soldiers put the boxes into tunnels, deep pits, or caverns scattered around the Cagayan Valley. Once Ben saw Filipinos bring boxes in trucks and stack them beside a road. After the Filipinos left, Japanese soldiers moved the boxes into a cave. Then the soldiers were ordered to leave, and Chinese slaves carried the boxes out of the cave and put them in a deep pit where they were covered with soil, which was then scattered with the flat cobbles typical of this region, and fast-growing papaya plants and bamboo were planted to complete the disguise. Some tunnels Ben saw led into big caverns that were enlarged by Kimsu's Japanese engineers. In the beginning Ben had no idea what was happening; he saw little violence, so his life with the Japanese was neither scary nor ominous.

He learned that he was to be Kimsu's water boy, cook, servant and valet, bringing him food, shining his shoes, doing his laundry, looking after his clothes, and keeping his living quarters spotless. Kimsu lived in a proper house in the midst of the camp, not in a tent. All Filipino residents of San Fernando barrio had been sent away. In Kimsu's house there was a bedroom with a single large bed, and a table holding a magnificent Shang bronze urn, looted somewhere in Southeast Asia. Ben thought it was a vase and supposed that Kimsu used it as a wash basin. But it was there only as an art object, to be admired. At night, Kimsu put a pillow in the middle of the bed and insisted that Ben sleep on one side, instead of on the floor. Kimsu slept on the opposite side. He warned Ben not to touch the pillow or – he drew his fingernail across his throat. Ben spent some restless nights at first, afraid to move at all, but later he got used to it. He was a handsome boy of 18, and Kimsu was a cultivated man in his early thirties, who looked even younger. As a Japanese aristocrat it would not have been unusual for him to have bisexual tastes. That cannot be ruled out, but there is no evidence whatever that there was any sexual side to his master-servant relationship with Ben. It was normal in Japan for aristocrats to have personal servants who slept nearby, to answer any command.

Kimsu obviously liked Ben, appreciated his sincerity and innocence, his loyalty to his parents and family. In the middle of an army camp with over a thousand soldiers, and nearly as many slave laborers, Kimsu was completely alone, a nobleman among serfs, most of whom did not dare raise their eyes to his face for fear of being blinded. In his complete solitude, Kimsu welcomed Ben's presence as if he were a younger brother, and was extremely kind. Both Kimsu and Colonel Adachi protected the boy from other Japanese, and when they traveled in convoy to other parts of Luzon, or to other islands in the Philippines, they looked after him attentively. Ben said he saw many Japanese officers and soldiers who behaved angrily and cruelly toward Filipinos, in particular toward POWs and slave laborers. But Kimsu avoided violence.

"Kimsu was always giving me his food," Ben said. "Chicken, pork, beef, sardines in tins."

In manners, Kimsu was elegant, and gentle. He spoke in a soft voice, so one had to listen closely. When nobody else was around, he spoke to Ben in English. Once when a lone Filipino guerrilla was captured and dragged into the San Fernando camp, Kimsu's top aides Brigadier General Kawabata and Colonel Kaburagi wanted to shoot him, but Kimsu said let him go. The guerrilla ran away screaming at the top of his lungs – afraid he would be hit by bullets in the back. All the Japanese laughed at his antics.

After Ben had been there one month, and felt braver, he asked Colonel Adachi why Kimsu was different. Adachi replied simply: "He's a prince." Kimsu heard this exchange and came in from the other room. Smiling, he put his two index fingers together and said in English, "Hirohito and I are like that." Ben said, "Are you a brother of the emperor?" Kimsu said, "No, that's Chichibu. I'm a cousin."

During one of many private conversations later, Kimsu told Ben that his secret name was Prince Takeda, but in the war he used the codename Kimsu Murakusi. He swore Ben to silence on these and many other matters.

Prince Takeda Tsuneyoshi (for that was his full name) was a grandson of Japan's Meiji Emperor, who had lived from 1852 to 1912. Meiji had four surviving daughters by imperial concubines, whom he married to four princes. These four princes were extraordinary characters, lifelong cronies – Prince Kitashirakawa Naruhisa and his brother Prince Takeda Tsunehisa, and Prince Asaka Yasuhiko and his half-brother Prince Higashikuni Naruhiko. These princes of the blood went to school together as boys, attended the same university, served in the army together, shared the same Geisha, went overseas together, and partied together as playboys. Two died young: Prince Takeda in 1919 when his only son was ten years old, and his brother Prince Kitashirakawa in 1923 when he wrapped his hand-made Bugatti touring car around a giant sycamore tree on the road from Paris to Deauville, following a liquid lunch. Thereafter, the two surviving playboy princes, Prince Asaka and Prince Higashikuni, took a special interest in raising young Prince Takeda. He also became a favorite of his first cousin, Crown Prince Hirohito, who was nine years older.

All male members of the imperial family received a military education. Young Takeda was educated first at the Gakushuin, or Peers' School, graduated from the

Military Academy in 1930, and became a sub-lieutenant in the Cavalry, quickly rising to lieutenant. He studied at Army Staff College, became a captain in August 1936, a major in 1940. In 1942, he went to Saigon as Hirohito's personal liaison to Count Terauchi, commander-in-chief of Japanese armies in Southeast Asia (son of General Terauchi, the Japanese viceroy in Korea who had looted tombs and terrorized civilians). Like other princes, Takeda was part of the military elite, whose presence in the field was a constant reminder of the emperor's supreme command. In his capacity as special emissary of the emperor, Takeda became second-in-command to Prince Chichibu in directing the operations of Golden Lily throughout Asia. Promoted to lieutenant colonel, he was listed as a staff officer in the Strategic Section of the Operations Division, under the alias 'Lieutenant-Colonel Miyata'. Although still officially posted to Saigon, he moved to the Philippines where he took charge of Golden Lily's field operations outside Manila. Prince Chichibu remained in overall command in Manila, and personally oversaw the most important treasure sites in and around the city, but he was often away on trips to Tokyo, Singapore or Jakarta. Ben saw Chichibu twice in Manila during 1943, when all the princes held a strategy conference. Chichibu, he said, was always referred to by other princes as 'Chako', as Prince Takeda always was called 'Kimsu'.

Prince Takeda based himself in the highlands at San Fernando to construct several very big cavern sites, the most important being immediately next to his camp. He also directed the work of chief engineers at each of 174 other imperial treasure sites throughout the islands. So he did not remain constantly in San Fernando. He traveled around the Philippines, flew to Singapore, Bangkok, Saigon and Jakarta to shepherd war loot on its way, and made frequent trips back to Tokyo. We know he was in Japan at least once a year because his wife bore him children in 1940, 1942, 1943, 1944, and 1945.

Whenever Kimsu walked around the camp at San Fernando, guards called out warnings to the next guard that a prince was coming. Everyone stared at the ground, avoiding looking him in the eyes. In previous centuries, Japanese commoners always threw themselves down and pressed their foreheads in the dirt. Ben observed all this, but he was not Japanese and did not know the rules. For some reason Kimsu was delighted to have Ben act toward him as he acted toward his own father, Esteban.

One evening, when Colonel Adachi sent him to fetch salt in the bomb shelter next to the house, Ben saw nothing resembling salt and wandered into the wrong tunnel, where he found boxes filled with gold bars, and many jars. Thinking one of the jars might be full of salt he opened it and found it packed with coins: gold sovereigns, silver dollars, all the hard currencies in circulation across Southeast Asia. He had never seen such coins. He opened other jars to see if they contained salt, and found more coins. Amazed to see so much money in one place, he stuck his hand in a jar and picked up a coin. Just then a Japanese soldier came in and asked Ben angrily what he was doing. He dragged Ben outside and Colonel Adachi took him to Kimsu. The prince questioned him, and Ben explained he was only looking for salt. Kimsu was amused and warned Ben mildly never to go into places where he was not supposed to go, and never to touch coins or other valuables.

Early the next morning, Ben awakened to find himself alone in the bed, lying in the midst of a lot of coins. He was afraid to move. He feared that he would be killed if he touched the coins. When he heard his name called, Ben called back that he was stuck in bed. Kimsu came in laughing and told Ben to pick up the coins and put them in a sack, then to harness a carabao to a wagon, get a cow and a horse, and put a new sewing machine in the cart with the coins. Kimsu said, "We're going to see your father." He had been thinking about Ben's fascination with the coins in the tunnel, and realized that the boy's family was completely impoverished. Along the way to Dulao barrio they passed a group of Japanese soldiers by a river, some digging a deep pit while others played with quantities of coins taken from earthenware jars standing all around the pit. Kimsu talked with them, examined some paperwork, and returned to the cart satisfied. They continued toward Dulao and came upon a barbed-wire compound where Ben saw prisoners chopping wood. He recognized one nearly naked and emaciated prisoner as Father Disney, the priest who had taught him to read and write at the church school in Bambang. He felt very sad and sorry for the priest, knowing he would die.

When they reached Ben's home, Kimsu told Ben's father through Col. Adachi that Ben had worked out so well as his valet that he wanted to keep Ben on and to give his father in trade the sewing machine, the cow, horse, carabao and wagon, and the big bag of coins. At first Ben and his parents thought he was being purchased as a slave, so Ben began to weep. His mother, looking at Ben, also cried openly. But Adachi explained that they just wanted to employ Ben. He told them that Kimsu was a prince of Japan, who liked Ben, protected him, and swore that when the war was over he would personally bring Ben back to his parents. They asked Ben what he thought. He told his mother she need not worry, because Kimsu treated him like a little brother. All of Kimsu's retinue were kind to him, he explained. The senior officers, Brigadier General Kawabata, Col. Adachi, Col. Kaburagi, Col. Kasabuchi, Navy Captain Honda and Navy Captain Takahashi, all were teaching Ben Japanese words and phrases. (By the war's end, Ben was modestly fluent, and could even read a few simpler ideographs.)

That settled, Ben and Kimsu got back in their cart and returned to the San Fernando camp. The sight of a grandson of Emperor Meiji riding around in a carabao cart was all the more remarkable because Kimsu always wore an immaculate white uniform, different from the army and navy officers in his retinue. Above the red disk on the left breast of his tunic, he wore a row of medals, and on his epaulets were insignias that meant nothing whatever to Ben. However, the red patch did have special significance. It was finely embroidered in bright red silk thread. Around the perimeter was a border of 18-karat gold thread worked in a scalloped pattern, creating a stylized 14-petal chrysanthemum, the emblem of princes of the blood. Once when Ben brushed the embroidery too hard and pulled out some gold threads, he was beaten by one of the other officers. This beating, and the scolding he got for messing with the coins in the bomb shelter, were the only times he was handled roughly. (Half a century later, when Ben first saw the British edition of our book *The Yamato Dynasty* with a gold chrysanthemum embossed on the dustjacket, he exclaimed: "That is what Kimsu had on his tunic!") A similar emblem on a pennant flew from a staff on the front fender of Kimsu's car, so wherever he went Japanese checkpoints and military guards realized that a prince was approaching.

Ben guessed that Kimsu was 24 or 25 years old (in 1943 he was 34, but looked younger). He was taller than Ben, about 5 feet 10 inches. His face was very smooth, his head shaved. He did have small quirks: a curious way of smoking a cigarette, holding it between his little finger and ring finger, as he blew smoke rings. As an aristocrat, his manner was languid, and he never hurried. He always carried a clean white handkerchief to pat the sweat off his face. His glasses were hinged so the lenses could be flipped up, unlike anything Ben had ever seen. Often he hummed Japanese folk songs like 'Sakura' ('Cherry Blossoms'), and he taught Ben the Japanese version of 'Lili Marlene', a song popular everywhere in the world during the war. Kimsu spoke elegant English, but only to Ben when they were alone. When officers were around, he spoke Japanese even to Ben, and this was translated into Ilocano by Col. Adachi.

The house where they lived at San Fernando was heavily guarded. Senior officers brought papers every day. Ben overheard them talking about ships full of treasure, which they had scuttled in places where recovery would be easy. For an office, Kimsu had a separate tent with a desk and a large blackboard, where he gave instructions to chief engineers who came to report from other sites throughout the Philippines. Eventually, Ben learned there were 175 imperial sites specially built for treasure belonging exclusively to Emperor Hirohito and the imperial family. Hiding it was Kimsu's main responsibility. Each site had a chief engineer, architect, mining expert, experts in mixing and molding ceramics, demolition experts for booby traps, and chemists for seeding each site with toxic chemicals and glass bottles of cyanide. They reported to Kimsu, he reviewed their progress, and when each site was ready, the prince came to inspect, inventory, and close it. Ben traveled everywhere with him, as far as the big southern island of Mindanao. In addition to his personal retinue, on these journeys Kimsu was guarded by three platoons of heavily armed soldiers who traveled in a convoy of trucks behind the staff cars. These common soldiers never spoke to the prince, and avoided looking in his direction. Beside him in the sedan, Kimsu kept a leather satchel packed with architectural drawings, inventories, maps and instruments, including drawing tools, a compass and a magnifying glass. Beside it lay his sword. Arriving at each site, Kimsu carried out a final inspection, scrutinizing maps and drawings prepared by the chief engineer, walking around above and below ground. When he was satisfied, the vault was sealed with all Allied POWs and slave laborers inside. Kimsu told Ben that Emperor Hirohito directly ordered him to seal each site with all the slave laborers and POWs inside, to guarantee that its location would remain secret till the treasure was recovered later by members of the imperial family. Kimsu said he had no choice but to obey. Ben believed him because he often saw the prince weeping as a tunnel was closed with men inside. (Ben did not like talking to us about this. Tears welled in his eyes as he described how even groups of Japanese soldiers were buried alive "so their spirits would guard the treasure". He was scared of being buried alive with them. Half a century later it still worried him that the Japanese might return to punish him.)

According to Ben, Kimsu was diligent and meticulous in all his duties. Once a Chinese slave escaped from a work crew just as a vault was about to be sealed. After it became evident that the Japanese could not catch him, Kimsu ordered the vault emptied, and all 270 bronze boxes full of gold bars were taken out and moved elsewhere. On another occasion, after inspecting a site, the prince concluded that the drawings and maps given him were not accurate, that the chief engineer had made crafty alterations to reserve the treasure for himself. Kimsu ordered the officer beheaded on the spot, and the order was carried out instantly.

Over three years, Ben accompanied him by plane and ship to islands as small as Lubang, where there were treasure vaults of different sizes in progress. At a small island off the north coast of Mindanao, Ben saw a ship strangely camouflaged with live trees that grew in big planters on its deck. Heavy boxes were stacked on deck, guarded by German soldiers. Kimsu's officers told Ben it was a German ship. They watched as all the boxes were unloaded and taken into a cave on the island. Ben was not sure what was in the boxes, but it was very heavy. During that period of the war, Japanese cargo submarines were taking gold bullion to the Nazi sub base at Lorient, France, to pay for purchases of uranium. This was part of Japan's secret project to develop its own atomic bomb. German U-boats and fast surface raiders delivered the uranium to rendezvous points in Indonesia and the Philippines, where the cargo was offloaded, then the uranium was taken by Japanese submarines to Tokyo. Ben may have witnessed one such exchange, in which uranium was offloaded in lead-shielded boxes, to await transfer to Japanese subs.

While Kimsu was the only one who did final inventories at any of the 175 imperial sites, Ben said there were other teams involved in earlier stages. One, he said, was headed by Hirohito's youngest brother Prince Mikasa. Ben insisted that Prince Mikasa was in Luzon for three years, which coincides with the period Mikasa was officially attached to Japanese headquarters in Nanking. So his presence in Luzon is certainly possible. (Similarly, Prince Takeda was officially assigned to Hanoi, but was actually in Luzon.) Another team, he said, was headed by young Prince Asaka Takahito, son of the Prince Asaka who ordered the rape of Nanking in 1937. We were surprised that Ben knew the correct names of these princes. In the 1990s, we conducted blind tests using photos taken seventy or eighty years earlier, in the 1930s, and he identified the princes correctly. He only failed to identify faces we inserted who were not princes. We prepared these blind tests using rare photographs provided to us by a curator of the Oriental Collection at the British Library, and we were scrupulous about removing all identification. Ben's ability to identify princes who were virtually unknown outside Japan, from period photos rarely seen outside Japan, is all the more significant when you realize that he never learned how to dial a telephone. He assured us that 'many men' in white tunics with red emblems came to visit Kimsu at San Fernando. Some were considerably older, including Prince Higashikuni and the older Prince Asaka, who came to Luzon by plane on inspection tours. Soldiers and officers, Ben said, were extremely careful when these senior princes visited. On two occasions, when he went with Kimsu to meetings in Manila, Ben observed Prince Chichibu at close range, and noticed that he spat blood into his handkerchief, a detail that made a deep impression on Ben then and later, when he saw Chichibu again near Bambang in the closing months of the war. Ben had no way of knowing that Chichibu had tuberculosis, aside from his own direct observation. During the intervening months, Ben said Chichibu returned to Japan for treatment because he was increasingly sick. He told us that during this period Prince Mikasa visited Kimsu several times at San Fernando. Independent witnesses, including Japanese who served with Golden Lily, told us they saw Ben in the company of Prince Mikasa when groups of princes were inspecting major sites. One Japanese source even assumed that Ben was Prince Mikasa's valet.

It was unusual for Ben to be allowed inside any of these vaults, whether they were deep pits, natural caves, or man-made tunnels. Around each entrance there was an area of ten meters or so that he was forbidden to enter, so he seldom got close enough to see exactly what was going on below ground. He remained nearby, ready to fetch food or water or cigarettes, but all he could see was the opening to a tunnel or cave, a hole in the ground full of hoisting gear, the convoys of trucks that came with treasure, or the boxes being lowered into a shaft, or carried into a tunnel. What happened inside was unknown to him till later. This is of particular significance because many Golden Lily tunnels went straight into a hill or mountain, and then twenty meters or so inside a deep pit often was dug in the floor of the tunnel. This pit was then lined with concrete, and filled with treasure, in certain cases solid gold Buddhas (what Ben thought of as 'the Japanese god'). Then a concrete slab one or two meters thick was poured, and disguised to look like the floor of the tunnel. Treasure hunters have searched such caves or tunnels fruitlessly, only to discover by chance that the vault was beneath their feet, or in a perfectly hidden branch tunnel off to one side. One of these was at a mountain Filipinos call Bantay Lakay. Another, at Cayapa, had a very large solid gold Buddha placed in a pit just inside the tunnel mouth. Ben watched as the Japanese rolled an enormous boulder into the mouth of this tunnel, packed three smaller boulders in the remaining openings, then covered everything with extra-hard ceramic cement, colored to look like local stone. At Montalban, east of Manila, were several Japanese military camps where a number of tunnels were dug into gently rolling terrain. Before these were sealed by Kimsu, Ben saw truckloads of treasure arrive all day every day for two weeks. During the Pacific War there were tall trees with dense foliage that hid the excavations. Today, Montalban has been deforested and much of it is covered with paddy fields. Recent efforts to recover treasure there have been stymied not only by thousand-pound bombs, but by ingenious water traps devised by the Japanese that can flood tunnels in a matter of seconds.

Unusual though it was, there were several occasions when Kimsu did take Ben into a tunnel or cave, including the Many Monkeys site in Aritao, south of Bambang. This was a curious place, a hillside covered with dozens of giant boulders weighing ten to twenty tons apiece. These cobbles, each several meters across, had been washed down the hillsides by typhoons and flash floods over the ages, especially severe in November each year. At Aritao, the jumble of boulders covered with vines and forest canopy, created natural vaults between the rocks, occupied by troupes of rhesus monkeys. The monkeys were scared away, and Kimsu's engineers burned the foliage and chose two large chambers about 46 meters deep in the hillside. These they reinforced with concrete. Each about twenty feet wide by thirty feet long, the chambers were filled with platinum and gold bars stacked in neat rows, plus five large urns filled with loose gems, which had been pried out of jewelry. Ben was surprised to see urns filled with thousands of watches, confiscated because they were gold studded with gems. The urns were carried down to the chambers by soldiers. A small quarter-ton solid gold Buddha was carefully encased in a concrete egg, then was dragged by a group of Korean slave laborers into the chambers, using a canvas sling. The whole operation of stocking and inventorying the site took a week, and Ben saw more than a hundred trucks come with treasure. It was then ready for Kimsu to make a final inspection. Ben watched in fascination as the prince admired a last urn filled with gems of all colors, dipping his hands into the stones and watching them cascade through his fingers. He then ordered a soldier to take the urn into the labyrinth, while he and Ben followed trailing a stout red cord in case they got lost. Once this urn was put beside the others, the passage leading to the chambers was blocked with a thick wall of concrete mixed with coloring agents so it looked like the local stone. Kimsu and Ben then followed the soldiers and engineers down the rest of the way through the boulders to the bottom of the valley, where they emerged from the hill beside a fast-flowing river. (We visited the Many Monkeys site with Ben, but made no attempt to enter because of an infestation of cobras; we include photos of the hillside in our CDs.)

One of the biggest treasure vault complexes in the Philippines was immediately adjacent to the San Fernando army camp where Kimsu was based. He had men working underground there for three full years, expanding three natural caverns, lining them with steel reinforced concrete, linking them with connecting tunnels. The large vault beneath San Fernando was called Tunnel-8, and was said to be the size of a football field. This was connected to two other caverns the size of gymnasiums. One, called Tunnel-9, was directly beneath another Japanese Army camp nearby. The third, called the Graveyard Site, was almost underneath Bambang cemetery. Tunnel-8 and Tunnel-9 were about a kilometer apart, while the Graveyard cavern was more than a kilometer and a half distant. This complex was one of the last to be inventoried and sealed before the war ended.

Standing by Prince Takeda's house in San Fernando, looking due east, the bucolic view was dominated by two cone-shaped mountains resembling a stout 1940s brassiere reinforced with whalebone. The right breast was 4,774-foot Mount Sehal, its near-twin on the left was 5,594-foot Mount Palau. Ilocanos called Mount Sehal by the name Nagkumbintuan, but the Japanese called it *Kisad*. That was where the sun rose each morning, so Kimsu always emerged then to bow at the mountain. A dirt secondary road passed by the San Fernando camp, heading east toward the cleavage between the two giant breasts. On the left side of this road was a spur of Mount Palau, and Tunnel-8 was beneath this spur. (The original red-series map is reproduced on our CDs.) On the north flank of this spur, about a kilometer distant, was another army camp with a separate entrance to Tunnel-9. Late in the war, during the winter and early spring of 1945, this became the headquarters of General Yamashita before he moved into the Kiangan Pocket for his final defense. Ben never learned about the separate 'Yamashita' entrance.

At Kimsu's headquarters in San Fernando, the only sign of Tunnel-8 was a hole in the ground with a crude open elevator like those that take miners into deep coal pits. This elevator carried Ben and Kimsu down 220 feet to the mouth of a lateral tunnel. Once below ground, Ben was unable to tell which way they walked. First they came to a circular chamber called the Conference Room, filled with bags. Ben did not know what was in the bags, and did not ask. Around its perimeter were six tunnels radiating in all directions like the spokes of a wheel. When they walked into one of these tunnels, Ben saw that it was stacked floor to ceiling with boxes well above Kimsu's head. After descending another thirty feet, they reached a much bigger chamber with concrete walls and ceiling, which Ben thought was as big as a football field. This was the main part of Tunnel-8, called the Commodity Room, already filled with gold bars. Originally a natural cavern, Ben said it took two years for the Japanese to enlarge and reinforce it, and more personnel and trucks were involved at this site than any other he ever visited. Here the ingots were not stacked in rows but in large islands, with aisles between them. When they reached the third chamber, it was sealed with steel doors, and he was not allowed to enter. This was Tunnel-9, or the Command Center. Kimsu and Ben walked on through another very long tunnel that brought them eventually to another vault the size of a gymnasium, adjacent to Bambang cemetery, which was stacked wall to wall with gold bars.

"What I saw," Ben told us, "was plenty of gold. There was a big statue of a boy, like a Buddha. There were two other large Buddhas, and maybe twenty-five smaller ones." All, he said, were solid gold, or they would not have been there.

•

By the summer of 1944 it was evident that an Allied invasion of the Philippines or Formosa was imminent. A great fleet of American ships was assembling at Hollandia in New Guinea. Japan would have to fight hard to hold on even to Luzon. General Shigenori Kuroda was relieved of his command in the Philippines, and replaced by Japan's finest fighting general, Yamashita Tomoyuki. He was to defend the northern Philippines at all cost, as part of an effort to block attacks on Guam and Okinawa, the loss of which would threaten the Home Islands.

Yamashita was a complex and interesting man. On the surface he seemed to be the ideal product of Japan's fascination with Prussian militarism. He was a big man, bull-necked, barrel-chested, head shaved, his face an expressionless mask so he seemed brutal and insensitive. In fact, he was a moderate who had opposed the explosive growth of fanatical militarism in Japan. In 1935, when one of the most dangerous fanatics, General Nagata Tetsuzan, was stabbed to death at Tokyo headquarters by Lt. Col. Aizawa Saburo, Yamashita stopped the assassin in the hallway, shook his hand vigorously and thanked him for his courageous act.

Because of his extraordinary victory at Singapore early in the war, Yamashita became such a public hero in Japan that he was feared and resented by Prime Minister Tojo, who recalled him and salted him away in Manchuria for the bulk of the war. By mid-1944, however, Tojo had been forced out of office, and the high command sent General Yamashita directly from Manchuria to Luzon, hoping that this military genius could produce another miracle. He arrived in Manila on October 6, 1944, too late to alter the outcome significantly. Thus Yamashita became involved with Golden Lily only during the final ten months of the war, when the princes and their helpers were hastily moving the last truckloads and freight cars of gold bullion and other treasure into the mountains north of Manila, where Yamashita planned to hold out as long as he could. As it happened, Yamashita was a personal friend of Prince Chichibu who, as a young officer in the early 1930s, had served in his regiment in Tokyo, so there was immediate rapport between them when they were brought together by circumstance in Manila. Ben saw them greet each other once and told us Yamashita was the only Japanese he ever saw who did not bow first to Chichibu, but instead welcomed him like a long lost brother.

That October, Ben accompanied Kimsu north of Bambang to Bagabag, where there was a Japanese airfield. They flew to Manila in a twin-engine army plane with twelve other passengers. First they went to Ft. Santiago, where POWs were hard at work lowering the Mosler safes into the old Spanish air-vent shafts. Next morning they visited the Six-Finger Site at San Augustin Church, and Manila Cathedral, where they watched bronze boxes of gold lowered into the treasure vaults one by one, followed by a solid gold statue. This was done by attaching a horse to one end of the ropes around the statue. While scores of men helped, the horse was slowly backed toward the pit as the statue gradually descended. At that moment, General Yamashita appeared. Unlike Yamashita's friendly greeting of Prince Chichibu, he and Kimsu seemed aloof.

During those last ten months, Yamashita had his driver, Major Kojima Kashii, take him to observe progress at more than a dozen Golden Lily sites between Baguio in the west, Bambang in the center, and Aparri at the northern tip of Luzon. There was no time to lose. In the Battle of Leyte Gulf in October 1944, the biggest sea battle in history, Japan suffered disastrous losses. Both sides blundered, but America less. U.S. forces then landed on Leyte. General MacArthur was still smarting from the way he had been taken by surprise in December 1941, humiliated in the months that followed, and forced to flee ignominiously from Corregidor, abandoning his troops in Bataan. He was taking no chances now. At Leyte his forces outnumbered the Japanese nearly ten to one. Victorious there, MacArthur prepared to invade Luzon.

Yamashita had more than 275,000 men on Luzon, including one armored division and six of infantry. But they were a mixed bag of convalescents, survivors, and service troops. The best he could do was to fight a holding action in the mountains, and drag it out as long as he could. It was impossible to defend Manila. He decided to withdraw from the city, and to declare it open, so it would not be destroyed pointlessly.

Unfortunately, Manila was actually controlled by the Japanese Navy, so Yamashita had no influence over 16,000 marines and naval forces there. When he ordered all Japanese to withdraw into the countryside, Rear Admiral Iwabuchi Sanji rejected the order without informing Yamashita. Iwabuchi had instructions to destroy all port facilities and naval warehouses. He also had his own plans. He had been involved personally in the hiding of large quantities of war loot on the island of Corregidor, also navy-controlled, and he knew all about the masses of treasure hidden in Manila by Prince Chichibu. With U.S. aircraft controlling the skies, there was no escape by sea. Iwabuchi could have withdrawn into the mountains, but he chose instead to play the cornered rat, and set his marines loose on a rampage against the civilian population of Manila.

Assuming that Manila was undefended, MacArthur ordered his forces to hurry south from their beachhead in the Lingayen Gulf, hoping to enter the capital on his birthday, January 26, 1945.

Iwabuchi commanded his 16,000 men to fight to the death. They panicked and turned Manila into a charnel house, fighting house-to-house, disemboweling thousands of non-combatants in the streets, including women and children – the worst such atrocity since the Rape of Nanking. One hundred thousand Filipinos were slaughtered, and a thousand Americans, and 80 percent of the city's houses were flattened. In the chaos, Iwabuchi himself slipped away through the tunnel network beneath Intramuros and was never seen again in public. Declared officially dead, his remains were never found. There are indications that he escaped from Luzon by submarine and lived to a ripe old age in Japan under a pseudonym, because he was posthumously promoted to vice admiral by Emperor Hirohito.

In the mountains to the north, Yamashita's defensive perimeter was built on a triangle with its points at Baguio, Bambang and Bontoc. These three points could be reached only by narrow roads through ravines and gorges, where his forces were dug in.

Ben had no idea what was happening. One day Kimsu and his staff crowded with him into a hut as many planes flew over. Ben thought the planes were Japanese, but Col. Adachi told him they were American. Ben said, "No, the Japanese are strong." Adachi and the others laughed, and said, "The Americans are coming, Benhameen." A few days later, the aircraft returned to bomb and strafe, and Ben saw Kimsu and his staff officers praying.

His relationship with Prince Takeda then went through a subtle change. Kimsu insisted that Ben go through a blood-oath ritual with him. This involved cutting the tips of their little fingers on the right hand, letting the blood drip together on a battle flag. (Indeed, we saw that the tip of Ben's right little finger was missing.) First, Ben was forbidden ever to talk about Prince Chichibu. Second, he must never reveal Prince Takeda's secret name. Finally, he must never reveal locations of any treasure sites, "not to Americans, to Filipinos, to guerrillas, to Chinese, even to Japanese". These sites, Kimsu told him, were reserved only for members of the imperial family. To provide for Ben in the future, Kimsu said he was hiding two steel trunks full of gold. So that Ben would not forget, he had one of his men tattoo two blue dots on Ben's hand, one for each box. The next day they went to the Pingkian Bridge, on the road leading from Aritao toward Baguio. On a high bank a few meters from the river, stood a huge mango tree. Soldiers already had dug a deep pit beneath the tree. Two large steel boxes were dragged into the pit by harnessed carabao. Five carabao were needed to pull each box, even though the

Japanese put steel pipes on the ground for the box to roll over. When both trunks were in the pit, the lids were opened and Kimsu called Ben over, to show what was inside. They were completely filled with chunks of gold cut off 75-kilo bars.

Speaking Japanese, Kimsu told Ben: *Kurene sabisu dayo taksan taksan goruda, Neh?* Freely translated, this means: "Here's what I'm giving you for your service – lots and lots of gold, Okay?" (The Japanese word for gold is *kin*, but when the English word 'gold' is used, Japanese pronounce it goruda. Half a century later, we had Ben write down what Kimsu said, and with his limited knowledge of Japanese he wrote: "Kurene sabis sayo kurei taksan taksan gorne.")

They would now sprinkle the boxes with poison, Kimsu told him, and close them. After the war, Ben was to come here by himself and recover the boxes. When he opened the pit, he must pour kerosene over the boxes and burn the powder off. When he opened the lids he should pour in more kerosene to burn off the powder inside each box. Then he could recover the gold safely. He was given small pieces of ingots, instead of whole ingots, because they would be easier to sell without attracting too much attention. Kimsu told him to buy land for a very big ranch, and to marry the pretty girl they had often watched in the village, and have lots of children to help him run the ranch. Ben was speechless.

While they finished filling the pit, they were surprised to see another Golden Lily team drive up at the other end of the Pingkian Bridge. The leader was Prince Chichibu himself, dressed like Kimsu in a white tunic with the red badge. Kimsu and Chichibu did not bow to each other, and showed no emotion. Chichibu looked very thin, coughing, and Ben said his handkerchief was red "like the battle flag".

In the days and weeks that followed, there was frenzied burying of remaining treasure. Yamashita had to abandon Baguio to the advancing Americans, and moved his Shobu Group headquarters to Bambang. But he never came to Kimsu's camp at San Fernando. Yamashita had his own separate entrance to the underground command bunker of Tunnel-9. He and his staff spent a lot of time below ground there, in the weeks before they withdrew to the Kiangan Pocket. In the meantime, at Kiangan, another big cavern was prepared as a hard base for Yamashita and his staff, to use during the 'fight to the death' that lay ahead. The Kiangan Pocket was a naturally formed geological rift, like the Rift Valley in Kenya, well-watered and full of caves, a natural fortress perfectly suited to the defensive purpose General Yamashita had chosen for it. Ben said most of this work was done by slave labor, supervised by disabled soldiers and service personnel unsuited to combat.

By May 5, 1945, American forces were advancing into the mountains so quickly that Yamashita also had to abandon Bontoc, giving up two of the three corners of his defensive triangle. He pulled his forces back between Bambang and Bagabag, and began to funnel them along the Asin River into the Kiangan Pocket. Although this terrain is extremely rugged, Bagabag is actually only 25 miles north of Bambang, and the edge of the Kiangan Pocket was only five miles west of Bambang. Supplies of food were in place there, including herds of carabao. Yamashita's troops also had gathered the early rice harvest throughout the Cagayan

Valley. A new crop would be ready in September, but by then the fighting would be over. Meanwhile, the rains would come, bringing typhoon deluges that would make life difficult for the Americans. Yamashita was counting on the rains and typhoons to discourage air attacks.

At the end of May, 1945, Kimsu took Ben on a secret trip north. They went first to Bagabag, where Prince Mikasa was awaiting them. The two princes and Ben were then driven north through the Cagayan Valley toward Aparri, then turned right along the coast to a small bay. There they boarded a fast patrol boat and made the crossing to the north side of Camiguin Island, where a Japanese submarine was lying low in the water. Kimsu went aboard to make arrangements with the skipper for a rendezvous at the same place the next week. Ben and Prince Mikasa remained in the patrol boat. Ben said it was the only time he was completely alone in the company of Prince Mikasa. He thought Kimsu took him along to be sure nothing bad happened to Ben in his absence.

In the first four days of June, Yamashita's antitank units south of Aritao (location of the Many-Monkeys site) fought a running battle with the U.S. 775th Tank Battalion, and from that moment pressure was acute to speed up withdrawal into the Pocket.

On the evening of June 1, all 175 Golden Lily chief engineers were summoned to a farewell party in the underground conference room of Tunnel-8. All remaining treasure had now been hidden. Tunnel-8, Tunnel-9 and the Cemetery Site were packed with gold bars. According to Ben, who was with Kimsu that evening, the engineers were drinking large quantities of sake, with many toasts and shouts of "Banzai!" Meanwhile, two hundred remaining slave laborers were herded into the Cemetery Site chamber, where they were kept under guard by Japanese soldiers with heavy machineguns on tripods.

Kimsu, who had built this place, spent an hour with the chief engineers, then took Ben for a final tour of the whole complex. They walked through the connecting tunnels for more than an hour, admiring stacked gold bars and other treasure. Kimsu repeatedly told Ben, "Be careful, do not step on the wires, we might be blown up." The wires led to bundles of dynamite here and there through all the tunnels. When they returned to the farewell party, Kimsu gave a rousing speech to the engineers, praising them for what they had achieved, thanking them in the name of the emperor. The red-faced men kept shouting, "Banzai!"

When the speech ended, it was near midnight. General Yamashita arrived. He said it was time for Kimsu to come out of the tunnel. Ben, he said, must remain inside.

"No!" Kimsu said. "I gave my oath that I would bring him home personally." He turned to Ben. "You go!" He pointed toward the exit tunnel with the crude elevator. Yamashita was angry, but unprepared to argue with the Meiji Emperor's grandson. We asked Ben why Yamashita wanted him inside. "Maybe so nobody will know about this one," Ben replied. With Yamashita leading, they walked to the pit elevator, and rose to the surface. Without a word, Yamashita stalked away into the night. As Kimsu and Ben walked quickly away from the pit, Ben heard what he thought was a bomb from a plane, and dived to the ground. Huge explosions shook the ground. (When the sun rose the next day, there would be a big sinkhole on the west side of the dirt road, fifteen feet deep, where connecting tunnels had collapsed.) We asked Ben if at that moment he knew all the engineers and slaves were trapped belowground? Ben looked at the ground. "I was very happy that Kimsu did not allow Yamashita to… I would be left here." A moment later he added: "I was afraid of Yamashita."

When the ground stopped shaking, Ben saw that Kimsu was weeping. "He did this," Ben said, "because the emperor gave him a direct order." Many members of Kimsu's staff, including Navy Captain Honda, had been buried alive with the engineers. Only when they reached Ben's house did Kimsu say it was time for him and Col. Adachi to leave. They would go that night to Camiguin Island, where the submarine would be waiting to take them back to Japan. Although it was dark, Ben could see tears in Kimsu's eyes. Ben also wept. "You must go in to your papa, Benhameen. He has only one eye and needs you on the farm. Don't join the guerrillas, or the Americans. Just stay with your papa and help him plant rice."

Kimsu put down his leather satchel and his sword, and took off his white tunic. He handed Ben the tunic, then handed his sword to Ben as well. He started to walk away, then made up his mind about something and came back to hand Ben the satchel, which held a full set of maps. Perhaps in his mind was the possibility that the submarine taking him back to Japan might not get there.

"Keep these for me. Put it in a wooden box and bury it in the ground, behind your house." Then he repeated the mantra: "Never forget your oath: You will not give the maps to anyone, no American, no Chinese, no Japanese, no Filipino, no guerrillas, just wait for me. Asha, Asha, Asha." (Repeating this, Ben counts on his fingers as he says the word Asha ten times.) "Wait, until I come back and get these from you. Wait thirty years. If I have not come back by then, take the maps to Japan. If I am dead, give the maps to my family."

Kimsu walked away a hundred yards, then came back. Again he repeated the mantra: "Benhameen, don't join the guerrillas or the Americans. If you do the Japanese will shoot you. Remember, no guerrillas, no Americans, no Chinese, no Japanese, wait for me."

This time, when he walked away, Kimsu did not come back. Ben stared after him for a long time, then he took the sword, the satchel, and the tunic, and went into the house.

At sunrise, Yamashita withdrew up the Asin River into the Kiangan Pocket, for the last three months of the war.

The sword Prince Takeda gave Ben had a blade of manmade steel folded and forged with darker metal from a meteorite, and a sheath of wood and leather. Made by one of Japan's 'living treasures' it was a gift from Kimsu's grandfather, Emperor Meiji, who collected fine swords. Not knowing its great value, Ben used it in the paddy fields to cut rice stalks at harvest that November and for many years that followed. When he plowed the fields the next Spring, he wore the white tunic with the red and gold chrysanthemum patch on the left breast. His father warned him not to wear it again in public, or he might be killed as a collaborator. Both the tunic and the sword lasted many years. While all those years passed, Ben kept his oath.

CHAPTER SEVEN

DOWN THE RABBIT HOLE

On September 2, 1945, after receiving official notice of Japan's formal capitulation, the tall bull-necked figure of General Yamashita Tomoyuki appeared along a mountain trail, his left hand holding his samurai sword, approaching American lines to surrender himself and his staff. During the last month, American forces had advanced only three miles. Under siege in the Kiangan Pocket, Yamashita had lost a lot of weight. He also had lost a lot of men. But he did not commit ritual suicide because, he said, "If I kill myself, someone else will have to take the blame." Behind his staff officers came his driver and others. They were met by a U.S. Army reception committee, including Military Police Major A.S. 'Jack' Kenworthy, who would make the arrest and escort the men to New Bilibad Prison just outside Manila. Yamashita stopped and waited for his officers to take positions behind him. According to Lt. Col. Leslie M. Fry, who was present, a number of younger Japanese bringing up the rear came forward carrying gold bars, which were stacked neatly by one side – altogether about half a metric ton. Yamashita unbuckled his sword, bowed deeply, and presented it to Major Kenworthy. Five months later, on February 23, 1946, after what many described as a grotesque miscarriage of justice, Yamashita was hanged.

No mention of plundered treasure, or of looting during the war, was made in the charges against Yamashita or during his trial. He was charged with war crimes because of the atrocities committed, against his explicit orders, by Admiral Iwabuchi's sailors and marines in Manila. It was the first time in history that the United States as a sovereign power tried a general of a defeated enemy nation for alleged war crimes. The tribunal in Manila was not composed of men with legal degrees, and only hearsay evidence was offered to link Yamashita to the crimes. Nonetheless, the prosecution was "badgered by MacArthur's headquarters to quicken its pace, to minimize court procedure and to allow hearsay evidence". Yamashita's defense team appealed to the U.S. Supreme Court. Two Supreme Court justices denounced the conduct of the trial. Justice Murphy said "The petitioner was rushed to trial under an improper charge, given insufficient time to prepare an adequate defense, [and there] was no serious attempt to ...prove that he committed a recognized violation of the laws of war. He was not charged with personally participating in the acts of atrocity or with ordering or condoning their commission. Not even knowledge of these crimes was attributed to him." Justice Rutledge, the other dissenter, concluded that the process had departed "from the whole British-American tradition of common law and the Constitution". He concluded with Thomas Paine's warning: "He that would make his own liberty secure must guard even his enemy from oppression; for if he violates this duty he establishes a precedent that will reach to himself."

Yamashita's conviction was not overturned. After a failed appeal to President Truman (who did not respond at all) Yamashita was hanged. Many thought he was railroaded because MacArthur was a vainglorious man who wanted revenge for being made to look incompetent.

But we now know there was a hidden agenda. Because it was not possible to torture General Yamashita physically without this becoming evident to his defense attorneys, members of his staff were tortured instead. In particular, his driver, Major Kojima Kashii, was given special attention. He had accompanied Yamashita everywhere since the general had arrived from Manchuria in October 1944 to take over the defense of the Philippines from General Kuroda Shigenori. In charge of the torture of Major Kojima was a Filipino-American intelligence officer named Severino Garcia Diaz Santa Romana, whose friends called him Santy. He was a big-boned man, tall, with a high, broad forehead, who looked like a judo black belt, or the Genie that popped out of an old green bottle. Because of the recent Japanese savagery in Manila, Santy was enjoying his work. Many Filipinos had been cruelly tortured and beheaded; women and girls were gang raped in the streets, many of them disemboweled and hacked to pieces. But Santy and his assistants were careful. They did not want to kill Major Kojima, or to damage his memory.

What Santy wanted to know was where the gold was hidden. He wanted the major to reveal each place where he had taken General Yamashita during the past year, where bullion and other plundered treasure was placed for recovery later. He wanted the major to take him to each site, to point out the entrance, and to describe the booby traps in detail.

This brutal interrogation of Major Kojima produced results that astounded everyone from General MacArthur all the way up to the White House, and became one of the biggest state secrets of the twentieth century. Even today it remains carefully obscured, by making all archival records on this topic inaccessible for 'reasons of national security'. It is no exaggeration to say that Santy's results greatly altered America's leverage throughout the world during the Cold War. So astonishing are the consequences that we must take a step back now, and be meticulous in examining every detail closely. For example, who was Santy, and for whom was he really working? Who ordered him to torture Major Kojima? Today, Santa Romana remains a legendary but mysterious figure at the CIA, and in Manila, where it is not unusual for people to deny that he ever existed. When they speak of him at all, senior CIA officials always say that Santy was 'an OSS agent', implying that he was working for America's wartime intelligence agency, the Office of Strategic Services headed by General William 'Wild Bill' Donovan. But that turns out to be a meaningless generality, for Santy never was an OSS agent, and when he tortured Major Kojima the OSS had officially ceased to exist.

We also must ask how Santy knew about the hidden treasure of Golden Lily. That is easier to answer.

America had realized for some time that Japan was hiding plundered treasure in the Philippines, although the details were not shared with Britain or other Allies. During the last year of the war, for example, Americans fighting alongside Filipino guerrillas observed a heavily laden Japanese hospital ship unloading bronze boxes at Subic Bay, near Manila. U.S. Navy Warrant Officer John C. Ballinger, disguised as a fisherman, secretly photographed the vessel from a brightly painted Filipino fishing pirogue. It was not a real hospital ship. After studying the ship's profile and comparing it with naval intelligence records, we were able to identify it as the fast liner *Fuji Maru*, built in 1937, which had been disguised with false superstructures, and huge crosses painted on her sides. As a fake hospital ship, the *Fuji Maru* was carrying war loot from Singapore to Manila for Prince Chichibu and Golden Lily. Ballinger's unit, led by the guerrilla hero Captain Medina, followed the convoy of army trucks carrying this odd cargo into the mountains. There they watched Japanese soldiers lug the very heavy boxes into a cave. Ballinger had no idea what was in them, but it was clearly something of great value. Four men were needed to move each box, using a sling harness. When the Japanese sealed and disguised the cave entrance and left, the guerrillas took several days to re-open the cave and found that the boxes inside contained 75-kilo gold bars. There were rows upon rows of boxes. Photographs of the ship, along with a report of the cave full of gold, were sent by submarine to MacArthur's intelligence headquarters in Australia, adding to many similar reports. According to Ballinger's son Gene, his father assumed that he was reporting to the OSS, but nothing was that simple.

Some months later, when American troops had landed on Leyte, Ballinger witnessed another movement of treasure by the Japanese. This time, a convoy of trucks carried heavy boxes out of Japanese Army headquarters in Baguio to a tunnel near a hospital on the outskirts of town. Ballinger's son Gene told us: "This was not nearly as big a secret at the time as the Japanese wanted it to be. They were in a big hurry and made the mistake of not paying attention. Medina's company kicked their ass and blew the tunnel shut – Japs and all." A report on this action also was passed up the line by John Ballinger to 'the OSS'.

Because of the intense secrecy surrounding this subject, trying today to trace any of those intelligence reports on war loot is like falling down a rabbit hole, entering a subterranean world full of lies, evasions, and Mad Hatters.

America's wartime effort to monitor movements of looted gold bullion was indeed a major responsibility of the OSS, a precursor of the CIA. There also were special intelligence units responsible for monitoring displaced and looted artworks: the Art Looting Investigative Unit, and the Monuments, Fine Arts and Archives Group. But these were much more effective in Europe than in Asia. Compared to Europe, Allied intelligence services in Asia and the Pacific were fragmented, and did not cooperate. In any case, efforts to keep track of looted art or shipments of precious metals in East Asia were unsatisfactory because of geographical, cultural and linguistic barriers. Nearly all those records kept by intelligence services of the United States have since been made to vanish. What has surfaced, did so accidentally.

In Europe, the OSS at times worked closely with other intelligence services, but competition and rivalry were intense. One of the fiercest turf battles over the tracking of Nazi loot went on inside the U.S. Government, waged between Secretary of the Treasury Henry Morgenthau and Allen Dulles, the OSS chief in Switzerland, a romantic who had a much more cavalier attitude about such things. Axis loot was being moved under the noses of the Allies into neutral safe havens. In one instance, American agents in Switzerland watched 280 trucks of Nazi gold move from Germany across France and Spain to the safe haven of neutral Portugal. Owned by private Swiss firms, the trucks were painted with the Swiss cross, allowing the gold to be moved under 'neutral' cover.

However, while the gathering of intelligence on war loot may have been disjointed, ultimately all such reports were passed up to the office of the Secretary of War, Henry L. Stimson. He had a special interest in the subject of looted bullion, and kept a group of financial experts thinking hard about it. Three of these men were Stimson's special assistants John J. McCloy, Robert Lovett, and consultant Robert B. Anderson.

The problem of how to deal with plundered treasure, and what to do with Axis gold after the war, was discussed in July 1944 when forty-four nations met at the resort of Bretton Woods, New Hampshire, to plan the post-war economy. These discussions, some of them extremely secret, revealed the flaws and loopholes that existed in the international financial system, making any clear-cut resolution unlikely. Among the delegates, trust was far from universal. Many of them believed that the Bank of International Settlements was secretly laundering Nazi loot. That distrust set the tone. Among other things, the Bretton Woods agreement (as it was made public) set a fixed price for gold of $35 an ounce, and banned the importation of gold to America for personal use. Neutral countries that signed the pact promised not to knowingly accept stolen gold and other looted assets, but Portugal forgot to include Macao in the list of its dependent territories. This was a convenient oversight, for during the rest of the war, as we saw in Chapter Four, Macao became a world center for trade in illicit gold and was heavily exploited by Japan.

Unlike Europe where the OSS was tolerated by General Dwight Eisenhower, in the Southwest Pacific General MacArthur resisted all attempts by the OSS to get a foothold in his territory. MacArthur and his staff intended to conduct their own brand of special operations from their headquarters in Australia, without any interference.

Intelligence-gathering in MacArthur's domain was under the command of Charles Willoughby. Born in Heidelberg, Germany, in 1892, he was the love child of Baron T. Scheppe-Weidenbach and Emma Willoughby of Baltimore, Maryland. By 1910 her romance with the baron had soured and Emma returned to the United States with her 18-year-old son, who immediately enlisted as a private in the U.S.

Army, rising gradually to sergeant. When he returned to civilian life in 1913, Willoughby enrolled at Gettysburg College where he was able to get a degree quickly. Re-joining the army as an officer, he served in France in 1917-1918, then taught machinegun tactics at Ft. Benning. The next few years he served as an army attache at U.S. embassies in Venezuela, Colombia and Ecuador, speaking Spanish with a heavy German accent. In 1940, after staff school at Ft. Leavenworth, he was sent to Manila to be MacArthur's assistant chief of staff for logistics. At the time, Douglas MacArthur was America's field marshal of the Philippine Army. Willoughby, who craved grandeur and authority, was awed by the patrician MacArthur. In mid-1941, when MacArthur became commander of the new U.S. Far Eastern Command, Willoughby stuck with his idol. This impressed MacArthur, who valued personal loyalty above all other qualities, and he made Willoughby his assistant chief of staff for intelligence, promoting him to colonel. When Japan attacked, Willoughby moved to Corregidor with MacArthur, and then accompanied him to Australia.

MacArthur wanted absolute control of intelligence-gathering and special operations in his zone of command. Willoughby's qualifications for such work have been seriously questioned. Repeatedly, he blundered in battlefield estimates, but was kept on because MacArthur liked to surround himself with admirers. According to military historian Kenneth Campbell, Willoughby was often given assignments "for which he was not remotely prepared", and his "attempts to conceal his mistakes are a violation of honor…". For Willoughby, truth was flexible.

In Australia, Willoughby set up the Allied Intelligence Bureau to run guerrilla operations in the Philippines. He also started the Allied Translator and Interpreter Section (ATIS), to monitor Japanese radio broadcasts, interrogate prisoners, and translate captured Japanese documents. Most men in ATIS were Nisei, second generation Japanese born in foreign countries, in this case born in America of Japanese parents. However, Willoughby's approach to guerrilla warfare proved to be too cautious for MacArthur, who craved audacity. Leaving Willoughby in charge of intelligence gathering, MacArthur gave special operations to his intimate friend and personal attorney Courtney A. Whitney. Willoughby was furious, but MacArthur soothed him by promoting him to general.

In this way, MacArthur's intimate crony Courtney Whitney became the key man running secret agents in the islands and reading reports of war loot, including those from John Ballinger. The OSS had no part whatever in this. Whitney was effective in special operations because he was well connected in Manila, a clever rich man on first name basis with all the politically powerful families in the Philippines. In the late 1920s when he had been fresh out of law school in Washington, D.C., MacArthur had got Whitney a job with the top Manila law firm of Dewitt, Perkins & Enrile, who handled MacArthur's financial affairs in the islands, and also handled Benguet, the biggest gold mining operation in the islands, in which MacArthur had investments. By Pearl Harbor, Whitney was intimately involved in all manner of political, legal, and financial intrigues, as played in the islands. He could call in favors from men like Santa Romana.

According to various CIA sources including former deputy director Ray Cline, Santa Romana was born in Luzon in 1907, one of several children of Marcelo Diaz

Santa Romana and Pelagia Garcia. As an adult, he used the names Garcia, Diaz, or Santa Romana interchangeably. Under the name Severino Diaz, he completed his university education in California where he married a wealthy young heiress, Evangeline Campton. Her family had owned a hotel on Stockton Street in San Francisco at the time of the great earthquake and fire of 1907. After the quake they rebuilt the hotel and sold it to new owners who called it the Drake-Wilshire. (Today the location still is called Campton Place; the hotel has been renamed the Campton Place Hotel.) In the 1930s, Santy took 'Angelina' back to the Philippines, where her inheritance got him started in business, and he became a fringe member of the social circle of MacArthur, Whitney and Andreas Soriano, owner of San Miguel Brewery and the wealthiest man in the islands.

Santy and Angelina had three children, named Peter Diaz, Mary Ann Diaz, and Roy Diaz. Angelina is said to have died in the early weeks of World War II when she was killed by a Japanese bomb, leaving the children what was left of her money. Her marriage to Santy had chilled out earlier. In the Catholic Philippines, divorce was illegal. Back in 1936, dropping the name Diaz and using the name Severino Santa Romana, Santy married a pretty schoolteacher named Julieta Huerto on the island of Mindoro, by whom he later had a daughter called Diana. In his marriage application, Santy claimed to be a schoolteacher himself. These deceptions were necessary because he was committing bigamy.

During the war, Santy stayed in the islands, becoming one of Whitney's most effective agents. Therefore only Whitney, MacArthur's attorney and intimate crony, could have authorized Santy's torture of Major Kojima in September 1945. Whitney never acted without MacArthur's approval, so there can be no question that it was done in the full knowledge of MacArthur and his inner circle. When Japan surrendered, the need for Whitney's special operations officially ceased. Willoughby's G-2 army intelligence unit continued to exist, pro forma, but both Willoughby and Whitney accompanied General MacArthur to Japan. The Philippines continued to be Whitney's personal power base, and one leg of MacArthur's power base. Whitney and MacArthur watched closely as the trial of General Yamashita got under way, and as we have seen they interfered often in the legal process. They also stayed informed of the interrogations of Yamashita's staff.

Another key figure in MacArthur's Manila circle was Joseph McMicking, whose father was a law partner of Courtney Whitney before the war. When the Japanese invaded, Captain Joe McMicking was made assistant G-2 to Major Willoughby. He was among the 'Bataan Boys' who fled with MacArthur by PT boat from Corregidor to the Dole Pineapple estate in Mindanao, and onward by plane to Australia. During the torture of Major Kojima in 1945, Colonel McMicking was the immediate G-2 superior of Santa Romana and was the interface between Santy in Manila and Whitney and MacArthur in Tokyo. When Major Kojima broke and Santy began recovering billions in gold, McMicking became fantastically wealthy seemingly overnight and married Mercedes Zobel, an heiress of the Zobel-Ayala clan of Spanish grandees in the Philippines. In the explosion of wealth in Manila that followed Santy's recoveries, Joe McMicking masterminded the Zobel-Ayala clan's acquisition of global real estate, helping create what has become one of the world's great fortunes. While the Zobel-Ayala clan certainly was not poor, their pockets were not as deep as McMicking's. The *Philippine Star* called McMicking the 'real moneybags' behind today's colossal Zobel-Ayala fortune. In the early 1960s, McMicking and his wife set up the Ayala Foundation to promote vocational education, arts and livelihood projects in the Philippines. It may be sheer coincidence, but in 1983 it was the Ayala Corporation that bought the rundown Campton Place Hotel in San Francisco, and turned it into an elegant and expensive boutique hotel.

The OSS only became involved in Santy's interrogation by sheer chance. Eight days after General Yamashita surrendered, Captain Edward G. Lansdale, formerly of the OSS, arrived in Manila by plane from San Francisco and began looking for something to do.

Lansdale was a deceptively engaging and colorful character, the elusive Cheshire Cat in our rabbit hole. Later, he became an icon of gigantic mythology, as one of America's most famous Cold Warriors (or infamous, depending on one's point of view). Many novelists including Graham Greene used him as the model for obsessive or pathological characters pushing the American Way in Asia. Lansdale was always on stage, acting various characters. So evasive was he about his life that the myth he contrived has overwhelmed the facts. There are two schools of thought – Lansdale as the savior of Asia, or Lansdale as war criminal and far-right hachetman. (Fletcher Prouty, a U.S. military intelligence officer and historian who shared office space with Lansdale for many years, positively identified Lansdale in photographs taken during the assassination of President Kennedy, identification confirmed by others. In the movie *JFK* Oliver Stone has a thinly-disguised Lansdale involved in the assassination of the president.)

How an advertising agency wordsmith like Lansdale became such an influential player during the Cold War remained a mystery until now. The missing key is the torture of Major Kojima.

When he landed in Manila in 1945, Lansdale was 37 and utterly insignificant. He had spent the entire war in San Francisco writing propaganda for the OSS, and having a good time.

Lansdale was born in Detroit in 1908, in a strongly religious middle-class family, his mother a driven Christian Scientist, his father a devout Presbyterian. As a child, Lansdale was taught by his father all kinds of religious sayings and Sunday School homilies of the sort used in Burma Shave signs along America's rural roads. "When the work has once begun/ Don't leave it until it's done/ Be the labor great or small/ Do it well or not at all." In his forties he could spout these like a whale for half an hour. As a CIA field agent, he taught the same cute sayings to assassins who worked for him in the Philippines, Vietnam, and Japan, used them as code phrases during covert operations, and recited them to Asian secret police bosses as a benediction. Over the years, Santy picked up this habit of Lansdale's and repeated the same signature homilies, even in his last will and testament.

During the Depression, Lansdale had studied journalism at UCLA where he was in the army reserve program. Following graduation he worked as a copywriter for ad agencies in Los Angeles and San Francisco, where his quirky jingles served him well. When he heard about Pearl Harbor, he quit his job and enlisted in the army, getting a choice billet dreaming up psychological warfare gimmicks for the Military Intelligence Service and then for the OSS. Sitting behind a desk in San Francisco, he passed his days thinking about how to demoralize Japanese troops. A pamphlet he wrote called *From The Serpent's Mouth* took old Japanese proverbs and used them to point out Japan's wartime blunders: "'The man who makes the first bad move always loses the game.' (Remember Pearl Harbor!)"

Chance entered Lansdale's life in a big way when President Truman ordered the OSS closed down at the end of September 1945. In the weeks remaining to them, General Donovan and his deputy, Brigadier General John Magruder, looked for ways to preserve personnel and OSS overseas networks by shifting them to other intelligence services, to other government agencies, in some cases even to private American corporations like General Electric that could afford to sustain clusters of secret agents in various parts of the world, for commercial intelligence, and as a favor to Washington. Captain Lansdale was one of fifty OSS office staff who were given a chance to transfer to General Willoughby's G-2 section in the Philippines, headed by Colonel McMicking.

When Lansdale arrived in Manila he was shocked by his first sight of war close up. The city was in ruins following the rampage by Admiral Iwabuchi's large force of marines and sailors. Lansdale heard grisly stories, and conceived a loathing for Japanese because of their excessive cruelty. In his journal entries from the 1940s, he told of this hatred. An entry dated November 10, 1946, says: "Many of the Filipinos were tortured …until they were just broken lumps of bleeding flesh." In his office at G-2, Lansdale discovered files describing gold being hidden by Japanese soldiers, and heard of Santy's interrogation of Major Kojima. Electrified, he seized the initiative, taking administrative control of Santy's interrogation. Lansdale was able to do this because most of MacArthur's team, including Willoughby's senior staff officers, were in Japan. In Manila, Lansdale had the G-2 office more or less to himself. He galvanized his Filipino and American clerical staff to make a painstaking search of the files for all mentions of Japanese war loot.

Later, all he was willing to say about it was: "The G-2's office at our headquarters held a treasury of reports… whose contents I had to master for my daily work. …I gave my intelligence group the task of sorting through what we already knew and obtaining further facts."

Santy was extracting those 'further facts' from Major Kojima.

Early in October, after many days of torture, Kojima broke and revealed everything he knew. Lansdale organized a convoy of cars and set out with Santy and Major Kojima to retrace the trips made by General Yamashita to 'more than a dozen' Golden Lily treasure vaults. These were all in the high valleys north of Manila, in a triangle from Baguio in the west to Bambang in the center, and Aparri at the northern tip of Luzon.

When they returned to Manila in mid-October, Lansdale reported to Colonel McMicking, then flew to Tokyo where he briefed Willoughby, Whitney, and MacArthur. At their instruction, he then flew to Washington to brief General Magruder, who still headed the Strategic Services Unit, a last vestige of the OSS just before the new Central Intelligence Group (CIG) was created under General Hoyt

Vandenberg. It was Magruder who had moved Lansdale to Manila two months earlier. Vandenberg or Magruder then sent Lansdale to the White House to brief President Truman's national security aide, Navy Captain Clark Clifford, and members of the Cabinet. President Truman decided to keep the discovery secret, and to recover as much of the Japanese loot as possible. At this stage, it is impossible to say precisely how these briefings unfolded, or exactly what President Truman did. The secrecy surrounding Santy's recoveries is nearly total.

What we do know, from two separate high-level sources in the CIA, is that Robert B. Anderson flew back to Tokyo with Lansdale, for discussions with MacArthur. After some days of meetings, MacArthur and Anderson flew secretly to Manila, where they were taken by Lansdale and Santy to some of the sites in the mountains, and to six other sites around Aparri at the northern tip of Luzon. In the intervening weeks, Santy's men, aided by hand-picked teams from the U.S. Army Corps of Engineers, had successfully opened several of these vaults, where MacArthur and Anderson were able to stroll down row after row of gold bars. Other sites were opened in subsequent months. In all, the recoveries took two years to complete, from late 1945 to early 1947.

From what was seen in these vaults, and also discovered by U.S. Army investigators in Japan, it became evident that over a period of decades Japan had looted billions of dollars' worth of gold, platinum, diamonds, and other treasure, from all over East and Southeast Asia. Much of this had reached Japan by sea, or overland from China through Korea, but a lot had been hidden in the Philippines.

Washington's 'official' (public) figure for recovered Nazi gold still is only 550 metric tons. But Anderson knew better. One of his business associates saw photos in Anderson's office of an American soldier "sitting on top of stacks of bullion that Hitler had stolen from Poland, Austria, Belgium and France. It ended up with the Allied high command and no one was allowed to talk about it." The same source said he was taken to the courtyard of a convent in Europe where 11,200 metric tons of Nazi looted bullion had been collected.

After the Nazi defeat, the OSS and other Allied intelligence organizations searched Germany and Austria for art treasures and looted gold. Soviet troops and special units did the same in the Russian zone. More is known of what happened to the recovered art than to the recovered gold. When one hundred tons of Nazi gold were recovered from a salt mine near Merkers, Germany, the truck convoy carrying it to Frankfurt vanished; it was said to have been hijacked, but the more likely explanation is that this gold was among the bullion stacked in the convent courtyard.

The reason for all this discretion was a top secret project sometimes called Black Eagle, a strategy first suggested to President Roosevelt by Secretary of War Henry L. Stimson and his wartime advisors, John J. McCloy (later head of the World Bank), Robert Lovett (later secretary of Defense), and Robert B. Anderson (later secretary of the Treasury). Stimson proposed using all recovered Axis war loot (Nazi, Fascist, and Japanese) to finance a global political action fund. Because it would be difficult if not impossible to determine who were the rightful owners of all the looted gold, better to keep its recovery quiet and set up a trust to help friendly governments stay in power after the war. This was informally called the Black Eagle Trust after the German black eagle, referring to Nazi bullion marked with an eagle and swastika, recovered from underground vaults of the Reichsbank.

According to some sources, the Black Eagle Trust could only have been set up with the cooperation of the most powerful banking families in America and Europe, including the Rockefellers, Harrimans, Rothschilds, Oppenheimers, Warburgs, and others.

A brilliant Wall Street attorney, Stimson was a man of immense experience who had served in various posts for five presidents – Taft, Coolidge, Hoover, Roosevelt, Truman – but he was nearing the end of his extraordinary career. He knew Manila intimately, having served as governor-general of the Philippines in the 1920s. President Herbert Hoover had then named him secretary of State. (Like Hoover, Stimson thought highly of MacArthur.) By Pearl Harbor, Stimson was already in his seventies. He managed his vast wartime responsibilities by delegating authority to four assistant secretaries of War: Robert Patterson, a lawyer and former federal judge; Harvey Bundy, Boston lawyer and Yale graduate; and two dynamos Stimson called his Heavenly Twins – John McCloy and Robert Lovett. What they all had in common was their close relationship to the Harrimans and Rockefellers. Lovett's father had been the right-hand man of railway magnate E.H. Harriman, who once tried to buy the South Manchurian Railway from the Japanese. Following in his father's footsteps, Robert Lovett worked with Averell Harriman at the Wall Street firm of Brown Brothers Harriman, handling international currency and lending operations. John J. McCloy, by contrast, was a poor boy from Philadelphia who graduated from Harvard Law School, joined the Cravath firm on Wall Street, and gained the admiration of Averell Harriman by helping get $77-million worth of bond issues for the Union Pacific railroad. (McCloy engineered such deals for everyone from the House of Morgan on down.) Working for Secretary of War Stimson, Lovett and McCloy became midwives at the birth of America's postwar national security establishment, which was closely interwoven with the financial community.

McCloy was a troubleshooter and expert fixer. He said his job was "to be at all points of the organizational chart where the lines did not quite intersect". He made endless trips around the world during the war, solving problems, working with statesmen, bankers and generals. He was intensely involved in backstage strategy and understood, to borrow from Cicero, that "the sinew of war is unlimited money". Money also was to be the sinew of the Cold War. A wheeler-dealer, McCloy knew all the ins and outs of international finance. After the war he became a partner in the law firm of Milbank Tweed, which handled the affairs of the Rockefeller family and its Chase Bank, became a leader of the Council on Foreign Relations, head of the World Bank, chairman of Chase, and head of the Ford Foundation. He may have been the key player in executing the Black Eagle Trust, the one who took Stimson's idea and turned it into a working reality.

By comparison, Robert B. Anderson got off to an inauspicious start. Born in Burleson, Texas, on June 4, 1910, he taught high school for a while before studying law at the University of Texas. He was elected to the state legislature and appointed assistant attorney general for Texas in 1933, and state tax commissioner the following year. Then something clicked, and Anderson left government to become an extraordinarily successful financial consultant to very rich people. By the early 1940s he was general manager of the enormously wealthy W.T. Waggoner estate, which owned ranch land and oil land all over Texas. Anderson was so deft at money management that President Roosevelt appointed him a special aide to Secretary of War Stimson with responsibility for keeping tabs on Axis looting. Navy Captain Clark Clifford, Truman's aide for national security matters who was briefed by Captain Lansdale, was Anderson's protégé and intimate friend. Together, Anderson and Clifford became major power brokers in postwar Washington.

Although Stimson retired from public life in 1945, and McCloy also left government service at that time, they and Anderson continued to be involved in overseeing the Black Eagle Trust. According to former CIA deputy director Ray Cline, the gold bullion recovered by Santa Romana was put "in 176 bank accounts in 42 countries". Anderson apparently traveled all over the world, setting up these black gold accounts, providing money for political action funds throughout the noncommunist world. Later we closely examine several.

In 1953, to reward him, President Eisenhower nominated Anderson to a Cabinet post as secretary of the Navy. The following year he rose to deputy secretary of Defense. During the second Eisenhower Administration, he became secretary of the Treasury, serving from 1957 to 1961. After that, Anderson resumed private life, but remained intimately involved with the CIA's worldwide network of banks, set up after the war by Paul Helliwell. Eventually, this led to Anderson becoming involved in BCCI, the Bank of Credit and Commerce International, an Arab-Pakistani bank with CIA ties that parlayed money-laundering and the discreet movement of black gold into ownership of the biggest bank in Washington, D.C. The collapse of BCCI in what the *Wall Street Journal* called "the world's largest bank fraud" also snared Anderson's protégé, Clark Clifford, who was indicted for fraud. Clifford and his associate Robert Altman headed First American Bankshares, the BCCI front in the nation's capital, and were accused of using political patronage to shield BCCI from full investigation.

Anderson's reputation began to crumble when it was revealed by Bernard Nossiter in *The Washington Post* that he had sought and received $290,000 from a Texas oilman while serving as Eisenhower's secretary of the Treasury. Anderson later pleaded guilty to federal charges of tax evasion and money laundering, and died in disgrace.

It is beyond the scope of this book to examine how Anderson, McCloy and the others administered the Black Eagle Trust from the top down. Because so much of the documentation is still sealed, we must content ourselves with evidence that has surfaced so far, and the players we know were involved in the field. But by looking briefly at what is known about the public side of the arrangements made at Bretton Woods, we find a window into the secret side.

Battered and bankrupt by their long war in Europe and Asia, America's allies had no choice but to stand aside as the U.S. Government set about the 'dollarization' of the global economy. Economists see the end of World War II as 'year zero' for the current system of international finance. Because of widespread suspicion that the Bank of International Settlements (BIS) in Zurich had been laundering Axis loot, Bretton Woods set up a new central financial clearinghouse called the International Monetary Fund (IMF), to act as the world's future financial clearinghouse and moneychanger. Gold was assigned a dollar value of $35 an ounce, and all other currencies were valued against the dollar. This removed any doubt about the relative position of the dollar and the British pound, for example. Although Britain was a partner in the plan, she was deep in debt to the United States. In 1941, in exchange for a $30-billion war loan, Britain had been obliged to take a backseat in postwar planning.

Each IMF member country agreed on a value for its currency expressed in terms of the U.S. dollar. Each member country deposited with the IMF an amount of gold and currency as reserves to be used to sustain the value of that currency. The main function of the IMF was to maintain stable values for these currencies by shifting funds temporarily from one to another. While it was a global organization, its most important backer was the U.S. Government. Federal statistics show that at the end of the war the United States held 60 percent of the world's official gold reserves, which put Washington in the position of being able to manipulate the other nations.

By 1960, however, it was evident to European members of the IMF that they would soon hold dollars far in excess of the official U.S. gold reserves. One solution would have been to devalue the dollar, but Washington blocked this. Instead, in 1961 the U.S. joined with the central banks of Europe, Great Britain and Switzerland to form the London Gold Pool, managed by the Bank of England. The idea was that the collective official reserves of these countries would give them enough gold to intervene in the private market for gold, to keep the price at $35 an ounce. It worked for a while. But by 1968, France had left the Gold Pool, the British pound had been devalued, and private demand for gold skyrocketed. In a last-ditch attempt to sustain the London Gold Pool, the U.S. Air Force made emergency airlifts of gold from Fort Knox to London. So much gold bullion was moved onto the weighing room floor at the Bank of England that the floor collapsed. It was an omen, for the Gold Pool itself collapsed shortly thereafter.

The invisible Black Eagle Trust set up by Stimson's team, beefed up by bullion from the Santa Romana recoveries, created a separate pool of black gold that put an extra floor under the postwar economy, and gave Washington and its allies covert financial leverage. There are certain similarities between this trust and the Diamond Cartel identified with DeBeers, or the Gold Cartel identified with the Oppenheimer family of South Africa. According to informed sources, these similarities exist for good reason and on many different planes. The Diamond Cartel was able to amass huge quantities of stones, and yet keep prices artificially high by limiting to a trickle the number of diamonds reaching the market, maintaining the impression of extraordinary rarity. In a similar way, the black gold cartel could hold many thousands of metric tons of gold bullion – far more than the official gold supply – keeping gold prices artificially high while discreetly using derivatives of this gold as a clandestine slush fund.

If the recovery of this huge mass of plundered gold was known only to a trusted few, those countries and individuals that had been robbed by the Nazis, the Fascists, or the Japanese, would not sue to recover it. Also, the argument was made that the existence of so much black gold, if it became public knowledge, would cause the fixed price of $35 an ounce to collapse. As so many countries now linked their currencies to the U.S. dollar, and the dollar was linked to gold, currency values throughout the world might then plummet, causing financial disaster. But so long as it was kept secret, gold prices could be kept at $35 an ounce, and currencies pegged to gold would be stable. Meanwhile, the black gold would serve as a reserve asset, bolstering the prime banks in each country, and strengthening the governments of those nations.

As a safeguard, the black gold placed in those banks was 'earmarked' or strictly limited in the uses that could be made of it. This enabled Washington to bring pressure, from time to time, on those governments, central banks and prime banks. So long as a country and its leaders cooperated with Washington, and remained allied to it in the Cold War, the sleeping bullion would provide the asset base for patronage. Gold bearer certificates and other derivatives could be given as gifts or bribes, without actually giving away the bullion itself. Beneficial trusts could be set up in behalf of certain statesmen, military leaders, or political figures, or their families. In the hands of clever men like Anderson and McCloy, the possibilities were endless. From time to time, as more bullion was recovered from Golden Lily vaults in the Philippines, quantities of the bullion would be offered in strictest secrecy to central banks, or to consortiums of private buyers.

In later chapters we will see numerous documented instances when these underground funds surfaced as huge bribes, or were used to buy elections, famously in Italy, Greece, and Japan, but probably in other countries as well. Some internationally famous banks appear to have become addicted to having billions of dollars of black gold in their vaults. So addicted that they refuse to surrender the bullion, and in some cases have stooped to swindling the original owners or their heirs, by denouncing their documents as counterfeit. Indeed, some owners claimed that not only were they told their documents were fake, but were given veiled threats of murder if they pressed their claims. In some cases the banks may have made such heavy use of these black gold reserves that they no longer are in a position to relinquish the bullion without going under.

In a certain sense, no one made better use of the Santa Romana recoveries than Lansdale. His role at first was strictly as a facilitator in Manila, supervising the recovery of Golden Lily vaults, inventorying the bullion, having it trucked to warehouses at the U.S. Navy base in Subic Bay, or the U.S. Air Force base at Clark Field. The bullion had to be moved under tight security, by armed convoy, military aircraft, and navy vessel. Preference went to the U.S. Navy because of the weight of the bullion. One source even insists that this was one of the reasons President Eisenhower appointed Anderson secretary of the Navy. The transfer of these big quantities of bullion is confirmed by documents, bills of lading, insurance covers, and a multitude of other paper that over the years revealed the names of the individuals and famous brokerages involved, and the prime banks to which the bullion was shipped. In later chapters, some of these shipments will be described. The documents are reproduced in full on our CDs.

General Willoughby, a man of limited imagination, detested Lansdale as a 'smartass', and blocked his promotion to major until 1947, when Lansdale also was made deputy director of G-2 in the Philippines. General Hoyt Vandenberg, chief of the new Central Intelligence Group, came to Lansdale's rescue by transferring him to the Air Force. After a few months at its Strategic Intelligence School in Colorado, where he rose to lieutenant colonel, Lansdale was sent back to the Philippines as a full colonel, working for Frank Wisner, the Mad Hatter of the CIA and head of its new dirty tricks division, called the Office of Policy Coordination (OPC). Lansdale's rise then became meteoric. This usually is attributed to his success in grooming Ramon Magsaysay to be 'America's Boy' in the newly independent Philippines, and Lansdale's much exaggerated success in suppressing the communist Huk 'rebellion' there. Because the Huks were only a rural protest movement of poor farmers, abused for generations by rich Spaniards and Overseas Chinese landowners, that scenario was never convincing to anyone who really knew the Philippines. Most of the Huks knew nothing about Marxism and would have joined any protest movement that helped them in their struggle against predatory landlords. Lansdale, always the huckster, had movie crews film phony attacks on villages staged by special units of the Filipino army, and the next day filmed the 'liberation' of the village led by a well-coached Magsaysay. It was pure Hollywood.

What really made Lansdale a great Cold War celebrity was something known only to a few: The way he capitalized on his secret role in the torture of Yamashita's driver, in the Santa Romana gold recoveries, and in the Black Eagle Trust. Having spent so much of his adult life as an ad agency man, Lansdale was easily able to con powerful men in Washington into believing that he had done this all by himself. His natural charm, his quaint Midwestern homilies, and his 'visionary' ideas about America's great mission to reform Asia, were taken seriously by Allen Dulles and John Foster Dulles, who had great power but little direct experience of Asia, and others in Washington who should have known better. Lansdale became an instant hit at the Sunday evening drinking parties thrown by the Dulles brothers. Writing to the U.S. Ambassador in Manila, Admiral Raymond Spruance, Allen Dulles called Lansdale "our mutual friend". When he sent Lansdale to Vietnam in 1954, Dulles told Eisenhower he was sending one of his "best men". Eisenhower enjoyed hearing about Lansdale's escapades in the Philippines, recounted with wry humor and heavy irony. Lansdale was also close to Richard Nixon, which led to a number of unsavory consequences.

Others noticed that Lansdale had a curious gleam in his eye, not unlike that of Elmer Gantry, and concluded that he was nuts, and must be stopped at all cost. Douglas Valentine, author of *The Phoenix Program*, said: "Lansdale used Madison Avenue language to construct a squeaky-clean, Boy Scout image, behind which he masked his own perverse delight in atrocity." Lansdale's Asian adventures were costly failures, without exception. In the early 1950s, Allen Dulles gave Lansdale $5-million to finance CIA operations in the Philippines, but after the money was spent Lansdale's protégé, President Magsaysay, died prematurely in a plane crash. As recounted in detail in *The Marcos Dynasty*, his widely publicized suppression of the Huks was fraudulent. In Vietnam he initially spread $12-million in black money in a misguided attempt to reverse the floodtide of events, by backing the Diem family. Like many of the other characters in this book, Lansdale loved the power he gained from having access to limitless covert funds, and (like Willoughby) he was largely successful in keeping his failures secret – the very essence of 'national security' cover. In the late 1950s, he was in and out of Tokyo on secret missions with a hand-picked team of Filipino assassins, including his favorite, a handsome cold-blooded killer named Napoleon Valeriano. The daughter of an American officer who knew Lansdale, told how he arrived in Japan with "characters who were known as his assassins – the ones he brought in from the Philippines. As a kid I was fascinated by him and his gun which everyone could see – unusual because no one in Japan had weapons… the whole idea of Lansdale and our government assassinating people struck me as shocking, weird."

In retrospect, recovering the Golden Lily treasure vaults and setting up the Black Eagle Trust were the easy part, because they only involved spending somebody else's money. Making intelligent use of so much invisible wealth during the Cold War, its original strategic purpose, was not so easy. In Japan and elsewhere, because of their extreme secrecy, these enormous political action funds soon got into corrupt hands, where they remain to this day. Along the way, it was necessary to do a lot of lying, and even some killing. Especially lying about Japan, which had stolen most of that gold to start with. To keep people from knowing about the Santa Romana recoveries, and the Black Eagle Trust, Washington had to insist that Japan never stole anything, and was flat broke and bankrupt when the war ended. This was the beginning of many terrible secrets.

CHAPTER EIGHT

DIRTY TRICKS

When pieces of the body were found before dawn in the rail yards of Tokyo's North Senju station, they were scattered along the tracks for a hundred meters. The corpse was so mangled you could not tell if it was man or woman. At sunrise that day in July 1949, identification cards were found by the rails, with a shattered wristwatch putting the time of death at 12:20 a.m. The victim was 49-year-old Shimoyama Sadanori, president of the Japanese National Railroads. He had made the mistake of trying to sack thousands of ex-soldiers who had been put on his payroll in return for kickbacks to the notoriously right-wing *yakuza*. Curiously, by the time his murder made the newspapers (controlled at the time by SCAP, MacArthur's occupation headquarters) it was all turned around to create the impression that Shimoyama had been slain as part of a conspiracy by the Japanese Communist Party. A few days later, a train was wrecked by sabotage, causing the death of three people. Again this was blamed on 'communists', and twenty workers were charged and tried (nineteen of them labor organizers or leftists of one sort or another). Over the next twenty years, their fate became one of Japan's biggest legal scandals. Their case remained before the courts until 1970 when the workers were exonerated and paid damages by the government, for having been framed. Many Japanese believed then, and still believe today, that Shimoyama's murder and the train wreck were both the work of American secret agents, helped by the *yakuza*. Half a century later, the truth still is not known because all records of the U.S. occupation remain tightly sealed. Shimoyama's corpse is a metaphor for many victims of a curious collusion between Washington and Tokyo during the six-year occupation, a collusion that continues to this day. Until now, it has been seen as the logical consequence of the anti-communist hysteria that gripped America after World War II, rising to its greatest pitch during the witch hunts of the McCarthy era. However, this hysteria did not subside even after the Soviet Union collapsed, the Berlin Wall crumbled, and China's communist party turned into capitalist-roaders. For those whose snouts were deep in the trough, it was too convenient to end. The hysteria is still apparent in America and Japan, seeking justification in new enemies with new labels.

Discovery of the Santa Romana recoveries suggests that anti-communist hysteria may not have been the only motivation behind the murders and collusion of the postwar years. Another factor may have been the great sums of money derived from this black gold, for which there was no need to account. Hard evidence now emerging shows that America set up secret political action funds in Japan that were used to influence the imperial family, the ruling elite, the underworld, and to support a rightwing regime and keep it in power. Documents show that these funds, originally under the control of senior U.S. Army officers at MacArthur's headquarters, were used to bribe witnesses at the Tokyo war crimes trials, and almost certainly were used to pay for the murder of liberal politicians and left-wing organizers. As we documented in *The Yamato Dynasty*, Japan's right-wing leaders were fully aware of America's anti-communist fears and cravings during that period, and responded to them with enthusiasm and cleverness. The democratization of Japan was reversed, its government given back to indicted war criminals – specifically the group surrounding Kishi Nobosuke. His political party, the Liberal Democratic Party or LDP, created and funded by underworld godfather Kodama from treasure he amassed during the war, was vigorously backed by Washington and kept supplied with virtually limitless unvouchered funds.

Once millions of dollars derived from black gold were in this covert pipeline, hidden by 'national security', nobody had to keep track of the way it was spent. Whatever the original strategic purpose of Presidents Roosevelt and Truman, the funds fell into the hands of corrupt people who could use them any way they wished, with little concern about discovery. Raising fears of communism at every turn did keep citizens of both countries from questioning deals that were made by the two governments. Invoking national security did allow officials making these deals to hide the documents, forbidding anyone to look at them until deep into the twenty-first century. Anyone protesting this in America was ridiculed as a Japan Basher, or more recently as a 'terrorist'. In Japan, anyone who might reveal too much became a victim of 'assisted suicide'.

Meanwhile, Japan and the rest of the world were flooded with news stories and other propaganda to create a false impression. Initially through the SCAP-controlled press, and through tame journalists beholden to MacArthur's backers on Wall Street, Japan was portrayed as a poverty-stricken country unable to pay reparations or compensation to its victims. Had Washington acknowledged the existence of the great mass of treasure it knew Japan had stolen, much of it slumbering in vaults throughout the Home Islands, it would have been obvious that Japan had plenty of money. (Not to mention all the stolen art and cultural treasures that could have been converted into cash, or returned in place of cash.) It now seems inescapable that the 1951 Japan Peace Treaty was falsely contrived to buy Tokyo's cooperation in the Cold War, by assuring Japan's elite that they would not be obliged to part with their private hoards of plunder. This was done by adding Article 14 to the Treaty, which says: "It is recognized that Japan should pay reparations to the Allied Powers for the damage and suffering caused by it during the war. Nevertheless it is also recognized that the resources of Japan are not presently sufficient. …[Therefore] the Allied Powers waive all reparations claims of the Allied Powers *and their nationals* arising out of any actions taken by Japan." [Our italics.] From this it became dogma that individual victims could not expect compensation for their years of torture and brutalization as POWs or as civilian slave laborers toiling for giant Japanese corporations like Mitsubishi, Mitsui, and Sumitomo. To this day the State Department and the Justice Department, shielding the government and *zaibatsu* of Japan, still invoke Article 14 of the 1951 Peace Treaty to block any attempt by victims to sue these immensely rich corporations. In fact, as the Santa Romana recoveries demonstrate, the Treaty is invalid because it is based on lies and deceptions.

Japan is not the only example of how Washington used Axis war loot for political action during the first years of the Cold War. The Italian elections of 1948 are another.

In postwar Italy, CIA agent James Jesus Angleton recovered Ethiopian treasure plundered by Mussolini's forces. Instead of returning this loot to the desperately impoverished Ethiopian people, it was appropriated by the CIA and used to finance pro-American and anti-communist candidates in Italy's 1948 elections. In addition, the Agency raised a great deal of money in Europe from the sale of surplus U.S. war materiel, and gave this money to the Vatican, earmarked explicitly for the war on communism in Italy. The Agency then arranged for the Pope to provide 100-million lira from this personal account to back the anti-communist ticket during the elections. This comes as no surprise because it is now known that the Vatican bank sheltered Hirohito's assets and Nazi assets during the war. It also is one of the 42 countries to which Ray Cline said the recovered Golden Lily bullion was shipped during 1945-1947. And it is one of the banks named as having accounts in Santy's various names.

By the 1960s, Angleton was back in Washington running the counterintelligence staff of the CIA, often wryly referred to as The Gestapo, which had its own "very secret slush fund …that was never audited". The CIA's 'historical intelligence budget information' (how it actually spent covert funds) remains one of its biggest secrets to this day, apparently on the premise that it can never reveal who was bribed, coerced, or paid off, no matter how many decades pass, or what misjudgments, folly, and corruption, were involved. We may well wonder whether this really is intended to protect the recipients, or the American officials who fiddled the funds.

Covert actions like manipulating the Italian elections of 1948 were the dark side of the so-called Truman Doctrine, the backbone of every U.S. administration's foreign policy since 1948, when President Truman declared America's commitment to global hegemony, and made it clear that the Cold War would set the tone of future U.S. foreign and military policy.

Similar U.S. covert intervention occurred in Greece, when Britain gave notice that her empty treasury compelled her to end all financial and military aid to the eastern end of the Mediterranean, quitting her role in Greece and Turkey. Fearing the spread of communism, London appealed to Washington to step into the vacuum. Greece was in the throes of civil war, and Turkey might be next to fall, in what

Secretary of State Dean Acheson called the 'rotten apple in the barrel syndrome' (later the 'domino theory'). Truman called a joint session of Congress and asked for $400-million in aid for Greece and Turkey. "At the present moment..." he said, "nearly every nation must choose between alternative ways of life. ...One way of life is based upon the will of the majority, and is distinguished by free institutions, representative government, free elections, guarantees of individual liberty, freedom of speech and religion, and freedom from political oppression. The second way of life is based upon the will of a minority forcibly imposed upon the majority. It relies upon terror and oppression, a controlled press and radio, fixed elections, and the suppression of personal freedoms."

Secretly, Truman simultaneously authorized the use of Axis war loot and other unvouchered funds to do precisely that – to interfere in the political life of sovereign nations, to buy elections, to undercut the rule of law, to control the media, to carry out assassinations, and to impose America's will on countries with whom it was not at war.

The man put in charge of these dirty tricks was Frank Wisner. He had an especially free hand in Asia. CIA director Allen Dulles knew little about Asia, so he gave that part of the world entirely to Wisner's Office of Policy Coordination, which included a group of maverick OSS 'China Cowboys'. Driven from China by the communist victory in 1949, the Cowboys regrouped in Japan, or Korea, or fled to Taiwan with Generalissimo Chiang.

Wisner was a pivotal figure in giving postwar U.S. covert operations the especially dirty qualities that have since come to haunt many Americans. He had spent the war with the OSS in Cairo, Istanbul and Bucharest where he was less interested in fighting the Nazis than in fighting the Soviets. Stationed in Germany after the war, Wisner came up with the idea of America hiring ex-Nazis to create an anti-Soviet fifth column. His powerful friends the Dulles brothers, George Kennan, Averell Harriman, Joe and Stewart Alsop, were so excited by Wisner's eccentric ideas for subversion, sabotage, and assassinations, they got him the job of running dirty tricks at the CIA. There Wisner hired all manner of unsavory characters who claimed to be anti-communist, which in those days was synonymous with pro-American. If they were far enough to the right, both Nazi and Japanese war criminals qualified for financial support. According to Evan Thomas, Wisner funded his covert teams in Europe by siphoning off funds from the Marshall Plan. He gave this 'candy' to his agents. "We couldn't spend it all," said one. "There were no limits and nobody had to account for it." By 1952, after only four years in the job, Wisner had set up forty-seven overseas stations, was running a staff of nearly three thousand, plus another three thousand contract personnel, with an official annual budget of $84-million. How big his *unofficial* budget was, we can only guess, because this was a secret empire of dirty tricks. Wisner recruited another old OSS hand to help him, Desmond Fitzgerald, who knew more than Wisner about Asia. One of their favorite agents was Lansdale, who was sent to Japan, Korea, Taiwan, Indochina, Thailand, and Indonesia with his team of Filipino killers headed by Napoleon Valeriano, to carry out gangland-style assassinations. Despite the resources available to Wisner and Fitzgerald, these covert operations were not a success. Never acknowledging his chronic failures, Lansdale was forced to retire from the CIA in 1963, at the same time that Wisner, the Agency's Mad Hatter, suffered what was called 'a nervous breakdown' and was hastily retired. Sources in the CIA said: "Wisner was showing increasing signs of insanity over previous months, and suddenly went nuts." New CIA directors and deputy directors came and went, as America became mired deeper and deeper in the muck of black operations.

Like Angleton's meddling in Italy, the political action funds set up by SCAP and the CIA in postwar Japan were based on stolen gold and other treasure. Some was treasure recovered by Santa Romana. The rest was loot discovered and confiscated by the U.S. 8th Army in Japan, which was kept as bullion or – in the case of diamonds – converted into liquid assets. According to Takahashi Toshio, a postwar student leader at Tokyo University law school with close ties to the CIA, General MacArthur was the key figure in setting up the M-Fund: "MacArthur realized, as General Marshall did in Europe, that a substantial sum of money would be needed to restore the economy of Japan. But whereas General Marshall had to go to Congress to get the money, General MacArthur found that the Imperial Army of Japan had very large resources that were not on the books of the country. They had occupied Korea for nearly half a century. They had occupied a large area of China for many years, Southeast Asia, the Philippines, and those areas produced very large resources, which the Army brought back to Japan. MacArthur set aside a substantial fund to be used for rebuilding the economy of Japan... But MacArthur also saw that some money would be needed for purposes that would not stand public scrutiny very well, for example, helping politicians... MacArthur decided that they would keep this fund confidential so that they could use it, in part, to help the democratic process get going in Japan after the war, and that involved making contributions to political parties and to individual politicians."

According to investigative journalist Takano Hajime, whose study of the M-Fund was published by *Nikei*, Japan's most respected financial journal, much of the cash derived from sale of confiscated stockpiles of diamonds, platinum, gold and silver, other strategic materials, and the blackmarket sale in Japan of U.S. foreign aid. Other sources were proceeds from the sale of several minor *zaibatsu* conglomerates that were broken up and sold to other entities, to set an example that was, in fact, the exception to the rule. The size of the M-Fund at its inception is not known precisely but some sources put it at $2-billion. It then grew quickly.

Long time Tokyo correspondent Robert Whiting described "a secret billion-dollar slush fund... equivalent to nearly 10 percent of Japan's 1950 GNP". Whiting told us, "The Japanese government also sold [on the blackmarket] great stockpiles of gold, silver and copper ...which they had concealed in early 1945 in anticipation of Japan's defeat."

Most of Japan's military supplies, stockpiled for the final bloodbath defense of the Home Islands, vanished.

Articles about the M-Fund published in the reputable Japanese weekly magazine *Shukan Bunshun* in 1979, said a lot of the money raised by the covert sale of these materials went to high government officials and politicians. The magazine said 800,000 karats of diamonds stored in the Bank of Japan inexplicably shrank to only

160,000 karats. "Even after the occupation ended, there was movement by the American side to deposit black money behind the scenes... [which was] used for political conspiracy."

Another source of underground funds was Kodama, who was reported to have amassed some $13-billion in war loot for his personal use. This included two truck-loads of diamonds, gold bars, platinum ingots, radium, copper, and other vital materials. In order to curry favor with MacArthur's men, *Skukan Bunshun* said Kodama turned the radium over to SCAP. In *Tokyo Journal*, John Carroll states that at war's end "Kodama had a good portion of [his] valuables transported to the vault of the Imperial Family in the Imperial Palace." Despite his lifelong involvement in murder, kidnapping, drugs and extortion, Kodama is said to have been regarded by Emperor Hirohito as a true patriot, possibly because of the great sums he generat-ed for Golden Lily. This may explain why Japan's top gangster was permitted to hide some of his loot in palace vaults. But it goes deeper to include narcotics.

In the spring of 1945, Kodama made a quick trip to Taiwan to see that its many heroin factories were dismantled for return to Japan, along with remaining stocks of heroin and morphine. On his return, Kodama was assigned to be a special advi-sor to the emperor's uncle, Prince Higashikuni, who served as Japan's prime min-ister briefly at the start of the U.S. occupation. According to Kodama's own mem-oir, immediately after the surrender, Higashikuni had "two or three of us councilors arrange a meeting and secretly, unknown to his cabinet ministers, [Higashikuni] visited General MacArthur in Yokohama". Kodama provides no details of what transpired at this meeting, or whether he accompanied the prince.

Kodama then spent two years in Sugamo Prison as an indicted war criminal, but was magically released in mid-1948 when he made a deal with General Willoughby to give the CIA $100-million (equal to $1-billion in today's values). This payment bought Kodama his freedom from prison and from any prosecution for war crimes. The money was placed in one of the secret slush funds controlled by the CIA sta-tion at the U.S. Embassy. Subsequently, Kodama was put directly on the CIA pay-roll, where he remained for many years, until his death in 1984. Tad Szulc of *The New York Times* wrote, "Kodama had a working relationship with the CIA." Chalmers Johnson said Kodama was "probably the CIA's chief asset in Japan".

While literally an employee of the U.S. Government, Kodama continued to over-see Japan's postwar drug trade. Heroin labs were moved back not only from Taiwan, but from North China, Manchuria and Korea. Chinese who had collaborated with Japan in drug processing and distribution, were given sanctuary and began operat-ing from Japanese soil. Two of the three major players in Asian narcotics soon died: Nationalist China's General Tai Li was assassinated in a 1946 plane crash; Shanghai godfather Tu Yueh-sheng died in Hong Kong of natural causes in 1951. Kodama was left as Asia's top druglord, while on the U.S. payroll. This could have been embarrassing, for Japan's dominant role in narcotics was widely known and undis-puted, but a Cold War hush descended over it like an Arctic whiteout. During the occupation, U.S. propaganda characterized Asia's drug trade as exclusively the enterprise of leftists and communist agents. In truth it was dominated by Kodama in Japan, and by Generalissimo Chiang through the KMT opium armies based in the Golden Triangle, who were under the direct control of the generalissimo's son, Chiang Ching-kuo, the KMT chief of military intelligence at that time. (The two top KMT opium warlords in the Golden Triangle, General Tuan and General Li, spoke to us openly of this.)

As for Japan, Professor H. Richard Firman, writing in *The Pacific Review* in 1993, said: "Occupation forces, as well as Japanese criminal organizations …seized stockpiles of …drugs produced during the war by the Japanese government. …[These] soon found their way onto the black market either through direct diversion by American servicemen or through indirect diversion by the Chinese, Taiwanese, and Korean middlemen contracted by SCAP officials to disperse drugs along with other medical supplies to the Japanese population. …Drawing on linkages with the leadership of Korean *yakuza* based in Japan, the Yamaguchi-gumi and Inagawa-kai [*yakuza*] developed a transnational, vertically integrated network of production and distribution between South Korea and Japan… tapping old organized crime networks with Taiwan, Korea, China."

•

In this context of intense corruption and artful misrepresentation, it was inevitable that the political action funds America set up in Japan would be diverted. But the corruption, dishonesty, and moral turpitude cannot be blamed only on the Japanese. Americans were involved in diverting the funds, benefited from their abuse, and may still be benefiting today in a multitude of ways.

Three underground funds were controlled by American officials during the occupation – the M-Fund, the Yotsuya Fund and the Keenan Fund. According to Takano Hajime, the M-Fund was named after General William Frederic Marquat, chief of SCAP's Economic and Scientific Section. In theory, Marquat headed America's program to punish and reform Japanese businesses that had gorged on war profiteering. In reality, Marquat's biggest public relations headache was how to help them *conceal* these obscene profits, which by custom were shared with the imperial family. Historian John Dower explains that Marquat "assumed responsibility for nothing less than supervising all developments in finance, economics, labor, and science, including the dissolution of *zaibatsu* holding companies and the promotion of economic deconcentration. Every major government financial and economic institution reported to his section, including the Ministry of Finance, the Ministry of Commerce and Industry, and the Bank of Japan".

Little has been written about Marquat, who usually is portrayed as an amiable nincompoop, unfit for the job. This hardly comes as a surprise. Like Willoughby and Whitney, Marquat was one of MacArthur's inner-circle 'The Bataan Boys', whose chief quality was undying loyalty. John Gunther said Marquat "pays little attention to the jargon of his present field; once he …turned to his first assistant during a heavy conference on economic affairs, saying 'What is marginal economy, anyway?'"

Marquat was supposed to dissolve the banks and conglomerates that financed Japan's war and profited from it. Despite purely cosmetic changes and the break-up and sale of several small conglomerates, the biggest war profiteers were let off without even a slap on the wrist. General Marquat was also in charge of closing down and punishing Japan's biological and chemical warfare service, Unit 731. Instead, the U.S. Government secretly absorbed Unit 731, moving most of its scientists, personnel, and documents to U.S. military research centers like Fort Dietrich in the Maryland countryside. All information about its activities, including biological warfare atrocities, and horrific experiments on fully conscious victims, was withheld by Washington from the American and Japanese public, and from the Tokyo War Crimes Tribunals. All Unit 731's records held by the U.S. Government are still top secret.

So while he was supposed to be making Japan more democratic, Marquat was doing the opposite. The M-Fund was created to buy elections for Japanese politicians so far to the right that they were solidly anti-communist. Japan was the most highly industrialized country in Asia; Washington wanted it to be a capitalist bastion against communism, for its economy to thrive so there would be no need for labor unions, leftist organizers, or revolution. This was the view of American conservatives who thought President Roosevelt was a communist, and believed that Britain should have allied itself with Germany and Japan, and gone to war against the USSR. As a consequence of this thinking, plans to reform Japan were truncated or aborted. (One major exception was land reform, successfully completed before it could be halted.)

The first big application of the M-Fund was in the late 1940s when a Socialist government happened to win election in Japan – a development that astonished, panicked, and galvanized SCAP. Immediately, great sums were distributed by SCAP to discredit the Socialist cabinet, and to replace it with a regime more to Washington's liking. Later, when Tokyo considered establishing relations with the People's Republic of China, sums again were disbursed to get Japan back on the right track. When Yoshida Shigeru became prime minister, Washington relaxed because Yoshida was trusted, conservative, and personally very rich. During his period as prime minister, the M-Fund was called the Yoshida Fund. After he ceased to be prime minister, the name reverted to M-Fund. (In a conversation in 1987, White House national security advisor Richard Allen said: "All my life I've heard of a thing called the Yoshida Fund – I think that's the same thing as the M-Fund.")

Very different from the M-Fund was the Yotsuya Fund. This was set up to manipulate and steer Japan's underworld, and to finance 'wet work' – extortion, kidnapping, and murder. General Willoughby, MacArthur's 'lovable fascist' and head of G-2 at SCAP, controlled the Yotsuya Fund and worked energetically with Kodama and his legions of *yakuza* to suppress any kind of leftist activity or public protest during the occupation. Because democracy tolerated dissent, the concept of democracy had long been regarded by Japan's ruling elite as 'a poisonous idea from the West'. In Japan, even the mildest kind of dissent was not tolerated. During the McCarthy era in America, the suppression of dissent became synonymous with anti-communism. But the witchhunt in Japan during that epoch was far more severe, and bloody.

Despite being head of G-2, at this late stage in his career Willoughby was involved in dirty tricks rather than intelligence-gathering or counter-espionage.

Among other things, his Yotsuya Fund financed a Korean Liaison Office that sent spies into North Korea, Red China and the far eastern USSR.

Yotsuya, the district for which Willoughby named his underground fund, was a seedy Tokyo tenderloin populated in the postwar years by gangsters, prostitutes, and bottom-feeders, a hub for the blackmarket, awake all night with illegal gambling casinos and attached brothels. (Today Yotsuya has changed, and is famous for bars frequented by university students and company executives.) Kickbacks from postwar dives like the Mandarin Club, a casino and brothel in Yotsuya run by American Ted Lewin, a pal of Kodama, funded the Cannon Agency, Willoughby's dirtiest and wettest operation in Japan. Named for U.S. Army Colonel J. Y. Cannon, this was a military version of Murder Incorporated, a death squad.

Jack Cannon arranged the beating and killings of student leaders, liberals, leftists, socialists, labor union organizers, scholars, journalists, and anyone else who got in the way. Cannon worked closely with Machii Hisayuki, Kodama's Korean lieutenant who headed the ethnic Korean Tosei-kai gang of *yakuza*. Jack Cannon initially worked for the U.S. Army's Counter-Intelligence Corps, or CIC. His job was to ferret out and to murder dissidents. A Nisei interpreter employed by Willoughby's ATIS, who once had helped Cannon blow open a safe, recalled that the colonel always behaved like 'a movie style gangster'. Once the Cannon Agency was set up, Jack Cannon became something that would have chilled the blood of most Americans. He is thought to have been behind the kidnapping of a prominent left-wing writer, Kaji Wataru. Also attributed to him was the torture, dismemberment, and murder of Shimoyama, the president of Japan's national railroads whose body was found scattered along the railway tracks. Whenever he needed a hand, Cannon called on Machii's Korean *yakuza*. He also was suspected of arranging plane crashes that took the lives of British and American diplomats and military officers who were investigating the links between Willoughby and indicted war criminals like Kodama and Colonel Tsuji Masanobu. When the job was so wet and dirty that it had to be completely divorced from Washington, Willoughby bypassed Cannon and brought in a murder squad called KATOH, the acronym of five Japanese Army officers who did surgical assassinations for money.

To be sure, what makes this even more disturbing is that Willoughby was judged by U. S. Army contemporaries to be incompetent, paranoid, and congenitally driven to cover up his misjudgments. As most documents relating to Willoughby's activities still are kept hidden by the U.S. Government half a century later, we may reasonably suppose that there is yet more disturbing information on his messianic activities.

The Keenan Fund, by contrast, was controlled by a civilian: Joseph B. Keenan, another MacArthur intimate who was chief prosecutor in the Tokyo war crimes trials. Previously, Keenan had been chief of the U.S. Justice Department's criminal division, where he acquired a reputation for 'gang-busting' and heavy boozing. His appointment as chief war crimes prosecutor in Tokyo was criticized because he was not considered a good enough lawyer, knew nothing of Asia, and was a shameless headline seeker. Many thought Keenan got the job because President Truman disliked him and wanted him out of Washington.

In Japan, Keenan's personal assistant was none less than General Tanaka Takayoshi, the bull-like *tairiku ronin* who was General Doihara's alter-ego in Manchuria, the cold-blooded manipulator of Pu Yi's young Empress Elizabeth. Tanaka spent the late 1930s and early 1940s in Shanghai with Doihara, running covert operations. Like Doihara, he personally carried out many individual murders. The idea that he was suited to babysit America's chief war crimes prosecutor in postwar Tokyo is black humor at its best.

It was common gossip among journalists in Tokyo (as it had been in Washington) that Keenan had a severe drinking problem, and 'liked the ladies' excessively. General Tanaka took charge of Keenan's date book, accompanied him to inns and brothels to carry out these assignations and, when Keenan passed out, got him safely home.

Unlike the broad mandates of the M-Fund and the Yotsuya Fund, the Keenan Fund had a narrow and specific function. Simply put, it was used to bribe witnesses at the war crimes trials, or to grease the intermediaries who persuaded the witnesses to falsify their testimony. Unlike the swift punishment meted out to Generals Yamashita and Homma in Manila, the War Crimes Tribunal in Tokyo dragged on for three years, while a lot of horse-trading took place. The Tribunal had been established to try General Tojo and other senior military and civilian leaders for complicity in Japan's cruel aggression. Although the Tribunal was labeled an international commission, the whole operation was carried out exclusively by MacArthur's inner circle. In the charter establishing the Tribunal, MacArthur invested himself with broad powers, and the Tribunal was kept under his sole and exclusive authority. As a final touch, the charter (written by MacArthur and Keenan) stated, "the Tribunal shall not be bound by technical rules of evidence".

Accordingly, MacArthur's men were able to control access to the defendants, to suborn whoever they wished, and to arrange omissions of evidence. Money changed hands secretly to assure scapegoats that their families would be cared for. As we documented in *The Yamato Dynasty*, the private papers of MacArthur's military secretary Brigadier General Bonner Fellers reveal that he personally suborned witnesses, got them to falsify their testimony, and made sure that Emperor Hirohito was not brought to trial. On January 25, 1946, MacArthur sent a secret telegram to Army Chief of Staff Dwight Eisenhower saying the 'investigations' conducted by SCAP could not support any criminal charges against Hirohito: "No specific and tangible evidence has been uncovered with regard to [the emperor's] exact activities which might connect him in varying degree with the political decisions of the Japanese Empire during the last decade…" Documents we found in the MacArthur Memorial in Norfolk, Virginia, show that MacArthur and Bonner Fellers conspired with former president Herbert Hoover to guarantee that Hirohito would escape punishment of any kind, and that General Tojo would falsify his testimony to take all responsibility for the attack on Pearl Harbor. Intermediaries, including Admiral Yonai, were paid large sums from the Keenan Fund to negotiate with Tojo and guarantee his perjury. In his papers, General Fellers proudly describes his meetings with Yonai to set up the false testimony. (During the war, incidentally, Admiral Yonai was the immediate superior of Rear Admiral Kodama.)

A number of key witnesses who resisted subornation died violently, or under suspicious circumstances. Fellers and MacArthur intensely disliked Hirohito's close advisor and one-time prime minister, Prince Konoe, one of the few statesmen who had tried to talk Hirohito into seeking an early peace. Fellers denounced the prince as "a rat who's quite prepared to sell anyone to save himself [and who had even called] his master the emperor 'the major war criminal'". Konoe was blackballed by MacArthur's men and hounded to despair by a campaign of backbiting, disinformation, and innuendo. For example, he was falsely informed that his name had been added to the list of war criminals, and that he faced imminent arrest, imprisonment, and hanging. On December 16, 1945, Prince Konoe was found dead in his home under suspicious circumstances. Most sources say he would not submit to the indignity of trial, and the official ruling was suicide, but it appears to have been one of the first postwar episodes of 'assisted suicide'. Scholars Meirion and Susie Harries, among others, believe that Prince Konoe was murdered because he represented a danger to the plans of MacArthur to exonerate Hirohito. Other crucial witnesses who died conveniently before the trials began were two of Prince Asaka's staff who had first-hand knowledge of Asaka's instructions for the Rape of Nanking. At the end of 1945, both these aides suddenly developed 'heart trouble' and died.

Bribes from the Keenan Fund also were used to prevent testimony about Japan's biological and chemical warfare program, and the vast scale of looting carried out by the imperial family's Golden Lily operation. We now know that the U.S. Government and other Allied governments browbeat POWs when they were liberated from Japanese slave labor camps. They were bullied into signing secrecy oaths before they were allowed to go home, forced to swear that they would not reveal anything they knew about war looting or about the chemical and biological weapons testing of Unit 731. Even men who had been victims of Japanese medical experiments were forced to take this oath. At the time, they were told it was their patriotic duty to remain silent. Today they are realizing that they were victimized by their own governments, which were less interested in justice than in staying in power, and preparing for the coming Cold War.

Willoughby also took on the job of falsifying the Japanese military history of the Pacific War, so that it would conform to the needs of America's Cold Warriors. On the Japanese side, Willoughby's 'historians' included those most notorious war criminals, Kodama and Tsuji (who masterminded the *Sook Ching* massacres in Singapore and Malaya). The historical monographs they prepared were first composed in Japanese, then translated with the help of Nisei in Willoughby's ATIS. The monographs were then laundered of anything remotely sensitive. Once sanitized, they were published by the U.S. Government, collectively titled *The Japanese Monographs* and *Japanese Studies in World War Two*. Not surprisingly, the series contains big gaps. As the official introduction states: "The paucity of original orders, plans and unit journals ... rendered the task of compilation most difficult... However, while many of the important orders, plans and estimates have been reconstructed from memory... they are believed to be generally accurate and reliable." According to Louis Morton, author of the official military history of the Philippines campaign, the reports prepared by Willoughby's office "constitute the most important single Japanese source on Japanese operations in the Pacific and Asia during World War II".

Willoughby persuaded Kodama to write a memoir guaranteed to please his new American clients. Disingenuously titled *I Was Defeated* in its English translation, it was published in 1951 by a CIA proprietary called Asian Publications. Listed as publishers were Harvey Fukuda, who did the editing, and Robert Booth, who did the bookkeeping. In 1952, the same publishers gave birth to the English-language translation of a memoir by Colonel Tsuji – a man who, readers will recall, also had been charged by British investigators with cannibalism. Tsuji's *Underground Escape* presented a falsified story in which he claimed he spent years after the war hiding from the Allies in Thailand and China, when in fact he was, like Kodama, an employee of General Willoughby and the CIA in Tokyo.

The purpose of these memoirs was to shift war blame away from certain politicians, so they could be groomed for political careers in postwar Japan. Kodama's memoir put blame for the war exclusively upon senior officers of Japan's army and navy, most of them dead, who he portrayed as fanatical war-crazed monsters. Everyone else was a helpless pawn.

Generously, Kodama provided funds from his own deep pockets to launch two postwar political parties headed by fanatical rightists, which eventually merged into the Liberal Democratic Party. The political views expressed in his memoir were designed for American audiences. "I feel supreme anxiety over the fact that the conservative forces in Japan – the strongest anti-Communist influence in the country – have been so thoroughly purged of so-called wartime collaborators. This was just what the Communist Party had hoped for. ... The main purport of the purge directive of the Occupation forces should have been the elimination of those who positively collaborated in the prosecution of the war of aggression." Kodama did not consider himself part of that group.

According to Kodama, in Japan only leftists engaged in bribery. At that moment, Socialist Party leaders were demanding a Diet investigation of widespread payoffs. Huffily, Kodama remarked that the Socialist Party was rudely "peeking into an occupied bathroom through a key-hole". It was wrong, he said, for the Socialist Party to "brazenly engage in underhand tactics to retain power".

For three decades, Kodama worked closely with Harvey Fukuda, the Nisei interpreter from ATIS who doubled as the publisher of Kodama and Tsuji. Born in Salt Lake City, Harvey Fukuda spent the war broadcasting anti-Japanese radio propaganda. In postwar Tokyo he was chosen by Willoughby to be Kodama's full-time amanuensis, English-language secretary and public relations man. Their collaboration was so successful that Fukuda was rewarded with his own CIA proprietary, a public relations company called Japan-PR, with Fukuda as the proprietor, and Kodama as the source of supplemental funds. Because Kodama spoke no English, Fukuda was his personal interpreter in all dealings with Americans. When America ran short of tungsten, Kodama offered to sell some of the tungsten he had looted from China – a deal Harvey Fukuda discreetly negotiated with U.S. diplomat Eugene Dooman. In the late 1950s, it was Harvey Fukuda who set up the original meeting between Kodama and Lockheed Aircraft executives, where Kodama agreed to funnel bribes to induce Japanese government officials to buy Lockheed airplanes. This climaxed in a major scandal in the mid-1970s when Kodama's role as bagman was revealed, and U.S. officials and business executives were charged with corruption.

Why was Japan's most powerful crime lord kept on the federal payroll by Presidents Truman, Eisenhower, Kennedy, Johnson, Nixon, Ford, Carter and Reagan, a payroll also reviewed by George H.W. Bush while serving as director of the CIA? The short answer is that Kodama also was Japan's most ardent anti-communist. And like an acupuncturist he knew all the points where pins of different types could be inserted, and pressure applied. His intimate knowledge of the Asian underworld made him an effective fixer at a time when Washington was alarmed by the perceived threat of the Soviet Union and Red China. In August 1949, Moscow tested its own first atomic bomb. In October 1949, the People's Republic of China came into being. Eight months later in June 1950, the Korean War broke out. Just before that war began, Kodama accompanied John Foster Dulles to negotiations in Seoul. The Dulles party also included Kodama's protégé, Machii Hisayuki, boss of the Korean *yakuza* in Japan. Efforts to discover under Freedom of Information what Kodama and Machii did during this trip with Dulles have run into a stone wall. In the MacArthur Memorial archive we discovered a personal letter from Kodama to General MacArthur offering to provide thousands of *yakuza* and former Japanese Army soldiers to fight alongside American soldiers in Korea. According to sources in Korea and Japan, the offer was accepted and these men joined the Allied force on the peninsula, posing as Korean soldiers.

It was in this highly polarized atmosphere that peace treaty negotiations with Japan proceeded in absolute secrecy, and a severely abbreviated treaty was signed in San Francisco in April 1951. While this treaty was midwifed by Secretary of State Dean Acheson, the terms were worked out in secret by special Republican Party negotiator John Foster Dulles in private talks with three Japanese including Miyazawa Kiichi, a ranking member of the Ministry of Finance and special aid to Prime Minister Yoshida Shigeru. Kodama also held private talks with Dulles to discuss the terms. Many countries were making demands for reparations, but Acheson said he made it clear to other signatories that Japan "could not pay monetary reparations". Although it pretends to be a treaty achieved jointly by the Allies, it was negotiated, written and executed exclusively by Dulles, based on agreements that remain secret to this day.

Years later, Acheson admitted in his memoir that "To accomplish the treaty negotiations… required … a determination amounting at times to ruthlessness," which clearly included lying. Acheson's assertion that Japan was bankrupt and unable to pay reparations, we now know, was totally false.

Despite propaganda to the contrary, Americans and Europeans who toured Japan immediately after the surrender were surprised that infrastructure, factories, utilities, and railways were largely intact, thanks to selective American bombing. Firebombing had destroyed tens of thousands of the tinderbox homes of ordinary Japanese, giving Tokyo the look of a devastated city, but most great estates, factories, and vital infrastructure seemed magically to have been spared. John Dower notes: "Vast areas of poor people's residences, small shops and factories in the capital were gutted...but a good number of the homes of the wealthy in fashionable neighborhoods survived...Tokyo's financial district [was] largely undamaged. Undamaged also was the building that housed much of the imperial military bureaucracy at war's end... Railways still functioned more or less effectively throughout the country ...U.S. bombing policy ...had tended to reaffirm existing hierarchies of fortune."

This information was not made public. SCAP censors made sure that newspapers and newsreels showed only a flattened, desiccated landscape.

Huge sums changed hands quickly just before the surrender. In the first two weeks following, before the Allies set foot in Japan, the government in Tokyo gushed money in all directions. Records discovered by Japanese journalists in the 1970s revealed that their government gave nearly 300-billion yen in war contracts, and stockpiled materials to the *zaibatsu* so these conglomerates realized 30 per cent of their entire war profits in the first four months after the surrender. All outstanding military contracts were paid. New contracts of all sorts were signed and paid in advance, many of them never to be carried out. For example, Tanaka Kakuei (later prime minister) was given a multi-million-dollar contract to move piston-ring factories to Korea, and was paid in full, knowing the work would never be done. Still a small-fry at the time, Tanaka was allowed to participate in a feeding frenzy in which the government threw money at well-placed individuals to get it out of the banks and into hiding. Tanaka was paid in scrip, but he was told to fly immediately to Korea where a Japanese bank would swap the scrip for gold bullion; he did this, and brought the bullion back to Japan aboard a navy vessel.

Once the Allies arrived, and it became evident that they were not really interested in what was going on under their noses, the gusher of government money continued. Dower says this represented something in the neighborhood of 300-million tons of goods – diamonds, gold, steel, rubber, chemicals, oil, salt, drugs and titanium, with a value of $20-billion 1945 U.S. dollars, or $200-billion in present values. The Allies themselves turned over ¥100-billion in stockpiles to the Japanese government: clothing, food and medicine for distribution to the civilian population. Instead these goods vanished into the blackmarket, where gangsters made fortunes. Stocks of opium, heroin and morphine were among the 'medicines' that disappeared.

Dower notes that at war's end there was another ¥264-billion in private bank accounts, much of which was hastily turned into goods through trade in the blackmarket. These figures do not include Golden Lily loot or profits derived from heroin trafficking, which had been $3-billion a year (in today's dollar values). Dower adds, "in the immediate wake of defeat, a great many individuals at the highest levels displayed no concern at all for the good of society. They concentrated instead on enriching themselves by the wholesale plunder of military stockpiles and public resources." During the occupation, many ordinary Japanese worked two jobs to earn enough to buy one potato each day. During the same period, Hirohito was earning $50-million a year in interest merely on his Swiss bank accounts.

Washington told the world again and again that Japan was bankrupt and her industries destroyed, so Tokyo absolutely could not pay compensation to war victims. The Cold Warriors had worked themselves into such a passion that they were prepared to abandon any sense of obligation to those who had died during the Pacific War, whether civilian victims, or military casualties, and those who were brutalized and enslaved, but somehow survived. The most enthusiastic users of wartime slave labor were Japan's *zaibatsu,* especially Mitsui, Mitsubishi and Sumitomo. More than 100,000 Allied prisoners and internees became slave laborers in wretched conditions at their mines, steel plants, construction sites, and factories, in Japan and elsewhere. Many died, others were crippled, few ever were paid any compensation. Despite what Japanese firms say today about having no connection to the wartime *zaibatsu,* there was no complete break after the war. Most of the capital amassed by the *zaibatsu* during Japan's colonial expansion from 1895 to 1945 survived the American occupation intact. As Dower remarks, "the wartime elites followed the lead of their sovereign and devoted themselves to obscuring their wartime deeds."

Strangely, nowhere in the official record of the U.S. occupation so far declassified is there any tally of Japan's national gold reserves, plundered art and cultural objects, looted religious artifacts, personal jewelry and heirlooms, no tally of what was stolen from safe deposit boxes in twelve countries, or from family burial vaults and imperial tombs. If all this hidden information were to be made public, it would make a public mockery of the 1951 Peace Treaty and of the secret negotiations conducted by John Foster Dulles.

During those negotiations, Dulles brazenly manipulated the Allies. In Britain's first draft proposal, Clause 39 read "Japan shall pay reparation in the amount of £60-million in monetary gold over a period of three years." (This is gold kept in central banks for use by national governments to protect their currency, or to buy foreign goods.) Clause 53 of Britain's draft, proposed that "Japan shall restore to Governments of the United Nations concerned all monetary gold looted or wrongfully removed." This sum was not specified in the text, but the statement does affirm that Japan did loot large quantities of gold, and not just from Britain's Far Eastern possessions. Neither clause 39 nor clause 53 mentioned anything about "non-monetary gold" – privately held gold stolen from museums, religious orders and private citizens of those countries, including jewelry, biscuit ingots, art and religious objects.

The British Treasury was far from happy with Washington's assertion that Japan's cupboard was bare. It took the following position regarding gold: "We regard the payment of Japan's 'gold pot' reparation as one of the points on which it is essential for us to be firm."

The following month, April 1951, however, after Dulles had a chance to react, the British Foreign Office asked for "authority to modify our attitude so that we can agree with the U.S. that the gold can remain in Japan. It is now quite clear that even if we could get the gold away from the Japanese (and agreement on this is by no means certain) there is for practical purposes no possibility of our obtaining a share of it." Britain's firm position was caving in, under American pressure. The official British record goes on to say that the view of the United States and SCAP was that the "gold should be left in Japan as an addition to foreign exchange resources in order to assist her general [economic] stabilization".

In the end, Britain capitulated: "We have agreed that gold should not be mentioned in the Treaty." Other allies followed suit.

Was Britain deceived about the true circumstance of Japan's postwar economy? Not likely. Britain was far from ignorant of the looting that had taken place, nor was it ignorant of what was done with the treasure. We know from high-level CIA sources that Britain's biggest financiers participated in setting up the Black Eagle Trust. Numerous documents in our CD archive accompanying this book show that large quantities of gold bullion recovered by Santa Romana ended up in the big gold trading houses of the City of London, and in the British Treasury. Bank documents and insurance cover documents from the gold movements carried out by Lansdale and Santa Romana also show bulk quantities of gold placed in accounts at various British commercial banks. Therefore, Britain did benefit in a multitude of ways from the Black Eagle Trust.

In its final form, the 1951 Peace Treaty tried to prohibit any future efforts by private individuals to claim reparations. It bears repeating that Article 14 reads: "It is recognized that Japan should pay reparations to the Allied Powers for the damage and suffering caused by it during the war. Nevertheless it is also recognized that *the resources of Japan are not presently sufficient.*" (Our italics.)

The Treaty did provide limited recourse for a tiny group of businessmen and diplomats such as U.S. Ambassador Joseph Grew. They could recover personal possessions and property forfeited when they were trapped in Japan after Pearl Harbor. If applicants failed to qualify within a tight deadline, Japan got to keep the property. Few people were informed of this clause, so many unclaimed properties remained in the hands of the Japanese government and were later sold for tremendous profits, and used by corrupt politicians to prop up Japan's LDP.

The Treaty stated that "Except as otherwise provided in the present Treaty, the Allied Powers waive all reparations claims of the Allied Powers, other claims of the Allied Powers and their nationals arising out of any actions taken by Japan and its nationals in the course of the prosecution of the war, and claims of the Allied Powers for direct military costs of occupation."

According to the British Foreign Office archives: "Canadian authorities had themselves felt that provision should have been made in the Treaty for compensation to civilian internees and indeed raised the question in Washington …but on meeting resistance did not press the point." In conclusion, the Foreign Office noted: "If Article 16 was widened to include civilians, the amount of claimants would be so far increased (by the inclusion of Asiatic claimants) that the amount available to each would be derisory."

So, with the sweep of a pen, the United States unjustly shut the door on the claims of comfort women, Asian slave labor, and Allied prisoners of war. Today there still are some 700,000 people alive who were victimized first by the Japanese and then by the San Francisco Peace Treaty.

Aside from the fact (often pointed out) that Washington improperly gave away the rights of individual citizens, there is a loophole in the Treaty's Article 26, which provides that should Japan make better deals with any country in the future, the signatories in the Treaty are entitled to file new claims for similar compensation. Ultimately, Japan did separately make better deals with other countries, including Burma, Holland, and Switzerland. So, by extrapolation, all Japan's victims are entitled to renegotiate, which should open the door to lawsuits currently being pressed in California.

While it is plain that the 1951 Peace Treaty is invalid because it is based on lies and deceptions, every American and British government since 1945 has vigorously blocked all efforts to right the wrongs done to Japan's victims. To this day the State Department, the Justice Department, and the Japanese Foreign Ministry invoke the 1951 Peace Treaty to block any attempt by victims to sue for the compensation so long denied them.

In the year 2000, when Germany's government and industry finally approved a $5-billion fund to compensate Nazi slave-labor victims, President Bill Clinton remarked: "It is an important day for those victims of Nazi-era wrongs who have waited 50 years for justice." A few months earlier, Clinton's ambassador to Japan, Thomas Foley, flatly rejected the claims of Japan's victims: "The peace treaty," Foley said, "put aside all claims against Japan." A Japanese Foreign Ministry spokesman intoned: "One does wonder why all this is taking place some 50 years after the war. All claims from World War II, including claims by nationals of the United States arising from actions taken by Japan and its nationals, have already been settled."

It is interesting that during his time in Japan, Ambassador Foley's wife was a well-paid consultant to Sumitomo, one of the main targets of slave-labor lawsuits.

Foley's denial of victims' right to sue was reinforced over and over by his Deputy Chief of Mission, Christopher J. Lafleur. And why not? Lafleur was the son-in-law of Miyazawa Kiichi, one of the Japanese who took part in the secret negotiations with John Foster Dulles to work out terms of the Peace Treaty – terms designed to block any form of reparations to Japan's victims. Since then, Miyazawa has remained a major figure in the LDP, its senior financial brain, closely identified with the M-Fund.

CHAPTER NINE

HEART OF DARKNESS

America lost control of the M-Fund in 1960 when it was given away by Vice President Nixon, in exchange for Tokyo's secret financial support of his bid for the U.S. presidency. For more than forty years since then, the M-Fund has remained the illicit toy of seven LDP politicians who have used it to keep themselves in power. Nixon effectively gave them the ultimate secret weapon, a bottomless black bag.

President Eisenhower was going to Tokyo to conclude revisions to the Mutual Security Treaty, but his trip was canceled after violent protests in Japan. Instead, Prime Minister Kishi Nobosuke flew to Washington, where the Security Treaty negotiations were conducted by the vice president. Nixon was obsessed by his craving to become president, and was willing to turn over control of the M-Fund, and to promise the return of Okinawa, in return for kickbacks to his campaign fund. Kishi, an indicted war criminal, a key figure in the wartime regime and in hard drugs, munitions and slave labor, thereby gained personal control of the M-Fund. According to Takano Hajime and other well-informed sources, Nixon justified the deal with the dubious excuse that Tokyo needed an emergency covert source of money in the event that war broke out in Northeast Asia. In theory, Japan's postwar constitution prevented it from creating a new army, so Tokyo could not allocate a huge defense budget – at least not publicly. Nixon argued that full LDP control of the M-Fund would accomplish the same thing covertly. In 1960, the M-Fund was said to have an asset base worth ¥12.3-trillion ($35-billion). How much of this Kishi agreed to kick back to Nixon is not known. It is important to note that Nixon did not turn the M-Fund over to the government of Japan, but to Prime Minister Kishi personally, putting the lie to his grandiose justifications. So a few months later, when Kishi ceased to be prime minister, he and his clique continued to control the M-Fund. It goes without saying that they never used it for the designated purpose, instead turning it into a private source of personal enrichment.

That Nixon made such Faustian bargains was widely rumored. Publication of *The*

Arrogance of Power: The Secret World of Richard Nixon, by Anthony Summers, shows that to advance his political career, Nixon even made financial deals with Meyer Lansky and other underworld figures. This is further supported by evidence first presented by Christopher Hitchens in "The Case Against Henry Kissinger" in *Harper's Magazine*, arguing that Nixon and Kissinger secretly manipulated American policy for their own personal ends in violation of the U.S. Constitution.

Nixon's M-Fund giveaway was not the end of the story – far from it. Under LDP control, the M-Fund spawned a number of exotic financial instruments that propagated through global financial markets like Ebola virus. Investors or their attorneys have been snared in amazing international sting operations, charged with negotiating fraudulent instruments, ending in wrongful convictions and prison sentences. It is now painfully obvious that some of these victims were holding authentic paper, and only were stung to shield Japan's government from its own folly – although more crafty political and financial motives also may be discerned.

How did Nixon's dirty deal lead to such a scandalous impasse decades later? To know that, we must see what happened when the M-Fund changed hands.

•

Until Nixon interfered, the M-Fund was controlled and administered by a small group of Americans in Tokyo close to MacArthur. In 1950, when the Korean War started, most U.S. forces in Japan were rushed to Korea, creating a security vacuum. Because the postwar constitution prohibited setting up a new army, the M-Fund secretly provided over $50-million to create what was characterized as a self-defense force. When the occupation ended in 1952 and Washington and Tokyo concluded their joint security treaty, administration of the M-Fund shifted to dual control, staffed by U.S. Embassy CIA personnel and their Japanese counterparts, weighted in favor of the Americans. The Yotsuya Fund and Keenan Fund were folded into it. The M-Fund's asset base was being invested in Japanese industry and finance, and the returns were used for political inducements. The M-Fund council interfered vigorously to keep Japan's government, industry, and society under the tight control of conservatives friendly toward America. This meant blocking or undermining Japanese individuals or groups who wished to liberalize Japanese politics, or unbuckle what Dr. Miyamato Masao called Japan's 'straitjacket society'.

In 1956, for example, the Eisenhower Administration labored long and hard to install Kishi as head of the newly-merged Liberal-Democratic Party and as Japan's new prime minister. This was the same Kishi who had been a member of the hard-core ruling clique in Manchuria with General Tojo Hideki and Hoshino Naoki, head of the narcotics monopoly. Kishi had also signed Japan's Declaration of War against America in December 1941. During World War II, he was vice minister of munitions and minister of commerce and industry, actively involved in slave labor. Along the way, he made a personal fortune in side-deals with the *zaibatsu*. Following Japan's surrender, he was one of the most prominent indicted war criminals at Sugamo, where he was a cellmate of Kodama. In 1948, when his release from prison was purchased by Kodama, Kishi began organizing the financial base of the LDP, using Kodama's black gold and injections of M-Fund cash. For ten years, Kishi was groomed as America's Boy by Harry Kern, Eugene Dooman, Compton Packenham and other members of Averell Harriman's group at the American Council for Japan (ACJ). They worked tirelessly to improve Kishi's mousy image, tutored him in English, and taught him to like Scotch. To them, Kishi was America's 'only bet left in Japan'. All this was done covertly, for if the Japanese public learned that Washington was using the M-Fund to replace one prime minister with another, the democracy fiction would collapse.

Despite all this manipulation, when the 1956 election results were in, Kishi was trumped by rival LDP faction leader Ishibashi Tanzan, regarded as 'the least pro-American among the major LDP leaders'. Ishibashi had won because Washington had paid off Kishi supporters, but had not given enough to his opponents. Annoyed, President Eisenhower personally authorized the CIA to destroy Ishibashi, and put Kishi at the head of the LDP. This meant paying very large bribes to all factions of the LDP, to shift their support to Kishi. In February 1957, after an extraordinary amount of grunting and snorting behind the folding screen, Kishi at last replaced Ishibashi as leader of the LDP, and was named prime minister. According to historian Michael Schaller, Kishi then took over from Kodama as 'America's favorite war criminal'.

"Washington heaved an audible sigh of relief," Schaller said. "Kishi reasserted his loyalty to America's Cold War strategy, pledging to limit contact with [Communist] China and, instead, to focus Japanese economic attention on exports to the United States and mutual development of Southeast Asia."

During Kishi's term as prime minister (1957-1960) the LDP received $10-million each year directly from the CIA, chiefly from the M-Fund. Alfred C. Ulmer, Jr., the CIA officer who controlled the M-Fund and many other operations in Japan from 1955 to 1958, said: "We financed them," because the CIA "depended on the LDP for information." When the party's coffers were depleted by the monumental effort to get Kishi named prime minister, Finance Minister Sato Eisaku (Kishi's brother) appealed to Ambassador Douglas MacArthur II (the general's nephew) for additional secret funds. In July 1958, Ambassador MacArthur wrote to the Department of State, providing details of this request: "Sato asked if it would not be possible for the United States to supply financial funds to aid the conservative forces in this constant struggle against Communism. ...This did not come as a surprise to us, since he suggested the same general idea last year."

The ball then was lobbed into Nixon's court.

A few months later, when Nixon renegotiated the Mutual Security Treaty in 1959-1960, he not only gave Kishi the M-Fund, he also promised that when he became president he would give Okinawa back to Japan, while retaining military base rights there. According to sources close to former Prime Minister Tanaka, "Nixon told Kishi that if Japan would assist him in becoming president, he would see to it that the U.S. withdrew from its role in managing the M-Fund, and upon his being elected Nixon would return Okinawa to Japan." Accordingly, when Nixon and Kishi concluded the revision of the security treaty in 1960, the M-Fund was turned over to Kishi. And in 1973, when Nixon at last was elected president, he returned Okinawa to Japan.

White House national security advisor Richard Allen later remarked that the Okinawa transfer had puzzled him. "In 1973, when Nixon gave Okinawa back to Japan, I was following very closely. I was in touch with the White House and I was always puzzled by that, not that it was really a strange thing to do, but there was no agitation for that. He just up and did it. I never quite understood why he did that. Now [in light of Nixon's M-Fund deal] this makes sense to me."

In Japan, the revised Joint Security Treaty was so unpopular that Kishi immediately lost control of his cabinet and had to resign as prime minister. So, only a matter of months after giving him control of the M-Fund, America lost much of the leverage gained by the huge bribe. Nixon may not have got all the kickbacks he expected. Years later, when the chance came to take America off the gold standard, weakening the dollar and strengthening the yen, making Japanese exports more expensive, Nixon chortled that he was "sticking it to the Japanese".

Nevertheless, Kishi remained an LDP kingmaker behind the scenes. Virtually every prime minister of Japan since then was picked by the clique controlling the M-Fund, because they had the most inducements to pass around. Sarcastically called The Magnificent Seven, the clique included prime ministers Kishi, Tanaka Kakuei, Takeshita Noboru, Nakasone Yasuhiro, Miyazawa Kiichi, deputy prime minister Gotoda Masaharu, and LDP vice president Kanemaru Shin. Compared to Japan's great dynastic families and financial shoguns, these were only politicians greasing the wheels. But as politicians go, they were in an unrivaled position to steer Japan's economy, politics and government at every level, without being accountable to the Japanese people. War loot provided the asset base, generating huge profits hidden in creative ways, or offshore. They were all clever men, but Tanaka was the cleverest. How he acquired personal control of the M-Fund from Kishi provides a rare keyhole view of money-politics in Japan.

One of Kishi's first acts when Nixon gave him the M-Fund, was to help himself to ¥1-trillion ($3-billion). This was nearly 10 percent of the fund's total assets in 1960. Although he was no longer prime minister, Kishi arranged the selection of Tanaka as minister of Finance in the new Ikeda administration, and in the next administration headed by Kishi's brother, Prime Minister Sato Eisaku.

As a high school drop-out, Tanaka hardly seemed qualified to head the Ministry of Finance. But he had other qualifications, including a superabundance of charm and an unparalleled instinct for financial scams. As a young draftsman for an architectural firm in the 1930s, he became the protégé of Viscount Okochi Masatoshi, a pal of Kishi and boss of a conglomerate called Riken Group, profiteering on military contracts. Riken was the center of Japan's unsuccessful attempt to create an atom bomb. The viscount set up Tanaka for life, by arranging for him to marry a rich divorcee. As part of the deal, Tanaka inherited her father's construction company. While most Japanese were losing everything to firebombing, Tanaka won vastly inflated military contracts, becoming one of Japan's wartime *arrivistes*. Immediately before the surrender, he was paid $73-million to transfer a piston ring factory to Korea to put it out of the range of American bombers. He did not move the factory, but converted the money into gold bullion and never had to account for it. Some of this windfall he contributed to the new Liberal Party, buying himself a seat in the Diet. When Kishi became prime minister of the merged Liberal-Democratic Party in 1957 he appointed Tanaka minister of Posts. (Tanaka boasted that he bought this first cabinet position from Kishi for ¥3-million in cash.)

Japan's postal system was ripe for plucking, because it included a national bank with postal gyro accounts for millions of citizens. Tanaka showed real genius by finding ways to dip into the savings of ordinary people. This gift for picking pockets is what persuaded Kishi to turn the M-Fund over to Tanaka, and to put him in charge of the Finance Ministry. In that position, Tanaka took personal control of all central government subsidies for local governments, and all national and local expenditures for public works, which total about US$400-billion each year. Controlling the M-Fund, the Ministry of Finance, and the Bank of Japan, Tanaka was able to loot both private citizens and the national treasury, and to move billions into the M-Fund – and into private accounts in Japan and Switzerland.

During the twenty-six years Tanaka ran the M-Fund personally, from mid-1960 to 1986, he described himself as 'governor of the private Bank of Japan'. By distributing patronage, he persuaded senior civil servants to help him enlarge the M-Fund. According to journalist Takano Hajime, Tanaka bought off the entire Ministry of Finance "from top to bottom".

It costs about $4-million to get elected to Japan's Diet, where a member's annual salary is less than $200,000. A 1989 survey of one hundred MPs showed monthly duties to constituents included attending an average of 6.6 weddings and 26.5 funerals. At each occasion an MP was expected to make a traditional gift of congratulations or condolence, which cost roughly $6,000 a month. So an MP could not stay afloat without support. In an off-election year, the LDP had to spend $200-million to assist MPs. By this reckoning, since the LDP was founded in the 1950s, it has had to spend around $10-trillion in bribes and patronage to remain in power. So Tanaka could not relax. He had to enlarge the M-Fund asset base to generate the interest needed to maintain continual injections of new cash. This made extraordinary demands upon his natural gifts.

It was not enough to raid the national treasury. In addition to rigged bidding for the construction industry, and straightforward kickbacks, Tanaka created government construction bond issues, without approval from the Diet. These bonds were sold at a discount to wealthy cronies, or simply were given away in exchange for secret donations to the M-Fund. When the bonds matured, cronies agreed to return most of the proceeds to Tanaka, who then kept the money for his own use or added it to the M-Fund.

Tanaka also came up with a scheme to sell real estate confiscated during the war from enemy aliens, who had failed to apply for postwar restitution. These 'unclaimed' properties were an outright gift to Japan under terms of Article 16 of the 1951 Peace Treaty, and when Tanaka discovered they still were unsold he recognized a pot of gold. Over ten years from 1960 to 1970, Tanaka sold 1,681 of these properties to cronies at absurdly low prices, depositing the proceeds to Ministry of Finance accounts. His cronies then re-sold the properties at Japan's greatly inflated open-market value, at a total profit of ¥7.9-trillion ($22-billion). In return for a small slice for their trouble, they remitted the bulk to Tanaka, who put some in his offshore accounts and put the rest in the M-Fund, increasing its value from around $35-billion in 1960 to what was said to be nearly $60-billion in 1970. That year, questions were raised in the Diet, and Tanaka's real-estate scam was closed down by Prime Minister Sato, to avoid public disclosure.

The most important source for Tanaka's 'private Bank of Japan' was the National Social Welfare Association he set up in 1964 (sometimes translated as the All Japan Welfare Council). The title is a private joke, since the club existed only for the welfare of Tanaka and his friends. It was really the Tanaka Club, and was in Tanaka's private home. According to U.S. court testimony and copies of original Japanese documents we reproduce on our CDs with translations, the original membership of the club was seventeen cronies. Eventually it grew to over thirty. All of them were men who had made fortunes in banking, commerce, real estate development, speculation and construction, including Sushi Bar king Ishii Ryuji, industrialists Kobori Takashi and Kondo Masao, and Yamashita Shigeo of Ocean Dome resorts.

Although these names may ring few bells outside Japan, two others are well-known worldwide. Tsutsumi Seiji's family holdings include national and international hotels, railways, resorts, and department stores. Among global financial moguls, the Tsutsumis rank with the Rockefellers.

The other was Osano Kenji, one of Japan's richest men and chairman of Kokumin Bank, nicknamed 'the Monster' for his ruthless business tactics. A Japanese of Korean descent, during the war he made a fortune selling auto parts to the military. At the surrender, Osano was involved in hiding the Imperial Army's huge stockpiles and profiteering by selling them off on the blackmarket. In the occupation, he was a big time dealer in blackmarket currency. In later decades, Japanese joked bitterly about the 'Tanaka-Osano Trading House'. In the 1970s, having secured Tanaka's approval to move gigantic sums overseas when most Japanese were forbidden to do so, Osano bought many Waikiki Beach hotels and made himself godfather of the Japanese-Korean mafia in Hawaii, which then extended its tentacles throughout the West Coast using tourism fronts.

Tanaka's biggest scam was specially contrived government bonds. Because he had them issued by the Ministry of Finance, they were technically legitimate with or without Diet approval. Each had a very big face amount, ranging from ¥10-billion to ¥50-billion ($50-million to $250-million at the time, but now worth almost double). In some cases, these bonds were purchased by core Tanaka clubmembers using their own money, or black money from the M-Fund. While their names appear as the designated payees, most were serving only as straw men for Tanaka. This allowed him to park very large amounts of illicit funds in the secure form of government bonds.

Interest paid on these bonds, and profits on their maturity, were to be kicked back directly to Tanaka, or split between Tanaka and the bondholders. These documents (some labeled 'Top Secret' or 'Very Important') bear the personal seals of Tanaka, Nakasone and Takeshita, and lesser lights, proving the arrangement was endorsed by the Ministry of Finance, by the leadership of the LDP, and by the top management of Dai-Ichi Kangyo Bank, responsible for some of the transactions, including interest payments.

For a while, the scam worked flawlessly.

In running the M-Fund, Tanaka was assisted by Kanemaru and Gotoda, two of the LDP's backroom boys. All three became very rich. Before ill health caused him to relinquish control of the M-Fund in 1986, Tanaka is thought to have helped himself to ¥10-trillion ($30-billion then, double that now), which Japanese sources say he invested offshore through Union Banque Suisse, as a trust fund to safeguard his family in future generations. (In 2001, Tanaka's daughter briefly served as Japan's foreign minister.)

According to Karl Van Wolferen, Gotoda was discovered by Tanaka, and became his brain. After graduating from Tokyo Imperial University in 1939, Gotoda entered the wartime secret service associated with Golden Lily, rising after the war to be chief of the National Police. When Tanaka became prime minister, he chose Gotoda as his deputy chief cabinet secretary, the most important bureaucratic post in the cabinet. As a former secret policeman and head of the national police, Gotoda was one of the most feared men in the country. His assignment from Tanaka was to keep bureaucrats nervous.

Their specialist bagman was Kanemaru, son of a sake brewer, who kept LDP politicians in line by distributing bribes and kickbacks from the M-Fund and other sources. Kanemaru ranked as one of Japan's top political fixers. Although elected to the Diet twelve times, he always contrived to remain invisible.

That was not Tanaka's style. A man of perpetual flash and vanity, Tanaka did not know where to stop. Once he became prime minister, in 1972, enemies began to leak information about his improprieties, and two years later a team of Japanese investigative journalists bravely published an exposé of his monumental corruption. The ensuing scandal forced Tanaka to claim ill-health and step down. He was not prosecuted, and continued backstage as a top LDP boss. In 1976, the U.S. Senate Foreign Relations Committee began hearings into the Lockheed bribery scandal, where it emerged that Tanaka was one of the government officials that Lockheed had bribed to win sales of its new plane to All Nippon Airways. Although the money came from Lockheed, it was conveyed by the CIA through godfather Kodama, still on the Agency's payroll, who also arranged for Japan to buy 230 Lockheed F-104 Starfighters. Tanaka was said to have been paid as much as $14-million by Lockheed, although when he was arrested the indictment was only for accepting $2-million. A Tanaka aide testified that his boss probably was unaware of the Lockheed bribe because it was so paltry. The trial lasted seven years, and Tanaka spent over $8-million on his defense. Meanwhile, he retained control of the M-Fund, oversaw the appointment of three prime ministers, and was returned to the Diet for the fifteenth time.

As the trial dragged on, there were the first signs of defection from the ranks. Prime Minister Nakasone (a leader of the LDP extreme right) begged Tanaka to resign from the party. Nakasone's disloyalty alarmed Tanaka and he began to worry that other members of his club might defect, taking their billions of dollars in bonds with them. Aside from the hardcore clubmembers, there was a second tier of rich men on the perimeter of the club, whose loyalty to Tanaka was not absolute. If several of them tried to redeem their bonds simultaneously, the Ministry of

Finance would be caught with its pants down. Tanaka and his clique had so thoroughly plundered the national treasury that the Ministry of Finance was able to maintain its sinking fund for the outstanding bonds only by selling the government's share of NTT (Nippon Telephone & Telegraph). A sinking fund is a special reserve account created by a government when it issues bonds; the government is obliged to put money into the sinking fund at regular intervals, in order to be able to redeem the bonds when they come due. If several of Tanaka's disloyal bondholders insisted on redeeming their bonds, the Ministry of Finance did not have sufficient funds and would have no choice but to default, which could cause the whole LDP house of cards to collapse.

Rather than cover this exposure by dipping into the M-Fund, or into his own 'private Bank of Japan', Tanaka and his clever associates at the Ministry of Finance came up with an ingenious dodge. They would roll over the original Japanese government bonds by exchanging them for new financial instruments called Certificates of Redemption. These were not the Ministry's usual bonds but a form of debt instrument or IOU specially designed, printed and issued by the Ministry of Finance in the fifty-seventh year of Hirohito's reign, so they often are called "57s" to distinguish them from regular government bonds. We will use that label in this book.

Bondholders who already were owed outstanding interest would be given specially designed and printed cashier's checks from the Dai-Ichi Kangyo Bank, serving as the Ministry's conduit for interest payments. Because many of the bondholders were considered politically untrustworthy, they were given no choice in the matter, and simply were told by the Ministry that the exchange of bonds for "57s" and cashier's checks would take place. While this might seem unusual in Europe or America, intimidation has been developed to such a high art in Japan that to defy the exchange would mean social ostracism or even assisted suicide.

Already the M-Fund appeared to have led to the death of Kishi's brother, Prime Minister Sato. Many Japanese believe Sato was poisoned in 1975 at the height of a contest with Tanaka for control of the M-Fund. A number of others associated with Sato in M-Fund financing of Fuji Steel also died mysteriously in the early 1970s. A major scandal over Sato's death was avoided when Tanaka paid Sato's widow ¥300-billion from the M-Fund. In 1984, Harvey Fukuda, Kodama's publisher and business partner, who knew where all the skeletons were hidden, died of 'heart failure' while in the hospital being dried out and treated for cirrhosis of the liver. He had expressed fear of being poisoned, and members of his family did not believe his death was from natural causes. In Japan, if you are afraid of being murdered, it is considered good advice to avoid hospitals, where the job can be done unobtrusively. The next assisted suicide was Prime Minister Takeshita's personal assistant, Aoki Ihei, who knew too much about the "57s". According to *The Wall Street Journal*, Aoki "slashed his wrists, legs, and neck and, when that failed, hanged himself with a necktie from a curtain rod."

Physically, the "57s" were unlike anything previously issued by the government of Japan. They were not offered to the public at large, nor were they to be traded on the international bond-market like normal government bonds, so only the holders actually saw them. The magic of this scheme is that by their very difference, it was possible for the Ministry of Finance later to declare all "57s" to be forgeries. Only certain ones were then selectively and very secretly renegotiated at a discount. Those who paid for their original government bonds, and then were forced to exchange them for "57s", were thus swindled twice.

Washington has backed Tokyo's assertion that the "57s" are counterfeit. But, as we will see, there is evidence both are lying. Because they were jointly involved in setting up the M-Fund with Golden Lily war loot, they both have reason to deny its existence.

According to American attorney Norbert Schlei, the "57s" were printed at the Ministry of Finance factory in Tokinogawa, on the order of Watanabe Michio, who was Minister of Finance under Prime Minister Suzuki. Watanabe told Schlei this privately. Schlei was unable to name his source because Watanabe would be murdered. Watanabe subsequently served as deputy prime minister, minister of foreign affairs, and minister of international trade and industry, dying in the late 1990s. Because he no longer is in danger, we are able to identify him here as the expert source of this confirmation.

Undeniable evidence of the authenticity of the "57s" has been painstakingly assembled by Professor Edmond C. Lausier of the University of Southern California's Marshall School of Business. For five years, Professor Lausier made it a hobby to study the M-Fund, and Tanaka's bond-manipulations. He patiently collected copies of bonds and related documents going back many years, finding groups of them in collections at different universities. Part of his research was a methodical comparison of the original bonds with the "57s" that replaced them. In his affidavit concerning these documents, he refers collectively to the "57s" as Certificates of Redemption:

"The Certificates," Lausier said, "acknowledge that the payees are due the proceeds of the bonds they have surrendered and state that this obligation is to be satisfied with the proceeds at maturity of 15-year bonds. Seven such bond issues thereafter were in fact issued by the Japanese government over a three-year period beginning in 1983. These bonds are unique in that they were the first and only 15-year obligations ever issued by the Japanese government until the maturity of issue #7 in the third quarter of year 2000. These seven issues of 15-year obligations were subjected upon issuance by the Ministry of Finance to restrictions prohibiting their assignment, transfer or conveyance throughout their term.

"The documents I have examined show that in 1982, a decision was made in the Ministry of Finance or at an even higher level in the Japanese government to call in the bonds held *by certain holders*, [our italics] together with the interest-passbook accounts at the Dai-Ichi Kangyo Bank held by them, and to issue Certificates ["57s"] in exchange for those items." The documents Lausier assembled included hundreds from the Ministry of Finance, Dai-Ichi Kangyo Bank, and the Liberal Democratic Party, identifying specific valid outstanding Japanese government bonds to be refunded. These documents, he said, provide a detailed, undeniable connection between the holders of the bonds, the Ministry, the Bank, and the "57s".

"The documents I have examined are so precisely in agreement in innumerable respects with the official published records of the government of Japan... that, in my opinion, it is quite impossible for them, or the Certificates that resulted from them, to have been the work of any counterfeiter. No person outside the government could possibly have had the requisite knowledge to prepare these documents with the requisite degree of accuracy, and indeed, a rather large number of knowledgeable government officials was needed to prepare them. It is, accordingly, my unqualified opinion that the Certificates are not counterfeit."

Lausier said the only plausible explanation was that "the government of Japan grew concerned about the fact that huge sums in verifiably genuine government bonds were held by potentially unreliable nominees, and therefore decided to replace those bonds with Certificates – a type of instrument previously unknown – which could much more plausibly be repudiated."

Beginning in 1982, Lausier said, and continuing for six years, the Japanese government lacked the funds necessary to redeem its outstanding bonds. The problem was solved, at least temporarily, by retrieving the outstanding bonds and replacing them with the off-book "57s".

In 1985, Tanaka suffered an incapacitating stroke. At first his condition was hidden even from close colleagues, but as it became apparent that he would be a permanent invalid, rivals began to quarrel over who would inherit the M-Fund. Nakasone saw himself and the far right of the LDP as the natural heir. Gotoda and Kanemaru tried to elbow Nakasone aside, bringing Takeshita in to strengthen their hands by forming a troika.

As this succession struggle got underway, a number of wealthy Japanese decided the moment had come when they had better cash in their "57s". Informed by the Ministry of Finance that all "57s" were counterfeit, they became enraged, and decided to fight back. Some tried to unload their certificates in private deals with foreigners, while others tried to pressure the LDP and the Ministry of Finance to privately acknowledge their claim, and to pay at least a substantial percentage of the face value.

Only those who were especially tight with the LDP leadership were successful. As the Ministry was unable to pay, members of the troika personally redeemed these privileged "57s" and related Dai-Ichi Bank checks, at what must have been a very deep discount. According to journalist Joseph Schlesinger, "starting in 1984, [Kanemaru] had regularly converted much of his assets into special bonds that allowed the purchaser to remain anonymous, and had never declared these holdings."

During the same period, Gotoda also apparently redeemed a number of "57s" and Dai-Ichi checks. According to Japanese sources, Gotoda held ¥60-billion worth ($600-million) of the Dai-Ichi checks. With so many on his hands, he decided to unload them back to Dai-Ichi. When he confronted bank officials, they tried to buy him off at a lower rate, but Gotoda stood firm and eventually was paid their full face value. The bank's directors apparently decided it was unwise to annoy the former secret policeman. We know of this transaction because government investigators gathering evidence on an unrelated matter had a wiretap on Dai-Ichi Bank, and purely by chance Gotoda's phone call came in on the tapped line.

That two very senior LDP party leaders, Gotoda and Kanemaru, were buying and selling "57s" and Dai-Ichi checks, makes it obvious they were not counterfeit.

Many of the Japanese holders of "57s" who were thwarted were working in America, Europe, or Southeast Asia. At such a distance, they could be stonewalled forever. Tanaka, paralyzed by his stroke, could not walk or speak, so they could not communicate directly with him. Some were afraid of what would happen if they returned to Japan to press their case. As a precaution, they made their approach through international bankers, attorneys, or other intermediaries, hoping this would embarrass the Ministry into redeeming their certificates. That was how Norbert Schlei became involved.

Schlei was an exceptional man. Born in 1929 in Dayton, a graduate of Ohio State, he was a naval officer during the Korean War. Going on to Yale Law School, he became editor-in-chief of its *Law Journal* and graduated *magna cum laude* in 1956. After serving for a year as a clerk to U.S. Supreme Court Justice John Marshall Harlan, Schlei entered law practice in Los Angeles. In 1962, at the age of 33, he was appointed Assistant Attorney General of the United States by President Kennedy. He was deputy to Attorney General Robert Kennedy in 1962 when the U.S. Army was sent to enforce the racial integration of the University of Mississippi. During the Cuban Missile Crisis, Schlei developed the 'quarantine' concept relied on by President Kennedy. He found himself in opposition to men like the aging Dean Acheson, who was all in favor of bombing Havana back to the Stone Age. Later, Schlei was the principal draftsman of the Civil Rights Act of 1964, the Immigration Act of 1965, and the Anti-Poverty programs of the Johnson Administration. In 1972, he joined the Wall Street law firm of Hughes Hubbard & Reed, establishing an office for the firm in Los Angeles, where he was a prominent trial lawyer representing clients like Howard Hughes and Morgan Stanley, handling business and securities law for clients such as Carlsberg and Arco petroleum.

Schlei became involved with the M-Fund and "57s" quite innocently, when he agreed to make inquiries for Asian clients of his California lawfirm. While acknowledging all along that the government of Japan *claimed* these Certificates of Redemption were counterfeit, his clients vigorously contended that these officials were lying in order to avoid redeeming them. They told Schlei how previously they had held normal government bonds, only to be forced to relinquish them for the "57s" and Dai-Ichi checks, deliberately printed to look unusual, which would allow them to be denounced as fraudulent. They asked Schlei to look into the possibility of persuading the Japanese government to redeem their certificates. Bringing in a lawfirm of the stature of Hughes Hubbard and Reed, they hoped, would put pressure on the Ministry of Finance and on Dai-Ichi Bank, who might agree to make an out-of-court settlement to avoid a public scandal. They told Schlei they did not seek to collect the huge face values, they only wanted the percentage promised them for acting as Tanaka's straw men.

As Schlei began his inquiries, he provoked an extraordinary reaction from an unexpected quarter, the U.S. Government, which ultimately set out to destroy him and his reputation. Schlei was convinced, as are many people on Wall Street and at various universities, that he became the victim of a sting operation that went out of control when Washington had to cover up its involvement in the M-Fund and Japan's black money politics. What happened to Schlei reveals a breath-taking depth of deceit, a measure of what is being kept hidden.

What Schlei could not foresee were the extreme measures the governments of Japan and the United States would be prepared to take to keep secret the historical origins of these financial instruments.

Schlei was surprised by his clients' allegation that Tanaka's M-Fund originally had been set up by General MacArthur with treasure looted from occupied countries by the Japanese. He was dismayed when he learned about the role played by Vice President Nixon. But as Schlei carried out his own due diligence he became convinced that it was true, at least in its broad outlines. His mistake was to assume this was all in the distant past, and he could discuss it with American diplomats and bureaucrats as a curious historical anomaly. Only much later did he realize he had intruded upon something still alive and very dangerous, in the heart of darkness.

Takahashi Toshio, one of his clients, while a student leader, had been given ¥40-million from the M-Fund ($500,000 today), in checks laundered through a CIA front, the Committee for a Free Asia. So he was familiar with the history of the M-Fund from its earliest days. More recently, Takahashi had become a member of the Tanaka Club, and bought several Tanaka bonds, later swapped for "57s". When he was then told he could not cash in the "57s" because they were counterfeit, he realized he had been swindled, and decided to fight back through Schlei.

Schlei went to Japan to investigate the story personally, interviewed twenty witnesses with the aid of interpreters, and reviewed records going back to the 1960s. While the LDP leaders claimed that the "57s" were fraudulent and the M-Fund never existed, Schlei saw enough evidence to conclude that they were lying.

"I formed the conclusion quite early that my clients' claims were at least 'honestly arguable' – the standard that governs whether a lawyer may ethically argue a client's case."

He said, "The whole thing was set up so that if anybody tried to do anything with these instruments the matter would be referred immediately to the Minister of Finance, and the Minister of Finance would be able to stop the transaction *or authorize it*, if it were one that the Ministry wanted to authorize."

Schlei talked to U.S. Government officials in a position to know, including Ambassador Mike Mansfield, CIA general counsel Stanley Sporkin, and President Reagan's national security advisor Richard Allen. Mansfield's embassy aides scoffed at any suggestion that Washington made covert payments to the LDP.

No one warned Schlei that he was on extremely thin ice with his own government. Schlei told Sporkin explicitly that he was going to try to negotiate these instruments in Japan and wanted to make sure the CIA had no objection. After looking into the matter overnight, Sporkin told Schlei he found the whole story 'extraordinary' but that the Agency had no interest in the proposed sale of the instruments because it was 'a private matter'. This was a very strange thing for Sporkin to say, and it can only be understood in light of what followed. Although Sporkin may have had no immediate personal knowledge of the "57s" and the M-

Fund, he must have asked CIA officers who knew all about them, including the CIA station chief in Tokyo. These CIA officers naturally would be determined to keep it secret, but by responding as they did they set in motion a process of entrapment, whether deliberately or otherwise.

As Chalmers Johnson points out, Washington's "manipulation of the Japanese political process during the Allied occupation and its evolution over the more than [fifty] years since the occupation ended… has not merely historical significance". As Schlei would learn the hard way.

When Schlei returned to Japan to press his clients' claims, the LDP bosses complained to the U.S. embassy. Without Schlei's knowledge, several of his clients in America then were approached by U.S. Treasury agents, who urged them to offer their "57s" for sale in the United States, which was illegal; whoever offered to buy them would be arrested and their "57s" seized. (As their attorney, Schlei then could be drawn in as a co-conspirator and prosecuted.)

Until Washington turned the full force of its ire on Schlei in 1992, the target of the U.S. Government sting was an elderly invalid named Barbara Jean Bravender Ah Loo, living in Los Angeles on Social Security benefits of less than $1,000 a month. A U.S. citizen of Caucasian origin, she had married a Hawaiian Chinese businessman named Ah Loo and spent long periods with him in Hong Kong, running a company called Transfield Investments. In 1987, Transfield was approached by Japanese clients, including Takahashi, looking for help in redeeming their "57s". Initial efforts by Transfield failed when the Bank of Japan took the position that all "57s" were fraudulent. During this period, Mrs. Ah Loo met Craig Ivester, a bounty hunter employed by Bancorp International as a finder of commodity transactions. They discussed the "57s" and Ivester sent a photocopy of one to Union Banque Suisse, which replied automatically that it was fraudulent, without bothering to examine the original.

Aging and seriously ill, Mrs. Ah Loo then returned by herself to Los Angeles, and was living in a single room borrowed from a terminally-ill friend, in a house facing foreclosure, when she again encountered the bounty hunter. At this point Craig Ivester was making his living as a U.S. Customs Service informer, looking for targets. Reminded of their previous discussions of the "57s" in Hong Kong, Ivester decided to persuade Mrs. Ah Loo to offer some "57s" for sale inside the United States, which he knew was illegal, earning him a finder's fee from the Customs Service.

Sick as she was, Mrs. Ah Loo still had gumption. She told Ivester she would never negotiate a "57" in the United States. Ivester approached the Customs Service, and offered to help entrap Mrs. Ah Loo by baiting her with the offer of a very large commission.

According to Schlei's investigators, the sting operation was mounted by U.S. Secret Service agent Jack Fox, and Customs Service agents Michael Sankey and Michael Noonan, acting on the tip from Ivester. Their plan was to offer Mrs. Ah Loo a big commission to coax her into obtaining a "57" to sell in America, and then to arrest her for 'intent', or merely contemplating a crime. Because she was so reluctant, Fox got credentials showing he was a vice president of First National Bank of

Chicago. Sankey would pretend to be a rich businessman. They rented a room in Reno that they wired, and asked her to come for a meeting. If they could get her to cross a state line, it could be construed as a federal offense, rather than a state offense. Mrs. Ah Loo could not come because she could not afford the airline ticket. The Secret Service sent her a free round trip ticket, the first concrete step in their entrapment. When she got to Reno, Mrs. Ah Loo said she was sorry, but she could not obtain any "57s". Anyway, she said, the Japanese government claimed they were fraudulent, and "People have gone to jail for selling these bonds...".

Fox, Sankey and Noonan persisted, browbeating Mrs. Ah Loo until finally she said she would try again to get a "57", but only if they could arrange a proper and legitimate transaction through a leading American securities firm – a firm that would make sure all laws were observed so nobody got in trouble. Secret Service agent Fox promised to bring Smith Barney into the deal. He faxed Mrs. Ah Loo a letter purporting to be from A. George Saks, Executive Vice President and General Council of Smith Barney, offering to purchase three "57s".

For the sting to work, it had to happen in a jurisdiction where there was a Smith Barney office, and a compliant judge. They decided to lure Mrs. Ah Loo to Tampa, Florida, where Smith Barney had an office, and where the U.S. attorney expected Federal district court judge Elizabeth Kovachevich to be cooperative, allowing him to go for the jugular.

Eventually, Mrs. Ah Loo heard about Roger Hill, a broker who had some of Takahashi's "57s" in his possession, hoping to find a potential buyer. But on the eve of the trip to Tampa, Mrs. Ah Loo suffered a heart attack, and asked her son – Bruce Hansberry – to go with Roger Hill in her place, to conclude the deal at Smith Barney. When they arrived in Tampa, on January 18, 1992, they were arrested.

Because she was not present, they had to rope in Mrs. Ah Loo by getting her on the telephone to discuss the fictitious closing, so she could be arrested in Los Angeles. This was done, and she was taken into custody. On the pretext that her earlier residence in Hong Kong meant she might try to flee the country, she was put in prison to await trial, and ultimately was convicted of conspiracy, wire fraud, money-laundering and securities fraud. Bewildered, Mrs. Ah Loo began to lose her mind, and was moved to a prison psychiatric ward. There she was found to have cancer of the throat, and died.

By January 1992, sixteen offices of the Secret Service were said to be involved in the Ah Loo sting. Mrs. Ah Loo was too insignificant to justify such an expenditure of taxpayers' money, so the vigilantes looked for someone else to lynch. One possibility was Takahashi, to whom the "57s" belonged, but when they broke into his Los Angeles apartment it was empty and he was out of the country in hiding.

Trophy hunting has become a feature of the American criminal justice system. Takahashi was not famous, so he was not a proper trophy for an ambitious U.S. attorney.

Norbert Schlei, on the other hand, was sticking his nose into Deep Black secrets, and alarming Tokyo. His high profile made him a perfect target. One year earlier, Schlei had written a memo about the M-Fund. It was not meant for general circulation but a copy was passed to U.S. Government officials, who became alarmed and angry. If they could snare Schlei, all branches of the U.S. Government would cooperate to stop his digging into the M-Fund, and the LDP leadership in Tokyo would be indebted.

How to snare him was the problem. Schlei had never tried to negotiate a "57" in America, only in Japan, on behalf of clients legally entitled to have an attorney make inquiries. Furthermore, Schlei had never accepted a penny from these clients. But Takahashi was so impatient to sell one of his "57s" that he had taken several of them back from Schlei and, without telling him, turned them over to Roger Hill to market. It was quite a stretch to argue that Schlei had anything to do with the independent marketing of the "57s" by Roger Hill. The government could try to get Schlei indicted as a party to the conspiracy of Ah Loo, Hansberry, and Hill, because he happened to be Takahashi's attorney and was admittedly trying to negotiate other "57s" in Japan. It would be absurd to assert that Schlei was involved in the Tampa transaction, but that could be covered by a little sleight of hand, misdirecting the jury so it did not notice. Finally, since Schlei freely acknowledged that the Japanese government regarded the "57s" as counterfeit, it could be argued that he was admittedly marketing certificates he knew to be false. This dodged the crucial point, which Schlei stated again and again, that he was convinced the Japanese government was lying to avoid payment.

In sum, the case against Schlei would depend on a trophy-hunting prosecutor, a compliant judge, a misdirected jury, a coordinated effort by Washington to block all Schlei's efforts at discovery, denial by the court of leave for Schlei to take depositions in Japan, intimidation of defense witnesses, and 'expert' prosecution witnesses brought in from Japan's Ministry of Finance and Dai-Ichi Bank, who seemed to have been coached to be evasive and to give false testimony.

Astonished to be named a party to the Ah Loo deal, of which he was not even aware, Schlei found himself the subject of Grand Jury proceedings in Tampa and was indicted. Immediately, clients holding "57s" scattered to avoid being drawn in, or – if cornered – became so frightened that they offered to testify against Schlei in return for immunity from prosecution.

In court, the prosecution 'proved' the certificates were fakes by bringing in two minor officials of Japan's Ministry of Finance and Dai-Ichi Bank, who had a vested interest in sticking to this story. Schlei's defense countered, "Corrupt Japanese officials were now falsely claiming that these financial instruments were not genuine." However, Professor Lausier insisted they were genuine (as quoted earlier): "The documents …are so precisely in agreement in innumerable respects with the official published records of the government of Japan …that, in my opinion, it is quite impossible for them, or the Certificates that resulted from them, to have been the work of any counterfeiter."

To demonstrate collusion between Tokyo and Washington, the defense attempted to locate any reports or documents showing covert payments by the U.S. Government to the government of Japan or any political party in Japan, from 1945 to the present. As we have seen, this has been confirmed by a number of sources including former CIA officials and U.S. diplomats. But, fighting for his life, Schlei needed all the documentary evidence available. As a former assistant attorney general of the United States, he was certain he would find these documents.

It was Schlei's legal right to make such discoveries, but federal agencies flatly refused to comply. News stories about the M-Fund and "57s" obliged the court to order the CIA, the Secret Service, National Archives, and State Department to conduct a search of their databases. Given the intense secrecy surrounding the Black Eagle Trust, the 1951 Peace Treaty, the M-Fund, and the disappearance of millions of documents concerning Japan, it would have been a great surprise if anything turned up. The jury was told that "search of the records of the CIA, the Secret Service, and the National Archives did not disclose any relevant or material documents or information that substantiated ...that the CIA gave money to employees or officials of the Japanese government, or any political party in Japan". The court record says, "The government searched hundreds of files of CIA paper records dating back to 1948 for any documents that might indicate that payments were made by the CIA to either the Japanese government, the Liberal Democratic Party, or individual party members. They also conducted computer searches for Marquat Fund... [and] the search ...did not discover any relevant or material documents or information."

The jury was not told that Acting CIA Director Admiral William O. Studeman had informed *The New York Times* in March 1995, that CIA was not about to divulge information on the subject of payola to foreign governments and politicos. Studeman said the Agency had an obligation to "keep faith" with politicians who "received legally authorized covert support from the United States".

This statement actually confirms that such payments were made, and merely refuses to give details. Japanese politicians bribed with huge sums of money had to be protected, which was more important than justice in American courts.

Schlei told the court, "I figured that if the Iran Contra case people like Ollie North and Admiral Poindexter and Mr. MacFarlane could be doing things and lying about it, then maybe people in the Japanese Government could be lying about some things, too."

Judge Kovachevich refused Schlei the right to take depositions in Japan, and brushed aside Schlei's protests that a key defense witness had been intimidated by the U.S. attorney. His attorneys alleged that the prosecution tampered with the witness, S.M. Han, who had an immunity agreement with U.S. attorney Mark Krum. Han swore that Krum told him if he testified for the defense, his immunity agreement would be nullified. Han also said Krum told him he had "better not give him any basis to withdraw the immunity because he would not hesitate to do so". Witness tampering is one of the most serious crimes in the U.S. judicial system and is grounds for disbarment. Judge Kovachevich denied a motion for a new trial based on the charge of witness tampering, and even refused to hold an evidentiary hearing to determine whether Han's allegations were true.

After six years of persecution, Schlei was convicted on one felony count of securities fraud, and one misdemeanor. Before the trial began, he had assets in the neighborhood of $10-million. During his trial, he was unable to practice law, and had enormous legal costs. He was professionally and financially ruined, left virtually bankrupt. He estimated that the U.S. Government spent over $45-million of taxpayers' money on the sting and the lawsuit.

Schlei appealed, and in September 1997 the Eleventh Circuit Court of Appeals reversed and vacated the conviction on the felony count and the misdemeanor, remanding the misdemeanor to the district court for a hearing on Schlei's motion for a new trial, based on government intimidation of witnesses. The three appeals court judges paid special attention to the way Kovachevich had handled the witness-tampering issue. In their decision they wrote that the transactions leading to the Schlei indictment were 'unusual, if not bizarre'. They found Kovachevich's handling of the witness tampering 'enigmatic'. They said, "We cannot determine whether Schlei was deprived of his right to due process ...because the [Kovachevich] court did not conduct an evidentiary hearing. ...Where defendants present evidence to the district court that the government intimidated a defense witness *a trial court must grant a hearing to determine whether the allegations of intimidation are true.*" (Our italics.)

So a case that was contrived to start with and dragged on for six years, resulting in Schlei's complete ruin, was overturned. Still insisting on his innocence, Schlei asked for a retrial, but the government knew he was broke. Nearly 70, and in no position to fight indefinitely to clear his name, he finally agreed not to press his charges of witness tampering, leaving the minor misdemeanor charge unresolved.

In Washington to this day he is slandered. An eminent libel lawyer, who should know better, recently insisted that Schlei's evidence was 'untrustworthy' because he was a 'convicted felon'. Others declared Schlei's unresolved misdemeanor conviction amounted to 'moral turpitude'.

It took further wrangling with the California bar to have this smear removed from the official record. In January 2001, the *California Bar Journal* announced that Schlei was once again 'an attorney in good standing'. But the harm had been done. In the Spring of 2002, while jogging on a California beach, Schlei suffered a major heart attack, collapsed and hit his head. A homeless man nearby called for help, but Schlei remained in a coma for many months. The last time we saw Schlei, he told us, "I now know how and why the jury convicted me. Until I figured that out, I was a very troubled man."

Other events unfolding in January 1992 may have led directly to Schlei's persecution. He was not the only target of M-Fund stings. Also arrested was James P. Sena, a 17-year veteran of the U.S. Secret Service, the agency that also investigates counterfeiting for the Treasury Department. Sena had examined M-Fund financial instruments in America and Japan, where he became convinced of the legitimacy of the "57s". He decided to sell some himself. He and Ian Yorkshire of Great Britain and Francis Cheung of Hong Kong were all arrested for attempting to market "57s" with a total face value of $50-billion. Abruptly, and for no apparent reason, in November 1995 the case against them was suddenly dismissed 'with prejudice', meaning the charges cannot be re-filed. Nevertheless, prosecutors refused to return the "57s" they had confiscated as evidence, calling them 'contraband'. If counterfeit, why were they contraband? We were told by a Wall Street source that Treasury is eager to get its hands on "57s" and other supposedly counterfeit derivatives, to negotiate them secretly.

Another prominent American who reportedly became involved in negotiating "57s" during the same period was the former Secretary of State, General Alexander Haig. Unlike Schlei, Haig was not arrested or persecuted, demonstrating how selective Washington has been in choosing its sting targets.

According to a detailed account we have from someone present at all the meetings, Haig was asked to intercede in behalf of Paraguay. The government of Paraguay had bought a single "57" with a face value of $500-million from First Hanover Securities in New York City on November 20, 1991, at the very moment the sting of Mrs. Ah Loo was going down. The same day, Paraguay asked MIC Debt Readjustment Company to arrange for the Japanese government to redeem this "57" – not for cash but for credit against ¥40-billion in foreign aid that Paraguay owed to Tokyo. This represented 80 percent of the face value of the "57", and Tokyo could keep the other 20 percent as a discount. (MIC is an organization backed by the Israeli government, which negotiates adjustments of national debt for governments in Eastern Europe and South America.) If successful, MIC was to be given oil exploration and development rights on Paraguayan territory. After considering former Secretary of State Henry Kissinger and former Ambassador Mike Mansfield, MIC chose Haig as their negotiator.

He was a good choice. Haig knew Japan because in 1947, fresh out of West Point, he had served as an aide to General MacArthur in Tokyo until the general's recall in 1951. As a MacArthur aide, working in a tight circle with men like Whitney and Willoughby, Haig doubtless heard a lot about black operations and secret funds set up in Tokyo during the occupation. While in Japan, Haig married the daughter of General Alonzo Patrick Fox, MacArthur's deputy chief of staff. Haig later served President Nixon on the national security staff, was White House chief of staff for both Nixon and Ford, and secretary of State for President Reagan.

At a strategy meeting in Miami, attended by our source, MIC and the Paraguayans asked Haig to negotiate personally with former Japanese prime minister Takeshita, a key man in the M-Fund and one of the LDP kingmakers. After being embarrassed by bribery scandals, including the Recruit scandal involving M-Fund kickbacks and war loot, Takeshita had been forced to resign as prime minister two years earlier, in 1989, but he remained powerful. Haig agreed to meet with Takeshita in Tokyo in January 1992. He reportedly told the Miami roundtable that the "57" should be negotiated 'underground' as quickly as possible.

To learn more about the background of the "57s" our source said Haig had discussions in Washington with the FBI and CIA, much as Schlei had done. One CIA official explained that Japan had a number of secret funds, including what he called 'the MacArthur Fund', apparently referring to the Sanwa Bank joint account in the names of MacArthur and Hirohito, which Japanese call the Showa Fund, referring to the reign title of Hirohito. He also explained how the Japanese government bonds had evolved into the "57s". Our source said Haig also paid a visit to the White House, to tell President Bush of his forthcoming meeting with Takeshita to negotiate the "57" for Paraguay. Explaining the give-and-take involved, he asked Bush for his support. To ease the way, our source said, Bush gave Haig a personal letter to Takeshita.

President Bush was on his way to Japan himself that January. He was in Tokyo a few days before Haig, a visit made famous when Bush vomited all over Prime Minister Miyazawa.

On January 13, 1992, Haig was informed that two weeks later he was to be guest of honor at a lunch in Tokyo's Imperial Hotel with the LDP Diet committee, after which he and Takeshita were to have a private talk in an adjoining room. MIC said Takeshita would probably start by saying all "57s" were counterfeit. Haig had to be prepared for this, and ready to say two or three things that would jolt Takeshita. He asked MIC to choose the three most impressive supporting documents to show Takeshita. One of these was an insurance policy issued by Yasuda Fire Insurance Company in Tokyo to cover transporting the certificate from the Ministry of Finance. This alone established the authenticity of the "57". MIC briefed Haig in detail about the significance of these supporting documents, and reviewed the differences between "57s" and ordinary Japanese government bonds.

Shortly before the meeting in Tokyo on the 27th, Haig was told that Takeshita had been acutely embarrassed by a recent series of major scandals, so what the LDP leader hoped to get from Haig was a promise to stop Japan-Bashing in America. If Takeshita could come out of their meeting with such an assurance, he might survive the scandals and resume power.

When the two men sat down privately at 2:40 p.m., our source said Takeshita opened as predicted, asking Haig to get U.S. companies and politicians to stop Japan-Bashing. Haig replied positively, handing Takeshita the personal letter from President Bush. Takeshita then said that any agreement on settling Paraguay's debt to Japan would have to include Japanese participation in developing oilfields in that country. With that on the table, Haig explained that one of the main reasons for his visit to Tokyo was to get Takeshita's assurance that Paraguay's "57" would be credited against its foreign aid debt. He showed Takeshita the "57" that Paraguay had purchased from Hanover.

Takeshita glanced at the document and said, "Mr. Haig, this paper is a forgery printed in Hong Kong."

"Then," Haig said, "please take a look at these documents." He handed Takeshita the Yasuda insurance cover document, and the two others. Reading each document in turn, "Takeshita's face turned pale and his voice faint."

"Mr. Haig," he said, "it seems to include a very delicate problem for the settlement."

"Yes," said Haig. "I agree. It's delicate."

"I cannot give you an immediate reply…"

The meeting ended, and minutes later, Haig reported all this to the MIC group in his suite. He said it was only when he saw Takeshita recoil in shock at sight of the insurance cover that he realized how serious was the secrecy surrounding the "57s". Our source said Haig turned angrily to the Paraguayans and said, "You're making me blackmail him!" Then he grinned and said, "That first missile hit the target!" He warned the Paraguayans and Israelis to be very careful about their personal safety while they were in Japan, because Takeshita was not happy, and he would certainly alert Japan's secret service.

Next day, our source said Takeshita's personal secretary came to see Haig. Insisting on talking in the hallway where they could not be monitored, he said: "Mr. Haig, the certificate and documents are not *formal*. So our government cannot repurchase it."

Haig squinted at him and said, "So we can make it public?"

Takeshita's secretary turned pale. He said he would speak again to Takeshita. The second missile also hit home.

The following morning, Takeshita's secretary came again. "As for the problem of the certificate, many inquiries are coming to our Ministry of Finance locally and overseas, and the administration is greatly perplexed." He paused. "We are ready to take certain measures on the certificate in question. You must treat this negotiation as strictly confidential. If a similar demand is made by another government, our administration would suffer because we are not prepared for it financially."

In short, Haig had succeeded, and the deal went down.

But how could Haig negotiate a "57" in Miami, Washington, and Tokyo, with discussions at the FBI, CIA and with President Bush in the White House, without being arrested and prosecuted like Norbert Schlei? Federal agents always insisted it was illegal to negotiate one inside America, or even to contemplate it.

If all "57s" are counterfeit, why did Haig succeed? If Haig's "57" was genuine, did he still do something illegal? Does the legitimacy of a Japanese debt instrument depend on your connections to the current occupant of the White House?

Norbert Schlei was drawn into the sting soon after Haig's Tokyo negotiation concluded. One of Takeshita's conditions about ending Japan-Bashing may have been that Schlei, who was asking so many embarrassing questions, must be silenced and removed from the field of play. If so, Haig certainly would have reported this to President Bush, which could explain why Schlei was then dragged into the Ah Loo case.

There is a lesson here for investors. Financial instruments growing out of the Black Eagle Trust continue to float around the global market, like magnetic mines left over from World War II that can blow up and sink any institution or individual that comes in contact with them. If some certificates are counterfeit while others are legitimate, investors and their attorneys have a right to inquire, without fear of arrest or intimidation, whether the documents they hold are real or fake, and not to be brushed off with falsehoods. Especially when the issuing government has a history of evasiveness, and is strongly suspected of lying. When Washington demonstrates that it has a greater sense of responsibility to corrupt foreign politicians than it does to its own citizens, we may rightly ask whom it really is protecting. Washington's main concern has been to protect and preserve a system of secret financial collusion with Japan, which has worked to its satisfaction for over half a century. And to protect the careers and reputations of U.S. Government officials involved in that collusion. In the end, how many billions went to Japanese politicians is less important than how much went into the pockets of American officials. As power corrupts, secret power corrupts secretly.

CHAPTER TEN

THE UMBRELLA

Today, the Philippine government denies that Santa Romana ever existed: "He's just a legend." Tell that to his family. We have interviewed his brother, his mistresses, and his children. We have visited his tombstone. We have amassed hundreds of documents, tapes, videos, eyewitness accounts, marriage licenses, confirmation from senior CIA officials, Marcos family members, Santy's business associates, bank records, and lawsuits – indisputable evidence from more than 60 years that Santa Romana is real, and that his vast fortune of cash and gold bullion sleeps in banks all over the world. The gold recovered by Santy became the asset base for many secret funds like the M-Fund. He was the gatekeeper of America's Golden Lily recoveries, until Ferdinand Marcos moved in, elbowed him aside, and took over as the new gatekeeper.

After Santy completed his recoveries in 1947, there was a lull of twenty years before Marcos began making similar ones. During the late 1950s, small groups of Japanese returned quietly to the Philippines to recover gold under various pretexts. Some claimed to be seeking the remains of dead soldiers for Shinto reburial in Japan. Tokyo offered to help Filipinos repair war damage with 'free' infrastructure projects, including irrigation systems and roads that took unlikely routes through the mountains. Japanese salvage firms offered to remove the hulks cluttering up Manila Bay, and to dredge and restore the battered bay front; in the course of this work they salvaged ships that had been scuttled at the docks with bullion aboard. Japanese corporations built factories in odd locations throughout the Philippines, on foundations requiring deep excavations. When these factories were completed, Filipino workers on their assembly lines put together TVs and tape recorders, computers, refrigerators and air conditioners, which were then shipped to Japan in remarkably heavy crates. According to a CIA source, the Agency knew that gold bullion was being smuggled out of the Philippines this way, but did not interfere.

The first time Marcos recovered gold was an accident, when he heard about two Japanese digging in Ilocos Norte, the home province of the Marcos family in the northwest corner of Luzon. Imperial Army veterans, they had hidden a small stash of their own. Marcos confiscated their gold biscuit bars.

As a sharp young politician, Marcos heard about Santy's recoveries and cultivated him aggressively. Being a lawyer, Marcos could make himself useful in many ways. Gradually, he began to take over parts of Santy's operation, called The Umbrella. When he was elected president in 1965, Marcos was approached directly by Japanese underworld fixer Sasakawa Ryoichi, offering to do joint recoveries of war loot. A crony of Kodama, Sasakawa knew the location of a number of major vaults. For a substantial cut, Marcos could grant presidential authorizations. It was typical of Marcos to scavenge this way, rather than do treasure hunting himself. He did not hesitate to grant import permits for canned sardines long past their shelf life, knowing many Filipinos could die from eating them. He was equally happy to make deals with Japanese gangsters to enrich himself, and impoverish the Philippine people.

•

In 1971, Marcos hijacked an extraordinary treasure that few people have ever seen, but is now world-famous.

In January of that year, a Filipino locksmith and amateur treasure hunter named Rogelio 'Roger' Roxas crawled into a tunnel dug by the Japanese Army and found a magnificent solid gold Buddha weighing one ton. The seated Buddha, 28-inches tall and distinctly Burmese in style, had been confiscated from a Buddhist order in Mandalay, to whom it represented the accumulated wealth of centuries.

What happened to Roxas after that is so bizarre that we took pains to base our narrative largely on the trial record of *The Supreme Court of the State of Hawaii, Roger Roxas and the Golden Budha [sic] Corporation v. Marcos*. This court case concluded with the award of $43-billion, the biggest civil award in judicial history. The court's 'findings of fact' were assembled from thousands of pages of testimony, transcripts, original documents, photographs, and videotaped depositions. Neither the Marcos defense attorneys nor the Roxas legal team disputed the summary.

Roger Roxas made a meager living at his trade in the mountain resort of Baguio, but in his spare time he was president of the Treasure Hunters Association of the Philippines. In that role, he was approached from time to time by visiting Japanese. One, Okubo Eusebio, told Roxas that as a young boy he had been an interpreter for General Yamashita. He said Yamashita had taken a large quantity of gold and silver bars from Manila to Baguio to pay and feed his troops during the last year of the war. Okubo said the ingots were in wooden boxes stacked in a tunnel near Baguio general hospital. He also told Roxas he saw a solid gold Buddha in the nearby convent that Yamashita used as his residence and headquarters.

A mestizo named Albert Fuchigami told Roxas his Japanese father had left him treasure maps. Fuchigami's family had a vegetable stand in the market. He said his father once took him into a tunnel behind Baguio Hospital, which had tracks for handcars, and side tunnels full of boxes of gold. Just before his father died, he gave Albert maps. A few years later, Albert started searching but found nothing, and in a fit of anger burned the maps. When his sister found out, she scolded him because the maps were to be seen reversed in a mirror.

Roxas was friends with the American John Ballinger, who had fought in Luzon during the war with Captain Medina's guerrilla unit. It was Ballinger who had photographed the fake hospital ship *Fuji Maru* unloading bronze boxes at Subic Bay, and followed the truck convoy into the mountains where the Japanese had placed the boxes in a cave and sealed the entrance. Later, when Medina's company infiltrated Baguio, Ballinger observed Japanese soldiers carrying heavy boxes into a tunnel near the hospital. The guerrillas attacked with grenades and machineguns, blowing the cave entrance shut and sealing some of the enemy inside. Ballinger had since gone back to live in New Mexico, where he and his son Gene started a newspaper for amateur treasure hunters. As often as they could, the Ballingers visited the Philippines. On one trip, John Ballinger told Roxas he remembered that the entrance to the tunnel they had blown shut was near a concrete pillbox. He could not pinpoint the location, because many years had passed and rainforest had grown over the pillbox.

With the different reports from Fuchigami, Okubo, and Ballinger, Roxas was sure the tunnel existed, but it took him a long time to find the pillbox. Because it was on public land, he applied for the necessary government permit to dig for treasure. By terms of this agreement, the Philippine government was entitled to 30 percent of any treasure recovered. The permit was granted by Judge Pio Marcos, an uncle of President Marcos, whose court was in Baguio.

In Spring of 1970, while Roxas and his team were digging near the pillbox, they found what they thought was the collapsed tunnel entrance. It took seven months of hard work to re-open, and they were sickened immediately by gas from dead bodies. They had to let the tunnel air out for a week before they could crawl inside. Near the entrance they found army radios, bayonets, rifles, and a human skeleton in Japanese uniform. After weeks of digging around a cave-in, they penetrated into a main shaft with tracks for handcars, and wiring for a crude lighting system, so they were sure it was the right tunnel. Off to the sides were branch tunnels. Beneath a layer of dirt in the floor of the main shaft, they discovered a ten-foot-thick concrete slab, and began pounding on it. On January 24, 1971, they broke through and discovered the Gold Buddha. Although less than three feet tall, it was extremely heavy and ten men were needed to raise it to floor level, using a chain block hoist on a steel A-frame. Even with rolling logs, they had to struggle to drag it outside. Roxas borrowed a truck and one night he and his friends moved the Buddha to his home, where they put it in a corner of his back bedroom, covered with a bedspread.

Resuming his exploration of the tunnels, he found a small wooden box on the tunnel floor. When he pried it open he found twenty-four small gold biscuit bars, one inch wide by two inches long, and half an inch thick. A 24-karat gold bar of this dimension would weigh about 30 troy ounces, and in 1971 would have been worth $1,050. So the whole box was worth over $25,000. Nearby, Roxas discovered a man-made chamber six feet wide by thirty feet long, filled with hundreds of neatly stacked wood boxes. Each box was the size of a case of beer cans, suitable for 75-kilo bars. He did not open any of these, because he knew what he would find – and he already had a small fortune in gold biscuits to deal with. Roxas took the twenty-four biscuits home, along with some samurai swords, bayonets and other arti-facts. He left the big boxes where they were. Several days later, worried that some-body else might chance upon his discovery, Roxas blew the tunnel mouth shut. He needed to raise money before he could continue the excavation in safety, and recover the rest of the treasure.

He sold seven of the biscuits and started hunting for a buyer for the Gold Buddha. This was his mistake. Word got around quickly. Two prospective buyers arrived and assayed the Buddha, drilling tiny holes in the body near the neck. Both determined that the Buddha was between 20 and 22 carats, typical of gold refined in Asia before 1940.

On April Fool's Day, 1971, a third buyer, Joe Oihara, came to inspect the Buddha. Oihara, who appeared to be Japanese, told Roxas that he was staying at the home of Ferdinand Marcos's mother, Josefa Edralin Marcos, who had a repu-tation for being crafty and predatory. Oihara examined the Buddha closely and said he was interested in buying it. He promised to return in several days with a partial payment of 1-million pesos. Roxas noticed that Oihara was especially interested in the Buddha's neck. When he left, Roxas and his brother Danilo tried to twist the head, placed a plank against it, and pounded with a hammer till it moved, unscrew-ing it. Inside was a cavity the size of a cookie jar, containing three handfuls of what turned out to be diamonds. Roxas removed the diamonds and stored them sepa-rately, screwing the head back on.

Four days later, at 2:30 in the morning on April 5, eight uniformed men armed with machineguns banged on the front door of the Roxas house. Claiming to be agents from the Criminal Investigation Service of the National Bureau of Investigation, they demanded entry and said they had a search warrant. Roxas was afraid to open the door. Two of the men broke the front window of the house, pointed their machine guns inside and told Roxas he had three minutes to make up his mind: Open the door or die.

He opened the door. Oihara was there, too. The men flashed a search warrant in front of Roxas. He saw something about "violation of Central Bank regulation and illegal possession of firearms". Signed by Judge Pio Marcos, the warrant ordered that the Buddha and other seized property be delivered to the custody of the clerk of the court forthwith.

Roxas was not alone in the house. His brother Danilo put up a struggle and was cruelly beaten with gun butts. Roxas, his family, and two friends who were his bodyguards were told to lie down on the floor while the armed men searched the house. When they left they took the Buddha, the diamonds, the remaining seven-teen gold biscuits, the samurai swords, a coin collection, and a child's piggybank. They also confiscated a broken .22 caliber rifle, left at his house by a friend, and later charged him with possessing an illegal weapon. They did not deliver the Buddha or anything else to the clerk of the court.

In the morning, Roxas reported the robbery to the local press, and police. Then he went to see Judge Pio, to ask why he had signed the search warrant. The judge said he had been ordered to do so by his nephew, President Marcos. He added that it was a shame Roxas had gone to the police and the media because now he probably was going to be killed. Undaunted, Roxas went back to the police station and signed an official complaint.

He took his family to Cabanatuan City, northeast of Manila, to enlist the aid of the provincial governor, who assigned four bodyguards and gave him a place to hide. Meanwhile, another judge in Baguio ordered the military to turn the statue over to court custody, as specified in the search warrant. The army delayed a fortnight, while a Manila artisan quickly cast a Buddha made of brass. The brass statue, its head not detachable and bearing little resemblance to the original, was deposited at the Baguio court.

A few days later, Roxas was tracked down in Cabanatuan by two agents of the president's mother. They offered him 3-million pesos to declare in public that the brass Buddha was the one he recovered. At the end of April, his safety "personally guaranteed" by the Philippine Secretary of Justice, Roxas returned to Baguio to examine the Buddha, accompanied by four bodyguards, two prosecutors from the Justice Department, his personal attorney, and a number of reporters and cameramen. At the courthouse, he examined the Buddha, and bravely (or foolishly) announced that it was not his. He pointed out that the color was different, the facial features were different, the head was not detachable, and there was no sign of the tiny assay drill holes.

The press was electrified by this simple man's challenge to the famously predatory Marcos clan. Everybody had heard about the ruthlessness of the president, his thugs, his wife and his mother. Members of the opposition Liberal Party, excited by a chance to damage Marcos at the polls, persuaded Roxas to testify before the Senate, in an investigation of 'The Gold Buddha Affair'. On May 4, 1971, Roxas gave a full account before the Senate. President Marcos immediately denounced the inquiry as a scurrilous, politically motivated attack, and threatened a 'personal vendetta'.

Fourteen days later, back in hiding in Cabanatuan City, Roxas was again tracked down and this time arrested. His captors were three Marcos agents in civilian clothing. They told him they were taking him to see the president. Instead he was taken to the home of a Philippine Constabulary (national police) officer, where he was beaten and kicked. Then they took him to Constabulary headquarters in San Fernando, Pampanga, north of Manila. In a dark, windowless cell, they showed him a picture of his wife and children. If he wanted to see them again, he must make a list of the senators who were encouraging him, and must reveal the location of the remaining treasure. Roxas refused. He was then subjected to electric shocks to all parts of his body, and burned with cigarettes.

They moved him next to a hotel in Angeles City, near Clark Air Base, where the torture resumed. This time he was beaten about the face and head with a large rubber mallet, until he passed out. His right eye was permanently blinded, and so misshapen that from then on he looked like Quasimodo. For two weeks he was kept in the hotel room, and told repeatedly to sign an affidavit that the raid on his house had been peaceful, and the soldiers were unarmed. A lot of the questions seemed insignificant, as if they were told to torture him, but ran out of ideas.

One day he was taken back to the Baguio court where he was photographed with the brass Buddha. That night, he picked the lock on his hotel window and escaped, seeking refuge at the home of his sister. He phoned a senator to tell him what had happened, and again was asked to testify before the Senate, which he did on June 30, 1971, reporting all that had befallen him since his last appearance, including the torture. When he returned to his home in Baguio, a man came with a letter summoning him to Malacanang Palace. At the palace, Roxas met Caesar Dumlao, a finance officer, who said President Marcos was now willing to pay him 5-million pesos for his Buddha (up from 3-million). Roxas was to come back to the palace that afternoon to get the money. By that point Roger was afraid for his life, and did not dare go back.

In early July, he was arrested for failing to appear at a hearing on the illegal weapon charge, which had been pending since January 28, 1971. At the hearing, he was ordered jailed for failing to appear earlier. After a month in jail, he was bailed out by an attorney sent by Senator Sergio Osmena, Jr., leader of the opposition Liberal Party, whose father once had been president of the Philippines. Roxas was flown to Manila in a private plane and taken in a truck to Plaza Miranda, where Osmena had asked him to speak at a political rally that evening. Organized by opponents of Marcos, the rally drew a huge crowd, and many prominent opposition leaders were on the speakers' platform. Roxas was asked to remain in the truck till he was called up to the platform. Minutes later, two grenades were thrown into the crowd. Ten people were killed and sixty-six wounded, including Osmena and seven other senatorial candidates. We were told by a member of the Marcos family that the grenades were thrown by men from the Presidential Security Command, on orders of Marcos, and that security chief General Fabian Ver threw one of them. Blaming the attack on communist terrorists, President Marcos suspended the writ of habeas corpus and jailed many of his opponents, calling them leftists. It was the first step toward martial law, which Marcos would declare a few months later in September 1972.

Thoroughly frightened by the carnage, Roxas fled Manila and went into hiding for the next twelve months. When he finally went home in July 1972, he was arrested immediately by two national security agents watching his house. They took him to a naval base in Zambales province, where he was confined in the stockade. There he was questioned by the provincial commander about his original discovery of the Gold Buddha. He was still imprisoned three months later when Marcos declared martial law. General Ver came personally to see Roxas in his cell. Ver said he had been in the raiding party that had come to the Roxas house to kidnap the Buddha.

In January 1973, Roxas was again taken to Baguio courthouse, where he was tried on the charge of possession of the illegal firearm. Convicted, he was sent to Baguio prison camp, where on at least two occasions he was beaten and questioned again about the location of the tunnel of gold. After serving nearly two years there, he was released and returned home. The next month, he was visited by men who said they were from Task Force Restoration and wanted his help on treasure excavations near Baguio General Hospital. Roxas refused.

Unable to get him to cooperate, Marcos relied on information his men obtained from torturing one of Roger's digging team, Olimpio Magbanua. Using pliers, they pulled out Magbanua's teeth one-by-one until he told them approximately where the tunnel entrance was. Army units were sent to probe the grounds behind the hospital, till they found the closed tunnel mouth. Nurses and patients in the hospital had ringside seats to watch the soldiers and their search. One day in 1974, hospital staff saw soldiers start carrying very heavy wooden boxes out of a hole in the ground, placing them in trucks. Each box required four to six men. In addition to men from the Presidential Security Command, there were cadets from the Philippine Military Academy. Several of the wood boxes were rotten, and when each crumbled three gold bars fell to the ground, the size of cigarette cartons – 75-kilo bars. A hospital employee estimated that ten boxes each day were loaded onto the trucks, over a period of one year, which would come to approximately 3,600 boxes, or 10,800 bars weighing 75 kilos each. During this time, armed guards were posted all around the site, keeping people away.

Roxas knew the soldiers had found his tunnel, and were stealing the gold he had discovered, but against a well-armed military force there was nothing he could do. In 1976, resigned to his fate at least for the time being, he moved to a secret location with his family, where they remained for ten years without further incident. Roxas only surfaced again in 1986, after Ferdinand and Imelda Marcos were removed from power by the U.S. Government, and taken to exile in Hawaii. The moment had come when Roxas could strike back – a story we resume in Chapter 15.

•

During the years when Roxas was being persecuted and tortured, President Marcos was pressing Santa Romana to turn over some of his big gold accounts.

The relationship between them went back a long way. A family source told us that Marcos and Santy first teamed up in the early 1960s, before Marcos became president. The same source insists that Santy was an intimate friend of Imelda when she was a beauty queen in Leyte, implying that she had been Santy's mistress, and that he was the first to introduce her to Ferdinand.

In those days, Santy was a ladies' man, handsome and vigorous. Tall, powerfully-built, with a shaved head, high cheekbones and Oriental features, he bore a strong resemblance to actor Yul Brynner. In one of the few photos we have, he wears a white Nehru suit and white shoes, towering over others in the picture, a big man with natural grace. A friend described him as "a good-natured gentleman …with a refined conduct and manner". His charisma made him attractive to women and men alike.

Santy had many identities, of which Severino Garcia Diaz Santa Romana was only the first. (A younger brother, Judge Miguel 'Mike' Santa Romana, now retired and living in Cabanatuan City not far from Santy's grave, uses the same family name.) When Santy married Evangeline Campton, he used his father's other name, Diaz. But in his 1938 marriage license to Julieta Huerto, he switched to Santa Romana.

His business aliases, which he started using in the late 1940s, appear on bank documents all over the world. These include Ramon Poirrotte, Jose Antonio Diaz, Jose Antonio Severino Garcia Diaz, J. Antonio Diaz, Severino Pena Garcia de la Paz,

Mateass Connea, Jose Almonte, Santy, and others. Using aliases is not illegal, or necessarily suspicious. The U.S. legal system does not regard an alias as illegal so long as it is not used for a fraudulent purpose. Pennames, stage-names, and other aliases have a legitimate place in life. As gatekeeper of the Japanese plunder recoveries, Santy used his aliases in behalf of the CIA and the Treasury Department, serving as controller and sole stockholder of a blizzard of front companies beginning with DNP Enterprises (Diaz-Nanette-Poirrotte), registered in Monaco. Because he was titleholder of bullion accounts in banks all over the world, one company was not adequate. Others included Nanette Enterprises, Collette Enterprises, Montizuma [sic], Diaz-Campton Enterprises, Poirrotte Enterprises, and Diaz-Poirrotte Enterprises. These were shell companies, set up to hide the movement of gold bullion from Manila to world banking centers.

Santy also set up a trust in Liechtenstein originally called the Santa Romana Foundation, which later evolved into the Sandy Foundation, or (in German) Sandy Anstalt. The German variant appears as a cryptic reference in letters from Wall Street firms, including Sullivan & Cromwell, the law firm of John Foster Dulles – as if Sandy Anstalt is the name of a client everybody knows and loves.

The corporate logo for Santy's flagship DNP Enterprises was an open umbrella, signifying 'umbrella organization'. But it was not just a logo. The Umbrella also was the codename for the group Santy relied on to move gold from the Philippines to foreign banks. On our CDs we reproduce a flow-chart, hand-drawn and annotated by President Marcos, showing how The Umbrella grew by the late 1970s into a powerful network mingling CIA agents, Mafia godfathers, Filipino secret police, and Marcos hitmen.

One part of The Umbrella organization was American millionaire ex-convict Wallace Groves, owner of Grand Bahama Island, whose casinos there and in Nassau were operated by mobster Meyer Lansky. One of Groves' partners in the ownership of Grand Bahama was the Wall Street firm, Allen & Co., run by Herbert and Charlie Allen, who also had control of Paramount Pictures. The Allens owned a big chunk of Benguet Mines in the Philippines, and Herbert was a golfing crony of Marcos. (The Allens once said, "We trade every day with hustlers, deal makers, shysters, con men... That's the way [America] was built.")

In a complex deal, Groves and the Allens swapped a piece of Grand Bahama to Marcos in return for nearly complete control of Benguet. This allowed The Umbrella to move war-gold out of the Philippines, masquerading as gold from Benguet Mines. Once the gold reached certain banks in Nassau, it served as part of an elaborate money-laundering scheme that included washing drug profits through the Groves casinos, then converting them into gold bars.

Santy knew all about the deal and wrote in 1973 – during his month-long visit to the CIA and The Enterprise in Washington – that, "the Benguet-Bahamas deal, a good grade major co. swap, made instant millions for X, Y, Z groups".

The Umbrella served as a conduit of gold bullion for many banks identified with the CIA. Paul Helliwell, an OSS-CIA associate of Bill Casey and Ray Cline, was involved in moving the first generation recoveries of Yamashita's Gold out of the Philippines. In 1951, Helliwell helped set up Sea Supply Corp., a CIA front used to run supplies to the Nationalists in China, which also ran Nationalist opium and heroin out of the Golden Triangle for the KMT opium armies. Helliwell then 'retired' to Nassau where he set up Castle Bank, and Mercantile Bank & Trust, and became an intimate of Groves. Helliwell's Castle Bank was one of a worldwide network of banks identified with the CIA, which allowed black money to move outside normal banking channels, providing offshore refuge for the ill-gotten gains of dictators, warlords, and dissident Asian military officers. Castle Bank was closely tied to the Cayman Island firm, ID Corp., whose sole owner was Japanese-American Shig Katayama, one of the key facilitators of Lockheed's huge payoffs to Japanese politicians. When Castle Bank became notorious, it was folded and superseded by one in Australia called Nugan-Hand Bank, which had a board packed with retired U.S. intelligence officials and Pentagon brass, with CIA director William Colby as its legal counsel. When Nugan-Hand collapsed, following several murders, BCCI moved into the picture. And when BCCI finally collapsed in 1991, the CIA admitted it used BCCI for years to pay for covert operations.

•

Because so much of the documentary record remains hidden, we must assume that Santy's role was as a gatekeeper, facilitator and cutout. CIA needed deniability, so it subcontracted much of the financial routine to Santy, who happily played the role of the mysterious Filipino billionaire. When black gold had to be moved from the Philippines to a bank in Hong Kong, Zurich, Buenos Aires, or London, documents we have including cargo manifests, waybills and insurance covers show that gold was moved from Clark Air Base on U.S. aircraft, or from Subic Bay aboard U.S. Navy vessels, or from Manila International Airport aboard Cathay Pacific and other airlines, or from the bayfront on American President Lines passenger ships. The Umbrella took care of security, accompanying the bullion to its destination. The Mafia first became involved after the war when a lot of Santy's gold was moved to banks in Italy, including the Vatican bank, as part of the CIA effort to keep the Italian Communist Party from coming to power, described earlier.

Each time a new account was opened, Santy's name or one of his aliases was entered as the account holder. Because he used so many aliases, he was referred to sometimes as 'The Man With No Name'. To access any of these bank accounts required the proper bank codes, passwords, and sheaves of documents, including Santy's own codes and jingles he learned from Lansdale.

On the face of it, Santy remained the titleholder of these accounts, yet the assets – or their derivatives – appear to have been used by various governments, through secret earmarking arrangements with the Federal Reserve, Bank of England, Bank of Japan, and Swiss banks.

In return for gatekeeping these accounts, Santy received a generous management fee that was never disclosed, probably a percentage of each account's net assets. A management fee of 1 percent per year for a $1-billion account would yield $10-million; a smaller fee of .1 percent would yield an annual fee of $1-million – and there were dozens and dozens of these accounts. By the early 1970s, the accounts closely linked to Santy, and considered by some sources to belong to him, were modestly estimated to total well over $50-billion. If these accounts were his personal property, he would have been one of the world's richest men. But he never became an international celebrity. We know that he visited Washington as a guest of a faction of the CIA in 1973, the year before he died, and continued to be employed by the CIA up to the time of his death. He had a good life with spacious homes in Manila and at Cabanatuan City, and kept a suite at the Manila Hilton. But he never bought Lear Jets, or Ferraris. He was unknown outside the Philippines, except to bankers and spooks, and was not prominent socially even in Manila. Nobody ever wrote an article about 'Manila's Mystery Billionaire'. His job was only one element in a very complex clandestine Cold War scenario.

Without access to CIA or U.S. Treasury documents, spelling out their relationship more clearly, and the internal documents of the banks involved, it is impossible to deduce exactly how Santy was positioned as titleholder of these accounts. But he clearly was.

What happened inside the Philippines is easier to grasp. Some of Santy's money helped get Ferdinand Marcos elected president. Marcos spent twenty years grooming himself for the post, and finally succeeded in 1965. Along the way, as we recounted in *The Marcos Dynasty*, he did favors for the CIA and Pentagon during the expansion of the Indochina War. When Marcos got the presidential nomination, all members of his campaign team previously had worked for Lansdale. Marcos was pushed into the palace as a 'new Magsaysay' – America's Boy.

Marcos convinced the White House that he could help sell the Vietnam War to other Southeast Asian leaders by funneling bribes from Santy's accounts at banks in Hong Kong, Tokyo, Taipei, Singapore and Sydney. These bribes were not in cash, which could be frittered away overnight, but in the form of derivatives including gold bearer certificates entitling the holder to interest on a large account. So long as the recipient behaved, he could continue to draw the interest. If he went sour, the certificate could be declared counterfeit, just as the LDP said the "57s" were counterfeit.

Once he was president, Marcos did support the American war in Indochina, but not for free. He traded public support of U.S. policy for America keeping him in Malacanang Palace. He remained a darling of the White House till he fell out with the Reagan Administration in 1986.

By the end of his first four-year term, he was getting terrible press. Imelda was mocked for blowing millions on weekend shopping sprees. In 1968, she spent $3.3-million on a single weekend in New York City with her daughter Imee. At the same time she opened a big account at Citibank in Manhattan, where tax office documents show that Santy also had large cash and bullion accounts. There were rumors – later proved true – that the Marcoses were salting billions in foreign bank accounts, while the salary of a Philippine president was minimal.

Despite the bad press, in 1969 Marcos won another four-year term by stuffing ballot boxes. According to the Philippine constitution, he could not run for a third term. Unable to get the constitution revised, in 1972 Marcos and his defense minister, Juan Ponce Enrile, launched a phony campaign of 'communist' insurrection to justify declaring martial law, so they could stay in office. One of its highlights was the grenade attack at the Plaza Miranda, terrorizing the opposition party and silencing Roger Roxas.

Extraordinarily cunning, Marcos persuaded Santy to name him deputy director of The Umbrella. Fatigued by twenty-five years of doing the same thing over and over, Santy was beginning to drink heavily. He was losing control to Marcos, which depressed him. What tipped the scale in favor of Marcos was the fickle nature of new people rising to the top of the CIA hierarchy, men who did not share wartime experiences in the OSS, memories of the good old days as China Cowboys, or of the formative years of the postwar CIA when everybody was a Cold Warrior engaged in dirty tricks. The Old Guard knew Santy first-hand, and valued him.

Marcos knew that some of Santy's accounts had lain dormant for years, as new people in the CIA lost track. He leaned hard on Santy to transfer these dormant accounts to him. Marcos was particularly fixated on the Sandy Foundation. Physical violence always was implicit at Malacanang Palace. It was widely known that people had been tortured and murdered in a part of the palace called the Black Room. Anyone who crossed the president was murdered in grisly fashion, corpses left by the roadside with eyeballs plucked out, hanging on their stalks – the signature of General Ver.

Worried, Santy began taking steps to protect himself, and to protect his personal accounts from seizure by presidential decree. Among the people he enlisted was a Filipina named Tarciana Rodriguez. He made her the official treasurer of all his shell companies, putting her in charge of billions in cash, bullion, gold certificates, stocks and other assets all over the world. In a deposition prepared for Philippine courts, Tarciana described how she first met Santy in August 1971. She was running a small accounting firm and secretarial service when she was introduced to him by her cousin, Luz Rambano, who was Santy's mistress during the last three years of his life. (Some sources said Luz was legally married to him, but divorce does not exist in the Catholic Philippines, so he was still technically married to Julieta Huerto.)

Luz brought him to Tarciana's office, figuring that he needed an accountant and bookkeeper he could trust. Later, when Tarciana came to his suite in the Manila Hilton as his chief accountant, she realized he was a significant figure in the financial world.

"It was in my mind then that he must be somebody because, to be billeted in a Five-star Hotel in the 70s was an indication of a symbol status of a person or VIP, especially he was only a Filipino. [sic] In my going to and fro to his Hotel accommodation, what amazed me so much, there were many people of different nationalities who often visited him …Bankers, Brokers, Business associates… he was a very famous personality especially to all the Banks concerned throughout the world."

From then on, Tarciana did all the bookkeeping and secretarial chores for Santy's shell companies. Although she never asked indiscreet questions, she was puzzled by his eccentric habits. If he could afford a year-round suite at the Hilton, just across the street from the CIA station in the Magsaysay Building, why did he dress in patched clothing? Then she discovered the patches were not covering holes. He was disguising himself to fool Manila street toughs, who watched people come and go from the hotel.

After Marcos stole the Gold Buddha and had Roxas beaten to a pulp, Santy took Luz Rambano with him to open an account at the Manila branch of First National City Bank (now Citibank). According to her deposition: "$43-million U.S. dollars in cash was deposited in the presence of bank officer James J. Collins. The transaction was unusual in that the cash was in small denominations and it took six (6) days for bank personnel to count it." Not something a banker would forget. When Luz later hired San Francisco attorney Mel Belli to sue Citibank and recover this and other money, "Collins had his deposition taken in New York City and denied that he was ever involved in establishing this account. Collins denied that the transaction ever took place, and stated that he did remember Severino Santa Romana coming into the bank on one occasion in 1971 'talking about borrowing some money for some venture'."

What was Santy doing with $43-million in small bills? Being a rich eccentric, with fake patches, he may have kept money in wall safes in offices and homes all over the Philippines. It may also have been currency confiscated by the Japanese Army from Southeast Asian banks, which never got back to Tokyo. When Marcos scared him, he and Luz put it in laundry bags and took it to National City Bank. If they thought it was safe there, they had surprises in store.

He also rented nine safety deposit boxes at the same bank, which Luz said he filled with cash and jewelry. According to a Marcos family source, just before martial law Santy transferred $800-million out of the Philippines, moving it from First National City Bank Manila to Citibank New York.

He did this none too soon. On February 27, 1973, Santy was brought to Malacanang Palace where, in the president's private office, Marcos made him sign a typewritten 'Will and Testament'. This document said Santy had been using various names "for personal reasons, security and preservation of my properties, real, personal, cash/money in different currencies, treasures and other forms of bank deposits." It goes on to say, "I had acquired various properties ...presently on deposit" in Manila, Hong Kong, California, Switzerland, New York, Argentina, Singapore, Taiwan, Germany, Australia, and various Asian countries.

This Will then named "my wife, Julieta Huerto, as my successor of all my properties as above-mentioned, with full power and authority that upon my death, may appoint other persons to act as my Administrator subject to the approval of the Court on probate". This Will was reluctantly signed by Santy and witnessed by his business partner Jose T. Velasquez, and two Marcos flunkeys, Gil de Guzman and presidential secretary Victor G. Nituda. Although technically it made Julieta Huerto his sole legal heir, on his death Marcos easily could oblige her to appoint him administrator of the estate, so he could gain control of all Santy's accounts.

A few months later, in March 1973, Santy had another attack of nerves and moved $500-million from Manila to the Hongkong & Shanghai Banking Corporation (HSBC) central branch in Hong Kong. This sum, plus the $800-million transferred to Citibank New York, meant he had now moved $1.3-billion in cash out of Manila. During the same period, records show that he also moved 1,640 metric tons of gold to a Hong Kong bank that was later taken over by Japan's Sanwa

Bank. Soon afterward, on a trip to Tacloban on the island of Leyte, Santy drank too much and spoke too loudly of his fears, for he and Luz were arrested. Martial law allowed Marcos to arrest anyone.

Tarciana received a long-distance call from Santy saying they were being held prisoner at Camp Bampus, an army base on the island. He told Tarciana they had been arrested for 'rumor-mongering' (talking about Marcos behind his back). He asked Tarciana to come to Leyte as soon as possible. When she arrived, he told her to deliver a letter personally to the Citibank vice president, and gave her a safe-deposit box key. The letter to Collins authorized Tarciana to open his nine safe-deposit boxes. Box One held keys to the other eight. Box Two contained cash, from which Tarciana was to pay the box rental fees. Box Three contained jewelry, which he wanted her to bring. When Tarciana got to Citibank with the letter and key, she was told Collins was out of the country, and to come back some other time.

Over the years, Santy had been protected by the CIA, and by General Lansdale in particular. But in 1973 the Agency was in turmoil. A number of senior people were sacked, or resigned in disgust rather than be posted to remote backwaters. These men were now intent upon setting up their own private covert organization, or 'shadow-CIA'. Where the CIA often was called The Company, the new shadow-CIA would be called The Enterprise. (In a later chapter, we will look more closely at the circumstances, and some of the curious consequences.)

In the midst of this turmoil, Santy was invited to Washington as a private guest of the disaffected old guard, including Lansdale, Helliwell, Cline, and others. For over a month, they regaled him with stories about OSS days, about the fight against Mao and the escape to Taiwan, how they turned Claire Chennault's Civil Air Transport (CAT) into Air America, and briefed Santy on CIA's other black ops in Latin America, Africa, and behind the Iron Curtain. Each night he went back to the Mayflower Hotel and sat down with a tumbler and a bottle of Scotch, to make notes. His sloppy handwriting, and occasional mistakes in dates and spellings, were attributed by Tarciana to the whisky. In the notes, Santy describes in striking detail many of the CIA's covert operations that did not become known to the American public until years later: How the CIA went about setting up proprietaries, like his own DNP Enterprises; how many of these companies were airlines and transport services, arms suppliers, or private mercenary forces, to support secret wars like the one in Angola. People, he said, were "paid pensions…to maintain silence". He commented on the moral dilemma posed by many of the Agency's operations: "While ethics of transaction are questionable, conflict of interest laws do not apply to CIA"; expenditures made "w/out regard to provisions of laws"; bankrolling agents "living up their cover". He seemed nervous that: "Langley headquarters sometimes only has vaguest notions of what certain proprietaries are up to". Near the end of his notes, Santy wrote that the CIA and the Nixon Administration were convinced that Asia as a whole was a mess, and this justified long-term interference by the United States: "…strongly implied continued open American intervention [in] internal affairs of Third World Asean Cartel members".

What the old guard wanted from Santy, now that they were setting up their own private CIA and private military forces, was access to some of the black bullion accounts that Washington had lost track of. They knew Santy also had a number of very large personal accounts that were dormant, and they wanted him to make these available.

Pressed hard by Marcos, by the CIA, and by this new shadow-CIA, Santy decided to take further steps to protect himself and his assets.

When he got back to the Philippines and had time to think it over, he phoned Tarciana on August 1, 1974, and asked her to come see him in Cavite City. When she arrived he gave her a document officially and formally appointing her National Treasurer of DNP Enterprises, "to have custody of and be responsible for all the funds, securities and bonds of the corporation" and "to deposit in the name and to the credit of the corporation" as advised by DNP National Chairman Jose T. Velasquez, Jr., his old friend and business partner. He also gave her instructions about what to do with Santy's accounts at Wells Fargo Bank and Hanover Bank. She asked why he had not chosen a more sophisticated person. He said, "You are the only person who can be trusted."

Santy was having a moral crisis. It was thirty years since he took charge of torturing Major Kojima, in the anguished period immediately following the rape of Manila. By 1947, his recoveries of Golden Lily vaults were concluded, and he began to enjoy big income from his commissions. Because he preferred a simple life, his assets grew until he had far more money than could ever be spent. A good man at heart, he became mellower as the years passed. The treachery and cruelty of Marcos had taken him by surprise. Then in Washington he had been confronted by old men he hardly knew, who regaled him with stories of assassinations, atrocities, political kidnappings, and grand deception that made a mockery of humanity. For them World War II had never ended. For the first time, Santy began thinking of himself as a paymaster for scoundrels and death squads, and it depressed him

As a safeguard, he had Tarciana, Luz, and Jose Velasquez sign specimen signature cards at HSBC's Manila branch, forwarded to the Hong Kong central branch, to open an account that could be accessed by all three. He obliged Luz and Tarciana to memorize all his aliases, his many companies, where they were registered, and all the banks where he had accounts. He gave them lists of the account numbers at each bank, code words and phrases, and all the paperwork needed to gain access to the accounts.

He was drinking more heavily, and his liver was in bad shape. By late August, Tarciana noticed "restlessness and uneasiness... he was very sick and short of [breath]". On September 13, 1974, he collapsed and was admitted to the San Juan de Dios Hospital in Pasay City. At his bedside, he told Tarciana it was time to open the safe-deposit boxes. He gave her the insurance policies of all the trust certificates, and handed her a piece of paper about the color code, plus "many instructions, quotations and stories about his exploits and adventures of his life".

In the hospital on September 21, he wrote out in long-hand a new four-page will: "I'm pressed for Time, so no matter how incoherent this peace [*sic*] of note may seem Please Take it in the light it is given." He makes reference to the terms of his Malacanang Palace will, which he was forced by Marcos to sign. In this new will he mentions a number of 'live' (active) bank accounts at HSBC's Hong Kong main branch, and others at Citibank Manila. He names fourteen people as beneficiaries of sums from several bank accounts. From numbered accounts at Citibank Manila he authorized distribution of over $65-million. From HSBC's Hong Kong branch, he authorized distributions in excess of $200-million, and another in excess of $80-million. Another $120-million at HSBC was set aside for 'the people of Leyte' and for 'all the people I've forgotten to mention'. There were also distributions to be made from his personal account in the Citibank branch in the Philippine city of San Juan, of over $50-million, plus another 10-million in pesos. The beneficiaries include his two sons by his first marriage, Peter and Roy Diaz, here called by their Spanish names Pedro and Rolando. (This holographic will has been probated before courts in the Philippines and the United States, and is reproduced in our CDs.)

After twelve days in the hospital, his daughter Flordeliza Tantoco Santa Romana (often called just Liza Tan), discharged her father into her own care. Santy was afraid to leave the hospital but Liza wanted him to die at home. She took him to his house in Cabanatuan City, where he died in bed a few days later. The cause of death was cirrhosis of the liver.

According to a knowledgeable source in the Marcos family, Major General Lansdale immediately arranged to move 'all of Santy's remaining gold bullion at Citibank Manila' to Citibank's main office in New York City. Exactly how he could do this is difficult to say, unless he was able to contrive a power of attorney in Santy's name. One motive certainly was to get the gold out of Manila before it could be expropriated by Marcos.

With another wave of the magic wand, some of Santy's big accounts at other banks, notably one at UBS Geneva said to contain 20,000 metric tons of gold and listing Santy as the holder of record, were changed to list Major General Lansdale as the holder of record. (UBS documents spelled his name Landsdale, evidently as part of the agreed coding.) Did Lansdale have these accounts moved to bring them under greater CIA control, or under greater control by The Enterprise and its powerful conservative backers, including the John Birch Society and the World Anti-Communist League? The answer is surely the latter.

If Marcos thought Santy's death would give him control of all those accounts, he was disappointed. His relationship with the CIA and the White House was becoming turbulent. He thought he could manipulate them. The White House and CIA thought they could manipulate him. They were both right, so long as there was more gold to recover, and Santy's dormant accounts were there to fight over.

CHAPTER ELEVEN

POINTING THE WAY

When Santy died in 1974, magazines and newspapers already were calling President Marcos the richest man in Asia, with holdings estimated from $10-billion to $100-billion. Curiously, the source of his wealth could not be explained. With a grin, Marcos told people he had found Yamashita's Gold. They thought he was joking. But a number of people were shown around Marcos vaults stacked with gold bars, some with strange markings. Maybe it was not a joke. General John Singlaub, one of the original CIA Cold Warriors who knew all about Santy's recoveries, added his assurance that "Marcos's $12-billion fortune actually came from [Yamashita's] treasure".

What greatly enlarged Ferdinand's assets was the reappearance of Ben Valmores, the Filipino valet of Prince Takeda, present during the inventory and sealing of many Golden Lily vaults during the war. It was Ben that enabled a Marcos team to find and recover treasure from Teresa-2, from the sunken cruiser *Nachi*, and other sites. We last saw Ben in June 1945 at Tunnel-8, the underground complex near Bambang where 175 Japanese chief engineers were given a farewell drinking party before being buried alive. At midnight, when General Yamashita and Prince Takeda ('Kimsu') were leaving the cavern, and dynamite charges were about to be set off, the prince refused to leave Ben inside. Over Yamashita's angry protests, he took Ben to the surface and led him to safety. Moments later, a huge explosion shook the ground.

"Kimsu had promised my papa that he would bring me home when the war was over," Ben told us. "So he would not let Yamashita leave me inside. When we were in front of my uncle's house, Kimsu told me he was leaving that night to go back to Japan on a submarine. He gave me his sword, and his tunic. He said I must never change my character. Always obey my father. He thanked me for being loyal to him. Then he gave me his satchel of treasure maps and told me to bury it in a box in the ground, and one day he would come back for it."

The prince then vanished into the night. As instructed, Ben buried the satchel behind Uncle Lino's house, inside a stout wooden box. General Yamashita surrendered to the U.S. Army three months later.

Many years passed before Ben dug up the satchel. In the meantime the roads around Dulao and Bambang were full of American soldiers. Ben befriended them, and was given a job working in a field kitchen. He sold the GIs rusty Japanese swords and campaign medals. Once he hitched a carabao to an abandoned Japanese Army truck, one of many hidden in the forest near Indiana barrio, and pulled it to Dulao where he sold it to some GIs for $5. He sold fifteen trucks in all. In those days, you could get a full meal of rice and pork for only five cents.

When the American soldiers had gone, and life in the Cagayan Valley returned to normal, Ben got out Takeda's sword and white uniform. The tunic fit him well. On the left breast still was the embroidered red chrysanthemum. Ben wore it a few times till his father warned him that people might call him a traitor. After that he only wore it inside their house. The samurai sword he used at harvest time, to cut the ripened stalks of rice, until there was nothing left of the blade. He did not realize that it had been given to Prince Takeda by his grandfather, Emperor Meiji. Twenty years passed, but Prince Takeda did not come back.

To provide for Ben's future, the prince had buried two large steel trunks full of gold ingots. It had taken five carabao and fifteen soldiers to drag each trunk into the pit under a giant mango tree near Pingkian Bridge. Takeda had told him, when the war was over Ben must dig up the boxes, buy a large ranch, marry the pretty girl who had caught their eye in Dulao, and raise lots of children. But until the American soldiers left, Ben was afraid to go near the bridge.

In 1949 a Manila attorney named Benitez, who knew Uncle Lino, came to Bambang. He said he was looking for the Filipino boy who had been with the Japanese at San Fernando during the war. Ben's uncle said that was his nephew. He said Ben was 'crazy' – always wanting to dig for treasure. "Let's go, Papa, let's dig there, and there," Lino mimicked. "He knows where they buried the treasure, but his father tells him not to mess with it because of the booby traps."

When Ben got home from working in the fields, he told Benitez that he knew nothing about treasure. Right in front of the attorney, Uncle Lino reminded Ben about the two steel trunks the prince had left for him. The attorney was excited and insisted that he and Ben go immediately to Pingkian to recover the trunks. Ben could keep one, the attorney the other. Early next morning they drove with a group of sturdy farm workers to the barrio by the Pingkian River. An old man was waiting for them, the headman of the barrio. Benitez pretended he was surprised to find the mayor waiting, and said: "You know, mayor, we have a really important business matter to discuss."

"Let's go upstairs," the mayor said. Ben was left downstairs with the other men to breakfast on cold boiled sweet potatoes. When the two conspirators returned, the headman told Ben, "You know, a civilian like you is not allowed to hold gold in his possession. That is why the partition of 50/50 is no good. Our government does not allow that. I will give you one bar, as your reward for pointing us to it."

Ben looked at Attorney Benitez, who nodded his head gravely.

"Okay," Ben said. "Let's go now. You don't have to give me anything. I just want to see what is in the boxes." He took them to an acacia tree by the river, instead of to the mango tree. He watched them dig all day, quietly chuckling to himself. When the sun went down and they had found nothing, Ben said, "Maybe the Japs dug it up and put it somewhere else."

Benitez looked up at the tree and said, "You told me it was under a mango tree. This is an acacia tree."

"I thought it was a mango tree."

On their way back to Dulao, Ben told the attorney, "It's a good thing I got to know you early, because you think you are smart enough to fool me." When they got home, Ben told his Uncle Lino what the two men had tried to do. Benitez had a lot of explaining to do. Ben left them to it, and went outside to have a good laugh by himself.

Afraid that the Pingkian mayor would capture and torture him, Ben did not go back for many years. The river was in NPA (New People's Army) territory, and Ben did not want to be kidnapped by the Marxists. When he finally went back in 1999 with a friend, they discovered that a huge typhoon had caused flash floods that swept away the Pingkian Bridge and the entire embankment where the two trunks were buried. Even the big mango tree was gone. Each of the trunks had weighed over one ton, worth millions of dollars. Now they were on the bottom of the Pingkian River, buried in the muck. So much for the ranch.

The pretty girl Kimsu fancied married somebody else. But Ben did marry and had children. When that first marriage ended, he married again and had two daughters, of whom he was very fond.

Twenty years after the war, Ben was still a poor rice farmer. He owned a little house in Dulao, smack in the midst of hundreds of Japanese hiding places, but he never had much luck finding them. When he did, he always was cheated or robbed. On quiet evenings, he sat looking at the cool mountain valleys dotted with cone-shaped hills. The maps Kimsu had given him were still buried behind the house. Ben had dug up the satchel several times to look for a map simple enough to decipher himself. They made no sense to him, so he put the maps back and re-buried the satchel, only keeping out a compass and magnifying glass.

Among treasure hunters it was common knowledge that such maps existed. There were three types: a white series showing the general location of each site; a red series like Ben had, coded with all the essential information needed to make a recovery if you understood the code; and a blue series of detailed engineering drawings in which all the information was presented in plain technical language. Some white series maps had been found in a church and were in circulation, but they did not give the coordinates needed to pinpoint a vault, or its depth.

In 1953, seven young Japanese came to see Ben, offering money for 'his' maps. They were too young to have been in the war, but somehow they knew the maps had been left with Ben, and they knew Ben lived in Dulao. Perhaps they were friends of Prince Takeda's children, or might have been the sons of the prince. They did not explain who they were. When Ben denied knowing anything about treasure maps and asked why they came to see him, they laughed, smiled and said, "We know you." Then they went away and never came back.

After the war, gold hunting became a cottage industry. Filipinos who claimed they knew where the Japanese hid gold were called Pointers. Every barrio had Pointers, gold junkies, con men, local priests or preachers, all with 'secret maps' and 'eyewitness' memory. For a substantial monthly retainer, they would take you to a secret site, and watch you dig. They had an uncanny sense of timing, and just before you were ready to give up, the Pointer would vanish to find another sucker.

Ben had no interest in being a Pointer. He kept his oath to Kimsu. He only talked with his father about sites around Bambang. Ben's visual memory was flawless. He remembered how he had gone with Kimsu to each of the sites, and how he watched while the prince walked around with the blue series engineering drawings, and did a final inventory before ordering the vault closed. The minute treasure hunters pressed Ben for details, he clammed up.

He was by no means the only eyewitness – there were POWs who survived, Taiwanese slave laborers who escaped, Filipinos and a few Americans like John Ballinger who saw the Japanese hiding gold. A family that owned pastureland at the Indiana site were rumored to have made a recovery. They became VIPs in Bambang, put up a three-storey building in town, and went into business providing cable TV shows downloaded from three large satellite dishes. Ben was the only one present at all 175 'imperial' sites, and he stayed poor.

Once he dug up a small gold Buddha, four inches tall. He could have bought a small ranch, but he did not know its value and traded it for a radio. He was just twenty-two years old then. He remained a humble, good-natured man, affectionate to his wife and children, kind, and quick to laugh.

Only in the mid-1960s, when Ferdinand Marcos began making onshore and off-shore recovery deals with the Japanese, was official hostility relaxed, and Japanese began coming back to the Philippines in significant numbers to hunt for treasure. Small groups came to the Cagayan Valley every year. One team searched around the Bambang cemetery where Ben had watched Kimsu's naked slave laborers dig deep pits and tunnels leading down to a very big circular vault rated as a 777 site – part of the complex that included Tunnel-8 and Tunnel-9. Ben did not recognize anyone in the group. One day they were gone. Villagers found a tree by the cemetery that had been cut down during the night with a chain saw, exposing the inside of the tree trunk. There they clearly saw where several gold bars had been hidden, leaving their impression in the wood as the tree grew around the bars.

At the end of 1968, President Marcos sent a team to Tokyo to make a deal for more effective joint recoveries. The team included Lieutenant Colonel Florentino Villacrusis, a senior intelligence officer; Brigadier General Onofre T. Ramos, comptroller of the Philippine armed forces; and two other officers. Their mission was to acquire a set of Golden Lily treasure maps in return for a share to Japan of whatever Marcos recovered. If Tokyo did not cooperate, Marcos warned that he would close down Japanese companies all over the islands.

In his first two years as president, Marcos had authorized offshore recoveries by a syndicate of Japanese and Korean gangsters, headed by Kodama and Machii Hisayuki, head of the *Tosei-kai*. Another partner was billionaire fixer Sasakawa Ryoichi, another of Kodama's Sugamo Prison cellmates, who staged speedboat races, one of Japan's favorite betting sports and a convenient way to launder money. His true wealth came from secret deals with President Sukarno and President Marcos to share in the recovery of war loot in Indonesia and the Philippines. "I was very close to Marcos," Sasakawa told journalists, "long before he became president." He pointed Marcos at several sites, including the sunken cruiser *Nachi* in Manila Bay, and in return was allowed to build cemeteries and memorials for Japanese war dead in the Philippines, on property that just happened to include Golden Lily sites. "I personally donated the biggest cultural hall in [the Philippines]," Sasakawa boasted, "as well as supplied the cement." Forty thousand sacks, to be precise.

When the Villacrusis team arrived in Tokyo in 1968, Kodama and Sasakawa told them that the head of Golden Lily, Prince Chichibu, had died of tuberculosis in the early 1950s. But they arranged for Villacrusis to have a private audience with another aristocrat who had worked for Prince Chichibu. According to members of the Villacrusis family, this was "a ranking Japanese officer who was a cousin of Emperor Hirohito". This shadowy figure, high up in Japan's intelligence services, told Ramos and Villacrusis that the Japanese had hidden over $100-billion worth of treasure in the Philippines and it would take 'more than a century' to recover it all. In his memorandum of the meeting, Villacrusis identified this Japanese aristocrat only as Ishihara, which Villacrusis – with his Spanish language background – spelled phonetically as 'Lord Ichibarra'. Many documents later recovered from the Presidential Security Command after Marcos lost power refer to secret contacts in Tokyo with 'Lord Ichibarra'. From these documents, it is evident that Ishihara was one of Prince Chichibu's key men, hiding loot in Luzon during 1942-1945, a walking encyclopedia of Golden Lily. He appears to have been a senior intelligence officer working with Kodama and Prince Chichibu during the war. But all our efforts to identify Ishihara have failed. It is a common Japanese name that can be spelled various ways. After the war, SCAP forced Japan to abandon its titled aristocracy, so the use of such a title in 1968 was anachronistic. He may not have been a prince, but a count or baron. Ishihara may have been a pseudonym to keep the Filipinos from knowing who he really was. Or he could have become a 'lord' after the war, among those privately given honors by Emperor Hirohito in recognition of wartime service. We considered the possibility that Ishihara was a pseudonym for Prince Takeda, but concluded that they were two different men. Ishihara's willingness to conspire with President Marcos does not square with the personal loyalties of Prince Takeda. 'Kimsu' would have kept Marcos away from Ben Valmores, but Ishihara steered him to Ben.

One Japanese source told us Ishihara might be the notorious Colonel Tsuji Masanobu, reviled for the *Sook Ching* massacres of ethnic Chinese in Singapore and Malaya, and for eating an Allied pilot's liver. After *Sook Ching*, he was sent to Manila as troubleshooter with the rank of 'Imperial Inspector General'. True to form, Tsuji became a key figure responsible for the Bataan Death March when he bypassed mild-mannered General Homma and urged field officers to murder Allied prisoners during the march. When he was in areas controlled by the Imperial Navy, Tsuji had the navy rank of captain. In areas controlled by the army, he changed uniforms and became a colonel. Although he made frequent trips to Tokyo by plane the next two years, and put in appearances at Guadalcanal and other battles, he is said to have spent most of 1943 and 1944 in Luzon working with Kodama and keeping an eye on Golden Lily treasure sites in and around Manila. Late in 1944, Tsuji moved to Burma and Siam, and was in Bangkok in August 1945 when Japan surrendered, eluding capture.

Tsuji or not, Ishihara arrived in Manila in mid-1942, wearing a naval uniform. Japanese ships were unloading plunder at the Manila docks, and it was then taken by truck convoy to Fort Bonafacio. Like Fort Santiago, Fort Bonafacio had a prison full of suspected spies and saboteurs. On a visit to Bonafacio, Ishihara came upon a prisoner hanging by his thumbs from a flagpole halyard, and made a wry remark in Japanese. To his surprise, the prisoner replied in fluent Japanese. Ishihara asked how he came to speak the language. The prisoner replied that his mother was Filipina but his father had been a Japanese officer attached to the embassy in Manila.

"What is your name?" Ishihara asked.

"Leopoldo Giga," the man answered. His friends called him Pol, he added.

"Giga is a Japanese name," the navy captain said. In fact, a Major Giga was famous for helping assassinate the Manchurian warlord, Chang Tso-lin, in 1928. This, it turned out, was Pol Giga's father. Major Giga had served as a Japanese intelligence officer all over East Asia. While stationed in Manila in the early 1920s, he had married a Filipino woman and had a son. The boy grew up speaking Japanese, English and Tagalog, but was left behind when his father went off to other postings in Shanghai and Mukden. In 1938, Major Giga himself was assassinated in Japan by agents sent by the murdered warlord's son.

Ishihara ordered soldiers to untie the prisoner and had Giga released into his custody. From then on he employed Giga as an interpreter and informant. To test Pol's loyalty and cold-bloodedness, Ishihara had him put on a hood and review all the prisoners at Ft. Bonafacio. Giga and Ishihara sat at a table while the prisoners walked by, and the hooded Giga nodded whenever he spotted a man who he thought was secretly working for the Americans. All those men were executed immediately. The word for a traitor in Tagalog was 'Makapili', but the hood hid Giga's identity.

From then on, Pol Giga was Ishihara's man in Luzon. It was Ishihara who worked with Japanese engineers to design four treasure vaults at Manila's Fort Santiago, including the booby traps. Pol arranged for a Filipino electrician from Cavite to help wire the booby traps.

When Ishihara moved his operations from Manila to the countryside, under army control, he changed into the uniform of a colonel and arranged for Giga to be given the rank of lieutenant in the Japanese 16th Army engineering corps. Giga said he was sent to Japan for six months to learn tunneling technology. But Giga proved to be such a chameleon, taking on whatever color suited the occasion, that his story changed constantly.

In Tokyo twenty-five years later, in 1968, Ishihara told Colonel Villacrusis that the best way to recover a full set of the Golden Lily treasure maps for President

Marcos would be by finding Pol Giga. Then Villacrusis could have Giga track down Ben Valmores, the wartime valet of Prince Takeda. The prince, he explained, had left a whole set of maps with Ben at the end of the war, in the event that the submarine taking him back to Japan was sunk. He told Villacrusis that Giga was employed by the Colgate toothpaste factory in the Philippines. So it is evident that Ishihara had been in contact with Giga since the war. Ishihara said that Giga supplemented his Colgate income by serving as a translator, pointer and fixer for Japanese groups digging for gold. Giga hired cars, drill rigs, generators, and jackhammers, so the Japanese did not attract unwelcome attention. Villacrusis asked how would they know that Giga had found the right Ben Valmores? Ishihara said they could put Ben on the telephone directly with Prince Takeda, and they could all listen to the conversation. If he were the right Ben Valmores, they would know immediately.

On his return from Tokyo, Villacrusis immediately sent security men to find Giga at Colgate, and had him brought to the Presidential Security Command. Giga was scared, ready to do whatever was asked of him. Finding Ben Valmores, he said, would not be difficult. He had seen Ben many times during the war, accompanying his prince, who had been based most of the time in the barrio of San Fernando, outside Bambang, and Ben's family had lived somewhere nearby. So Giga took time off from Colgate and caught a bus into the mountains.

When Giga knocked on his door in Dulao early in January 1969, Ben Valmores had no idea who he was. Giga claimed that during the war he and Ben had spoken often at different Golden Lily sites, where Giga claimed he was personally involved in the inventories. Ben knew this was not true because only Prince Takeda did inventories, and he was certain he had never seen Giga before. Giga said he always had worn a Japanese uniform, so how could Ben remember him among all the other soldiers? Their relationship was strained from the beginning, because Ben sensed that Pol was a devious and unreliable character. Later, Ben discovered that Pol was telling everybody that he – Giga – had been the prince's valet, and the prince had given the maps to him, not to Ben. Giga claimed to have buried the map satchel, then dug it up after the war, and that only he had the true copies. For a retainer of a thousand dollars a month, Giga would show people where to dig. (When our researcher tracked down Giga in 1986, he insisted that Ben had died the previous year; that both he and Ben were mestizo, half Filipino, half Japanese, which also was untrue. Then he recounted how he and Ben had "stolen the maps from General Yamashita's headquarters in Baguio" in the closing weeks of the war. It was only later that we discovered that Giga had lied to keep us from talking to Ben.)

Giga stayed in Dulao several weeks, trying to win Ben over. To fend him off, Ben pretended he spoke only Ilocano, but Giga switched to Japanese, saying he knew Ben had learned basic Japanese during the war. Giga said he came as an emissary from President Marcos who wanted Ben's maps to make gold recoveries that would permanently lift Filipinos out of poverty. Ben doubted this, because the reputation of Ferdinand Marcos was evil, and Imelda's million-dollar shopping sprees were making headlines. Finally, Giga dropped all pretence and said if Ben refused to turn over the maps, soldiers from the Presidential Security Command would take him and his whole family to Bilibad Prison, where they would be tortured, Ben's daughters would be abused, and all of them killed. Ben still refused.

He was frightened for his wife and children, but he had given his oath to Kimsu. Twenty-three years had passed since Prince Takeda had gone back to Japan. Ben had sworn to guard the maps for thirty years, so there were seven years to go. The prince had never returned, and had never contacted Ben. For all he knew, Kimsu was dead. Nevertheless, Ben had never revealed Kimsu's real name to anyone. Not once had he mentioned the names of Prince Chichibu, Prince Mikasa, and Prince Asaka. Finally, Ben decided on a compromise to protect his family.

Early one morning, he dug up the satchel again. First he set aside the blue series maps, which were the engineering drawings. He wrapped these in plastic, placed them in a strong box and immediately reburied them. Next he studied the red series maps. There were 175 red series maps in all. Ben set aside his three favorite sites for himself. These were the maps of Tunnel-8 and Tunnel-9, near Bambang, and Montalban east of Manila. The red series maps were on sheets of stout paper, heavily waxed after the drawings were finished. They provided a 3-dimensional view of the terrain. Movie audiences who watched Akira Kurosawa's classic film, *Seven Samurai,* saw a similar map drawn by the samurai as they prepared to defend the village from bandits. Added to the stylized drawing was vital coded information – a Japanese flag flying to the right or left showed whether the map must be read the way it was or in a mirror; a clock-face with two or more hands provided information about compass orientation, depths and booby traps; other icons showed exactly what treasure was in which part of each site. Most important, the red series maps indicated the fulcrum point for each site. Without knowing the fulcrum point, you would never know the correct depth or bearings. (We reproduce several red series maps on our CDs.) Of the remaining 172 red series maps, Ben selected forty that he thought were minor, or very difficult. If he was pressed, and his family was in peril, he could give this bundle of forty to Giga to take to Marcos.

A few days later, Colonel Villacrusis himself came to Ben's house, banging on the door in the middle of the night, yelling: "Ben, Ben!"

Ben let him in. Villacrusis said he was on a special mission for the president, to get the maps. Ben said he could not comply, because of his oath to Kimsu. Villacrusis said, "We will honor your words!" He would not take the maps by force. But Ben had to come with him to Manila to show the maps "only to the president – and then we will give them back to you".

Realizing he had no choice, Ben handed Villacrusis the map bundle of forty minor sites. Villacrusis was so fascinated that he did not ask to see the others.

Thoroughly scared, Ben rode down from the mountains with Villacrusis in his chauffeured army staff car, carrying the maps in an old leather case. Instead of going to Malacanang Palace, they drove to the home of Brig. Gen. Onofrio Ramos, the army comptroller who had gone with Villacrusis to Tokyo, to see Kodama, Sasakawa and Ishihara. In the general's secure basement office, a group of overweight cigar-smoking cronies were waiting, including several Marcos cabinet ministers. Mrs. Ramos served drinks as the men lit cigars and talked. They were mightily pleased with themselves. The next question was whether to take Ben immediately to Malacanang Palace to meet Marcos. Mrs. Ramos butted in: "If I were you I would not surrender this Ben, because you already have the key. Why are you going to give this Ben to the president when you already have the key?"

Unable to make up their minds, and reluctant to admit that she was right, they climbed into their cars and drove to the private hideout of Defense Minister Ernesto Mata, in the heights of Antipolo, east of Manila. Villacrusis showed Mata the forty mysterious maps. Mata took the leather folder and rooted around inside it like a wart-hog. Mata was one of the bully-boys of the Marcos regime, with a lot of blood and drool on his hands. He examined several of the maps, comprehending nothing, then said to Ben: "You killed the person who owned these."

"No, sir, I didn't kill for this."

"Then why is the portfolio in your hands?"

"Because he leave it to me."

"No, you killed him." Ben was very scared. He whispered to Villacrusis that he wanted to go home. Ben asked to have the maps back, as Villacrusis had promised, but they said President Marcos needed to see them. Villacrusis told Ben that after the president saw the maps they would be returned to Ben.

Mata had direct lines to the switchboard at Malacanang Palace. Using the secure palace switchboard, they placed the long-anticipated phone call to Ishihara in Tokyo. He had the call patched through to Prince Takeda at his ranch on the east side of Tokyo Bay. While the entire Marcos group listened in, the phone was handed to Ben. The next thing Ben heard was Kimsu's voice, out of the past:

"Benhameen." Their conversation was short but emotionally charged. When Kimsu started speaking to him in simple Japanese, Ben told us he could tell from the sound of his voice that Kimsu was choked with emotion, probably weeping. Kimsu reminded him of his oath never to give the maps to anyone but an imperial prince, repeating the Mantra: "Benhameen, please, no Filipinos, no Americans, no Japanese, no Chinese, just wait for me." Defense Minister Mata grabbed the phone away from Ben and put it in its cradle. It was to be Ben's last direct contact with Kimsu. The Marcos men cheered, waved their cigars in the air, and began high-fiving. This was the right Ben. They decided not to take him to Marcos, now that (as Mrs. Ramos said) they had the key. After all their posturing, Villacrusis, Ramos and Mata never did show a single one of the red series maps to Marcos.

When they left Mata's hilltop hideaway, Villacrusis kept the bundle of forty maps to study, giving Ben the empty old leather folder. He also gave Ben some travel money. This was only one of many flashes of kindness Villacrusis displayed. He was not as ruthless as the others. He was content to have forty of the maps. If you could not understand forty, what was the point of having more? He knew he could get the rest from Ben any time he wished, because Ben was afraid for his wife and children. Thankful to be alive, Ben fled back to Bambang.

In this clumsy, oafish, bullying manner began the big Marcos gold recoveries of the 1970s and early 1980s. Equipped for the first time with real Golden Lily maps, which none of them could understand, Marcos and his lieutenants thought it would be easy. They were wrong.

Initially, Villacrusis was successful in excavating a site at Santa Mesa Rotunda, where he recovered a mixed variety of gold bars from various Asian countries, and a number of small solid gold Buddhas looted from temples and pagodas. Encouraged, President Marcos put together a special unit of army engineers and set them to work digging at a site in Laguna, where they uncovered several concrete vaults filled with gold bars. (See Chapter Fifteen.) Marcos's first really big recovery as president was from a Golden Lily vault beneath the flagpole at Camp Aguinaldo. Next, Marcos sent his soldiers to the officers' club at Fort Bonafacio – previously called Ft. McKinley – where he had them dig down to General MacArthur's bomb shelter. There they discovered one end of the 35-miles of tunnels under Manila. After two years of exploring these tunnels, they found only one gold bar in the back of an abandoned army truck. The spur tunnels and treasure vaults hidden by Golden Lily were too well disguised.

Ishihara continued to be helpful. When the Marcos protégé Dr. Gil Gadi ran into trouble digging at Ft. Santiago, he turned to Ishihara for expert advise. A memo to Marcos from Brigadier General Santiago Barangan reports: "Dr. Gadi says because of difficulties he encountered at the Ft. Santiago site, he wrote to Lord Ichibarra in Tokyo, and Lord Ichibarra told him to contact Pedro Lim from Laguna, who had worked with Colonel Yagura and Captain Yamaguchi, who were members of Lord Ichibarra's team in the hiding of the war loot in Luzon. Pedro Lim then referred Dr. Gadi to Benjamin Irruquia, the Filipino electrical engineer who installed and rigged the explosives [booby traps] at Ft. Santiago for Lord Ichibarra."

For Ben, who knew where all the gold vaults were, life in Dulao and Bambang continued in its cyclic pattern of wet rice planting and harvest. The one exception was when Ben became friends with Roger Roxas, the Baguio locksmith who came to Bambang periodically to hunt for buried loot. Over the years Roxas and Ben became friends, and one day Ben agreed to give Roxas a Golden Lily map showing the location of the warren of tunnels behind the Baguio hospital. When Roxas discovered the Gold Buddha, he also found a magnificent gold model of the famous Cathedral of Reims, in France, and gave it to Ben as his share in the recovery. The cathedral was nearly half a meter tall, as big as a wedding cake, beautifully hand-crafted, and correct in every detail of the original medieval church, except that in place of the big round stained glass window over the main entrance, the gold model had a finely-made clock. Nobody knew its provenance, except that it came from Vietnam. Such treasures have their own secret lives. But it was clearly the work of a master goldsmith, made for a wealthy patron of the Catholic Church in Hanoi, Hue, or Saigon. As a work of art at auction in London or New York, its value would doubtless exceed its gold content. When he saw what then happened to Roxas and the Gold Buddha, Ben re-buried the cathedral in a box in the yard of his house in Dulao. Later, when General Fabian Ver heard from Pol Giga that Ben had recovered a solid gold cathedral, Ver sent thugs to Ben's house and threatened to terrorize his wife and children if Ben did not give it to them. Ben complied. Ten years later the only thing Ben still possessed, given to him by Kimsu, was a Japanese campaign medal, showing an airplane, carabao, thatch hut, coconut tree and paddy field. Everything else had been stolen, 'confiscated' or lost. "All they ever gave me,"

Ben said about Marcos and his cronies, "was cigarettes." Children were born, treasure hunters came and went, Ben remained poor.

In 1972 Ben heard that a group of Japanese had arrived in Bambang, and were working with bulldozers and backhoes in the area where General Yamashita's camp had been, more than half a mile from Kimsu's camp at San Fernando. Ben laughed that they were digging in the wrong place. He was mistaken. When Ben had toured the underground complex with Kimsu, they had gone down through the Tunnel-8 entrance, which Ben thought was the only one. He did not know there was a separate entrance for Tunnel-9. In 1945, the connecting tunnels were blown up, but the main vaults, lined with steel-reinforced concrete, were intact.

These Japanese re-opened the Tunnel-9 entrance, leading down to Yamashita's bomb-proof command center. In daylight hours they stayed out of sight belowground. A neighboring farmer said that at night empty trucks arrived that left loaded before dawn. With Marcos making moves on other Golden Lily sites, Prince Takeda may have authorized the recovery of part of the Bambang complex. It is unlikely that they recovered all, because that would have involved re-opening the connecting tunnels to Tunnel-8 and the Cemetery site.

We do know that Takeda personally returned to Manila two years later, in 1974, by which time the Tunnel-9 recovery was complete.

Since leaving Ben and returning to Japan by submarine in June 1945, Takeda had been warmly received by his cousin Hirohito for having successfully completed his mission. He was then sent to Manchuria as chief financial officer of the Imperial Army there for the last months of the war. At war's end, he was given the assignment of ensuring that the Kwantung Army in Manchuria complied with Hirohito's order to surrender. After that, Takeda went home to his wife and children in Tokyo. When the peerage system was ended, Takeda forfeited his hereditary title and became simply Mister Takeda Tsuneyoshi. This brought an end to one of Japan's great princely houses, Takeda-no-miya, founded in 1906 at the wish of the Meiji Emperor, Takeda's grandfather. Like other former princes, to avoid having his properties seized by the Allies, Takeda sold his estates to the wealthy Tsutsumi family, to whom he remained closely allied for the rest of his life. He kept only one estate, a sprawling ranch in Chiba Prefecture on the eastern side of Tokyo Bay. Like other princes, he tried to become a businessman, starting the Takeda Knitting Machines Company, but it soon went under. When the Americans went home, Takeda quietly resumed his life as one of Japan's top aristocrats. Money was never a problem. After all, he had helped enrich the entire Japanese establishment, a debt that could never be repaid. Tiring of the ugliness of Tokyo, he spent most of his time at his Chiba ranch, where he raised prized thoroughbred horses, one of the world's most expensive hobbies. He became president of the Japan Olympic Committee in 1962, and was a member of the International Olympic Committee from 1967 to 1981. (His son continues this IOC tradition.)

A profile of Takeda in the *Japan Times* in April 1964 concluded with these remarks: "If it were possible to sum up Takeda in a single word, the adjective for him would be 'relaxed'. Completely free from self-consciousness and tension, he breathes genuine warmth and generous friendliness. A text by his desk urging

adherence to truth, fairness, and goodwill in everyday actions suggests the principles by which he is guided... If you wanted to espouse the cause of royalty, you
need look no further for the perfect model..."

In 1974, Takeda flew to the Philippines when a Japanese straggler, Second
Lieutenant Onoda Hiroo, was discovered hiding on 74-square-mile Lubang Island,
70 miles southwest of Manila Bay. Back in 1945, all but three Japanese soldiers on
Lubang had been killed or surrendered during a four-day battle with the Americans.
Onoda and two comrades fled into the jungle and for the next thirty years kept up
sporadic guerrilla warfare. In the 1950s, leaflets were dropped telling them the war
was over, but they thought it was a trick. Both of Onoda's companions eventually
died of tropical diseases, and Onoda himself was declared legally dead in Japan.
Lubang villagers said otherwise. When a young Japanese named Suzuki Norio
tracked Onoda down in the jungle in February 1974, he still carried his rifle, 500
rounds of ammunition, and several hand grenades.

Onoda refused to surrender unless released from duty by his commanding officer. Ben heard all about Onoda from television news. He knew Onoda personally,
having spent weeks on Lubang during the war with Prince Takeda, closing a treasure vault. Ben knew it was Takeda who had ordered Onoda to guard the site at
Lubang, so only the prince himself could rescind the command. A few weeks later,
a group of Japanese officials arrived in the Philippines to persuade Onoda to surrender. Attention was focused on Major Taniguchi Yoshima, who was presented to
TV audiences as Onoda's commanding officer. But among the Japanese delegation
in the background Ben saw Prince Takeda's unforgettable face and knew that he had
come personally to release Onoda from his oath. A few days later, Onoda returned
to Japan. (Claiming that he could not adjust to life in modern Japan, Onoda was
then sent to Brazil, to a big Japanese-owned ranch in the Mata Grosso. There bodyguards made sure nobody came to quiz him about the Lubang treasures, until they
were recovered.)

The Lubang recovery was done by Sasakawa, under the guise of developing
Lubang into a resort for wealthy Japanese tourists. Sasakawa said he was doing this
'at the request of Marcos'. Eventually, when hotels and golf courses had been built,
the resort was stocked with African wild game and exotic birds for rich Japanese
hunters, who were provided with young male or female 'private companions' for
sexual sport. At the same time, President Marcos made Sasakawa an honorary citizen of the Philippines, in recognition of his many donations to Imelda's highly-
publicized relief projects, and for his efforts to pave over residual ill-feeling about
the war by establishing the Japan-Philippines Friendship Society. Nothing was said
of Sasakawa sharing war loot with Marcos.

Although Prince Takeda did not go back to see Ben after the war, he did send an
emissary. In 1984, while Ben was living temporarily in Manila, a Japanese resembling a sumo wrestler got off the bus in Bambang one morning, lugging a heavy
suitcase. It was Colonel Kasabuchi, one of Takeda's staff officers during the war.
Now an old man with white hair, he was suffering from the heat, wiping the sweat
from his face with a soggy handkerchief. In a small town like Bambang there were
no taxis, just motorized trikes. The only trike at the bus stop was owned by Rangho,

who made his living hauling people and goods. Kasabuchi asked Rangho to take him to the barrio of San Fernando. When Rangho tried to help with the suitcase, Kasabuchi would not let it go. He held it on his lap all the way to San Fernando. He told Rangho he was looking for a man named Benhameen. Kasabuchi could not remember Ben's last name. Nor could he remember which barrio Ben came from originally. He told Rangho that Ben had been a valet for a Japanese prince during the war, here at San Fernando. Kasabuchi had come all the way from Tokyo to bring Ben a gift from the prince. Several times, Rangho offered to carry the suitcase, but the colonel would not let him touch it. They spent the day riding around in the trike, trying to find anyone who knew Ben. If they had gone to the barrio of Dulao, only a kilometer and a half away, everyone would have known Ben and they could have told the colonel exactly where to find him in Manila. At the end of the day, when he and Rangho decided they had exhausted all the possibilities, Kasabuchi reluctantly got aboard the last bus to Manila, taking the suitcase of gifts with him. Ben stayed poor.

CHAPTER TWELVE

SANCTIFYING THE GOLD

Already a billionaire with his own tropical paradise, Marcos had a pathological streak – too much was never enough. He wanted everyone to know he was as rich as the Rothschilds, Saudis, and Oppenheimers. This would do him in.

He knew the Japanese were ripping him off, steering him away from big vaults. Without their help, recovering the best Golden Lily sites was difficult. Even with true maps and an eyewitness like Ben Valmores, you could not just pick a spot and start digging. Ben could take you there, but he knew nothing of the underground configuration. Even above ground, Ben could not be precise; trees had toppled, rivers changed course, new construction obliterated landmarks. If you missed by a few inches, months were wasted. Marcos decided to bring in a famous psychic and a clever mining expert. The mining expert would reverse-engineer Ben's maps, and the psychic could determine the precise position of the gold. Once their jobs were done, they could be eliminated.

Marketing the gold was another headache. By 1974, it was legal for the first time since 1933 for private American citizens to purchase gold. Accordingly, world gold prices started to rise. This put Marcos in an enviable 'long position' with a lot of gold to sell – if he could get the gold into the market. But the bars he recovered were not standard in size, purity, or hallmark, and had no legalizing paper trail. Aside from blackmarket deals where anything goes, gold normally is traded in standard size, weight and purity acceptable to the London gold market. Legitimate gold bars must have recognized hallmarks and identification numbers. They must be accompanied by proof of ownership, called a statement of origin, with a paper trail showing the record of transportation, security, insurance, and so forth. Almost all the treasure stolen by Golden Lily did not meet London standard. It came from Asian countries where gold was of inconsistent purity, usually 22 karats or less, not only from banks and treasuries but from the hoards of Overseas Chinese tycoons, Malay Moslem datos, Buddhist sects, druglords, triads, gangsters, ancient tombs, jewelry and artifacts. Ingots were all shapes and sizes, marked with odd signs and symbols, stamped or engraved in different languages. Each contained minerals and impurities, like a fingerprint, so an assay would reveal where it had been mined. At the end of World War II in Europe, the Allies got around this problem by re-smelting Nazi gold, erasing the fingerprint and any trace of ownership.

In the past, Marcos had avoided this problem by marketing the gold he recovered through the Japanese, or the CIA. Both would take irregular ingots, but only at a deep discount. In effect, the CIA would pay Marcos a finder's fee, as they had paid Santa Romana during his time as gatekeeper. Marcos tried blackmarket deals, swapping non-standard gold to Panama for cocaine, and to Thai druglords for heroin, but that created marketing headaches of another kind, when he had to find buyers for the narcotics.

If he was going to bypass the CIA and the Japanese and sell his gold on the world market, it had to be physically altered – a process called sanctifying – to conform to London gold standard. A member of the Gold Cartel would only do this for him at a deep discount, so Marcos had to find a private individual who could sanctify the gold and add the right impurities to prove it was legitimate gold from Philippine mines.

One possibility was a mining expert and metallurgist in Nevada named Robert Curtis. When Marcos attended a presidential conference at Cancun on the Gulf of Mexico, he discussed his gold problem with Costa Rica's president, Jose Figueres. Costa Rica also had gold mines, so Figueras was well informed. He told Marcos that Robert Curtis had developed a process to extract more gold from previously mined ores, and also could change gold's fingerprint to make it look as if it came from the Philippines. To track down Curtis, Marcos called in Norman Kirst, a hustler from Wisconsin who was doing him favors.

Ferdinand already had made contact with a famous psychic, Olof Jonsson, a Swede who had become a naturalized American citizen and was living in Chicago. Jonsson had helped the American deep-sea treasure hunter Mel Fisher locate the wreck of a seventeenth century Spanish galleon that sank with New World gold worth $140-million. Jonsson also had been hired by the U.S. Government to conduct experiments in telepathy with astronauts during the Apollo moon missions. In his work with NASA, Jonsson met a U.S. Air Force colonel who asked him to come to the Philippines to check out a treasure site on Clark Air Base. While Jonsson was a guest at Clark, word got around, and Colonel Villacrusis came to see him. He told Jonsson that treasure hunting on Clark was strictly forbidden. But Jonsson could be of great service to President Marcos, treasure hunting off the base.

Marcos always had imagined himself to be psychic, so when they met at Malacanang Palace he was deeply impressed by Jonsson. He told the psychic that his help was needed to find World War II treasure for the benefit of the Filipino people, to lift them out of poverty. He said he already knew many locations of hidden Japanese gold, but his men did not know exactly where to dig. Olof could be a great asset pinpointing the targets. Colonel Villacrusis was putting together an expert team, he said, called the Leber Group, for Rebel spelled backwards. Marcos wanted Olof to be a leading member of the Leber Group, and he would share generously in the rewards. Jonsson was charmed, and fascinated, and readily agreed.

Meanwhile, late in 1974, Robert Curtis received the first of a number of calls from Norman Kirst, phoning from the Philippines.

Curtis was the 44-year-old owner of a successful mining and refining business in Sparks, Nevada, near Reno. Starting out as a banker in San Francisco, he became fascinated by old silver and gold mines along the California-Nevada border. He acquired a number of these old mines, and built a factory in Sparks where he reprocessed the ore and developed new techniques to extract more gold, and other precious metals such as platinum and iridium. Most people did not know there was platinum to be mined in America, because the Gold Cartel discouraged hunting for platinum in order to control quantities and prices of the metal from its own mines in Africa. But Curtis independently developed processes to extract platinum from the ore he was recovering in the Sierras. This made him a modestly wealthy man.

Norman Kirst asked Bob Curtis if he would fly out to Manila to discuss setting up a refinery for President Marcos. He explained that Marcos wanted Curtis to re-smelt gold bars, change the hallmarks to Philippine official numbers and stamps, and alter the chemical composition so the gold would appear to have come from Philippine mines. What was staggering to Curtis was the amount of gold mentioned. Kirst said Marcos was hoping to process at least 300 metric tons of gold a year for the next ten years, or some 3,000 metric tons, for starters.

Thinking it over, Curtis did some homework. Historically, there was no way to account for so much gold coming from Philippine mines. In 1939 those mines produced their greatest quantity ever, one million troy ounces, or just over thirty-one metric tons. In the 1970s the Philippines were producing only 22 metric tons of gold each year. Because gold mine operations in the islands were sluggish and inefficient, it would be difficult to explain a sudden ten-fold jump in annual production. However, with a little patience, Marcos could slip small quantities into the market over a period of time. If the ingots were sanctified, he could sell them readily to private buyers.

After turning Kirst down several times, Curtis changed his mind when he got a long letter from him on February 22, 1975, revealing that the real source of the gold was Japanese loot. Kirst said: "There is a buried treasure on [American] Embassy grounds, Clark Air Force Base, Subic Naval Base ... there are exactly 34 locations of major importance and 138 locations of lesser importance. The Leber Group has retrieval plans for all 172 locations, but wish to only work on the 34 [major] locations, knowing that if they retrieve several of the 34 sites they will have done an excellent job." (This figure of 172 sites became fixed because Marcos did not know Ben had set aside three maps for himself, of Tunnel-8, Tunnel-9, and Montalban.)

"You will be taken to these sites, shown their original Japanese drawings."

"There is 777 billion Yen based on AU [gold] values in 1940... It is buried in Mosler vaults in tunnels... There is a 999 billion... There is an 888 billion Yen treasure..." On and on. Such numbers were nonsensical. The Marcos inner circle based these guesses on map markings with the yen sign followed by three digits and a long row of zeros. Without stopping to ask whether there might be a deceptive code involved, as in most other markings on the maps, they jumped to the conclusion that it meant a site held 777-billion yen worth of gold. Marcos was so excited he named his yacht the '777'. A more rational assumption would be that nobody knows how much treasure is in any of these sites. Some individual items are identified in the maps, such as gold Buddhas, or drums filled with gemstones, but values are not assigned. Whatever the current gold price, to find a single 75-kilo ingot would gratify all but the unhinged. For a multitude of reasons most treasure hunters, with or without maps, come up empty handed. Only a few succeeded, among them Marcos, thanks to Robert Curtis.

Curtis recalls: "I was incredulous. I had every reason not to believe in the treasure." He could not reconcile what Kirst said with accepted beliefs about total world gold production. Curtis was fascinated by the idea that there were big vaults of World War II treasure waiting to be reverse-engineered, with ingenuity and luck. He had to learn more before he decided what to do. He told Kirst he would fly to Manila for three days.

When he arrived at the end of February 1975, Curtis was met by Kirst and introduced to Marcos aides and associates, including General Fabian Ver. They were so friendly he had no way of knowing that half of them, including Ver, were professional killers. That would come later.

"In three or four days, I was convinced," Curtis told us. He had intended to stay three days, but stayed a month. What convinced him was the overwhelming physical evidence he was shown. He saw rooms full of gold bars, at Malacanang Palace in Manila, and at other locations. In one room alone, he calculated that he had seen $60-million in gold bars. As a banker, and a metallurgist, he knew it was real.

Marcos went out of his way to be a gracious host, and Curtis was impressed by his intelligence. Only later did he discover that Marcos was also 'a very ruthless man'. At their first meeting, Marcos said he needed help because international law held that any identifiable World War II treasures recovered must go back to the countries from which they were taken. He told Curtis he had recovered an enormous amount of gold, and would have to forfeit it unless the gold could be disguised.

On March 11-12, 1975, he took Curtis and other guests on a night cruise aboard the presidential yacht, a converted minesweeper. The ship took a hundred guests around Manila Bay while there was a banquet, followed by a dance. When the dance ended at midnight, the guests were dropped at the bay front, and the yacht cruised out into Manila Bay again with only the core members of the Leber Group and several foreign visitors. In addition to Robert Curtis, Olof Jonsson, and Norman Kirst, Curtis remembers 'an aide to [former] President Nixon' and 'an aide to President Ford' who took part in these secret meetings about the recovery of war loot. Nixon had resigned seven months earlier, succeeded by Ford. The Republican Party seemed likely to lose the 1976 presidential election because of the Watergate scandal. From the presence of the two aides, Curtis guessed that both Nixon and Ford somehow were participating in Marcos gold recoveries. Curtis wondered whether the two aides were government agents, or representing Nixon and Ford privately.

Curtis and Marcos spent much of the night in deck chairs under the stars, talking about the problem of black gold. Marcos portrayed himself as the president of a pro-American democracy who was fighting the good fight to improve the lot of his people, and to be a good ally to Washington in the Cold War. He explained the difficulty he was having, getting rid of the gold. Curtis said he thought the best idea was for Marcos to set up his own gold bank in Manila, rather than be involved in the hazards of selling it to other gold banks. With his own gold bank, Marcos could keep the gold and just lend derivatives, profiting hugely. This did not interest Marcos because it did not fit his flashy self image as the world's new Oppenheimer. Curtis asked him whether he had tried swapping the gold to Arab countries for oil, which he could then sell to Japan, ending up with clean money. Marcos liked the idea.

In the morning the yacht anchored off the presidential summer palace at Mariveles in Bataan. Curtis, Jonsson, and Kirst were taken ashore to Marcos's study where they saw the real Roxas Buddha. Curtis inspected the Buddha closely, satisfying himself that it was solid gold. There were nicks and scratches and tiny drill holes on the neck, making it obvious that it was not plated lead. Marcos showed how the head unscrewed. Even with help from Olof Jonsson, Curtis was unable to budge the massive weight. Next, Curtis was taken by General Ver to a large room in the basement, to examine rows and rows of gold bars. On their return, Marcos stood on the terrace and pointed to the hill behind the summer palace. He said he wanted Curtis to design underground vaults for that hill, each 80 feet wide and the length of a football field, where Marcos could store between 200,000 metric tons and 500,000 metric tons of bullion. He said the vaults he was using in Manila were already overflowing.

Again Curtis was astonished by the quantities Marcos mentioned, many times the amount of refined gold commonly thought to be in existence. But he had seen enough to convince him that the myth of gold being scarce was just like the myth of diamonds being scarce – to keep prices high.

On March 25, 1975, Curtis signed the Leber contract along with Olof Jonsson and others. They agreed "to pool their capabilities and resources together in order to search for, research, recover and retrieve …said treasure troves" in return for a share of the gold recovered "on Philippine land and waters".

As part of his participation, Curtis would provide two smelters from his Nevada factory. These would be shipped to Manila. One smelter would be installed at the National Development Co-op adjacent to Malacanang Palace, where it would be used to sanctify the gold to London standard, with appropriate hallmarks and numbers. The other smelter would be installed in a refinery to be built to Curtis's specifications on land next to an eel farm in Bataan. There, large quantities of previously refined ores, and new ores, could be subjected to the more efficient extraction process that Curtis had developed. The increased yield of gold from this new process would provide a plausible explanation for the overall increase in gold being sold from the Philippines. Some of the Marcos gold would be downgraded to look like crude miner's ingots, by adding silver and other metals to about 800 fineness. Miner's bars did not need to be registered and hallmarked, so they could enter the market in a trickle, without raising suspicion.

While Curtis was in Manila the first trip, Marcos put Olof Jonsson to the test.

General Ver took Jonsson and Curtis on a coast guard PT boat to the sector of Manila Bay where the Japanese heavy cruiser *Nachi* was sunk on November 5, 1944, to see if Jonsson could find it. There is controversy about the *Nachi* and various stories of how (and where) she met her end. One version is that after being damaged in a collision, needing extensive repairs in Japan, she was loaded with 100 metric tons of Golden Lily bullion at Cavite on Manila Bay, and then as she steamed out was deliberately torpedoed in Manila Bay by a Japanese submarine lying in wait. Crewmembers who rose to the surface were machine-gunned by the sub's crew. By this account, the *Nachi* was also towing a barge loaded with oil drums full of silver and gold coins, bound for Tokyo. A second torpedo hit the barge, which split in half, dumping the coins over a broad area of sand and mud bottom. Like other treasure ships intentionally scuttled by the Japanese, the *Nachi* went down in shallow water – about 100 feet. The official U.S. Navy report affirms that it was sunk in Manila Bay on November 5, 1944, but attributes the sinking to Allied aircraft. A Golden Lily map left with Ben Valmores showed the location of the hulk, and the precise nature of the treasure on board, but Marcos divers had not been able to find it in the murky water. Olof Jonsson was expected to find it with his psychic powers.

Tension surrounded this effort to pinpoint the *Nachi*, because Japanese divers also were searching for it. Marcos earlier had granted permits to Japanese salvage companies, but he did not want them diving on the *Nachi* now. As a safeguard, he nationalized the Luzon Stevedore Company, which he knew was working for the Japanese. General Ver ordered coast guard patrol boats to watch for any sign of Japanese divers.

As if Tokyo knew what was going on, Japan's prime minister chose this very moment to pay an informal visit to Marcos, bringing with him a delegation of relatives of the *Nachi* crew, including the widow of the ship's commander, Captain Kanooka Enpei. Saying they hoped to recover the human remains, the prime minister requested permission for Japanese salvage teams to search for bodies from the *Nachi*, and also to search for approximately four hundred other Japanese ships sunk in Philippine waters. Marcos refused.

Also aboard the PT boat with Curtis and Jonsson were Ben Valmores and Pol Giga, plus a group of Filipino divers and Ver's security men. Anchoring over the site indicated on Ben's map, the divers spent hours searching fruitlessly in the murky water. Jonsson waited patiently till they gave up, then insisted that they move starboard several hundred yards. The divers went down again and surfaced in minutes to shout that Jonsson had found the *Nachi*. As proof, they brought up the ship's bell. They attached floating buoys to the bow and stern of the hulk.

When they all returned to the site the following afternoon, the marker buoys were gone. Currents might have broken the lines, but it was too late in the day to relocate the ship. On the third day, Jonsson again found the *Nachi*, new buoys were securely attached, and Ver promised to leave a patrol boat to guard against intruders. But three days later when they returned to begin the physical recovery, the buoys again were gone. Something was fishy. Curtis hinted that Ver's own men had removed them. Ver claimed that his patrol boat had been obliged to leave the scene to escort the presidential yacht.

Actually, Curtis was getting his first taste of the real Ferdinand Marcos. Now that he knew exactly where the *Nachi* was, Marcos had no intention of sharing the recovery with anyone. He told Curtis and Jonsson to forget the ship and turn their attention instead to the most promising on-shore treasure sites.

According to several sources in the Marcos circle, he did recover the *Nachi* gold. The Leber Group's Amelito Mutuc, a former ambassador to the United States, told Curtis that the gold Marcos recovered from the *Nachi* was worth $6-billion in 1975, when gold was selling at $65 an ounce. This figure was confirmed to us by another Marcos source.

At the end of March, Curtis flew back to Nevada to wind up pressing business and to ship his smelting equipment to the Philippines. He had already decided, after studying some of the maps, that he could make a fairly quick recovery at Manila's Fort Santiago, then turn to a major site called Teresa-2, just southeast of Manila. According to Ben's Golden Lily map, Teresa-2 contained over $8-billion in gold bars in the back of a number of Japanese Army trucks that had been driven into one of the tunnels, plus three large solid gold Buddhas, and many oil drums filled with loose diamonds. Teresa-2 was only one part of a multi-tier complex. Once they were inside Teresa-2 they could penetrate the others.

Curtis had several employees in Nevada with engineering backgrounds. He planned to take them with him to Manila to assist in opening the treasure sites. This would cost him a lot up front for salaries, transportation, and the overseas living expenses. He had to foot the bill for shipping his two 6-ton smelters to the Philippines. He also would lose income otherwise generated by his Nevada operations. Marcos refused to pay the expenses of any Leber Group partners, so Curtis had to pay for everything out of his own pocket. From the Marcos point of view, Curtis was being given the chance of a lifetime – a sure thing for which Curtis should be prepared to sacrifice everything. Now he was hooked, Curtis wanted things to go smoothly. He had a lot of money tied up in his mines and in his Sparks factory and equipment, which he did not want to disturb. He would have to get a loan to cover expenses in the Philippines until he started pulling gold bars out of the ground. Since this venture was both extraordinary and secret, he could hardly approach a bank. So he contacted the John Birch Society. He knew its inner circle were heavily involved in precious metals. Several years earlier, they had approached Curtis.

"When the Hunt Brothers were trying to corner the world's silver production in the early 1970s," Curtis told us, "they sent Colonel Herbert F. Buchholtz to me… later came Jerry Adams… Robert Welch, founder of the Birch Society; Congressman Larry McDonald, and Jay and Dan Agnew, and Floyd Paxton."

The Birch Society was started in 1958 by a group of wealthy businessmen and far right politicians convinced that every closet in America contained communists, Jews, wetbacks, Afro-Americans, liberals and homosexuals. The Birchers also were dedicated gold and silver bugs. They had a longstanding grudge against U.S. presidents, starting with FDR, who had intervened to make private ownership of gold in America a crime, with penalties of heavy fines, confiscation and imprisonment.

They also believed that Nixon had sold the United States down the river twice – first by taking America off the gold standard, second by his recognition of Red China. On the other hand, Nixon's actions made it possible for the first time since 1933 for Americans to purchase and own gold legally. So Nixon opened up avenues for the Birch leadership to acquire gold overseas, and sneak it into America through the back door of Canada, where it added to the Society's fund for anti-communist activities. Like other ultra-conservative groups in America, and individuals like General Lansdale – one of their own – who had been forced out of the CIA and Pentagon by liberals, the Birchers had a long-term strategy to create their own right-wing vigilante force. Not something crude like Hitler's Brown Shirts or Gestapo. More like a private FBI, assisted by elite private military forces. This would cost money, hence the need for large amounts of privately held gold.

Although he was a conservative, and a patriot, Curtis was not a Bircher. But he shared their fascination with precious metals. Once he joined the Marcos gold hunt, Curtis told the Birch Society board confidentially about the hidden Japanese loot. He described his role in the Leber Group, and his participation with Marcos in sanctifying the gold, and in finding discreet channels to market it.

Curtis did not realize that the inner circle of the Birch leadership already knew about the Santa Romana recoveries, and the role of Robert B. Anderson and John J. McCloy in setting up the Black Eagle Trust. They also knew about the roles of Generals MacArthur, Whitney and Willoughby in the M-Fund, and all the financial manipulations in postwar Tokyo. They knew this because one of the founding members of the Birch Society was Colonel Laurence Bunker, a humorless fellow who had succeeded General Bonner Fellers on MacArthur's personal staff in Tokyo. Bunker became MacArthur's chief aide and spokesman in Tokyo from 1946-1951 – the years of witch-hunting in Japan that made the McCarthy witch-hunts in America look bland.

The Birch Society money men who arranged the loan for Curtis were Washington State senator Floyd Paxton and his son Jerry, who ran Kwik Lok Corporation, makers of the ubiquitous plastic clips used to close plastic bags in supermarkets. Another participant, Curtis said, was Jerry Adams of Atlanta, head of the Great American Silver Corporation, a precious metals company associated with the Hunt brothers. Curtis said he was informed by Congressman McDonald and Robert Welch that the loan for Curtis to work with Marcos had been 'cleared' by them personally. They told Curtis he was to deal directly with multi-millionaire Samuel Jay Agnew, who sat on the national council of the Birch Society.

They agreed to give Curtis three loans totaling $375,000 to cover his expenses in the Philippines. These loans were unsecured except for a promise from Curtis of 22.2 percent of his Leber share, and a 10 percent share in his Bataan refinery near the eel farm.

Buoyed by his success in getting financial support from the Birchers, and confident that he could easily pay it back in a few months with recovered gold, Curtis returned to the Philippines in the middle of April 1975. He was counting on making a quick recovery at Ft. Santiago, so it was only a matter of weeks or months before he would be a very rich man. He took along his partner John MacAllaster and John's wife Marcella, engineer Wes Chapman, and psychic Olof Jonsson. In a burst of generosity, Curtis bought first class plane tickets not only for his own people, but also for Jonsson.

During their reunion in Manila that April, Curtis told Marcos that he wanted to start by recovering the Mosler safes from the air vent at Fort Santiago, a straightforward recovery. This would allow him to pay off the Birch Society and get his own company back into production in Nevada.

Marcos did not care if Curtis ever paid back the Birch loan. If Fort Santiago was going to be so easy, why should he let Curtis do it?

Marcos lied to Curtis that Fort Santiago would require a special permit because it was a historic site, and told Curtis to choose a site outside Metro-Manila. He pressed Curtis again to engineer the two underground vaults behind the summer palace at Mariveles. Curtis gave that job to Wes Chapman, who did engineering drawings for two tunnels, each 80 feet wide by 300-feet long. Both tunnels were built, and visitors – one a full-time CIA officer – later attested that they were packed with gold.

Curtis was disappointed that he could not do the quick recovery at Ft. Santiago, but he was excited about working on Teresa-2, or another target. Col. Villacrusis took him to checkout forty treasure sites, with Ben Valmores and Pol Giga in tow, to determine which would be their first target. Each night he returned to the Philippine Village Hotel, a four-star hotel near Manila airport, where he shared a penthouse with John and Marcella MacAllaster, Wes Chapman, and Olof Jonsson.

When he was not visiting sites with Ben, Curtis spent most of his time in the penthouse studying the maps, finding the fulcrum points and trying to crack the codes. Each time he wanted to study a particular site, Ben traveled the long distance back to Bambang, where he retrieved the desired map and brought it to Manila. Eventually, Ben got tired of making the trip, and brought all the rest of the maps to Curtis, except the three he always kept for himself. It was a fateful decision.

The Leber Group now had a number of specialists studying the maps with Curtis, including Japanese language experts. Each map contained a drawing of at least one clock face, sometimes two or three. Some clocks had no hands, others had up to four hands. The numbers on each clock were sometimes conventional, sometimes in odd sequences, sometimes reversed. In all cases, markings between the numbers on the clocks were always different. Each map was a riddle.

With so many field trips during the day, Curtis had less and less time to linger over the maps, and no way to be sure they would not be taken away from him. So he photographed all 172 – taking first Polaroid, then 35 mm color shots. Because of his mania for record keeping, Curtis was accumulating piles of papers, photos, and tape recordings. He worried that the cleaning ladies might dispose of them. One day Marcella MacAllaster came back from a shopping trip with a three-tier lazy susan, hand carved from Filipino hardwoods. Curtis went to the same shop to send one to his wife in Nevada. As he watched the clerks packing old newspapers into the shipping crate, to pad the lazy susan, he asked if he could substitute his own paperwork. It would save him the expense of sending a separate package. He hurried back to the hotel and returned with three boxes of documents, notes, audiotapes, and photographs, including the photos he had taken of Ben's maps. It was a spur-of-the-moment decision that would save his life, and that of John MacAllaster.

Next day, Curtis recommended to Marcos that they tackle Teresa-2. According to Ben's maps, this was a 777 site, a big one. An army team sent by Marcos had already tried and failed to excavate Teresa-1. Both Teresa-1 and Teresa-2 were by an army base at a barrio called Teresa, a sleepy provincial town in Rizal, southeast of Manila. Here was an elaborate tunnel complex carved out of a limestone hill shaped like a sugarloaf, holding billions of dollars' worth of gold, platinum, diamonds, and three solid-gold Buddhas. Teresa was dug in 1943 by some 2,000 American, Australian, Dutch and Filipino prisoners of war. When the Japanese Army took over the existing military base, all local Filipino residents were moved away, and a prison camp was built. Just outside Teresa stood the peculiar sugarloaf, which was a calcium karst formation sticking up over 200 feet. This limestone was a fine-grained, dark grey rock, which Filipinos cut into building bricks they call adobe. Because the stone was strong but easy to cut, tunneling was possible without shoring or concrete reinforcement. Japanese engineers developed a plan for several tiers of tunnels in the sugarloaf and beneath it. There would be five layers in all (Teresa-1 through Teresa-5). The top layer resembled a stick figure with curved tunnels like carabao horns at either end. The left-hand horns were Teresa-1, the right-hand horns Teresa-2. Other layers were beneath that. To ventilate the tunnels during construction, the map showed that six vertical airshafts were dug. Curtis hoped to locate one of the larger vents as a point of entry.

During the war, there were six excavation teams here, each with 200 POWs, working around the clock from different starting points. The men wore only loin clothes and dog-tags, and were sustained only by bowls of thin rice gruel. Those who collapsed and died were replaced. There was no shortage of slaves.

When the tunneling was complete, five of the six tunnels were sealed twenty feet inside each mouth, using a special mixture of porcelain clay, fine sand, crushed rock and cement. An officer from Ishikawa prefecture in northern Honshu – a region famous for its ceramic industries – was in charge of blocking the entrances. One secret of Ishikawa ceramics was clay from North China. When it was mixed with marine sand, cement and crushed local rock, it did not shrink as it cured, and became exceptionally hard. It could be colored to blend with the local limestone, leaving no visible trace of an opening. When these plugs had cured, the remaining twenty feet of each entrance were backfilled with dirt, planted with shrubs, bamboo, and papaya. Papaya trees grow fast, so the patches soon were indistinguishable from adjacent terrain.

Meanwhile, convoys of Japanese Army trucks made their way to Teresa from Manila Bay warehouses, carrying gold bullion, oil drums of gems, and the three solid gold Buddhas – one three feet tall, one eight feet tall, and one thirteen feet tall. According to plan the treasure was dispersed in various parts of the complex. In Teresa 1 and 2 there were six locations for the gold bars. Two smaller lots of gold were placed in pits dug in the floor, like the pit discovered by Roger Roxas. Other spaces were filled with drums of mixed gems or diamonds. Over many days, bronze boxes of gold were carried into the tunnels and placed in designated locations. All these areas were then backfilled with dirt carried in wicker baskets by the POWs. Next the two smaller gold Buddhas were pushed into the tunnels using a bulldozer. Each Buddha was shoved into position on top of a slab of plate steel, resting on top of a 1,000-pound bomb that had its nose sticking out one side. Once the trigger mechanism was primed, the bomb would explode if anybody disturbed the Buddha. The third Buddha, thirteen feet tall, was so heavy that two bulldozers had to be used to get it into the tunnel, one pulling while another pushed. When the Buddha was in place, the bulldozer that had pulled could not leave. So the Japanese removed its engine, putting two boxes of gold bars in its place, then drained the fuel tank, and filled it with loose gems. When this was done, a final convoy of trucks arrived at Teresa. These 23 trucks were driven straight into the remaining space in the carabao horns. The tires were deflated and the vehicles, weighted down with gold, sank to their hubs. A Shinto priest came to bless the treasure. All POWs were ordered into the tunnels, on the pretext that they were to unload the trucks. When all 1,200 were inside, bulldozers began shoving earth over the last entrance. As the POWs realized they were to be buried alive, they started yelling and running for the entrance. Machine guns already positioned at each entrance shot them down. Once the first ranks died, others half-dead from starvation and overwork did not have the strength to get past the bodies blocking their way, or to climb over the mound of dirt already shoved in by the bulldozers. They kept yelling and clawing at the barricade of dirt and bodies as they were entombed.

This entrance was then sealed with the special ceramic cement, booby-trapped with 1,000-pound bombs and small glass vials of cyanide. Finally, the Japanese closed the three airshafts over Teresa-1 and the three over Teresa-2. In each group, two vents measured only two feet in diameter, while the third shaft measured eight feet in diameter, ventilating a deeper tunnel. The small vents were filled with soil, rubble, and rocks. The eight-foot-wide vents were filled layer-by-layer, with dirt, rocks, charcoal, bamboo, broken glass, and human bones – mostly skulls and hands. (As punishment, the Japanese chopped off hands first, and then the head, in front of all the other prisoners.) The red series treasure map included exact details about the fill in the main airshafts, because this was to be the point of access for the team that would return from Japan someday to recover the treasure. The last touch was to replant the top of the hill and its surroundings, so villagers would detect no changes when they returned.

Curtis had a hunch that he and Ben Valmores could find one of the big airshafts, which could make recovery easy. Visiting the site with Ben and Pol in April 1975, Curtis discovered local men quarrying limestone blocks from the top of the hill. He asked General Ver to have them removed with the excuse that the army was going to take soil samples here for a military installation. A few squatters were evicted from their shacks. Curtis, Ben and Pol soon found the main airshaft, because the fill had settled somewhat, leaving a circular depression. Marcos arranged for the Age Construction Company (pronounced Ah-gay) to do the excavation, and they began digging into the airshaft. Just as the map indicated, they encountered layers of human bones, bamboo, broken glass and charcoal. At thirty-one meters depth they hit a porcelain-cement barrier. When they jackhammered through it, everyone smelled a terrible stench and began vomiting. The workers broke out in sores and rashes and had to be hospitalized. Some believed the escaping gases came from the putrefaction of over a thousand bodies sealed with the treasure. Curtis thought it might be methane gas, or poison from canisters dropped into the shaft before it was sealed. Whatever the source, it included gases of decay, for within days the mouth of the airshaft was surrounded by large ugly flowers, called Death Flowers.

Once the shaft aired out, digging resumed down to thirty-six meters. There the diggers found a large round stone 60 inches in diameter with a six-inch hole bored in its middle. It was a millstone, another of the symbols shown on Ben's treasure map, proving the legitimacy of the maps in his possession. After five weeks, on June 8, 1975, the diggers jackhammered through another thick porcelain-cement layer and broke into the vault containing the trucks loaded with gold. Olof Jonsson climbed down and had a look, then climbed frantically out in a state of wild alarm. He told Curtis that he had an intense sense of the spirits of all the men buried alive there – he even felt fingers clutching at him. After that Olof would not go back inside.

Curtis climbed down himself, and began collecting dog-tags to notify next of kin, but Ver's men demanded he turn them over.

Had Curtis been psychic like Jonsson, he would have been alarmed by this behavior, and by new demands suddenly laid on him by the John Birch Society. Out of the blue, the Agnews suddenly demanded additional security for the loan. Over the phone, Curtis offered them the titles to his heavy equipment in Nevada. He was obliged to sign a new document, giving the Birch Society exclusive rights to market up to $20-billion worth of any gold recoveries he engineered for Marcos. Curtis was told the Birchers would do this through an offshore company in the Bahamas called Commonwealth Packaging Ltd., owned by Kwik Lok. Marcos gold would be sold in Nassau, which is a major center for gold trading. The proceeds would be deposited in the Nassau branch of the Royal Bank of Canada. Then, using accounts controlled by senior members of the Birch Society, the money would be credited to the Royal Bank of Canada branch in Kelowna, British Columbia, east of Vancouver. There it would be deposited to an account controlled by one of the key financial experts of the Birch Society, who would retrieve the money and smuggle it across the border personally. Curtis said the Birchers boasted to him about smuggling very large sums into the United States in this fashion.

Curtis should have been suspicious, because these new demands signaled that something was happening behind the curtains, while he was occupied with Teresa-2.

Recovery was near. Well in advance, Curtis had sent Marcos a memo about security precautions, and how treasure recovered from Teresa-2 should be removed. As it came out of the tunnels, he proposed that it should be inventoried by five men, including Curtis, Villacrusis, and Ver's deputy, Colonel Mario Lachica. Then it should be placed in numbered containers. Curtis suggested that the loose jewels be stored in the National Defense Command. Artifacts could be sent to a bonded warehouse along with foreign currency and all paper money that was no longer in circulation.

"The heavy inventory [gold bullion] would best be stored at or near the laundering facility so that military escorts will not be necessary to move the material to and from the laundering equipment."

Marcos had told Curtis that when the three Buddhas were recovered, they must be cut into pieces and re-smelted. Otherwise, they might be identified.

At 4 a.m. on the morning of July 5, 1975, Curtis was awakened at the penthouse suite in the Philippine Village Hotel by a phone call from one of the security guards at Teresa-2. A job foreman had just stopped all digging because the diggers had hit a truck fender and the nose of a 1,000-pound bomb. By prior agreement, if they came upon a bomb, Curtis was to remove all construction workers, and contact a Colonel Gemora who would arrange for a bomb removal squad to be rushed to the site. Excited by news of the truck fender, Curtis and MacAllaster drove to the army base to wake Gemora, who tried to reach General Ver but failed to get through. They all drove to Quezon City to alert General Cannu, who located Ver by phone. Ver told Curtis he would take care of everything, and that Curtis and MacAllaster should go back to their hotel. He would send a car for them later, to have a victory meeting with President Marcos.

When Curtis and MacAllaster returned to the penthouse they found Olof Jonsson in the sitting room with bags packed, deeply worried. Olof told them he sensed they were in mortal danger and must leave the Philippines immediately. Although Olof had a very gentle nature, there was nothing weak or eccentric about him. Curtis had never seen him so agitated: "You could actually sense his fear, as he spoke to us." He and MacAllaster tried to calm Olof, saying they were about to become very rich, but Olof was adamant. He was leaving the Philippines as fast as he could get to the nearby airport.

Curtis reminded him that with martial law in effect, there was no way he could get the necessary exit permit and still make that day's flight to Hawaii. Olof was not dissuaded. He left immediately for the airport.

"I still do not know how Olof made that airplane." Curtis told us. "The flight was delayed for three hours. When I asked him later if he had influenced that delay with his psychic powers, Olof would only smile."

Curtis and MacAllaster remained elated. They knew they had hit the fender of one of the twenty-three military trucks loaded with gold bars. They were going to be very rich.

"We thought we were all going to celebrate at Malacanang Palace with the President," Curtis said. It seemed a shame that Olof would miss the festivities.

That afternoon, as promised, a car came to pick up Curtis and MacAllaster. Instead of taking them to Malacanang Palace, it took them to the American war cemetery at Ft. Bonafacio. Colonel Lachica was waiting for them, sitting in a jeep with Major Olivas. He was holding a .45 caliber automatic, Olivas a .38 caliber revolver. Lachica ordered Curtis out of the car and took him into a patch of rhododendron. Olivas led MacAllaster to another cluster of rhododendron. Behind the bushes, Lachica motioned for Curtis to look down – there was a freshly dug grave three feet deep. Curtis realized it was his. Lachica put his .45 behind Curtis's right ear and said: "I am sorry Bob, but I have been ordered to do this. This is nothing personal." Curtis began to talk fast: "I can't stop you from pulling that trigger

Mario, but if you do, I am sure you will be laying in a hole right next to me very soon. Kill me and Marcos won't have the treasure maps."

Lachica thought it was bluff, but he was uncertain. He called Olivas, and they walked back to the jeep to radio Ver. While they waited for instructions, Ver sent men to ransack the penthouse suite and the conference room next door, which had been used by Curtis and his team. Marcella MacAllaster watched, terrified. The searchers confiscated every piece of paper, every picture, every drawing, every roll of film. These were taken to the palace and examined, but the red series maps were not among them. When it was clear the maps were missing, Marcos told Ver to postpone the executions.

At the cemetery, Lachica said: "President Marcos and the general want to meet with you for dinner in a few days to make amends and in the meantime I am to return you to your hotel." Curtis simply replied, "Good."

By then it was after sunset. When Lachica and Olivas dropped them at the hotel, Lachica said, "President Marcos and General Ver are very sorry about this incident. It has all been a serious misunderstanding."

Curtis did not know until later that the misunderstanding had to do with a man named Primitivo Mijares.

Mijares had been Imelda Marcos's press secretary for many years. An intelligent man, he knew more than most people what was really going on in the Philippines, and about the torture and murders taking place in security chambers at Malacanang Palace called the Black Room. He had finally been sickened, and was convinced by anti-Marcos partisans to speak out. Like Roxas, Mijares would suffer terribly for his courage. Seeking the biggest stage available, Mijares had flown to the United States, where it was arranged for him to testify before a committee of the U.S. Congress holding hearings about the Marcos regime. There were already strong indications that U.S. aid to the Philippines could be drastically cut if Marcos did not mend his ways. When Mijares gave his testimony on Capitol Hill a diplomatic storm broke. At the same moment, columnist Jack Anderson reported on July 4 and 5, 1975, that Marcos was hunting Japanese war loot with the help of several Americans.

Marcos suspected that Bob Curtis had leaked this information to Jack Anderson, so he decided to have Curtis and MacAllister murdered the moment treasure was found at Teresa-2.

At the penthouse the night of July 5, 1975, Curtis knew only what Lachica had told him: That there had been a leak to Jack Anderson's column, and Curtis and MacAllaster were blamed for it. They had narrowly escaped having their heads blown off. He now understood Olof's terrible premonition. Marcos would not hesitate to have them killed once he regained possession of the maps.

In fact, the maps were there in the penthouse the whole time, and Curtis was astonished that Ver's men did not find them during their search.

Weeks earlier, Curtis had been confronted by the problem of what to do with the 172 waxed maps while he was away working at Teresa-2. Each map was priceless and irreplaceable. Yet there were maids cleaning these rooms each day. Looking around the conference room, he noticed that there was a plumber's panel under the sink in the wet bar. On the spur of the moment, Curtis unscrewed the panel and saw that the maps would fit neatly inside. From then on he kept the original maps there around the clock, only taking out the ones that currently interested him.

Now, after his near-death experience in the American cemetery, Curtis realized that Ver soon would have a more thorough search made of their rooms. He took the maps out of their hiding place and roused John MacAllaster.

"Forget the treasure," he told MacAllaster, "let's save our lives." The only way to do that, Curtis explained, was to destroy the maps. If the maps were found, they would be murdered. So long as Marcos and Ver were unable to find them, they would assume that Curtis had hidden them, and avoid doing anything to risk losing the maps. Curtis explained to MacAllaster that he had photographs of the maps, showing all details, and had sent these already to Nevada. He knew they had arrived safely with the lazy susan. So the original maps no longer were absolutely necessary. MacAllaster agreed. The problem was how to destroy them. He suggested burying them. Curtis said they were being watched closely, so there was no way to get out of the hotel with a bundle, buy a shovel, and find some inconspicuous place to bury them. Better to destroy them right there in the hotel. Because the maps were heavily coated with wax, they couldn't tear them up and flush them down the toilet. The best solution was to burn them. On the balcony of the conference room was a small hibachi used by hotel caterers to grill cocktail snacks.

At three in the morning, Curtis and MacAllaster dragged heavy bedspreads out onto the conference room balcony and draped them over the railings. That blocked any view of the balcony from watchers in the hotel gardens far below. Lighting the hibachi, they burned all 172 maps, one by one. It took over an hour.

Once the maps were destroyed, they still needed an exit visa to get out of the Philippines. That had to come directly from Ver or Marcos.

Curtis sent an encrypted telex to Jim Duclos, a trusted aide in Nevada. Duclos was instructed to telex back in clear that Curtis was needed for an urgent board meeting of his company. He also asked Duclos to contact a friend, Nevada Governor D. N. O'Callaghan, who was on the board of *The Las Vegas Sun* newspaper. Curtis did not dare use phones in the hotel, certain they were monitored. When the clear telex arrived at the hotel from Nevada, Curtis called Colonel Lachica at the palace and read him the message. He told Lachica that MacAllaster had suffered a heart attack because of the stress caused by the incident in the cemetery, so MacAllaster must also return immediately to the United States for medical attention.

Although Ver and Marcos certainly realized that these were only contrived excuses, they were stymied by not knowing how to recover the maps. Marcos was so alarmed by the Jack Anderson columns, and so worried that the U.S. Congress would cut his foreign aid, that he had to keep a low profile till this blew over. If he wanted to go after Curtis and MacAllaster in America, he could do so easily, or simply send a hit team. He decided to play for time, and told Ver to okay their departure.

Curtis and the MacAllasters received their exit permits at the hotel immediately. They booked reservations on the next United Airlines flight. While they waited they worried that Ver might try to plant drugs in their luggage, so they left everything behind except small carry-on bags. At the airport they were in a nervous sweat, expecting to be grabbed by security men.

"We finally boarded the plane," Curtis said, "and taxied down the runway. I was beginning to think we had pulled it off, when the pilot eased back on the throttle and announced that we were returning to the gate. We were in first class. I whispered to MacAllaster that we might be in trouble. We were. The door opened and two colonels in uniform entered. The stewardess called me to the cabin door. I went. The colonel in charge was talking on a portable radio. He told me that he had been ordered to search me and my carry-on bag. I was certain they would plant something on me such as drugs, money or gold and then claim we were trying to exit with contraband. I raised holy hell, screaming I am an American, on an American airplane and that I had gone through all of the airport security. I refused to submit to a search and said in a loud voice that I would consider that an illegal international act. The colonel got on the radio and spoke to someone in Tagalog. Whoever it was, he was outranked and kept saying 'sir' in English. Finally, after what seemed like an eternity, he said 'You may take your seat.' After about five minutes the door was again closed, and we started taxiing down the runway again. We were safe, for the time being…"

Villacrusis never took the precaution of photographing or photocopying the maps. To protect himself after Curtis fled, Villacrusis drew fourteen maps from memory, which he passed off successfully as red series originals that he had kept aside. The only red series map Marcos had ever seen was one shown him by Curtis, so the ruse worked. Marcos put the Villacrusis reproductions in his office vault at Malacanang Palace, where they were found after he was removed from power.

From one of Ver's officers, Colonel Orlando Dulay, Curtis learned later that Marcos proceeded with the Teresa-2 recovery, but only recovered the gold bullion from the army trucks. He then ordered the main air duct closed. He did not recover the oil drums of diamonds and loose gemstones, nor did he try to recover the three solid gold Buddhas. According to Dulay, the gold was trucked from Teresa to a private home owned by Marcos in the town of San Juan where it was assayed and inventoried. Dulay said the gold bullion in the trucks totaled 22,000 metric tons, while a member of the Marcos family who helped inventory the gold bullion said it was 20,000 metric tons. In either case, they said this put the value of the gold in mid-1975 at around $8-billion, give or take a few million in change. Add this $8-billion in gold from Teresa-2 to the $6-billion in gold from the *Nachi* and in a matter of six months Marcos had been enriched by around $14-billion, thanks chiefly to the efforts of Olof Jonsson, Robert Curtis, and Ben Valmores. But during the next five years gold prices shot up to over $800 an ounce, making the Marcos hoard worth about fifteen times as much. Why, then, did Marcos not pay Curtis and the others their share in the Leber Group recoveries, to keep them silent and to ensure their cooperation for future recoveries? The short answer is that Marcos was pathologically greedy, and would rather kill you than pay you. The bad press he was getting in America was making him anxious, and he had to kill, destroy, or bankrupt somebody just to ease his discomfort.

Although Curtis was still alive, his problems had only begun. When his plane took off from Manila International Airport, he thought he was safe. But when he reached Nevada he discovered that Marcos already had double-crossed him – before he hit the truck fender at Teresa-2.

Curtis told us that while he was working on Teresa-2, the Gold Cartel had approached Marcos with a Mafia-type offer – "either kill Curtis and let the Cartel do the business of [gold] distribution, or he [Marcos] would be in trouble". By Gold Cartel, he meant the alliance of prime banks, gold processing companies, and national treasuries (including the Federal Reserve and Bank of England) that dominate the official world gold market. While it is impossible to document what Curtis said in this instance, it is supported by subsequent events. His smelters and gold-sanctifying function in Manila were taken over by a member of the Cartel called Johnson-Mathey Chemicals, part of Johnson-Mathey Bank (JMB), one of England's gold banks. A few years later, after a number of scandals provoked by what brokers in the City of London called 'Marcos Black Eagle deals', JMB collapsed and was absorbed by the Bank of England.

Marcos also sent Ambassador Mutuc to San Francisco, to start the process of destroying everything Curtis was involved in. Curtis told us, "Mutuc contacted all of my managers and stockholders, and had a meeting in San Francisco where he told them I wasn't coming back. [Mutuc] made them very large cash offers, to destroy my company and file civil suits. Most of them bought the package and Marcos made some of the key people very rich... As a result I was hit with a Civil Suit, Grand Jury, and Indictment. They literally destroyed my five plants [in the United States]. – Bulldozed down a wall, stole all my equipment, precious metal, and emptied out our bank accounts. We owned every piece of equipment free and clear, including trucks, drills, earthmovers, etc. They were all stolen and, since the safes had the titles, they sold them. We were forced into bankruptcy... We had no money for a trial defense and in fact were destitute. Not much threat to Marcos or the Gold Cartel."

Jay Agnew of the John Birch Society took Curtis to court to recover the money loaned to him through Commonwealth Packaging. Curtis was unable to repay because Marcos now had bankrupted him, with Birch Society help. A Marcos family source told us that before they sued Curtis, the Birchers already had made a deal with Marcos to market the $20-billion in gold they originally intended to get through Curtis, so the Birch board of directors achieved all that they originally sought. The Agnew lawsuits against Curtis, we were told, were a price demanded by Marcos to clinch the deal.

"A bullet in the head would have been easier, quicker, and less painful," Curtis said.

The FBI, which previously took no interest in Curtis, now ordered an investigation. The Bureau did not seek to indict the Agnews for their part in the scheme, which was to sell the black gold in the Bahamas and smuggle the proceeds into America by way of Canada. Instead, Curtis and MacAllaster were indicted for discussing the details by cable or telephone, based on evidence provided by the Birchers. Their trial was to begin on August 14, 1978, but Curtis and MacAllaster were broke. They also believed their public defender was not up to the job. At a hearing, Curtis pleaded no contest, and was placed on probation for five years.

Fighting back, Curtis sent his full story and all his evidence (over three hundred hours of taped phone conversations and two thousand pages of documents) to Senator Paul Laxalt of Nevada, head of the U.S. Senate Intelligence Committee. Laxalt's office told Curtis nothing could be done, and passed copies of all his material to the Birch Society. Years later, Curtis discovered Laxalt was one of the main links between President Marcos and the White House, and one of the chief reasons why so many Marcos cronies had second homes in Nevada.

Curtis now had no alternative but to go public. He contacted editor Hank Greenspun of *The Las Vegas Sun,* and columnist Jack Anderson. They broke the story in articles that began running in April 1978. Steve Psinakis, a Filipino exile in California, published a 24-part series in the *Philippine News* that June, adding more to the anti-Marcos outcry. Marcos responded by calling Yamashita's Gold a hoax. But from these articles, Marcos learned that Curtis had burned the red series maps, and was the only one with copies.

Through an intermediary, Curtis offered to return the copies to Marcos one by one, in exchange for installments of the money owed to him under the Leber agreement. In October 1980, Marcos replied, offering to buy back all the maps by sending Curtis $5-billion in gold, as full payment of his Leber share. The gold would be flown directly from Manila to the airport at Reno, Nevada. By state law, Nevada is a free port, so gold and other imports can be brought in without taxes. That October, the loaded planes took off from Manila. Half way across the Pacific, Marcos abruptly diverted them to Zurich. According to Philippine ambassador Trinidad Alconcel, who cleared the flight in Washington, Marcos was warned by his future son-in-law Gregory Araneta, by General Ver, and by his friend Adnan Khashogyi, that he was making a big mistake. If he paid the $5-billion, Curtis would have proof that he was telling the truth all along.

CHAPTER THIRTEEN

THE PALADINS

Once it was proved in U.S. courts that massive gold shipments did come out of the Philippines during the twenty years Marcos was president – gold that did not originate in the Central Bank, or in mines like Benguet – the remaining mystery is where did it go?

To be sure, the gold was shipped covertly, usually after re-smelting in Manila by Johnson-Mathey Chemicals, using equipment Marcos stole from Robert Curtis. Before it left Manila some was re-papered by Johnson-Mathey Bank, then made its way to buyers through the gold pools in New York, Zurich and London. Other black bullion was sold privately to Saudi princes and Middle Eastern syndicates, or to discreet groups of Europeans through Luxembourg and Liechtenstein.

Documents including waybills show that some shipments went to America aboard commercial ships and planes, while others went out on CIA aircraft to Hong Kong or to an American military base in Australia. So far as anyone can tell, the gold that went to America did not end up in Fort Knox. If it did, the U.S. Government is not admitting it. So where did it go? Who was shielding and helping Marcos, other than the CIA and Pentagon? Who else benefited from all this recovered plunder? Was the leverage of the federal government used to get some of this gold bullion into private hands?

The answer is that Marcos had connections beyond the CIA, to a shadowy network called The Enterprise, a cluster of private intelligence organizations (PIOs) and private military firms (PMFs). These were staffed by former CIA and Pentagon officers who saw themselves as Paladins of the Cold War. Many PIOs and PMFs got their start in the 1970s during shakeups at the CIA. They mushroomed in the 1980s after Jimmy Carter stirred up the anthill, and strongly motivated men had to continue their careers elsewhere.

At the end of 1972, when he replaced Richard Helms as CIA director, James Schlesinger made it clear that he intended to forcibly retire hundreds of agents who were dead wood, or part of a Dirty Tricks clique under Helms long engaged in operations that violated American laws, including assassinations. When it then became known that the CIA was involved in the Watergate break-in and other domestic break-ins, Schlesinger ordered an internal investigation and preparation of a complete list of all Agency projects that might embarrass the government. The resulting 693-page report, called 'the Family Jewels', led to leaks about assassination programs like Mongoose, death squads like Phoenix, and other wet-work hidden by national security. Over a thousand CIA agents were sacked or obliged to take early retirement.

When Nixon resigned, President Ford set up the Rockefeller Commission to investigate CIA wrongdoing, but staffed it with hardline conservatives who would avoid revealing things that would "blacken the name of the United States and every president since Truman".

Congressional hearings into Phoenix, the Lockheed bribery scandal, and later Iran-Contra, resulted in additional housecleaning at CIA and the Pentagon.

Added to these purges were disputes between CIA officials like Ray Cline and President Nixon over rapprochement with China, and between Jimmy Carter and top military officers like Major General John Singlaub, and Air Force General George Keegan. When Carter got rid of so many professional soldiers and spooks, he does not appear to have given much thought to what they might do to keep busy in private life. No Roman emperor would have been so careless in disbanding a legion.

Many of these clever and aggressive men regrouped privately, with funding from hard-right organizations like the Birch Society, Moonies, World Anti-Communist League, and wealthy conservative tycoons. Like Santy's Umbrella organization, The Enterprise grew into a powerful and influential network during the late 1980s. Although they were now private citizens, these men continued to have close ties to serving military officers, to top men in the CIA and the armed services. This overlap made it nearly impossible to distinguish between official U.S. Government operations and those that had private objectives. This was especially true because so many of these individuals had long experience in covert operations, deception, and the clandestine use of government resources and secret funds. They were accustomed to working with CIA proprietaries that had every appearance of being legitimate companies in private industry but were actually Trojan Horses for the intelligence community and, by extension, for the armed forces. In fact, some of the PMFs were little more than fronts set up so that generals, admirals, and former spooks could continue to draw salaries and pensions as if they had never left government service. Many CIA agents spent years or even decades under various covers, so it was hard to establish beyond any doubt whether they ever left the Agency, or merely went underground.

A perfect example is William Casey.

Casey was one of the original OSS crowd. After law school, he went to work for an accounting firm but kept in touch with fellow lawyer John 'Pop' Howley, who worked for Wild Bill Donovan's law firm, Donovan Leisure Newton & Irvine. When Donovan became head of OSS, Casey and Howley joined him. Casey was John Singlaub's case officer in the war, while Paul Helliwell was Singlaub's direct superior. Casey also was a close friend of Allen Dulles and John Foster Dulles, worked with Ray Cline, and became involved with Lansdale as Santa Romana's torture of Major Kojima was bearing fruit. This put Casey in a position to know a great deal about the Black Eagle Trust, and one source insists that Casey's financial skills made him one of the key players, along with Paul Helliwell and Edwin Pauley, in implementing the Black Eagle Trust under the guidance of Robert B. Anderson and John J. McCloy. Following the war, Casey and his old friend Howell founded their own Wall Street law firm. But what made Casey really wealthy was his involvement with other former intelligence officers in setting up the media holding company Capital Cities, in 1954. According to many investigators, during this period the CIA poured millions into setting up front companies for covert operations in broadcasting and publishing, and it is alleged that Casey funneled some of these funds into Capital Cities to acquire failing media companies and turn them around. It is likely that Casey never left the Agency, but only moulted into one of its financial butterflies. It would not be the first time a senior CIA agent has had a double career on Wall Street, Allen Dulles being but one of many others. From 1971-1973, Casey was Nixon's appointee as chief of the Securities and Exchange Commission, where he worked closely with SEC attorney Stanley Sporkin (later appointed by Casey as CIA general counsel, and involved in the Schlei case). Casey also served as Nixon's Under-Secretary of State for Economic Affairs, and chairman of the Export-Import Bank. In 1978, Casey founded a think tank called the Manhattan Institute that absorbed a number of former CIA officers, and funneled money from conservative foundations to conservative authors. When Casey left Capital Cities to head the Reagan presidential campaign and then to become Reagan's director of the CIA, he is said to have been its biggest single stockholder with $7.5-million in Capital Cities stock. He was still its biggest stockholder, and CIA director, in 1985 when Capital Cities bought ABC.

A man who was involved in covert financial operations throughout his entire career, Casey had links to all the key players in this book; his DNA is all over the place, from pre-Santy to post-Marcos. He was one of the men who dreamed up the privatization of the CIA, and as CIA director he showed President Reagan how to implement it.

One of Reagan's first acts was to sign Executive Order 12333, which authorized the CIA and other government agencies to enter into contracts with PMFs, "and need not reveal the sponsorship of such contracts or arrangements for authorized intelligence purposes". This put Casey back in harness with Cline, Singlaub, Shackley, Lansdale and many others purged earlier, while obscuring their activities, keeping them – theoretically at least – in the private domain. Simultaneously, Casey personally took over handling President Marcos, pressing him to provide black gold for covert purposes, and finally masterminded the downfall and removal of Marcos, and his bullion.

•

Eventually, Iran-Contra revealed the intimate bonds between members of The Enterprise and unelected officials of the National Security Council, Pentagon and CIA.

Such overlap can be useful to the government when, for example, it had Lansdale subcontract to the Mafia the assassination of Fidel Castro. Having PMFs train death squads in other countries enabled the White House to carry out secret foreign policy objectives including murder, and proxy military operations inside countries with which the United States was not at war. It is like putting on surgical gloves and a condom to carry out the dirty side of foreign policy, without leaving fingerprints or DNA. Should bureaucrats be allowed to get away with murder-for-hire? Does this not lead to serial killing, and other addictions?

Along the way, a surprising number of retired generals, admirals, and senior officials from the National Security Council, became involved in treasure hunting in the Philippines, and the covert movement of gold from Manila. Overlap in this case may have been used both to advance foreign policy objectives, and to enrich and finance private military forces whose secret agenda is exclusively that of the far right.

Some of the best known figures in The Enterprise like Lansdale, Ray Cline, and John Singlaub began their careers with OSS in World War II, and rose rapidly during the Truman and Eisenhower Administrations, when Nazi and Japanese gold first was used to set up black bag operations like the M-Fund. Their political views as Cold Warriors were shaped as they tried to rescue Generalissimo Chiang, put the Shah in power in Iran, sought to remove Sukarno and Castro, helped arrange the overthrow of Allende in Chile, and had carte blanche to dispose of inconvenient civilians in Cambodia, Laos, and Vietnam. Lansdale, while still a colonel on active duty, ran Operation Mongoose, the effort to kill Castro. When Lansdale was forced to retire by President Kennedy, he simply went private, becoming a charter member of The Enterprise, and remained a ringleader till his death in 1987.

Operation Phoenix was overseen by Ted Shackley, CIA station chief in Saigon from 1969-1972; later CIA deputy director for operations. Some sources have claimed that Singlaub was involved in Phoenix on the military side, although he denies this vigorously. He certainly was close to many people involved, including Shackley. William Colby told a Senate hearing that Phoenix killed over 20,000 Vietnamese civilians (men, women and children) suspected of being communists; others put the total over 70,000. Congressional hearings declared that Phoenix was a 'totally unlawful operation'. Yet Phoenix continued in rogue violation until the U.S. pulled out of Saigon in 1975.

"Phoenix was the creation of the old-boy network," says Colonel Stan Fulcher, who was part of the operation, "a group of guys at highest level – Colby and that crowd – who thought they were Lawrence of Arabia." The same old boys were in El Salvador, this time using proxies, including Taiwanese officers trained by Ray Cline's special warfare academy. Journalist Douglas Valentine explains: "What these 'old Phoenix boys' all have in common is that they profit from antiterrorism by selling weapons and supplies to repressive governments and insurgent groups like the contras. Their legacy is a trail of ashes across the third world."

Both Singlaub and Shackley later left the Agency, and became closely identified with The Enterprise network. Singlaub went private after a well-publicized dispute with President Carter in 1978. Shackley went private the next year after a dispute with Carter's CIA director, Admiral Stansfield Turner. Singlaub and Lansdale then joined the Reagan campaign, headed by William Casey.

The combined effect of the Family Jewels purge by Schlesinger and the subsequent housecleaning by President Carter therefore backfired, in the sense that it drove the hard right underground, into the private sector, where it could operate without peer review to an even greater degree, while continuing to make free use of the government's covert assets. If The Enterprise wished to use Air Force planes, Navy ships, SEALs or Special Forces, there were ways these could be put at their disposal without anyone being the wiser. *The New York Times* journalist Seth Mydans quoted a well-placed source that "Singlaub comes in and out of the [Philippines]. He can even land at Clark without our knowing it." We have established that senior Special Forces officers took brief leaves from duty in order to participate in Philippine treasure hunts with groups of PMFs linked to Singlaub, Cline and others. This erases a vital line between government service and private gain, and makes it impossible to enforce ethical standards.

Freedom from peer review is addictive. Under Presidents Reagan and Bush, the PIOs and PMFs multiplied and became a virtual private extension of the White House. To this day, leaders of The Enterprise and advocates of PMFs insist that the White House needs a private clandestine service run by experienced intelligence officers turned entrepreneurs. Accordingly, PMFs were involved in South Africa, Angola, Colombia, Croatia, Eritrea, Ethiopia, and Sierra Leone, to name only a few. When not engaged by the White House, they work under contract to regimes whose human rights record is as bad as it gets. The Vinnel Corporation, PMF subsidiary of Dick Cheney's Haliburton, worked with the army dictatorship in Myanmar, which has one of the worst human rights records on the planet.

Some of their motives are of questionable constitutionality. We reproduce letters from members of The Enterprise network, describing how they intend to use recovered Japanese war loot to set up a private FBI-style security force to police the American public, and a separate military-industrial complex 'controlled by us'.

This costs money. Groups like the Moonies and Birchers, and wealthy individuals, put up only a portion of what is needed. One obvious solution was to divert existing Black Eagle funds, such as the dormant accounts controlled by Santa Romana. This is why Santy was brought to Washington in 1973, and pressed to make over funds to which he held title. When Santy died the following year, this may explain why several of his biggest accounts at Citibank and UBS were quickly transferred to Lansdale's control. How they were used is unknown.

When Marcos began making his second-generation recoveries in the 1970s and needed help getting the black gold to market, he and The Enterprise made common cause. Because members of The Enterprise had access to CIA aircraft, U.S. Air Force planes, and U.S. Navy ships, when Marcos gold left Subic or Clark it was impossible to tell whether this was done officially by the White House or privately by The Enterprise. In Chapter Fourteen, we will see episode after episode where this overlap is demonstrated.

•

Increasingly, Marcos found himself in a tug-of-war with the Reagan White House for control, disbursal, and management of the gold he recovered. He resorted to every trick to bypass U.S. Government channels. This would be his downfall.

When international monetary authorities decided to allow central banks to buy gold directly from private sources, Marcos decreed that all gold mined in the Philippines had to be sold directly to the Central Bank. This enabled him to sell some of his gold, and the bank could then move it overseas without raising eyebrows. In November 1981, Manila announced it would place 'excess locally derived gold reserves' on the international market. Over three months, some 300,000 ounces of gold were shipped to Hong Kong, New York, London, and Zurich. It was earmarked as Philippine government gold, but the commercial banks involved were allowed to play with it, meaning it could be traded over the short term. For this privilege, the banks paid 1 percent commission on these earnings, which went to Marcos.

According to a former Filipino diplomat, Ferdinand's personal plane made many round trips to Switzerland. Commercial airlines also were used, as evidenced by waybills. Twelve secret shipments were said to have taken place aboard KLM, PAL, Air France, and Sabena. In September 1983, for example, a KLM flight from Manila to Zurich carried seven tons of bullion. Another 1.5 tons were shipped to London at the same time. Meanwhile, CIA pilots and Pentagon cargo planes periodically airlifted Marcos gold to Australia and Hong Kong.

While the Agency was physically moving Marcos bullion, it actively encouraged the Marcoses to salt their profits in America. This became clear during the Honolulu fraud trial of Ronald Rewald in 1983-85, which revealed that his investment firm, Bishop, Baldwin, Rewald, Dillingham & Wong, was a conduit for CIA funds in general. The firm helped Marcos and other wealthy Filipinos invest illicit funds in America. When Imelda later was tried in New York on charges of racketeering, her defense attorneys told us she and her husband had been encouraged to do so "by their friends in the White House".

According to court testimony in Honolulu, the pipeline was set up by Rewald with help from Filipino billionaire Enrique Zobel, a friend of the Marcoses. Rewald ran a polo club in Hawaii, and Zobel was a world-class player. Rewald testified that Zobel was, like him, a CIA confederate. Through such joint ventures as Ayala-Hawaii, they and the CIA would "shelter monies of highly placed foreign diplomats and businessmen who wished to 'export' cash to the United States, where it would be available to them in the event of an emergency".

The Zobel connection goes back to 1945 when Colonel Joe McMicking was the immediate G-2 superior of Santa Romana and Captain Lansdale as they tortured Major Kojima. Flush with money thereafter, McMicking married Don Enrique's aunt Mercedes and helped the Zobel-Ayala clan become one of the world's great fortunes. In this tightlipped milieu, Enrique Zobel is something of a renegade. After studying at UCLA, he made a name for himself developing Manila's posh Makati financial hub. His relations with the Marcos family were complex and shifting. In the early 1980s he was mentioned as a possible successor as president. When Marcos crony Eduardo Cojuangco mounted an aggressive takeover of San Miguel Corporation, brewers of San Miguel beer, one of Ayala Corporation's premier holdings, the family thought Don Enrique gave in too easily. This so displeased Aunt

Mercedes and Uncle Joe that they stripped Zobel of his control over Ayala and handed it to his first cousin. Don Enrique went his own way thereafter.

Zobel knew a lot about Marcos efforts to recover war loot. In 1975, Ambassador Mutuc of the Leber Group notified Zobel that there was a Golden Lily vault under the control tower of Nelson airfield where Zobel was building the Peninsula Hotel. On June 3, 1975, Mutuc wrote: "I am with a group which has the necessary maps and eyewitnesses to the effect that in the premises in and around the old control tower ... there is a buried treasure trove allegedly consisting of jewelries [*sic*] and gold bullions in a staggering amount of at least several hundred million dollars! We have noticed that the said building has been vacated and we fear that some construction work might be done in the premises. ...any project you plan to do there can afford to wait until after we shall have located and retrieved the treasure trove."

In 1983, Zobel was a patron of the lavish wedding of Irene Marcos to sports star Gregory Araneta, stepson of Lansdale's top hit man, Napoleon Valeriano. It was reported that Imelda spent $20-million on the wedding. Austria's Kurt Waldheim provided a silver carriage, pulled by seven white Arabian stallions provided by Morocco's King Hassan. In return, the Marcoses deposited a very large dowry in Austrian and Moroccan banks. (Evidence of this dowry resurfaced in 2001, when the German government accused Irene and her husband of attempting to move some $13.4-billion illegally from Swiss banks to German banks.)

Flaunting money like this was part of the Marcos psychosis. He could have set up a charitable trust like the Ayala Foundation, and retired to his estates in Ilocos Norte. Andrew Carnegie once said, "The man who dies rich dies a fool." Marcos had no time for charity because he was pressed continually by the Reagan White House to supply more black gold for its foreign policy objectives. According to a well-informed source in the Marcos family, "Bill Casey told Ferdinand the White House would keep him in power forever if he agreed to put his black gold in banks designated by the CIA".

One deal said to have resulted is the so-called China Mandate. Our Marcos family source insists that in 1972 President Nixon and Henry Kissinger made a secret deal with Premier Chou En-lai to keep China out of conflict with the United States over Taiwan, in return for access to a large quantity of gold provided by Marcos. We have not been able to confirm the political details. However, bank documents that have surfaced over the years clearly demonstrate that large quantities of gold bullion were moved into Chinese mainland banks during this period, including bullion accounts in the names of Santa Romana, Ferdinand and Imelda Marcos, and other members of their family and circle of rich cronies. Since all these people were loudly anti-communist, there is no plausible reason for them to transfer gold bullion to Chinese banks in the midst of the Cold War. For that reason alone, the story may well be true.

According to this source, in 1971-1972 the economy of the People's Republic was in very bad shape, its foreign currency reserves were flat, aggravated by the worldwide oil crisis and famine in the countryside, all of which is correct. As pressure mounted on the Politburo, party hawks gained a stronger voice, pushing for invasion of Taiwan to gain control of its assets, and as a much-needed distraction. CIA and Pentagon analysts concluded that Beijing was about to invade, while America had its hands full in Vietnam. This could lead to nuclear war. A way had to be found to defuse the situation, and a novel solution proposed by a CIA analyst was to help Beijing stabilize its economy with a huge infusion of black gold from Marcos, reducing the pressure for war. If America helped China out of this domestic crisis, it could bring a period of peace that would benefit the Philippines as well.

As our source tells it, Nixon and Kissinger secretly offered Beijing $68-billion in gold (an amount they knew Marcos had), to be moved into PRC banks in a number of tranches over several years. This would not be an outright gift. It would be deposited incrementally in various PRC banks in Hong Kong and major cities inside China. There the bullion would remain as an asset base, earmarked for various purposes negotiated in advance. The Chinese banks would be strengthened, the PRC economy would be stabilized, moderates in the Politburo would regain their leverage, and hawks pushing for an invasion of Taiwan would be silenced. No U.S. funds were involved.

"It was only Japanese war loot," our source said, "recovered by Marcos, being put to good use."

Chou En-lai, ever a pragmatist, reportedly pushed it through. The temptation for Marcos to agree was great; he would be fully supported by Washington, and rewarded in many ways. The White House sweetened the deal by assuring Marcos that he and Imelda could make state visits to Beijing, which would enhance their stature throughout the world. Additionally, Beijing would reciprocate by providing agricultural aid to the Philippines.

In 1974, Imelda and her son Bong-Bong did make a state visit to Beijing, where they were photographed grinning goofily with a startled and frail Mao Tse-tung clamped between them, one of the strangest photographs of Mao ever made. Ferdinand went to Beijing the following year, a curious thing for him to do as an outspoken Cold Warrior. In a subsidiary development, Imelda's brother Kokoy Romualdez, noted more for his loyalty than for his intelligence, became Manila's ambassador to Beijing.

Our Marcos source insists the China Mandate was the foundation for Nixon's historic visit to China and establishment of diplomatic relations with the Peoples Republic.

Documents do show that beginning in 1972 and continuing over a period of years, Marcos gold was moved to PRC-owned banks including Po Sang Bank and Bank of China in Hong Kong, and to other Chinese banks in Xiamen. Documents from those banks show very large accounts in the names of Santa Romana, Ferdinand Marcos, Imelda Marcos and others. Among related documents we reproduced on our CDs are letters from gold brokers asking for commissions to be paid after these transfers were successfully carried out. The Marcos family and wealthy friends subsequently traveled to Xiamen to inaugurate a new building for the PRC bank holding these accounts. Xiamen is adjacent to Amoy, home of the Hokkien dialect group long associated with the natural father of Ferdinand Marcos.

Further evidence came in 2000, when Imelda was accused by Hong Kong government authorities of hiring a Chinese woman to obtain access to some of these gold accounts by bribing bank officials. In December 1999, according to Hong Kong government prosecutors, Imelda agreed to pay the bounty hunters 35 percent to recover $2.5-billion from accounts at Bank of China, HSBC, and PRC banks in Xiamen. Imelda's lawyers said she was only trying to raise money to help the poor. When news then came of yet another secret Marcos bullion account at UBS in Switzerland, containing $13.4-billion, Imelda sighed, "I wouldn't be surprised. I know we used to have money."

When the existence of these bullion holdings in China was revealed, nobody seemed at all curious how they came to be there, some since the early 1970s, when the Cold War was still on. Nobody connected them to Nixon's 1972 state visit to Beijing.

•

In the early 1980s there was another bizarre development, when Ferdinand and Imelda learned of an extraordinary secret account set up with Golden Lily plunder after the Pacific War.

This was the billion-dollar gold bullion trust at Sanwa Bank in Osaka, set up in the names of General MacArthur and Emperor Hirohito, mentioned in Chapter Nine. Japanese call it the MacArthur Fund, while Americans call it the Showa Trust, using the name of Hirohito's reign period. Sanwa Bank is one of Japan's oldest, and Hirohito owned a large chunk of its stock from before World War II. The trust appears to have been set up by Robert B. Anderson shortly after he toured the Golden Lily treasure sites in the Philippines with MacArthur and Lansdale. Although MacArthur's name is identified with it, it does not appear to have been intended to benefit MacArthur, at least not directly.

As for Hirohito, according to journalist Paul Manning who had access to SCAP records during an early stage of the U.S. Occupation, the emperor had $1-billion in gold and currencies hidden in overseas accounts since before the war. The emperor was pulling in $50-million a year in interest from overseas investments during the U.S. occupation, and SCAP financial advisors were aware of these income-producing assets. Significantly, Sanwa Bank was one of three Japanese banks left untouched by General Marquat's Economic and Scientific Section of SCAP. The other two were Tokai Bank and Dai-Ichi Kangyo Bank, involved in the Tanaka Club disbursements growing out of the M-Fund. Today, Sanwa Bank advertises its worldwide banking operations with the slogan "We've come a long way". Indeed.

Ferdinand and Imelda learned of the Showa Trust at Sanwa Bank while combing through Santy's papers after his death. According to documents we reproduce, by 1981 the Showa Trust was generating over $300-million in interest every quarter, or over one billion dollars of interest annually. As one of the bank's owners, the emperor was doubtless getting a favorable rate of interest. (These documents were found in Marcos's private safe in Malacanang Palace after he was removed from power, and confiscated by the Philippine government.)

The Marcoses imagined that if they played their cards right, they could gain access to the Showa Trust, or at least divert some of its interest payments in their direction. It would be acutely embarrassing to Tokyo and to Washington if news of the joint account leaked, for several reasons. First, Tokyo still maintained the pretense that Hirohito was so impoverished at war's end that the Diet had to vote him an annual salary of $22,000 to keep him afloat. Second, Japan's LDP was at that moment wallowing in yet another great scandal involving Tanaka's bribe-taking and bribe-giving. As for Washington, disclosure of a Hirohito-MacArthur joint trust since 1945 would require fancy footwork, given repeated declarations that Japan had been flat broke.

A Marcos team, including negotiator Natividad M. Fajardo, flew to Tokyo for private talks with Japanese government officials, including three trustees of the Showa Trust (one Japanese and two Americans). Fajardo was a broker who acted for the Marcoses in a number of gold transfers. His trip to Tokyo occurred within days of Ronald Reagan's first presidential inauguration. Reagan was an important friend of the Marcoses. He and Nancy first went to the Philippines in 1970 as President Nixon's personal representatives at the opening of Imelda's Cultural Center in Manila. It was the beginning of a long friendship in which Marcos and Reagan flattered each other.

Only when Fajardo and his team arrived in Tokyo did they reveal the true purpose of their visit. In short, the Marcoses offered to keep quiet about the Showa Trust in exchange for giant payments disguised as a financial aid package for the Philippines. They demanded that the quarterly interest from the trust be turned over to them.

This sounded something like extortion. The Japanese government was so alarmed that they kept Fajardo and his delegation sequestered under armed guard in their rooms at the Miyako Hotel the entire time they were in Japan. They had to eat all their meals in their rooms.

According to Fajardo's letter to Imelda from Tokyo dated February 22, 1981, "The Japanese financial aid [for the Philippines] consists of accumulated interest income of dollar fund [sic] left in trust by General MacArthur to the Imperial family. ...We are devising a means of how to bring out the money to Hongkong under the authority of the Ministry of Finance of Japan... It shall be made to appear that the money will be loaned to a Japanese company doing big business in the Philippines and they [the Japanese government] found that Kawasaki is qualified. The Trust money in the hands of the Imperial Family has already been deposited with Sanwa Bank in Osaka and is ready for transfer to Hongkong. To do this, it shall be made to appear that it is a loan to Kawasaki without any interest for a period of 30 years. It will be Kawasaki that will release the money to finance the massive economic development projects of the Philippines of the First Lady."

We do not know if the deal negotiated by Fajardo went through. But bank documents show there are a number of Marcos accounts today in the Hong Kong branch of Sanwa Bank.

Tokyo probably complained to Washington about this threat, and it probably contributed to the downfall of the Marcoses soon afterward. But the main reason Washington finally gave up on Marcos was the failure of Reagan's Rainbow Dollars.

President Reagan declared at the beginning of his administration that he would restore the gold standard, abandoned by Nixon in 1971, and introduce a new gold-backed currency called Rainbow Dollars. In the decade since Nixon's action, the United States had experienced periods of raging inflation, recession, and killing interest rates. Reagan's remedy was to go back on the gold standard. Treasury Secretary Donald Regan said this would bring about a 'roaring boom'.

So many dollar banknotes were in circulation that if they suddenly became convertible to gold, as was the case before 1933, Washington could be swamped with demands for bullion. The solution was a two-tier system. Rainbow Dollars would replace greenbacks gradually, but ordinary people could not walk in and exchange them for gold. There would be special issues of Rainbow Dollars, convertible to gold when held by central banks.

To make this work, America needed a large stock of gold, enough to manipulate gold prices. If the price fell too low, Washington would buy gold to keep currency values stable. If the price rose too high, and central banks demanded bullion from Washington, the government would release bullion into the market, depressing the price. This was Reagan's essential plan.

The change to Rainbow Dollars also would mean that people hoarding illicit cash, such as heroin and cocaine druglords, would have to exchange their old currency for new, so money would come out of hiding. The result could help reduce the federal deficit.

President Reagan privately asked Ferdinand to lend part of his hoard of black gold to back Rainbow Dollars. As usual, he could charge a commission for lending his gold to Reagan. Unfortunately for Marcos, he demanded a higher commission than the White House thought fair.

According to our sources, including one who was on the White House staff at the time, Reagan was dismayed that his old friend had let him down.

Given the concurrent attempt to blackmail Tokyo over the Showa Trust, Reagan's advisors – particularly Casey – argued that Marcos had gone too far. The time had come to depose him, and in the process divest him of the mass of bullion he still had salted away. Casey swung into action. In the months that followed, People Power took to the streets of Manila, mobs demanding that Marcos step down.

As popular clamor increased in the streets, Casey is said to have flown to Manila with Treasury Secretary Regan, CIA economist Professor Frank Higdon, and attorney Lawrence Kreagar. The purpose of the meeting, according to a Marcos aide, was to convince Ferdinand to turn over 73,000 metric tons of gold. Casey and Regan were giving Marcos a last chance. Regan reportedly told Marcos that he must sign over the gold in return for 80 percent of the value in U.S. debt instruments, 20 percent in cash. Sensing that the end was nigh, Marcos wanted 80 percent in cash, only 20 percent in debt instruments. When haggling proved fruitless, Professor Higdon is said to have told Marcos he would be out of power 'in two weeks'. Indeed, weeks later Marcos was in Hawaii, effectively under house arrest.

According to the same Marcos aide, the next move in the endgame came a few days after the meeting with Casey, Regan and Higdon, when an emissary from the Trilateral Commission hand-delivered a confidential request to Marcos asking him to contribute $54-billion in gold bullion to a global development fund. Our source, who was present, said Marcos glanced at the ornate document and tossed it contemptuously into his out-basket. The emissary hurried back to the office of the Trilateral Commission in Makati, to report.

Three days later, Marcos was given a last ultimatum by Nevada Senator Paul Laxalt, President Reagan's go-between. By then Marcos was effectively under siege at Malacanang Palace. A very sick man, suffering from lupus, failing kidneys and liver, Marcos gave in, forfeiting 'his' gold in return for being rescued by U.S. Army helicopters. That evening, barges were towed up the Pasig River to the palace, and great quantities of gold bars were loaded on them from palace vaults, and other vaults at the Presidential Security Command compound and other buildings adjacent to the palace. This went on all night and was witnessed by many people. At dawn the laden barges were towed out into Manila Bay, their ultimate destination Subic Bay naval base where the gold is said to have been put first into munitions bunkers, and then aboard U.S. Navy vessels. (What happened to the gold thereafter is hard to say because the U.S. Government has not publicly audited its gold stocks since 1950, and only admits to having 8,000 metric tons.)

That evening U.S. Army choppers swarmed into the gardens of Malacanang Palace and took aboard the Marcos family and their minions.

To their surprise, the Marcoses were not taken from Malacanang Palace to the family stronghold in Ilocos Norte, where they planned to mount a defense of their realm. They were taken to house arrest in Hawaii.

"We were not rescued," Imelda snapped, "we were kidnapped."

On their arrival in Honolulu, she said U.S. Customs agents seized billions of dollars worth of gold certificates she was carrying. The official list prepared by Customs did not mention them. Subsequently, she claimed that the U.S. Treasury admitted confiscating the certificates, but said its experts had determined that all of them were fakes. As we have seen, it is routine procedure to denounce gold certificates as counterfeit, even when they are real. This is a universally practiced form of confiscation. Under the circumstances, one wonders why wealthy people continue to entrust their gold to banks, if there is a very strong likelihood that sooner or later the banks will tell them their paperwork is fraudulent. In such a climate of deceit, it would be interesting to know precisely what Treasury did with the confiscated gold certificates.

Treasury Secretary Regan certainly was not telling. He and CIA Director Casey had to resign in disgrace for their part in money laundering and gunrunning during Iran-Contra. Casey's prominence in the Iran-Contra scandal kept us from fully appreciating his other role in making clandestine use of Japanese plunder to manipulate foreign governments, and to finance right-wing militias in America.

The fleecing of the Marcoses and the confiscation of their gold certificates on arrival in Hawaii may have been richly deserved, but many questions remain unanswered.

To begin with, why did Imelda and Ferdinand insist upon moving their black gold to banks controlled by other people, when in so doing they forfeited everything? In Hawaii, they discovered they could no longer access the bullion they had taken such pains to hide offshore. Their accounts were blocked on the pretense that, as a corrupt fallen dictator, it might turn out that these were ill-gotten gains.

This was the position of the U.S. Government, which had been in bed with Marcos for more than thirty years. The Swiss government took a more realistic position by simply denying that Marcos had any money in Swiss banks. Bankers all over the world said they knew nothing about Marcos accounts.

When they could no longer pay their bills in Honolulu, Ferdinand asked old friend Don Enrique Zobel for a small loan of $250-million to tide them over. According to Zobel, Marcos showed him gold certificates to prove he could pay the loan back – certificates that had not been seized by the U.S. Customs. These, too, were later pronounced fraudulent by the U.S. Treasury.

A few months later, looking increasingly puffy and jaundiced, Marcos sent out for a large order of McDonald's burgers and fries for himself and his friends. In the midst of his meal, Marcos began to choke on a piece of Big Mac, coughing violently. The next morning, January 15, 1989, he was hospitalized at Honolulu's St. Francis Medical Center for a collapsed lung, remaining on life support until his death that September. And so ended one of the most corrupt relationships in Washington's history. Or so it seemed.

Santy was dead. Marcos was dead. In May 1987 Casey was dead. But leaders of the many private organizations that make up The Enterprise knew lots of war-gold remained in the ground in the Philippines, and lying dormant in Santy's worldwide bank accounts. They decided to see if they could recover some from the ground, or from the banks. Not knowing exactly where to look, the John Birch Society urged them to approach Robert Curtis, to see if by-gones really could be by-gones.

CHAPTER FOURTEEN

LOOSE CANNONS

Robert Curtis had paid a very high price for becoming involved in gold recoveries with Ferdinand Marcos. But Curtis was stubborn, and he still had the only full set of Japanese treasure maps to surface since the war. Slowly putting his ruined life back together, he moved from Sparks to Las Vegas, where he became sales manager of a big Chevrolet dealership. In his spare time, he studied the maps, figured out many of the coded riddles of Golden Lily cartographers, and decided how he would approach a recovery next time – if there ever was a next time. So when the phone rang one day in 1978, he could hardly believe his changed luck. A man he knew and trusted asked Curtis to meet privately with a foreign diplomat whose government wanted to sponsor a big clandestine recovery of war gold from the Philippines. The rendezvous took place in a Las Vegas hotel, where Curtis was put in direct contact with the prime minister of a major Western nation, prepared to put everything including a submarine at his disposal, for a fifty-fifty split. On the condition that we would not reveal the name of the country or the prime minister, Curtis recounted what follows:

The prime minister was well informed about earlier Marcos recoveries, and the crucial role Curtis had played. He wanted Curtis to pick a target suited to a midnight recovery from a sub. Curtis chose the island of Corregidor, where he knew of three substantial vaults. To avoid an international incident, the prime minister's own navy would not put men ashore to open the vault, because they could be captured. A navy cruiser would stand off Luzon in the international waters of the South China Sea. A sub would come in fairly close to shore, but remain submerged until night when commandos would launch inflatables to retrieve the gold bars from the beach. It was up to Curtis to open the vault, and get the ingots down to the beach.

As Marcos was still in power, Curtis could not go to Manila himself for he would be arrested and murdered. Instead, he would send men to recover the gold, and carry the ingots to the beach. Then his men could be extracted by the sub.

"This was exciting," Curtis told us. "I was mad at Marcos and this would let me get even, although I would never be able to talk about it." Getting rich would heal a lot of wounds.

"I chose the south end of Corregidor, which is the head of the tadpole-shaped island, because there was deep water for the sub. To get down the cliffs to a very narrow beach, my guys would have to traverse one of two ravines." At high tide, the beach was submerged, so timing would be crucial. When the commandos came in their rubber rafts, it would have to be a moonless night, with a low tide.

Corregidor lies in the mouth of Manila Bay, off the Bataan Peninsula, where President Marcos had his summer palace at Mariveles. The island lies east-west, with the head of the tadpole – Topside – on the west. The low-lying eastern tail was called Bottomside. In 1978, the only residents of Corregidor were half a dozen people living in the town of San Jose in Bottomside. But each morning a tourist boat arrived from Manila.

As his target, Curtis chose a concrete bunker beneath the Crockett Battery, a mortar emplacement off the beaten path for tourists. The U.S. Coast Guard had built these mortar emplacements in 1901. Beneath a concrete slab, two intersecting tunnels originally served as a munitions magazine. During the defense of Bataan and Corregidor in early 1942, a direct hit on Crockett by an incoming round blew up the powder magazine and destroyed most of the bunker. After the Japanese gained control, Prince Chichibu saw the concrete-lined tunnels beneath the ruined emplacement, and decided to hide a mass of 65-pound gold bars there, covering it with a six-foot-thick slab of concrete, making the mortar emplacement look undisturbed. It was unlikely that anyone would remember Crockett blowing up.

As a metallurgical chemist, Curtis thought he could burn a man-sized hole through that slab using thermite, if he could enhance it enough. Thermite is a simple compound of equal parts powdered aluminum and powdered iron oxide. Once it ignites, it burns at around 3,000 degrees centigrade. Thermite was used as an incendiary weapon during World War II. Today it is used to pierce armor, or as a thermal decoy for heat-seeking missiles. It takes a lot of heat to ignite thermite. The simplest method is to use a match to light a fireworks sparkler, which burns hot enough to ignite the thermite.

In the Nevada desert, Curtis set up a test bed with a six-foot thick concrete slab, and found that ordinary thermite worked too slowly. He added other ingredients, enhancing the thermite till he had a blend that would burn at close to 5,000 degrees centigrade. This, he said, burned through six feet of concrete in forty minutes, making a hole big enough for a man to crawl through.

Curtis figured two men could make the recovery and carry the gold to the beach. He knew two, who seemed right for the job, and they were enthusiastic. Both had served in the Special Forces with Colonel 'Bo' Gritz, so Curtis figured they could handle just about anything.

"One was a big macho military type," Curtis said, "who was head of security for a large company in Las Vegas. He had a friend with similar background who was the son of a former sheriff of Las Vegas." We will call them Gary and Mike. Both men needed to learn how to use the enhanced thermite, and to toughen up physically so they could make repeated trips up and down the ravine, lugging ingots to the beach. For this job, Curtis had a saddler make two heavy-duty backpacks shaped for the gold bars. After many weeks of strenuous training, Gary and Mike decided they could each manage two bars at a time. Two 25-pound bags of enhanced thermite would do the job with plenty to spare. Because thermite is an incendiary, it cannot be carried on airliners. So the special enhanced mixture was taken to Manila in a diplomatic pouch.

Gary and Mike assembled everything needed to live two weeks in a patch of rainforest on Corregidor, including machetes, food and water, high-tech sleeping bags, mosquito nets, medicines, and cobra anti-venom. Two weeks would give them time to carry down enough gold bars to satisfy the prime minister. As cover for Philippine immigration, Curtis obtained credentials attesting that Gary and Mike were Mormon missionaries on their first evangelical assignment. They flew to Manila and were lodged by the embassy in secure diplomatic quarters.

For reconnaissance, they took the tour boat to Corregidor. Crockett Battery was much as they expected, and Topside was empty of people. Returning to Manila with the other tourists, they gathered their gear and were driven by a diplomat to Bataan. There, at a harbor town called Cabcaben opposite Corregidor, they rented a *banca*, a brightly painted Filipino dugout with outriggers and a good-size outboard motor, paying a hefty deposit to use the boat without a paid skipper. Once their gear was aboard, the banca looked overloaded, but its owner assured them it was safe. They told him they were going camping.

It would have been wiser to let the sub put them ashore in a rubber boat, but for some reason that was not considered.

An hour and a half before dark, taking a casual fix on the small notch in Corregidor that was their destination, Gary and Mike shoved off. It would take an hour to get there; they would loiter offshore like fishermen, and make a run for the beach when darkness came.

Gary and Mike were soldiers, not sailors. They knew little about the sea. Every sailor knows Sod's Law: If it can go wrong, it will. With tide racing out of Manila Bay, they should not have headed straight toward their target. They should have headed up into the tide, and let it carry them back to their destination. In the mouth of Manila Bay, fighting the tide proved too much for their outboard motor, which died. They tried desperately to restart it, as the *banca* was swept far out into the deep swells of the South China Sea. Several breaking waves hit them broadside, foaming over their low freeboard, nearly swamping them and carrying away the backpacks and thermite. This area was notorious for sharks scavenging on dog bodies and garbage flushed out from Metro Manila, and both men were now desperately afraid. To lighten the boat, they jettisoned the rest of their equipment.

Providentially, the motor then roared into life. They were able to turn the banca and make their way back to Bataan. After midnight they stumbled ashore, found a phone and called Curtis in Nevada.

Curtis was stunned and deflated. He wanted to abort the mission, but once back on dry land Gary and Mike were recovering from their fright, and needed to save face. They would try drilling through the concrete using a star drill and a sledgehammer. Curtis knew it would fail, but Gary insisted, so Curtis reluctantly agreed. Shock and disappointment were so great all around, it never occurred to them that Gary and Mike could lie low while a diplomat brought more enhanced thermite.

Returning to Manila, Gary and Mike purchased new supplies and tools, and again hired the troublesome *banca*. This time they made it to Corregidor. As Curtis foresaw, drilling the concrete proved hopeless. In two days they made a hole only three inches deep. They called Curtis again from Bataan and said they were giving up. He phoned the embassy in Washington and passed word to the prime minister. The sub lurking off Bataan was called home.

•

Not all recovery efforts were such failures. Successful recoveries did happen during the 1980s. Japanese groups were well organized and their security was good because they kept their mouths shut. One group was headed by a man we will call Toshi, resident of a Tokyo suburb, who had been an intelligence officer with Golden Lily during the last year of the war, when he was in his early twenties. Toshi told his story on the condition that his name would not be revealed. During 1944-45 he said he was often in the company of Prince Chichibu, Prince Mikasa, Prince Takeda and Prince Asaka Yasuhiko, the butcher of Nanking. Toshi said he observed Ben Valmores bringing tea and cigarettes to the princes, while they toured Golden Lily sites. After the war Toshi returned to university and inherited money from his father. A handsome, cosmopolitan man, fluent in English and French, Toshi decided to devote himself full time to recovering the gold he had helped hide. He bought a small house set in gardens on the outskirts of Manila, and went about his recoveries with singleminded dedication and total secrecy. When his son graduated from university, Toshi set him up in the gold business in Tokyo. In 1981, Toshi was one of a group of Japanese involved with President Marcos in a very large recovery from a vault in the Santa Maria mountains. The gold was sanctified by Johnson-Mathey Chemicals, at the refinery Marcos had built with equipment stolen from Curtis in 1975. When Marcos sold a mass of gold in May 1983 through one of the leading international banks in Luxembourg, Toshi said some of the gold came from his recoveries. The first tranche alone was for 716,045 bars, at a sale price of $124-billion. The deal was signed by a number of attorneys representing the buyers, who were members of the London gold pool. The memorandum of agreement on Philippine presidential letterhead was signed by one of the Marcos 'trusted gold ladies', Konsehala Candelaria V. Santiago. (See our CDs.) These papers were notarized by the U.S. Consul, who photocopied them and passed them to the CIA. According to Norman 'Tony' Dacus, who was paid a commission on the deal, the gold was flown out of the Philippines to Hong Kong by U.S. Air Force planes from Clark, at sixty tons a week. Even if only the first tranche went down, this was one of the biggest single deals Marcos ever made.

Toshi used his share from the Luxembourg deal to buy real estate in Japan. Among other acquisitions, he bought some prime land opposite a suburban Tokyo railway station, and built a large apartment block where he installed all his relatives on the top floors, and rented out all the flats on lower levels. He made trips to

America where he bought electronic devices for detecting metal in the ground, including a Filter King Plus, and an underground scanner, paying for everything from a big roll of crisp new hundred dollar bills. Genial and easygoing, Toshi was happy to pull out color photos showing him at various digs, including before and after photos. We have some of these color photos, but cannot reproduce them without identifying Toshi.

There were offshore recoveries as well. In 1976 Curtis was contacted by a group of Americans who wanted to salvage the fake Japanese hospital ship *Awa Maru*, lying off the coast of China. The *Awa Maru* was sunk in April 1945 by the U.S. submarine *Queenfish*. The sub's skipper, Commander Charles Elliott Loughlin, was court-martialed because Japan claimed he had sunk a genuine hospital ship, implying that 2,009 people who died were mostly patients. (The only survivor was an illiterate crewman blown off the fantail and picked up by the sub.) After the war Commander Laughlin was vindicated when records were discovered showing that the *Awa Maru* was a fake hospital ship that had carried munitions, crated fighter aircraft, and VIP families to the South Seas, and was bringing war loot and VIPs back to Japan. The *Awa Maru* was, in fact, carrying over $5-billion worth of treasure when it was sunk. She had aboard 40 metric tons of gold, 12 metric tons of platinum, 150,000 carats of diamonds, large quantities of titanium and other strategic materials. Astronaut Scott Carpenter and Jon Lindbergh, son of Charles Lindbergh, had found a copy of the sub's log in naval archives showing exactly where the sinking occurred, and confirmed this with the sub's executive officer, who was still alive. Because the hulk was lying close to Chinese territorial waters, they tried unsuccessfully to make a deal with Beijing to carry out a joint venture and share the recovered treasure. When they started their own salvage operation, pinpointing the site, they were run off by the Chinese navy. Beijing then carried out the recovery itself.

A more intriguing recovery was that of the Dutch liner *Op ten Noort*, whose capture off Java was described in Chapter Five. Her name was changed several times, including *Tenno Maru* and *Hikawa Maru*. She spent the rest of the war as a fake hospital ship in the service of Golden Lily, carrying treasure to Manila and Yokohama. Just before the war ended, she arrived in Yokohama with 2,000 metric tons of gold. A few days later she was moved to Maizuru Naval Base on the west coast of Japan. Maizuru is an almost landlocked bay, meaning that any ship sunk there will remain near where she goes down, instead of being moved by strong ocean currents and tsunami. There she took on more treasure from underground bunkers in the hills around the naval base. Late one night, the ship was taken into the bay, her captain and twenty-four crewmen were murdered, and the ship was scuttled by opening its Kingston valve, which flooded the hull. The murderers were a group of high-ranking Japanese Navy officers who were anxious to keep this treasure to themselves. They liked to boast that some day the treasure would be used to rebuild the power of the Imperial Navy.

The *Op ten Noort* recovery got off to a bad start in 1987 when the last survivors of this group of officers approached underworld fixer Sasakawa, who had worked with Kodama in the 1930s and 1940s, then made recoveries in Indonesia and the Philippines in partnership with President Sukarno and President Marcos. Efforts

were made to bring in underwater recovery specialists and other equipment neces-
sary for deep diving. But quarreling over Sasakawa's share caused negotiations to
break down. In 1990 the recovery began again, with the participation of big
Japanese corporations including the huge sea-crane ships of the Moricho
Corporation. Also enlisted were international experts in deep sea recovery. They
brought along a submersible belonging to Divcon International, carried aboard an
Australian salvage vessel called the *Torrens Tide*, owned and managed by Tidewater
Port Jackson Marine Pty. Ltd., of Sydney. (See color photos on our CDs.)
Participants in the recovery told us that once the treasure was safely aboard the
Torrens Tide, the Japanese went ashore that night to celebrate. During their absence,
our sources said, the Australian ship slipped anchor and made it to international
waters with the treasure before her disappearance was discovered at sunrise.

The most publicized treasure hunters of the last thirty years were the Nippon Star
group of General John Singlaub, one of The Enterprise network of PMFs. Singlaub
first became a national hero near the end of the Pacific War when he parachuted
into Hainan Island and released hundreds of POWs from Japanese concentration
camps. After that, he became one of the China Cowboys who holed up in Korea
while Mao Tse-tung's forces took over the mainland. Singlaub was involved in setting up the Korean CIA (KCIA), which developed a particularly nasty reputation
backing military dictatorships over the decades. In the course of his long CIA
career, Singlaub worked with all the most famous Cold Warriors, including Ted
Shackley, Cline and Lansdale. In the 1970s he was America's top military commander in Korea, when he had the first of several public differences of opinion with
President Jimmy Carter and was forced to take early retirement.

He remained a hero of the far right, one of the PMF paramilitary proxies supporting bloodstained regimes around the world. Many of his ex-CIA associates in
The Enterprise, such as Lansdale and Cline, knew all about Santa Romana's recoveries in the late 1940s, and the Marcos recoveries of the 1970s.

After Marcos was removed from power, Singlaub and two PMFs called Nippon
Star and Phoenix Exploration came to Manila to hunt for gold, with CIA knowl-
edge and cooperation. Nippon was incorporated in Hong Kong, Phoenix in
London. Along with Helmut Trading, registered in Liberia, they were all based in
Colorado and closely tied to Phoenix Associates, founded by Colonel Robert
Brown, publisher of *Soldier of Fortune* magazine and close friend and neighbor of
Singlaub.

"Normally," Singlaub said, "I would not have been interested in buried-treasure
schemes, but the Nippon Star group were not naïve beachcombers. And I knew
from past experience that stories of buried Japanese gold in the Philippines were
legitimate." He added: "Marcos's $12-billion fortune actually came from [this]
treasure, not skimmed-off U.S. aid. But Marcos had only managed to rake off a
dozen or so of the biggest sites. That left well over a hundred untouched." Singlaub
would be the security advisor, in return for Nippon Star giving a percentage of the
take to his U.S. Council for World Freedom.

Through the mid-1980s, many newspaper stories appeared about the misadventures of Nippon Star digging for treasure in the Philippines, with zero luck.

Continued failures led their financial backers to propose calling in Robert Curtis.

Early in January 1987, Curtis received a phone call from someone named Alan Foringer in Seattle. Foringer said he wanted to come to Las Vegas the next morning to see Curtis about "the Philippine treasure".

"How do you know about that?" Curtis asked.

"I'm with Jack Singlaub and Nippon Star," Foringer replied.

"You guys are CIA," Curtis said, "and I'm not interested." He slammed down the phone.

When Curtis arrived for work at the Chevrolet dealership the next morning, just before 9 a.m., two men waiting in his office were Foringer and his deputy, John Voss. They said they were actually with an outfit called Phoenix Exploration in Denver, associated with Nippon Star. Later, Curtis said he learned that Phoenix Exploration was a CIA front, and that Foringer was really the administrative head or office manager of the CIA station in Manila, in the Magsaysay Building. He was not the CIA station chief, which is a separate post at the embassy usually held by the first secretary or deputy chief of mission.

Curtis was about to throw them out of the showroom when Foringer pointed at the clock and said, "In three minutes you will get a very important call from the Pentagon switchboard, which will explain why this is so important." Exactly at 9 a.m. the phone rang and Curtis found himself talking to Major General Robert L. Schweitzer, until recently President Reagan's senior army advisor at the National Security Council in the Executive Office Building beside the White House. In 1986, as the Iran-Contra arms scandal was breaking, Schweitzer retired from active service and joined Singlaub in The Enterprise network. But he still had an office at the NSC, and remained the man President Reagan turned to for advice on military matters. Schweitzer kept his hand in through his NSC deputy, Colonel Dick Childress, who had the Far East portfolio. Others in this circle were General Daniel Graham, former head of the Defense Intelligence Agency; General Jack Vessey, former chairman of the Joint Chiefs of Staff; and former CIA deputy director Ray Cline, who now headed the Center for Strategic Studies at Georgetown University.

Curtis said General Schweitzer told him he was calling from the Executive Office Building. He said President Reagan – "the old man in the funny house next door" – had personally endorsed the effort by Nippon Star and Phoenix Exploration to make new war loot recoveries in the Philippines. Because the White House and the CIA had to maintain deniability, Reagan could not give the project official sanction, but General Schweitzer said the U.S. Embassy in Manila was fully briefed, along with the U.S. commanders of Subic Bay Naval Base and Clark Air Force Base, who would provide support in the form of men and helicopters, and secure storage for the gold in underground bunkers. Schweitzer played heavily on patriotism, urging Curtis to meet in Hong Kong with Schweitzer, Singlaub, Foringer, Voss, and other 'big hitters'. That very morning Schweitzer said Reagan had received a message from President Cory Aquino saying, "she would cooperate one hundred percent".

Curtis had been so badly burned by the John Birch Society and by U.S. Government agencies colluding with Marcos and the Birchers that he wanted nothing to do with any of these characters. Since 1975 he had learned a lot about CIA/Enterprise involvement in moving Marcos gold out of the Philippines. He collected thousands of pages of documents proving this to his satisfaction. He had an uneasy feeling that he was going to be shafted again. But he was a patriot, and if this meant he could get back on his feet financially, it might be worth the risk. At least he could listen to what the generals had to say, and what President Reagan had to say through the generals. Reluctantly, Curtis agreed, and on February 11, 1987, he checked into the Mandarin Hotel in Hong Kong, where the others were waiting. Over the next four days they met in a hotel conference room, and ate their meals together. To protect himself this time, Curtis insisted upon taping the entire conference from start to finish. (He gave us copies of all the tapes from which we have drawn much of what follows.) As a further safeguard against being railroaded again, Curtis brought along as his partner Dennis Barton, chief criminal investigator for the Internal Revenue Service in Nevada. If anybody could make sure that Curtis did not get falsely accused of anything this time around, Barton could. Later in the week, they were joined by Olof Jonsson, the Swedish psychic, who Curtis regarded as indispensable.

As the conference began, Singlaub told the group their greatest danger was that Japan's victims would band together to get the World Court to freeze further recoveries of war loot until its true ownership could be established. He said thirty-two countries in all claimed to have been looted of thousands of metric tons of gold. He did not say where he got these figures, but his group had access to U.S. Government archives that are not accessible to the public.

To Curtis's astonishment, anger and dismay, it now emerged that Singlaub had persuaded the John Birch Society to take over funding Nippon Star, and it was Jay Agnew's son Dan who had Foringer recruit Curtis. Foringer's first phone call to Curtis was from the office of Agnew's attorney in Seattle. This was truly bizarre, because it was the Agnews who had destroyed Curtis financially and professionally in 1975, bringing criminal charges against him, as recounted in Chapter Twelve. Having ruined Curtis, the Agnews told Singlaub they would only finance Nippon Star recoveries in the Philippines if he and Foringer recruited Curtis, to gain access to his maps and reverse-engineering.

"The Agnews ruined my life," Curtis said, "and now they wanted my help. You don't forgive something like that. I had been called the biggest criminal of the twentieth century, or words to that effect. If I was, I am certainly the dumbest. I was flat broke when I came back from the Philippines in 1975, and I remain flat broke today."

At the Mandarin Hotel in Hong Kong, Generals Singlaub and Schweitzer worked on Curtis, whitewashing the Agnews' involvement. They told Curtis they were offering him his best chance ever to make a major recovery, with President Reagan and the entire U.S. Government backing them all the way, including the American Embassy and the commanding officers of Subic and Clark. You could not do better than that, they said. These were the big hitters. It was a powerful argument. In 1975, the whole U.S. establishment had come down on Curtis like a Mack truck, flattening him like road kill. Now the same American establishment was pleading with the road kill to give them access to all his secret maps and special knowledge. Curtis felt sickened, but having come this far, he decided reluctantly to see where it led.

He liked Singlaub in particular, but he thought they all were nuts. Singlaub admitted spending upwards of two million dollars during the previous thirteen months, trying and failing to make recoveries at several sites. He was steered to these sites by two Pointers, a Filipino dentist named Dr. Cesar Leyran and his side-kick Pol Giga. They had given maps to Nippon Star claiming they were authentic. When Curtis saw the maps he knew immediately they were fakes. Curtis had worked with Pol Giga in 1975 and recognized that Giga had some first-hand knowledge of Japanese treasure sites from the war, but did not trust Leyran at all. If the two were working together, fobbing off fake maps like these, they were simply conning the gullible generals. But how do you tell two American generals they are fools?

Alan Foringer, an earnest, nice-looking man in his mid-thirties, of considerable intelligence, told Curtis: "Our game plan all along has been to hit a small site we control which is under water, on private property, and take a bar from there and demonstrate it to Cory [President Cory Aquino]. That should give us the full and complete blessings of the [Aquino] administration for all other sites."

Problem was, Curtis discovered that this was the Anchor Site on a reef in Calitagan Bay, which Giga and Leyran had been flogging to gullible people for years, like selling the Brooklyn Bridge. Those two hustlers claimed that a solid platinum anchor had been pushed off the fantail of a Japanese naval vessel, chained to a bronze box filled with gold bars, and the anchor and box were lying on the reef. Curtis knew this was a lie, but he did not know how to tell a man like Cold Warrior John Singlaub that he had been conned by a couple of experts. When Nippon Star's divers found nothing on the reef, Giga insisted that the anchor and box "must have slipped down into a crevice". Investors were told that a Japanese concrete slab covering the treasure was too hard to penetrate, and tides kept shifting Nippon Star's dive platform.

Once Curtis realized the generals had been duped on the anchor site, he pressed them to tell him about the onshore site they were working. They had been taken to this site at Alfonso, a town outside Cavite, by Cesar Leyran, who owned the property. When Foringer described it, Curtis could not believe his ears. Leyran had told Nippon Star that as a boy he had seen the Japanese hide treasure in a deep pit they dug under the house next door, which also belonged to the Leyran family. The excited generals put Leyran on a big monthly retainer and started to dig. When they found nothing, they figured it was deeper, so they kept digging. Over thirteen months they dug straight down 400 feet under the kitchen, bagging the dirt and hauling it away at night so neighbors would not guess what was going on. By this time the generals had spent so much money that they could not give up. Because the water table was only a hundred feet down, the next 300 feet had to be dug under water, so the generals had to bring in deep-sea divers from the U.S. Navy. At those depths, the divers had to use a decompression chamber each time they came up.

"Imagine," Curtis said, "diving down more than 300 feet inside a 6 foot by 6 foot shaft, then digging underwater at that depth and hauling the mud and rocks up to be bagged. They never asked themselves, 'How did the Japs dig this in the forties?' It was sheer folly. According to their financial records they spent $1.5-million on this one hole. I had to argue with them to get them to stop throwing money away on that typical Leyran scam."

Curtis also was amazed by the backbiting in Hong Kong. Although they claimed to be old pals, the tape recordings show that Generals Singlaub and Schweitzer were privately at each other's throats.

Singlaub insisted on taking charge of security personally. He said the only Filipino he trusted was Teodoro 'Teddy' Locsin, President Aquino's minister of information. Singlaub said Locsin also was tight with U.S. Ambassador Stephen Bosworth.

"Cory really doesn't do anything," Singlaub said, "without consulting Bosworth."

Singlaub swore he had legal contracts with the Aquino government to dig any treasure site in the country, including federal property. He showed Curtis his authorization, written on Presidential Task Force stationery and signed by Wilfredo P. San Juan. (Later, it turned out that San Juan had no authority to issue treasure agreements of any kind.) Singlaub boasted about bribing people in Malacanang Palace, the Presidential Security Command, the mafia boss of Cavite, and – for extra security – guerrilla leaders of the leftist New People's Army. When so many people are bribed, word gets around. As a result, a great many Filipinos knew about the activities of Nippon Star and Phoenix.

While Foringer was intelligent and rational, Curtis said, he had not commanded whole armies, so he was shouted down by the generals. When they wanted Foringer's opinion, they would give it to him.

They urgently wanted Curtis to rescue them from their folly. He could tell them where to dig, and they would give him a percentage of the recovery. It sounded a lot like the offer Curtis had got from Marcos.

For starters, they asked Curtis to give them an easy site where they could make a quick recovery, to regain credibility in Manila and Washington. Assuming that Singlaub really did have permission from President Aquino to do a recovery on federal land, which was a big if, Curtis suggested targeting sites on Corregidor. He explained that there were several big sites there, and a small one that would be easy – although it was out in the open. They were sure to be seen, so a permit was absolutely essential. Singlaub claimed his permit was correct. He had the men in place to carry out this recovery. By this time, Singlaub had brought in thirty-seven U.S. Special Forces and Delta Force officers, who arrived at Manila International Airport in groups of two or three, traveling with false names and passports.

While the generals prepared a game plan, Curtis went back to Nevada to resume his nine-to-five job as Chevrolet sales manager. On the plane, he realized he had joined a ship of fools. Singlaub and Foringer were charming and personable in different ways, but Curtis seriously doubted they could ever achieve their goal. A week later he received a hand-written letter from Foringer. Addressed to his codename

'George' it began: "Following are some quick notes I would prefer not to have to relate to you over the phone. Board of Directors of Nippon have met and decided that Singlaub must stay out of the Philippines for the foreseeable future and should publicly be disassociated from Nippon. That will be a hard pill for him to swallow …we may find ourselves dealing with a hostile takeover attempt by investors loyal to him…" He told Curtis that all three of Singlaub's existing gold recovery projects were being closed down. Nippon Star would continue as a club for super-patriots from the CIA, Pentagon, State Department, and National Security Council – people like Singlaub and Schweitzer – but its main purpose would be to divert attention from what was really going on. In its place the Paladins were setting up a new Philippine-American Freedom Foundation (PAFF) that would seriously pursue recoveries of war loot in the islands, and its sale on the world gold market. Foringer said they would use the first ton of gold they recovered to complete their purchase of Benguet, the top Philippine gold-mining company, which Marcos had used to export re-smelted war loot with help from the Mafia based in Miami and Nassau. Benguet would serve as PAFF's conduit for moving black gold into the world market. Foringer said the bulk of the proceeds would go to funding defense projects like the B-1 bomber and Reagan's Star Wars program, "in effect to build a new military industrial complex controlled by us". Accompanying his letter, Foringer had drawn a chart showing the relationship of all these people and organizations. (See our CDs.)

As partners with Phoenix Exploration and Nippon Star in this joint venture, Foringer said he hoped Curtis and his friend Barton – calling themselves C&B Salvage – would endorse this political strategy.

Curtis desperately wanted to make a gold recovery for his own sake, to get back on his feet financially. But he had serious misgivings about working with this bunch. He urged Foringer to concentrate on making a quick recovery at the movie theater site on Corregidor. This was the easiest, simplest, quickest site Curtis could give them. He would have done it himself years ago, but this site was right out in the open, so it required official sanction to dig on government property. Any child could do it. But could generals do it?

Opposite General MacArthur's headquarters at Topside, there was a bombed-out movie theater. Beside it was a small cache – eighteen ingots – simple to reach with a shovel at a depth of only 15 feet in soft soil, if you knew where to dig. Eighteen 75-kilo bars meant millions of dollars. Curtis had learned about it in 1975, when he and President Marcos flew by helicopter to Corregidor for sightseeing. One photo taken that day shows them strolling by the movie theater, its walls peppered by shrapnel. When Colonel Villacrusis saw the photo he told Curtis an amusing story he had heard from an eyewitness in Tokyo, while meeting with Prince Takeda and Ishihara. The eyewitness said he was at Corregidor visiting a senior Japanese naval officer in the headquarters building, when American forces began their assault to recapture the island on the morning of February 16, 1945. A heavy bomb landed across the street by the theater, blasting a crater fifteen feet deep. The navy commander still had eighteen 75-kilo gold bars in his office, and saw his chance. He had his office staff drop the gold bars into the bomb crater. A small bulldozer nearby was used quickly to fill in the crater. A few minutes later, paratroopers of the 11th Airborne Division and the 503rd Parachute Regimental Combat Team began hitting the ground. Fighting was fierce and the navy officer was among those killed. After thirty years the eyewitness could recall that the crater was next to the theater, but not exactly where. In 1975, while he was working with the Leber Group, Curtis went back to Corregidor to visit the Pacific War Memorial. The walls of its rotunda displayed vintage black and white aerial photographs showing the 1945 bombardment and the assault, each taken by reconnaissance planes a few minutes apart. One taken at 10:16 a.m. showed the crater by the movie theater and one taken at 10:38 showed that the crater had been filled in. So Curtis knew exactly where those eighteen bars were hidden, if they were still there. These ingots could liberate Phoenix Exploration and Nippon Star from their most troublesome financial backers, and enable several years of big recovery projects at other sites Curtis had in mind.

When all was set, ten Americans from Phoenix and Nippon Star arrived on Corregidor. They brought with them a group of Filipino soldiers to guard the perimeter, led by a sergeant from the Presidential Security Command. Among the Americans were Foringer, President Reagan's man General Schweitzer, five colonels, a U.S. Navy Seal, and Curtis's associates Dennis Barton and John Lemmon. One of the five colonels was Eldon Cummings, a veteran of CIA covert operations in El Salvador. Two others were Colonel 'Rock' Myers, and Colonel James York, both legendary characters. The Seal was the equally iconic Tom Mix, now attached to a shadowy company called GIMCO or GEO-Innerspace, who worked closely with Nippon Star on offshore recoveries of Japanese treasure hulks. These were big guns. That day, they were all heavily armed in case of trouble. Leaving the five colonels in charge of work at the movie theater site, Schweitzer returned to their safe house in Alabang, south of Manila.

First the colonels got out an earth resistivity sensor. By the 1980s, these had advanced to a point where they could detect masses of gold down thirty feet, so the colonels knew the ingots were still sleeping there.

Over the next five days, they dug a hole ten feet deep. They expected to hit the gold bars the next day, or the day after – when all of a sudden there was a whoosh and three big Philippine Army Huey helicopters came whopping in over their heads, bristling with heavily-armed soldiers in flak jackets. While the other Hueys hovered menacingly, one landed and a squad of soldiers jumped down with light machineguns, followed by a Philippine Army general. He told the Americans brusquely that he had been sent by General Fidel Ramos, head of the armed forces, to throw them off the island, which was federal property. Foringer showed him the letter Singlaub had been waving around, giving presidential authority to be on federal land. The general looked at the signature and said, "That's not legitimate. This man San Juan has no authority to issue such a permit." He repeated his command to get off the island, immediately.

The Americans broke camp and left.

General Schweitzer, informed that his handpicked team had been expelled from Corregidor, was livid with rage. He threatened to phone President Reagan and have him intervene personally with President Aquino. He was persuaded by Curtis that this was not a good idea.

A lot of people in the Philippine government and armed forces were offended by the highhanded behavior of Nippon Star. Manila journalists learned that Nippon Star was funded by John and Joan Harrigan with Moonie money. When Nippon Star first set up in Manila, Singlaub had bought weapons on the blackmarket, including Armalites and grenade launchers for which he then was unable to get licenses, because they turned out to be stolen goods. He also bought a fleet of cars cheap, which turned out to be hot. They had belonged to Marcos secret police boss General Fabian Ver, and when Ver fled into exile the cars were sold privately and Ver pocketed the money. When Singlaub tried to get the cars registered, it emerged that they were missing government property. These episodes were all it took for Juan Ponce Enrile and other artful dodgers in the Philippine Senate to claim that Nippon Star was riding roughshod over the islands, defiling national heritage sites. One impassioned journalist wrote, "If the Philippines is to remain a free and democratic society, and to not fall into the abyss of CIA engineered and created civil conflict, to prepare the stage for the forced intrusion and deployment of American troops, to force a retention of U.S. bases, the movements and activities of these enemies of democracy should be closely monitored and curtailed."

When Phoenix and Nippon Star were booted off Corregidor, Singlaub was in Washington testifying before Congress about the Iran-Contra mess.

"I liked Jack Singlaub," Curtis told us emphatically, "but he just couldn't keep his mouth shut."

When Curtis sent word to Foringer that he was pulling out of the joint venture, the nucleus of Phoenix and The Enterprise descended in a rush on his home in Las Vegas, including Generals Schweitzer and Singlaub. They pleaded with him to reconsider. At one point, Foringer asked to speak to Curtis privately. They went outside to sit in his Chevy Blazer with the air conditioner running and the radio on.

"He explained to me that he had to deliver me back into the fold, or they would 'eliminate' him. I asked: 'You mean the CIA?' He said, 'No, not just them.' He said GeoMiliTech had threatened him, saying that he should have forced me to stay in. He also said Agnew was giving him problems."

But Curtis had made up his mind. The clincher was his discovery that the house next door to Nippon Star's safe house in Alabang, where Generals Schweitzer and Singlaub and all the big guns had lived when they were in Manila, had been rented by KGB agents from the Soviet embassy, and they were monitoring and recording everything.

"We had all the windows open," Curtis told us, "so they just sat by their windows and heard everything we said, including our radio communications, which were decoded there. I went bonkers over this."

In the months that followed, Foringer contacted Curtis again and again, pleading with him to reconsider. Singlaub and Schweitzer also phoned. Curtis was adamant. The generals did not blame themselves. Everyone blamed Foringer.

Not long afterward, in Hawaii on his way back to Manila, Foringer was strolling in his bathing suit along the crowded beach at Waikiki after a swim, when his bare leg was nicked by a passerby holding something sharp. Later that day, he was rushed to a hospital in agony, having difficulty breathing. Doctors suspected shellfish toxin. For a while he was near death. Gradually, his condition improved, and he returned to Manila to recuperate at his own apartment, which he was sharing with a Filipino named Jun Mitra. When a friend came to visit one morning, Foringer had lost a lot of weight and was again complaining of breathing problems. He did have some appetite, and asked his friend to get them Italian food. When the man returned an hour later, Foringer was having a seizure. They rushed him to a nearby clinic. He had severe bronchial pneumonia and something was very wrong with his immune system. When another seizure soon followed, his heart stopped, and all attempts to resuscitate him failed.

Referring to the episode on Waikiki Beach, Curtis said, "One of Alan's associates told me later that it could have been an assassination attempt." Whatever happened in Hawaii, the Manila hospital's clinical abstract does not indicate foul play. But absence of evidence is not evidence of absence.

Foringer had been under tremendous pressure. Strain was taking its toll on Curtis as well. On a trip to San Francisco in July 1987, in which he broke off all remaining ties to the generals, he had severe stomach trouble and had to undergo immediate surgery. When he came out of the anaesthetic, he was kept on painkillers that made him groggy. One of his visitors at the hospital was a total stranger named Charles McDougald, who said he was writing a book about Yamashita's Gold. A former Green Beret, McDougald had studied for a while at the University of the Philippines, where he said he became a close friend of the dean, Noel Soriano, who was now President Aquino's national security advisor. On repeated visits to the hospital, McDougald talked to Curtis about various treasure sites. In his fuzzy state, Curtis began to think that McDougald might be a suitable partner, assuming that his connection to Soriano was solid. They discussed going after one of the treasure vaults in Ft. Santiago, under cover of a restoration project. McDougald said he broached the idea to Soriano, who discussed it with President Aquino, and she approved. They would go after the gold Prince Chichibu had placed in the third basement of the fort, at the bottom of one of the airshafts. The project would be carried out by a new company headed by Curtis called International Precious Metals (IPM). McDougald would participate and share in the proceeds after the Philippine government had taken its cut off the top. The excavation would proceed in stages, with President Aquino's approval required at each new stage. They would tunnel through the backfill the Japanese had placed in the way, then drill down in hope of striking the gold and getting a core sample with the drill bit, producing evidence that Aquino needed before they could continue.

Work began with teams of young Filipinos digging around the clock, sections of wood shoring going in to protect against cave-ins. There were four types of booby-traps. Most obvious were 100, 250, 500, or 1000-pound aerial bombs, activated by disturbing a spring. Bottles of cyanide placed in the backfill were easily broken. At some sites there were terra cotta pipes that easily broke and flooded a tunnel. Least expected were sand traps, made by alternating layers of clay and very fine sand. If a worker disturbed it, the clay would collapse and trap the digger, while the fine sand suffocated him. Stout shoring was essential.

Curtis gave strict orders that shoring would be placed as digging proceeded. But he could not be on-site around the clock. As pressure mounted to reach the target, workers and supervisors became careless. Three men working deep in the tunnel after midnight one night, moving well ahead of the shoring, suddenly burst a sand trap. Sand poured down, and clay slabs crushed two men. The third man, his feet protruding from the debris, was pulled out alive.

Curtis and security chief Soriano were notified, but nobody was prepared for the public outcry. Journalists crowded into Ft. Santiago, and the Philippine Senate demanded an investigation. Marcos cronies led the attack, blaming Curtis for the deaths, and for 'desecrating a national monument'. He countered that the gold they were on the verge of recovering would pay the Philippine national debt. President Aquino backed Curtis. She authorized IPM to continue for ninety days more.

Curtis knew he was only a few meters from hitting the gold vault. To prove it, he brought in a drill rig and bored down. Drill hole number twelve paid off. On April 23, 1988, the bit came up with fragments of gold, marble, wood. The Golden Lily map showed gold bars in wood crates on marble slabs. Curtis had hit paydirt.

His electronic sensors also detected a small but significant target just to the left of this drill hole, probably the oil drum of loose treasure that Ben said was added to the backfill at the last moment. It could be worth millions. President Aquino was elated.

Once again, however, there was mischief backstage. Fundraiser George Wortinger returned from Nevada with Ernie Whittenburg, who claimed to be a building contractor. Whittenburg's money actually came from drug-traffic; he would later be convicted and imprisoned. Soriano and McDougald both knew that Wortinger was feeding Whittenburg's drug money into this project all along, but nobody told Curtis.

When Curtis protested, Whittenburg countered by offering to buy a controlling interest in the project for $500,000 cash, on the condition that Curtis be removed and sent home. Now that Curtis had located the gold, he was no longer needed – Teresa-2 all over again. Any goldbug who wanted to make a recovery in the Philippines needed Curtis, because he had the maps and understood them. But once Curtis identified a target, he was expendable. This is typical of treasure hunting, as parodied in the book and movie *Treasure of the Sierra Madre*. Greed feeds narcissism, and narcissism feeds greed.

"Soriano begged me to take Whittenburg's money," Curtis told us. "It was drug money, and I wanted no part of it."

Soriano then asked Curtis to turn over to him personally the treasure maps for Ft. Santiago, and for another important site in Manila at the Bonafacio Bridge. When Curtis flatly refused, the national security chief dropped the bomb. He told Curtis that unless he left the Philippines immediately, he would urge President Aquino to cancel the IPM permit. If Curtis cooperated, Soriano would let Curtis come back later. If he refused to leave, he would be arrested, and charges would be filed against him. Grimly, Curtis packed his bags and flew home.

According to Grand Jury testimony, the moment Curtis had gone, Soriano and McDougald took on Whittenburg as a full partner and moved ahead with the recovery at Ft. Santiago. A member of their team testified that they recovered an oil drum packed with 24 small gold bars, gold and silver coins, and loose jewels. The main target, which Curtis had drilled into, was several meters below that, but they would be on top of it soon.

They also started digging at Bonafacio Bridge, where they put Whittenburg in charge. In 1942, this railway bridge over the Pasig River was blown up during the American retreat. The bridge had collapsed but its big concrete abutments were still in place. Subsequently, Golden Lily had dug a deep vault beneath one of the concrete abutments, placing 340 metric tons of 50-kilo gold bars inside Mosler safes (worth about $4.5-billion in 1988). The cache was hidden with a slab resembling the original concrete. Unfortunately for him, Curtis had revealed to his partners that it would be simple to penetrate the vault by excavating from the side. What always kept him from doing the site himself was the adjacent highway that made it too conspicuous. Now the Aquino administration had conveniently re-routed the highway, so Whittenburg, McDougald and Soriano could use drill rigs without being observed by every passing car or truck. Soriano arranged the official permit, and a few squatters were moved away.

Work at Bonafacio Bridge proceeded quickly when Craig Nelson, a California investor, gave $100,000 to bring in a drill rig able to bore a hole six feet in diameter. By November 30, they were down 170 feet below the bridge abutment. When Nelson arrived at the site that morning to check on progress, he found Ernie Whittenburg in a state of great excitement. "I touched a Jap!" Whittenburg shouted, an agreed code phrase meaning they had hit their target.

Nelson later testified: "Ernie Whittenburg told us that when he went down the hole in the elevator, he saw and touched two of the eight safes that were visible." Soriano, Nelson said, had a plan to bring in army trucks to haul the gold away at night. Because of their weight, only twenty-five bars could be brought up the elevator each time, and there were more than six thousand bars.

Soriano immediately made a trans-Pacific phone call to McDougald, who cut short a trip to California and flew back to Manila. The next day, Nelson said, "McDougald told me… that I must have misunderstood Ernie Whittenburg …he said that Ernie Whittenburg didn't actually see the safes." Nelson said McDougald insisted they had not yet reached the chamber containing the safes. Realizing he was being lied to, Nelson returned to the site to see for himself and discovered that he was not allowed to enter, although he had paid for the drilling rig. All Filipino workers had been sent home, and security at the bridge was taken over by two heavily-armed members of the U.S. Special Forces, friends of McDougald, one of them a full colonel who reportedly took leave from active duty for this purpose. McDougald told all those involved that water had flooded the hole, so they had to abandon the project.

According to Colonel Canson, head of the constabulary in Rizal province, he assigned two army trucks to McDougald for five nights, December 2-6, 1988, from midnight to 6 a.m. Other sources said a number of armored cars also were involved.

Eyewitnesses claim the trucks and armored cars carried heavy loads from Bonafacio Bridge to Ft. Santiago, where the cargo was loaded onto barges in the Pasig River. Subsequently, word got around that 325 metric tons of gold were for sale in secure storage at Manila International Airport – less 15 metric tons that were not accounted for.

Remaining partners in the venture now turned on each other. Fundraiser George Wortinger told a federal Grand Jury in Nevada that a total of $1.5-million in drug money had been poured into the digs at the fort and the bridge, by Ernie Whittenburg. Wortinger testified that McDougald and Soriano both knew it was drug money: "[McDougald] said 'You know, if this ever breaks in the press …he [Soriano] will be in lots of trouble.'

"It was drug money," Wortinger stated. "I mean, if that broke in the press over there, we would be crucified."

Indeed, when Manila newspapers reported that some Whittenburg drug money was transferred to Soriano's personal account, President Aquino demanded his resignation as national security advisor, effective February 15, 1989. Wortinger also testified that Whittenburg paid for $50,000 of furniture to equip a new house McDougald purchased in Manila, and helped to finance a new house McDougald bought in San Francisco. He said Whittenburg also gave Soriano and McDougald each $50,000 in cash. The Grand Jury then called in McDougald.

Government prosecutors initially sought forfeiture of McDougald's new San Francisco home. But McDougald was persuaded instead to prepare a report on his partner. Thanks in part to McDougald's testimony, Whittenburg was tried and sentenced to life in prison for drug trafficking.

Like Humphrey Bogart and his partners in the Sierra Madre, all these men were obsessed with gold, and turned on each other. But they are small fry compared to international bankers who accept the gold on deposit then, in the manner of magicians, make it vanish.

CHAPTER FIFTEEN

CONNECT THE DOTS

After half a century of disinformation to hide the war-gold recoveries and secret slush funds, incontrovertible evidence is emerging from investigations, lawsuits, leaks and blunders. Until Marcos lost power, Japan's looting was fobbed off successfully as isolated instances. If it rarely happened, why ask what became of the plunder?

Once on American turf, however, the Marcoses were hit by lawsuits accusing them of theft and conversion of recovered treasure, human rights abuse and racketeering related to that treasure. Ensuing revelations in court lifted the veil of secrecy and provided an unexpected glimpse of Washington's furtive conduct. The Reagan Administration's inept damage control, especially during Iran-Contra, revealed black-bag operations previously unknown, and a network of private military and intelligence companies intended to privatize U.S. foreign policy and national security. It became obvious that their true purpose was to get around laws, and to avoid peer review.

For twenty-five years, Santa Romana's heirs also were stonewalled, but they too filed suit to recover masses of bullion hidden in American banks – much of it still there, as we now demonstrate.

For hard evidence, the keystone case was the Gold Buddha, because it proved certain elementary things about Japan's looting of Asia and the postwar recoveries of this loot. This evidence was presented to a jury in a U.S. court in Hawaii, which awarded the largest sum in history.

It happened this way: After years in hiding, Roger Roxas resurfaced in 1988. With Marcos under house arrest in Honolulu, Roxas thought he could safely press a suit to reclaim the Gold Buddha and bullion stolen from him in 1971. He contacted Felix Dacaney, a childhood friend living near Atlanta, Georgia, who had prospered in America and had two sons attending the Annapolis Naval Academy. To protect Roxas, he and Dacaney formed Golden Budha [sic] Corporation, or GBC, and Roxas assigned his interest in the treasure to GBC. As Roxas no longer had control over the claim, it was less likely that he would be threatened or tricked out of his interest. Dacaney's Georgia attorney sought outside help, and reached an agreement with Daniel Cathcart's influential firm in Los Angeles. In February 1988, Cathcart filed suit against Marcos in Honolulu, asking for damages, including injuries from beatings and torture. The suit asserted that Marcos had stolen the Gold Buddha, diamonds, and gold biscuits from Roxas, then removed a lot more gold from the tunnel Roxas had spent years discovering. Technically, Roxas was the finder not only of the Gold Buddha, diamonds and gold biscuits he took home, but of all other Japanese war loot later recovered from the site by Marcos soldiers.

In Hawaii the Marcoses scoffed, and military aid Arturo Aruiza told the press the whole idea of Yamashita's Gold was "a fantastic story that came out 16 years ago and there was an investigation by the [Philippine] Senate... Nothing came out of it. We dismissed the story 16 years ago, and don't want to talk about it."

Cathcart's firm took seven years to gather evidence of eyewitnesses establishing that there *was* Japanese plunder in the Philippines, that Roxas had found a solid 22-karat Gold Buddha and ingots, and that Marcos had stolen the Buddha and ingots, then tortured Roxas in a conspiracy to hush it up.

In the course of tracking down witnesses, a great deal of evidence emerged concerning the overall nature of Japan's looting, how the loot was hidden in the islands, how it was recovered by Marcos, and how Marcos had used subterfuge to move the gold into the global market, clearly with help from the U.S. Government. All this was assembled in documents and depositions, many of them on videotape, eventually filling a large room.

Much of the legwork was done by Arlene Friedman, a feisty Los Angeles private detective employed by Cathcart. To her, the story Roxas told at first seemed utterly fantastic. Yamashita's Gold involved quantities so huge, dollar figures so enormous, it was hard to believe. To convince a jury, Cathcart and Friedman had to track down gold brokers who shun publicity, treasure hunters who crave secrecy, eyewitnesses scared of being murdered. Petite but relentless, Friedman pulled off what had daunted and eluded most investigators since World War II, and in the process made startling discoveries bearing on the Tokyo-Washington cover-up.

"As long as it's legal and it won't give me a disease," she told us, "I will do anything to get information. If it means playing dumb woman or flirt, or putting on my Shirley Temple outfit, I'll do it."

When Cathcart called her in to meet Roxas, she was startled by his lumpy, misshapen face and bulging blind left eye (souvenir of the beatings by Marcos thugs using a rubber mallet reported in Chapter Ten).

Cathcart interviewed Roxas exhaustively for five days. Prying details from his memory, Cathcart concluded that ten people might still be alive who knew what really had happened. He asked Friedman to track them down one by one. Many years had passed. It would not be easy.

Roxas remembered an American GI stationed in the Philippines who visited his home in Baguio and took photos of Roxas with the Gold Buddha just before it was stolen. His name might have been 'Tim' or 'Chitem'. Friedman began the tedious process of poring over Pentagon records. After more than a year, she tracked down

Ken Cheatham, working as a night security guard for a Las Vegas hotel. "It was," she said, "like, *Eureka!*" According to what Cheatham later told the jury, in the early 1970s, age 26, he had been an Air Force intelligence officer stationed at Clark Field. An amateur treasure hunter, he was intrigued by stories of Yamashita's Gold, and drove up to Baguio to search for Japanese artifacts. This was the very moment Roxas recovered the Gold Buddha and took it home, and the resort town was buzzing with rumors that a local man had found something amazing. Cheatham knocked on the door and introduced himself. It turned out they were members of the same treasure-hunting club run by Gene Ballinger. Roxas took Cheatham to his back bedroom and removed a bedspread covering the seated Gold Buddha, still coiled in heavy ropes. Cheatham got out his camera and took photos, including a shot of himself with Roxas and the Buddha – irrefutable proof that Cheatham was there, and the Buddha existed. Back at Clark Field, he wrote a letter to Gene Ballinger enclosing prints of his photos. Ballinger published an article on the discovery in his treasure-hunters' newsletter, wrongly identifying Cheatham as Roxas' partner. The story was picked up by news wires, and carried in the U.S. military paper, Stars and Stripes.

When Marcos saw the story, he hit the roof. Cheatham was summoned to base security where he was confronted by a CIA officer and Marcos agents. He told Arlene Friedman, "The CIA guy told me to say the statue wasn't made of gold and to downplay the whole thing, so Marcos would lose interest in me. If I got involved in this, he said they'd ship me out to Vietnam." Cheatham was scared. At the insistence of the CIA officer, he signed an affidavit certifying that the Buddha was not made of gold. He told Cathcart that he lied about the Buddha from then on, saying it was brass or, anyway, not gold. At the trial in Hawaii, Cheatham's photographs provided definite physical proof that Roxas did possess a Buddha with a removable head, totally unlike the brass Buddha with a fixed head hastily substituted by Marcos.

Next Cathcart and Friedman had to establish that it was Marcos who stole the Gold Buddha. In Las Vegas she made contact with Robert Curtis, who eventually gave a long videotape deposition describing how in 1975 he had spent many hours with Marcos and had seen a seated Buddha of solid gold, with a removable head, in the office of the president at his summer palace in Mariveles. Curtis testified that he had examined the statue closely, unscrewed the head, and determined to his satisfaction as a metallurgist that it was solid gold. Examining the Cheatham color photos, Curtis testified it was exactly the same Buddha he saw in the summer palace. (There are unique qualities to the shape, color, and detail of this Buddha that are unmistakable.)

Psychic Olof Jonsson then was located. Jonsson testified that when he was in the Philippines helping Marcos pinpoint gold treasure vaults, he, too, had examined the Gold Buddha in the summer palace, and corroborated the testimony of Curtis that it was identical to the one in Cheatham's photos, with a removable head.

Daniel Cathcart also had to establish beyond doubt that the statue really was solid gold. The answer came from Luis Mendoza, a Filipino goldsmith who had assayed the statue at the Roxas house in 1971, drilling tiny holes in the back near the neck to produce powder that he could run through the necessary tests. Mendoza testified that his test showed the Buddha was solid 22-carat gold, normal in Asia at the time.

Aside from the Gold Buddha, there also was the theft of the small gold biscuit bars, and thousands of other gold ingots that Roxas sealed in the tunnel for his own later recovery. A Filipino army cook, Juan Quijon, testified to the Honolulu court that he had been assigned to Task Force Restoration, an army unit created in 1972 by Marcos and General Ver to secretly excavate treasure sites in the Philippines. Quijon spent nearly a year (1974-1975) with other soldiers excavating the tunnel behind the hospital in Baguio, where Roxas had found the Gold Buddha. Quijon watched three or four men at a time carry out heavy wooden boxes and, when some rotten boxes broke, he saw big gold bars fall to the ground, three to a box. He said an average of ten boxes of gold a day were removed from the tunnel during that twelve-month period. Hospital staff, who were watching during these months, confirmed this. Igorot tribesmen did the heaviest work, Quijon said. When all the gold was removed, he said the Igorots were taken into the tunnel and shot, to eliminate them as witnesses.

As evidence that Marcos was in possession of enormous quantities of gold bullion far in excess of known Philippine reserves, Friedman tracked down two Australian brokers who in the early 1980s had negotiated nine contracts with Marcos to sell a total of $1.63-trillion in gold. They established for the court record, and to the satisfaction of the jury, that the deals were made, and were not a fiction. The documentation they provided established beyond any doubt that Marcos did have in his possession and did sell $1.63-trillion worth of gold bullion. The Australians would also testify that while visiting Marcos they were blindfolded and taken to a warehouse where the blindfolds were removed, and they saw that the warehouse was full of gold bars.

Norman 'Tony' Dacus, a Las Vegas investor, told Friedman that on a visit to the Philippines he was taken to Mt. Apo where Marcos was building a Mt. Rushmore style memorial to himself. Dacus said the president's son Bong-Bong took him into secret tunnels in Mt. Apo, where he was shown boxes of gold bars and other treasure. Dacus said Bong-Bong told him this gold was waiting to be flown out of the country by the U.S. military, at the behest of the CIA. Dacus was an expert source because he was linked by marriage to one of the senior Marcos intelligence officers, Colonel Pimentel, who arranged a number of these gold deals and personally escorted the gold to its destinations as a senior member of The Umbrella. Dacus also helped Pimental and Marcos broker the huge Luxembourg gold deal, described in Chapter Fourteen, for which he was paid a hefty commission.

A lot of Friedman's investigation in the Gold Buddha case was paper-chasing in libraries and archives, where she plowed through tens of thousands of pages of assets and business records. What had started as archival research became dangerous. One morning as she entered the stairwell of a parking garage, a man grabbed her from behind.

"We just want your help," he hissed. She punched her way free, escaping with a few cuts and bruises.

Cathcart's eighth floor office suite in a glass tower at Century City was broken into and bugged. Security experts told him the bugging was not done by Marcos, but by Washington, because the equipment was far too high-tech for anyone but the U.S. Government. His law office was under constant surveillance from teams in a high-rise opposite.

The Gold Buddha trial finally was set for May 25, 1993. As the trial date approached, Cathcart told Roxas to lie low and arranged for bodyguards to escort him from Manila to Honolulu. On May 24, he called Roxas and told him to catch a plane to Hawaii immediately. "An hour and a half later, he was dead," said Cathcart. His widow and many others believe Roxas was poisoned. As she explained, her husband had been looking tired and anemic. When she went to a bakery, downstairs from the apartment where they were hiding, she was approached by a well-dressed man who offered to give her some free medication for her husband. When he took the pills, Roxas died.

A few hours later, a CIA informant known to Cathcart and Friedman phoned his law office from Manila and told Friedman, "Your client is dead. He was poisoned. Imelda ordered it, and we did it."

The news stunned Cathcart.

"I told [Mrs. Roxas] to get the remaining pills and FedEx them to me immediately. But when the package arrived, the envelope was empty."

Cathcart tried to arrange an immediate autopsy, but this proved impossible. Roxas was hastily cremated.

"The coroner never conducted a toxicology test," Cathcart said, "and never opened [Roxas] up. He ruled that [Roxas] died of tuberculosis."

After many delays, the trial got underway in Honolulu, and the jury heard eye-witnesses describe the Gold Buddha, rooms full of gold bars, deals involving thousands of metric tons of gold. At one point, during a discussion of various Japanese imperial treasure sites in the Philippines, Imelda Marcos herself said the gold Marcos had in his warehouses "could have come from any of those sites".

Members of the Roxas family testified that Roger's brother Jose was paid thousands of dollars by Imelda Marcos to lie and perjure himself by stating that the Roxas Buddha was not gold but only brass. During trial, the jury were shown photos of Jose's tattooed back with the words in large letters:

BRO. OF FOUNDER OF THE GOLDEN BUDDHA.
INT'L NEWS PHILIPPINES

From all this testimony, it became evident to the jury that Japanese war loot definitely had been hidden in the Philippines, Roger Roxas definitely discovered a major cache of it, the Gold Buddha definitely was solid gold, Marcos definitely stole the treasure, and Marcos definitely made major gold deals to sell billions of dollars worth of this recovered plunder. The jury decided in favor of Roxas and his heirs, and awarded GBC a judgment of $43-billion against the Marcos estate, the biggest civil judgment in history to that date. ($22-billion plus 10 percent simple interest since the theft).

Later, on appeal, this award was reduced to $22-billion flat, based on the contention that nobody knew beyond question what was in every last one of the wood boxes recovered by Marcos soldiers from the Roxas tunnel. This is now being appealed by Cathcart to the Hawaii Supreme Court.

The estate of Roger Roxas was separately awarded $6-million for his imprisonment and torture, an award that stood up on appeal.

As for the Gold Buddha itself, the chief government prosecutor in Zurich, Switzerland, assured journalists that it was in a Marcos gold bullion vault in a special repository beneath Zurich's Kloten Airport.

While an American jury judged these to be incontrovertible facts, Tokyo and Washington continue to deny them.

•

Encouraged by the Roxas lawsuit, other victims came forward. In 1999, the Filipino soldiers who removed the gold from the Roxas tunnel and other sites in the Philippines prepared lawsuits against the Marcos estate. According to an affidavit signed by nearly a hundred of these men, they carried out 'massive diggings' while pretending to restore national monuments, and recovered thousands of metric tons of gold, other precious metals and large quantities of loose gemstones. Marcos came to the sites, they said, often in the company of Japanese.

Their first major success was in 1973 near Lake Caliraya in Lumban, Laguna, where one of their backhoes struck what turned out to be the first of several concrete vaults. Repeated banging of the backhoe broke open a corner of one vault, exposing 75-kilo gold bars. Marcos told them, "You will all share in everything that's here, but you have to wait for the right time." That time never came.

As other concrete vaults were unearthed – each 6 feet x 5 feet x 5 feet – a large crane hoisted them on to a massive army tank transporter, which took them to a secret destination.

From 1974 to 1979, the soldiers stated, they dug at Montalban, Antipolo, Baras, and Teresa, all Golden Lily sites in Rizal province. It was their failure to open Teresa-1 in 1974 that led to Robert Curtis successfully opening Teresa-2 the next year. They shifted operations to Intramuros, the old walled city in Manila, and to Ft. Santiago, where they said they recovered more than a hundred boxes of treasure.

According to their affidavit, crates of gold bars were shipped out of the Philippines from Manila International Airport using C-130 military aircraft. They said some of the gold was transported commercially by Cathay Pacific Airlines, and by American President Lines, through arrangement with Tamaraw Security Service, owned and operated for Marcos by General Ver, as part of The Umbrella.

This is independent corroboration by the recovery team itself of what we recounted in earlier chapters, and what was stated by Robert Curtis and others in their separate testimonies.

•

Santa Romana's dormant bank accounts were of special interest to his heirs – but also to The Enterprise, to the U.S. Treasury, and to major banks holding his cash and bullion. As these various parties bickered, maneuvered, and backstabbed, they became involved in very interesting lawsuits. Seen at random, the bits and pieces are curious. Seen altogether they are astounding, and supported by government records.

When he died, Santy left to fourteen heirs a fortune estimated by their attorneys to be worth over $50-billion. All their efforts to recover his assets from banks have been blocked or, more often, evaded.

The three main heirs were Santy's corporate accountant, Tarciana Rodriguez, acting for the estate; his common-law wife, Luz Rambano; and his adult daughter, Flordeliza. After a few false starts, they turned for help to the famous San Francisco lawyer Melvin Belli, New York attorney Eleanor Jackson Piel, former CIA deputy director Ray Cline, and one of America's best-known bankers, Citibank CEO John Reed. Also engaged in these efforts were Florida lobbyist George Depontis, former Bahamas supreme court justice Sir Leonard Knowles, and Washington attorney Robert A. Ackerman.

Because of the size of Santy's estate, and its secretive nature, Luz, Tarciana, and Flordeliza seem to have had every conceivable obstacle put in their path. The U.S. Government, and American banks, would like Santy's assets to remain where they are. So would the Swiss government and Swiss banks, banks in Hong Kong, and in other financial centers. In a few more years, everybody connected to Santy will be dead, so custody of his cash and bullion will remain in the banks, like Holocaust gold.

For Washington, stonewalling is imperative not only because of the gigantic assets involved, but to block attorneys from pursuing discovery (as in the Schlei case), which could reveal far more than Santy's financial data. Potentially, discovery could result in disclosure of the whole subject of covert war-gold recoveries, the Black Eagle Trust, diversion to corrupt purposes of secret funds like the M-Fund. This could damage reputations and careers, and make unavoidable an investigation by the General Accounting Office of Congress. President Ford had addressed a similar problem in 1975 when he set up the Rockefeller Commission to pacify interest in the CIA Family Jewels affair, remarking that he did not want information getting out that could blacken the reputation of every U.S. president since Truman.

Ironically, Santy's heirs were only interested in ending their poverty, not in exposing corruption, so it would have made sense to placate them with generous settlements in return for signed agreements never to raise the matter again. Yet both banks and governments have remained doggedly opaque and obstinate in blocking the heirs – a sure sign that they have much to hide.

Although the three principal heirs showed these banks probated wills, passbooks, bank statements, receipts, all the necessary passwords, code-words, and secret account numbers, provided to them by Santy, the response was the same. With four exceptions, the banks flatly denied having such accounts, whether the account in question was a safe-deposit box, or a huge gold bullion deposit.

For example, according to the Union Banque Suisse documents reproduced on our CDs, Santy's biggest single account there was 20,000 metric tons of gold bullion. This is the account on which the title-holder was magically changed at the moment of Santy's death, from his Crown Commodity Holdings to Major General Edward G. Landsdale [sic], bearing in mind that spelling errors made by Swiss banks are part of deliberate authenticity codes. One possibility is that on this monster account Santy was merely a straw man, being replaced by another straw man: Lansdale. We might ask, who else but a government would have sufficient leverage to make such a change at the biggest bank in Switzerland? Had UBS alone made the change, they are unlikely to have chosen the eccentric Lansdale as the new title-holder. However, by 1974 Lansdale had been out of government for a decade, and was one of the founding fathers of The Enterprise network, and an intimate colleague of some of America's wealthiest conservative moguls. If Lansdale and Santy always had shared control of this big UBS account, Lansdale might have been able to have UBS transfer title to his name, whereafter it could be accessed by his circle. The U.S. Government may not have been involved.

At $300 an ounce, this account would be worth $192-billion dollars, a lot more than the net worth of Bill Gates. Is this sum believable? Yes, if it is a covert U.S. Government account containing a mass of black gold. Just as no serious counter-feiter makes silly spelling mistakes, no conman in his right mind would dream up an account so big. Recall that the jury in the Roxas Gold Buddha case saw convincing evidence that $1.63-trillion in gold was sold by Marcos through his Australian brokers.

Documents we reproduce on our CDs bearing the signatures of a number of top Swiss bankers show that UBS has other accounts, including gold bullion and platinum, which are even larger. Such giant accounts are not out of the question for immensely wealthy men like King Fahd of Saudi Arabia, whose family have been banking bullion in Switzerland for decades. According to Gemini Consulting, worldwide private bank assets were $4.3-trillion in 1986, and were closing in on $14-trillion in 2000. So this account at UBS is not impossible.

UBS documents show that Crown Commodity Holdings was a subsidiary of Santy's Crown Enterprises. The group representative was Alfredo P. Ramos, an executive of Santy's company Diaz & Poirrotte Enterprises, registered in Monaco. Ramos states in an affidavit that "I know the late Don Severino Garcia Sta. Romana, Ramon Poirrotte or Jose Antonio Diaz, under the code 'From Father My Old Man... that once the work has begun, don't leave it until it's done, be the labor great or small, do it well or not at all'." This homily, as we've seen, is one that Santy learned from Lansdale in 1945. It is the same homily Santy quoted in his holographic will. It is used as a code phrase consistently in Santy's bank accounts. Such recurrences, over half a century, are not accidental.

According to videotaped interviews with Tarciana, immediately after Santy's death Lansdale also was involved in the mysterious movement of gold bullion from Santy's accounts at Citibank Manila to Citibank New York, possibly done to get the assets out of the Philippines before Marcos could attach them. Because the accounts were in Santy's names, such transfers would appear to be illegal without authorization from a recognized trustee of his estate, or someone holding his power of attorney, such as chief accountant Tarciana. If Lansdale had such a power of attorney, for whom was Lansdale acting?

Once these assets left the Philippines, they joined other bullion and cash accounts that documents show Santy already had in America at Citibank, Chase, Wells Fargo, Hanover Bank, and other banks.

Soon after his death, Santy's holographic will was probated in Manila, and Tarciana, Luz and Flordeliza were named by the court as legitimate heirs. Luz went to America hoping to gain access to the accounts at Citibank in Manhattan. There she enlisted the help of attorney Eleanor Jackson Piel, giving her Letters of Administration issued by the Philippine court. These had to be recognized by New York courts. Piel proceeded in Surrogate's Court for the issuance of Ancillary Letters of Administration, which would give Luz right of access to his accounts at Citibank, Chase, and Hanover. This took time.

While Luz pressed her case elsewhere, Piel wrote letters to the head offices of all the banks concerned, asking about the Santa Romana accounts. Not a single bank replied.

Luz flew to Switzerland, visiting UBS in Geneva with two American friends. According to one of the Americans, Jim Brown: "I sat with Luz and another American… while she gave a vice-president of Union Banque Suisse [Santy's] master gold account number with them [Master Gold Account 7257]. This banker not only admitted that it was a correct account, but also said he was familiar with the account." Brown insists the bank vice president then told Luz "he wouldn't recommend her trying to claim this account while she was in Switzerland, because before the bank or even the government of Switzerland would agree to allow her to take what this account represented, they would not be beyond having her killed first. He also went on to tell her, that he wouldn't recommend her hiring any Swiss attorneys, because the bank would simply buy them off."

We might scoff at the notion that a UBS vice president would make murder threats, but what of Christophe Meili? A student working nights as a security guard at UBS in Zurich, in January 1997 he discovered very old documents and books waiting to be shredded. They concerned assets of depositors who died in Nazi death camps. He knew that, a few months earlier, the Swiss government had ordered banks not to destroy archival material. He took some documents and gave them to the Hebrew Congregation of Zurich. When asked later why he did it, Meili replied that he had recently seen the movie *Schindler's List*.

"I knew I had to do something."

A month later, when the documents were made public by others, Meili was fired from his $18,000 job at UBS. Robert Studer, president of UBS, insinuated that Meili was financed by an international Jewish conspiracy. "This issue of so-called unclaimed Jewish money in Swiss banks rears its head again and again. For us it is no issue at all. The problem was thoroughly discussed after the Second World War and we conscientiously investigated then what money in our bank might have belonged to Holocaust victims because we wanted to settle the question once and for all. For us the case is closed."

Much as the State Department insists the 1951 San Francisco Peace Treaty closed the door on compensation and reparations for Japan's war victims. Much as Washington and the Marcoses insisted the Yamashita Gold story was only a myth.

UBS passed off the shredder incident as 'unfortunate' saying, "no one in our senior management would ever have approved such a decision." Robert Studer was removed from all official duties, but remained the bank's Honorary Chairman.

Meili received over 100 death threats, and threats to his wife and children. They fled to America where they were given asylum. Meili testified before U.S. Congressional committees investigating the hiding of Nazi assets by Swiss banks. Senator Anthony D'Amato called Christophe Meili an international hero. "The criminals are the ones who ordered the shredding of the documents."

•

Scared and deflated, Luz returned to the Philippines. Three years later she and Brown went back to Switzerland to approach a different bank. This time, Brown told us they were successful in recovering the accumulated interest from one of Santy's accounts, but the bank would not release the bullion itself. Another source told us Luz kept this recovery secret, feeling that she had been stonewalled so long that it would be absurd to forfeit any of it in taxes.

Meanwhile, Tarciana – Santy's corporate treasurer – tried to access his accounts at HSBC in Hong Kong. Following the advice of attorney Artemio Lobrin who had been Santy's tax consultant, she asked HSBC to verify the existence of the accounts mentioned in Santy's holographic will. After showing them all the necessary codes, passwords, and documents, a bank officer told her the accounts had not matured, were therefore inaccessible, and to come back in 1988.

In turn, Flordeliza sought access to Santy's accounts at the Hong Kong branch of Sanwa Bank. She had a passbook showing large cash deposits to that branch in March 1973. At first Sanwa denied it had a branch in Hong Kong in 1973. Then, despite all the documentation, they claimed they had no client called Santa Romana or any of his pseudonyms.

When Cory Aquino became president, her staff asked Australian financial expert Peter Nelson for help. He was shown computer sheets and forty passports bearing Santy's photo. "The passports matched details on the numerous bank accounts… Most transfers had originated in Hong Kong before being moved to other parts of the world. I added up the amounts mentally as I went along and lost count at around forty billion dollars! I was shown photos of crates and some of these were open. I of course could not vouch for this bullion but there were certificates to match."

The Aquino aides explained that Santy had left the majority of his estate to his daughter, which would make Flordeliza one of the richest women on earth, but when she tried to present the probated will to banks, she was told to prove that the man in the photo on all the passports with all the different names was in fact her father.

Meanwhile, the banks would sit profitably on the money.

Nelson said: "I told my Filipino friends there was a way out. If [Flordeliza] agreed to hand the money back to the government in the Philippines for a finder's fee of say five percent, that would give her more money than [she] could spend in a lifetime and the government would lend their weight in pushing for its return. They thanked me and I flew back to Sydney." Nothing came of it, and Flordeliza stayed poor.

•

Ultimately, all efforts fixed on Citibank, where John Reed was chairman and CEO. Under Reed's direction, Citibank became richly involved in offshore private banking. With offshore deposits worth over $100-billion it was ranked third after

UBS with $580-billion and Credit Suisse with $292-billion. By shifting money from country to country, offshore assets are protected from litigation by creditors, ex-spouses, or heirs. Except for cases involving moneylaundering, securities fraud or narcotics, most foreign courts will not recognize a U.S. court order. So a claimant must fight for access through courts in the nation where the account is held, only to discover the money already has been moved to another jurisdiction. This is key to what follows.

In December 1990, Tarciana went to Citibank's head office in Manhattan, with a friend acting as financial advisor and witness.

"We were taken in to see John Reed," her friend said. "When we showed him our documents, passwords and code-phrases, the magnitude of it suddenly hit Reed. He went white, and panicked. You could see it in his face. He left the conference room in a hurry. A few minutes later he returned with several Citibank lawyers." They told Tarciana to come back the following day.

"When we walked into the conference room the next day," Tarciana's friend recounted, "we found Reed sitting there with twenty lawyers. They told us these accounts did not exist."

Again Tarciana and her friend went away. On inspiration, they flew to Albany where they visited the New York State Tax Office. In its public records archive, they obtained a list of all the accounts Santy had at Citibank and other banks in New York State under his own name and aliases, and his company names. (Reproduced on our CDs.) They also discovered that all state and federal taxes had been waived on interest generated by these very big accounts, a curious exemption.

Returning to Citibank, they were confronted once again by Reed and his phalanx of attorneys. Tarciana and her friend showed them a copy of the New York State tax records list, demonstrating that the bank had lied, and the accounts did exist. According to Santy's own records and documents Tarciana had with her, Citibank held 4,700 metric tons of gold bullion belonging to Santy's estate.

No longer denying they had the accounts, the attorneys blandly told the two women to bring in 'the real party'. They refused to identify whom they meant – possibly Santy's corpse. They also said Tarciana needed 'legal' papers, which she already had shown them. They said Citibank wanted a statement from the Philippine government that it would not hold them responsible for releasing the money (again implicitly acknowledging the bank did hold the assets). This inferred that the funds might be claimed by Manila as gold stolen by Marcos, although the accounts were set up by Santy long before Marcos came to power. The attorneys also said they wanted a waiver from Imelda Marcos, implying that the Marcos family might make claims (real or imaginary) to some of Santy's assets. Finally they said they also needed a waiver from the U.S. Embassy in Manila, apparently meaning a waiver from the U.S. Government. All this doubletalk was clearly to fend off Tarciana while the bank decided what to do next. That did not take long.

The solution was simple: Citibank would move all Santy's assets offshore, from Citibank New York to Cititrust in the Bahamas. This would have the effect of putting the bullion outside the jurisdiction of New York courts, blocking any lawsuits contemplated by the heirs. Legally, such assets could not be moved out of New

York jurisdiction without authorization of the account holder or his heirs, or assigns (meaning Tarciana as corporate treasurer). But, if the gold were moved off-shore without the knowledge of the account holder or his heirs, the burden would be upon them to recover it. Large shipments of gold bullion also cannot take place without the knowledge and approval of the U.S. Treasury Department and the Federal Reserve. Nor could the bullion enter Nassau without approval of the Bahamian authorities. But there appear to have been ways to get around such obsta-cles, perhaps by attributing ownership of the gold to Citibank itself, which some attorneys might argue qualifies as 'wrongful conversion'.

This offshore maneuver was underway by the close of 1990, when word of it was leaked by a bank officer to members of The Enterprise. A counterploy to halt Citibank was initiated by former CIA Deputy Director Ray Cline and George Depontis, the Florida lobbyist with powerful connections in Nassau, including friendship with retired former Bahamas Chief Justice Sir Leonard Knowles. In case they needed help in Washington, Cline called in Robert A. Ackerman, a former Justice Department attorney. To get him up to speed, Cline gave Ackerman many documents including letters, memos and faxes. According to a letter written by Ackerman in January 1991, Cline explained how "in Gen. Lansdale's Philippine days" Santy had recovered a lot of Japanese war loot and moved it "to 176 bank accounts in 42 countries". These accounts, Cline said, included "large amounts of bullion [and] cash". He told Ackerman he was interested in brokering "an agree-ment between the Philippine claimant [Tarciana] and the USG under which most of any money belonging to the USG would go back to it".

It is unclear why any of this war-gold belonged to the U.S. Government rather than to the people from whom it was stolen, unless it was claimed as a war prize – in which case, why would it have been kept secret for over half a century? Nor is it clear how Cline could separate what belonged to the U.S. Government from what belonged to Santy's heirs; although, with Cline's close CIA connections, it is like-ly that he could work out a split. According to Alan Foringer, "Ray Cline told us he had made it a point to read all Agency files on Santy and Lansdale's recoveries." Foringer said Cline knew all about the secret accord at Bretton Woods and the Black Eagle Trust growing out of them, how General MacArthur and Robert B. Anderson had toured the Golden Lily sites with Santy and Lansdale, and how John J. McCloy had been the key man setting up the M-Fund and other political action funds.

Cline's long career in the CIA lends authority to what he told Foringer, Ackerman and others. At the end of World War II, Cline was a young OSS analyst in what remained of Nationalist China. He then spent three years as the CIA's chief analyst on Korea, dealing with John Singlaub, Paul Helliwell, and Bill Casey (who had moved to Wall Street but still was part of the Dulles brothers' circle). During 1958-1962, Cline was CIA station chief in Taiwan, a job he got through the chief of dirty tricks, Frank Wisner, just before Wisner went insane. In Taipei, Cline was responsible for clandestine operations all over Southeast Asia. He set up a Political Warfare Cadres Academy where trainees from the Philippines and elsewhere were taught: "to defeat communism, we had to be cruel." While Chiang Kai-shek was alive, Cline befriended the generalissimo's hard-drinking son, Chiang Ching-kuo (CCK), who controlled the KMT intelligence services. Cline became "his main drinking companion". When CCK succeeded his father as president of Taiwan, Cline's star rose accordingly. He returned to Washington as CIA's deputy director for intelligence gathering.

Cline understood the historical context, was expert on the financial side, and knew the personalities. He was personally acquainted with the wartime KMT secret police boss General Tai Li, Shanghai druglord Tu Yueh-sheng, *yakuza* boss Kodama, fixer Sasakawa, prime ministers Kishi and Tanaka, the CIA's Wisner and Casey, Helliwell, Lansdale, Santa Romana, Marcos, Singlaub, and Schweitzer. In 1966, after clashing sharply with President Johnson over Far Eastern policy, Cline was forced out of his job as CIA deputy director and exiled to the U.S. Embassy in Bonn. When Johnson decided not to run again, Cline was able to return in 1969 to become director of State Department's Bureau of Intelligence and Research, where part of his job was to keep tabs on the black money movements of President Marcos. Like Bill Casey, Cline always had a special interest in financial intelligence. He had impressive academic credentials from Harvard and Oxford. In 1973, with his extremely close ties to Taiwan, Cline quarreled with President Nixon over rapprochement with China, and was forced to retire from government, becoming head of a conservative think-tank at George Washington University. Now a key player in the shadow network of The Enterprise, Cline became a special advisor to President Reagan, closely tied to Casey, Schweitzer, and Singlaub. In audio tapes of the Hong Kong meetings where Curtis was cajoled into helping Nippon Star, Cline's name was invoked many times.

When Cline testified before Congress in the Iran-Contra hearings, he was asked if he visited General Singlaub in the Philippines. Cline said Singlaub met him at the airport. "I had it very fully explained to me, by both him and General Schweitzer, that he was there exploring for the recovery of gold and precious objects that had been buried in CENSORED which I knew about, and that he had found clear indications that he could recover this treasure, and that he was representing a group of people there who were trying to do so. ...I discussed nothing with Singlaub except the treasure. ...He showed me a lot of... told me things that made me believe that, that he felt he would be able to recover from several buried sites CENSORED a lot of bullion, money, and that was his sole objective, as far as I know."

From this testimony, it is obvious that Cline was evasive with Congress, not revealing what he told Ackerman. Basic historical and geographical details of his testimony were censored out, because they could not be shared with the American public.

•

According to Ackerman's letter, Depontis initially suggested that Tarciana deposit several small checks into Santy's corporate accounts at Citibank, which would not cause alarm. If Citibank accepted the deposits, it implicitly acknowledged Tarciana's role as corporate treasurer. She could then ask the bank to send her regular statements regarding any activity on the account. If the bank did so, she would have established her legal right of access, and could begin withdrawals.

When this did not work, Depontis prepared to file suit in Bahamian courts to block the transfer to Nassau. Before filing suit, he said he offered Citibank a deal. In a tape-recorded telephone conversation with Robert Curtis, Depontis related that if Citibank agreed to this deal, he expected to receive a 15 percent commission that would come to $7,287,937,000. At 15 percent, this meant the deal as a whole was for approximately $50-billion – the amount Citibank was trying to move off-shore. He said on the tape that he needed this much money, because "I have to pay off Ray Cline, Ackerman, this guy, that guy…"

To gain leverage, Depontis sought powers of attorney from Tarciana and Luz. In September 1991, Tarciana agreed to a ten-page personal services agreement with him, and a power of attorney. But when Depontis proposed offering Citibank a deal where she would settle for a mere $25-million, Tarciana said she broke off with Depontis. She was chasing billions of dollars in a dozen banks, so to accept such a small deal with Citibank would set a dangerous precedent.

Thereafter, Depontis apparently put all his effort into getting a settlement for Luz. On June 3, 1992, he told Robert Curtis, "Citibank is really hung out on this. I think Citibank is going to go down big time."

Weeks later, in July 1992, Tarciana and her financial advisor were back at Citibank again facing John Reed across his conference table. They demanded that the gold and cash accounts that had been moved to the Bahamas be returned to New York. According to Tarciana, when Reed realized that the two women knew the assets had been moved, he again "turned white and panicked" – and called in his attorneys.

Once more the ladies left empty-handed.

This affront persuaded Tarciana to go after Citibank. She restored to Depontis her power of attorney. Eleanor Piel received a call from Depontis, telling her that he would now represent Luz and Tarciana in the lawsuit in the Bahamas. On July 25, 1992, a joint agreement was drawn up by Tarciana, Luz, Eleanor Piel, Depontis, Sir Leonard Knowles, and Philippine attorney Zosimo Banaag, authorizing Depontis to offer Citibank a last deal before filing suit: They would allow Citibank to buy from them the $50-billion in gold it had moved to the Bahamas, at a favorable rate of $305 an ounce, $50 less than the market rate at that time; Citibank could then turn around and sell the gold at the market rate, making a significant profit while avoiding a lawsuit for wrongful conversion.

When Citibank turned down the offer, Depontis and Sir Leonard filed suit in Bahamian courts. Eleanor Piel flew to Nassau where she met Depontis and Sir Leonard. Piel told us Sir Leonard opened his files to her, and told her his position was that, by denying everything, Citibank was simply playing for time.

Attorney Mel Belli joined the fracas, mounting a flanking attack on Citibank at state courts in California where the bank had branches. In a $20-billion lawsuit Belli filed for Luz, John Reed was named as a defendant wrongfully converting Santy's assets for Reed's personal use. According to friends, Belli was in ill health, and relished the idea of climaxing his career with a stunning victory over Citibank and Reed. Belli wrote Brian Greenspun, editor-in-chief of *The Las Vegas Sun*, "It may

sound wild, and it did to me at first, but I'm now convinced that some very important banks around the world did have deposits of [Santy's] money. We've taken several depositions of banking officials around the world who have denied deposits
being made with them although we presented the receipts and passbooks." Belli
said he had reason to believe that Santy's wealth could be "an offshoot of the
Yamashita treasure".

Belli's suit was based on wrongful conversion of personal property. After listing
specific Citibank accounts belonging to Santy, the suit went on to say: "Defendant
John Reed, the Chairman and Chief Executive Officer of defendant Citibank, has
spearheaded Citibank's conversion of the gold bullion which was owned by
[Santy]." The crux of the lawsuit lay in the charge that "Reed and Citibank have
systematically sold and are selling said gold bullion to buyers and converting the
sales proceeds to their own use."

Belli's suit also brought charges of wrongful conversion against Chase Manhattan
Bank, HSBC, Bank of America, and Wells Fargo Bank, all of which had offices in
California.

The banks fought back through an impressive array of San Francisco law firms:
Folger & Levin representing Chase; Heller Ehrman White representing Wells Fargo;
Landels Ripley Diamond representing HSBC; Steefel Levitt Weiss representing
Citibank as corporation and John Reed as personally named defendant. Bank of
America was represented by its own general counsel. They were circling their wag-
ons.

After further investigation and discovery, Belli concluded that he had chanced
upon a major state secret. He told friends he now believed that Citibank's John
Reed had joined in a plot with President Reagan, James Baker, Bill Casey and Prime
Minister Margaret Thatcher, to use Yamashita's Gold to finance covert operations
by America and Britain. He referred to the plan as 'The Purple Ink Document'.

Unfortunately, Belli's health deteriorated sharply over the next two and a half
years, and he died in 1996 before the case could make much progress. Those who
succeeded him at his law firm did not pursue the case with similar vigor, but the
Belli suit against Reed and these five major banks is still pending.

•

In 2000, after years of delay, upheaval, interference, threats, and reversals,
Eleanor Piel filed new papers in the New York Surrogate's Court to empower Luz
and Piel as co-administrators of Santy's estate, allowing them to move forward in
locating Santy's assets in New York State. Piel told us she now had "the right to
recover any Santa Romana gold in the banks in New York State, or gold that previously was in those banks but had been moved elsewhere".

All was not well at Citibank. It was accused of moneylaundering. In December
1998, the General Accounting Office concluded that Citibank had laundered $100-
million dollars for Raul Salinas, brother of disgraced former Mexican President
Carlos Salinas. The GAO report described how Citibank helped Salinas create "a
money-managing system that disguised the origin, destination and beneficial owner
of the funds involved". In December 1996, CIA Director John Deutsch resigned

under a cloud and immediately joined Citibank's board of directors. In November 2000, just before another scandal broke at Citibank, John Reed resigned as CEO. This time the bank was embarrassed by the revelation that it had moved $800-million for Russian tycoon Irakly Kaveladze, who set up 2,000 dummy corporations in Delaware to which Citibank and others had been funneling his money for nearly a decade. Two other Citibank private clients were the sons of the late Nigerian dictator General Sani Abacha, accused of having siphoned off more than $4-billion from taxes, phony contracts and bribes. When Abacha's son Mohammed made an urgent demand of Citibank for a $39-million overdraft, Citibank disbursed the funds to him through three different accounts. Curiously there has been no similar investigation by the GAO into what was done with Santy's $50-billion at Cititrust.

Why are banks so evasive, and how can they deny having accounts? The answer is that there is much money to be made by delays. Merrill-Lynch sat for many years on $35-million in Marcos assets, and said not a word until the end of 2000 when they were ordered by a court to relinquish the funds. During those years, significant profits were made on the dormant funds. Swiss banks adamantly deny having Marcos accounts, but early in 2001 Irene Marcos and her husband were accused by the German government of attempting to launder $13.4-billion by moving it from Swiss banks to Deutsche Bank in Frankfurt. For decades, the same Swiss banks denied sitting on the assets of Holocaust victims. Heirs may show all manner of evidence, only to be told their documents are false. If they press, they risk arrest for negotiating 'counterfeit' instruments. But who says the documents are counterfeit?

For example, a document we reproduce on our CDs is a certificate that assured President Sukarno of Indonesia that quantities of gold and platinum he deposited in Swiss banks were guaranteed by all the members of the Swiss banking trust, whose signatures are conspicuously displayed and easily validated. Yet every effort by Sukarno's heirs to access the account failed, and the very idea that a Sukarno estate exists is derided. While some Sukarno precious metal certificates indeed may be counterfeit, how can you know for sure until an expert opinion is rendered? As the bank in question has a vested interest in claiming fraud, it is hardly the proper judge of validity. Only by testing the document in a court of law can that judgement be made, but as we saw in the case of Norbert Schlei, that avenue is subject to abuse.

Where can you turn? If you tell a bank you only want to know whether a document is real or counterfeit, you are almost certain to be arrested on the spot just for asking. You may be arrested even when you do not ask.

Take the bizarre case of Australian broker Peter Johnston, who was asked by a client to negotiate a UBS gold certificate in Europe. While traveling, Johnston did not want to carry the certificate, so he left it in 'safe custody' with the London branch of Australia's Westpac Bank. He often lodged such certificates with Westpac. He did not ask Westpac to attest to its being genuine. Yet the branch manager felt 'uneasy', and without asking Johnston faxed copies to UBS in Switzerland, asking if it was genuine. Without ever examining the original, UBS 'informally' declared it a forgery. It is UBS policy to call all such documents forgeries, but to avoid doing so formally by Tested Telex because that is equivalent to sworn testimony in a court of law. An informal opinion casts doubt, while avoiding liability. UBS does this routinely to scare away people hoping to negotiate gold certificates. Normally, the City of London Fraud Squad would refuse to pursue a charge based on an informal opinion, but this time the Fraud Squad set up a sting, and when Johnston walked in to the Westpac office on March 6, 1995, he was arrested and charged with attempted fraud – because the certificate *might* be phony and Johnston might try in the future to negotiate it. Amazingly, Johnston was convicted on this specious charge and languished in prison for 18 months. At no time did UBS actually establish that the certificate was a forgery, only saying it was not issued by UBS in Zurich. This was a blatant dodge, because UBS gold bullion deals are not done in Zurich but by their subsidiary, Warburg Dillon Read, at Glattbrug near Zurich airport. In short, Johnston appears to have been falsely imprisoned on false testimony, for something he did not attempt to do. There are many similarities to the Schlei case.

An expert on gold certificates, Wolfgang Jentsch, explains that these instruments "may take many forms and quite possibly will not be in the banking form. They are by their very nature private banking documents and will not be in the public domain. …the larger the amount concerned, the closer becomes the circle of those who know. …it is rare that the main structure of the bank itself would ever know of their existence… The owner of the funds…would be given a number of other documents in order to secure the certificate. He would be given a letter which would provide the details of only those persons who would be able to verify the existence of the certificates and he would be given coded security numbers." Jentsch said coding typically includes "what would appear to be severe spelling or grammatical errors…" Such errors enable the bank, when it wishes, to denounce the certificate as counterfeit.

In this chapter we have seen how Santy's heirs presented all the necessary documentation and codes, but still were stonewalled. We saw in Chapter Nine that Japan's Ministry of Finance deliberately contrived the "57s" to look different from ordinary Japanese government bonds so they could be denounced as forgeries, allowing the Ministry to dodge payment. That UBS, Citibank and other banks might do the same must come as no surprise. When a client dies, it matters little whether he was an inmate at Buchenwald or president of Indonesia – the bank will do all it can to retain the gold. Here is a an example of what John Kenneth Galbraith meant when he said, "The study of money, above all other fields in economics, is one in which complexity is used to disguise truth or to evade truth, not to reveal it."

Against this background, it is revealing to see how quickly the U.S. Secret Service rushes to the aide of a Swiss bank, when a customer walks in asking if a gold certificate is genuine.

In March 1996, Filipino attorney Ben Aragones met retired Wall Street broker W.R. 'Cotton' Jones. Aragones was trustee of a big estate with bullion deposits in Switzerland. He told Cotton how he had been arrested by Swiss authorities for trying to negotiate a gold certificate, spent three months in jail, and was forbidden to

return. On another trip to Zurich he said he and his wife were kidnaped and terrorized. He was told that UBS did this to scare him off forever.

Cotton, being a romantic, offered to test the water by seeing if the New York
branch of Swiss Bank Corporation would tell him whether one of Ben's certificates
was real. Cotton would not try to negotiate the 'cert', which could be dangerous. If
he only took a notarized photocopy, the original would not be confiscated. To be
cautious, he chose the cert with the smallest denomination, only $25-million.

"On March 20, 1996," he told us, "I walked into the Swiss Bank Corporation in
New York City and asked that the bank verify and authenticate a $25-million
Certificate of Deposit issued by their bank and bearing the Federal Reserve Seal."
They asked him to leave it for examination and come back in two days. When he
returned on March 22, three men posing as bank officers demanded the original
and made threatening noises. When Cotton tried to snatch his photocopy back, all
three men jumped up and identified themselves as U.S. Secret Service Agents, dis-
playing badges and ID cards. They blocked his way and said if he forced the issue
he would be assaulting a Federal Agent.

"I kept denying and still deny that I ever knew whether the documents were valid
or not. They told me I would be in jail twenty-two years… that I had better cooperate with them so it would go easier on me."

After ninety minutes of bullying, Cotton was taken downtown and issued two
U.S. District Court Grand Jury subpoenas and ordered to be in Secret Service
Agent Tom Atkinson's office at 10 a.m. Monday. When Cotton appeared, he suffered more browbeating. Yet not once did anyone call the certificate false. He was
told to appear before the Grand Jury the next day.

Cotton arrived on time, only to be informed that his presence was unnecessary.
Astounded, he went home and wrote to his U.S. Senator, Phil Gramm, telling him
how the Secret Service had violated his rights, and asking for help clearing up the
matter. The Justice Department told Senator Gramm that "Mr. Jones' claims are the
subject of his suit against the United States Department of the Treasury, Office of
the Comptroller of Currency, which is now pending before the Second Circuit
Court of Appeals … legal and ethical considerations preclude any further comment
concerning it." This was not true; there was no suit. Either the Justice Department
was lying to Senator Gramm, or being misinformed by the Treasury Department.
In July 1999, the Justice Department told Senator Gramm, "The matter was closed
some time ago. Regarding Mr. Jones' allegations that his civil rights were violated,
I suggest that he contact the local Federal Bureau of Investigation for information
and assistance." When Gramm persisted, he was told by the Controller of the
Currency "…there is no indication the Swiss Bank Corporation was ever under the
regulation of the OCC. All future correspondence… should be directed to the
Federal Reserve." It was a classic runaround.

Cotton was miffed: "How does any bank in the U.S. have any Federal Agency
intervene on their behalf and confiscate (steal) personal possessions? What right did
the Secret Service have to detain, interrogate, intimidate, and threaten me on the
bank's behalf, issuing me a Grand Jury subpoena?" Senator Gramm, knowing
Washington well, did not press the matter further. He had his hands full elsewhere.

Professor Lausier argues that the reason for these sting operations, for seizing such documents and declaring them counterfeit, is that they are worth a great deal of money. Once Treasury has them, they can be negotiated discreetly on a government-to-government basis.

If so, it is a novel form of armed robbery by one's own government.

Footdragging does the job less dramatically. Mel Belli died before his lawsuit progressed far in court. In March of the same year, 1996, Ray Cline also died, removing another player in the legal maneuvers. When the health of Sir Leonard Knowles deteriorated, the lawsuit he filed in Nassau for Tarciana, Luz, Depontis and Cline ran out of steam. Knowles left Nassau to stay with his son in Macon, Georgia, where he died in 1999. In November 2001, Luz Rambano died in the Philippines. Like Swiss banks sitting on Holocaust gold, American banks had only to wait long enough and all contenders for Santy's estate would be dead.

In the meantime, the message is: Do not ask too many questions or you may go to prison. According to Douglas Valentine, in 1976 when Congressional committees were investigating the Agency's role in criminal activities, CIA director George H.W. Bush's representative before the Congressional committees, Donald Gregg, gave them an ultimatum: Back off or face martial law. Today, this has a more ominous resonance. In July 2002, determined to stop continuing leaks of classified information to journalists, CIA official James B. Bruce declared, "We've got to do whatever it takes – if it takes sending SWAT teams into journalists' homes."

CHAPTER SIXTEEN

CONFLICT OF INTEREST

In March 2001, only weeks into the new Bush Administration, two U.S. Navy ships arrived in the Philippines carrying teams of SEAL commandos. According to a source at the U.S. Embassy, they were sent to the Philippines to recover gold as part of a plan to enlarge America's reserves. This gold, the embassy source said, would come from two places: – New excavations of Yamashita Gold vaults, and the purchase (at a deep discount) of Japanese loot already recovered and held in private vaults by wealthy Filipinos. One of the two ships sailed on to Mindanao to take on a load of bullion the embassy source said was owned by the family of the new president, Gloria Macapagal Arroyo. President Bush, the source said, was 'being aggressive'.

The buzz among gold hunters in Luzon was that associates of President Bush and his family were privately in the market to buy some of the bullion still being recovered from Golden Lily sites. One of the names being dropped by goldbugs in Manila was that of East Texas oil billionaire William Stamps Farish, an intimate friend and fishing companion of the Bush family. Will Farish, who raises horses in Kentucky and is board chairman of Churchill Downs where the Kentucky Derby is staged, had just been nominated by President Bush to be America's new ambassador to the Court of St. James's, where he was a personal friend of Queen Elizabeth. The buzz had special resonance because Will Farish is said to be the manager of President Bush's blind trust.

It should come as no surprise that yet another U.S. president may be taking an interest in Japanese plunder, while shielding Japan's biggest corporations from lawsuits by POWs and other victims. Every president since Harry Truman has been involved in covering up the looting and the slush funds. Even Jimmy Carter played a role, becoming a personal friend of the great fixer, Sasakawa, who was up to his knees in dog-tags.

Bluntly put, the terrible secret is that for over half a century some officials of the U.S. Government – not least of them Nixon – greatly advanced their careers by receiving stolen goods, made unscrupulous use of covert funds, and continue to collude with Tokyo. Justification always has been the Cold War and national security. As federal officials, this meant *their* security. In plain English, this is conflict of interest, and double standards. Politicians, diplomats, bureaucrats, military officers and businessmen have been involved in falsification and manipulation of facts and records. Whether cynical or misguided, they aided and abetted extraordinary corruption.

A quote from Chalmers Johnson bears repeating: "The Cold War is over. Whatever the United States may have believed was necessary to prosecute the Cold War, the Cold War itself can no longer be used to justify ignorance about its costs and unintended consequences. The issue today is not whether Japan might veer toward socialism or neutralism but why the government that evolved from its long period of dependence on the United States is so corrupt, inept, and weak."

The answer is that one thing leads to another. When Truman chose to keep secret the recoveries of Japanese war loot, he then had to endorse the cover-up, followed by a phony Peace Treaty based on fraudulent claims about Japan's postwar poverty. As contrived by John Foster Dulles in total secrecy, this peace treaty blocked POWs, and civilian victims including Comfort Women, from any compensation for their suffering. Their suffering continues to this day because the Department of State and Justice Department still block all legal recourse by Japan's victims in American courts. We may rightly wonder whether this really is what Truman had in mind.

President Eisenhower then authorized the use of war-gold to set up the LDP, interfering in the domestic political process in Japan, putting the Japanese people back under a one-party dictatorship, under a man – Kishi – who had been involved in armed robbery, narcotics, and slave labor since the 1930s.

How much did the LDP secretly contribute to Nixon's presidential campaigns, in return for exclusive control of the M-Fund? What were aides of President Nixon and President Ford doing with President Marcos in 1975 during his shipboard discussions of war loot recoveries?

Was President Carter oblivious to Sasakawa's participation with Marcos in recovering treasure vaults where hundreds of Allied POWs were buried alive?

How could Lansdale transfer Santy's assets at UBS into his own name, while transferring other Santy assets from Citibank-Manila to Citibank-New York? Why did Citibank first deny having Santy's accounts, later concede they had them, then move them offshore when his heirs fairly demanded access? What was Ray Cline really up to, trying to grab some or all of Santy's $50-billion that Citibank moved to Nassau?

What happened to all the bullion that was removed from Malacanang Palace when President Reagan had CIA Director Bill Casey kidnap the Marcoses? Is it in Fort Knox, or has it vanished into a black hole?

Why was Reagan's NSC advisor General Schweitzer using U.S. Army colonels, Navy Seals, and Navy deep-divers to recover war loot from the Philippines – is this normal, and if so, why be so evasive?

Was Clinton also playing games with black gold? Yes, according to the Gold Anti-Trust Action Committee. In September 2001, *The Economist* reported, "it has uncovered evidence that the American government, assisted by others, has somehow 'lent' thousands of tons [of gold bullion] to speculators and bullion banks, notably Citibank and J.P. Morgan Chase, to depress the gold price."

Conflict of interest is evident in all these instances.

As E.L. Doctorow remarked not long ago, "I try to think of a President in my life-time who has not lied to the American people."

•

These are not things that happened long ago, that can be swept under the rug. When Japan was exonerated by Dulles of its duty to pay reparations, it was allowed to keep the artworks, cultural artifacts, and other plunder stolen from its Asian neighbors since 1895. Little of this has been returned; the rest remains in Japanese vaults, enriching the ruling elite and continuing to impoverish those cultures, and individuals, from whom it was stolen. Thus the crime continues to be perpetrated to this day. Because justice has not been done, the victims continue to be victim-ized. There is no statute of limitations on guilt.

Washington's role is all too clear, in the way the Peace Treaty was bullied through. Professor John Price sums up: "The U.S. monopolized and abused the treaty prepa-rations."

As we now know, Japan was *not* bankrupted by the war. By 1951, six years after the war, Japan's economy was stronger than it had been during the best business years before the war. Carlos Romulo, head of the Philippine delegation to the peace conference, "demolished the U.S. argument that Japan lacked the ability to pay for economic reasons". Japan's industrial activity was 32 percent above pre-war levels, its fiscal position showed a surplus, and its balance of trade had moved into the black. In discussions between U.S. monetary experts and Japan's Finance Minister Ikeda Hayato just before the peace conference, he admitted to a budget surplus of over 100-billion yen and planned to use 40-billion of it as a tax-rebate to Japanese citizens. The governor of the Bank of Japan pleaded with U.S. authorities to take custody of $200-million worth of gold holdings because he feared "the Filipinos might try to attach the gold as reparations".

Dulles allowed certain other nations such as the Netherlands to make secret deals with Japan on reparations. These agreements were so sensitive that Washington clas-sified these documents as top secret for the next fifty years. The Dutch gambit only came to light in 2000.

The problem with the treaty terms laid down by Dulles, as the Dutch govern-ment expressed it, was that "it would appear the Dutch Government was, by the act of signing… giving up without due process the rights held by Dutch subjects." Dulles grudgingly agreed to give Dutch citizens the right to make separate claims against the Japanese government. Speaking of this secret deal, a U.S. Senator remarked, "Dulles classified it and kept it classified for 50 years to keep these [vic-tims] from having the right to go to court. That is what he did. That is what the U.S. Government did. That is wrong, and we need to correct it." Then he added: "Our own government would not give these documents to our own soldiers. What an outrage that is."

Subsequently, the Dutch government secretly negotiated a deal with Japan that resulted in Tokyo paying $10-million in 1956 – a drop in the bucket. In 1952, the U.S. Senate Foreign Relations Committee admitted that claims of Asian nations alone could total "as much as $100-billion" (1952 values).

Washington has much to hide. It played an active role in covering up Nazi looting, until its feet were held to the fire in the mid-1990s by Senator Alfonso D'Amato, backed by the deep pockets of Seagram's billionaire Edgar Bronfman, a leader of the World Jewish Congress. In an effort to redeem himself in the eyes of that important segment of the electorate – the Jewish community – President Clinton finally let the investigation proceed. But before then Washington dragged its feet, and was neither conscientious, nor honest, with Holocaust victims. Much of the documentary evidence was hidden, lost, or destroyed. The deputy archivist of the United States told D'Amato that the Reichsbank gold records (once in possession of the U. S. Government) 'have been lost'. Other records, the archivist admitted, were returned to the German government and, strangely, no copies were retained by the U.S.

There also is clear evidence of outright U.S. collusion with German business, bankers and former Nazi leaders, in strong parallels to Japan.

In December 2000, President Clinton signed into law the *Japanese Imperial Army Disclosure Act* to declassify documents about World War II in Asia and the Pacific. This bill originally required the government to open all classified documents from World War II that have bearing on Japanese war crimes, which include looting. But before the bill was passed, a filter was added providing for an interagency task force to review all the records and remove any that the CIA director thinks are too sensitive and might compromise national security. For Nazi records, withholding any information was specifically *disallowed*. For Japanese records it was specifically allowed.

Remarked one observer, "It arouses suspicion when the U.S. Government has a double standard in treating such issues with the two countries."

What could possibly be in Japanese war records to compromise American security sixty years or more after the fact? Who will be shamed by such disclosures? As it stands, the interagency task force was given three years to decide which records to declassify, which makes a joke of the whole process. A lot of outrage has been expressed about moneylaundering. This is historylaundering.

By the time these archives finally are opened, those that reveal the true nature of U.S.-Japanese collusion will have been 'lost' like the Nazi gold archives.

Destroying the evidence actually began before Japan's surrender.

Before the Occupation began in 1945, Japan burnt great quantities of war records and documents. Skies all over the islands were filled with smoke and ashes. In 1946, millions of pages of Japanese government and military records that remained were transferred to Herbert Hoover – peculiar, as Hoover was not a government official. However, as we revealed in *The Yamato Dynasty*, he was a chief mover in whitewashing the emperor, suborning General Tojo, and putting the war criminals back in power. Hoover shipped these records to the Hoover Institution in California, but half a century later their location remains a mystery.

Another huge collection of Japanese documents was transferred to the CIA in the late 1940s. After 'sensitive' documents were removed, the rest were turned over to the National Archives. The State Department then decided, amazingly, to return them all to Japan. Despite protests from scholars, only 10 percent were microfilmed first, and these were bleached of any evidence of looting and collusion.

When we did Freedom of Information queries on Yamashita's Gold in 1987, the Treasury Department, the Defense Department, and the CIA, dodged all our requests, claiming these records were exempt from release. In other words, the records *did* exist, but could not be seen. Yet during the Schlei lawsuit in the 1990s, the government claimed it carried out a thorough search of all government agencies and archives for any records related to Japan's looting of Asia, and postwar slush-funds, declaring to the court that no such written evidence could be found. What had happened to it in the intervening years?

While Germany has paid more than $45-billion in compensation and reparations, Japan has paid only $3-billion. Even today, Germany continues this program of compensation and reparations, but Japan has dug in its heels and said it was all settled in 1951. Its position is backed adamantly by the State Department, which is determined to block compensation payments even to U.S. citizens, even to former POWs.

Britain, having parroted Washington by declaring that all this was 'settled' in 1951, finally reversed itself. In 2001, the British government agreed to pay – from its own tax revenues – a £10,000 one-time settlement on former British POWs of Japan and their heirs. This may seem humane, but it sidesteps the real question of why Japan continues to be shielded from paying. It also does not satisfy the demands of British POWs and internees for an official apology from Japan.

Since the war, Tokyo has passed fifteen laws giving its own nationals compensation of $400-billion. Among those receiving compensation and pensions were indicted war criminals. Japanese sociologist Tanaka Hiroshi said, "We are generous with ourselves, stingy with others, [and] our policy on war compensation is manifestly unfair to foreigners, and unrepentant of the past."

Washington has paid compensation to Japanese civilians interned unjustly in America during the war. Each internee, even babies born at the end of this period, was awarded $20,000. Most of them were complete innocents and their lives were, in many cases, damaged or destroyed by the internment. But not one was forced to perform slave labor.

Since 1999, more than thirty lawsuits have been filed in California courts by survivors of the Bataan Death March and other POWs who were forced to provide slave labor for Japanese companies. They were focused in California because the state legislature had extended the period when such claims could be filed. The U.S. Government then had the cases transferred to a federal court in San Francisco, where most of these suits then were rejected in September 2000 by Federal Judge Vaughn Walker. Judge Walker said they were 'barred' by the terms of the 1951 Peace Treaty, the same stonewalling used by Tokyo and Washington.

Hard as it may be to believe, the State Department argued on the side of Japanese corporations in these cases. Walker summed up his decision by stating that the San

Francisco Peace Treaty had "exchanged full compensation of plaintiffs for a future peace. History has vindicated the wisdom of that bargain."

Chalmers Johnson reacted by pointing out that since the treaty was signed, at least ten million people and 55,000 Americans have died in Asian wars. By those facts alone, he rightly called Judge Walker's statement "one of the more abysmal moments of denial".

Some fought back. In March 2001, U.S. Congressmen Mike Honda (D-San Jose) and Dana Rohrabacher (R-Huntington Beach) introduced a bill, "Justice for Prisoners of War Act" before the U.S. Congress. The bill had strong bipartisan support and by August 2002 had 228 co-signers including House whips for both parties. Honda's bill called for "clarification of the wording of the 1951 Peace Treaty between Japan and the United States" to keep the State Department from deviously interfering in victims' lawsuits.

If this bill became law, it could open a window for compensation to POWs who were forced to perform slave labor for Japanese companies like Mitsui, Mitsubishi and Sumitomo, which are among the richest on earth. The bill would remove a key legal barrier used in Judge Walker's rejection of the slave-labor lawsuits. Article 26 of the 1951 treaty reads: "Should Japan make a peace settlement or war claims settlement with any State granting that State greater advantages than those provided by the present Treaty, those same advantages shall be extended to the parties to the present Treaty."

In other words, if Japan were ever to give another country greater advantages for war claims than those granted in the treaty, then it has to extend such terms to all forty-eight countries that signed the treaty. And as we now know, a secret deal was arranged by Dulles for the Dutch government to receive $10-million from Japan. Both Switzerland and Burma also negotiated compensation to their citizens that would today be worth about $50,000 each. While Burma was occupied by Japan, Switzerland was not even a belligerent during the war. When these settlements with Burma and Switzerland went through, the British government (confronted by demands from its own POWs) decided *against* reopening negotiations, although it was entitled to do so by the terms of the treaty. In fact, none of America's closest allies deviated from Washington's instructions not to meddle with Article 26.

Judge Walker, possibly under considerable pressure, sided with the State Department and ruled that Article 26 cannot be invoked by private citizens, but only by their government. The Honda-Rohrabacher bill would get around that bizarre ruling by having Congress act for the victims.

The State Department's unelected bureaucrats, aghast at the temerity of America's elected lawmakers, realized that Honda's bill cannot be thrown out by the exercise of political pressure over federal judges. Instead, State took the high moral ground by claiming that passage of Honda's bill "would be an act of extreme bad faith".

Bad faith toward Japan's biggest corporations and its extraordinarily corrupt and incompetent LDP bosses.

Since spring 2001 this bill has been stalled in committee. Once through the House of Representatives, the battle for the bill would have to be fought again in the Senate. Thereafter, the presidential veto could be (and probably would be) invoked. In which case, President George W. Bush would be honoring the tradition of cover-up by every American president since Truman.

Another Congressional effort to force State and Justice Departments to let justice take its course, was an amendment to an appropriations bill. This made it illegal for the State and Justice to spend any of their 2002 budget "to file a motion in any court opposing a civil action against any Japanese person or corporation for compensation or reparations in which the plaintiff alleges that, as an American prisoner of war during World War II, he or she was used as a slave or forced labor". This amendment was passed with overwhelming bi-partisan support one day before the World Trade Center attack.

Of course, nothing prohibits State or Justice from 'advising' courts against favorable settlements for POWs, or putting pressure on judges in federal courts. The bill was only valid for twelve months, after which it would have to be reintroduced, so it is popular, patriotic, but toothless.

Sadly, this judicial gridlock is like France before the Revolution, when a two-tiered system of justice was in place – one for nobility, one for ordinary people.

However, it may be too late for Washington to save Japan's LDP from its own ineptitude and venality. Japan's financial collapse has been predicted by scholars at Massachusetts Institute of Technology, on the premise that the LDP would refuse to undertake the serious reforms needed. In fact, all Japan's top banks failed long ago, but – as in a silent movie – the edifice collapsed without the audience hearing any sound.

Japan's banks had $1-trillion in bad loans on their books, in sweetheart deals for men like Prime Minister Tanaka, or zero-interest loans to the *yakuza*. Among the banks hit hardest were Sanwa Bank and Tokai Bank. Together with Dai-Ichi Kangyo Bank they are the three that were exempted by General MacArthur and General Marquat from reorganization in 1945.

Former prime minister and finance minister Miyazawa proposed a painless bailout – painless, that is, for the banks. They would be bailed out by Japanese taxpayers. After which the banks could resume their bad habits. Whether taxpayers would stand for it is questionable.

If anyone knew how to arrange such a magic trick, it was Miyazawa. Few other men have been so intimately and continually involved in the inner workings of the Ministry of Finance since the early 1940s. He began his career in the Finance Ministry in 1942 and was one of the three Japanese who negotiated the secret terms of the 1951 Peace Treaty with John Foster Dulles. Thanks to cachet he gained in those warped negotiations, Miyazawa entered politics where he remains to this day as a man of phenomenal leverage. He served as minister of finance in the Nakasone, Takeshita, Obuchi and Mori cabinets. Over all those decades, Miyazawa was chief of accounting for the LDP, so he had intimate knowledge of all the slush funds. He held many other ministerial posts, such as chief cabinet secretary to Prime Minister Suzuki when the M-Fund "57s" first were issued. When minister of finance for Takeshita, Miyazawa had to resign along with Takeshita in the Recruit insider-trading scandal tied to the M-Fund. In 1991, thanks to his rescue by M-

Fund controllers Kanemaru and Gotoda, Miyazawa became prime minister. He then named Gotoda as his deputy prime minister and made Kanemaru the LDP vice president, giving Kanemaru the informal role of 'co-prime minister'.

At a drunken celebration of this collaboration in a posh Tokyo restaurant, Miyazawa pledged to Kanemaru that, "I will not do anything that differs from [your] intentions. I will consult you on everything." The honeymoon was brief, as in 1992 Kanemaru became involved in the great scandal of the Sagawa Parcel Company, which was delivering war-gold bribes to politically influential people. Before his trial was concluded, Kanemaru conveniently died.

If anyone knows the truth, Miyazawa does. But he is not talking, nor is his son-in-law, Christopher J. Lafleur, a career U.S. Foreign Service officer who for years has been the most powerful diplomat at the American Embassy in Tokyo, as deputy chief of mission, or DCM.

In 1986, the 38-year-old Lafleur was dispatched to Tokyo, ostensibly to negotiate sales of the FS-X fighter plane (the same year Schlei came to Tokyo to negotiate his client's "57s"). Miyazawa, then minister of finance, was Japan's FS-X negotiator, under a cloud in the Recruit scandal, linked to the "57s" and M-Fund moneys.

One unexpected outcome of the friendship that bloomed between Lafleur and Miyazawa was that Lafleur married Miyazawa's daughter.

In September 1997, Lafleur was made Deputy Chief of Mission at the U.S. Embassy in Tokyo – called the 'defacto boss of the embassy'. A few months later, in 1998, Miyazawa was back in the drivers seat as finance minister in the Obuchi cabinet. Like his earlier appointments to this job, Miyazawa was returned to office to practice damage control. According to Professor Lausier, this time Miyazawa was put back in as minister of finance because a large number of "57s" were coming due – documents that the LDP and the government of Japan could ill afford to redeem, and therefore denounced as counterfeit.

Lausier believes that Miyazawa was there to decide which of these IOUs would be honored and which would not.

During the same period, the U.S. Embassy's Lafleur was vocal in claiming that the "57s" were fraudulent, and arguing against victims' rights to sue Japanese corporations, on the basis of the 1951 treaty negotiated by Lafleur's father-in-law.

Not only Lafleur but a string of ambassadors he served also showed conspicuous conflict of interest.

Many people were troubled to learn that Ambassador Tom Foley's wife was a paid consultant to Sumitomo Heavy Industries, one of the primary targets of the POW lawsuits for slave labor. The State Department declared that it saw no conflict of interest in Mrs. Foley's job and the simultaneous appointment of her husband as ambassador to Japan. However, in that post Foley vigorously denied the right of American POWs to sue Japanese corporations including the one his wife worked for.

After retiring as ambassador and returning to Washington, Foley openly became a paid lobbyist for Mitsubishi Corporation as a member of its advisory panel on strategy. Mitsubishi was among the biggest employers of American slave labor during the war.

When he was appointed DCM under Foley, foreign correspondents in Tokyo joked that Lafleur was a member of Japan's 'dream-team'.

In 2001, when news of Lafleur's special status as Miyazawa's son-in-law became more widely known, making the issues of conflict of interest and double standards too obvious to ignore further, Lafleur was recalled to Washington and made Deputy Assistant Director to the Bureau of East Asian and Pacific Affairs at the State Department. This removed him from potential embarrassment in Tokyo, but put him in a prime position to monitor and guide Congress, as well as to oversee any legal actions in U.S. courts.

The low point of this farce came in late September 2001, when a letter appeared in *The Washington Post* written by three former ambassadors to Tokyo – Thomas Foley, Michael Armacost and Fritz Mondale. The letter linked the claims of American POWs against Japan to the terrorist attacks on the World Trade Center:

"Why would Congress consider passing [the Rohrabacher Bill], which could abrogate a treaty so fundamental to our security at a time the president and his administration are trying so hard…to combat terrorism?"

In other words, Honda and Rohrabacher, and America's POWs, were no better than terrorists!

Even Japan's government winced at the Foley-Armacost-Mondale attack. A Japanese Embassy spokesman in Washington told the media that the government of Japan regarded the claims of POWs and the problems of world terrorism to be 'different issues'.

As a dissident State Department official quipped, "Sometimes it [seems] that Japan [has] two embassies working for them – ours and theirs."

CHAPTER SEVENTEEN

GRAND LARCENY

After the first edition of this book was published, we were contacted by new sources, with thousands more pages of documentary evidence, and answers to many remaining questions.

We now have photographic proof that Ben Valmores was, in fact, the valet of Prince Takeda during the Pacific War, and was in direct contact with General Yamashita. This is verified by a photo taken by a Japanese Army photographer in occupied Manchuria in the summer of 1944. It shows General Yamashita standing next to Prince Takeda, with young Ben Valmores immediately behind the general. The prince went to Manchuria to brief Yamashita, who had just been ordered by Emperor Hirohito to take over command of all Japanese troops in the Philippines. A few days after this photograph was taken, the general flew to Manila. Although the photo was published in 1944 in Japanese newspapers, Ben was not identified. The picture was one of Ben's treasures, kept hidden in a tin box until two years after his death.

More surprising, we located Yamashita's chauffeur, Major Kojima Kashii, the man who gave Santa Romana and Lansdale the secret locations of twelve imperial treasure vaults in 1945. At the time, Kojima was 31 years old, serving as an aide to the general, and as his driver. He was captured separately from Yamashita, and put in Bilibad Prison where Santy and Lansdale had him tortured to reveal the locations of treasure sites the general personally visited during the last year of the war. Later, the story was put about by Lansdale that Kojima committed suicide in his prison cell. In fact, we now know that Kojima readily gave in and agreed to show Santy and Lansdale a dozen treasure vaults in return for his freedom and a large bribe. Returning to Japan, where he kept a low profile with his family until the end of the U.S. occupation in the early 1950s, Kojima (travelling under various pseudonyms) began making discreet trips back to the Philippines, with various partners. Posing as businessmen, they recovered treasure from imperial vaults and "officers' stashes", where gold and gems had been hidden in the closing months of the war. Many of these recoveries were made on Clark Air Force Base, with the full knowledge and permission of the U.S. Government. (A brief summary of these recoveries on the base appears in our Annotations.) For more than fifty years, these recoveries kept Kojima a rich man. Our Filipino source, who met Kojima in Manila in the 1990s, knew nothing of his past. He said Kojima at that time used his name openly, but it meant nothing to him. Gradually, Kojima revealed more and more about his background, and how he knew the locations of so many vaults, through travelling by car with Yamashita. On our CDs we have a color photo of Kojima at age 88, taken on his last visit to Manila in 2002, still looking dashing and handsome. Kojima had told his Filipino friend that this would be his final trip to Manila, and his last recovery, because of his age and health. When he did not return, Kojima's friend gave us the photo, and recounted their adventures treasure hunting together.

On his final trip, Kojima and his Japanese partners recovered two metric tons of small gold biscuit bars. They were in such high spirits they became careless and had their Filipino helpers drive them directly to a Japanese shipping line in Subic Bay. At a warehouse beside the pier, the Filipinos were allowed to watch from a distance as Kojima and his associates slipped the small ingots through a hole in the massive front cylinder of a steamroller, typically used to flatten gravel aggregate during highway construction. The opening at the end of the roller was then welded shut and the machine was lifted by crane onto a Japanese freighter, to be taken to Yokohama for "repairs".

In a moment of nostalgia afterwards, while celebrating the recovery with a bottle of Suntory whisky, Kojima told our source what happened in late spring of 1945, when General Yamashita moved with his troops into the wild mountains of the Kiangan Pocket for their last defense of the war. Having no further need of an automobile, Yamashita ordered Kojima to go to Dingalan Bay to oversee the unloading of treasure from a Japanese ship for hiding in a tunnel ashore. Yamashita was giving his aide a chance to escape capture by U.S. troops, which is why Kojima was eventually captured separately.

The riddle of Santa Romana's true allegiance also has been revealed. We were always puzzled by whether he was really a CIA agent, when he seemed (until the early 1970s) to know so little about the Agency's history and covert activities. Authoritative sources in Spain with strong ties to the Philippines have now confirmed that Santy was actually a secret agent of the Vatican. Santy did have ties to the wartime U.S. underground in the Philippines, overseen for General MacArthur by General Whitney, General Willoughby, and Colonel McMicking. After the war, Santy did work in harness with Lansdale and the CIA. But his real loyalty was to the Vatican. Sources close to the Manila archdiocese always insisted that Santy was "working for the Vatican", and was not a CIA agent.

Our Spanish sources have now told us that Santy was "training for the Church" before the war. Given that he had been married twice already, with children from both marriages, in a country where divorce was illegal, he was a bigamist. So he was clearly not training for the priesthood. Instead, long before the Japanese invasion, Santy became a lay member of one of the Vatican's militant orders. There are a number of these, the most prominent being the Jesuits, the Dominicans, and Opus

Dei. The sources refuse to be explicit about which order Santy directly worked for, arguing that ultimately he was working for the bishops and cardinals in charge of the Vatican's financial office. But we have established that he was with Opus Dei.

After decades of shrinking Vatican influence in world affairs, the austere Eugenio Pacelli, Pope Pius XII, reached an accommodation with Hitler that gave the Pope and the Vatican increased control over traditionally independent Catholics in Germany. Also under Pius XII, the Vatican was the only state to officially recognize Japanese control of Manchuria. Even before the attack on Pearl Harbor, Emperor Hirohito's emissaries were pressing the Pope to negotiate an eventual peace settlement to Tokyo's advantage, allowing Japan to keep the lands it had conquered. After invading the Philippines, however, Japanese brutality destroyed any hope of Vatican support. So, while the Vatican's relationship with the Nazis remained ambiguous, its relationship with Japan chilled. As churches and cathedrals were desecrated to dig underground vaults for war loot, and priests and nuns were murdered, agents like Santa Romana worked against the Japanese and kept logs of which churches and cathedrals now hid hoards of treasure.

In Luzon, Leyte, Cebu, and other islands during the war, Santy ran his own underground consisting of hundreds of agents, including priests, bishops, and street rabble. Court documents show that it was during the Japanese occupation that he first invented his many pseudonyms, to avoid disclosing his real name. Because of his high-level connections in the Church and in the underground, Santy's network also included members of the influential family of Jose P. Laurel (1891-1959), pre-war head of a political clique in Luzon, who became Japan's wartime puppet president of the Philippines.

This intimate connection between the Laurels and Santa Romana started in the 1920s, ran like a bloody thread through the war, through the gold recoveries after the war, through the secret movement of black gold to banks around the world, through the dictatorship of Ferdinand Marcos, and today runs right up to the White House Oval Office in Washington.

Before the war, Jose Laurel was a Superior Court judge in Manila, a judge with a grudge going back decades. The grudge began early in 1898 when America sank its own battleship, the *Maine*, in Havana harbor in order to provoke the Spanish-American War, enabling it to divest Spain of much of its overseas empire. In 1901, when the United States had seized the Philippines from Spain, and was harshly suppressing the Filipino people's struggle for independence, Laurel's father was tortured by American soldiers. Later, when Jose studied law at Yale University, he was snubbed and abused by racist Yankee classmates. He went on to study in Tokyo, becoming fluent in Japanese. Setting up a law practice in Manila, he detested the American colonial government, and began organizing his own mafia, modelled on the traditional pirate syndicates of the archipelago.

Laurel was at heart a nationalist, keen to cultivate acolytes, and quick to make deals with the super-rich Overseas Chinese families who controlled the Philippine economy and the underworld. Some of these Hokkien and Fukien Chinese families, adopting Spanish names, were the biggest landowners in Luzon, other than the Church itself. Like Laurel, the Chinese wanted independence for the Philippines, independence from America as well as from Spain. During four centuries of Spanish colonial rule, rich Chinese had been victims of official extortion, had their property seized, and were expelled back to China. They fared no better under American rule, which pandered to the interests of Chiang Kai-shek's corrupt Kuomintang regime. So the Laurels and the Chinese had similar passions.

When Jose Laurel was first appointed a judge in Manila, he became an ally of Judge Ferdinand Chua, head of one of the six richest Chinese clans in Luzon. Because of an affair with a chambermaid, Judge Chua had the odd distinction of being the natural father of the future Philippine dictator, Ferdinand Marcos. Although his paternity was never admitted, Chua found a husband for the chambermaid, and paid for the child's education, including putting Marcos through law school. In 1928, when young Marcos faced murder charges for shooting a political rival, Judge Laurel took over the case, dismissed all evidence of Marcos's guilt, and personally handed the accused his law degree. In this way, Laurel created a blood debt that had to be repaid by Judge Chua. Six years later, the debt was repaid with a massive quantity of Chinese and Filipino gold – 1,665 metric tons, to be exact – loaned to the U.S. Federal Reserve in exchange for Federal Reserve bonds.

Why this same gold has become a matter of bitter contention and embarrassment to the U.S. Government seventy years later has everything to do with the corruption spawned by the Black Eagle Trust and the Federal Reserve System. Its similarities to the scandal of the M-Fund in Japan are astonishing. Ultimately, the ghosts of Santa Romana and Jose Laurel have come back to haunt Washington along with the ghost of Norbert Schlei and other victims of its grand larceny.

What lies behind this scandal and mischief is surprisingly simple: Once citizens of a country relinquish control of their money to private bankers, they are at the bankers' mercy – which is the whole idea. When citizens are then deprived of the right to keep precious metal like gold – which has true value because of its rarity – they have no alternative but to make do with the paper money printed and manipulated by private bankers – literally monopoly money. In return for printing all the paper money they wish, to profit by manipulating money-supply to cause inflation or deflation, bankers get to hold all the gold as their monopoly. Once the gold is in their vaults, some is retained on display. But most of the gold vanishes offshore, or into private accounts in Switzerland. The Swiss, in turn, keep some of it under Zurich Airport, where it is in transit like petty cash, but most precious metal goes into underground vaults deep in the Alps that are also strongholds of the Swiss Army, secure against nuclear war.

Account holders may think some gold or platinum is theirs because they have title to it in bonds or certificates, with lots of supporting paperwork provided by the bank. But – as we've seen again and again in this book – if they try to redeem the bonds or certs, chances are they will end up arrested, imprisoned, or murdered, and their bonds and certs will be confiscated and vanish. The story of Graham Halksworth, which we briefly recount in this chapter, is a case in point. Even when the certs are denounced as counterfeit, instead of being destroyed on the spot they are confiscated and held in secure government facilities, indicating that they are not, actually, counterfeit.

A journalist at the *Financial Times* told us: "It has now reached a point where you can go into one of the big banks in New York, London or Zurich, give them half a metric ton of gold in return for a certificate of ownership, walk around the block for ten minutes, re-enter the same bank, and they'll deny ever seeing you before, and have you arrested for presenting them with a counterfeit certificate." He was not joking.

In Europe and Asia, this has been the case for centuries. Rulers whose armies and police gave them a monopoly on violence enjoyed squandering the money they stole or confiscated, but they knew nothing about manipulating money and making it grow. So they gave this job to clever financial advisers who served as their bankers. Thereafter, these bankers influenced all policy decisions. When bankers gained too much influence, or rulers found themselves too deep in debt, they put the bankers to death, or sent them into exile, thus cancelling the debt. (There are obvious equations between murdering people and imprisoning them, as in both cases they are removed.) A perfect example was Europe's first banking network, created by the Knights Templar in the eleventh and twelfth centuries. They lent the king of France a lot of money, which made him realize they probably had much more hidden away. He ordered his police and army to arrest all the Templars in a single day, and had their leaders tortured to reveal where the Templar treasure was hidden. When they refused, he had their leaders burned alive at the stake. The king never found the Templar treasure, and the Nazis were still looking for it in the 1940s when they occupied France.

Such wicked behavior by ruthless rulers and cunning bankers, is why America's Founding Fathers tried to do things differently.

From the moment the United States became independent of Britain, it was liberated from British currency and taxation. Money was to be backed by gold and silver and kept under the control of the central government, on behalf of all citizens. But the Federalist clique of Alexander Hamilton, which had strong financial and emotional ties to Old Europe, began lobbying to put U.S. currency in private hands. U.S. Presidents Jefferson, Madison, Adams, and others fought this, and two early attempts to set up a pseudo "United States Bank" that was actually in private hands were reversed. In 1816, President Jefferson warned that: "Private banking establishments are more dangerous than standing armies; and the principle of spending money to be paid by posterity, under the name of funding, is but swindling posterity."

During the Civil War, however, the Federal government went so deep in debt that the number of profiteering millionaires in America mushroomed. J.P. Morgan, for instance, sold 5,000 defective weapons to the Union Army, which he purchased for $3.50 each and sold for $22 each. Railways, steel, oil, and other monopolies grew into what was called The Octopus, controlled by the Rockefellers, Harrimans, Mellons, and others, who also founded their own banks. They learned how to do this with guidance from Morgan and Paul Warburg, who were agents in America of Europe's enormously rich and powerful Rothschild family. Morgan made another fortune in 1895, selling U.S. gold bonds in Europe, through his alliance with the House of Rothschild. By 1902, Morgan interests controlled 5,000 miles of railway track in the U.S. How he ruined thousands of farmers and rivals is related in the contemporary Frank Norris novel, *The Octopus*.

Andrew Mellon, while Secretary of the Treasury in the 1920s, took advantage of federal tax loopholes and refunded $3.5-billion to rich cronies. When Treasury Secretary Morganthau later tried to bring tax evasion charges against Mellon, the grand jury refused to indict him.

After a very secret meeting at Morgan's Jekyll Island estate in 1910, the Robber Barons followed Warburg's gameplan to take control of all U.S. currency and gold. As Warburg said at that secret meeting, it was essential not to let American citizens know that the Federal Reserve was a cartel of private banks, and to persuade them that it was a government agency. In other words, there was nothing "federal" about it, and all control of currency and gold was "reserved" to the private bankers who owned its stock. The majority of that stock was held by banks now called Morgan-Chase and Citibank.

This grand larceny began with the carefully contrived election of the bankers' presidential candidate, Woodrow Wilson, whose administration was "marked by the acquisition and exercise of 'dictatorial powers'." In short, Wilson was put into the White House by a consortium of bankers and Robber Barons, including Warburgs, Rockefellers, Morgans, Schiffs, Kahns, Harrimans, and Europe's Rothschilds, who wanted private control of America's money supply. By that point the bankers practically owned a majority of the U.S. Congress. These carefully coached lawmakers drafted the Federal Reserve Act of 1913, pretended to argue for and against it, then when many of its serious opponents left town for the Christmas holidays, President Wilson hastily signed it into law the day before Christmas Eve, while public attention was elsewhere.

The private banking powers of the Federal Reserve were further increased during World War I, in 1917, when President Wilson pushed through the Trading With The Enemy Act, which gave the president the right to "regulate ... [the] export [and] ... earmarkings of gold or bullion." Simply put, this meant whenever there was any sort of emergency all the government's gold could be moved around secretly, and earmarked or designated for whatever purpose Wilson wanted, without any kind of public oversight. Since Wilson had been put in the White House by the big bankers who owned all the stock in the Federal Reserve, this meant they – the private bankers – could thereafter make the gold vanish, and nobody would be the wiser.

So much government gold vanished during the Hoover Administration that when Wall Street crashed in 1929, the vaults were nearly empty.

In 1933, President Franklin Roosevelt used Wilson's legal precedent to declare another state of national emergency (this time the collapse of the U.S. economy in the Great Depression). Roosevelt urgently needed gold to underwrite social programs for millions of jobless people. Later – in the event of war with either Germany or Japan, or both – he would need a great deal more gold to finance expansion of the U.S. military and its armaments. In those days, money spent on social programs and armaments still had to be backed by gold. The quick way to increase gold reserves was to force citizens to turn over their private gold holdings, and to force all gold-mining operations to sell only to the U.S. Government. In return they got paper money.

The government's newly acquired public gold would be held by the private Federal Reserve (the Fed). Because the Fed is a private banking cartel, whose books are not open to the public, it is impossible to know precisely how much gold was acquired in the 1930s. The Fed is famous for being Delphic, which means it lies by evasion. This is the reason for the public's great ignorance about how much gold there is, to whom it belongs, where it is really kept, and how it got there. Bankers, economists, judges and attorneys pretend to know exact details, but it is easy to demonstrate that they twist the facts to suit themselves.

Secretary of the Treasury Henry Morganthau continually found himself in conflict with the Federal Reserve and the State Department. As he put it, "There is one more issue to be settled ... whether the Government through the Treasury should control ... monetary policy or whether the control should be exercised through the Federal Reserve banks, which are privately owned." He complained that J.P. Morgan had more power than the State Department, and added: "You can rape me if you want to, but I won't like it." The Federal Reserve was even issuing gold bearer bonds and certificates with Morganthau's signature, without Morganthau's knowledge.

FDR's Executive Order 6102 made it illegal for private American citizens living in the United States to hold gold coin, gold bullion, or gold certificates. Interestingly, this applied only to American citizens in the continental United States. The Philippines and other U.S. possessions such as Hawaii, Guam and Samoa were excluded. U.S. citizens resident in those places could continue to hold gold, other precious metals, and gold certificates.

All citizens in the continental U.S. had to turn in their gold ingots and gold certificates in return for Federal Reserve paper dollars at an official price of $20 an ounce. To make it look fair, private banks in America were also obliged to turn over their gold reserves and certificates. This looked like they were giving it to the government, because few people knew the Fed was private. American mining companies (and foreign mining companies, foreign governments and foreign citizens) were all given a special break and could sell their gold to the Fed for $35 an ounce.

Because of legal challenges in the courts, it took a few months for Roosevelt's executive order to become law. But by 1934 the Fed became the legal custodian of all of America's gold, and of much foreign gold as well. Gold poured into Fort Knox, and other Fed vaults in New York City; West Point, New York; and former U.S. Government mints in San Francisco, Philadelphia, and Denver.

A huge influx of European gold, to repay U.S. loans to foreign governments during and after World War I, soon made America the world's biggest repository of "official" monetary gold. This flow of gold from overseas was further stimulated by gathering war clouds in Europe, and by Japan's annexation of Korea and Manchuria, and its incursions into North China. As Hitler became more aggressive, even the British crown jewels were moved to the Fed's vaults in New York City.

The notion that all this gold somehow belongs to the American people is a carefully cultivated myth. Most people think Ft. Knox is a government vault, but while it is built on government land it is managed by the Fed. Since the creation of the Federal Reserve System all the gold vaults of the Fed have been guarded by America's largest domestic private security organizations like Diebold, Inc., an Ohio-based security firm established in 1859. In each vault the gold is kept in numbered chambers, and its actual ownership is known to only a handful of Fed officials. The largest of these rectangular lockers are 10 feet by 10 feet by 18 feet, so each locker is big enough to hold $17.1 billion-worth of bullion, given a market price of $400 per ounce.

Not everyone was convinced that the United States was the safest place for their gold, least of all Asians who had an ancient distrust of governments and banks. FDR and his advisors understood that in South Asia, East Asia and the Pacific, a lot of gold was held by Overseas Chinese individuals, family-associations, and trading networks; by local warlords and criminal syndicates; by wealthy Indians; by Buddhist sects; by Dutch, French, Portuguese and Spanish colonial families, and by the Catholic Church, which had dominated the Philippines for four centuries. Large quantities of gold had been moved out of Europe for safekeeping during World War I, and during the Spanish Civil War, and were sleeping in vaults in the Philippines.

Wealthy Chinese families, victimized by dynasties and warlords for thousands of years, held their precious metal in secret places, or in banks they owned or controlled in Manila, Hanoi, Bangkok, or Singapore. They expected Japan's conquest to spread south to the islands. Through Jose Laurel, Judge Chua and other Chinese clan elders knew that Roosevelt's Treasury Secretary Morganthau was offering to buy gold from rich individuals and syndicates in Asia and the Pacific in exchange for Federal Reserve bonds or notes.

In 1934, Laurel's circle pooled their resources and offered to sell Morganthau 1,665 metric tons of gold. In return, they would be given 250 separate Federal Reserve bearer bonds, each in a $100-million denomination. So at the time of issue in 1934 this transaction had a total face value of $25-billion. But, on maturity after thirty-two years – i.e., after 1966 – the 250 bonds could be redeemed for a total of $100-billion. Instead of an outright purchase, the gold was being acquired by the Federal Reserve Bank in Chicago, as a loan, paying slightly over $10 an ounce (half the existing private gold price) in return for interest over thirty-two years that would result in a total of $100-billion at maturity.

This is supported by documents that accompanied the original transaction, reproduced on our CDs. One document, a Federal Reserve Bond Global Immunity, signed by Morganthau, said the purchase was arranged this way "to enable the government of the United States of America to determine the contract in a manner appearing as a loan, which shall be known as Federal Reserve Bond issued by the Bank of Chicago series of 1934." Each bond had coupons attached so the bearer could collect the interest annually, or let it accumulate until maturity. Essentially, the Fed was borrowing the gold for $10 an ounce rather than buying it outright for $20 an ounce.

When the deal was concluded, the 1,665 metric tons of gold was transported by ship from Manila to San Francisco, then carried by train to the Federal Reserve

Bank in Chicago, where the ingots were placed in its vault. The 250 Fed bonds, meanwhile, plus supporting official documents, were received in exchange by Laurel. He shared them out among his partners, who put them in the safest places they could find: some in Swiss bank vaults, others in Argentina or Chile.

When the Japanese invaded, Laurel, fluent in Japanese, was ordered by President Quezon – on instructions from Washington – to offer himself to the Japanese as their puppet president during the occupation. Quezon then fled to the U.S. (After the war, Washington hypocritically denounced Laurel as a quisling, to rig the 1949 presidential election in favor of General MacArthur's crony Jose Quirino; MacArthur said he wanted Quirino elected "or else" all U.S. aid and loans would be cancelled.)

During the Japanese occupation, Laurel's son Pedro Palafox Laurel, a close friend of Santa Romana from before the war, secretly became part of Santy's Opus Dei underground. In 1945, when Santy and Lansdale tortured and bribed Major Kojima, Pedro Palafox Laurel participated in the gold recoveries.

Because of the key role played by Santy, as the gold was recovered and moved to banks throughout the world, a major portion went to the Vatican bank and other banks tied to the Vatican, as we describe in Chapters 4 and 8. It is now clear that this is why Santy was treated with such respect by bankers who came to see him at his Manila Hilton suite, although he remained a secretive figure and was never the subject of a magazine profile in the Philippines or anywhere else. It was not his connection to the CIA that gave him invisibility, but his position as an agent of the Vatican secret services, filling the coffers of the Vatican bank. Diagrams of the "Umbrella" organization that moved much of the gold, which we reproduce on our CDs, show that security was provided both by the CIA and by the Italian Mafia. Collaboration in Europe between the Mafia and the OSS began on the eve of the war, and continued throughout. OSS agents were smuggled into Italy through Sicily. In return, at the end of the war, top Mafia figures were released from American prisons and allowed to return to Italy, where they helped the CIA and the Vatican promote candidates of the Christian Democrats, to prevent the Communist Party from gaining control of Italy's government.

Santy's stature in the Vatican financial hierarchy must have been assured by his role in restoring solvency to banks linked to the Vatican. This resolves the puzzle of why his visit to Washington and his tour of the CIA complex in 1973 was his first acquaintance with the Agency headquarters and many of its covert operations, noted in his diary each evening. Had Santy been an agent of the CIA all along, he would have received training at the Farm in Virginia like other agents, and known all about the headquarters in Langley and its mythology. But as a lay member of the Vatican secret services, his orientation was to Europe, not the U.S.

It was the rise of Ferdinand Marcos (saved from prison by Jose Laurel) that undercut Santy, took the Umbrella organization out of his hands, broke up his personal network, and turned Santy into an alcoholic. A photograph of Santy taken during this period shows him slouching in an armchair, with a paunch, and a full head of hair – not the tough, sleek, shaven-headed Yul Brynner of the immediate postwar years.

After President Magsaysay's death in a plane crash, and his replacement by a conspicuously corrupt President Macapagal, Marcos came to be seen by Washington as "our boy". America was bogged down in Vietnam and anxious for the commitment of more Filipino troops. Marcos was already senate president, made all the right pro-American noises, and his campaign for the presidency was financed by the CIA, the Overseas Chinese, and lavish contributions from Chiang Kai-shek's Nationalist regime in Taiwan. He won a landslide victory and entered Malacanang Palace on December 30, 1965.

Even in the Philippines where life is cheap, Marcos was uniquely predatory and murderous. Once in the palace, he began hijacking all the private wealth he could get his hands on.

Jose Laurel had died in 1959, and the Laurel clan was now headed by one of his sons, Pedro Palafox Laurel, Santy's pal and business partner, and fellow Vatican agent. Unfortunately for the Laurels, when their Federal Reserve bonds reached maturity in 1966, the election of Marcos as president made it too dangerous to bring the bonds out of hiding and present them to the U.S. Treasury and the Federal Reserve for redemption. Marcos would learn about it immediately, and stop at nothing to confiscate the bonds and sell them to Washington for his own profit.

Marcos had long known about Santy's gold recoveries with Lansdale, and knew that Santy had hundreds of accounts in banks all over the world – many as a strawman for the Vatican, the CIA, or the Black Eagle Trust. But Marcos also knew that Santy had personal accounts at Citibank and other banks in Manila and Hong Kong, where he salted gold for his own use. (As there is no evidence of extravagance in his personal life, Santy seems to have diverted gold into many offshore private accounts because that is what everyone else was doing. It is astonishing that the CIA and other U.S. Government agencies and individuals have claimed that those accounts contained money or gold that was somehow the property of the United States, rather than the property of the people from whom it was stolen, or of Santy's heirs, or of the Vatican that employed him, or of the Filipino people from whom some of it was stolen, or in whose national soil it remained for years or decades, and who need it a great deal more than bankers.)

Once Marcos became president, he went after Santy, forcing him to sign over powers of attorney, and using extortion to deprive him of several large gold accounts, including all those at Manila banks that were vulnerable to pressure from Malacanang. All of Santy's efforts to defend himself failed, and in September 1974, driven into a deep alcoholic depression, he collapsed, was hospitalised, and died several weeks later at home with members of his family in Cabanatuan City. Marcos quickly looted Santy's few remaining accounts in the Philippines, and went after others in New York, Hong Kong and European capitals.

In 1983, when Marcos heard rumors that the Laurel family had a hoard of Federal Reserve bonds and gold bearer certificates on deposit at UBS, he had Pedro Palafox Laurel and his business partner Domingo Clemente arrested and brought to the Black Room at the palace. There, over a period of weeks, the two men were slowly tortured to death by General Ver. Clemente knew nothing about the bonds, and Laurel refused to reveal their locations.

Pedro's widow, Loretta, subsequently fled to Spain to live.

From then on, the Laurels lived in fear. It was only in 1986, when Ferdinand Marcos was removed from power by the Reagan Administration and put under house arrest in Hawaii, where he later died, that Laurel's heirs and the surviving members of his circle dared begin to recover the bonds from their hiding places.

Unfortunately, at this very moment, another large stash of Federal Reserve Notes (FRNs) and Federal Reserve Bonds (FRBs) began coming on to the market, recovered from U.S. military planes that had crashed long ago in the jungles of Mindanao.

According to reliable sources who visited the wrecked aircraft and recovered the dog-tags of the crew, the truth is as follows: In May 1948, four U.S. Air Force planes on their way from California to Malaysian Borneo, refuelled at Clark just north of Manila, then continued on their way toward Borneo. A typhoon that had been brewing in the western Pacific moved directly into their flight path, and all four planes crashed into the mountains of Mindanao. In the doomed flight were two B-29 Superfortresses of the type that had dropped atomic bombs on Hiroshima and Nagasaki, plus a new modified version of the same plane called a B-50, and a much smaller twin-engined B-26. The lead B-29 had the serial number 7695132. Among the dead on board were General Frank Reagan, Colonel John Reagan, and crewmen named Colling, Dalton, Johnrey and Withor. The two B-29s were carrying thousands of FRNs and FRBs, in boxes from the Chase Manhattan and Wells Fargo banks. The B-29s were wearing the livery of General Claire Chennault's Civil Air Transport (CAT), partly owned by the CIA through a front in Delaware named Airdale Corporation. In 1948, the CIA was using CAT to fly four million tons of supplies each month to Generalissimo Chiang Kai-shek's forces, which were rapidly losing all of China to the communists. These two CAT B-29s, loaded with billions of dollars' worth of FRNs and FRBs, were on their way to Malaysia on a roundabout route to southwestern China by way of Thailand and Burma.

The B-50, which had recently been built by Boeing to carry nuclear weapons for the Strategic Air Command (SAC), had a cargo of 117 canisters of uranium. At this time Washington was seriously considering dropping "dirty bombs" on Red China and North Korea. The B-26 was escorting the B-50 to a secret airbase in Thailand, which was being prepared by SAC in the event of such a nuclear war.

What concerns us here is the mission of the two B-29s with all the Fed notes and bonds. Professor Richard Aldrich of Nottingham University, co-editor of the journal *Intelligence and National Security*, described the strategic situation in 1948 in testimony before a British court in 2003: As Chairman Mao's forces advanced through China in 1948, Dr. Aldrich said, Britain and the U.S. dreaded the prospect that one of the world's largest stocks of gold – worth $83-billion at current prices – would fall into communist hands. So it was decided to extract the gold reserves from China before the communists could seize them. The CIA provided the means for this bullion rescue mission, flying in B-29 bombers disguised in the livery of its CAT, later renamed Air America. CAT flew numerous missions to bring huge shipments of gold out of Mainland China.

Where did the FRNs and FRBs fit in? Professor Aldrich said they may have been used "for persuading managers of major banks in the interior of China to part with their vast stocks of gold." Printing FRNs and FRBs with a face value much greater than that of the gold they were to replace, he said, served to encourage the banks or wealthy individuals to swap their gold for the bonds and notes, which would be easier to hide and later smuggle out of China to be cashed in the West. As Aldrich said, the U.S. almost certainly had no intention of honouring them anyway.

Professor Aldrich explained that the CIA was only emulating Britain's Special Operations Executive (SOE), which printed and circulated massive quantities of counterfeit currency and bonds during the war. "Foreign Office files also show that the CIA was involved in other currency issues, including the movement of printing plates for Chinese currency," Aldrich testified.

But why were such huge quantities of FRNs and FRBs flown out to China?

"Because of the possibility of operational loss," Aldrich told the court, "surplus amounts of FRNs were required. Regional banks [in China] receiving FRNs in return for their gold were aware that the FRNs were likely to be redeemable for only a proportion of their face value. Therefore a much larger value in FRNs would have been required than the total value of the gold that the Americans and Chinese Nationalists were trying to extract from China."

Aldrich was adamant that the FRNs being flown to China were authentic. However, he was uncertain whether the FRNs involved in the 2003 lawsuit were of the same provenance.

"I cannot prove that *these* FRNs were part of the operation to extract gold from China," Aldrich said. "But there is absolutely no doubt that such an operation took place."

We interviewed pilot Eric Shilling, one of the original Flying Tigers in the American Volunteer Group (AVG) in 1941, who went on to fly for CAT and the CIA after the war. Shilling told us he made numerous flights from Guam and Clark, ferrying FRNs and Nationalist secret agents as far into China as Chengtu in Sinkiang Province, and flying boxes of gold out to Taiwan. The B-29 had a range suited to long round-trips, and Shilling was skilled at flying the aircraft at thirty or forty feet above the ocean to enter and leave Chinese airspace without being picked up by radar. He told us Generalissimo and Mme. Chiang Kai-shek were fully informed of the flights, and that once on his return to Taipei, Shilling was invited to the presidential palace where Mme. Chiang praised him, telling him: "I did not go to bed until I knew that you had landed safely."

Whether the FRNs and FRBs found in the crashed CAT aircraft in Mindanao should be considered real or counterfeit raises interesting legal, moral and ethical questions, since they were printed by the U.S. Government at the Bureau of Engraving and Printing in Washington, where the CIA has an office occupied full-time in such activities, according to a CIA source we interviewed who worked there for years.

If a promissory note is created by the U.S. Government and exchanged for gold by the U.S. Government, it can reasonably be argued that it is a legitimate document, and therefore binding upon the government to redeem it. For, if a government can freely create false financial documents at whim, for whatever purpose, how do you know what to trust and what not to trust? The same question might be raised about U.S. currency printed by a Federal Reserve that exists for private profit. For the government and the banks owning stock in the Fed to renege on redeeming such bonds would be the equivalent of grand larceny.

In the late 1980s, just after Marcos died, the wreckage in Mindanao was discovered by a tribe of aboriginals, who found the B-29s full of incomprehensible Fed notes and bonds. Most of the boxes were still sealed with wax and official stamps, but some had broken open on impact. When these were carried out to a district town, and translated into Tagalog, it was understood that the Fed notes were important, and in astronomical denominations.

Quantities of these Fed notes suddenly appeared in the market as everyone and his brother tried to cash them in. The Fed was not buying, and neither was the U.S. Treasury, which automatically denounced them all as counterfeit. Secret Service agents were sent to Manila to pose as buyers so they could entrap brokers trying to sell the bonds. Assassins were also sent. An Australian private investigator was warned, "If I persisted in pursuing these items, I would most likely receive a visit from some very unpleasant men whose job it is to secure the safety of the USA against any threats to the stability of its economy. I was informed that if I ever tried to redeem them, I would not see another birthday. A CIA friend told me that these FRNs were all over the world, not only in the Philippines. He said Chiang Kai-shek's family owned large quantities. Some Chinese families involved with secret societies such as the Cherry Blossom and the Maple Leaf also had them in certain number sequences that had been assigned to those networks. Ferdinand Marcos had large quantities of FRNs that he was given by President Nixon in return for gold – which were referred to as 'Tricky-Dickie Notes'."

Unfortunately for the Laurels, this was the same period when President Reagan talked of putting the U.S. back on the gold standard. President Nixon had taken the dollar off the gold standard in 1970 and made it legal for the first time in nearly forty years for private American citizens to own gold. As a result the official price shot up – going above $800 an ounce during the early Reagan years. If at that moment the Laurels had demanded payment in full for the 1,665 metric tons of gold they had "loaned" to the Federal Reserve in 1934, that amount of gold would have been worth over $35-trillion. However, the Laurels were bound by the terms of their original agreement, which had a face value on maturity of only $100-billion. But even $100-billion was more than Washington could face paying. In fact, Washington had never really intended to redeem any of the 1934 Morganthau issue bonds, except at very deep discounts of 1% to 10%, and then only to "favored" individuals.

If the dollar was going to be put back on the gold standard, the White House had to block any attempts to redeem gold certificates and Fed bonds. No new administration likes to be held accountable for huge debts incurred by previous administrations. Redeeming those bonds would represent a huge drain on U.S. assets. So Reagan's team had to come up with a strategy to block any attempt by owners or bearers to redeem the bonds.

Curiously, it was also in 1986 that the Federal Reserve decided to recast all the gold bars in its vaults, changing "good delivery" bars from traditional rectangular ingots into trapezoidal-shape. Why this was done was never satisfactorily explained, but it allowed the Fed to change the hallmarks, serial numbers, and all other identification, which included re-papering and earmarking, effectively erasing all record of ownership of many thousands of tons of gold in its different vaults.

For a government that was up to its ears in the Iran-Contra swindle, Death Squads, October Surprise, Swiss numbered accounts, and lying to Congressional committees, the answer was obvious: Declare all the Fed notes and bonds floating around Asia counterfeit, including both the Laurel bonds and the bonds found on the crashed planes.

Here was a fraud that had been used many times by banks all over the world. When a gold certificate was issued in exchange for bullion placed on deposit, embedded codes were used including misspelled words, to "assure" that the owner's certificate matched the bank records exactly. These misspellings were later easily cited as "evidence" of fraud.

In Japan, Prime Minister Tanaka had gone one step further in designing his notorious "57s" to look completely different from normal Japanese government bonds. If he wanted to redeem one for an ally, he could. If he didn't, he could declare it a counterfeit, and point out that it didn't even look like a government bond.

The Reagan Administration's answer was similar. A large number of Fed bonds and gold certificates were printed at the Bureau of Engraving and Printing, on the wrong type of paper, with a comic variety of deliberate errors. Many were engraved with the wrong faces, the wrong mottos, the wrong designs, the wrong signatures. Some were even engraved and printed in traditional Chinese characters. This would be a hilarious disinformation campaign, flooding Asia with blatant forgeries, to make the whole idea ridiculous. It would cut the legal legs off anyone trying to redeem legitimate gold certificates or legitimate Fed bonds. They could be laughed out of court.

Special engraving plates were sent to Manila where the CIA already had presses to run them off. To confuse the issue in Mindanao, where the planes had crashed, two "missionaries" set themselves up with high-tech presses saying they were going to print Bibles, but instead ran off conspicuously bogus Fed notes and bonds, which added to the impression that they were all false.

•

It is crucial not to confuse the bogus Fed notes flooding Asia and the Pacific in the 1990s with the Fed notes issued to the Laurel family in 1934 by Treasury Secretary Morganthau and the Federal Reserve. These, which we have examined very closely, and which have been judged authentic by scientists at one of Spain's leading universities, and groups of experts elsewhere, are printed correctly in every detail on precisely the paper used for the Morganthau issue in 1934, with the same colored threads running through the fabric visible under a microscope. (The entire notarized forensic investigation of the Laurel family bonds, in both English and

Spanish, appears on volume three of our CDs of documentation.) In sum, these Fed notes were not created for a covert CIA operation in China, but are authentic in every respect.

Because they are authentic, the Fed and the U.S. Treasury are ethically bound to redeem them. However, there are mitigating factors. Banks, prosecuting attorneys and trusted judges always discover mitigating factors. For one thing, ideally these bonds should have been redeemed in the decade following their maturity in 1966. But that would have been suicidal, because Marcos was murdering people to get his hands on them, and Marcos was "America's Boy". One of those murdered was Pedro Palafox Laurel, Loretta's husband. So she was terrified, and therefore late in seeking to redeem them.

As Loretta Laurel's inheritance represented the largest part of the bonds, the Laurel circle decided to have a prominent Spanish attorney approach the U.S. Treasury, the FDIC (Federal Deposit Insurance Corporation) and the Federal Reserve Bank of Chicago. They chose Santiago Vila Marques, member of a wealthy Catalan family owning thousands of acres along the Costa Brava, north of Barcelona. Vila Marques, who had family ties to the Philippines going back generations, agreed on one condition: Half of whatever was recovered must go to projects to help raise living standards of the poor in the Philippines.

Vila Marques enlisted Chicago attorney Carey Portman, and Texas attorney Laurence J. Friedman (a friend of George W. Bush), to represent Loretta Laurel if the case came to trial in the U.S. They repeatedly contacted the Board of Governors of the Fed, the FDIC and the Treasury Department during 2000-2001, presenting them with authenticated copies of one of the bonds, plus all related documents in the 1934 transaction.

Eventually they received a response, different from Japan's response to Norbert Schlei and his clients trying to get Tokyo to redeem the "57" IOUs. Interestingly, the Fed, FDIC and Treasury stopped short of denouncing the Laurel bonds as counterfeit and fraudulent. Instead, they said they "could not verify" that they were real. This is a crucial distinction.

"After carefully reviewing the documents that you and your client have submitted, we are unable to verify that the Federal Reserve bond and related documents … are authentic. In addition, as I indicated to Mr. Portman by telephone, Chairman Greenspan is not available to meet or speak with you or your client concerning this matter." The Chicago Federal Reserve Bank also claimed to be "unable to verify" their authenticity. An affidavit from Mark Taylor, manager of accounting at the Chicago Fed, stated, "There was no record of the issuance or the existence of these bonds whatsoever." William G. Curtin, a financial specialist at the U.S. Treasury, stated: "the Treasury Department has no record that it issued any of the documents in question, and the Treasury has never issued any Federal Reserve bearer bonds of any kind."

Why were both the Fed and the Treasury claiming they had no record of such a transaction? Why did they not claim that the documents were forgeries, or counterfeit, and bring criminal charges against Laurel and her attorneys? Why were they merely "unable to verify" anything?

They were stonewalling. They did not say records of their issuance did not exist, only that they "could not be found". They'd gone missing. They stopped short of saying the documents were fake, just that they were "unable to verify" if they were real. This was doubletalk, like that at the trial of Norbert Schlei, where U.S. officials insisted they could find "no record" of America ever bribing Japanese politicians, and "no record" of Yamashita's Gold.

By not claiming the documents were forgeries, the Treasury and the Fed avoided having to bring criminal charges, which would enable Laurel's attorneys to pursue "discovery" – eventually finding the evidence the Fed and the Treasury were hiding.

The statement of William G. Curtin quoted above is sheer bunkum. Of course the Treasury never issued Fed bearer bonds – they were only issued by the Fed, a private banking cartel, not a government agency.

Of course the Fed could insist that no records could be found, because the Fed's ledgers have never been open to public scrutiny – so how could anyone challenge such a statement?

In September 2001, the Laurel case came to trial at the U.S. District Court for the Northern District of Chicago, before Judge Harry D. Leinenweber.

The judge was an interesting man, married to an interesting woman. A graduate of the University of Chicago law school, he established a practice in the famous Mafia stronghold of Joliet, Illinois, where he represented U.S. Government agencies, and became a GOP state politician serving in the Illinois House of Representatives. In 1986, President Reagan rewarded Leinenweber for loyal service to the GOP by appointing him to the federal bench. When Reagan was succeeded by President George H.W. Bush, Leinenweber's wife, Lynn Martin, a U.S. Congresswoman, was given a Cabinet post as U.S. Secretary of Labor. Because she used her maiden name, most people did not immediately connect her to the judge she was married to.

While his wife was Secretary of Labor, Judge Leinenweber presided over many lawsuits involving labor discrimination. Many people who knew they were married felt he should have disqualified himself because of his wife's Cabinet position as Labor Secretary. When confronted by journalists, Lynn Martin claimed that she never discussed court cases with her husband.

When the new Clinton Administration took office, Lynn Martin lost her Cabinet post but became a richly paid consultant to the Mitsubishi Corporation, specifically to defend Mitsubishi in a lawsuit charging sex discrimination at a factory in Normal, Illinois, not far from her husband's court. Journalists reported that for this Lynn Martin was paid $2-million by Mitsubishi, to oversee a case in a state where her husband was a federal judge specializing in labor discrimination cases, raising serious questions about conflict of interest. Despite Martin's intervention, Mitsubishi lost the case and paid a record settlement.

Subsequently, Judge Leinenweber became involved in hearing cases about a network of CIA-owned savings and loan companies, used to launder dirty money, then looted and allowed to go bankrupt. One was Libertyville Savings and Loan. On its board was Charles Hunter, who was also chief financial officer of the nationwide Walgreen drugstore chain. Hunter and others were accused of mismanaging and causing the downfall of the CIA-owned S&L, resulting in damages of more than $42-million. At Libertyville Savings and Loan, between $20-million and $42-million was lost by account holders (depending on who tallies the figures) while several wealthy directors including Hunter were allowed to settle a lawsuit quietly for only $6-million. Investigative journalists alleged in public that Judge Leinenweber received a gift of some $17-million to rule in favor of Hunter. The judge did not sue the journalists for slander or libel.

Therefore, Federal Judge Leinenweber hardly seemed to be a disinterested party in the lawsuit between the Laurels and the Chicago Federal Reserve Bank, a claim of $100-billion by a foreigner against a local institution that was the taproot of Chicago's financial structure. A loss of $100-billion would be like cutting that taproot.

Predictably, Judge Leinenweber showed a bias against Mrs. Laurel and in favor of the Chicago Fed. When it became evident to Laurel's attorneys that the case was rigged, and they were being blocked in the same manner as Norbert Schlei, they sought to present additional evidence that would overcome the stonewalling of the Fed and Treasury. Neither the Fed nor Treasury wanted additional evidence presented, so they filed a motion saying this new information was inadmissible, because it should have been presented earlier. Judge Leinenweber immediately ruled in favor of the Fed and Treasury. No surprise.

Stymied, Laurel's attorneys filed a "notice of voluntary dismissal" telling the court they wished to drop the case. The same day, attorneys for the Chicago Fed also made a motion to dismiss. Because of the court's slovenly record keeping, it was unclear which side made the move first.

Attorney Portman immediately filed an appeal to the U.S. Court of Appeals for the 7th Circuit. This was a three-judge panel headed by Judge Richard Posner, who soon made it clear that he knew little of the financial history of his country, had no idea what the true relationship was between the federal government and the Federal Reserve, did not have the vaguest idea what the Treasury and the Fed had done covertly in the 1930s, and thought he was being exceedingly witty by calling the entire lawsuit "nonsense". Judge Posner is said to be closely associated with the Federalist Society, established in 1982 by a clique of extreme right-wing Christian-Zionist grand inquisitors including Robert Bork, William Rehnquist, Edwin Meese, William Kristol and John Ashcroft. The organization was underwritten by the Mellon family, which had been involved in setting up the Fed in 1913.

Judge for yourself: In July 2002, Posner gave his opinion of the Laurel case as follows: "The suit is preposterous. There is no record of any such bond issue, and as the national debt of the United States was only $28-billion in 1934, as a year later the entire stock of gold owned by the United States had a value of only $9-billion, and as no securities issued by a U.S. Government entity exceeded $100-million before 1940, the claim that in 1934 a Federal Reserve Bank issued bonds that virtually doubled the national debt and added $25-billion in gold to the government's holdings can only cause one to laugh." Whoever gave Judge Posner this disinformation, the laugh is on him.

Economist Dr. Martin A. Larson, an expert in this field, gave totally different facts: "Between 1934 and 1941," Larson stated, "18,000 metric tons of gold were purchased by the Federal Reserve system and placed in the vaults of Ft. Knox. It was owned by the Federal Reserve, and the government was simply the custodian thereof, and American taxpayers paid the storage fee."

Judge Posner claimed to be stating self-evident facts, but he did not know the facts. If 18,000 metric tons of gold were purchased by the Fed during the 1930s, the amount purchased from the Laurels (1,665 metric tons) was a mere drop in the bucket. For Posner to say such a gold purchase would have "virtually doubled the national debt" is nonsensical because what the Fed's private banking cartel bought had nothing to do with the national debt.

Had Judge Posner proceeded with due diligence, he would have known that in 1952, Congressman Wright Patman of the House Banking and Currency Committee said: "These funds are expended by the Federal Reserve system without an adequate accounting to the Congress. In fact, there has never been an independent audit of either the twelve [Fed] banks or the Federal Reserve Board that has been filed with the Congress, where a member of Congress would have an opportunity to inspect it. The General Accounting Office does not have jurisdiction over the Federal Reserve. For forty years the system, while freely using the money of the government, has not made a proper accounting."

As a Court of Appeals judge, Posner should have known that in 1982, the 9th District U.S. Court of Appeals said: "Federal Reserve Banks are not federal instrumentalities ... but are independent, privately owned, and locally controlled corporations, in light of the fact that direct supervision and control of each bank is exercised by a board of directors, Federal Reserve Banks, though heavily regulated, are locally controlled by their member banks, banks are listed neither as 'wholly owned' government corporations nor as 'mixed ownership' corporations; Federal Reserve Banks receive no appropriated funds from Congress, and the banks are empowered to sue and be sued in their own names."

On the other hand, Posner showed true insight when he went on to say: "The [Chicago Fed] bank's lawyer told us without being contradicted that the Department of Justice has declined to prosecute the persons involved in the fraud because no one could possibly be deceived by such obvious nonsense. We are puzzled by this suggestion." Having been led to believe by the Fed, the Treasury Department, and others, that the whole Laurel case was a scam, Posner couldn't figure out why the Justice Department didn't burn them all at the stake, or at least arrest them. In this, Posner had rightly been "puzzled" – tripping over the truth hidden by a swamp of disinformation and character assassination.

The Department of Justice refused to prosecute because it knew the bonds were genuine, and so could not prove that they were false. The Department of Justice also now knew that Vila Marques had a thick stack of additional evidence and forensic analysis to prove the validity of the bonds, which Justice had not been aware of during the first trial before Judge Leinenweber. To prosecute would permit Vila Marques to present this additional evidence and would also enable "discovery", allowing Vila Marques and his American colleagues to delve into the archives.

So the Department had deceived Judge Posner into thinking the Laurel case was "obvious nonsense", only to pull the rug from under the judge by refusing to prosecute. Posner was left with no choice but to dismiss the Laurel suit "without prejudice" – leaving undecided whether the bonds were real or not.

Where the case went from there depended on whether Vila Marques and his allies felt they had strong enough evidence (and deep enough pockets) to force the issue in favor of their clients. For strategic reasons, Vila Marques had held back important information proving beyond question the authenticity of the bonds – so that unless the Treasury and the Fed were able to steal the bonds from where they were hidden, or to damage his reputation by further character assassination, they might have to negotiate a settlement. The U.S. Treasury and the Fed were known to have paid off several earlier cases involving legitimate bonds. This was done secretly to avoid establishing a legal precedent.

The Laurel group had adequate money to fight the case in court for years, but that depended on where it was tried – in the U.S. where judges could be manipulated by Washington, or in continental Europe where they could not. Did Washington and the Bush Administration have the stomach to be humiliated yet again?

Given the cowed media in America, and compliant journalists in the U.K. of Tony Blair and the Spain of José Aznar, lies could be spread and repeated so often that the public would begin to believe them. This was how one forensic expert, the U.K.'s Charles Halksworth, was railroaded in British courts and media, and put in prison for six years. One of the zany allegations endlessly repeated in the U.K. media was that Halksworth had verified Fed notes printed on an inkjet printer. In fact, government agents had scanned the documents and printed them on an inkjet printer themselves, then substituted these for the originals to make Halksworth look like a fool. The accusation that such a well-known forensic expert, who had previously helped Scotland Yard develop finger-printing technology, would verify paper printed on an inkjet was so laughable, no self-respecting journalist should have given it credibility; but in the U.K. of Tony Blair the silly allegation was given heavy play in media throughout the country. This was the sort of abuse of power that Vila Marques was facing. But he was rescued by the Madrid bombing in March 2004.

In the months following the dismissal of the Laurel case in Chicago, the U.S. Secret Service, which has authority to operate overseas in cases of currency counterfeiting and fraudulent financial instruments, informed a branch of Spain's intelligence service that there had been no legitimate legal proceedings about the Laurel bonds brought by Vila Marques in the United States. This was a lie that could easily have been verified by going online to court records on the Internet. However, at the time, Spain's government was headed by the conservative Aznar, who was close to President George W. Bush. Instead of determining the facts first, the intelligence service was ordered to come down hard on Vila Marques. He found himself subject to surveillance, wiretaps and indirect threats to his personal safety and that of his family. Following the Madrid bombing, which led to the downfall of the Aznar government, and the installation of a liberal new government headed by

José Luis Rodriguez Zapatero, Vila Marques fought back by presenting evidence to Madrid of his legal procedures in the U.S. This led the new Spanish government to rebuke the U.S. Secret Service – a victory for Vila Marques.

This was not the only time Washington had targeted Vila Marques. In 2001, he discovered that four boxes of Laurel bonds, in safe-keeping with a security firm in Germany, had been seized by the U.S. Secret Service. When challenged by the German government to justify the seizure, the Secret Service was unable to establish that the documents were fraudulent. They were rebuked by the German authorities, and the four boxes of documents were recovered and put into safekeeping by the Superior Court in Berlin.

While Vila Marques was in Berlin to press for the recovery of the boxes, he left his hotel room for a few minutes only to discover on his return that U.S. agents had intimidated the hotel maid and gained entry to his room, where they stole his private papers.

One of the boxes of Laurel bonds, which had been left in the custody of document forensic expert Halksworth in London, was confiscated by the British police when they took Halksworth into custody in connection with an entirely different investigation. In the opinion of most independent observers, Halksworth's conviction for fraud in 2003 was false. In September 2004, Vila Marques received a scurrilous letter from the British police at 37 Wood Street, London, saying they were preparing to move the box to another location and would proceed to destroy the billions of dollars' worth of Loretta Laurel's Federal Reserve bonds, "because of lack of space at the new facility." The behavior of the British police in this instance can only be understood in light of the incestuous relationship between current regimes in the U.K. and U.S.

Over the years, as we have seen in this book, many individuals and groups have attempted to redeem gold certificates, FRNs and FRBs, or personal and family gold deposits, at banks or other financial institutions. A few have succeeded, but the vast majority have been threatened and intimidated, and some have even been murdered. Nevertheless, when all else has failed, the U.S. Treasury and the Fed have agreed to redeem such notes for a very deep discount – 2 percent or 5 percent of their face value. In view of the failure of the Secret Service to steal the Laurel bonds, and its failure to damage the reputation of Vila Marques, such may turn out to be the case with the Laurel bonds. But the deal will be kept secret to avoid a stampede of similar legal challenges. As for the Laurel group, as little as 2 percent would still mean many billions of dollars.

If an agreement of some kind is not reached with the Laurel group, the U.S. Treasury and the Fed will be looking at major lawsuits in Madrid and Berlin – the Central Court of Madrid is already closely reviewing the case. This could expose all the accumulated evidence, establish precedents, and spawn similar lawsuits all over a planet awash with bonds and certificates deceitfully issued by the U.S. and U.K. Governments in past decades with no serious intention of redeeming them.

Unlike others who have tried to redeem such notes or bonds, Vila Marques went to unusual lengths to document their authenticity at one of Spain's top universities. Forensic experts from many disciplines examined the bonds, the paper on which they were printed, the inks, the boxes and other materials enclosed in the boxes, and collectively arrived at the conclusion that they were absolutely authentic in every detail. Unlike the U.K., which easily railroaded Halksworth as a solitary forensic expert, the U.S. could not do the same to a team of scientists from across the scholastic spectrum; especially not today, in Madrid courts famous for the tenacity of their magistrates, in a new Spain that is not intimidated by Washington, and in a new Europe that has begun to talk back.

MEN IN BLACK

We cannot blame private banks and government agencies for these crimes of grand larceny without identifying some of the spiders that wove the web of influence. That General Haig successfully redeemed a "57" in Tokyo, thanks to a personal letter from President George H.W. Bush, reveals the vital role of influence-peddling at the highest levels of state. Becoming the American president, or the British prime minister, is no longer the climax of a career. More important is whether the president or prime minister can look forward, on retirement from office, to becoming a board member of the foremost influence-peddlers in Washington, such as The Carlyle Group. As U.S. Supreme Court Justice Felix Frankfurter wrote: "The real rulers in Washington are invisible, and exercise power from behind the scenes." As far back as 1922, New York Mayor John Hylan said: "The invisible government is like a giant octopus that sprawls its slimy length over ... the nation. At the head of this octopus are the Rockefeller ... interests and a small group of powerful banking houses ... who virtually run the U.S. Government for their own selfish purposes." He got it right.

The corruption evident in the Federal Reserve system, the gold cartel and the big banks, has turned America into a nation most of the world no longer respects – a nation driven by greed, greased by influence-peddling, controlled by fear and misled by lies. Since 1945, its all-consuming greed has been hidden by the veil of National Security. Despite the collapse of the "communist menace" that justified excessive secrecy during the Cold War, the corrupt Bush administration has shown how new enemies can always be found to scare Americans into submission and compliance.

The Carlyle Group is only one of many organizations whose boards are composed of former presidents, former prime ministers, and other top government officials, employed for their advance knowledge of future government defense contract requirements and their ability to arrange mergers and acquisitions. Unless you are part of this network, your prospects in life range from being cannon-fodder in Iraq to being a serf in the pseudo-Puritan feudal society of the Neo-Cons.

In the Puritan ethic, wealth is evidence of God's approval of you as a person. The richer you are, the more God approves of you. Once private bankers gained monopoly control of gold and the supply of money in 1913, America's Robber Barons moulted into Puritan nobility, a new aristocracy based on money in a country that had totally rejected aristocracy of any other type.

Not content to be merely super-rich, the monopolists saw themselves as "The Illuminati", symbolized by the all-seeing eye at the top of the pyramid on U.S. currency. Many of the richest families in America learned to avoid drawing attention to themselves – among the Rockefellers for example, only Nelson courted publicity and involved himself personally in covert operations, becoming an intimate friend of General Lansdale and other spooks. As a consequence of this low profile, the label "The Octopus" has since been relegated to their cadre of servants, who do the dirty work in the hope of someday joining the overlords.

Among the most successful of these servants were Allen and John Foster Dulles, whose father gave Sunday sermons at a church in a community of Illuminati. In due course, the Dulles brothers became powerful servants of the Harrimans, Morgans, Mellons, Warburgs and Rockefellers, from the 1920s to the ends of their lives. The Bush family climbed similarly. Another comer was John J. McCloy, who rose from relative poverty to become a top Rockefeller man and head of the World Bank. These were some of the spiders who wove the web linking the Fed to the Black Eagle Trust, the M-Fund, Project Hammer, the CIA, a string of CIA black banks around the world, and CIA savings and loan companies inside America. James Jesus Angleton once told a journalist bitterly that the only reason he was named chief of counter-intelligence at the CIA was because he had taken an oath that he would never subject the Dulles brothers to lie-detector tests about their collusion with Nazi Party bankers in the 1930s. Men in black need to remain unseen.

As they put the black economy in place, behind the curtain of National Security, they found ways to make most gold reserves disappear into coffers only they could access – as illustrated by the numbered Swiss accounts held by White House staffers during the Iran-Contra scandal, and the way Santa Romana's gold accounts have been blocked, or moved offshore, by banks that refuse to acknowledge the rights of his heirs.

Look closely enough, however, and the hand does *not* move faster than the eye. Just follow the filaments in the web. For example:

Currently, when "black gold" is recovered from Japanese treasure vaults in the Philippines it enters the world market through an agency in Australia with genetic ties to the Bank of England. First the ingots are taken to Manila where they are assayed by international gold buyers (one of whom is our source). Once satisfied with the assay, the broker buys the gold at a deep discount, then airlifts or sealifts it to Australia where it is "sanctified" by Johnson Mathey Bank (JMB), the UK gold bank that worked with President Marcos. Following a major scandal leading to questions in Parliament, JMB was absorbed in late 1984 by the Bank of England. Two years later, in April 1986, the JMB bullion operation was sold to the biggest Australian banking, mining and bullion syndicate, Mase-Westpac. Our gold broker source swears that upon reaching Australia the gold is re-smelted to London standard by JMB and re-papered by JMB, and then simply joins the flow of newly mined gold shipped from Australia to the City of London, where it enters the world market. That at least appears to establish a link between gold laundering and the Bank of England.

Sources in Manila also insist that Sir Evelyn de Rothschild, whose family is so closely identified with the Bank of England and the U.S. Fed, is the true majority owner of the Benguet gold mines in the Philippines. There is nothing startling about that, in and of itself, but the Benguet board has long been dominated by members of Imelda Marcos's Romualdez family, and still is today. Imelda's children had the use of a Rothschild mansion in London when they were attending school. As the biggest gold mine in the Philippines, Benguet has always been one of the primary channels for war-looted gold leaving Manila. During the Marcos years, a big piece of Benguet was acquired by a group of Wall Street venture capitalists who shared property ownership and a casino in the Bahamas with the Mafia's Meyer Lansky. So there are interlocking directorships that reveal more when seen together than when seen apart. Let's follow the filaments further:

Lansky, in turn, was closely associated with top CIA banker Paul Helliwell, also based in the Bahamas, who created the chain of CIA black money banks throughout the world, including Castle Bank in the Bahamas, Nugan Hand Bank in Sydney and Honolulu, and BCCI (Bank of Credit and Commerce International), now said to be reincarnated as Pinnacle.

Helliwell's ultimate boss during and after World War II, was Wall Street attorney and former OSS chief William "Wild Bill" Donovan, who also was the boss of Allen Dulles, William Colby, Bill Casey – and others who later became heads of the CIA – and an intimate friend of Meyer Lansky.

"Almost every key man in the OSS had direct connections with large international industrial and banking interests; among those listed as having been key OSS executives were Julius Spencer Morgan, and Henry Sturgis Morgan, sons of the late J.P. Morgan, who were special assistants to Donovan…"

The front man for Helliwell was banker General Erle Cocke, a Grand Commander of the Knights of Malta – to which Donovan and many other OSS and CIA brass belonged – which was, in turn, closely linked to Vatican secret services. Knights of Malta membership is dominated by reactionary European aristocracy and Americans whose names read like a Who's Who of the Black Eagle Trust: Former OSS chief Donovan, former CIA top brass William Colby, John McCone, William Casey, George H. W. Bush, James Jesus Angleton and Vernon Walters. Also on the roster were General Douglas MacArthur's intimates, General Charles Willoughby and General Bonner Fellers. Last but not least, former Secretary of State Alexander Haig who negotiated the "57" in Tokyo with the help of the first President Bush, described in Chapter 9.

Donovan was the chief spider – America's original man in black. It was Donovan, working behind the scenes with John J. McCloy and the Dulles brothers, who set up the global network of secret funds and black banks that made creative use of the Black Eagle Trust, and laundered drug profits before they entered U.S. banks to bolster the American economy. This was racketeering on a global scale, run by covert agents of the U.S. Government, with proceeds so huge the only way to hide them was by claiming National Security was constantly at stake.

Far more effective than two sets of accounting ledgers, National Security kept everything off the record. To protect BCCI, Nugan Hand, and other black banks, people were murdered, including Frank Nugan, journalist Danny Casolaro, and former CIA Director William Colby, "legal counsel" to the black banks, whose body was found floating in the Potomac River estuary in 1996.

Like the careers of the Dulles brothers, Donovan's life wove gold, drugs, espionage, underworld and global politics together using personal connections. In 1923, he was a little-known Assistant U.S. Attorney in the state of New York, who became friends with super-rich Albert Lasker, one of the heads of the General American Tank Car Company, which had the first patent for a welded petroleum railway tank car (without rivets) and dominated the shipment of Rockefeller petroleum on Harriman railways. This, plus Lasker's tight family connections with Germany, and his financial cronyism with most of the Robber Barons, allowed him to introduce Donovan to all the right people. With Lasker's encouragement, Donovan became a celebrity when he and Federal Bureau of Narcotics agent Ken Oyler cracked a major drug ring in Buffalo, and made a huge drug seizure in Canada, making America look virtuous just before the 1924 Geneva Opium Conference. The seized drugs were traced to the Golden Triangle, where the borders of Burma, China, Laos and Thailand meet. Lasker introduced Donovan to the Rockefellers and Harrimans. Oyler introduced Donovan to FBN chief Harry Anslinger, who got his job as drug czar because he married the niece of Coolidge Administration Treasury Secretary Andrew Mellon. Mellon was one of the Robber Barons who had set up the Federal Reserve system. Mellon's son-in-law, diplomat David K. Bruce, later helped Allen Dulles, Anslinger and Donovan organize the OSS. It was practically a Mellon family enterprise.

Once OSS was set up, Donovan became heavily involved in opium and heroin, mingling narcotics with espionage during the war. He learned a lot from the Brits. In China, he worked with SOE's William and John Keswick of Jardine-Matheson, Britain's biggest opium cartel in Asia, with a controlling interest in the Hongkong & Shanghai Banking Corporation and ties to the Oppenheimer family through the giant mining firm Rio Tinto Zinc. (HSBC was one of the main repositories of Santy's gold, and has blocked all efforts by his heirs to access it.) Together, Donovan and the Keswicks arranged deals with KMT spy-boss General Tai Li and his underworld business partner, druglord Du Yueh-sheng. So did Commander "Mary" Miles of SACO, the Sino American Cooperative Organization set up by Donovan's old friend Navy Secretary Frank Knox, as cover in China for the Office of Naval Intelligence (ONI). Their currency in covert operations was drugs, gold and diamonds.

Donovan also set up a special office in OSS called X-2, which spied on foreign insurance companies – many of the biggest being in Nazi Germany. His partner in running X-2 was Cornelius Starr, who started out selling insurance in Shanghai in 1919 and went on to build American International Group (AIG), into one of the largest insurance companies on earth today. Early in the war, Donovan sent James

Jesus Angleton to Rome as chief of X-2 and other OSS black operations there. Angleton paid Sicilian and Calabrian Mafiosi to smuggle OSS agents into Sicily and across to the toe of Italy. In appreciation, Angleton and Donovan put Sicilian gangsters in positions of political leverage in Palermo and Rome, and kept them supplied with gold and guns. In America, the Mafia helped government agents keep an eye out for Nazi spies along the Atlantic and Gulf waterfronts, on the understanding that when the war ended, Mafia dons currently serving time in federal penitentiaries would be freed and "deported" back to Sicily.

In effect, Donovan and his circle of intimates wove a web linking the underworld in Asia, Europe and America to U.S. banks and the U.S. Government. This would pay off richly during the Cold War.

In 1946, when the OSS was shut down by Truman, to be succeeded by the CIA, Donovan pretended to resume private practice as a Wall Street attorney, but in reality spent most of his time helping Paul Helliwell set up black banks to make use of the Black Eagle Trust. To disguise these postwar operations, Donovan founded World Commerce Corporation (WCC) with financial backing from the Rockefellers, particularly Nelson Rockefeller. One of WCC's main objectives was to buy and sell surplus U.S. weapons and munitions to foreign underworld groups, like the Chinese and Italian mafias, in return for their cooperation against communist and socialist political parties or labor unions. Author Douglas Valentine called it a sort of private Marshall Plan, a cross between "an import-export combine and a commercially oriented espionage network".

To maintain secrecy, WCC was registered in Panama. Many of its operations involved the Nationalist Chinese in Asia, and the Sicilian and Calabrian Mafia in Europe. The Nationalist Chinese provided the hard drugs, and the Sicilians moved them into the U.S. through Meyer Lansky in Havana and Santo Traficante in Tampa, or through Mexico to Bugsy Siegel in California.

Mixing drugs and espionage in Italy, Donovan and Angleton forged a three-way alliance with the Mafia, the postwar Christian Democratic Party and the Vatican. New York narcotics boss Frank Coppola was recruited to be Donovan's liaison with Sicilian godfather Salvatore Giuliano. In May 1947, paid by Donovan and provided with guns by Coppola, Giuliano's men murdered eight people and wounded thirty-three in a Sicilian village that had made the mistake of voting for Communist Party candidates. Coppola's main mission was to get Mafiosi into the Christian Democratic party, and the party's deputies into government, while eliminating rival Communist candidates, killing them if necessary. Their reign of terror was so successful that by 1948, Italian Communist Party boss Palmiro Togliatti accused the U.S. of subverting Italy's elections, not the first or last time that accusation was voiced.

The point here is that it was not strictly a CIA operation, it was a Donovan operation supported by the CIA, and Donovan's WCC had been set up with Rockefeller money. Where do you draw the line?

In Asia, Donovan was a registered agent of the Thai government, creating an alliance between the disgraced Nationalist regime on Taiwan and crooked Thai generals. Together, they moved opium and heroin out of the Golden Triangle, bypassing old French channels of the Union Corse, which had gone through Laos and Vietnam. To dominate the Asian drug trade, remnant Nationalist Chinese armies stranded in southwest China crossed the border into Burma where they seized control of the Golden Triangle. They were lavishly supported by Washington on the pretext that they were carrying out guerrilla operations against the Chinese Communists. These KMT forces became the main movers of drugs into the international market, aided by the CIA airline Air America, and the CIA shipping line Sea Supply, set up by Helliwell and Donovan.

Air America was dreamed up by Donovan and Old China Hands William Pawley, Whiting Willauer and General Claire Chennault. In the 1930s, Pawley had set up the Central Aircraft Manufacturing Company (CAMCO) for Madame Chiang Kai-shek, to assemble planes for what were later called the Flying Tigers. Pawley was paid lavishly by the Chiang regime, the Soong family and druglord Du Yueh-sheng. In 1950, Donovan and Pawley bought out Chennault, having persuaded the China Lobby to pay him $5-million for his beat-up airline. Pawley then "retired" to Havana where he went into business with Meyer Lansky. He spent lavishly, buying sugar plantations, an airline and a bus company. When Fidel Castro seized control of Cuba from the Batista regime, Pawley escaped to Miami where he continued his alliance with Lansky, using a Miami bus company as his front. Meanwhile, Pawley helped Donovan persuade right-wing Texas oil man H.L. Hunt to support the KMT regime with millions of dollars for covert operations. Valentine points out that Pawley and Donovan were aided in all this by the CIA's Allen Dulles, Admiral Charles Cooke, ambassador William Bullitt, Brooklyn publisher M. Preston Goodfellow, former SOE agent William Keswick and Satiris Fassoulis, vice president of Commerce International China, a subsidiary of Donovan's WCC.

Donovan kept up his close ties to General Chennault and former Flying Tigers' physician Dr. Margaret Chung, said to be a key link between the KMT drug generals and Bugsy Siegel. While the China Lobby insisted that all narcotics came from Communist China, the KMT's General Tuan and General Li assured us over dinner in Chiangmai that they were the ones moving the drugs. We observed their opium-laden mule trains, trucks and planes, and airdrops over the Gulf of Thailand to waiting Taiwanese cargo and fishing vessels.

One of Donovan's top financial allies was Helliwell's front man General Erle Cocke, whose family had been in banking for generations. After World War II, Cocke served in the World Bank and IMF, and as head of the American Legion, but also on the board of CIA banks such as Nugan Hand. In April 2000, just two weeks before he died of pancreatic cancer, General Cocke agreed to give a legal deposition to the attorney of six plaintiffs who said they had been swindled by former intelligence agents of the South African Apartheid regime. The scam was typical of many rackets run under a part of the Black Eagle Trust called Project Hammer, in which unsuspecting investors were encouraged to put up money for projects in the Third World, which then collapsed, swallowing their money.

In his deposition, reproduced on our CDs, General Cocke said he knew a lot about the Black Eagle Trust's Project Hammer because he had been a part of the

Donovan spider's web for decades. He testified that by the 1990s, he knew person-ally that Project Hammer had assets exceeding $1-trillion. Cocke testified that no Project Hammer transaction could take place without the personal approval of Citibank CEO John Reed. General Cocke explained that Reed was "the cheese" (the Big Cheese, boss, or overseer) of Project Hammer. "I had no problem seeing the president of the United States, but I could never get in to see John Reed." Reed was third in a string of Citibank CEOs groomed by Donovan, each the mentor of the next, starting with George Moore who was an OSS agent during the war. Rising quickly to head Citibank after the war, Moore trained Walter Wriston as his replacement, who in turn trained John Reed.

Ties between Citibank and the CIA were always close, and a number of top spooks joined the bank when they left the Agency, such as former DCI John Deutsch, who left Langley under a cloud to immediately become a member of Citibank's board. John Reed, who denies knowing anything about Project Hammer, has since left Citibank, also under a cloud, and is now head of the U.S. Stock Exchange.

It is curious that in the 1990s – while Reed and Citibank were being sued for moving $50-billion in Santa Romana's gold from New York to the Bahamas, and General Cocke testified that Reed was overseeing Project Hammer with assets of over $1-trillion – Citibank claimed to be going bankrupt. It was not the only player in the game of musical chairs by major banks, as various Rockefeller Holdings absorbed each other and their offshore holdings companies like hungry amoebas.

By this time, Spain's Santiago Vila Marques was also serving as the attorney for Alberto Cacpal's huge gold deposits, many of them at Citibank. Before John Reed retired, Vila Marques cabled him asking for a meeting to "clarify" Cacpal's assets in Citibank, which totalled hundreds of millions of dollars. Reed never replied. In effect, Reed was succeeded at Citibank by President Clinton's Treasury Secretary Robert Rubin, the new chairman of Citigroup, who has been equally opaque and evasive.

As documented in earlier chapters, Santy's Bengal Trading stashed most of his gold at UBS in Zurich, in the name of Pedro Palafox Laurel. UBS, which first acknowledged that these bonds were redeemable in 2003, then reversed itself by claiming they were now considered false. This is odd because when Santy's daughter Diana Luatic visited UBS as an adult, the official in charge of the gold repository said in front of witnesses that he remembered first meeting her as an ado-lescent when he had taken her prints as part of security measures for her gold accounts. Vila Marques, as attorney for Loretta Laurel, is preparing to launch a legal battle with UBS, as soon as he has washed his hands of the U.S. Fed.

Seen as a giant spider's web, the involvement of a great many organizations and individuals becomes apparent.

Of one thing we can be sure: Since the Federal Reserve system was established in 1913, privatising the money supply and making gold vanish, it has served "The Illuminati" and their servants in "The Octopus" far better than it has served the great majority of American citizens. Interlocking directorships and personal networks reveal an astonishing variety of racketeering between the moneymen, the spooks, the druglords and the underworld. National Security hides little from America's enemies. But it hides a great deal from U.S. citizens.

The fact that the U.S. Government has been able to pull in all this gold, both Japanese and Nazi war loot and gold from a large number of endangered banks and desperate individuals, and then renege on redeeming their holdings, has enabled the U.S. to acquire companies and properties throughout the world that represent an American financial global empire by massive fraud. One is tempted to speculate that these maneuvers were part of what put the Clinton Administration in the black. U.S. imperial policy pretends to occupy a theological and moral high ground compared to Old Europe and Old Asia, but it is a farce.

It was all summed up brilliantly by Henry Ford: "It is well enough that the people of the nation do not understand our banking and monetary system for, if they did, I believe there would be a revolution before tomorrow morning."

ACKNOWLEDGEMENTS

Many people helped us with documents, information, and eyewitness accounts over nearly twenty years of research bearing on this subject. Most of our Japanese and Filipino sources, fearing retribution, asked not to be identified. Our sources in the CIA, and in American embassies, also could not be named. Members of the Marcos family gave us unique insight, as did members of the family of Santa Romana. Former POWs in the U.S., U.K., New Zealand, the Netherlands, and Australia, were very helpful, as were former civilian slave laborers, and other victims of Japan, in Asia as well as in the West. In England, we thank in particular Arthur Titherington, Ron Bridge, and Keith Martin; in New Zealand, Hank Zeeman; in the U.S., Gil Hair and Ed Jackfert. Among the attorneys who helped us in America were Daniel Cathcart, Eleanor Piel, Anthony D'Amato, Jerome Garchik, and Hartley Paul; in England, Martyn Day, Gina Baylin, and Mark Stephens.

A number of journalists and scholars in different countries were very generous with their assistance and insights, including Bertil Lintner in Thailand, Glenn Schloss and Charmaine Chan in Hong Kong, Robert Whiting in Japan, Hamish Todd and Elizabeth Murray in the U.K., Anneliese Graschy in Germany, Michel Gurfinkiel, Henri Eyraud, Roger Faligot, Alain Coulon, and Julien Holstein in France.

We are especially indebted to Iris Chang, Ignatius Ding, and Jesse Hwa, for their unstinting support and encouragement throughout, and to our colleague Joel Legendre, correspondent in Japan of RTL and numerous French and Swiss journals, whose comprehension of what goes on behind the folding screen has been a great help on this and previous books.

Above all, we wish to thank Yolanda and Robert Curtis in Nevada, for giving us unlimited access to their incomparable archive of documents, videotapes, audiotapes, maps, and photographs, and for always being prepared to discuss background, details, and clarifications. Norbert Schlei in California provided invaluable documentation, and many hours of discussion. Professor Edmond Lausier in California shared his files and insights on Japanese financial transactions, and the

LDP personalities involved. Blair Baker provided perspectives from Wall Street. Gillian Tett, Tokyo bureau chief of *The Financial Times*, gave us her lucid perceptions and encouragement. Dr. Lambert Dolphin, formerly scientific director of Stanford Research Institute, shared his exceptional understanding of Golden Lily treasure vaults in the islands. Bill Luttig, Norman and Matilda Haynes, and Claude Cochran, kindly relayed countless messages to and from Ben Valmores and his family. James Raper spent many days tape-recording Ben's answers to our lists of questions. John Foringer gave us his insights on the life and thoughts of his brother, Alan Foringer.

In the Netherlands, investigative journalist Jos Hagers of *De Telegraaf* helped us with financial background and historical materials, and shared her unique contacts with other victims of Japan in Indonesia. Henk Hovinga kindly gave us access to his excellent book on the Death Railway in Sumatra. We owe special thanks to Dutch nautical historian Albert Kelder for his outstanding research into the grim subject of the Hell Ships, and for helping us identify many of the people and events surrounding the saga of the *Op ten Noort* and the eventual recovery of its sunken treasure.

Thanks as well to Michael Dorr, Robin Mackness, Helen Ellis, Cotton Jones, Bill Conklin, Edward Leslie, Melissa Saurborn, Neill Graham, John Easterbrook, Laura and Michael Capps, Clarence 'Jim' Brown, Jacques and Lucette Mustin, Drs. Joan and Brian Pengilly, Ted and Jocelyn Fundoukos, and Micheline and Yvon Martinez.

For their encouragement on this and other books, we are much in debt to Annik Zambetti, Jean-Francois Hiebler, Yves Michalon, Sophie Mairot, and Stephane Pasadeos.

Special thanks to author Douglas Valentine.

BIBLIOGRAPHY

Readers interested in knowing more about similar American covert intervention in Europe, before and after WWII, are encouraged to read Christopher Simpson's excellent books, *Blowback*, and *The Splendid Blond Beast*. The first is an account of CIA collusion with Nazis after World War II. The second is a groundbreaking new look at how the Dulles brothers and other Wall Street operators, including John J. McCloy, saved German financiers and other elite from being tried for war crimes and genocide, which they had helped to carry out in return for favors from the Nazi regime. In Germany as in Japan, international law was manipulated cynically, to rescue bankers and industrialists linked to the Wall Street firms and American corporations closely identified with the Dulles brothers and their circle. Because the Dulles brothers headed both the CIA and the State Department, these devious manipulations remain in place today and continue to thwart justice for war crime victims. This explains why the State Department continues to block victim lawsuits, and both CIA and State refuse to release documents going back half a century.

"A. Frank Reel Death Notice." *Virginia-Pilot*, April 11, 2000. www.pilotonline.com/news/nw0411obt.html.

Acheson, Dean. *Present at the Creation: My Years in the State Department*. New York: W.W. Norton, 1969.

Adams, James Ring and Douglas Frantz. *A Full Service Bank: How BCCI Stole Billions around the World*. London: Pocket, 1992.

Agee, Philip. *Inside the Company: CIA Diary*. NY: Bantam, 1976.

Akashi Yoji. *Watanabe Wataru: the Architect of the Malaya Military Administration, December 1941-March 1943*. Aichi Shukutoku University. Paper presented at the Second International Malaysian Studies Conference, 2-4 August 1999, Institute of Postgraduate Studies and Research, University of Malaya, Kuala Lumpur.

Allen, G.C. *A Short Economic History of Modern Japan: 1867-1937*. London: George Allen & Unwin, 1945.

Alletzhauser, Albert J. *The House of Nomura: the Inside Story of the Legendary Financial Dynasty*. New York: Arcade Publishing, 1990.

"Allies Sent Millions to Ease the Plight of Japanese Prisoners." *The Sunday Telegraph*, November 30, 1997.

Anderson, Scott and Anderson, Jon Lee. *Inside the League*. New York: Dodd, Mead & Company, 1986.

Andrew, Christopher. *For the President's Eyes Only: Secret Intelligence and the American Presidency from Washington to Bush*. London: Harper-Collins, 1995.

Angle, Robert. "The Mutual Understanding Industry. " *JPRI Working Paper*, No. 2, September 1994.

Anslinger, H.J. *The Traffic in Narcotics*. New York: Funk & Wagnalls, Co., 1953. Available online at the Schaffer Library of Drug Policy.

Appeal to the International Labour Organization Regarding Violation of Convention No. 29 by Japan during

Wartime. December 8, 1997, Tokyo, Japan. Available at International Labor Organization website.

Armour, Andres. *Asia and Japan: the Search for Modernization and Identity*. London: The Athlone Press, 1985.

Axelbrook, Albert. *Black Star over Japan: Rising Forces of Militarism*. London: George Allen & Unwin, 1972.

Aziz, M.A. *Japan's Colonialism and Indonesia*. The Hague: Martinus Nijhoff, 1955.

Bamforth, James. *The Puzzle Palace: inside the National Security Agency*. New York: Penguin, 1983.

Barber, Laurie. "The Yamashita War Crimes Trial Revisited." At www.waikato.ac.nz/history/journalfolder/waimilhist2folder/yamashita.html.

Barber, Noel. *Sinister Twilight: the Fall of Singapore*. London: Fontana, 1970.

Barnes, Kathleen. "Controversial U.S. General Joins Fight in Philippines." *Toronto Star*, 17 February 1987.

Barnhart, Michael A. *Japan Prepares for Total War: the Search for Economic Security*, 1919-1941. Ithaca: Cornell, 1987.

Bartholet, Jeffrey. "Gold is Losing Its Glitter." *Newsweek*, July 19, 1999.

Bartu, Friedemann. *The Ugly Japanese: Nippon's Economic Empire in Asia*. Tokyo: Yenbooks, 1993.

Beasley, W.G. *The Rise of Modern Japan*. New York: St. Martin's Press, 1990.

Beasley, W.G. *Japanese Imperialism: 1894-1945*. Oxford: Clarendon Press, 1987.

Beasley W.G. *The Meiji Restoration*. Stanford: Stanford, 1972.

Behr, Edward. *The Last Emperor*. New York: Bantam Books, 1987.

Belluck, Pam. "General's Mystery Philippines Trip." *San Francisco Chronicle*, February 18, 1987.

Benedict, Ruth. *The Chrysanthemum and the Sword*. Tokyo, Charles E. Tuttle Company, 1954.

Bergamini, David. *Japan's Imperial Conspiracy*. UK: Heinemann, 1971.

Berger, Major D.H. "The Use of Covert Paramilitary Activity as a Policy Tool: An Analysis of Operations Conducted by the United States Central Intelligence Agency, 1949-1951." Available online.

Bernstein, Peter L. *The Power of Gold*. New York: John Wiley, 2000.

Bidwell, Bruce W. *History of the Military Intelligence Division, Department of the Army General Staff: 1775-1941*. Frederick: University Publications of America, 1986.

Bingman, Charles F. *Japanese Government Leadership and Management*. London: Macmillan, 1989.

Birnbaum, W.E. "Dollar Instability and World Economic Growth." October 1996, Presentation before Joint Economic Committee of the U.S. Senate. Available at www.senate.gov

Bisson, T.A. *Prospects for Democracy in Japan*. New York: Macmillan, 1949.

Bix, Herbert. *Hirohito and the Making of Modern Japan*. New York: Harper Collins, 2000.

Bix, Herbert. "Inventing the 'Symbol Monarchy' in Japan, 1945-1952." *Journal of Japanese Studies*, Vol. 21. No. 2, pp. 319-363 (1995).

Bix, Herbert. "The Showa Emperor's 'Monologue' and the Problem of War Responsibility." *Journal of Japanese Studies*, Vol. 18, No. 2, pp. 295-363 (1992).

Bix, Herbert. "Emperor Hirohito's War." *History Today*, Vol. 41 (December 1991), pp. 12-19.

"Blast Killed 524 Korean Laborers." *Japan Times*, January 27, 2001.

Blum, William *Killing Hope: US Military and CIA Interventions Since World War II*. Common Courage Press: Monroe, Maine, 1995. This is the revised edition of the book as originally published in 1986 under the title *The CIA: A Forgotten History*. London: Zed Books, 1986. Blum's work can also be found on the internet.

Boegheim, L.M.J. "De Japanse Muntenroof in Nederlandsch-Indie Gedurende de Tweede Wereldoorlog." *De Beeldenaar*, No. 5, 1995.

Botting, Douglas. *The Aftermath: Europe*. Time-Life Books, Alexandria, Virginia: 1983

Bower, Tom. *Blood Money: the Swiss, the Nazis and the Looted Billions*. London: Macmillan, 1997.

Brackman, Arnold C. *The Other Nuremberg: the Untold Story of the Tokyo War Crimes Trials*. New York: William Morrow and Company, 1987.

Breuer, William B. *Shadow Warriors: the Covert War in Korea*. New York: John Wiley, 1996.

Breuer, William B. *MacArthur's Undercover War*. New York: John Wiley, 1995.

Broker, Stephen. "Hominoid Evolution [Peking Man]. Yale-New Haven Teachers Institute, Curriculum Unit 79.06.02 at www. Yale.edu/ynhti/curriculum/units/1979/6/79.06.0s2.html

Brook-Shepherd, Gordon. *Ironmaze: the Western Secret Services and the Bolsheviks*. London: Pan Books, 1999.

Browne, Courtney. *Tojo: the Last Banzai*. New York: Da Capo, 1998.

Bruce, David. *The Future and the Fighting Generations*. London: W.H. Allen & Co., 1943.

Bulletin on Narcotics, 1953 Issue 2. Available at the United Nations website www.undcp.org.

Bunyai, Richard. *Money and Banking in China and Southeast Asia during the Japanese Military Occupation*. Taiwan: Tai Wan Enterprises Co., 1974.

Burress, Charles. "Japan's War Time Atrocities." *San Francisco Chronicle*, October 1, 2001.

Burnell, Elaine H. (ed.). *Asian Dilemma: United States Japan and China*. Santa Barbara: Center for Democratic Institutions, 1969.

Buruma, Ian. *Wages of Guilt: Memories of War in Germany and Japan*. London: Vintage, 1995.

Buruma, Ian. *Behind the Mask: on Sexual Demons, Sacred Mothers, Transvestites, Gangsters and other Japanese Cultural Heroes*. New York: Pantheon Books, 1984.

Byas, Hugh. *Government by Assassination*. New York: Alfred A. Knopf, 1942.

Cahn, Anne. *Killing Detente: the Right Attacks the CIA*. University Park: The Pennsylvania State University Press, 1998.

Callon, Scott. *Divided Sun*. Stanford: Stanford University Press, 1995.

Cameron, Rondo (ed.). *Banking and Economic Development: Some Lessons Of History*. London: Oxford University Press, 1971.

Campbell, Kenneth J. "Major General Charles A. Willoughby: A Mixed Performance." *American Intelligence Journal*, Vol. 18, No. 1-2 (1998) pp. 87-91. Available online.

Carpozi, George Jr. *Nazi Gold: the Real Story of How the World Plundered Jewish Treasures*. Far Hills, New Jersey: New Horizon Press, 1999.

Carroll, John. "The Enigma of Yoshio Kodama." *The Tokyo Journal*, July 1988, pp. 90-94.

Chamberlin, William Henry. *Japan Over Asia*. Boston: Little, Brown, 1937.

Chang, Iris. *The Rape of Nanking*. New York: Basic Books, 1997.

Chapman, F. Spencer. *The Jungle is Neutral*. London: Corgi, 1957.

Checkland, Olive, Shizuya Nishimura and Norio Tamaki (eds). *Pacific Banking*, 1859-1959. New York: St. Martin's Press, 1994.

"Cheney Says Haliburton Did Not Support Myanmar Regime." CNN.com: Larry King Live, October 27, 2000.

Choate, Pat. *Agents of Influence: How Japan Manipulates America's Political and Economic System*. New York: Touchstone, 1990.

Clemons, Steven. "Recovering Japan's Wartime Past and Ours." *The New York Times*, Sept. 4, 2001.

Colby, William and Peter Forbath. *Honorable Men*. New York: Simon & Schuster, 1978.

Collins, James. "Gold People." *The New Yorker*, July 17, 2000.

Cook, Haruko Taya. "Nagano 1945: Hirohito's Secret Hideout." *MHQ: the Quarterly Journal of Military History*. Spring 1998, p. 44-47.

Cook, Haruko Taya and Theodore F. Cook. *Japan at War: an Oral History*. New York: The New Press, 1992.

Coox, Alvin D. *Nomonhan: Japan Against Russia*, 1939. Stanford: Stanford University Press, 1985.

Cornwell, John. *Hitler's Pope*. London: Penguin Books, 1999.

Craig, William. *The Fall of Japan*. New York: Galahad Books, 1967.

Crump, Thomas. *Death of an Emperor*. London: Constable, 1989.

Cumings, Bruce. *Parallax Visions: Making Sense of American-East Asian Relations at the End of the Century*. Durham, N.C.: Duke University Press, 1999.

Cumings, Bruce. *Korea's Place in the Sun: a Modern History*. New York: W.W. Norton, 1997.

Cumings, Bruce. "Korean Scandal, or American Scandal?" *JPRI Working Paper*, No. 20, May 1996. Available at the JPRI website.

Davis, Glenn and John G. Roberts. *An Occupation Without Troops*. Tokyo: Yenbooks, 1996.

Daws, Gavan. *Prisoners of the Japanese*. New York: Morrow, 1994.

Dingman, Roger. *Ghost of War: the Sinking of the Awa Maru*. Annapolis: Naval Institute Press, 1997.

Dixon, Karl Hale. *The Extreme Right Wing in Contemporary Japan*. Dissertation: Florida State University College of Social Sciences, 1975.

Doran, Alan. *Trends in Gold Banking*. World Gold Council: Research Study 19, June 1998. Available at WGC website.

Dower, John. "The Showa Emperor and Japan's Postwar Imperial Democracy." *JPRI Working Paper,* No. 61, October 1999. Available at JPRI website.

Dower, John W. *Embracing Defeat: Japan in the Wake of World War II*. New York: W.W. Norton, 1999.

Dower, John W. *Japan in War and Peace*. HarperCollins, 1995.

Dower, John W. *Empire and Aftermath: Yoshida Shigeru and the Japanese Experience 1878-1954*. Cambridge: Harvard, 1988.

Dower, John W. with Timothy S. George. *Japanese History and Culture from Ancient to Modern Times: Seven Basic Bibliographies*. Princeton: Markus Weiner Publishers, 1995.

Downer, Lesley. *The Brothers: the Saga of the Richest Family in Japan*. London: Vintage, 1995.

Drea, Edward J. *In the Service of the Emperor: Essay on the Imperial Japanese Army*. Lincoln: U. Nebraska, 1998.

Drea, Edward J. *MacArthur's ULTRA*. Lawrence: U. Kansas, 1992.

Driscoll, David. "What is the International Monetary Fund?" External Relations Department, International Monetary Fund, September 1998. Available at the www.imf.org

Duus, Peter. *The Abacus and the Sword: the Japanese Penetration Of Korea, 1895-1910*. Berkeley: U. Cal., 1998.

Duus, Peter, Romon H. Myers, and Mark R. Peattie (eds). *The Japanese Informal Empire in China, 1895-1945*. Princeton: Princeton, 1989.

Edwards, Duval A. *Spy Catchers of the U.S. Army in the War with Japan*. Gig Harbor: Red Apple Publishing, 1994.

Edwards, Bernard. *Blood and Bushido: Japanese Atrocities at Sea, 1941-1945*. New York: Brick Tower Press, 1997.

Elphick, Peter. *Far Eastern File: the Intelligence War in the Far East, 1930-1945*. London: Hodder & Stoughton, 1997.

Endicott, Stephen and Edward Hagerman. *The United States and Biological Warfare: Secrets from the Early Cold War and Korea*. Bloomington: Indiana University Press, 1998.

Enriquez, Marge. "The Mother of All Luncheons." At www.inquirer.net/issues/jan2000/jan14/lifestyle/lif_7.htm

Eringer, Robert. *The Global Manipulators*. Bristol: Pentacle, 1980.

Fallows, James. *Looking at the Sun: the Rise and Fall of the New East Asian Economic Political System*. New York: Pantheon Books, 1994.

Fay, Stephen. *Portrait of an Old Lady*. Middlesex: Viking, 1987.

Federal Reserve Bank of San Francisco Economic Letter. August 28, 1998. "How Do Currency Crises Spread?" Available at Federal Reserve Bank website.

Final Report on Zaibatsu Dissolution: Report by the Holding Company Liquidation Commission. Tokyo: July 1951.

Financial Action Task Force on Money Laundering Annual Report 1997-1998. Financial Action Task Force website.

Fingleton, Eamonn. "The Anomalous Position of Christopher Lafleur." *Unsustainable*, May 15, 2001. Online at www.unsustainable.org.

Firman, Richard. "Awaiting the Tsunami? Japan and the International Drug Trade." *The Pacific Review*, Vol. 6, No. 1, 1993

Foreign & Commonwealth Office. *Nazi Gold: the London Conference 2-4 December 1997*. London: Stationery Office, 1998.

Foreign Relations of the United States 1945-1950: Emergence of the Intelligence Establishment, "The National Security Act of 1947." Washington, D.C.: Department of State, 1996.

Foreign Relations of the United States 1946: the Far East. Volume VIII. Washington: Government Printing Office, 1971.

Forty, George. *Japanese Army Handbook*: 1939-1945. Gloucestershire: Sutton Publishing, 1999.

Frank, Richard B. *Downfall: the End of the Imperial Japanese Empire*. New York: Random House, 1999.

Freeman, Laurie. "Japan's Press Clubs as Information Cartels". *JPRI Working Paper*, No. 18, April 1996. Available at JPRI website.

Fu, Poshek. *Passivity, Resistance and Collaboration: Intellectual Choices in Occupation Shanghai, 1937-1945*. Stanford: Stanford University Press, 1993.

Fulford, Benjamin. "Japan's Dirty Secrets." *Forbes*, October 30, 2000.

Gerlach, Michael L. *Alliance Capitalism*. Berkeley: U. Cal., 1992.

Gilley, Bruce. "After the Party." *Far Eastern Economic Review*, December 30, 1999 & January 6, 2000.

Gold, Hal. *Unit 731 Testimony*. Tokyo: Yenbooks, 1996.

Gomer, Robert, John W. Powell and B. V.A. Roling. "Japan's Biological Weapons: 1930-1945." *The Bulletin of the Atomic Scientists*, Vol. 37, No. 8, p. 43-53 (October 1981).

Grabbe, J. Orlin. *International Financial Markets* (3rd Edition). Englewood Cliffs, N.J.: Prentice Hall, 1996.

Grabbe, J. Orlin. "The Gold Market". At www.aci.net/kalliste/gold1.htm

Grabbe, J. Orlin. "The Rise and Fall of Bretton Woods". At www.aci.net/kalliste/gold1.htm

Grant, Zalin. *Facing The Phoenix*. New York: W.W. Norton, 1991.

Green, Timothy. *Central Bank Gold Reserves: an Historical Perspective since 1845*. World Gold Council, November 1999.

Greenspan, Alan. "Can the U.S. Return to a Gold Standard?" *The Wall Street Journal*, September 1, 1981.

Grew, Joseph. *Ten Years in Japan: a Contemporary Record Drawn from the Diaries and Private and Official Papers of Joseph C. Grew*. Westport: Greenwood Press, 1973.

Grew, Joseph. *Turbulent Era*. Boston: Houghton Mifflin, 1952.

Grose, Peter. *Gentleman Spy: the Life of Allen Dulles*. Amherst: University of Massachusetts, 1994.

Guevara, Jose. "Gen. MacArthur also Looked for Yamashita Treasure." November 7, 1999. At www.mb.com.ph/OPED/Jose/1999/jg991107.asp

Guillain, Robert. *I Saw Tokyo Burning: an Eyewitness Narrative from Pearl Harbor to Hiroshima*. New York:

Doubleday, 1981.

Gunther, John. *The Riddle of MacArthur*. New York: Harper, 1951.

Gunther, John. *Inside Asia*. New York: Harper, 1942.

Gutman, Roy and David Rieff (eds). *Crimes of War*. New York: W.W. Norton, 1999.

Guy, George F. "The Defense of General Yamashita", 1950. The article was originally published in the *Wyoming Law Journal*. At www.supremecourthistory.org/myweb/81journal/guy81.htm

Guyot, Dorothy. "The Uses of Buddhism in Wartime Burma." *Asian Studies*, Vol. VII, No. 1.

Hager, Nicky. *Secret Power: New Zealand's Role in the International Spy Network*. Nelson, New Zealand: Craig Potton, 1996.

Hane, Mikiso. *Eastern Phoenix: Japan Since 1945*. New York: Westview, 1996.

Hane, Mikiso. *Emperor Hirohito and His Chief Aide-de-Camp: the Honjo Diary, 1933-1936*. Tokyo: University of Tokyo, 1967.

Harmston, Stephen. *Gold as a Store of Value*. World Gold Council, Research Study No. 22. At the World Gold Council website.

Harries, Meirion and Susie Harries. *Soldiers of the Sun: the Rise and Fall of the Imperial Japanese Army*. New York: Random House, 1991.

Harries, Merion and Susie Harries. *Sheathing the Sword: the Demilitarisation of Japan*. London: Hamish Hamilton, 1987.

Harris, Sheldon H. *Factories of Death: Japanese Biological Warfare, 1932-1945 and the American Cover-Up*. London: Routledge, 1994.

Heppner, Ernest G. *Shanghai Refuge: a Memoir of the World War II Jewish Ghetto*. Lincoln: University of Nebraska Press, 1993.

Hicks, George. *The Comfort Women*. Tokyo: Yenbooks, 1995.

Higashinakano Shudo and Fujioka Nobukatsu. *Exploding the Myth of the Rape of Nanking*. 1999. (An unpublished manuscript written by Japanese professors who claim that the Rape of Nanking never happened.)

Hitchens, Christopher. "The Case Against Henry Kissinger: Part One." *Harpers Magazine*, February 2001.

Hogan, David W. Jr. "MacArthur, Stilwell, and Special Operations in the War against Japan." *Parameters*, Spring 1995. Available online.

Hogan, David W. Jr. *U.S. Army Special Operations in World War II*, CMH Publication 70-42, Washington, D.C. Department of the Army, 1992.

Holmes, W.J. *Double-Edged Secrets: U.S. Naval Intelligence Operations in the Pacific During World War II*. Annapolis: Naval Institute, 1979.

Holzer, Henry. *How Americans Lost Their Right to Own Gold and Became Criminals in the Process*. Committee for Monetary Research and Education, 1981. Available at CMRE website.

Hoover Institution Public Policy Inquiry: International Monetary Fund. *The Bretton Woods Conference*. Available online.

"Hirohito's Brother Tells of War Crimes." *The Times*, July 7, 1994.

Horowitz, David. *From Yalta to Vietnam*. London: Penguin, 1967.

Hoyt, Edwin P. *Three Military Leaders: Togo, Yamamoto, Yamashita*. Tokyo: Kodansha International, 1993.

Hunziker, Steven and Ikuro Kamimura. *Kakuei Tanaka: a Political Biography of Modern Japan*. Singapore: Times Books, 1996.

Huthmacher, J. Joseph (ed.). *Herbert Hoover and the Crisis of American Capitalism*. Cambridge: Schenkman, 1973.

Ienaga Saburo. *The Pacific War: 1931-1945*. New York: Pantheon, 1968.

Immerman, Richard H. *John Foster Dulles*. Wilmington: A Scholarly Resources Inc. Imprint, 1999.

Implementation of the Japanese Imperial Government Disclosure Act and the Japanese War Crimes Provisions of the Nazi War Crimes Disclosure Act: an Interim Report to Congress, July 1, 2002. National Archives and Records Service. Available online.

Innis, W. Joe and Bill Bunton. *In Pursuit of the Awa Maru*. New York: Bantam Books, 1981.

Inside the Shadow Government. Declaration of Plaintiffs' Counsel, filed by the Christic Institute, U.S. District Court, Miami, March 31, 1988.

International Narcotics Control Strategy Reports. Available at www.usis.org

Inventarisatie Rapport Onderzoek Indische Tegoeden. Amsterdam, 1998.

Iriye Akira. *The Origins of the Second World War in Asia and the Pacific*. London: Longman, 1987.

Iriye Akira. "The Ideology of Japanese Imperialism: Imperial Japan and China." In Goodman, Grant K. (Compiler) *Imperial Japan and Asia: a Reassessment*. New York: Columbia University, 1967.

Irokawa Daikichi. *The Age of Hirohito: in Search of Modern Japan*. New York: The Free Press, 1995.

Isaacson, Walter and Thomas, Evan. *The Wise Men: Six Friends and the World They Made*. New York: Simon and Schuster, 1986.

Isenberg, David. "Regulated Private Military Firms." *Defense News*, March 11-17, 2002.

Isenberg, David. "The Pitfalls of U.S. Covert Operations." *Policy Analysis*, No. 118, April 7, 1989. Available online.

Ishida Takeshi. "Pressure Groups in Japan." *Journal of Social and Political Ideas in Japan*, Vol. 2, No. 3, pp. 108-111 (December 1964).

Iwata Taro. "Blurring Boundaries in Manchuria: Japanese Colonialism." Conference Paper presented at the Association of Asian Studies Annual Meeting, San Diego, March 2000. Available online.

Jackson, James. "Diamonds: Is Their Luster Fading?" *Time* International, March 6, 1996. Available at elibrary.com

Jakub, Jay. *Spies and Saboteurs: Anglo-American Collaboration and Rivalry in Human Intelligence Collection and Special Operations, 1940-1945*. London: Macmillan, 1999.

"Japan Allegedly Sank Ship Carrying 5,000 Koreans (Ukushima)." *Korean Times*, October 15, 1999. At NAPSNet Daily Report, October 15, 1999.

"Japan Diverted Allied Funds from Secret Accounts." *Japan Today*, August 14, 2002.

"Japan Must Pay Up Say Protesters." *Hongkong Standard*, December 25, 1998. Available at elibrary.com

Japan Biographical Encyclopedia and Who's Who. Tokyo: The Rengo Press, 1958.

"Japanese Gold." *Drafts of 1951 San Francisco Peace Treaty*, 1951, British Foreign Office, series FO 371, 1951 at Public Records Office, Kew. See FO 371/83828-83839; 92529/92600; 92529-92539 and 92589-92600.

Japanese Imperial Government Disclosure Act of 2000. National Archives and Records Service, available online.

"Japan's Murky Past Catches Up." *The Economist*, July 8, 2000, p. 73-74.

Jeffreys-Jones, Rhodri. *The CIA and American Democracy*. New Haven: Yale University, 1989.

"John G. Roberts on Mitsui and the Opium Monopoly Bureau." At www.vikingphoenix.com

Johnson, Chalmers. "Why Are American Troops Still in Okinawa?" *JPRI Critique*, Vol. 4, No. 2, April 1997. Available at JPRI website.

Johnson, Chalmers. *Japan: Who Governs?* New York: Norton, 1995.

Johnson, Chalmers. *Conspiracy at Matsukawa*. Berkeley: University of California, 1972.

Johnson, Chalmers. "American Intelligence Services Lose Credibility." *JPRI Critique*, Vol. 6, No. 6. June 1999. Available at JPRI website.

Johnson, Chalmers. "Japan Should Pay for Individuals' Suffering." *Los Angeles Times*, March 31, 2000.

Johnson, Chalmers. "The 1955 System and the American Connection." *JPRI Working Paper*, No. 11, July

1995. Available at the JPRI website.

Kaiser, David. *American Tragedy*. Cambridge: Harvard, 2000.

Kanfer, Stefan. *The Last Empire: De Beers, Diamonds, and the World*. New York: Farrar, Straus and Giroux, 1993.

Kaplan, David E. and Alec Dubro. *Yakuza*. Reading, Massachusetts: Addison-Wesley, 1986.

Kaplan, David. "The Golden Age of Crime: Why International Drug Traffickers are Invading the Global Gold Trade." *US News and World Report*, November 29, 1999.

Kaplan, David. "U.S. Propaganda Efforts in Postwar Japan." *JPRI Critique* Vol. 4, No. 1, February 1997. Available at JPRI website.

Kataoka Tetsuya (ed.). *Creating Single-Party Democracy: Japan's Postwar Political System*. Stanford: Hoover, 1992.

Kawahara Toshiaki. *Hirohito and His Times: a Japanese Perspective*. Tokyo: Kodansha International, 1990.

Kawai Kazuo. *Japan's American Interlude*. Chicago: The University of Chicago, 1960.

Kawasaki Ichiro. *Japan Unmasked*. Tokyo: Tuttle, 1969.

Kazuya Sakamoto. "Securing the 'San Francisco System'". Harvard University Asia Center, Triangular Relations Conference. At opatrick@fas.harvard.edu

Keith, Agnes. *Three Came Home: a Woman's Ordeal in a Japanese Prison Camp*. London: Eland, 1985 (reprint of 1948 edition).

Kernan, Michael. "Around the Mall." *Smithsonian Magazine*, May 1995. Available online.

Kesler, Ronald. *Inside the CIA*. New York: Signet Books, 1992.

Kim Choong Soon. *A Korean Nationalist Entrepreneur*. Albany: State University of New York Press, 1998.

Kim Yong-mok. "Whither Japan-Korea Relations." *JPRI Critique*, Vol. 5, No. 9 (October 1998). At the JPRI website.

Kodama, Yoshio. *I Was Defeated*. Tokyo: An Asian Publication, 1951.

Kodansha Encyclopedia of Japan. Eight volumes. Tokyo: Kodansha, 1983.

"Korean Opium for Japan's War." At www.kimsoft.com

Kratoska, Paul H. *The Japanese Occupation of Malaya 1941-1945*. London: Hurst, 1998.

Kratoska, Paul H. (ed.). *Food Supplies and the Japanese Occupation in South-East Asia*. London: Macmillan 1998.

Kriek, D.W.N. *43 Special Mission*. 1998. Available online.

Kruze, Uldis. *San Fransciso and the 1951 U.S.-Japan Treaty Conference*. San Francisco: University of San Francisco, 2001.

Kurzman, Dan. *Kishi and Japan: the Search for the Sun*. New York: Ivan Obolensky, 1960.

Lamont-Brown, Raymond. *Kempeitai*. Gloucestershire: Sutton; 1998.

Lanciaux, Bernadette. "The Influence of Economic Thought on the Political Economy of Modern Japan." *Journal of Economic Issues*, Vol. 30, No. 2, pp. 475-482 (June, 1996).

Lansdale, Edward Geary. *In the Midst of Wars*. New York: Fordham University, 1991.

Large, Stephen S. *Emperors of The Rising Sun: Three Biographies*. Tokyo: Kodansha, 1997.

Large, Stephen S. *Emperor Hirohito and Showa Japan: a Political Biography*. London: Routledge, 1992.

Large, Stephen S. "Imperial Princes and Court Politics in Early Showa Japan." *Japan Forum*, Vol. 1, No. 2 pp. 257-264 (October 1989).

Lasserre, Philippe and Helmut Schutte. *Strategies for Asia Pacific*. London: Macmillan, 1995.

Lebor, Adam. *Hitler's Secret Bankers: How Switzerland Profited from Nazi Genocide*. London: Simon & Schuster, 1999.

Lintner, Bertil. "Friends in Need." *Far Eastern Economic Review*, December 30, 1999 & January 6, 2000.

Livingston, Jon, Joe Moore, and Felicia Oldfather (eds). *Postwar Japan: 1945 to the Present*. New York: Pantheon, 1973.

Lord Russell of Liverpool. *The Knights of Bushido: a Short History of Japanese War Crimes*. London: Corgi, 1958.

Lowe, Peter. *The Origins of the Korean War*. UK: Longman, 1997.

Mabon, David W. "Elusive Agreements: The Pacific Pact Proposals of 1949-1951." *Pacific Historical Review*, Vol. LVII, No. 2, May 1988.

MacArthur, Douglas. *Reminiscences*. New York: Crest Books, 1964.

MacDougall, Terry Edward (ed.). *Political Leadership in Contemporary Japan*. Ann Arbor: Center for Japanese Studies, The University of Michigan, 1982.

Mackay, James. *Betrayal in High Places*. Auckland: Tasman, 1996.

Mackay, James. *The Allied Japanese Conspiracy*. Durham: The Pentland Press, 1995.

MacKenzie, Donald A. *China and Japan*. London: Studio Editions, 1994.

MacKinnon, Stephen R. and Friesen, Oris. *China Reporting: an Oral History of American Journalism in the 1930s and 1940s*. Berkeley: University of California, 1987.

Maeda Tetsuo. *The Hidden Army: the Untold Story of Japan's Military Forces*. Chicago: Edition Q, 1995.

Mainchi Daily News. *Fifty Years of Light and Dark: the Hirohito Era*. Tokyo: The Mainichi Newspaper, 1975.

"Maj. Gen. Courtney Whitney, 71, Adviser to MacArthur is Dead." *The New York Times*, March 22, 1969, p. 33:2.

Manchester, William. *American Caesar: Douglas MacArthur, 1880-1964*. Boston: Little, Brown, 1978.

Manchester, William. *Goodbye Darkness: a Memoir of the Pacific War*. New York: Dell, 1979.

Mangold, Tom. *Cold Warrior: James Jesus Angleton*. London: Simon & Schuster, 1991.

Manning, Paul. *Hirohito: the War Years*. New York: Bantam, 1989.

Marchetti, Victor and John D. Marks. *The CIA and the Cult of Intelligence*. New York: Dell, 1980.

Marshall, Jonathan. "Opium and the Politics of Gangsterism in Nationalist China, 1927-1945." *Bulletin of Concerned Asian Scholars*, Vol. 8, No. 3, pp. 19-48 (July-September, 1976.)

Marshall, William. *Shanghai*. London: Pan Books, 1980.

Martin, Brian G. *The Shanghai Green Gang: Politics and Organized Crime, 1919-1937*. Berkeley: University of California, 1996.

Maruyama Masao. *Thought and Behavior in Modern Japanese Politics*. London: Oxford, 1969.

Masland, John W. "Commercial Influence upon American Far Eastern Policy, 1937-1941." *The Pacific Historical Review*, Vol. 11, pp. 281-299.

Mason, Mark. *The Origins and Evolution of Japanese Direct Investment in East Asia*. Yale: School of Management.

Mayers, David. *The Ambassadors and America's Soviet Policy*. Oxford: Oxford University, 1995.

Mazzocco, Dennis. *Networks of Power*. Boston: South End, 1994.

McClintock, Michael. *Instruments of Statecraft*. New York: Pantheon, 1992.

McCoy, Alfred W. (ed.) *Southeast Asia under Japanese Occupation*. New Haven: Yale University, 1985.

McCoy, Alfred W. with Cathleen B. Read and Leonard P. Adams II. *The Politics of Heroin in Southeast Asia*. New York: Harper & Row, 1972.

McCullough, David. *Truman*. New York: Simon & Schuster, 1992.

McDougald, Charles C. *The Buddha, the Gold, & the Myth*. San Francisco: San Francisco Publishers, 1997.

McDougald, Charles C. *Asian Loot: Unearthing the Secret of Marcos, Yamashita and the Gold*. San Francisco: San Francisco Publishers, 1993.

McDougald, Charles C. *The Marcos File*. San Francisco: San Francisco Publishers, 1987.

McGehee, Ralph. *Deadly Deceits*. New York: Ocean Press, 1999.

McGhie, Stuart. "Private Military Companies: Soldiers, Inc." *Janes Defence Weekly*, May 22, 2002.

McNaughton, James C. "Nisei Linguists and New Perspectives on the Pacific War: Intelligence, Race, and Continuity." A paper at the 1994 Conference of Army Historians. Available at www.army.mil/cmh-pg/topics/apam/Nisei.htm.

Mears, Helen. *Mirror for Americans: Japan*. Boston: Houghton Mifflin, 1948.

Miller, Joseph M. *Monetary Gold*. Luckow Group, Inc. n.d. Available at Luckow website.

Miller, Merle. *Plain Speaking: an Oral Biography of Harry Truman*. Berkeley: Putnam, 1973.

Miller, Nathan. *Spying for America: the Hidden History of U.S. Intelligence*. New York: Dell, 1989.

Miller, Roy Andrew. *Japan's Modern Myth: the Language and Beyond*. Tokyo: Weatherhill, 1982.

Minear, Richard H. *Victor's Justice: the Tokyo War Crimes Trial*. Princeton: Princeton University, 1971.

Mishima Akio. *Bitter Sea: the Human Cost of Minamata Disease*. Tokyo: Kosei, 1992.

Miyamoto Masao. *Straitjacket Society*. Tokyo: Kodansha International, 1993.

Montgomery, Michael. *Imperialist Japan: the Yen to Dominate*. London: Christopher Helm, 1987.

Moon, Thomas N. and Carl F. Eifler. *The Deadliest Colonel*. New York: Vantage, 1975.

Moorehead, Caroline. *Dunant's Dream: War, Switzerland and the History of the Red Cross*. New York: Carroll & Graf Publishers, 1998.

Morikawa Hidemasa. *Zaibatsu: the Rise and Fall of Family Enterprise Groups in Japan*. Tokyo: University of Tokyo Press, 1992.

Morton, Louis. *United States Army in World War Two: the War in the Pacific: the Fall of the Philippines*. Washington, D.C. : Government Printing Office, 1953.

Moser, Michael. "Machiavellian Politics and Japanese Ideals: The Enigma of Japanese Power Eight Years Later." *JPRI Occasional Paper* No. 10, 1998. Available at JPRI website.

Mosley, Leonard. *Dulles: a Biography of Eleanor, Allen and John Foster Dulles and their Family Network*. New York: Dial Press, 1978.

Moss, Stanley. *Gold is Where You Hide it: What Happened to the Reichsbank Treasure?* London: André Deutsch, 1956.

Moyers, Bill. *The Secret Government*. Seven Locks Press, 1988.

Mundell, Robert. *A Reconsideration of the Twentieth Century*. At www. columbia.edu

Mydans, Seth. "Singlaub Asserts he Seeks Treasure." *The New York Times*, February 22, 1987.

Mydans, Seth. "Mystery in Manila: Singlaub's Quest." *The New York Times*, February, 18, 1987.

Nakamura Kaju. *Prince Ito: the Man and Statesman, a Brief History of His Life*. NY: Japanese-American Commercial Weekly, 1910.

Nakamura Masanori. *The Japanese Monarchy: Ambassador Joseph Grew and the Making of the Symbol Emperor System, 1931-1991*. New York: M.E. Sharpe, 1992.

Nakane Chie. *Japanese Society*. Harmondsworth: Penguin, 1973.

Nash, Lee (ed.). *Understanding Herbert Hoover: Ten Perspectives*. Stanford: Hoover Institution, 1987.

Nashel, Jonathan. *Edward Lansdale and the American Attempt to Remake Southeast Asia*. New Brunswick: Rutgers UMI, 1994.

Neary, Ian (ed.). *War and Revolution and Japan*. Sandgate, Folkestone, Kent: Japan Library, 1993.

Nelson, Peter. *Anatomy of a Bank Job*. Dar es Salaam, Tanzania: Nelson International Limited, 1995.

Neumann, A. Lin. "Ex-General Tied to Arms Deals in Philippines." *San Francisco Examiner*, February 18, 1987.

"The New Mercenaries." *Wilson Quarterly*, Summer 2002.

Nishara Masashi. *The Japanese and Sukarno's Indonesia: Tokyo-Jakarta Relations 1951-1966*. Honolulu:

University of Hawaii, 1975.

"No Peace for South Africa's Wand'ring Warriors." *Bulletin of the Atomic Scientists*, May/June 1996, Vol. 51, No. 3.

"Norbert Schlei." *California Bar Journal*, January 2001. Online.

North, Gary. "Gold Bears are Now Trapped; John Exter's 1974 Prophecy is Coming True." November 10, 1999. At www.garnorth.com

Numnonda Thamsook. *Thailand and the Japanese Presence, 1941-1945*. Research and Discussion, No. 6, Institute of Southeast Asian Studies.

O'Brien, Kevin A. "Interfering with Civil Society: CIA and KGB Covert Political Action during the Cold War." *International Journal of Intelligence and Counterintelligence*. Winter 1995, p. 431-456. At www.kcl.ac.uk/orga/icsa/intel.html

Okazaki Hisahiko. *A Grand Strategy for Japanese Defense*. Lanham, Maryland: University Press of America, 1986.

Onoda Hiroo. *No Surrender*. London: Transworld, 1975.

Ooi Keat Gin. *Japanese Empire in the Tropics: Selected Documents and Reports of the Japanese Period in Sarawak Northwest Borneo, 1941-1945*. Volume One and Two. Athens: Ohio University, 1998.

O'Toole, G.J.A. *Honorable Treachery*. New York: The Atlantic Monthly Press, 1991.

Parillo, Mark P. *The Japanese Merchant Marine in World War II*. Annapolis: Naval Institute, 1993.

Parks, Lawrence. *The Near Death and Resurrection of the Gold Mining Industry*, July 17, 2000. Advancement of Monetary Education. Available at www.fame.org

Pauley, Edwin W. *Report on Japanese Assets in Manchuria to the President of the United States July, 1946*. No publisher.

Penders, C.L.M. *The Life and Times of Sukarno*. Rutherford: Fairleigh Dickinson University, 1974.

Persico, Joseph E. *Nuremberg: Infamy on Trial*. NY: Penguin, 1994.

"Policing the Moneymen." *The Economist*, December 12, 1997.

Pomeroy, Charles (ed.). *Foreign Correspondents in Japan*. Tokyo: Charles E. Tuttle, 1998.

Pool, James. *Hitler And His Secret Partners: Contributions, Loot and Rewards, 1933-1945*. New York: Simon & Schuster, 1997.

Post, Peter and Elly Touwen-Bouwsma (eds). *Japan, Indonesia and the War: Myths and Realities*. Leiden: KITLV Press, 1997.

Potter, John Deane. *The Life and Death of a Japanese General*. Toronto: Signet, 1962.

Powers, Thomas. "Department of Dirty Tricks." *The Atlantic Monthly*, August 1979, Vol. 244, No. 2, pp. 33-64.

Powers, Thomas. *The Man Who Kept the Secrets: Richard Helms and the CIA*. New York: Pocket Books, 1979.

Powles, Cyril H. "The Myth of the Two Emperors: A Study in Misunderstanding." *Pacific Historical Review*, Vol. 37, pp. 35-50.

Prados, John. *Presidents' Secret Wars: CIA and Pentagon Covert Operations from World War II through the Persian Gulf*. Chicago: Elephant Paperbacks, 1996.

Price, John. "A Just Peace? The 1951 San Francisco Peace Treaty in Historical Perspective." *JPRI Working Paper*, No. 78: June 2001.

Price, Willard. *The Son of Heaven: The Problem of the Mikado*. London: William Heinemann, 1945.

Pu Yi. *From Emperor to Citizen*. Peking: Foreign Languages, 1979.

Pyle, Kenneth B. *The Japanese Question: Power and Purpose in a New Era*. Washington, D.C.: AEI Press, 1992.

Ramsayer, J. Mark and Frances M. Rosenbluth. *Japan's Political Market Place*. Cambridge: Harvard University, 1997.

Ramseyer, J. Mark and Frances M. Rosenbluth. *The Politics of Oligarchy: Institutional Choice in Imperial Japan*. Cambridge: Cambridge University, 1995.

Reid, Anthony and Oki Akira. *The Japanese Experience in Indonesia: Selected Memoirs of 1942-1945*. Athens: Ohio University Center for International Studies, 1986.

Report on the Mission to the Democratic People's Republic of Korea, the Republic of Korea and Japan on the Issue of Military Sexual Slavery, January 4, 1996. Available at the United Nations website.

Reports of General MacArthur. MacArthur in Japan: the Occupation: Military Phase. Volume I Supplement. Prepared by his General Staff, Library of Congress Card Number 66-60006, Facsimile reprint, 1994, Center for Military History.

Richelson, Jeffrey T. *The U.S. Intelligence Community*. New York: Ballinger, 1989. Excerpts are available online.

Roberts, John G. *Mitsui: Three Centuries of Japanese Business*. New York: Weatherhill, 2nd edition, 1989.

Roberts, John G. "The Lockheed-Japan-Watergate Connection." *Ampo: Japan-Asia Quarterly Review*. Vol. 8, No. 1, March 1976; pp. 6-15.

Robertson, Eric. *The Japanese File: Pre-War Japanese Penetration in Southeast Asia*. Hong Kong: Heineman, 1979.

Robinson, Jeffrey. *The Laundrymen*. New York: Pocket Books, 1995.

Roling, B.V.A. and Antonio Cassese. *The Tokyo Trial and Beyond*. Cambridge: Polity Press, 1993.

Rubin, Evelyn Pike. *Ghetto Shanghai*. New York: Shengold, 1993.

Saga Junichi. *Confessions of a Yakuza*. Tokyo: Kodansha, 1991.

Sakaiya Taichi. *What is Japan?: Contradictions and Transformations*. Tokyo: Kodansha, 1993.

Salerno, Joseph T. "The Gold Standard: an Analysis of Some Recent Proposals." *Policy Analysis*, No. 16, September 9, 1982. Available online.

Sansom, George. *A History of Japan*. Tokyo: Tuttle, 1974.

Sanchez, Henry. "Why Do States Hire Private Military Companies?" Online.

Sayer, Ian and Douglas Botting. *Nazi Gold*. Edinburgh: Mainstream, 1999.

Sayer, Ian and Douglas Botting. *America's Secret Army*. London: Grafton, 1989.

Schaller, Michael. *Altered States: the United States and Japan since the Occupation*. Oxford: Oxford University, 1997.

Schaller, Michael. "America's Favorite War Criminal: Kishi Nobusuke and the Transformation of U.S.-Japan Relations." *JPRI Working Paper* No. 11, July 1995. Available at the JPRI website.

Schaller, Michael. *Douglas MacArthur: the Far Eastern General*. Oxford: Oxford University, 1989.

Schaller, Michael. *The American Occupation of Japan: the Origins of the Cold War in Asia*. Oxford: Oxford University, 1985.

Scherer, James A.B. *Three Meiji Leaders: Ito, Togo, Nogi*. Tokyo: Hokuseido Press, 1936.

Schlei, Norbert A. "Japan's 'M-Fund' Memorandum, January 7, 1991," *JPRI Working Paper*, No. 11, July 1995. Available at the JPRI website.

Schlesinger, Jacob M. *Shadow Shoguns*. Stanford: Stanford University Press, 1997.

Schonberger, Howard. "The Japan Lobby in American Diplomacy." *Pacific Historical Review*, Vol. 44, No. 3, pp. 327-359, August 1977.

Schrecker, Ellen. *The Age of Mccarthyism*. Boston: Bedford, 1994.

Schreiber, Mark. *Shocking Crimes of Postwar Japan*. Tokyo: Yen Books, 1996.

Scott, Otto. "On the Role of Gold." *USAgold, the Gilded Opinion*. Available online.

Scovel, Myra. *The Chinese Ginger Jars*. New York: Harper, 1962.

Seagrave, Sterling. *Lords of the Rim: the Invisible Empire of the Overseas Chinese*. New York: Putnam, 1995.

Seagrave, Sterling. *The Marcos Dynasty*. NY: Harper and Row, 1988.

Seagrave, Sterling. *The Soong Dynasty*. NY: Harper and Row, 1985.

Seagrave, Sterling. *Soldiers of Fortune*. Alexandria: Time-Life, 1981.

Seagrave, Sterling and Peggy Seagrave. *Dragonlady*. NY: Knopf, 1990.

Seagrave, Sterling and Peggy Seagrave. *The Yamato Dynasty*. New York: Broadway Books, Random House, 2000.

Sergeant, Harriet. *Shanghai*. New York: Crown Publishers, 1990.

Seth, Ronald. *Secret Servants: a History of Japanese Espionage*. New York: Farrar, Straus and Cudahy, 1957.

Sheldon, Charles D. "Japanese Aggression and the Emperor, 1931-1941, from Contemporary Diaries." *Modern Asian Studies*, Vol. 10, No. 1, 1976.

Shiroyama Saburo. *War Criminal: the Life and Death of Hirota Koki*. Tokyo: Kodansha International, 1977.

Silverstein, Josef (ed.). *Southeast Asia in World War II*. New Haven: Yale University, 1974.

Simpson, Christopher. *Blowback: America's Recruitment of Nazis and Its Effect on the Cold War*. New York: Crowell-Collier, 1989.

Simpson, Christopher. *The Splendid Blond Beast: Money, Law, and Genocide in the Twentieth Century*. Monroe: Common Courage Press, 1995.

Singer, P.W. "Corporate Warriors: The Rise of the Privatized Military Industry and Its Ramifications for International Security." *International Security*, Winter 2001-02.

Singlaub, John K. *Hazardous Duty: an American Soldier in the Twentieth Century*. New York: Summit Books, 1991.

Sklar, Holly (ed.). *Trilateralism*. Boston: South End Press, 1980.

Smith, Joseph B. *Portrait of a Cold Warrior: Second Thoughts of a Top CIA Agent*. New York: Ballantine Books, 1976.

Smith, Robert. *United States Army in World War II: the War in the Pacific: Triumph in the Philippines*. Washington, D.C.: Office of the Chief of Military History, Department of the Army, 1963.

Spector, Ronald H. *Eagle against the Sun: the American War with Japan*. Harmondsworth: Penguin Books, 1984.

Srodes, James. *Allen Dulles: Master of Spies*. Washington, D.C.: Regnery, 1999.

Steinberg, David Joel. *Philippine Collaboration in World War II*. Manila: Solidaridad, 1967.

Steinberg, Rafael. *Return to the Philippines*. Alexandria, Virginia: Time-Life Books, 1979.

Stockwell, John. *In Search of Enemies: a CIA Story*. New York: W.W. Norton, 1978.

Storry, Richard. *A History of Modern Japan*. Harmondsworth: Penguin, 1990 reprint.

Storry, Richard. *Japan and the Decline of the West in Asia, 1894-1943*. London: Macmillan, 1979.

Storry, Richard. *The Double Patriots: a Study of Japanese Nationalism*. Westport: Greenwood Press, Publishers, 1973.

Sugita Yoneyuki. "Transfer of Policy Initiative and its Implications: U.S. Occupation Policies Towards Japan, 1946-1948, U.S.-East Asian Relations in the Truman Era." Society for Historians of American Foreign Relations, 1996 Annual Meeting, Boulder, Colorado. Go to www.sugita.org/SHAFR.htm

Sugita Yoneyuki. "The International Military Tribunal of the Far East and Emperor Hirohito – Justice Undone." Osaka University of Foreign Studies. Available at Sugita's website.

Summers, Anthony. *The Arrogance of Power: the Secret World of Richard Nixon*. London: Victor Gollancz, 2000.

Sun Kungtu. *The Economic Development of Manchuria in the First Half of the Twentieth Century*. Cambridge: Harvard University, 1969.

Swinson, Arthur. *Four Samurai: a Quartet of Japanese Army Commanders in the Second World War*. UK:

Hutchinson, 1968.

Takeyama Michio. *Harp of Burma.* Rutland: Charles E. Tuttle Co., 1966.

Tamaki Norio. *Japanese Banking: a History, 1859-1959.* Cambridge: Cambridge University, 1995.

Tanaka Hiroshi. "Why is Asia Demanding Postwar Compensation Now?" *Hitotsubashi Journal of Social Studies.* V. 28, No. 1, July 1996.

Tanaka Yuki. *Hidden Horrors: Japanese War Crimes in World War II.* New York: Westview, 1998.

Tetsuya Kataoka (ed). *Creating Single-Party Democracy: Japan's Postwar Political System.* Stanford: Hoover, 1992.

Thomas, Evan. *The Very Best Men: Four Who Dared – the Early Years of the CIA.* New York: Touchstone, 1995.

Thompson, Gary. "Search for the Tiger's Treasure." *The Las Vegas Sun,* a multi-part series that appeared in 1993.

Time-Life Books. *Japan at War.* New York: Time Inc., 1980.

Tipton, Elise. *Japanese Police State: Tokko in Interwar Japan.* London: Athlone Press, 1991.

Titus, David A. "The Making of the 'Symbol Emperor System' in Postwar Japan." *Modern Asian Studies,* Vol. 14, No. 4 (1980), pp. 529-578.

Tobias, Sigmund. *Strange Haven: a Jewish Childhood in Wartime Shanghai.* Chicago: University of Illinois, 1999.

Tokudome, Kinue. "POW Forced Labor Lawsuits Against Japanese Companies", *JPRI Working Paper,* No. 82, November 2001. Available at the JPRI website and also at www.expows.com/position1.htm.

"Tokyo in 1931 Poison Plot." *Independent,* July 7, 1994 at elibrary.com

Toland, John. *Infamy: Pearl Harbor and its Aftermath.* New York: Berkeley, 1983.

Toland, John. *The Rising Sun: the Decline and Fall of the Japanese Empire.* New York: Bantam, 1970.

Tregonning, K.G. *A History of Modern Malaya.* London: Eastern Universities, 1964.

"Trial of General Tomoyuki Yamashita. " *Law Reports of the Trials of War Criminals.* Selected and Prepared by the United Nations War Crimes Commission. Volume IV. London: HMSO, 1948. Online at www.ess.uwe.ac.uk/WCC/Yamashita

"Tribute to the Late Lt. Col. Richard Sakakida" U.S. Senate January 30, 1996.

Troy, Thomas F. *Wild Bill and Intrepid: Donovan, Stephenson, and the Origin of the CIA.* New Haven: Yale University, 1996.

Tsuji, Masanobu. *Japan's Greatest Victory, Britain's Worst Defeat.* New York: Sarpedon, 1997.

Turk, James. "We Have a Right to Know – Ft. Knox Audits." *Freemarket Gold and Money Report.* Letter No. 256, December 13, 1999.

United Nations Information Office. *Japan's Records and World Security.* New York, 1943.

Urban, Mark. *UK Eyes Alpha: the Inside Story of British Intelligence.* London: Faber and Faber, 1996.

"U.S. Probe of Citibank Could Widen." Reuters, June 21, 1996.

U.S. Supreme Court: Application of Yamashita, 327 U.S. 1(1946) Yamashita V. Styer, Commanding Genreal, U.S. Army Forces, Western Pacific. Argued Jan. 7,8, 1946, Decided Feb. 4, 1946. Available online at caselaw.lp.findlaw.com

Valentine, Douglas. *The Phoenix Program.* New York: William Morrow, 1990.

Van Wolferen, Karel. *The Enigma of Japanese Power: People and Politics in a Stateless Nation.* London: Macmillan, 1989.

"Vatican Drawn into Scandal over Nazi-era Gold." CNN Interactive Edition, July 22, 1997.

Vincent, David. *The Culture of Secrecy: Britain 1832-1998.* Oxford: Oxford University, 1998.

Wakeman, Frederic Jr. *Policing Shanghai 1927-1937.* Berkeley: University of California, 1995.

Ward, Ian. *The Killer They Called a God*. Singapore: Media Masters, 1992.

Ward, Robert E. and Sakamoto Yoshikazu (eds). *Democratizing Japan: the Allied Occupation*. Honolulu: University of Hawaii, 1987.

Wasserstein, Bernard. *The Secret War in Shanghai*. London: Profile Books, 1998.

Watts, Anthony J. *Japanese Warships of World War II*. New York: Doubleday, 1966.

Waycott, Angus. *Sado: Japan's Island in Exile*. Berkeley: Stone Bridge, 1996.

Weber, Ralph E. *Spymasters: Ten CIA Officers in Their Own Words*. Wilmington: Scholarly Resources, 1999.

Weiner, Tim. "CIA Spent Millions to Support Japanese Right in 50s and 60s." *The New York Times*, October 4, 1994.

Weitz, John. *Hitler's Banker: Hjalmar Horace Greely Schacht*. New York: Warner Books, 1999.

West, Nigel and Oleg Tsarev. *The Crown Jewels: the British Secrets Exposed by the KGB Archives*. London: HarperCollins, 1999.

Wetzler, Peter. *Hirohito and War*. Honolulu: U. of Hawaii, 1998.

Wheeler, Keith. *The Road to Tokyo*. Alexandria: Time-Life, 1979.

Whiting, Robert. *Tokyo Underworld: the Fast Times and Hard Life of an American Gangster in Japan*. New York: Pantheon, 1999.

Whitney, Courtney. *MacArthur: His Rendezvous with History*. New York: Knopf, 1956.

Whymant, Robert. *Stalin's Spy: Richard Sorge and the Tokyo Espionage Ring*. London: I.B. Tauris, 1996.

Willoughby, Charles and John Chamberlain. *MacArthur: 1941-1951*. New York: McGraw-Hill, Inc., 1954.

Wilson, Garret. "Global Purse Strings; The Implications of the IMF on Traditional International Order". University of London, School of Oriental and African Studies, *International Relations*, Essay 2, March 26, 1999. Available online.

Woodward, Bob. *Veil: the Secret Wars of the CIA, 1981-1987*. New York: Pocket Books, 1987.

Woodward, William P. *The Allied Occupation of Japan, 1945-1952 and Japanese Religions*. Leiden: Brill, 1972.

Wright-Nooth, George with Mark Adkin. *Prisoner of the Turnip Heads: the Fall of Hong Kong and Imprisonment by the Japanese*. London: Cassell, 1994.

Wu Tianwei. "The Failure of the Tokyo Trial." At www.centurychina.com

Yamakawa Akio. "Lockheed Scandal: What Do the People Make of It?" *Ampo: Japan-Asia Quarterly Review*. Vol. 8 No. 2, April -September 1976.

Yamamura Kozo and Yasukichi Yasuba (eds). *The Political Economy of Japan: Volume One, the Domestic Transformation*. Stanford: Stanford University, 1987.

Yanaga Chitoshi. *Big Business in Japanese Politics*. New Haven: Yale University, 1968.

Yasutomi Ayumu. *Money and Finance in Manchuria, 1895-1945*. Japan: School of Information and Science, Nagoya University. Available online.

Yeh Wen-hsin (ed.). *Wartime Shanghai*. London: Routledge, 1998.

Yeung, Bernice. "Slave Wages." *Bay View*, July 5, 2000. At sfweekly.com

Yoshida Shigeru. *The Yoshida Memoirs: the Story of Japan in Crisis*. Boston: Houghton Mifflin, 1962.

Yoshitake Oka. *Konoe Fumimaro: a Political Biography*. Lanham, Maryland: Madison Books, 1992.

Yoshitake Oka. *Five Political Leaders of Modern Japan*. Tokyo: University of Tokyo, 1986.

Young, Louise. *Japan's Total Empire: Manchuria and the Culture of Wartime Imperialism*. Berkeley: U. Cal, 1998.

Yu Maochun. *OSS in China: Prelude to Cold War*. New Haven: Yale University, 1996.

Zeiler, Thomas W. "US Foreign Economic Policy and Relations with Japan, 1969-1976." University of Colorado, Working Paper No. 1, U.S.-Japan Project.

Zhao Jianmin. "Looting Books: Unforgettable Facts in History on the Issues of Looting Books in the Nanking Massacre and the Return of These Books." Paper presented at Tokyo International Citizen Forum December 10-12, 1999.

Ziegler, Jean. *The Swiss, the Gold and the Dead: How Swiss Bankers Helped Finance the Nazi War Machine.* Harmondsworth, Middlesex: Penguin Books, 1997.

ANNOTATIONS

The purpose of this book is to reveal why so little is known about Japan's industrial-scale looting of Asia, and the devious role Washington played in the cover-up that continues to this day. Many people may be shocked and dismayed by our revelations, or think them fantastic. Starting with the eye-witness account of the live burial of Japanese engineers who were responsible for creating treasure vaults in the Philippines, readers will want to see the proof. Those who have read our previous books know they are thoroughly documented with up to 200 pages of annotations, and will recognize continuing themes we have investigated over thirty years. Like the bones of dinosaurs or the fragments of the space-shuttle Challenger, the evidence is widely scattered but abundant. In putting together these bits and pieces of historical debris, a thoroughly convincing body of evidence has emerged. The detailed annotations that follow are backed up with another 1500 megabytes of documentation on our three CDs, which readers are welcome to examine.

AUTHORS' NOTE

x–Jean Ziegler's indictment for treason for revealing secrets about the Swiss government and Holocaust gold. See Ziegler, *The Swiss, the Gold and the Dead*, pp. 280-281.

x–Henry Liu's murder was the subject of a book by David Kaplan. See *Fires of the Dragon*.

xii–It is CIA's James Bruce, chairman of the Foreign Denial and Deception Committee, who wants to send "SWAT teams into journalist's homes". See *Village Voice* on-line. July 31 – 6 August 2002.

PROLOGUE

(Because it is a summary, limited citations are given for the Prologue. For individual chapters, readers will find full and exhaustive annotations for all statements, quotes and statistics. Readers who want more detail, and full reproductions of documents, may obtain from our website www.bowstring.net the two compact discs we have prepared, containing over 900 megabytes of additional documentation.)

1–Yamashita's holding action. By May 5, 1945, U.S. forces were advancing into the mountains so quickly that Yamashita had to write off Bontoc and Baguio (two corners of his defensive triangle). He began pulling his forces back between Bambang and Bagabag, to funnel them along the Asin River into the Kiangan Pocket. Between 1 and 4 June,

Yamashita's antitank units south of Aritao fought a running battle with the US 775th Tank Battalion, and pressure became acute to speed up withdrawal from Bambang into the Pocket. It was at this point that entombment of the engineers occurred. See Chapter 6.

2—Ben Valmores was interviewed by us extensively. See Chapters 6 and 12 (both text and endnotes) for more details. Evidence has emerged that the Japanese High Command routinely authorized live-burials and exterminations of Allied POWs, starting in August 1944. Orders such as the following were passed down from the Ministry of War in Tokyo to regional commands throughout Japanese-occupied Asia: "Whether they are destroyed individually or in groups, or however it is done, with mass bombing, poisonous smoke, poison, drowning, decapitation or whatever, dispose of the prisoners of war as the situation dictates. In any case, it is the aim to annihilate them all and to leave no trace." Thousands of prisoners were mass-murdered by Japanese soldiers following these orders. For example, on July 30, 1945, the same month as the live-burial witnessed by Ben Valmores, a similar event took place at mining works at Loa Kulu in Borneo. One hundred Dutch POWs, along with their wives and children, were murdered on orders of the camp commandant, obeying instructions from Tokyo. The wives and mothers were the first to die, while their helpless husbands and terrified children watched. Hands tied behind their backs, the women were individually hacked to death with swords and bayonets and their bodies hurled down the 600-foot mine shaft. The screaming children were tossed *alive* into the pit. Finally, the men were decapitated, their heads and bodies dumped on top of the corpses of their wives and children. Three days later, at Mitsubishi's Sado Island gold mine, off the west coast of Japan, 387 Allied POWs were entombed alive in the tunnels. The Japanese soldiers herded their prisoners into the mine shaft laterals, at a depth of 400 feet, then detonated explosives that sequentially collapsed the tunnels at depths of 300 feet, 200 feet, and 100 feet. Not one POW made it out alive. This information, and the sworn testimony of one of the Japanese officers who directed the mass murder at Sado Island, was then suppressed by U.S. occupation authorities as part of their campaign to shield bankers, financiers, and corporate leaders in Japan and Germany, including the management of Mitsubishi.

3—Yamashita's surrender. See Chapter 7.

3—Kojima Kashii. See Chapter 7.

3—Lansdale. See Chapters 7, 8, 10, 13, 15.

4—Stimson had resigned his wartime post by this date, but still was actively involved. The Black Eagle Trust is covered in Chapters 7, 8, 9.

4—There is no public record of MacArthur making this flight to the Philippines, but we have confirmed it with numerous sources, who said MacArthur was in Luzon with Anderson during that period. It would have been a simple matter for MacArthur to make the flight secretly from Atsugi airbase in Japan to Clark airbase near Manila. See Chapter 7.

4—Santa Romana, his role in the gold recoveries and what happened to this treasure. See Chapters 7, 10, 13, 15.

6—Nixon and the M-Fund. See Chapters 9, 15.

6—Japan's looting of Asia is the subject of Chapters 1, 2, 3, 4, 5, 6.

8—Allied recovery of Japanese loot. See Chapters 7, 8, 15.

8—The role of John Reed, Citibank and the Santa Romana gold recoveries. See Chapters 10, 13, 15.

9—M–Fund and Alexander Haig. See Chapter 15.

9—Norbert Schlei's legal battle. See Chapters 9, 15.

9—Roger Roxas's story. See Chapters 10, 15.

10—Robert Curtis's involvement. See Chapters 11, 12, 13, 14.

10—Sanwa Bank. See Chapter 13.

11—*Op ten Noort.* See Chapters 5 and 14.

11—General John Singlaub and General Robert Schweitzer. See Chapters 13, 14.

12 –The San Francisco Peace Treaty and the coverup. But see Chapter 16.

CHAPTER ONE

14—thirty assassins: diplomat Horace Allen advised the Department of State that on his way to a royal audience he observed thirty "evil-looking Japanese with ... long swords, and sword canes" running from the palace. National Archives, *Dispatch Book*, Seoul, Allen to Olney, Oct. 10, 1895.

14—Minister of the Royal Household: Yi Kyong-sik. Duus, *Abacus and the Sword*, p. 111.

14—General Dye and the Japanese gloss, both from Duus, *Abacus and Sword,* pp. 111-112.

14—Min's murder: Lensen, *Korea and Manchuria between Russia and China,* p. 92. Duus, *Abacus and Sword,* pp. 101, 108-112. Seagrave, *Dragon Lady,* Chapter 10.

14—control the king: Japan's puppet regent was the Taewon'gun, an aging Confucian.

14—Japanese-trained Korean soldiers: the 'hullyondae'.

14—Black Ocean: Roberts, *Mitsui,* p. 268, and Duus, *Abacus and Sword,* p. 111. Mitsui and other top Japanese corporations often employed agents of secret societies.

14—drugs and Japanese secret societies: Montgomery, *Imperial Japan;* Kaplan, *Yakuza;* Whiting, *Tokyo Underworld,* Duus, *Abacus and Sword* and Cumings, *Korea's Place in the Sun.*

15—professional assassins: Many Black Ocean agents were professional bullies called *soshi.*

15—security men: Duus, *Abacus and Sword,* p. 111.

15—foreign observers: Queen Min's murder was witnessed by American and Russian advisors. Cumings, *Korea's Place in the Sun,* p. 12. Duus, *Abacus and Sword,* pp. 108-112.

15—high-end estimate of dead, 300,000. Cumings, *Parallax Visions,* p. 44.

15—Itami: had first-hand experience of the underworld when he was attacked by thugs and had his face slashed. Buruma, *Behind the Mask* for the role of the outlaw as a pillar of Japan's power structure.

16—Korean ancestors of Japan's imperial family. Of the three ancient Korean kingdoms, Pakche may have had the strongest cultural influence on Japan. Cumings, *Korea's Place in the Sun,* pp. 31 note 19, 33.

16—mutual loathing of Japanese and Koreans. "a severe anti-Japanese allergy". See Cumings, *Korea's Place,* p. 89.

16—feuding: The northernmost kingdom, Koguryo, stretched from what is now Port Arthur, all the way to Vladivostok, and south nearly to Seoul. Down the east coast of the peninsula, facing Japan, sprawled the rich kingdom of Silla. The third kingdom, Pakche, in the southwestern corner, is known today as the Cholla Provinces, famous for its dissidents. Of these ancient states Koguryo was the most powerful, protecting the entire peninsula from Chinese incursions. Cumings, *Korea's Place,* p. 39.

16–movable type: Cumings, *Korea's Place*, pp. 64-65.

16–most advanced. Cumings, *Korea's Place*, pp. 33-39.

16–paranoid style: Duus, *Abacus and Sword,* p. 16.

16–erase the culture: Cumings, *Korea's Place*, pp. 31-41. Duus, *Abacus and Sword.*

16–Turtle ship: Cumings, *Korea's Place,* p. 76.

16–Toyotomi Hideyoshi: Cumings, *Korea's Place,* p. 77.

16–Ri Sam-pyong: One of Korea's most famous porcelain artists was kidnaped by Hideyoshi's culture squads and taken to Japan. Ri, working for his kidnappers, would later find the right kind of clays in Kyushu that produce the famous Imari ware. Looting and kidnapping: Cumings, *Korea's Place,* p. 78.

16–'wild animals.': Cumings, *Korea's Place,* p. 101.

16–Korea never recovered: Cumings, *Korea's Place*, pp. 81-82.

16–China's defeat by Britain during the Opium War "was a profound shock to the [Japanese] elite who had long seen the country as a source of culture and learning". Duus, *Abacus and Sword*, p. 21.

16–"The modernization of Japan with new technology permitted the Meiji leaders to crush opposition within Japan and then to project Japanese power outward." Duus, *Abacus and Sword*, p. 18.

17–Japan's new conscript army was created to suppress internal conspiracies and uprisings. With those under control the general staff now turned their attention to a military and logistical buildup for conquest on the Asian mainland, and possible war with China. Duus, *Abacus and Sword*, p. 61.

17–first target: Korea was rich in rice, wheat, mineral resources, and manpower, all of which Japan needed. Duus, *Abacus and Sword*, p. 35. Ito Hirobumi, "two-thirds of the men in the Imperial Guard lean toward the view that Korea should be subjugated," Duus, *Abacus and Sword,* p. 40 note 21.

17–Korea: several false starts were made, as Japan provoked incidents. China gamely countered. In 1884 Tokyo tried again, paying Korean radicals to attempt a coup. Chinese troops intervened, but not before the Korean coup leader, Kim Ok-kium escaped to Japan with the help of Black Ocean. Later, in 1894, Kim was lured to Shanghai where Chinese agents shot him dead. His murder was the catalyst that brought about the Sino-Japanese War of 1894-95. Seagrave, *Dragon Lady*, pp. 177-178.

17–Tonghaks: Duus, *Abacus and Sword*, p. 66.

17–*Kowshing:* A precedent followed in later decades. See Roberts, *Mitsui*, p. 148.

17–1894-95 Sino-Russian War: Japan's victory brought unexpected dividends. The Chinese indemnity, $150 million paid in gold bullion, enabled Japan to go on the gold standard. Roberts, *Mitsui*, p. 148. Tamaki, *Japanese Banking*, p. xv. Checkland, *Pacific Banking,* Chapter One.

17–February 4, 1904: War was declared six days later. Roberts, *Mitsui*, p. 156, Duus, *Abacus and Sword*, p. 180.

17–Japan's gains from the Sino-Russian War. Roberts, *Mitsui*, p. 162.

18–Japan's annexation of Korea... in 1910...[was] the result of two ...interlinked process-es... The political process entailed ...control over the Korean state...; the economic process entailed ... penetration of the Korean market by ...Japanese traders, sojourners, and settlers. " Duus, *Abacus and Sword*, p. 23.

18–Korea, a secret police state under Japan: Duus, *Abacus and Sword*, p. 186.

18–"Ah, how wretched". Duus, *Abacus and Sword*, p. 195.

18–Ito Hirobumi's quote. Duus, *Abacus and Sword*, p. 190.

18–fully incorporated: Tokyo justified the annexation of Korea because "the existing system of government in [Korea] has not proved entirely equal to the duty of preserving public order and tranquility." Duus, *Abacus and Sword*, p. 338. The Treaty of the Annexation is available online at the USC-UCLA Joint East Asian Studies Center at isop. ucla.edu/eas/documents/kore1910.htm

18–crush all resistance: The elimination of all anti-Japanese activities and activists is from *Kodansha Encyclopedia of Japan*, Volume 8, p. 12.

18–'scorpions': Lowe, *Origins of the Korean War*, p. 4.

18–"torture was a matter of course": Lowe, *Origins*, p. 10. The common forms of torture employed by the *kempeitai* were described in a 1928 report contained in Lamont-Brown, *Kempeitai*, p. 19.

18–Chrysanthemum crest: *kempeitai* plain clothes men with a chrysanthemum-crest pin hidden under their jacket lapels. Lamont-Brown, *Kempeitai*, p. 34

18–35,000 *kempeitai* at the height of the Pacific War. Lamont-Brown, *Kempeitai*, p. 17, p. 34.

18–Black Ocean; *kempeitai*. Lamont-Brown, *Kempeitai*, p. 24. *Kempeitai* schools were in Tokyo, Seoul, Singapore and Manila. Training included espionage, explosives, fifth-column organization, code breaking, burglary, disguise, and torture. Foreign language study was downplayed, so in the field *kempeitai* officers used interpreters. Forty, *Japanese Army Handbook*, p. 236.

18–Black Ocean; appointments of *kempeitai*: Lamont-Brown, *Kempeitai*, p. 74.

18–arrests of Koreans in 1912, and 1918. Cumings, *Korea's Place*, p. 147.

18–Japanese school teachers in uniform: Cumings, *Korea's Place*, p. 152.

18–rice and police: Cumings, *Korea's Place*, p. 152.

19–one-fourth: Korean/Japanese wage disparities. Cumings, *Korea's Place*, pp. 168-169.

19–porcelain: William B. Honey, quoted in Cumings, *Korea's Place*, p. 42.

19–Korean celadon. Cumings, *Korea's Place*, p. 42.

19–Tokyo Art Museum catalogue for an exhibition of 152 Korean treasures. *Masterpieces in Koryo and Choson Ceramics* held at Japan's Tokyo Art Museum from September to November 1992.

19–Korean royal tombs looted: See Kim Ji-ho, Korean Central News Agency, "N.K. Raises Stolen Cultural Asset Issue in Talks with Japan". *Korean Central News Agency*, April 10, 2000. "Japan Urged to Own Its Responsibility" KCNA, April 27, 2000. Online.

19–wholesale theft: Yang Sung-jin, *Hankookilbo*, October 21, 1998, "Special Exhibit Commemorates 60 Anniversary of Kansong Museum", on-line. UNESCO's World Heritage List, Convention for the Protection of Cultural Property in the Event of Armed Conflict (1954), Convention on the Means of Prohibiting and Preventing the Illicit Import and Transfer of Ownership of Cultural Property (1970), Convention for the Protection of the World Cultural and Natural Heritage (1972). Japan has refused to sign United Nations conventions that would force her to repatriate looted cultural properties taken from Asia between 1910-1945. See also Kim Yong-mok, "Whither Japan-Korea Relations", *Japan Policy Research Institute Critique*, Volume 5, No. 9 (October 1998), available at the JPRI website.

19–classic literary texts, finest books: See above articles from the *Korean Central News Agency*.

20–Prince Yi Un. Cumings, *Korea's Place in the Sun,* p. 145, and Bix, *Hirohito and the Making of Modern Japan*, pp. 34-35. Yi was married to Princess Masako, once front-runner to become Hirohito's bride. The couple survived the Pacific War and lived in wealth and security until their deaths years later. See Seagrave, *The Yamato Dynasty*, pp. 92-94, p. 332.

20–Nakada: See the *Korean Central News Agency* and Yang Sung-jin cited above. Some rich Koreans managed to acquire whole lots of antiquities from Japanese dealers operating in Korea. They paid hugely inflated prices, but in this way they preserved some of Korea's patrimony. The most famous was Chon Hyong-pi, who eventually built the Kansong Art Museum to house his collection, the first private museum in Korea. Kim, *A Korean Nationalist Entrepreneur: A Life History of Kim Songsu.*

21–*Ukishima. The Korea Times*, "Japan Allegedly Sunk Ship Carrying 5,000 Koreans", Seoul, 15 October 1999. The ruling by a Kyoto court in August 2001 granting 3-million yen to a handful of *Ukishima* survivors (but no apology) was reported in *Mainichi Shimbun*, 23 August 2001.

21–Korean girls, comfort women: Why Japanese non-professional women were not forced to become sex slaves. "Korean Military Comfort Women" on *Postwar Compensation.* Online max@twics.com.

21–"erased history" vanished records. Cumings, *Korea's Place in the Sun*, p. 139.

21–Taiwan: Cumings, *Parallax*, pp. 77-82.

22–Kookayama Mountain Japan First Air Fleet headquarters: Kodama, *I Was Defeated*, pp. 144-145.

22–conscript labor on Taiwan. See Cumings, *Parallax*, p. 84.

CHAPTER TWO

23–Racing through the streets: riots organized by the Black Dragon Society in protest of Harriman's plans to buy the South Manchuria rail lines. Roberts, *Mitsui*, pp. 152, 163-4, 181, 211, 216, 385.

23–Manchuria's historical background: Seagrave, *Dragon Lady*.

24–Russian families: one predator was Konstantin Ivanovich Nakamura, a Japanese who claimed to have embraced the Russian Orthodox religion. He ran a barbershop, a front for a 'drugstore' dispensing morphine, heroin and opium. Down the street he had a brothel. Lamont-Brown, *Kempeitai*, pp. 66-68.

24–Port Arthur: the Chinese name was Lushun.

24–Russian-built railways: The railroad lease included a land corridor on either side of the track, towns adjacent to important stations. The narrow railway zone that traversed Southern Manchuria, and served to open the whole region to Japanese penetration. Roberts, *Mitsui*, p. 166.

24–Emperor Hirohito was the largest private stockholder in the Mantetsu (South Manchurian Railway). Roberts, *Mitsui*, p. 166. He also held nearly 25 percent of Yokohama

Specie Bank shares. See Gunther, *Inside Asia,* and Stephen Large, *Emperor Hirohito.*

24–research offices of the South Manchurian railway is from Young, *Japan's Total Empire,* p. 280. "the single most powerful center for China studies" is quoted from Young, *Japan's Total Empire,* p. 270. The career of Hirano Sakae, who started off in Manchuria and then ended up in Sumatra during World War II, is a good example of how the Manchurian researchers came to work with the military. See Hirano Sakae, "Memories of Sumatra" in Reid and Akira, *The Japanese Experience in Indonesia,* pp. 289-296. Mitsui offices used as cover for secret operations is from Roberts, *Mitsui,* p. 348. Kodama also used Mitsui offices in Shanghai and also offices of the Oji Paper Company. See Kodama, *I Was Defeated,* p. 70.

25–fifty Japanese officers: Young, *Japan's Total Empire,* p. 31.

25–Taiping Company: "the treasure house of the army." Roberts, *Mitsui,* p. 187.

25–The low army pay scales make it clear that 'private enterprise' was the only way many Japanese military officers accumulated great fortunes. Forty, *Japanese Army Handbook,* p. 85.

25–Manchuria a separate power base. Young, *Japan's Total Empire.*

25–Chang Tso-lin: See Behr, *The Last Emperor,* p. 145, Seagrave, *Soong Dynasty,* pp. 233-234.

26–Komoto Daisaku and rogue adventurers: Rightwing author Okawa Shumei spent ten years in China as an agent of Black Dragon. The sadistic secret policeman, Amakasu Masuhiko, was another. Young, *Japan's Total Empire,* p. 16. One of the most famous *tairiku ronin* was Colonel Tomiya Kaneo, a zealot who hated Russians and pushed for the establishment of strategic hamlets on Manchuria's northern frontier as a first line of defense against Soviet attack. He was a cult hero in Japan's popular press in the 1930s, a wild-eyed samurai with goatee and disheveled hair. See Young, *Japan's Total Empire,* p. 385.

26–Killing Chang Tso-lin: Our account blends elements from numerous sources, including Young, *Japan's Total Empire;* Pu Yi, *From Emperor to Citizen*; Roberts, *Mitsui;* Behr, *The Last Emperor*; and Brackman, *The Other Nuremberg.*

26–Hirohito personally sanctioned: a Japanese scholar makes this point about Hirohito. See Seagrave and Seagrave, *The Yamato Dynasty,* p. 144.

26–Major Giga: Behr, *The Last Emperor,* pp. 168-169.

26–"inverting roles.": Young, *Japan's Total Empire,* p. 145.

27–Spring 1931: Consequences of warlord's murder. Young, *Japan's Total Empire,* p. 38.

27–farmers riot and Nakamura incident, Young, *Japan's Total Empire,* p. 39.

27–lightning campaigns: Again, Hirohito did not punish the Kwantung Army commanders, according to the diary of his chief military aide. "The army was to be more careful in the future." See Seagrave and Seagrave, *The Yamato Dynasty,* p. 144.

27–laced with cholera: Japanese secret agents attempt to kill the Lytton Commission with cholera germs is from Terry McCarthy, "Tokyo In 1931 Poison Plot", *Independent,* 7 July 1994, Gwen Robinson, "Hirohito's Brother Tells of War Crimes by the Army", *The Times,* 7 July 1994.

27–war fever: In 1932, thirty-six articles and seventeen books appeared in Tokyo on the subject of a coming war with the United States.

27–"All Chinese": Japanese charges against Chang and his troops. See Young, *Japan's Total Empire,* p. 143.

27–two pairs of panties: Young, *Japan's Total Empire*, pp. 99-100.

28–basket of fruit and an unexploded bomb. See Brackman, *The Other Nuremburg*, p. 155.

28–Pu Yi's drug addiction. Harries and Harries, *Soldiers of the Sun*, p. 245. Pu Yi also describes his need for 'medicine' and 'injections' (though never describing this as heroin). Pu Yi, *From Emperor to Citizen*.

28–Pu Yi received messages of congratulations from the underworld bosses of Shanghai. Pu Yi, *From Emperor to Citizen*, Volume 2, p. 276. A secret Kwantung Army document said, "Officials of the Manchukuoan lineage shall outwardly assume charge… officials of Japanese lineage must … [control] its substance." Kwantung Army directive establishing the principles for Pu Yi's reign. Brackman, *The Other Nuremberg*, p. 156.

28–Pu Yi's description of how he and Pu Chieh removed treasures from the Forbidden City. Pu Yi, *From Emperor to Citizen*, Volume 1, p. 129.

28–"small white building" and details of the storage of the objects in Changchun is from Chinese-art.com "Zhang Xian's Ten Odes" and "Puyi's Legacy" at Chinese-art.com

28–"I spontaneously gave": Pu Yi's donations to the Army. *From Emperor to Citizen*, Vol. 2, p. 303. Objects described by Pu Yi started showing up at Christie's and Sotheby's in 1991. Disappearance of the treasures after the surrender, see Pu Yi, *From Emperor to Citizen*, Volume 1, p. 129.

29–Manchurian experiment: Manchurian incident gave the army increased influence over Tokyo. Young, *Japan's Total Empire*, p. 115. *Kodansha Encyclopedia of Japan*, Volume 2, p. 126.

29–*Ni-ki-san-suke* clique. Roberts, *Mitsui*, p. 312.

29–forty-eight new cities: Young, *Japan's Total Empire*, p. 245.

29–sequestration of banks: Yoshimasa, "The Monetary Policy in the Netherlands East Indies under the Japanese Administration", in Post and Touwen-Bouwsma (eds), *Japan, Indonesia and the War*, p. 181.

29–Kwantung Army sequestered funds to start the Central Bank of Manchukuo. See Yasutoni, "Money and Finance in Manchuria, 1895-1945", School of Information and Science, Nagoya University, Nagoya Japan. Online.

29–Bank of Chosen. Cumings, *Parallax Visions*, p. 76.

29–Simon Kaspe: kidnapping and murder. Lamont-Brown, *Kempeitai*, pp. 79-80.

30–Opium production in Manchuria 1911 and 1926. Wakeman, *Policing*, p. 272.

30–Hoshino and the Opium Monopoly Bureau. Roberts, *Mitsui*, pp. 311-313.

30–The Manchukuo Opium Monopoly, the world's largest single venture in illicit drugs. Wakeman, *Policing*, p. 272.

30–Narcotics dens operated by the *kempeitai* and Special Section 8. Harries and Harries, *Soldiers of the Sun*, p. 244.

30–90 percent of the world's illicit opium and morphine of Japanese origin. Harries and Harries, *Soldiers*, p. 246.

31–Pu Yi learned about Unit 731 installations. Pu Yi, *Emperor to Citizen*, Vol. Two, p. 289.

31–"tied to posts": Prince Mikasa reported Japanese Army atrocities during the Pacific War, but his report was kept secret and only found in 1994. *The Times* of London on July 7, 1994. In point of fact, we found a story in *The New York Times* in 1951 in which Prince Mikasa had expressed his dismay over the army conduct in the field.

31–Manchuria was an expensive failure: Young, *Japan's Total Empire*, pp. 218, 235.

31–"unopened treasure house": Young, *Japan's Total Empire*, pp. 229 and 230 note 104.

CHAPTER THREE

32–bite off parts: As far as many Chinese were concerned "Japan seemed bound and determined to 'colonize' China." Wakeman, *Policing*, p. 187.

32–Shanghai in the early 1930s. Seagrave, *The Soong Dynasty;* Sergeant, *Shanghai*, Chapter.5; Wakeman, *Policing*, p. 187.

32–90,000 troops in Shanghai, Hirohito's approval. Wakeman, *Policing*, pp. 187-192, 194; Sergeant, *Shanghai,* pp. 184-189; "Tales of Old Shanghai," online contains many contemporary quotations from observers.

33–The fact that Chinese were themselves great collectors of antiquities was observed by many Western visitors. See for instance Juliet Bredon, *Peking*, Chapter XIX, and Mrs. Archibald Little, *Intimate China*, p. 295.

34–Tu Yueh-Sheng. Though Kodama and General Doihara offered Boss Tu a chance to work full-time for Japan, Tu was no fool. He maintained tight connections with Generalissimo Chiang and the KMT secret police boss, General Tai Li. As the fighting moved beyond Nanking, Tu fled to Hong Kong, and made his roundabout way to Chungking, where he sat out the war. Seagrave, *Soong.*

34–prosperous foreign enclaves: Wakeman, *Policing*, p. 9.

34–Britain's $1-billion investment in China. Wasserstein, *Secret War*, p. 6.

34–Japanese in Shanghai were the single largest foreign community by the end of World War One. Wasserstein, *Secret War in Shanghai*, p. 6.

35–Japan's secret tunnel connecting commercial wharves to the Japanese military headquarters. Wakeman, *Policing*, p. 188.

35–Green Gang dominated illegal activities in Shanghai. Wakeman, *Policing*, p. 25, Seagrave, *Soong.*

35–Tu Yueh-sheng's abduction of Mayling Soong. Seagrave, *Soong,* pp. 269-270. Tu's early life and the triumph of the Green Gang over the Red and Blue gangs. Seagrave, *Soong*, pp. 150-152.

35–gambling, the Canidrome. Wakeman, *Policing*, pp. 97- 98, 103.

35–100,000 prostitutes. Wakeman, *Policing*, p. 115.

35–Farren's and Del Monte's. Wakeman, *Policing*, p. 107.

35–Tu Yueh-sheng's drug business moved into the Chinese area of Shanghai, his temporary loss of his private dope business and his re-invention as a government approved drug dealer; Tu's morphine and heroin factories supplied with KMT government. Wakeman, *Policing*, pp. 203-205, 263.

35–Japanese narcotics trafficking. Anslinger, *The Traffic in Narcotics*, p. 9, online. Japan's dope centers in Tientsin and Hankow, United Nations Information Office, *Japan's Record and World Security*, p. 35-36. International Red Cross and the League of Nations studies in the 1930s show that the entire legitimate medical practice in China and Manchuria required only 15 kilos of heroin per year. Under Japan's rule, Korea produced over 2600 kilos of heroin a year. See *Bulletin on Narcotics*, 1953 Issue 2, online at the United Nations website. China Affairs Board: Prince Konoe and the other officials associated with the

China Affairs Board. See "Korean Opium for Japan's Wars" at www.kimsoft.com. For other details on the China Affairs Bureau and drugs, see Marshall, p. 40.

36–Japan and drugs in Manchukuo. Wakeman, *Policing*, pp. 272-275.

36–Chiang Kai-shek purchased drugs from Japan's Manchurian cartel. See Marshall, "Opium and the Politics of Gangsterism in Nationalist China, 1927-1945".

36–contest for control of drug traffic between Chiang Kai-shek and the Japanese. Marshall, p. 24.

36–imaginary insult: Bix, *Hirohito and the Making of Modern Japan*, pp. 319-320.

36–"finished up in two or three months." Bix, *Hirohito*, p. 320.

36–Japan "bankrupt...on the verge of revolution." Seagrave, *Soong*, p. 363.

36–embargoes: Roosevelt's call for economic quarantine against the Japanese "epidemic". Seagrave and Seagrave, *The Yamato Dynasty*, p. 165.

36–Chiang's pre-emptive strike: Wasserstein, *Secret War*, p. 15.

37–Asaka Yasuhiko: Later, one of Prince Asaka's aides claimed that he had issued this instruction himself, not the prince, but it is obvious that this was only an attempt to shield his master. Historically, aides to Japanese princes were not in the habit of pre-empting the authority of their masters. The U.S. Occupation coerced many 'witnesses' to take the fall for the imperial family. Iris Chang, *The Rape of Nanking*. Seagrave and Seagrave, *The Yamato Dynasty*, Chapter Nine, "The Exorcists".

38–By 1937, Japan's gold reserves had shrunk by half. Barnhardt, *Japan Prepares for Total War*, p. 109.

38–tons of gold. Iris Chang, *Rape of Nanking*.

39–nightmares: Prince Takeda spoke of these nightmares to his Filipino valet, Ben Valmores, who did not know at the time where Nanking was. Authors' interview with Ben Valmores.

39–Special Service Units, details on the Japanese "book-squads" dispatched to China to loot books and manuscripts comes from Professor Zhao Jianmin, "Looting Books: Unforgettable Facts in History" a paper presented at the International Citizens' Forum On War Crimes And Redress, Tokyo 10-12 December, 1999.

40–Sumitomo Kichizaemon's collection of bronzes. Roberts, *Mitsui*, p. 380.

41–Kodama and Black Ocean, Black Dragon. Roberts, *Mitsui*, p. 348; the autumn assassination plan goes awry. Kodama, *I Was Defeated*, p. 43. April 1937. Kodama, *I Was Defeated*, p. 57.

41–Toyama a guest at Hirohito's wedding. Montgomery, *Imperialist Japan*, p. 274.

41–"wanton spending of secret funds." Kodama, *I Was Defeated*, p. 64.

41–"heads of Buddhas." Kodama, *I Was Defeated*, p. 65.

41–Shanghai Harbor Boss Ku: Ku had extraordinary family connections. He was the brother of one of Generalissimo Chiang's top army generals, Ku Chu-t'ung. The Ku brothers had evil reputations. In 1940, General Ku became one of China's most hated men. When the Chinese communist New Fourth Army passed through his territory on their way to attack the Japanese held railway between Nanking and Shanghai, Ku ambushed them and massacred all but the headquarters contingent, including many women cadres. All these women were subjected to mass rape and kept in KMT army brothels for the next 18 months, where a number of them committed suicide. As his reward, General Ku was promoted to commander in chief of the KMT armies.

41–Ye Ching-ho and Kodama. Marshall, "Opium and the Politics of Gangsterism".

42–Chinese smugglers and pirates working for the Japanese navy. Marshall, "Opium and the Politics of Gangsterism", p. 42.

42–Myra and Fred Scovel." You are not to leave the house. Everything you formerly owned." Scovel, *Chinese Ginger Jars*, p. 59, 98.

42–Peking Man: "Losing Peking Man" at www.peking-man.org. The National Archives of Canada. Charles Roland, "Davidson Black: Peking Man 1884-1943" online. Foley confided his story to Coggins, who has served with U.S. occupation forces in Japan. Coggins then told us.

43–Peking Man fossils recovered in Tokyo after the war. Stephen Broker, "Hominoid Evolution", Yale-New Haven Teachers Institute, Curriculum Unit 79.06.02. www.yale.edu/ynhti/curriculum/units/1979/6/79.06.02.x.html

CHAPTER FOUR

44–gambled on advancing further south: How loot from Manchuria and China financed Japan's Strike South. Bix, *Hirohito*, p. 396.

44–few Japanese officials believed Japan could win the war. Prince Fushimi told Hirohito to "avoid war with Britain and the United States". Bix, *Hirohito*, p. 402.

44–Hirohito and the Pope: Hirohito told Tojo in late October 1941 to contact Pope Pius XII. The Pope was an ardent anti-communist like Hitler and Hirohito. Bix, *Hirohito*, p. 421. Pius XII wanted to make the Vatican a greater force in world affairs, and had already reached a political accommodation with the Nazis giving him greater control over Catholics in Germany. Cornwell, *Hitler's Pope*. Hirohito hoped to cut a similar deal in Asia, in return for the Pope's intercession for a peace settlement. (The Vatican had been the first sovereign power to recognize Japan's puppet regime in Manchuria.) The imperial family's connection with the Vatican continued after the war. Prince Asaka, overseer of the Rape of Nanking, was baptized a Catholic in the early 1950s. The announcement of the baptism appeared in *The New York Times*. As Christopher Columbus once remarked, "Gold is a wonderful thing. Whoever possesses it is lord of all he wants. By means of gold one can even get souls into Paradise." Harmiston, "Gold as a Store of Value".

44–$45-million: Hirohito's secret overseas assets. Mackay, *Allied Japanese Conspiracy*, p. 214. Manning, *Hirohito: The War Years,* pp. 169-182, 224-226.

45–The Imperial Headquarters Liaison Conferences as "the device". Bix, *Hirohito*, p. 329.

45–"Principles for the Implementation of Military Administration in the Occupied Southern Areas" was the Imperial blue print for the occupation of the south Asia. Akashi Yoji, *Watanabe Wataru: The Architect of the Malaya Military Administration, December 1941-March 1943.*

45–"We can do anything we want." Hoshino quoted in Ienaga, *Pacific War*, p. 155.

45–Archival records of Japan's looting. See *Japanese Imperial Government Disclosure Act.* Reproduced in full on our CDs. It is interesting to note that the State Department received a letter from Tokyo's ambassador in Washington asking for "access" and "review" to any documents that had been designated for public release. The State Department's answer is not known. We say much more about the disappearance of Japanese records in subsequent chapters. See Tokudome Kinue. "POW Forced Labor Lawsuits", *JPRI Working Paper*, No. 82.

46–The 'official history' of Prince Chichibu's life during the war is Princess Chichibu's *The Silver Drum*.

47–Dutch colonials were ordered to stay put. Dutch citizens were forbidden to leave Indonesia or to move their assets overseas. The Dutch government meanwhile moved official gold reserves to safety. Hagers, *De Telegraaf*, 20 November 1999, from documents in the Algemeen Rijks Archief, The Hague.

47–National City Bank holdings. Edward Michaud, "Gold Is Also Ballast", online.

47–Philippine National Treasury. Some sources say it was taken by sub to Australia, others to the USA.

48–The Willoughby account comes from Michaud.

48–Philippine bullion and currency seized by the Japanese Army and remitted to Tokyo. Steinberg, *Philippine Collaboration in World War Two*, p. 88.

48–There are many eyewitness accounts of civilians stripped bare by the Japanese forces. One of those is Scovel, *Chinese Ginger Jars*, p. 148.

48–"All their loot was taken on ships to Japan": Romulo's quote United Nations Information Office, *Japan's Record and World Security*, p. 43.

48–Civilian women and girls forced into prostitution by the Japanese. At the Seagrave Hospital in northern Burma, several staff nurses were taken away by *Kempeitai* officers, remaining sex slaves for the next three years.

49–Japanese liquidation of Indonesian banks was carried out by Yamamoto Hiroshi. L.M.J. Boegheim, "De Beeldenaar", September 1995. Kratoska, *Japanese Occupation of Malaya*, pp. 214-215.

49–Amounts seized by the Japanese from Java banks and import-export firms. See Boegheim.

50–Jos Hagers was contacted by Geeromsz with his story. She kindly passed along her findings to us.

50–Tjikotok mine D.W.N. Kriek, Sr and Philip Clark, *43: Special Mission*, online.

50–The increased gold production under Japanese occupation, especially at the Benkalis island mines. See Boegheim.

50–Japanese military scrip. We reproduce originals on our CDs. The examples from Hong Kong are especially beautiful and intricate. Other occupation scrip was drab. But all promised backing and redemption.

50–Because some of the scrip was so simple, counterfeiters would not have much difficulty reproducing it. They were warned against their craft: "Tremble and Obey" read the warnings. Kratoska, *Japanese Occupation of Malaya*, p. 210.

50–"Guaranteed" "Giant reserve". These are the words appearing on the Hong Kong scrip we reproduce on our CD. Thanks to the Reparation Association of Hong Kong for its description of the Japanese military yen backing in materials they presented at a Tokyo Conference in 1999. They are deeply involved in efforts to force the Government of Japan to redeem the scrip, but have so far failed.

51–Japan exercised automatic "withholding" of POW "salaries." Ooi, *The Japanese Empire in the Tropics*, Vol. 2, p. 347.

51–"Even Japanese militarists": Grew quote is from United Nations Information Office, *Japan's Record and World Security*.

51–Japanese lotteries. See Ooi and Kratoska.

51–Japanese selling rationed goods to rake in foreign currency. See Akashi, "Watanabe".

51–Hirohito's share of Yokohama Specie Bank was reported by John Gunther, *Inside Asia*. See also Seagrave, *Yamato Dynasty*.

51–Hirohito's assets at the end of the war. See Manning, *Hirohito: the War Years*. On August 14, 2002 *Japan Today* reported the discovery of more than $3.5 billion in secret Japanese accounts in Switzerland. These were designated as "Special Account No. 1" and "Special Account No. 2". It helps explain why American official Edwin S. Pauley could say with a straight face at the end of the war that "no Swiss accounts had been discovered in the name of the Imperial family". See Chapter 7.

52–How Macao, through the 'oversight' of Allied governments meeting at Bretton Woods, became the center of the world's unofficial gold trade during the Pacific War. See Bertil Lintner, "Friends in Need", *Far Eastern Economic Review*, December 30, 1999, p. 15. The secret Swiss accounts referred to in the above note were set up just after the Bretton Woods conference.

52–Ho Yin's gold syndicate in Macao. Lintner, "Friends in Need".

52–Manning described how Hirohito's wealth moved to neutral safe havens. Manning, *Hirohito: The War Years*, pp. 171-181. When money was collected to aid Allied POWs it was placed in a special account at Swiss National Bank. The Japanese insisted on 'converting' the Swiss francs into local military scrip currency, and thereby realized a 'profit' on the exchange of more than 3,200 per cent. See *Japan Today*, "Japan Diverted Allied Funds from Secret Accounts", August 14, 2002.

52–The Vatican was also active in laundering loot for the Nazis. See "Vatican Drawn into Scandal over Nazi-era gold", CNN Interactive Edition, July 22, 1997.

53–Watanabe Wataru and his career in China. Akashi, " Watanabe".

53–Takase Toru met Watanabe through Tsuji Masanobu. Takase's expertise in overseas Chinese and his position as a Special Service agent Imperial Headquarters, Intelligence, Section 8. See Akashi.

53–Colonel Tsuji, the "treasure house of the Far East". Tsuji, *Greatest Victory*, p. 238.

53–terror and coercion as Watanabe's way of dealing with the Chinese. See Akashi.

54–*Sook Ching* and Tsuji's key role in the atrocity are well documented. See McCoy, *Southeast Asia Under Japanese Occupation*; Goodman, *Imperial Japan and Asia*; Seagrave, *Lords of the Rim*, Chapter 10; and Ward, *The Killer They Called God*. Tsuji hosted a dinner party in Burma where the main course was the liver of a captured American pilot. See Seagrave, *Lords*, p. 124.

54–Hirohito's birthday gift of 50 million yen and Takase's role. See Akashi; McCoy, *Southeast Asia under Japanese Occupation*; Seagrave, *Lords of the Rim*.

54–The figure of 140,000 Allied POWs. Daws, *Prisoners of the Japanese*, p. 17.

54–civilian internment camps as 'spartan'. Wasserstein, *Secret War*, p. 140.

54–North Korea claims Japan 'conscripted' 6-million Koreans during the war. Hicks, *Comfort Women*.

54–Kishi's use of nearly 1-million slave laborers. Roberts, *Mitsui*, pp. 357-358. Kishi became Japan's Prime Minister in the 1950s with the help of Eisenhower, Nixon and generous secret 'aid' from the U.S. Government. Indonesian slave laborers, who the Japanese called volunteers or conscript laborers, the 'romusha', were buried in railway embankments. Hundreds of thousands of romusha died or disappeared under the Japanese regime. Daws, *Prisoners of the Japanese*, p. 211.

55–treated worse than draft animals: Roberts, *Mitsui*, p. 358.

55–Taiwanese slave laborers. Valmores said there were Taiwanese slaves, as distinct from Chinese. Officially, Japan had no Taiwanese slave labor, but convicted criminals would have been an exception.

55–slave labor and *zaibatsu*: In November 2000, one of Japan's biggest construction companies, Kajima, agreed to pay $4.5-million in compensation to survivors and relatives of Chinese slaves who died at its Hanaoka copper mine in northern Japan. Conditions there were so brutal that the slaves rose up in rebellion in June 1945.

55–Allied POW death rates of 30 per cent in Japanese camps compared to 4 per cent in Nazi POW camps. Daws, *Prisoners*, pp. 360-361. Russian POWs in Nazi camps fared far less well, however.

55–Beriberi and intentional withholding of vitamins and food from POWs by the Japanese. Singlaub, *Hazardous Duty*, p. 94. Daws, *Prisoners*, pp. 121-122.

56–Hell Ships. Ignatius Ding and the Global Alliance provided this new research on who really owned and operated the Slave Ships and Hell Ships.

56–Bigelow was a slave laborer in Mitsui coalmines. He told his story at the age of 78, at hearings of the U.S. Senate Judiciary Committee, chaired by Senator Orrin Hatch of Utah on June 28, 2000.

56–The Japanese government still denies involvement of the military in the comfort stations and in the "recruitment" of Comfort Women. Hicks, *The Comfort Women*, p. 142.

56–*Kempeitai* and Comfort Women in Korea 1904, Manchuria 1931. Lamont-Brown, *Kempeitai*, p. 44. *Kempeitai* did the 'recruiting'. Hicks, *The Comfort Women*, p. 21. *Kempeitai* sold licenses for brothels. Hicks, p. 2. *Kempeitai* directly controlled comfort stations in Shanghai from 1932 on. See Hicks, p. 19. Physical description of a comfort station. Hicks, p. 20. United Nations *Report on the Mission to the Democratic People's Republic of Korea, the Republic of Korea and Japan on the Issue of Military Sexual Slavery*, 4 January 1996. Online at the UN website. *Yakuza* maintained security at comfort stations. Hicks, p. 47. Ethnic preferences and the fees. Hicks, p. 22. Records for each woman's performance. Hicks, p. 59. 200,000 women forced into sexual slavery. Margaret Scott, "Making the Rising Sun Blush", *Far Eastern Economic Review*, March 30, 1995, p. 50. Fifteen partners a day. See Hicks, p. 32. Comfort women's theoretical salary of 800 yen a month. See Hicks, pp. 63-64. In 1994, denying that any involvement by military or civilian officials in the sex slavery racket, the Japanese government encouraged private citizens to set up a fund, to compensate these women. Very few have accepted this money because it is just another dodge of responsibility by the Government of Japan.

57–"not to allow the escape of a single one, to annihilate them all and not to leave any trace": Exhibit "Q", Document No. 2701, Affidavit of J.T.N. Cross. Reproduced in Mackay, *Betrayal in High Places*.

CHAPTER FIVE

Much of what we know about the Golden Lily treasure sites in the Philippines comes from documents found in the safe of President Ferdinand Marcos after he was deposed in 1986. Other information comes from Robert Curtis. In 1975, Nevada mining expert Robert Curtis was brought to the Philippines by President Marcos to study the Golden Lily treasure maps, reverse-engineer them, and begin recoveries. Aside from Ben Valmores, Robert Curtis was the only non-Japanese to study and photograph all 175 maps before all but three of the originals were deliberately destroyed. Over a period of six months, Curtis visited the most important sites in and around Manila, and explored the 35-miles of tunnels under the city, often in the company of Ben Valmores and others who were eyewitnesses to particular urban sites. Curtis had the help of a team of scholars to analyze the Japanese ideographs and coding on each map, and the help of geologists and engineers in studying the lay of each site. The purpose was to select the most promising vaults for recovery by Filipino army units under the direct control of President Marcos. As a result, Curtis gained a rare firsthand appreciation for the thinking behind many of these sites. Later he was able to apply this to analyzing other sites. We revisited many of the sites ourselves to verify his logic, and became convinced that Curtis got it right. Our site descriptions are based on the Curtis reconstruction of the Japanese engineering. A vast number of documents and photographs related to treasury recovery by Curtis, Marcos and others are reproduced from the originals on our CDs.

58–Japan gained an overland route from Southeast Asia to China following the success of Operation Ichigo in late 1944, but held it only briefly.

58–Readers interested in learning more about these phony hospital ships are directed to the extensive literature on the *Awa Maru*, which was sunk by a U.S. submarine, provoking an international incident and a court martial of American officers. Had the truth been known at the time about Japan's true use of such ships, the court martial might not have taken place.

59–*Op ten Noort*: In our CDs we include documents and photographs covering the ship's whole career including her capture, the fate of her crew and medical complement, her scuttling, and salvaging of her gold cargo in the early 1990s. We include many color photographs of the recovery operation, the ships involved, and the Japanese and other participants.

59–The ship was named after Laurens *Op ten Noort*, a pioneer in Dutch merchant shipping in the early age of steam.

59–specifications, photos, and drawings of the *Op ten Noort* in her first incarnation. Talbot-Booth, *Merchant Ships*.

59–details of the Battle of the Java Sea are from Toland, *Rising Sun*, pp. 322-324.

59–*Op ten Noort* was intercepted by the *Amatsukase* and the *Murasame*. F.C. van Ooosten, *The Battle of the Java Sea*, p. 74.

60–The *Hikawa Maru* had served as a hospital ship previously. It is still a tourist attraction at Yokohama today.

60–eyewitness details of the capture and treatment of the crew and passengers are from the recollections of Dr. A. W. Mellema, chief medical officer and second in command of the *Op ten Noort*. Reproduced on our CDs.

60–Captain Tuizinga wrote a letter of protest on 21 August 1943 to the Japanese chief of police at Mioshi, itemizing abuses they suffered. After that, their treatment improved. Crewmember interviewed in 2001 by Albert Kelder.

60–scuttling of the *Op ten Noort* in Maizuru Bay. Recounted by members of the crew. Recollections reproduced on our CDs.

60–Dutch looted guilders: At war's end, the U.S. Government set up the Far East Commission (FEC) to trace looted property. In a matter of months, it became clear to members of the FEC that they were being sidetracked by Washington, which had its own reasons for blocking close scrutiny. The Dutch delegation to FEC, headed by Dr. G. A. P. Weijer, managed to interrogate a number of Japanese who had served in the Indies during the occupation. One of these was Yamamoto, the chief liquidator of all banks in the Dutch colony during the war. He was interrogated in January 1946, and submitted a summary of the coinage in public circulation in March 1942. Yamamoto's April 1944 report to the Ministry of War listed total coinage seized from Java banks between October 1942 and March 1944 at 18,242,000 guilders. This did not include coinage seized on Sumatra and other islands. The Javasche Bank filed a claim for the return of 20-million guilders worth of silver coin.

61–Kokusho loot processing center. Ed Jackfert's description of Kawasaki #2 and the loot stored there. Jackfert email letter to the Center for Internee Rights, Inc. (CFIR), November 2, 1999. He gave similar testimony before the Hatch Hearings in 2000.

61–Hirohito's bunker at Matsushiro: Cook, "Hirohito's Secret Hideout", *Military History Quarterly*, Spring 1998, Vol. 10, No. 3, pp. 44-47. Cook and Cook, *Japan at War: An Oral History*.

62–Mitsubishi goldmines, POWs and the Sado investigation: Captain J.G. Godwin, Investigating Officer, 2nd Australian War Crimes Section, 16 December 1949; BMP Report of Investigating Officer, File 125M, quoted in Mackay, *Betrayal In High Places*, pp. 249-251.

62–vanished Koreans on Sado Island at Mitsubishi mining works. Japan's secret was found in records of cigarette rations. Mitsubishi officials burnt other incriminating evidence about the Sado operations and the murders of the Korean slave laborers. Waycott, *Sado: Japan's Island of Exile*.

62–war loot discovered by Army Occupation Forces in Japan: "One of the spectacular tasks". *Reports of General MacArthur: MacArthur in Japan: The Occupation: Military Phase*, Volume One Supplement, p. 223. Selected pages of the original report are reproduced on our CD.

62–Sado Island gold mines. The description of the POW massacre is drawn from Mackay, *Betrayal in High Places*, pp. 249–252. Mitsubishi owned the main Sado gold mine which had over 250 miles of tunnels, some as much as 2500 feet deep. Japanese sources told us that some of these tunnels were used to hide quantities of gold, platinum and gems during and after the war. Much of the treasure looted in China was shipped to Japan through occupied Korea, and then carried by ship across the strait to the Japanese Home Islands, for which Sado provided a convenient offshore haven. As a penal colony and gold mine, Sado Island always was a stronghold of the Japanese underworld and smugglers. It is in Niigata prefecture, Prime Minister Tanaka's home district. Just before the end of the war, Tanaka made a fortune trading Japanese scrip for gold bullion held by Japanese banks in occupied Korea. Tanaka then smuggled this bullion back to Japan by ship, apparently stashing it on Sado where he could access it after the occupation ended. Today Sado is a tourist destination and theme park for gold jewelry and ornaments, with a very dark history. The Allied POWs who died horribly there have never been vindicated.

63–MacArthur's discovery of $50-million in diamonds and Edward Henderson's assessment of the hoard. Michael Kernan, "Around the Mall", *Smithsonian Magazine*, May 1995.

63–800,000 carats of diamonds disappeared. Whiting, *Tokyo Underworld*, p. 19.

63–5-ton stash of silver in the Mitsui warehouse. Roberts, *Mitsui*, p. 377. Mitsui was the largest employer of forced labor and had few scruples about burying alive employees trapped in mining accidents. Roberts, *Mitsui*, p. 358. There were also reports in the U.S.

press at this time about this loot and other caches of valuables like narcotics.

63–Kodama stashed his loot in the Imperial Palace. Carroll, "The Enigma of Yoshio Kodama", *Tokyo Journal*, July 1988, p. 94. Stephen Barber, a financial consultant who worked on *The House of Nomura* wrote: "I have a friend who works at the top of a Swiss private bank. [He] told me recently that he was approached by a Philippine general who claimed that tons of Japanese [war] gold was buried underneath the Philippine embassy in Tokyo and wanted to do a deal to transfer it to Switzerland. He was dismissed as a crackpot. Perhaps not?" Barber, email to the authors November 30, 1999.

64–Mel Gutierrez. Yeung, "Slave Wages", from *Bayview*, July 5, 2000, online. Today few Filipinos know that the great tunnel systems still exist. Most entrances have been covered over by new construction.

65–Japanese Army staff cars. This comes from Forty, *Japanese Army Handbook*.

65–treasure sites in and around Manila. Many color and black and white photographs of recovery efforts made by Marcos in the mid-1970s are included on our CDs. In addition nearly 100 pages of correspondence, contract, and discussions of these treasure sites are also reproduced on our CDs.

67–bodies in the Manila monastery discovered by American troops in Intramuros: Robert Trumbell in *The New York Times*, November 7, 1945. The article is quoted online at www.artist.zq.com.

68–Six-Finger Site: See Chapter Eleven. Curtis discovered what has become known as The Six-Finger Site.

69–Dr. Gadi's role in the recovery. See Chapter 9. Documents and memos found in the Presidential Security Command headquarters after Marcos lost power are reproduced on our CDs.

69–Imperial treasure maps. We reproduce several photos and an explanatory drawing of these on our CDs.

70–Prince Chichibu was in the Philippines for periods of six months, coinciding with the dry season. Sources in his entourage confirmed his presence in Manila in mid-1942, again at various locations during the spring of 1943, and he was positively identified at the Pingkian River bridge in Nueva Viscaya during the winter of 1944-1945, when he encountered his first cousin, Prince Takeda. MacArthur was outraged when he retook Manila and discovered that the departing Japanese had burned and looted his apartments, although for reasons that are not clear, many of his most precious possessions survived the war and were returned to him in Tokyo during the occupation.

CHAPTER SIX

We and our researchers and associates spent a great deal of time with Ben Valmores over three years, much of it recorded on over 100 hours of video and audiotape, and still photos (some reproduced on our CDs). This gave us repeated opportunities to verify his story and to resolve apparent contradictions. He showed us around major sites in the Bambang region including Tunnel-8, the 'Many Monkeys' site at Aritao, and others described in our text. We repeatedly interviewed people who worked with Valmores at treasure sites from 1975 to 2001. In the end, we were satisfied that Valmores was telling the truth. To keep his oath to Prince Takeda, he never revealed the prince's real name until he learned from us in 1999 that Takeda was dead. Until that moment, he insisted that he knew his wartime master only as 'Kimsu Maracusi'. This ruled out any possibility that Valmores was leading us on. See our CDs also for documents including legal contracts and affidavits pertaining to Valmores, Prince Chichibu, Prince Takeda, Golden Lily, and treasure sites in the Philippines. In addition, we were given access to Ben's wartime diary. Through mutual friends, as Ben's health began to fail, we were able to check details, and to conduct long written interviews with Ben through his daughters. This gave us many opportunities to examine fine points. For example, when we learned that Ben's father was blinded in his left eye during military training, we asked Ben if his father was left-handed. When Ben confirmed this, we asked if his father was blinded when he fired his training rifle from the wrong shoulder. Ben said yes. Rifles are built so the spent shell is ejected to the right, for precisely this reason. Ben confirmed that this was exactly how his father was blinded. Ben always described the red and gold badge on Prince Takeda's tunic simply as 'a red circle'. We thought it might be the stylized imperial crest of a 14-petal chrysanthemum. When we gave Ben a copy of the British edition of *The Yamato Dynasty* with such a crest on the dustjacket, Ben looked startled and immediately said, "That's what Kimsu had on his tunic."

71–Natural caverns in the Cagayan Valley. Wasson & Cochrane in Bartstra & Casparie, *Modern Quaternary Research in Southeast Asia*. Durkee & Pederson, *Geology of Northern Luzon*, in the *Bulletin of the American Association of Petroleum Geologists*, February 1961.

71–Japanese *zaibatsu* sent their agents and secret agents to all of Asia in this period. Manchuria was not the only target. See Roberts, *Mitsui*, for more.

72–Ben's early life comes from his interviews and recollections of his family.

72–January 1943: Ben's diary gives the date of January 1943 for the encounter with Kimsu, who we now know was Prince Takeda, Hirohito's first cousin.

73–Kimsu's tunic had a 14-petal chrysanthemum emblem. This was an official imperial designation for princes of his rank. Robert Curtis told us: "I do remember Ben telling me about being whipped by one of the Prince's staff for brushing his summer tunic with too stiff a brush. Ben said he unravelled an emblem on the pocket. He never mentioned a red circle or sun, only that the emblem was sewn in gold thread, and that his brush had pulled some of the threads out. I asked him if it was his [the prince's] rank and he said no, it showed he was an Imperial Prince."

73–Kimsu's intervention on behalf of the woman being assaulted by Japanese troops. Valmores interviews.

74–Slave laborers observed by Valmores. Valmores interviews.

75–The family relations of princes Kitashirakawa, Takeda, Asaka and Higashikuni are from *The Imperial Family of Japan* online at geocities.com. On May 12, 1934, Takeda married Sanjo Mitsuko, (born November 6, 1915) youngest daughter of Prince Sanjo Kiteru. See also Seagrave, *Yamato Dynasty*, for a detailed discussion of these princes.

75–Kimsu was only one of Takeda's aliases. Another alias Lt. Col. Miyata. Harris, *Factories of Death*, p. 143.

76–Chichibu: Valmores bears witness to Prince Chichibu being in the Philippines continually for at least six months in 1943, and saw him again at the Pingkian Bridge near Bambang in late May 1945.

76–Takeda's children: Prince Tsunetada, born 1940; Prince Tsunekazu 1944; Prince Tsuneharu 1945; Princess Motoko 1942; Princess Noriko 1943, Prince Takeda Tsunekazu, the second son, has served as chairman of the Japanese Olympic Committee.

76–Chichibu's and Takeda's fellow officers: From Ben's diary and Pol Giga's list provided by Robert Curtis: Kimsu Murakoshi, Record Custodian; Norio Ishihara, Navy Captain,

Naval Architect; Hideo Matsuda, Colonel, Civil Engineer; Terud Morita, Colonel, Mechanical Engineer; Saisho Sasaki, Colonel, Chemical Engineer; Toshio Adachi, Colonel, Ceramics & Design; Eike Kaburagi, Colonel, Ceramics & Design; Saburo Susuki, Colonel, Architect; Hideki Tanaka, General, Commanding east of Manila; Sato; Cato

79—Strangely camouflaged ship: Valmores told us that this small island where he saw the Nazi ship was on the north coast of Mindanao and was called Camiguin Island, the same name as the island on the north tip of Luzon.

79—There was no reason for Valmores to have known after the fact that Prince Chichibu had tuberculosis, unless he actually saw him spitting up blood. He repeatedly told Robert Curtis that he observed this. Tuberculosis was a serious and dangerously contagious disease at that time. Valmores would have been seriously concerned about contracting the disease himself. Curtis to authors, email 19/07/98.

80—Valmores saw the greatest number of gold Buddhas at a site in Santa Mesa Rotunda in Manila and at Oguwan. He said Marcos recovered treasure from both those sites in the 1970s. He said there was one large gold Buddha at Many Monkeys site in Aritao, encased in cement before it was hidden in underground chambers. At another cave site he saw a Buddha of about a ton, another of three or four tons, and twenty small ones.

81—Tunnel-8: It is the largest underground complex in the Philippines, although in terms of natural caverns Yamashita's "Surrender site" at Kiangan is nearly as big. Ben said that both Prince Takeda and Prince Chichibu gave him maps to keep for them, and that Tunnel-8 and Tunnel-9 were reserved for the princes. In 1994 Ben finally showed Curtis an original Red Series waxed map of Tunnel-8. A photograph of the Tunnel-8 map is reproduced on our CDs.

82—Background on Yamashita comes from a variety of sources. See Seagrave, *The Yamato Dynasty*, text and notes.

83—Ft. Santiago: recovery of treasure at Fort Santiago is detailed in Chapter 11. On our CDs we produce photographs of the treasure recovery and many documents related to the Ft. Santiago operations.

83—Rear Admiral Iwabuchi and the rape of Manila. Seagrave, *Marcos Dynasty*, pp. 310-314.

85—"Kurene sabisu" and other statements in Japanese, which Valmores rendered phonetically, have been read by several Japanese-language experts who have provided these translations.

85—Tunnel-9: Valmores said a Japanese group recovered Tunnel-9 in the 1970s using bulldozers and other heavy equipment. At first he thought it was comic as they were excavating half a mile from Tunnel-8 (which he thought was their target). Only later did he realize that they were excavating Tunnel-9. By the time President Marcos and several of his senior officers also became aware that the Japanese were recovering Tunnel-9, in the summer of 1975, the recovery was already finished and the Japanese had hauled away the treasure, loading their trucks at night. Valmores later discovered that General Yamashita and his staff spent a lot of time in the "secret room" with steel doors, during the winter of 1944-1945. This was Yamashita's underground command bunker in Bambang in the last months of the war. It was entered through the main portal of Tunnel 9, which Valmores at the time did not know existed. Today, the underground headquarters at Kiangan is referred to as the "Surrender site".

86—Sayonara Site: Norman Haynes told us : "Sayonara is covered by the two tunnels you mentioned" — [T-8 and T-9.] "We were to go to the other [T-9] when Ben became ill."

Norman Haynes email to authors 3/12/2000. Valmores drew a map for Norman Haynes showing the underground layout of Sayonara site. Our description is based on Valmores's drawing and his verbal accounts, plus details obtained from Robert Curtis, who had the maps. Curtis gave us copies of the maps for T-8 and the Graveyard site, but retained the map for T-9.

87–Prince Takeda also gave Valmores a Japanese Philippine campaign medal. Valmores had it gilded. A color photograph of this medal that Valmores kept for the rest of his life is reproduced on our CD.

CHAPTER SEVEN

Some people are under the impression that General Yamashita was tried in Japan during the Tokyo war crimes trials, which began after the start of the Nuremberg trials, and concluded after the end of the Nuremberg trials. In fact, General Yamashita was tried in the Philippines, not in Japan. He was arraigned with General Homma on 8 October 1945, and his trial began on 29 October 1945, weeks before the Nuremberg trials began on 20 November 1945, and months ahead of the Tokyo trials. Yamashita was hanged on 23 February 1946, eight months before the Nuremberg verdicts were handed down on 1 October 1946. So whether you draw your conclusion from the time the court case started, or from the time the verdicts were handed down, the conclusion is exactly as we express it here – Yamashita was the first general of a defeated nation tried by the United States for war crimes. This point has been made by several scholars, of whom we are only the most recent. Observers at the trials were puzzled why Yamashita's case was hurried through, why he was convicted exclusively on hearsay, and why he was hanged so quickly. It is now evident that Washington was anxious to eliminate Yamashita as fast as possible, to avoid any possibility of word getting out about the war-gold recoveries.

88–Yamashita's surrender: George F. Guy, "The Defense of General Yamashita", in *Yearbook 1981 Supreme Court Historical Society*. Guy was on Yamashita's defense team.

88–Yamashita's gold bars: Lt. Col. Fry's battalion was at the surrender site. Fry, an attorney from Reno, Nevada, had a long and distinguished career after the war.

88–Yamashita was hanged: There are theories that a double was hanged in Yamashita's place, as part of a deal between MacArthur and Hirohito. See Chapter 14. Yamashita was said to have been spirited off to Brazil, where Japan owned an immense ranch. Many people think this is unlikely, but some who knew Yamashita well said the man shown surrendering in the famous photo taken in the Kiangan Pocket is not Yamashita but a stand-in. Even so, such a ranch exists, and other war survivors are known to have gone there to live, including the famous holdout Lt. Onoda Hiroo. See Onoda, *Never Surrender*.

88–Charges against Yamashita: On 26 September 1945 he was served with a "generic" charge of war crimes: "Between October 9, 1944 and September 2, 1945 in the Philippine Islands, … he unlawfully disregarded and failed to discharge his duty as commander to control the operations of the members of his command, permitting them to commit brutal atrocities and other high crimes … and thereby violated the law of war." The charge brought against Yamashita is quoted in Laurie Barber, "The Yamashita War Crimes Trial Revisited". About Yamashita's guilt or innocence there are partisans on both sides – those who saw him as a major war criminal, and those who thought he was railroaded. The same can be said of General Homma. But things are never that simple. In Malaya and in the Philippines, Yamashita commanded men who carried out a range of grisly atrocities as if they were normal, everyday practice in Japan. While Yamashita was still in Manila, massacres of Filipino civilians took place just south of the city in Batangas and Laguna – with a death toll equal to that of the Rape of Manila a month later. And there is little solid evidence that Yamashita actually did order Manila to be spared. Both Yamashita and Homma were complex characters. (Homma was a playwright whose friends, including Prince Chichibu and his wife, thought he was a 'very gentle' man). In recent years, it became fashionable to blame the worst atrocities of the Bataan Death March not on Homma, but on Tsuji, who sought to inflame Japanese soldiers wherever he was, in order to inflate his image as Japan's most celebrated hot-head. However, research by Fred Baldessarre has shown that Tsuji left the Philippines on 10 April, a few hours after the Death March began. The notion that Homma was unaware of the brutality of his men, Baldessarre says, is nonsense. Responsibility for moving more than 60,000 American and Filipino POWs from Mariveles, Bataan, to Capas, Tarlac, was placed by Homma on Major General Kawane Yoshikata, and staff officer Colonel Takatsu Toshimitsu, whose preoccupation with other responsibilities contributed to the tragedy. Homma was under intense pressure from Tokyo to overwhelm resistance on the island of Corregidor. Takatsu had to rush equipment and men into position for the Corregidor offensive. The trucks set aside by America's General King for the purpose of moving POWs, were instead used to rush Japanese soldiers and equipment to the front. So the sick and malnourished POWs were forced to march overland, at a killing pace, many of them collapsing. Their guards became impatient, grew meaner, until an orgy of barbarism ensued. Along the way, other Japanese units massacred large groups of POWs in revenge for their stubborn defense of Bataan in preceding months. Homma was fully aware of this, for the Death March passed directly in front of his field headquarters. Homma admitted at his trial that he had driven along the route and seen the prisoners. "The result," Baldessarre says, "was a blend of Japanese incompetence, frustration, and sadism. In the 1980s and 1990s, there was a great need to beatify Homma and Yamashita, and to show that it was not the Japanese people, government, or culture to blame, but rather a few rotten apples whose behavior was 'most regrettable'. The ultimate villains were Hirohito and the Chrysanthemum Club." (Hirohito personally oversaw and approved strategic and policy decisions of the Imperial General Headquarters, including orders the high command issued to mass-murder POWs; the emperor's hands-on responsibility was neatly summed up by his former prime minister, Prince Konoe: "The emperor was [Japan's] major war criminal.")

88–First time in history: Yamashita's trial was precedent breaking. Guy, "Defense of General Yamashita". The prosecution was "badgered" by MacArthur. Barber,"Yamashita War Crimes Trial". See also Brackman, *The Other Nuremberg*.

89–Dissenting opinions of Supreme Court Justices Murphy and Rutledge: Barber, "Yamashita War Crimes Trial". The Yamashita appeal and the Supreme Court decision is available online. The current Bosnian war crimes trials have brought Yamashita's case back into the limelight.

89–Major Kojima: The name of Yamashita's driver, and the circumstances of his torture, were given to us by a source close to Santa Romana and confirmed by retired CIA sources who asked not to be named. When we interviewed Lansdale for *Soong Dynasty*, he said at one point, "Everything changed after we debriefed Major Kojima." When we interviewed Lansdale for *Marcos Dynasty*, he became evasive, and changed the subject. Robert Curtis was told the same story by Colonel Villacrusis. Villacrusis said he was told about Kojima during his 1968 meeting in Tokyo with Ishihara. See Chapter 10. Curtis to authors, April 2, 2001. Throughout his career, Lansdale justified his own use of torture and atrocity against "the enemy" and prisoners of war because it was "an appropriate response" to their "glum and deadly practices". See Lansdale, *In the Midst of Wars*, p. 72. He cut his teeth on the interrogation of Japanese prisoners of war and then moved on to the Huks in the

Philippines and then to the Vietnamese. All the while, he chanted his quaint Burma-shave jingles and concocted Madison Avenue-spin "to construct a squeaky-clean Boy Scout image, behind which he masked his own perverse delight in atrocity". See Valentine, *Operation Phoenix*, p. 26.

89—Severino Garcia Diaz Santa Romana. Santa Romana's photographs, documents written by and about him, his will, his marriage certificate, bank certificates, New York State tax office documents, and statements from CIA Deputy Director Ray Cline concerning Santa Romana appear on our CD. Much more on Santa Romana is found in Chapters Ten and Fifteen.

89—Torture of Kojima: It seems likely that Yamashita was kept informed of the torture of Kojima, and that this was used a form of 'torture by proxy'. He would have been pained to know that he was being spared physical torture, while Major Kojima was taking a terrible beating.

90—The United States government had full knowledge of Japan's looting of Asia. In fact, it would have been unusual for the Japanese not to loot the conquered countries. What was not then known, however, was the systematic nature of the looting as well as the involvement of the extended imperial family. *Reports of General MacArthur: MacArthur in Japan: the Occupation: Military Phase, Volume One, Supplement,* describes "Japanese-owned gold and silver", "property that was acquired by Japan under duress, wrongful actions of confiscation, dispossession or spoliation", "property found in Japan and identified as having been located in an Allied country and removed to Japan by fraud or coercion by the Japanese or their agents", "Great hoards of gold, silver, precious stones, foreign postage stamps, engraving plates", "precious metals and diamond stockpiles owned or controlled by the Japanese", and "the discovery of 30,000 carats of diamonds and 52.5 pounds of platinum". Relevant pages of this original document are reproduced on our CDs. Looting is one of the issues that are to be examined by the terms of the *Japanese Imperial Government Disclosure Act*. But the restraints already being imposed on the review and release of such documents give little hope that the governments of Japan and the United States are going to willingly divulge the secrets. See the *Japanese Imperial Government Disclosure Act* reproduced in full on our CDs.

90—Ballinger's story was related to the authors by his son. Gene Ballinger letters of May 4, 5, 1999. Ballinger was with a guerrilla unit with 25 men under the command of Captain Jesus Medina of the Philippines Scouts. Medina was captured by the Japanese, tortured and beheaded.

90—We identified the ship as the *Fuji Maru* by comparing Ballinger's photograph with ship profiles from the U.S. naval intelligence database. The ship is disguised with false superstructures to alter its profile. Ballinger's photograph of the ship appears on our CDs.

90—Ballinger had no idea what was in the boxes from the *Fuji Maru*. Gene Ballinger emails to the authors 1999. Medina's guerrillas following the Japanese inland. Gene Ballinger to authors.

90—Records of the loot. Of course, the Japanese records have vanished as is reported by the Interagency task force charged with the review of records under the *Japanese Imperial Disclosure Act, Interim Report,* reproduced in full on our CDs. This of course fails to take into consideration documents *that never reached* Washington like those given to Herbert Hoover. General Bonner Fellers, MacArthur's assistant in Tokyo wrote on June 23, 1967 that "[Herbert] Hoover had no trouble in securing ...a tremendous amount of documentation from the Japanese War Office... He sent back an enormous number of documents from Japan." These too have disappeared.

91–The intense competition between Secretary of the Treasury Henry Morgenthau and the Office of Strategic Services. Bower, *Blood Money*. Foreign & Commonwealth Office, *Nazi Gold: The London Conference 2-4 December 1997.*

91–The OSS was well-informed about the movement of Nazi loot through Europe. The instance of the 280 trucks passing through Switzerland: Ziegler, *The Swiss*, p. 71. It was useful to watch the loot, not necessarily because it was going to be repatriated to the looted countries or individuals, but because to the victor go the spoils. In subsequent chapters, we discuss how this actually happened when the OSS took over Axis assets after the war.

91–Macao as a loophole for the international gold trade was an oversight of the Bretton Woods agreements. Like the trucks passing through Switzerland, Macao's gold trade was being closely monitored by all of the Allied governments who had agents placed in this neutral haven. See Lintner.

91–That the Bank of International Settlements engaged in money-laundering. Finding Aid to Record Group 238, Records of the Joint Chiefs of Staff, National Archives and Records Service.

91–Macao was forgotten. See Bower, *Blood Money*, p. 73. Lintner, "Friends in Need".

91–The Office of Strategic Services was blocked from the Pacific. Hogan, *U.S. Army Special Operations in World War II*, CMH Publication 70-42, Department of the Army, 1992, p. 63.

91–Biographical details about Willoughby: Campbell, "Major General Charles A. Willoughby: A Mixed Performance" in *American Intelligence Journal*, Volume 18, Number 1-2 (1998), pp. 87-91. Willoughby's private papers are at the Gettysburg College, Musselman Library. There is a dearth of material from the occupation period, obviously sensitive records were purged.

91–MacArthur's absolute control of intelligence in the Pacific. See Hogan, pp. 104-115.

92–"not remotely prepared": Willoughby's blunders cost tens of thousands of lives. MacArthur's need for adulation: Campbell, "Major General Charles A. Willoughby".

92–The Allied Translation and Intelligence Service (ATIS) was created in September 1942. Campbell, "Major General Charles A. Willoughby". The ATIS was given primarily responsibility for assembling, translating and reviewing captured Japanese documents. The recollections and postwar careers of many ATIS are available online through Japanese-American veteran associations. It is evident that some of them were not happy about what they observed about secret operations of SCAP during the occupation. Some ATIS veterans returned to live in Japan on a permanent basis with jobs on the U.S. embassy staff in Tokyo.

92–Courtney Whitney: In 1940, MacArthur got Whitney commissioned as a major in the Reserve Officers Corps and found him a job in Washington as assistant chief of the legal division of the Army Air Force. Whitney was still in Washington when the Philippines came under Japanese attack, but soon joined MacArthur in Australia. Whitney's career 1917-1943 "Maj. Gen. Courtney Whitney, 71, Adviser to MacArthur Is Dead", *The New York Times*, March 22, 1969, p. 33:2. The switch to Whitney was made while Willoughby was in Washington in June 1943, lobbying unsuccessfully for the selection of MacArthur as the Republican Party's vice presidential candidate. Willoughby's promotion: Schaller, *Far Eastern General*, p. 80.

92–Whitney was MacArthur's personal lawyer in Manila. Gunther, *The Riddle of MacArthur*, p. 71.

92–Dewitt, Perkins & Enrile: This Enrile was the father of Juan Ponce Enrile, Marcos crony and defense minister who remains prominent in the Philippine Senate. *The New York Times* obituary says Whitney went to the Philippines in 1927. Philippine Supreme Court shows Whitney admitted to the Philippine Bar in 1925. Whitney worked for DeWitt, Perkins and Enrile. Seagrave, *The Marcos Dynasty.*

92–Santa Romana's birth date and names of his parents: Wedding Certificate. His brothers, sisters and some of his children are named in his holographic will. The wedding certificate and holographic will are reproduced on our CDs.

94–Information on the Campton family comes from members of Santa Romana's family, and has been difficult to confirm because records predating the San Francisco earthquake are incomplete.

94–Santy always told friends he was with the OSS because that saved a lot of explaining. Santy, like Lansdale and others officially assigned to Army G-2, actually were part of the Counter Intelligence Corps (CIC). In the Pacific, the CIC was under the control of General Charles Willoughby. *The Counter Intelligence Corps History and Mission in World War Two*, published by The Counter Intelligence Corps School, Ft. Holabird, gives some details about the creation and organization of the CIC and is available online at the Military History Center, Carlisle Barracks. CIC records are scattered throughout the U.S. government because its agents and special agents were given assignments with many different branches of the military and non-military as well. Tracking down the records of the CIC is a hit-or-miss proposition. The official 30-volume history of the CIC exists in two forms–classified and declassified–but this too is incomplete because the U.S. Army stopped the history project in the 1950s. A few books have been written about the CIC, but they are fragmentary and contradictory. At different times, CIC records were routinely burned, eliminating evidence about its agents and activities.

94–Joseph McMicking. His father was admitted to the Philippine Bar in 1907.

94–McMicking's global real estate: McMicking acquired and built the 4,400-acre luxury resort at Sotogrande, Spain, which includes a big yacht harbor and a world-class golf course. McMicking bought the acreage for Sotogrande in 1962, and it is now a haven for wealthy exiles. In the 1960s, Marcos invested in the resort. This information comes from W. Scott Malone's memo of investigation for Frontline, October 24, 1986, "CIA Document Analysis", p. 3. Malone's memo states that Marcos children were nominees in the project. But Malone was unaware of the McMicking/MacArthur/Santa Romana connection.

95–McMicking as the real moneybags is from *The Philippine Star.* philstar.com/datedata/d23_fed23/edi6.htm McMicking's Ayala Foundation at www.fillib.org.ph/afi

95–Ayala, Campton Place Hotel and its multi-million-dollar refurbishment is from the hotel's online sites.

95–Two schools of thought about Lansdale. Nashel, *Edward Lansdale.* Photos, documents, and bank documents naming Lansdale are included on our CD. "Lansdale becomes a multiple 'missing link' between all cold war events and their supposed sources, between elites and the general public, between fact and fiction." Nashel, *Edward Lansdale*, pp. 6, 13. See Valentine, *Operation Phoenix* for an unvarnished view of Lansdale as a man intrigued with torture and atrocity for the power it brought him.

95–Lansdale's ditty: "When the work has once begun": Santy wrote this same ditty in his holographic will. It must have been very important to Santy to include this clue as he had only a few days to live. The holographic will is reproduced on our CD.

95—Lansdale birth, background, UCLA days, ROTC intelligence officer. Nashel, *Lansdale*, pp. 36, 40.

96—Lansdale had advertising accounts of Wells Fargo Bank, the Union Trust Company and Levi Strauss and Company. Nashel, p. 37. The Wells Fargo bank later received Santa Romana assets and was named in a lawsuit filed by Melvin Belli in 1993, which is reproduced in full on our CD.

96—Pearl Harbor: Lansdale was then working for an ad agency. See Lansdale, *In the Midst of Wars*, p. 4.

96—Lansdale psy-ops and *The Serpent's Mouth* quoted from Nashel, pp. 53-54.

96—The course of Lansdale's career. "I served with the OSS for a time, then became an army intelligence officer." Lansdale was carefully vague about details of his career but he was a captain at the end of WWII, assigned to Intelligence Division of the G-2 in Manila, and later was promoted to major as Deputy G-2 of the army command before he returned to America in November 1948. He told a Congressional hearing: "I served in the Philippine Islands towards the end of World War II, and stayed in the Philippine Islands and organized the Philippine Islands Intelligence Service." Actually, he did not get sent to the Philippines until September 1945, when the war had already ended. Nashel, pp. 4, 11, 134, 170 note 31.

96—Lansdale's hatred of the Japanese, and the terrible things he saw in Manila. His journal entry. Nashel, pp. 189-190, 220 note 30. Lansdale justified his own use of torture and atrocity as an 'appropriate response'. See Lansdale, *In the Midst of Wars*, p. 72.

96—"treasury of reports": Lansdale's team roving the Philippines happened between September 1945 and July 1946. Lansdale, *In the Midst of Wars*, pp. 5-6.

97—We know about the secret trip of MacArthur and Anderson from Tokyo to Manila, and the tour they were given by Lansdale and Santa Romana, and other details we describe, from separate sources in the CIA that independently confirmed each other. We are satisfied that these sources are reliable. Alan Foringer (see Chapter 14) also knew about the Anderson trip and told Robert Curtis about this. One day, when Foringer was giving Ray Cline a tour of some treasure sites in the Philippines, Cline remarked to Foringer that "it reminded him of the Anderson tour". Curtis to authors, April 2, 2001. These basic details were confirmed independently by Gary Thompson of *The Las Vegas Sun*, in discussions he had with senior CIA sources. It appears that Mike Mansfield learned of these things when he paid a visit to Tokyo in 1947. That was also the year that Alexander Haig became a personal aide to MacArthur. See Chapter 9.

97—We do not know the fate of Major Kojima. We were told he committed suicide in his prison cell using a sharpened butter knife obtained from another prisoner, but we have been unable to confirm this. But see Chapter 17.

97—Officially there were 550 tons of Nazi gold recovered. But 11,200 tons of "unofficial" Nazi gold. See Thompson, "Search for the Tiger's Treasure", *The Las Vegas Sun*, 1993.

97—Stimson, Hoover and MacArthur. Schaller, *Far Eastern General*, pp. 12-13.

98—Patterson, Bundy, McCloy and Lovett. Isaacson and Thomas, *The Wise Men*, pp. 191-192. Lovett died in 1986. Isaacson and Thomas, *The Wise Men*, p. 736. Lovett and Brown Brothers Harriman: Isaacson and Thomas, *The Wise Men*, pp. 21, 111-112.

98—McCloy's work for Cravath before World War II, friendships with Harriman and Lovett: Isaacson and Thomas, *The Wise Men*, pp. 119-125. McCloy and Lovett central role in the post-war national security establishment. Isaacson and Thomas, *The Wise Men*,

p. 192.

98–"To be at all the points" is McCloy: Isaacson and Thomas, *Wise Men*, p. 192. McCloy became the U.S. High Commissioner for Germany and by 1951 had arranged for clemency to be granted to a number of Nazi war criminals, including every single German industrialist who had been convicted at the Nuremberg trials. Simpson, *The Splendid Blond Beast*, p. 271.

98–McCloy went to work for Milbank, Tweed which handled the affairs of the Rockefeller family and the Chase Bank. Isaacson and Thomas, *The Wise Men*, p. 336.

98–McCloy in the Council on Foreign Relations: Isaacson and Thomas, *The Wise Men*, p. 336. McCloy died in 1989. His papers are at the Amherst College Archives, purged of secrets.

98–Ray Cline on Santa Romana's 176 bank accounts. See the Ackerman letter reproduced on our CDs.

98–Paul Helliwell set up CIA banks, including Nugan-Hand. Seagrave, *The Marcos Dynasty*. BCCI is mentioned in Santa Romana documents reproduced on our CDs.

98–Details on BCCI and First American Bankshares are from *The Wall Street Journal*, 9/29/98. See also "Robert B. Anderson" at www.history.navy.mil; www.treas.gov; L.J. Davis, "The Name of the Rose", in *The New Republic*, April 4, 1994. "BCCI's Criminality" at sun00781.dn.net/irp/congress/1992.

98–Indictment of Clifford. Anderson pleaded guilty and died in disgrace. Adams, *The American Spectator*, December 1996. Available online.

98–"year zero": Grabbe, "The Rise and Fall of Bretton Woods", www.aci.net/kalliste/bretton_woods.htm.

99–Bretton Woods: Grabbe, "The Gold Market" Part 1. At www.aci.net/kalliste/gold1.htm

99–Britain followed the U.S. lead for a $30-billion war loan. Grabbe, "Rise and Fall of Bretton Woods".

99–The original purpose of the IMF: Wilson, "Global Purse Strings".

99–U.S. held 60 percent of the world gold stock. Grabbe, "Rise and Fall of Bretton Woods".

99–U.S. emergency airlifts of gold to London, collapse of the weighing room floor of the Bank of England: Grabbe, "Rise and Fall of Bretton Woods".

101–Lansdale's promotions. Lansdale, *In the Midst of Wars*, p. 12.

101–Lansdale arrival in Manila in 1950 to work with JUSMAG: Lansdale, *In the Midst of Wars*, pp. 15, 17. Lansdale was a full colonel in the Air Force by 1950. Evan Thomas, *Best Men*, p. 57. Lansdale's assignment by Wisner to Philippines: O'Toole, *Honorable Treachery*, p. 455.

101–Lansdale's confidential relationship with the Dulles brothers: Nashel, p. 7. Allen Dulles told Eisenhower that Lansdale was one of his "best men": Nashel, pp. 79, 81, 111 notes 90, 91, 96.

101–"Lansdale used Madison Avenue language …behind which he masked his own perverse delight in atrocity." See Valentine, *Operation Phoenix*, p. 23.

102–Lansdale's search for power and problems with the State Department. Nashel, p. 21. Lansdale's black money in Vietnam: $1-million delivered in a suitcase. Thomas Buell interview. Nashel, pp. 73, 88, and 113 note 114. Lansdale "manipulating and preserving":

Nashel, p. 130.

102–Lansdale and his assassins in Tokyo: Nashel, pp. 137, 170 note 35. Lansdale's Filipino assassins would "slit their grandmother's throat for a dollar eighty-five". See Valentine, *Operation Phoenix*, pp. 25-27. For more on Napoleon Valeriano see Seagrave, *The Marcos Dynasty*. In 1983, Valeriano's stepson, Greggy Araneta, became Ferdinand Marcos's son-in-law. Lansdale may have played the match-maker.

CHAPTER EIGHT

103–The definitive study of the murder of Shimoyama Sadanori is Johnson, *Conspiracy at Matsukawa*. Johnson calls it "the biggest criminal conspiracy case of postwar Japan". Takano Hajime called it "the greatest riddle" of the Occupation. Schreiber, *Shocking Crimes of Postwar Japan*, p. 80.

105–U.S. Ambassadors to Tokyo, Mondale, Armacost and Foley after the September 2001 World Trade Center wrote a letter to *The Washington Post*, charging that American POWs were tantamount to terrorists by their efforts to obtain compensation from Japan. See later chapters in this book. These are all manifestations of a trend to curtail America's civil liberties. In July 2002, CIA official James Bruce spoke publicly of the need for SWAT teams to be sent into the homes of American journalists to stop leaks of classified documents. For many, this evoked memories of the 1930s in Germany, during the rise of the Nazi Party.

105–Angleton, the Italian elections, and Operation Segun. Mangold, *Cold Warrior*, p. 21. In 1948, $10-million dollars in Axis loot was laundered by the CIA; see Andrew, *For the President's Eyes Only*, p. 172. The money was channeled through the National Civic Committee, a Vatican-supported political action group. Botting, *Aftermath Europe*, pp. 141-143. Cornwell, *Hitler's Pope*, p. 329. Angleton left the CIA in the purges of 1974 following the Family Jewels report.

105–Vatican sheltered Hirohito's accounts. Manning, *Hirohito: The War Years*.

105–Angleton's "very secret" slush-fund. Mangold, *Cold Warrior*, p. 31.

105–The CIA's "historical intelligence budget information" remains classified. See Federation of American Scientists, letter to the CIA Inspector General, December 21, 2000. Online.

105–Greece, Britain's withdrawal, Acheson's "rotten apple": Botting, *Aftermath Europe*, pp. 128-129.

106–"At the present moment": quotes from Truman Doctrine. McCullough, *Truman*, pp. 547-548.

106–China Mission/ China Cowboys. Thomas, *Very Best Men*, p. 154.

106–Wisner's jobs during World War II. Thomas, *Very Best Men*, pp. 19-24. Wisner worked with Helliwell, Casey and Singlaub. See Singlaub, *Hazardous Duty*.

106–Wisner's jobs 1947-48: friendships, lobbying for the Office of Policy Coordination (OPC). Thomas, *Very Best Men*, pp. 27-30. May 1948 OPC established, NSC directive 10/2. Jeffreys-Jones, *The CIA and American Democracy*, pp. 55-56.

106–Wisner recruits' unsavory. Thomas, *Very Best Men*, p. 33-35.

106–"We couldn't spend it all", Wisner's slush fund and the Marshall Plan. Thomas, *Very Best Men*, p. 40.

106–"no limits…nobody had to account". Wisner drew on a web of New York and State

Department connections to gain support for OPC's activities. "In this context, operational tasks, personnel, money and material tended to grow in relation to one another with little outside oversight." U.S. Senate report quoted in Mosley, *Dulles*, p. 245.

106—Wisner's OPC : 47 stations, budget, personnel. Mosley, *Dulles*, p. 245 footnote.

106—Wisner hires Desmond Fitzgerald. Thomas, *Very Best Men*, p. 43.

107—Wisner's mental breakdown and subsequent suicide are discussed in Thomas, *Very Best Men*.

107—Takahashi Toshio quoted by Norbert Schlei. We reproduce over 600 pages of Norbert Schlei court testimony on our CDs.

107—According to Takano Hajime, the M-Fund was financed from war loot, from the sale of stockpiles of industrial diamonds, platinum, gold, and silver plundered in occupied countries. Also from sales of shares of the several *zaibatsu* dissolved after the war, and GARIOA 'counterpart funds' derived from the sale of U.S. aid. Johnson, "The 1955 System and the American Connection".

107—"A secret billion-dollar slush fund". Whiting, *Tokyo Underworld*, p. 31.

107—"The Japanese government also sold great stockpiles of gold." Whiting, *Tokyo Underworld*, p. 31. The Japanese public has been familiar with the history of the M-Fund since the 1970s. It only began to surface widely in the American press in the mid-1990s with the publication of Norbert Schlei's "M-Fund Memorandum" by the Japan Policy Research Institute. Whiting kindly supplied us with materials from the three-part series that appeared in 1979 in the *Shukan Bunshun*, a reputable weekly magazine. Titled "M-Shigen No Ura No Sinjutsu" (The Truth Behind the M-Fund), the articles ran on October 4, October 25 and November 1, 1979. Whiting gave us the following synopsis: Almost all of the military supplies and valuables held by the Japanese Army at the end of World War II disappeared. Referring to an article that appeared in *Newsweek* in early 1948, these items were disposed of by military leaders for as much as 200-billion yen and "there is evidence that the profit went to political parties as election funds". The *Shukan Bunshun* criticized *Newsweek* for omitting to mention that "the major portion of the profit created by the hidden materials went to high officials of MacArthur's headquarters". Regarding GARIOA and EROA funds, which amounted to nearly 2-billion dollars during the Occupation, it was discovered that about 10 percent of supplies shipped out from the U.S. went personally to Japanese government officials, Occupation officials, and politicians. They disposed of these on the black market and enjoyed high profits. The materials officially handed over to the Japanese government were sold to trusted dealers, and the profit was reserved in the "special trade account" which was later put under the umbrella of the U.S. Aid Counterpart Funds, officially inaugurated by SCAP in April 1949. *Shukan Bunshun* said, "Even after the Occupation ended, there was movement on the American side to deposit black money behind the scenes that was generated from legitimate enterprises like cinema houses and oil-sales, but also from smuggling and other illegal businesses." *Shukan Bunshun* reported that the illegal business profits were used for political conspiracy. In the mid-to-late 1960s, according to *Shukan Bunshun*, when Mikio Mizuta was head of the Ministry of Finance, $12.8-billion was flown into Japan by a financial clique centered on the Rothschild consortium. It was decided that the Tokyo branch offices of Chase Manhattan Bank and the Bank of America would use this money to finance major business through four big Japanese banks, including Industrial Bank. The credit term was said to have been "20 years and interest low". *Shukan Bunshun* confirmed these banking arrangement after talking with a number of prominent Japanese financiers: "most top-class financial brokers [in Japan now] believe that some kind of new account was established during the second Sato cabinet." An apparent reference to the M-Fund. Robert Whiting, email to the authors, July 6, 2002.

108–Kodama hid Golden Lily loot in the Imperial Palace. Carroll, "The Enigma of Yoshio Kodama", *Tokyo Journal*, July 1988, p. 94.

108–Narcotics in the immediate postwar period in Japan. See Anslinger, *The Traffic in Narcotics*, and Firman, "Awaiting the Tsunami".

108–March 1945, Kodama was private assistant to Prince Higashikuni, Hirohito's uncle and Prime Minister immediately after the war. See Kodama, *I Was Defeated*, p. 151.

108–Prince Higashikuni's secret meeting with MacArthur was arranged by Kodama. See Kodama, *I Was Defeated*, p. 179. Because Kodama's book was written with the blessing of MacArthur and Willoughby and published by a CIA proprietary company, we can be sure that this meeting took place. Another overview of Kodama's criminal career and his involvement in criminal undertakings with the U.S. government comes from Richard Halloran, "Little-Known Japanese Wield Vast Power", *The New York Times Biographical Edition*, July 1974, pp. 988-989, Kaplan, *Yakuza*, is another thorough source. Also see Roberts, "The Lockheed-Japan-Watergate Connection", Johnson, "The 1955 System", and Sampson, *The Arms Bazaar*.

109–KMT and Chiang Kai-shek's control of drugs in the Golden Triangle: McCoy, *The Politics of Heroin*.

109–General Tuan and General Li were both interviewed extensively by Sterling Seagrave in the 1960s when he was a journalist in Southeast Asia. See *Lords of the Rim*.

109–Japan's postwar drug-trade: "The initial efforts of SCAP and the Japanese government to control the drug problem were limited. SCAP officials placed little emphasis on controlling the growing black market in drugs." Firman, "Awaiting the Tsunami? Japan and the International Drug Trade", in *The Pacific Review*, Volume 6, Number 1, 1993. Tons of narcotics were discovered in Nagano, near Hirohito's Matsushiro imperial bunker by SCAP authorities and reported in *The New York Times*, October 31, 1945. See also Anslinger, *The Traffic in Narcotics*.

109–General Frederic Marquat's domain: Dower, *Embracing Defeat*, p. 210. Intelligence, Government and Economic Sections were the most important areas of SCAP. Schaller, *Altered States*, p. 9. After he left Tokyo, Marquat was chief of the Army Audit Agency, Office of Civil Affairs, overseeing occupation properties. His personal papers, purged of sensitive materials, are at the Marquat Library in Ft. Bragg.

109–"a marginal economy". Marquat's lack of financial expertise. Gunther, *The Riddle of MacArthur*, pp. 73-74.

110–Unit 731 Information on Japan's medical experiments and biological warfare programs was withheld from the Tokyo War Crimes Tribunals. Casesse and Roling, *The Tokyo Trials and Beyond*. For a comprehensive treatment of the subject, see Harris, *Factories of Death*. Unit 731 records are part of those to be reviewed for release under the Japanese Imperial Government Disclosure Act, reproduced on our CDs.

110–M-Fund: "All my life", Richard Allen to Norbert Schlei. Schlei had long conversations with Nixon's security advisor Richard Allen, Ambassador Mike Mansfield, and CIA general counsel Stanley Sporkin about the M-Fund. Schlei testimony reproduced on our CDs.

110–Willoughby dubbed "lovable fascist" by MacArthur: Schaller, *Far Eastern General*, p. 121.

110–Yotsuya Fund and the black market. Johnson, "The 1955 System and the American Connection". Whiting, *Tokyo Underworld*. Yotsuya tenderloin: this description comes from Joel Legendre, to the authors July 13, 2000.

110–liberalism as a poisonous idea from the West. General Yamagata Aritomo spoke of democracy and communism being the head and tail of liberalism.

111–Willoughby's "Korean Liaison Office": Schaller, *Far Eastern General*, pp. 163, 170, 174.

111–Ted Lewin: Whiting, *Tokyo Underworld*, p. 45. Seagrave, *The Marcos Dynasty*, pp. 161, 164, 329-330, 334. Daws, *Prisoners of the Japanese* for the easy life Lewin led as a Japanese prisoner of war.

111–Cannon Agency's dirty work in Japan. Johnson, "The 1955 System and the American Connection". Jack Y. Cannon (some sources insist that the last name is properly spelled Canon) spent most of his career in the U.S. Army as a CIC agent. With a team of other CIC agents, "Cactus Jack" was sent to Biak Island, New Guinea in July 1944. Roaring around Biak island in a jeep with a machine-gun mounted on it, Cannon discovered a cache of 3,500 pounds of 'Japanese documents' for which he was awarded a Bronze Star (according to some sources it was a Silver Star). According to Greg Bradsher of the National Archives, the citation indicates that he has "with great risk to his life made reconnaissance in a number of caves which had been occupied by the Japanese…[and] recovered more than 11 cases of enemy documents vitally needed for the successful conclusion of the operation". As we have said earlier, evidence and information about CIC operations is vague and often contradictory. Of Cannon's discovery of documents, Duval Edwards, who was serving with Cannon at the time, said: "CIC contributed little of value on Biak." Edwards, *Spy Catchers of the U.S. Army*, p. 141. We conclude that Cannon discovered a large cache of war loot hidden by the Japanese, which would explain his being given a medal. At that stage of the war, documents would have been of no use, and normally would have been burned. Cannon, who sported a handlebar moustache and went everywhere heavily-armed, was regarded by his contemporaries as a dangerous nut case, of the type satirized by Colonel Kurtz in *Apocalypse Now*. He ran his outfits with an eccentricity that alarmed his men and many of his superiors. He took delight in welcoming new recruits by setting off grenades behind their backs. Men who refused to obey his bizarre orders found themselves facing court martial. But Cannon was protected by General Willoughby and in return did Willoughby's dirty work and wet work. During the occupation of Japan, Cannon organized a hit team that went after anyone Willoughby labeled a 'communist'. After Willoughby left the U.S. Army to work for the Spanish Fascist dictator General Franco, Cannon quickly ended up in the stockade at Fort Sam Houston. After that, he became a contract hit man for the CIA, working for his old pal General Lansdale in operations against Fidel Castro. According to his former comrade-in-arms, Duval Edwards, Cactus Jack committed suicide in Texas in 1981. Given his record, he may have had help. Edwards failed, as did we, to find official confirmation, but Cannon was never seen again. Edwards, *Spy Catchers*, p. 147.

111–Cannon and Machii Hisayuki. Kaplan, *Yakuza*, p. 61. Machii helped Korean CIA kidnap activist (and future president) Kim Dae Jung in Tokyo in 1973. Kaplan, *Yakuza*, p. 183. Machii headed Tosei-kai. Whiting, *Tokyo Underworld*, p. 80. Aside from being the Osabun or godfather of the Toseikai underworld, Machii also was president of Toa Sogo Kigyo Company and operated the ferry company called Kanpu linking Shimonoseki, Japan, to Pusan, Korea. He died of heart failure on September 14, 2002.

111–"movie style gangster". Recollections of ATIS translator on Japanese American Veterans Association website.

111–Cannon Agency in the kidnapping of Kaji Wataru see Johnson, *Conspiracy at Matsukawa*.

111–Cannon and Shimoyama. Schreiber, *Shocking Crimes*, pp. 66-80. Johnson, *Conspiracy at Matsukawa*. Cannon established the Japan Special Operation Branch (JSOB) under G-2, Far East command. Recollections of a former ATIS translator cited above.

111–Cannon arranged plane crashes: According to Professor Yu Maochun of the U.S. Naval Academy, American intelligence agents were responsible for the crash that killed Tai Li. Chief of the OSS Research and Development section designed a bomb that exploded when a plane carrying the device reached 5,000 feet altitude. Most of these bombs were shipped into the China theater. Yu, *OSS in China*, p. 256. Tai Li was apparently the victim of such a bomb. A similar crash in Hong Kong killed Captain James Godwin, who was investigating Tsuji Masanobu. Mackay, *Betrayal in High Places*. Another apparent victim was George Atcheson, senior State Department advisor in Japan, who tried to guide the occupation along more liberal lines. He and his colleagues were constantly harassed by General Whitney, General Willoughby and Colonel Bunker. In August 1947, when MacArthur's inner circle was making the final turn to the far right, Atcheson decided he had to go back to Washington personally to report to the Secretary of State and the White House. His plane crashed in mid-Pacific. See Seagrave, *Yamato Dynasty*, pp. 236-237.

111–KATOH Agency. Kaplan, *Yakuza*, p. 60.

111–Willoughby's incompetence and paranoia. Campbell, "Major General Charles A. Willoughby".

111–Willoughby's files hidden. There is not enough information available to the public to assess Willoughby's performance. Campbell, "Major General Charles A. Willoughby". Willoughby's official files and sensitive personal documents disappeared: Kaplan, *Yakuza*, p. 58. Willoughby's personal papers, purged of all sensitive material, are at Gettysburgh College, Musselman Library.

111–Joseph Keenan profile and background, boozing. Brackman, *The Other Nuremberg*, pp. 54-56 and *Kodansha Encyclopedia of Japan*, Volume 4, pp. 185-86.

112–Tanaka Takayoshi as Keenan's assistant, providing women. Behr, *The Last Emperor*, p. 180. His role in the drug addiction of Empress Elizabeth. Harries and Harries, *Soldiers of the Sun*, p. 245.

112–Shall not be bound by technical rules of evidence: The Charter of the International Military Tribunal Far East (IMFTE). Brackman, *The Other Nuremberg*. pp. 59-61.

112–suborning of Tokyo War Crimes Trials witnesses and perversion of justice. See Seagrave and Seagrave, *The Yamato Dynasty*, Chapter Nine "The Exorcists", pp. 197-219, 341-347.

112–MacArthur's telegram to Eisenhower about the failure to uncover evidence linking Hirohito to war crimes is from *Foreign Relations of the U.S. 1946*, Volume VIII, *The Far East*, pp. 395-97.

113–mysterious deaths of hostile witnesses who might have condemned Hirohito or Prince Asaka. See Seagrave and Seagrave, *The Yamato Dynasty*, p. 207, and Chang, *The Rape of Nanking*.

113–American soldiers released from Japanese POW camps were debriefed and forced to sign oaths of secrecy. This is the standard report from veterans and this information came to us from members of the CFIR.

113–"ATIS ... most prolific of the three analytical agencies in the SWP theater." From Military Intelligence Corps Hall of Fame, "Col. Sydney Forrester Mashbir", at huachuca-usaic.army.mil/mipg/jul-sep/HOF/HOF.html. The role of ATIS is explained in the

Japanese Imperial Government Disclosure Act reproduced in full on our CDs. The ATIS had responsibility for collecting and interpreting the captured documents, used (or withheld) as evidence in the Tokyo War Crimes Trials.

113—There were 185 *Japanese Monographs* generated by Willoughby's war criminal "historians". These are starting to appear on website www.metalab.unc.edu/pha/. Most of these 'historians' were men who had committed grave atrocities in the field. See Morton, *U.S. Army in World War II: The War in the Pacific, The Fall of the Philippines*, "The Sources."

114—English-language editions of Tsuji Masanobu's memoirs list Robert Booth and H. Fukuda as publishers. The title pages include the logo for An Asian Publication. This was a CIA proprietary, and the same publisher that produced Kodama's memoir, *I Was Defeated*, in English-language editions.

114—Tsuji hid in Tokyo under Willoughby's protection while he was being hunted by the government of Great Britain, for war crimes committed in Burma, Singapore, and elsewhere. Ward, *The Killer They Called a God*. Cannon's group solved the problem by arranging the murder of Captain James Godwin, the chief war crimes investigator trying to bring Tsuji to trial. Mackay, *Betrayal in High Places*.

114—When reading extracts from Kodama's memoir, readers are reminded that the English phrasing came from Harvey Fukuda.

114—"I feel supreme anxiety": Kodama, *I Was Defeated*, pp. 202-203. "positively collaborated ": Kodama, *I Was Defeated*, p. 203.

114—The 1947 Diet investigation into M-Fund moneys and Kodama's transfer of $174-million to finance the creation of the Liberal Party is discussed in Schlei, "Japan's 'M-Fund Memorandum": JPRI website.

114—"peeking into an occupied bathroom", "brazenly engaged": Kodama, *I Was Defeated*, pp. 197-199.

114—Harvey Fukuda met Kodama when he was a prisoner in Sugamo. Fukuda was assigned as a translator to work in Sugamo prison with Japanese war criminals. Roberts, "The Lockheed-Japan-Watergate Connection".

114—Fukuda worked for ATIS, and had his own CIA funded publishing, public relations and translation business. Yamakawa Akio, "The Lockheed Scandal: What Do the People Make of It?" Roberts, "The Lockheed-Japan-Watergate Connection". In 1960 Fukuda published a second volume of Kodama's memoirs *Sugamo Diary*. Whiting, *Tokyo Underworld*, p. 351. It was part of the CIA's push to popularise Kodama as its man in Tokyo. By that time, Kodama was full-time on the CIA payroll.

114—Japan-PR was a CIA proprietary company. Both Kodama and Fukuda worked for the CIA.

114—Eugene Dooman's deals in looted tungsten, which he purchased from Kodama's war-loot stash: Whiting, *Tokyo Underworld*, p. 317. Seagrave and Seagrave, *Yamato Dynasty*, p. 272.

114—Fukuda as Kodama's closest aide: Yamakawa, "Lockheed Scandal". Fukuda introduced Kodama to Lockheed in the late 1950s. Roberts, "The Lockheed-Japan-Watergate Connection".

115—Dulles was in Korea June 18-22, 1950: Schaller, *Far Eastern General*, p. 178.

115—Kodama and Machii were reported to be in Dulles's official group that went to Korea: Whiting, *Tokyo Underworld*, p. 86.

115–Kodama as CIA's chief asset in Japan. See Johnson, "The 1955 System".

115–Miyazawa's secret mission to John Foster Dulles. Prime Minister Yoshida sent Minister of Finance Ikeda, Miyazawa and Shirasu Jiro to Washington. Schaller, "Reversals of Fortune", Harvard University Asia Center, Triangular Relations Conference. It is worth noting that while the *Japanese Imperial Government Disclosure Act* is supposed to result in the release of Japanese documents, no similar legislative act enforces the release of U.S. Government-generated documents, such as those related to the San Francisco Peace Treaty negotiations. The U.S. Government continues to hide these documents under the seal of national security.

115–Acheson said "Japan could not pay reparations": Acheson, *Present at the Creation*, p. 539.

115–"To accomplish the treaty negotiations": Acheson, *Present at the Creation*, p. 539.

115–Japan's economic infrastructure and *zaibatsu* wealth as well as homes and private property of Japan's elite were undamaged by strategic bombing: Dower, *Embracing Defeat*, pp. 46-7.

116–300 billion yen in money and materiel was quickly cycled to the *zaibatsu* between August and November of 1945. The deal made by the Japanese government after the surrender. Mainichi, *Fifty Years of Light and Dark*, p. 215 and Roberts, *Mitsui*, p. 377. This also was discussed in the three-part series that appeared in 1979 in the *Shukan Bunshun*. Titled "M-Shigen No Ura No Sinjutsu" (The Truth Behind the M-Fund), the articles ran on October 4, October 25 and November 1, 1979.

116–Tanaka's deals at war's end. Seagrave and Seagrave, *The Yamato Dynasty*, pp. 271, 354, Hunziker, *Kakeui Tanaka*, and Schlesinger, *Shadow Shoguns*.

116–300-million tons of goods. Dower, *Embracing Defeat*, pp. 117, 188.

116–Yen-dollar conversions. This is always tricky, so we give the reader a number of sources to draw upon. The *Final Report on Zaibatsu Dissolution* gives us a rate of about 15 yen to $1.00. According to Bower, *Blood Money*, p. 33, $1 USD in 1940 is the equivalent of $10 U.S. dollars today.

116–The disappearance of 100-billion yen worth of stockpiles: Dower, *Embracing Defeat*, p. 114. This jibes with the 1979 report of *Shukan Bunshun*.

116–264 billion yen in private savings: Dower, *Embracing Defeat*, p. 114.

116–The $300-million ($3-billion in today's dollars) annual revenues from the Japanese drug-trade. Harries, *Soldiers of the Sun*, p. 246. Roberts, *Mitsui*, p. 313.

116–Hirohito's earnings of $50-million a year from his secret bank accounts was known to SCAP. See Manning, *Hirohito: The War Years*, pp. 175, 224. By the early 1930s, before looting most of Asia, Hirohito's personal fortune, according to Cambridge scholar Dr. Stephen Large, was worth $15-million in the values of that time. See Seagrave, *Yamato Dynasty*, pp. 222-224.

116–Japan's elite concentrated on enriching themselves: Dower, *Embracing Defeat*, p. 26.

116–potatoes sold for 4 yen a pound: Dower, *Embracing Defeat*, p. 64. Hirohito's investment income is from Manning, *Hirohito: The War Years*, p. 224.

117–The *zaibatsu* were the most enthusiastic employers of forced labor. *The Economist*, "What's in a Name?" July 8, 2000, p. 74.

117–Like Hirohito, the Japanese elite were only concerned with enriching themselves during the occupation. They "followed the lead of their sovereign". Dower, *Embracing Defeat*,

p. 39. The Nuremberg war crimes trials included Secondary Procedures for the prosecution of German industrialists who had contributed to the Nazi war effort and to mass murder. In Japan, no such trials of the *zaibatsu* industrialists were permitted. The planned trials of German industrialists were, however, cut short because of Washington's decision to completely exonerate all Japanese and German war criminals. To do so, Washington simply cut off funding to the prosecuting offices. See Simpson, *The Splendid Blond Beast*. General MacArthur assured advisors George Kennan and William Draper, at secret conversations in March 1948, that the heads of the *zaibatsu* were "elderly incompetents" not worth prosecuting. MacArthur said: "The brains of Japan had been in the armed forces. He regretted that it had been necessary to eliminate all those brains from public life." With his blessing, they were soon restored to public life, evading any kind of punishment for their war crimes and involvement in mass murder. *Recommendations with Respect to U.S. Policy toward Japan: Memoranda of Conversations with General of the Army Douglas MacArthur, March 1, March 5, March 21, 1948. Top Secret.* National Archives and Records Service.

117–Britain's first treaty draft, clause 39, is quoted from Foreign Office Records 371/92532 p. 109. Public Records Office. Keith Martin and Ron Bridge of the ABCIFER found these documents. They are available online at the ABCIFER website.

117–Britain's first treaty draft, clause 53, is Foreign Office Records 371/92533 p. 118, March 7, 1951. Public Records Office. $200-million in gold in Japan is from Britain's first treaty draft, clause 53, quoted from Foreign Office Records 371/92545 p. 66, reporting on a meeting in Washington D.C. which took place on April 26, 1951.

117–Britain's Treasury remarks about Japan's gold. Foreign Office Records 371/92533 p. 118. Public Records Office.

117 –"authority to modify our attitude". British Foreign Office Records 371/92540.

118–"We have agreed that gold should not be mentioned in the Treaty" is quoted from Foreign Office Record 371/92555 p. 115.

118–The 1951 San Francisco Treaty provided recourse for the well-connected: "Upon application made within nine months of the coming into force of the present Treaty between Japan and the Allied Power concerned, Japan will, within six months of the date of such application, return the property, tangible and intangible, and all rights or interests of any kind in Japan of each Allied Power and its nationals which was within Japan at any time between 7 December 1941 and 2 September 1945…Property whose return is not applied for by or on behalf of the owner or by his Government within the prescribed period may be disposed of by the Japanese Government as it may determine." Most eligible people simply were not apprised of this clause and missed their chance, so the government of Japan got to keep the properties. State Department cronies were alerted to this opportunity, and cashed in. Unclaimed properties, including very expensive land around Tokyo, later feathered the nest of Prime Minister Tanaka in extremely lucrative real-estate deals, discussed in Chapter Nine.

119–The Japanese government, colluding with neutral Swiss banks, siphoned off millions of dollars intended for the care of Allied prisoners of war. Even Red Cross parcels were looted and sold on the black market. See Henk Zeeman, "Don't forget the Japanese" in *Sunday Star Times*, June 16, 1996.

119–Canadian efforts to provide compensation for her citizens in the 1951 Treaty and the way in which this was thwarted by the U.S. Government is from the British Foreign Office 371/92591, p. 48, 27 August 1951. Public Records Office.

119–British Foreign Office discussions about extending Article 16 benefits to include civilians is found in Foreign Office 371/92591 p. 4. Public Records Office. See abcifer.com/ww2/newpage1.

119–In 1996, some 700,000 victims were still alive. Zeeman, "Don't Forget the Japanese". Their numbers have been drastically reduced, as they die off. Japan's strategy of stalling is obviously the best solution. All Japan has to do is to wait until all the claimants are dead.

119–Clinton's remarks about "an important day" were quoted in Jonathan Wright, "U.S. Germany Clear Way for Slave Labor Deal", Reuters, June 13, 2000.

119–"The peace treaty put aside": Ambassador Foley's remarks were widely reported in the international press. Kinue Tokudome, "POW Forced Labor Lawsuits Against Japanese Companies", *JPRI Working Paper*, No. 82, November 2001, available on the JPRI website. Since leaving government, Foley has now become a paid advisor to Mitsubishi, one of the giant companies being targeted by former slave-laborers. Foley and his wife, who is a paid consultant of Sumitomo, another firm involved in these lawsuits, see no "conflict of interest" in their employment by Japanese industry. The U.S. State Department officially supported the Foleys' "rights" while denying the rights of victims.

119–Christopher Lafleur's marriage to Miyazawa's daughter. Eamonn Fingleton, "The Anomalous Position of Christopher Lafleur", *Unsustainable*, May 15, 2001 on the web. For many years after World War II, as Fingleton points out, American diplomats were automatically disqualified from serving in Tokyo if they were married to Japanese nationals. This rule applied even to officials of low rank and in the case of marriages to Japanese nationals who had no connection to the Tokyo establishment. Although Foley left the State Department to become a Mitsubishi lobbyist, and Lafleur was recalled to Washington after a storm of protest over his personal relationship to Miyazawa, the Chrysanthemum Club is alive and well. Three former U.S. ambassadors, Thomas Foley, Walter Mondale and Michael Armacost, denounced American POWs in the wake of the World Trade Center bombings – likening them to terrorists in an Op Ed piece that appeared in *The Washington Post*, September 25, 2001. They defended the rejection of POW demands for compensation, saying this "would undermine our relations with Japan, a key ally. It would have serious, and negative, effects on our national security". They accused Congress and POWs of endangering White House efforts "to forge a coalition to combat terrorism". The story was widely reported. See *San Francisco Chronicle*, October 1, 2001. Their stance has been denounced by many, including John Dower. See Kinue Tokudome, "POW Forced Labor Lawsuits Against Japanese Companies", *JPRI Working Paper*, No. 82, November 2001, available on the JPRI website and also at www.expows.com/position1.htm.

CHAPTER NINE

120–Today, the M-Fund has assets in excess of $500-billion dollars. It had $35-billion in 1960. See Schlei, "Japan's M-Fund Memorandum, January 7, 1991", *Japan Policy Research Institute, Working Paper No. 11*, May 1995. Obviously, this is an educated guess, based on many indicators, not a documented figure.

120–Kishi: Schaller, "America's Favorite War Criminal: Kishi Nobusuke", *Japan Policy Research Institute*, Working Paper No. 11, May 1995. For Kishi's wartime criminal involvement with the *Ni-ki-san-suke* clique, including opium monopoly boss Hoshino Naoki, Mantetsu president Matsuoka Yosuke, and Nissan boss Aikawa Gisuke, see Roberts, *Mitsui*, p. 312.

121–Christopher Hitchens, "The Case Against Henry Kissinger: Part One: The Making of a War Criminal", in *Harper's Magazine*, February 2001. Verso later published a book by Hitchens expanding on this.

121–"M-fund was made subject to joint U.S.-Japanese joint control": Schlei, "Japan's 'M-Fund' Memorandum". Schaller, *Altered States*, p. 55. Schaller does not make any direct connection between the Procurement Coordination Subcommittee and the M-Fund.

121–Kishi's personal fortune acquired during the war: Schlesinger, *Shadow Shoguns*. Kishi, a war criminal, Kodama's financial backing of, and co-signing the declaration of war: Schaller, "America's Favorite War Criminal".

122–Kishi groomed by Kern, Dooman, Packenham and other ACJ members: Schaller, *Altered States*, p. 125, Seagrave *Yamato Dynasty* pp. 231, 237, Whiting, *Tokyo Underworld*. Dooman's tungsten deals with Kodama. See also Weiner, "CIA Spent Millions", *The New York Times*, October 9, 1994.

122–Kishi's English lessons: Schaller, "America's Favorite War Criminal"; Scotch: Schaller, *Altered States*, p. 125.

122–John F. Dulles said Kishi was America's last bet: Schaller, "America's Favorite War Criminal". Kishi was 'our boy.' Schaller, *Altered States*, p. 144.

122–Ishibashi Tanzan "the least pro-American": Schaller, "America's Favorite War Criminal".

122–U.S. Government backed Kishi with secret funds. An American diplomat said that the U.S. had put its "money on Kishi, but the wrong horse won": Schaller, "America's Favorite War Criminal". See Weiner.

122 –audible relief: Schaller, "America's Favorite War Criminal".

122–$10-million secretly supplied to the LDP by the CIA. Schaller, *Altered States*, p. 136, Weiner.

122–Alfred Ulmer quoted in Schaller, *Altered States*, p. 136, and Weiner.

122–Douglas MacArthur II, U.S. ambassador to Japan 1956-1961. He married the daughter of Truman's Vice President, Alban Barkley.

122–Finance Minister Sato Eisaku's appeal to Douglas MacArthur II. "[Sato] has tried to put the bite on us". Tim Weiner, "CIA Spent Millions to Support Japanese Right in 50s and 60s", *The New York Times*, October 9, 1994. (online at www.geocities.com)

122–Nixon told Kishi: testimony of Norbert Schlei reproduced on our CDs.

123–Richard Allen told Norbert Schlei: "I was always puzzled." Schlei testimony on our CDs.

123–"sticking it to the Japanese": Nixon quote in Schaller, *Altered States*, p. 211.

123–CIA officials say that covert aid to the LDP stopped in the early 1970s, because "By that time, they were self-financing." This was the result of Nixon's transfer of the M-Fund. See Weiner, "CIA Spent Millions", *The New York Times*, October 9, 1994.

123–Tanaka's 3-million yen bribe to Kishi. Schlesinger, *Shadow Shoguns*, p. 110.

123–Riken and the atomic bomb. Schlesinger, *Shadow Shoguns*, p. 28-29.

124–Tanaka as "governor of the *private* bank of Japan". Schlesinger, *Shadow Shoguns*, p. 110.

124–Tanaka "bought ministry of Finance": Schlesinger, *Shadow Shoguns*, p. 132.

124–Cost of being member of Diet. Schlesinger, *Shadow Shoguns*, pp. 224-225.

124–Tanaka's role in raising funds for the M-Fund from the sale of confiscated properties is from Schlei, "Japan's 'M-Fund' Memorandum".

125–National Social Welfare Association. Dozens of pages of documents from this association are reproduced on our CDs. See Fifty-Seven Folder.

125–Tsutsumi family: Downer, *The Brothers,* and Havens, *Architects of Affluence.* Seagrave, *The Yamato Dynasty,* pp. 278-282. See also Tsutsumi Seiji's "57" documents reproduced on our CDs.

125–Osano Kenji. Schlesinger, *Shadow Shoguns,* p. 73, Havens, *Architects,* p. 212. Some sources told us Osano was not ethnic Japanese, but the richest Korean in Japan, with the Korean family name Choi.

125–Tanaka Club members of the National Welfare Council are listed in documents reproduced in the Fifty-Seven Folder on our CDs. Tanaka Club had an inner circle of just over thirty billionaires, and an outer circle of mere mega-millionaires. Once the inner circle had exchanged their government bonds for "57s" and Dai-Ichi Bank cashier checks, Tanaka could not resist selling other "57s" to the outer circle. These sales were handled for him by an assistant named Miss Aoyagi Hatsu, who had worked for Tanaka since the 1950s. Aoyagi persuaded hundreds of wealthy Japanese to purchase "57s". Without telling anyone, she is said to have charged the buyers a substantial surcharge that she put into her own private accounts, pocketing more than 2.8 billion yen ($28-million). In 1985, Aoyagi and a colleague were arrested and convicted of fraud. At their trial, no "57s" were produced as evidence. The convictions were based solely on 'confessions' by Aoyagi and her co-defendant. Apparently, Aoyagi and her colleague took the fall, in exchange for condolence gifts from people endangered if the truth about the "57s" had come out. Their conviction was a fortuitous one, for it enabled the Ministry of Finance, the LDP, and the government of Japan to declare (falsely) that all "57s" were fraudulent and counterfeit. Letter of Norbert Schlei to U.S. Ambassador to Tokyo, Mike Mansfield. No evidence was produced at the Aoyagi trial. Lausier affidavit, 10 January 2001. Both documents reproduced in full on our CDs.

126–Gotoda discovered, brain. Von Wolferen, *Enigma of Japanese Power,* pp. 143, 151.

126–Gotoda secret policeman. "Japan Starts Search for Next Prime Minister", *Minneapolis Star Tribune,* Feb. 4, 1996. Gotoda said "I had a deep relationship with the CIA." See Weiner.

126–Kanemaru Shin: Seagrave, *Yamato Dynasty* pp. 269-70, 275-78. Schlesinger, *Shadow Shoguns.*

126–Lockheed, Kodama and Tanaka. Seagrave, *The Yamato Dynasty,* pp. 272-274, Roberts, Whiting. CIA Paul Helliwell and his off-shore Bahama's Castle Bank appear to have been involved in the transmission of the bribe money to Kodama.

127–Prime Minister Sato's death by poison, and his widow's benefit. Schlei, "Japan's 'M-Fund' Memorandum". Mrs. Sato's name appears on documents in "57s" on our CDs.

127–Mysterious circumstances of Harvey Fukuda's death. Whiting, *Tokyo Underworld,* p. 200. Aoki Ihei's 'suicide'. Schlesinger, *Shadow Shoguns,* pp. 236-37, Schlei, "Japan's M-Fund Memorandum".

128–Affidavit of Professor Lausier, 10 January 2001. Reproduced on our CDs.

128–Printing of the "57s" and the Japanese government involvement. See Lausier affidavit and Schlei to *The National Law Journal.* Letter of 12 April 1996.

129–Kanemaru backing Takeshita for prime minister. Takeshita and Kanemaru linked by the marriage of their children; 'the hatchet' and 'the fileting knife.' Schlesinger, *Shadow Shoguns.*

129–Nakasone took over control of M-Fund. See Schlei, "Japan's M-Fund".

129–Kanemaru Shin negotiated for "57s". Schlei to authors, email 21 September 2000. Kanemaru's "57s" see Schlesinger, *Shadow Shoguns*, pp. 246-47. Schlesinger does not call them "57s". Gotoda's 60-million yen in checks. Schlei letter to Mike Mansfield. Reproduced in full on our CDs

130–Dean Acheson wanted to bomb Cuba. Authors' interview with Schlei, March 18, 2001. Schlei was a legal advisor to President Kennedy on Cuba.

130–How Takahashi and others became Schlei clients. Schlei to *The National Law Journal*. Schlei court testimony reproduced on our CDs.

130–Built-in flaws allowed the Ministry of Finance to decide, case by case, whether or not to honor the 57s. Schlei testimony reproduced on our CDs.

131–Takahashi's background, his student organization funded by M-Fund money funneled through the CIA's Committee for a Free Asia. From Schlei's trial testimony, reproduced on our CDs. For readers unfamiliar with literature on CIA proprietaries, the Committee for a Free Asia was part of Lansdale's Office of Policy Coordination operations in Manila, set up under Frank Wisner. There was a parallel outfit called the Free Europe Committee. Schlei did not know the CIA connection until we explained this to him in 2001. Seagrave, *Marcos Dynasty*, p. 147.

131–Schlei meeting with Mansfield was covered in a memo he wrote to the ambassador, reproduced in full on our CDs. Schlei's conversations with Stanley Sporkin and Richard Allen are from his court testimony reproduced on our CDs.

132–foreign manipulation. Johnson, "The 1955 System and the American Connection".

132–Bravender Ah Loo. We drew her story from court testimony and appeals. Reproduced on our CDs.

133–The Smith-Barney letter used to entrap Ah Loo is reproduced on our CDs.

133–Ah Loo: documents and appeals from U.S. court records. Bank of Japan reply to John Blomfield of Merrill Lynch conveyed to Mrs. Ah Loo at Transfield, from p. 8: Decision on Schlei's Appeal, *US Court of Appeals 11ᵗʰ Circuit #95-3004 USA vs Norbert Schlei Sept 18, 1997*. Switzerland reply to Ivester, from p. 10: Decision on Schlei's Appeal, *US Court of Appeals 11ᵗʰ Circuit #95-3004 USA vs Norbert Schlei Sept 18, 1997*. Reproduced in full on our CDs.

135–That the court found "no evidence" to support Schlei's assertion that the U.S. Government gave money to officials and politicians in Japan. See *US Court of Appeals, Eleventh Circuit. No. 95-3004 United States of America v. Norbert Schlei*. For some irony in this assertion by the court, see *Japanese Imperial Disclosure Act* and *Interim Report*. All three documents reproduced in full on our CDs.

135–Studeman's response to *The New York Times*: Johnson, "The 1955 System".

135–Schlei never was arrested. He knew Federal prosecutors intended to stage his arrest in a melodramatic fashion as soon as the Grand Jury proceedings were concluded and an indictment was handed down. Schlei's Tampa attorney, Peter George, tried to negotiate a voluntary surrender. The Feds were not having any of that because they wanted to arrest Schlei and interrogate him at FBI Headquarters without an attorney present. Schlei and George cleverly outwitted them by going out of their way to cooperate with the Grand Jury. Schlei took a seat in the Tampa courtroom, while George sat by the door of the Grand Jury chamber upstairs. When the indictment was handed down, and the Feds emerged, George rode down in the elevator with them to the courtroom where Schlei was waiting, and Schlei voluntarily submitted to the indictment, so it was not necessary to arrest him. The Feds were suitably deflated. Letter to authors from William Schlei, son of Norbert Schlei, 16 August 2002.

136–Charges of tampering with a witness, and the reaction of the Appeals court. See September 1997 Appeals decision reproduced in full on our CDs.

136–Sena arrest and release. David Sommer, "$50-billion case dropped", *Tampa Tribune*, December 7, 1995; "Japanese Bond Fraud Hits Tampa" n.d. *Tampa Tribune*; Bruce Vielmetti, "Secret Service Agent Targeted in Bond Fraud Investigation", *St. Petersburg Times*, December 8, 1995. Schlei to authors, email 21 September 2000.

137–Schlei testified that he wrote to Takeshita while he was Minister of Finance in January 1968, "telling him that I represent these people who hold these financial instruments, that I'm going to be in Japan and I would like to have an interview with him to discuss the matter." Takeshita did not reply. See Schlei court testimony reproduced on our CDs.

137–Alexander Haig: When contacted by the *Financial Times* for information about his part in arranging the deal with Takeshita, Haig refused to be interviewed. Haig's background in Douglas MacArthur's staff, and with Kissinger, Nixon, and other details, are from a variety of other sources: State Department Electronic Research Collection, Seymour Hersh, "Cambodia: The Secret Bombing", excerpted from *The Price of Power*, 1983, available online at Third World Traveler.

137–According to the eyewitness, those present at the meeting included Haig, an aide to the president of Paraguay, the governor of Paraguay's central bank, top MIC executives from Israel, and various financial and legal advisors. Haig is also said to have talked by phone to Paraguay's president.

CHAPTER TEN

When the Marcoses fell from power, we were asked to do a multi-generational biography of the family along the lines of *The Soong Dynasty*. The result, published in 1988, was *The Marcos Dynasty*. (They hoped to found a dynasty, but failed in its execution.) We knew the Philippines well, visiting it first in 1947, and making many subsequent visits to all parts of the archipelago including Imelda's home in Leyte. At the time, we were not aware of the torture of Major Kojima and the Santa Romana recoveries. However, sources we developed then later proved useful for research on this book, including members of the Marcos family, senior Filipino military officers, leaders of the Overseas Chinese community, U.S. Government officers at the embassy under several administrations, and CIA agents then and now. We also benefited from being acquainted since the early 1960s with Lansdale, Cline, and many of their deputies in the field in China, Korea, Japan, Thailand, Laos, Vietnam, Indonesia, and the Philippines. All those contacts were useful in this chapter.

140–It is comic that the Philippine government should persist in claiming that Santa Romana is only an imaginary character like Peter Pan, when Philippine courts have probated his will, when his brother Miguel is a retired judge, and when the Aquino administration sent financial experts loaded down with Santa Romana's multiple passports and many bank statements to meet in Hong Kong with Australian financial expert Peter Nelson. Nelson wrote about his meeting with these officials. See Nelson, *Anatomy of a Bank Job*.

140–General John Singlaub was informed by CIA sources that Japanese were excavating and smuggling gold back from the Philippines in this manner. Audio tapes of the conference in Hong Kong, provided to us by Robert Curtis.

140–Singlaub confirmed that the Marcos fortune came from Japanese war loot recovered in the Philippines. See Singlaub, *Hazardous Duty*, p. 499. Singlaub's involvement and close friendship from OSS days with William Casey, Paul Helliwell and Ray Cline is well documented in his memoir. Today, Singlaub is the only one of this group still alive. It is not difficult to grasp why he is so popular with Special Forces and other elite military groups. He is a genuine war hero, famous for his audacity. One of us spent several hours talking with Singlaub one evening and found him immensely likeable.

141–Our account of what happened to Roxas is based on "*The Supreme Court of the State of Hawaii, Roger Roxas and the Golden Buddha Corporation v. Marcos, November 17, 1998. No. 20606, Appeal from the First Circuit Court Civ. No. 88-0522-02.*" The "Factual Background" was pieced together by the Court from thousands of pages of testimony, transcripts and hundreds of hours of videotaped testimony. Neither defense nor plaintiff disputed this summary. We reproduce this document in full on our CDs and hereafter refer to it as the *Roxas Court Case*. Except where noted, all details about Roxas come from this document. In addition, Daniel Cathcart very generously gave us access to the files of his law firm, which run to hundreds of thousands of pages.

142–Gene Ballinger provided us with the detail about how Roxas located the tunnel entrance by first finding the Japanese bunker. He also gave us the photographs reproduced on our CDs showing Roxas at the bunker, and with the Gold Buddha. This was only one of several tangents pursued by Roxas in finding the tunnel. Daniel Cathcart provided us with the other tangents.

142–gas from bodies, recollection of Roxas from Gene Ballinger in conversation with the authors.

143–Pio Marcos, paternal uncle of Ferdinand. Seagrave, *Marcos Dynasty*, p. 39.

143–Roxas and Ken Cheatham in a photograph made just after Roxas's discovery with the real Gold Buddha. Photograph reproduced on our CDs.

144–Fabricating the fake Buddha. Letter of April 24, 1986, to the Presidential Commission on Good Government, from Justo Tariga reproduced on our CDs.

144–Marcos threatened a personal vendetta. See Louis Trager, "Finder of Gold Buddha", *San Francisco Examiner*, November 17, 1986.

144–Roxas blinded by the beatings. See *Filipino Reporter*, 01-30-1997. From Ethnic News Watch. Daniel Cathcart's dossier provides grim reading on the brutal beatings of Roxas.

145–Plaza Miranda bombings, and sequence of events from Plaza Miranda to Martial Law: Seagrave, *Marcos Dynasty*, pp. 237-246. We also have a recent videotaped testimony of a source in the Marcos clan, lasting several hours, but have been asked not to reveal the identity for reasons of personal safety. We have assigned this source the pseudonym Doctor Peso. Daniel Cathcart provided us with clarifications on details of Plaza Miranda, from his interviews of Roxas.

145–Daniel Cathcart is the source on torture of Olimpio Magbanua.

146–Our source in the Marcos clan told us Marcos and Santa Romana became associated in the 1960s and that Imelda previously had known Santa Romana. This is supported by information on the Sandy Anstalt (Santa Romana Foundation) in Liechtenstein.

146–Santy's physical description is drawn from photographs we reproduce on our CDs. One was provided by Tarciana Rodriguez, the other two by his family during interviews in 2000-2001.

146–good-natured. See Tarciana's sworn 1995 statement on our CDs.

146–Santy's brother, Judge Miguel 'Mike' Santa Romana, listed in the Philippine Bar Records, available online. Interviewed in 2000-2001.

146–Santy's aliases are listed in the Tarciana affidavit, Malacanang Will, Santa Romana correspondence and documents, Ackerman letter, and the affidavit of Alfredo R. Ramos reproduced on our CDs. Most of these documents are part of the material found in Marcos's personal safe at Malacanang Palace after he fell from power. Palace shredder machines broke down in the final days, so Marcos was unable to destroy all his documents.

146–Santy's marriage license to Julieta Huerto is reproduced on our CDs. It was one of the documents found in Marcos's personal safe at Malacanang Palace.

147–DNP Enterprises. Document of August 1, 1974, signed by Santy (as J. Antonio Diaz), appointing Tarciana Rodriguez National Treasurer of the DNP. Reproduced on our CDs.

147–DNP Umbrella logo. Included in the Tarciana sworn statement. Handwritten flow-chart of the Umbrella and how it worked, including CIA agents, Mafia figures, and other organizations, as set out on paper in the handwriting of President Marcos. This came into our hands from Doctor Peso, a close blood relative of Ferdinand who was intimately informed and authoritative.

147–The story of Wallace Groves, the Allens and Benguet: Seagrave, *Marcos Dynasty*, pp. 31, 77, 214, 228, 335-336, 364.

147–"made instant millions for X, Y, Z". See Santy's CIA memo reproduced on our CDs.

147–Paul Helliwell and Castle Bank. See Seagrave, *Marcos Dynasty*, pp. 361-364, Jonathan Marshall, *Drug Wars: Enforcement as Counterinsurgency*, interview with Alfred McCoy, November 1991 by Paul De Rienzo Marble Collegiate Church conference on *Causes And Cures: National Teleconference on the Narcotics Epidemic*, available online.

148–Shig Katayama and Lockheed. See Marshall.

148–William Colby and Nugan-Hand. See Alfred McCoy.

148–BCCI, the third in the string of CIA banks after Castle Bank and Nugan-Hand. See Alfred McCoy.

148–CIA Deputy Director Richard Kerr on BCCI and its relationship to the Agency. See Adams and Frantz, *Full Service Bank*, p. 325.

148–It may seem improbable to the reader that Santy's assets were moved about so invisibly and fluidly. But since 1970, as much as $1-trillion dollars a day has been moved electronically around the world "with the speed of light and with unsurpassed secrecy" by the New York Clearing House Interbank Payment System (CHIPS). Moving Santy's millions was a hardly noticeable drop in the bucket. See Adams and Frantz, *Full Service Bank*, p. 111.

148–Other CIA alumni like Santy were virtually invisible and enormously wealthy. Sam Cummings, who started Interarmco in the 1950s, later became an expatriate living in Monaco. Starting without any visible assets, by the time of his death in the mid-1990s he was described as a billionaire. See Patrick Brogan and Albert Zarca, *Deadly Business: Sam Cummings, Interarms and the Arms Trade*. W.W. Norton, 1983. It is interesting to note that Santy learned all about Sam Cummings in his 1973 Washington meeting and wrote the following: "Samuel Cummings creation Inter-Armco – International Armaments Corporation private (agency) arms dealer for advanced and sophisticated military hardware and equipment; with warehouse and offices in the waterfronts of Alexandria, Virginia; Manchester England; Monte Carlo of Monaco; Singapore – Raffles; Pretoria South Africa for untraceable with STERILE arms and weapons which are always available for quick immediate use. This is the agencies second most important source after Pentagon of military material for special operations Secret Wars, interventions and limited guerrilla pocket wars. [all *sic*]" Santy's memo is scanned and reproduced in full on our CDs.

149–The size of Santa Romana's fortune. $20-billion for Santy's 'personal fortune' – apparently referring to his fortune in American banks. Melvin Belli lawsuit reproduced on our CD. $20-billion is also a figure sometimes cited for assets of the Sandy Anstalt/Santa Romana Foundation accounts. $50-billion is a figure given by one of Tarciana Rodriguez's associates who confronted Citibank's John Reed with passbooks and account numbers. $50-billion is the amount mentioned in connection with the lawsuit described in Chapter Fifteen against Citibank for moving Santy's assets from New York to Nassau. All these figures refer to Santy's 'personal fortune' as opposed to other accounts for which he was title holder and, presumably, just the gatekeeper.

149–Details about Marcos rise to political power and the role of Lansdale men, CIA, and the U.S. Government in assisting with his election, see Seagrave, *Marcos Dynasty*, Chapter Eight.

149–Imelda's $3.3-million shopping spree and Citibank account: *Marcos Dynasty*, p. 197.

150–Information on the Sandy Anstalt includes documents from Dulles brothers' law firm Sullivan and Cromwell reproduced on our CD.

151–Mention of the Collins deposition is contained in the lawsuit filed by Melvin Belli. It was New York attorney Eleanor Piel who took the Collins deposition. Eleanor Piel, correspondence with the authors. The $43-million cash deposit transaction overseen by Collins of Citibank. Belli lawsuit reproduced on our CDs. Tarciana fails to meet with Collins. From Tarciana's 1995 sworn statement reproduced on our CDs. That the threesome did not know exactly what was in the account. Tarciana noted "we were not given any document pertaining to what we had opened." Tarciana sworn statement, on our CDs.

151–The lawsuit filed by Belli on behalf of Luz in 1993 lists the Hongkong & Shanghai Banking Corporation, as having "an account representing cash deposits in the name of J. Antonio Diaz using customer identification number 0000001246137". Reproduced on our CDs. There is quite a file on the court case available at the Superior Court of California, County of San Francisco website. Go to sftc.org and type in the Court Case number 955366. Some of these documents also are reproduced on our CDs.

151–Santy's Malacanang Will is reproduced on our CDs.

152–Santy imprisoned for rumor mongering. Tarciana's 1995 sworn statement.

152–Santy was invited to Washington and handwrote many pages of notes about the CIA's global activities as he learned of them during his visit in 1973. The notes are reproduced in full on our CDs.

152–The disarray of the CIA at the time Santy was called for the secret meeting to Washington in 1973: a good summary is Thomas Powers, "The Department of Dirty Tricks", *Atlantic Monthly*, August 1979, Volume 244, No. 2. Available online from the *Atlantic Monthly* website.

153–Tarciana's description of her appointment as National Treasurer on August 1, 1974, her sworn 1995 statement. The letter signed by J. Antonio Diaz appointing her is reproduced on our CDs.

153–Santy's heavy drinking. His death certificate(s) list cirrhosis of the liver as the cause of death. Both certificates are reproduced on our CDs.

153–Tarciana's knowledge of the Hanover and Wells Fargo accounts is from her sworn statement of 1995. Santy lists Hanover and Wells Fargo in his memo of August 5, 1974, reproduced on our CDs. Lansdale worked on the Wells Fargo advertising account in the 1940s. Wells Fargo is one of the banks listed in the Mel Belli lawsuit.

153–Tarciana received instructions – verbal and written – from Santy during the last days of his life. From Tarciana's sworn statement. The written instructions for dispersal of his assets include the memo signed by Santy dated August 15, 1974 on our CDs.

153–Santy's holographic will is reproduced in full on our CDs.

154–Santy/Lansdale UBS account. Documents of the UBS account with Lansdale's name. Reproduced on our CDs.

154–Lansdale was now in disfavor. When President Kennedy forced him to retire, he was promoted to major general as a sop. CIA sources said he had shown signs of insanity, but that depends on your political views. During the Bay of Pigs fiasco, he proposed sarcastically that a U.S. nuclear sub off Havana could shoot fireworks into the night sky and all Cubans would lay down their guns thinking it was the second coming of Christ. A likelier explanation, with Washington turning into Camelot and the Kennedys filling posts with Ivy League liberals, is that Lansdale was too involved with the extreme right, including the John Birch Society, the Hunt brothers, and others. However, the Kennedys were active in pursuing aggressive policies against Castro and appear to have been fully aware of plans by the Agency to assassinate him. Lansdale was the intermediary in giving the assassination job to the Mafia.

CHAPTER ELEVEN

155–"Marcos's \$12-billion fortune came from Yamashita's gold." John Singlaub, *Hazardous Duty*, p. 499.

155–Eyewitnesses saw Marcos's gold. See *Roxas Court Case* (reproduced on our CDs); Robert Curtis's sworn deposition, *Roxas Court Case* (these six hours of videotape are in our archives); Cathcart legal archives; Seagrave, *Marcos Dynasty*, Chapter 18.

155–Ben's narrative comes from interviews we did with him at Tunnel-8 and Tunnel-9 near Dulao, Nueva Viscaya, January 2000. This particular interview continued for four days. It was conducted for us by James Raper, who was managing editor of the *Virginia Pilot* in Norfolk, Virginia, when it won a Pulitzer Prize for investigative reporting. Some small details, and the dialogue, were drawn from Ben's diary and recollections he wrote down in the 1950s.

158–This is the date Ben Valmores gave for the Villacrusis trip. Ben told us that several months later, in 1969, he met Pol Giga for the first time. Villacrusis sent Giga to find Ben, and soon afterward Villacrusis came to Bambang personally. Raper interview, Tape 3 Side A, January 2000. Authors' archives.

158–Villacrusis trip to Tokyo. Justo Tariga said Brig. Gen. Onofre T. Ramos, comptroller of the Philippine armed forces for Marcos, went to Tokyo with Villacrusis and two other army colonels, where they were given a treasure map by "a ranking Japanese officer who was…a cousin of Emperor Hirohito". Tariga's letter is reproduced on our CDs. Villacrusis said he was told that the Japanese had hidden \$100-billion worth of treasure in the Philippines and it would take over 100 years to recover it all. He discussed this with Robert Curtis, who confirmed the details as recalled by Tariga, Villacrusis, and his widow.

158–Marcos and Sasakawa: Seagrave, *The Marcos Dynasty;* Kaplan, *Yakuza*.

159–Sasakawa's boast that he was 'very close to Marcos': Sasakawa interview with

Guardian correspondent Robert Whymant, 6 September 1975. Document provided to the authors by David Kaplan, who at the time was with the Center for Investigative Reporting in San Francisco.

159–Ishihara: Documents recovered from Presidential Security Command after Marcos lost power refer to secret contacts with Lord Ichibarra in Tokyo. So far, all our efforts to identify this man have failed. It is a common Japanese name, with various renderings including Ishivara, Ishiwara, Ishihara, Ishibara. According to Pol Giga, a Navy Captain Ishihara Noburo arrived in Manila in late February 1943 with the special assignment of Imperial Inspector General. After Japan's surrender, the U.S. occupation authorities forced Japan to abandon a titled aristocracy, outside of the first tier of the imperial family. A Japanese journalist, who asked not to be named, told us that a number of intelligence officers were privately honored by the emperor at the end of the war, without their honors being made public, and this may explain why Ishihara remains a ghost. One of the possibilities is Colonel Tsuji Masanobu. There are other clues that suggest Ishihara was not Prince Takeda. For example, it was Ishihara who told Villacrusis to find Giga, and to send Giga to look for Ben Valmores, something Prince Takeda is not likely to have done. Also, it was Ishihara who later set up a phone conversation between Ben and Prince Takeda, so everyone would know whether this was the correct Ben Valmores.

159–Details about Tsuji's life. Tsuji, *The Fall of Singapore*, Ward, *The Killer They Called a God.* Seagrave, *Lords of the Rim.*

160–Chang Tso-lin and Major Giga. Behr, *The Last Emperor.*

160–Giga screening prisoners for the Japanese secret service came from a source that has known Giga for thirty years. The *kempeitai* used turncoats in this fashion all over Asia. In Singapore and Manila thousands of men were executed on the nod of a turncoat. Giga claimed he had no choice but to do this to keep from being killed himself. Dale van Atta and Don Goldberg of Jack Anderson's investigative staff were hired by us in the mid-1980s to go to Manila. When they interviewed Giga, he claimed that he had been the valet of a Japanese general, and "stole" the treasure maps from General Yamashita's headquarters in Baguio in the last months of the war. Giga told Goldberg that he and Ben Valmores were both half-Japanese turncoats working as valets to a Japanese general, and in the last weeks of the war they had together stolen the maps from Yamashita's headquarters in Baguio. When Goldberg tried to confirm this with Valmores, Giga told him that Ben was dead. Some of Giga's false histories were thus related in *The Marcos Dynasty*. We now are correcting them

163–Ernesto Mata. Seagrave, *Marcos Dynasty*, p. 193.

163–Benhameen: We asked Ben if Kimsu seemed happy to speak to him on the phone. He replied: "Yes, he cried. I can feel that he cried because according to his voice."

164–General Barangan's report is reproduced on our CDs.

165–In 1974, Ben recognized Prince Takeda on television among a delegation of Japanese who came to Manila to persuade Lt. Onoda Hiroo to surrender. After his 'rescue' Onoda wrote his memoirs, which were immediately translated into English. See Onoda, *Never Surrender.*

165–In 1987, Prince Takeda published a memoir titled *Above and Below the Clouds.* (The title refers to his early life as a Japanese godhead above the clouds, and as an 'ordinary person' after the war, below the clouds.) These and other biographical details of Prince Takeda's postwar life were provided to us by a Japanese journalist, who culled them from the clip files of Tokyo newspaper archives.

165–"If it were possible to sum up Takeda" the *Japan Times* quoted in Harris, *Factories of Death*, pp. 143, 263 note 58.

166–The story of Onoda is from his memoirs *Never Surrender.*

166–Sasakawa and the Lubang island resort. See Seagrave, *Marcos Dynasty*, pp. 323-324.

166–Kasabuchi. Ben's recollections, diary, interviews.

CHAPTER TWELVE

We first began researching the story and archives of Robert Curtis in the early 1980s. By then Curtis no longer lived near Reno. He was tracked down and interviewed for us by Don Goldberg, an investigator on the staff of columnist Jack Anderson. Goldberg later became an investigator for the U.S. Congress. Our findings from the Goldberg interviews were published in *The Marcos Dynasty.* Some years later, when we discovered the personal involvement of Prince Chichibu and other imperial princes in Golden Lily, we began a personal correspondence with Robert Curtis and this time made a far more thorough review of his archives, which include over 60,000 documents related to Japanese looting, hiding the treasure, and what became of the gold after it was recovered. During the last four years, we have been in frequent contact with Curtis, and he and his wife have been extraordinarily generous in allowing us to study their collected maps, photos, documents, audiotapes and videotapes. We have re-researched and cross-checked all of Curtis's recollections and the documentation supporting them. Curtis was so thorough in keeping records that we became convinced his version of events was highly accurate. Curtis died of heart failure in 2004.

169–The Allies re-smelted all recovered Nazi gold with the exception of a single gold bar. See *Nazi Gold: The London Conference, 2-4 December 1997*, p. 32. This report says Allied record-keeping about recovered gold was sloppy – both with regard to the amounts of gold found and the hallmarks on the gold: "all bars [were] melted and re-refined into good [London] delivery. The identity of the original bars was, therefore, lost." President Truman appointed Edwin S. Pauley, a rich oil man and one of the conservative oligarchs in the Democratic Party, to head commissions charged with reparations for Germany and Japan. Pauley brushed aside the whole issue of Japanese reparations and hidden assets. In fact, Pauley was closely linked to the oil interests of Robert O. Anderson, father of Robert B. Anderson, one of the brain-trust behind the Black Eagle Trust. Seagrave, *Yamato Dynasty*, p. 294.

169–So long as gold purchased in Costa Rica had the right mineralogical fingerprint, no questions were asked about its origin, even though there always seemed to be a discrepancy between Costa Rican gold-output, gold reserves and gold sales. See "Country-watch Costa Rica" for information on gold production 1993-1997. Country-watch is available on the Internet.

169–Gold as the perfect vehicle for laundering. Journalist David Kaplan described how dirty money becomes clean gold: "Top refiners in Switzerland sell their gold to jewellery makers in Italy, the world's largest supplier of fine gold jewellery. The Italian jewellery is sold to... Panama [buyers]... Once in Colon, ...the Italian gold is sold to Colombian front men for the cocaine industry... The gold is then smuggled back to Colombia, where some dealers ... melt down the jewellery, recast it into ingots, and sell the gold to refiners in the United States or Switzerland, producing a stream of income that looks legitimate. ...Investigators have found that in some cases, the launderers even buy back the same gold they've just sold for refining in the United States, paying for it with yet more drug money.

... The [gold] industry's bookkeeping practices can be nightmarish, and gold traders often are shielded by ethnic and family bonds. ...So much of the international gold trade operates 'off the books' that it is an easy target for organized crime. While many gold companies operate legitimately... law enforcement officials depict an industry riddled with money laundering, tax fraud, smuggling, and dubious bookkeeping. Gold has become the money laundering mechanism of choice." David Kaplan, "The Golden Age of Crime". *US News Online*, November 29, 1999. If keeping track of the trillions moving through CHIPS everyday is impossible, gold, once it loses its fingerprint, is the easiest of all things to launder.

169–Jonsson's invitation from the U.S. Air Force colonel: Robert Curtis to the authors. Curtis and Jonsson remained close friends until Jonsson's death.

170–Information about Curtis and Jonsson, and their involvement with Marcos, is from the *Roxas Court Case*, reproduced on our CDs, except as otherwise noted.

170–There are roughly 32,000 ounces in a metric ton of gold.

170–Norman Kirst to Robert Curtis, February 22, 1975. Letter reproduced on our CDs.

171–Curtis was incredulous. Curtis to authors. See also Curtis's narrative of his involvement with Marcos on our CDs.

171–"I was convinced." Curtis to authors.

171–Curtis called Marcos very ruthless. This remark was made by Curtis on Philippine television, a show called "Probe". Curtis sent us a videotape.

171–The presidential yacht was named for a 777 site that Marcos recovered at Camp Aguinaldo.

171–aide of President Nixon and aide of President Ford: from the Curtis video deposition for the *Roxas Court Case*. Photographs of these two men with Curtis and Marcos aboard the Marcos yacht in 1975 are reproduced on our CDs.

172–Curtis inspection of Roxas Gold Buddha at the Summer Palace. Curtis video deposition, *Roxas Court Case*. Photographs of Curtis at the Summer Palace with Marcos, Ver, Villacrusis and other members of LEBER group reproduced on our CDs.

172–The signed Leber Contract is reproduced on our CDs.

172–This refinery was supposed to be built on land next to a deep-water harbor, allowing propane carriers to discharge fuel for the furnaces, and freighters to ship the gold out. The site was on the tip of Bataan opposite Corregidor. On our CD we reproduce original correspondence, shipping bills and telex-messages concerning the transfer of the refinery to the Philippines by Curtis.

173–*Nachi* sinking by Allied air strike on 5 November 1944. See Tully, Anthony P., *The Nachi-Mogami Collision,* online. The deliberate sinking of the *Nachi,* see Seagrave, *The Marcos Dynasty.* Details about the *Nachi*'s depth and treasure maps. Robert Curtis to authors, March 21, and June 2, 2000. According to Ben Valmores, he and Prince Takeda watched the sinking of the *Nachi* from shore, and observed the survivors being machine-gunned by the crew of the submarine.

173–Japanese efforts to salvage the *Nachi* in the early 1970s as discussed by Villacrusis and Curtis, April 5, 1975. Transcript of the conversation is reproduced on our CDs. Machii was in the oil business with California assemblyman Kenneth Ross, who was later questioned about money-laundering. Machii's role in the recovery of the *Nachi* is from Seagrave, *Marcos* Dynasty, p. 315. Machii's club and Ross, see Whiting, *Tokyo Underworld,* pp. 185-187, p. 292.

173—Marcos nationalized the Luzon Stevedore Company. Curtis to authors March 29, 2001.

173—*Nachi* survivors coming to Manila. Robert Curtis to the authors. Captain Kanooka Enpei, see Tully. Tully says that 807 men died when the *Nachi* went down and that 220 survived.

174—*Nachi* recovery represented $6-billion worth of gold in 1975 prices of $65 an ounce. In 1992, this represented $42-billion U.S. dollars. See Curtis lawsuit against the Marcos Estate reproduced on our CD.

174—Colonel Buchholtz had been Col. Bunker's assistant in Tokyo. Bunker was still active in the Birch Society when Curtis came to them with his loan proposal. When he was introduced to Bunker, Curtis asked in mild jest whether he was any relation to Bunker Hunt. The colonel snarled: "Bunker is my last name." Curtis to the authors September 7 2000.

174—The Hunt Brothers. Robert Curtis to the authors, email of August 29, 2000. Robert Welch, Larry MacDonald, Jay Agnew, Larry Bunker and Herbert Buchholtz are all dead. Contracts Curtis made with the Birch Society are reproduced on our CD. Seagrave, *Marcos Dynasty*, pp. 307-309. It is curious that nearly all the Americans involved in treasure hunting in the Philippines are on the far right politically.

174—Buchholtz had a degree in mechanical engineering from the University of Kansas, so he understood technical details that were over the heads of the Birch moneymen. Buchholtz worked for Curtis as an engineer, keeping an eye on operations for the Birchers. He died May 16, 1992.

175—Col. Laurence Bunker, a charter member of the John Birch Society. Bunker obituary, *The New York Times*, October 11, 1977.

175—Curtis's agreements with the Birch Society are reproduced on our CDs.

176—Curtis was taken to 35 or 40 of the treasure sites selected from Ben's maps. Curtis videotape deposition, *Roxas Court Case.*

177—Marcos tried and failed at Teresa-1, according to an army sergeant who was given the job of guarding the site.

177—Ishikawa was one of the centers of Japanese ceramic production.

177—Map and interpretation of carabao horns at the Teresa site is reproduced on our CDs. See also Seagrave, *Yamato Dynasty.*

178—Age Construction Company. Correspondence between Villacrusis and the Age Construction Company, Age Company payrolls for the excavation work and a photograph of Robert Curtis with Age Construction employees are all reproduced on our CDs.

178—Teresa-2 massacre of POWs. All 1200 prisoners of war at Teresa were ordered into the tunnels and buried alive using bulldozers to seal the opening. See the annotation to page 2 (above), which discusses the policy of the Japanese Ministry of War to exterminate POWs and other examples of men buried alive. Regarding POWs who were murdered individually and in groups, we will never know exact figures. Official military records record such deaths only as KIA (killed in action) or MIA (missing in action). Where bodies were recovered, regardless of the cause of death—battle wounds or massacres of defenseless prisoners—the man was listed as KIA. MIA covered all the other categories where remains were not found. Therefore, no official records exist of the POWs who were buried alive at Teresa-2, Sado Island, and elsewhere, or otherwise were exterminated by the Japanese. Major Richard Gordon, of Battling Bastards of Bataan, explained these points to us.

179–death flowers: There are many varieties of stinky or carrion flowers in the islands, such as the species *Amorphophallus paeoniifolius*, sometimes known as *A. campanulatus*.)

179–The agreement Curtis signed with Commonwealth Packaging specifically cites his association with the Philippine treasure hunts of Ferdinand Marcos, naming all eleven members of the Leber Group, in which Mike Alonzo was Ferdinand Marcos and Jimmy de Veyra was General Ver. The agreement also included mention of "the treasure trove". This contract is reproduced on our CDs.

179–Security precautions outlined by Curtis. See Curtis to General Ver, memorandum May 31, 1975. Reproduced on our CDs.

179–In the end Marcos only took the gold bars his men found in the old army trucks in the tunnel, leaving the rest for later. According to two people who participated in the inventory, one a military officer, the other an economist, Marcos recovered 20,000 metric tons. Curtis video deposition, *Roxas Court Case*.

180–Curtis and his colleagues were nearly murdered. Jack Anderson's syndicated stories about Marcos and his gold recoveries appeared on July 4 and 5, 1975. Marcos thought Curtis was the source, so he ordered his men to ruin Curtis financially and to bankrupt his company in America. To do so, Marcos reached an agreement with the John Birch Society, which collaborated in ruining Curtis, and for good measure also filed lawsuits against Curtis. Not satisfied with all this, in early September Marcos ordered his men to murder Curtis and his partner MacAllaster. Anderson's source actually was Primitivo Mijares. Curtis recollections of his trip to the Philippines, *Roxas Court Record*, and Curtis video-deposition. See Seagrave, *Marcos Dynasty*, for background on Mijares.

191–Primitivo Mijares requested political asylum in the United States, which the State Department refused. It then became known that Marcos tried to bribe Mijares to reverse his Congressional testimony, which brought the U.S. Justice Department into the case. Before the bribe could be investigated, Mijares vanished, telling journalists that he was returning to the Philippines on a 'daring sortie'. Mijares was escorted on this trip by General Ver, passing through Guam. In Guam, according to our sources, Mijares was taken to an isolated beach where he was murdered by Ver. According to his widow, Judge Priscilla Mijares, two years later their sixteen-year-old son Luis received a phone call saying his father was alive and inviting the boy to come see him. Luis insisted on going. His body was later found dumped outside Manila, his eyeballs gouged out, his chest perforated with stab wounds, his head bashed in, and his genitals mangled. We were told that this gouging out of the eyeballs was the signature of General Ver. See Seagrave, *Marcos Dynasty*, pp. 268-275.

184–International Gold Cartel's Mafia-style approach to Marcos is from Curtis to authors.

184–Black Eagle Trust. See Seagrave, *The Marcos Dynasty,* Chapter Eighteen.

184–Marcos maneuvered Curtis into bankruptcy. Curtis to the authors, email 25 August 2000.

184–Curtis's law suits. Curtis provided us with court documents.

185–Curtis, Laxalt and the Senate Intelligence Committee. See Seagrave, *The Marcos Dynasty*, p. 309.

185–Marcos's offer to buy back the maps, and the shipment of gold to Curtis. One of the participants at this meeting confirmed to us that the planes had left for Nevada, but were diverted at the last moment. Videotape interview with confidential Marcos source, Doctor

Peso.

CHAPTER THIRTEEN

186–Johnson-Mathey Chemicals, Johnson-Mathey Bank. For a detailed account of JMB's involvement with Marcos, see *Marcos Dynasty*. See documents reproduced on our CDs.

186–Because of their influence behind the scenes, members of The Enterprise sometimes are called a 'shadow government'. In Britain, the party out of power is considered to have a shadow cabinet with a shadow foreign minister or shadow health minister. There is nothing sinister about European shadow cabinets, but America's shadow government has a sinister connotation because its agents meddle in domestic and foreign affairs, without any kind of peer review. The emergence of numerous Private Military Firms (PMFs) in America in recent years reportedly is intended in part 'to privatize foreign policy and national security'. This means conducting foreign policy and national security without peer review by Congress or the American people.

186–PIOs (private intelligence organizations) and PMFs (private military firms). Interested readers can do an online search for companies such as MPRI (Military Professional Resources, Inc.), Executive Outcomes, Sandline International, Vinnel Corporation, Control Risks Group, DynCorp, Kroll Associates, Saladin Security. See *Bulletin of the Atomic Scientists*, "No peace", May/June 1996; Henry Sanchez, "Why Do States Hire Private Military Companies"; Stuart McGhie, "Private Military Companies". Douglas Valentine took a look at the role of PMFs and their outgrowth from Operation Phoenix in his book *Operation Phoenix*. See also "The New Mercenaries", *Wilson Quarterly*, Summer 2002, p. 88. And P. W. Singer, "Corporate Warriors: The Rise of the Privatized Military Industry and Its Ramifications for International Security", in *International Security* (Winter 2001-02), MIT Press Journals.

187–The recycling of conservatives back into government. President George W. Bush's appointment of Eliot Abrams to the National Security Council in June 2001 is a case in point. As assistant secretary of State, Abrams was a figure in the Iran-Contra scandal. He was convicted of withholding information from Congress, and was also involved in obtaining secret funds for the Contras. He was pardoned by President George H.W. Bush on Christmas Eve 1992. See Tom Bowman, "Iran-Contra Figure Returns to Government as NSC official", *Detroit News*, June 30, 2001, online. He worked closely with Singlaub and other "private" citizens. See Singlaub, *Hazardous Duty*, pp. 503-504.

187–Family Jewels. See Powers, "The Department of Dirty Tricks".

187–Singlaub was president of the American chapter of the World Anti-Communist League. The Philippine chapter was known as the MacArthur Foundation.

187–Details about William Casey and his career come from a variety of sources including Senate hearings on his appointment as director of the CIA, available online. Other sources McGehee, *Deadly Deceits*; Princeton Alumni Association; McClintock, *Instruments of Statecraft*.

187–Casey started off working for the accounting company RIA, founded in 1935 by Carl Hovgard. Today the company is a unit of Thomson Tax & Accounting of the Canadian Thomson Corporation. RIA maintains a website.

187–John 'Pop' Howley. An obituary was found at the Princeton University website, providing much of this information.

187–Singlaub talks about Casey and Helliwell in his memoirs *Hazardous Duty*.

188–Information about Capital Cities and Casey. Mazzocco, *Networks of Power*.

188–The Manhattan Institute has a website.

188–Executive Order 12333 can be found online. Reagan Presidential Library.

188–Ted Shackley and 'privatization' of clandestine services. See James Goulden, "Aldrich Ames and the CIA's darkest hour", in *The Washington Times*, September 25, 1995, elibrary.com. McClintock, *Instruments of Statecraft*.

189–Operation Phoenix. See Valentine, *Operation Phoenix*.

189–Colonel Stan Fulcher quote and "legacy of ashes". See Valentine, *Operation Phoenix*, pp. 420, 421, 428.

190–"Singlaub comes in and out". Mydans, "Mystery in Manila", *The New York Times*, Feb. 18, 1987.

190–Special Forces officers took part in Singlaub's treasure hunts. Singlaub brought with him at least 37 Americans, Asians and other nationals who served with the U.S. Special Forces in Vietnam. They came in in groups of two and three travelling under false names. Kathleen Barnes, "Controversial US General Joins Fight in Philippines", *Toronto Star*, Feb. 17, 1987. *Philadelphia Inquirer*, Feb. 15, 1987. C.S. Mangold, "US General Said Behind Mercenaries". Pam Belluck, "General's Mystery Philippines Trip", *San Francisco Chronicle*, Feb. 18, 1987.

190–Secret gold shipments. Seagrave, *Marcos Dynasty*. W. Scott Malone did research on this for BBC, including nearly 100 pages of information. Arlene Friedman did additional investigation into the shipments. Information and witnesses discovered by her were crucial to the Roxas Court Case. Dan Cathcart provided us with many details.

191–CIA, Rewald, Zobel and Marcos. See Seagrave, *Marcos Dynasty*, pp. 196, 304. During the same period, we now know that the Sultan of Brunei (another ardent polo player) was lending millions to the Agency as part of the secret Iran-Contra arms deal of Lieutenant Colonel Oliver North. Eliot Abrams was involved in these loan deals from the Sultan. See Bowman.

191–McMicking acquired and built a 4,400-acre luxury resort at Sotogrande, Spain, including a large yacht harbor and world-class golf courses. He bought the acreage in 1962, before Marcos became president. The Zobel clan tried, even at that time, to interest Marcos in investing in the resort. It is a favorite haven for political exiles from around the world.

192–Nelson Airfield and Peninsula Hotel site. Mutuc wrote to Zobel about this Golden Lily site. Curtis was anxious about recovering it before construction work interfered, and wrote to Villacrucis on April 4, 1975: "The observation tower of the Jap air field was to be contracted by the Ambassador [Mutuc]. Has that been accomplished?" Both documents are reproduced on our CDs.

192–Gregorio Araneta III married Irene Marcos in June 1983. Gregorio is the stepson of Lansdale's professional killer, Napoleon Valeriano. The wedding cost $20-million. Waldheim and King Hassan. See Seagrave, *Marcos Dynasty*, p. 391.

192–Some of the $13.4-billion appears to be part of the Sandy Foundation accounts.

192–Documents on the China Mandate and related bank accounts and transactions are reproduced on our CDs.

193–Imelda's trip to China with Bong-Bong. Seagrave, *Marcos Dynasty*, and Bonner, *Waltzing with a Dictator*.

193—On our CD, we reproduce a hand-written list itemizing accounts Santy and Marcos hid in various banks in Hong Kong and mainland China. Imelda maintained that all of her own secret accounts already had been recovered. *Philippine Daily Inquirer*, "2 banks linked to Marcos Loot Tan's Tenants", August 4, 2000. The deal Imelda signed giving 35 percent to bounty-hunters for their part in retrieving her hidden assets in HSBC, Bank of China and other mainland banks. *South China Morning Post*, "Group Conspired to Bribe HSBC Chief" July 28, 2000. The accounts Imelda was trying to access were the same ones Peter Nelson was asked about in the 1980s, vis-à-vis Santa Romana.

193—Help the poor. In Imelda's case, charity begins at home. She needed the money to pay court judgments. See Frank Longid, "Marcos Millions Destined for Victims", *South China Morning Post*, August 1, 2000.

194—$13.4-billion Swiss account and Imelda's "I know we used to have money" are from AP Online, "Marcos Says $13.4B May Be Hers", August 23, 1999.

194—By 1945, MacArthur was a wealthy man, though by no means in the same class as Hirohito. Early in 1942, when he was under siege on Corregidor, MacArthur was given half a million dollars by Philippine President Quezon – apparently to stiffen his resolve. Although a senior U.S. military officer could not accept money, President Roosevelt let MacArthur keep it. He also had prewar investments made by him, and in his behalf, by Whitney and McMicking, who were his investment advisors in the Philippines. These included substantial holdings in Benguet gold mines and the Ayala group of companies including San Miguel Beer. When MacArthur returned to the United States in 1951, his personal baggage included a large collection of Japanese medieval armor and other antiquities now on display at the MacArthur Memorial in Norfolk, Virginia. He also shipped over a chest filled with gold and jewels, which was confiscated by the U.S. Treasury and has since disappeared. Nobody really knows how much MacArthur was worth at his death, and our efforts to examine the will of his widow, who died in 2001, were thwarted. Scholar Petillo discovered the 1942 'gift' to MacArthur, Schaller, *Far Eastern General*, p. 59. See also Seagrave, *Yamato Dynasty*, pp. 182-183. Information about MacArthur's chest of treasure came from news clippings provided to us by the MacArthur Memorial Library.

194—Hirohito's assets and income, and SCAP's knowledge. Manning, *Hirohito: The War Years*, p. 224.

194—"We've come a long way". Sanwa website: sanwabank.co.jp/English

195—Showa Trust. Natividad Fajardo's letter to Imelda Marcos on the Showa Trust. Reproduced on our CDs.

195—Marcos's Treasure Lady listed Natividad Fajardo as the account holder for bullion moved to the Hang Lung Bank in Hong Kong in the early 1980s.

195—Reagan's plan for Gold Standard. Joseph T.Salerno, "The Gold Standard", *Policy Analysis*, No. 16, September 9, 1982. www.cato.org/pubs/pas/pa016.html. See also Alan Greenspan, "Can the U.S. Return to a Gold Standard?" in *The Wall Street Journal*, September 1, 1981.

196—Before joining the U.S. Government, Treasury Secretary Regan had been chief executive officer of Merrill Lynch. Among the many secret Marcos accounts that later surfaced was a $35-million account at Merrill Lynch, carried under the name of Arelma, a shell-company. See Blanche Rivera, "Rights Victims Will Focus on Arelma Fund", *Philippine Daily Inquirer*, Jan. 4, 2001. Online. Regan was forced to resign during the Iran-Contra scandal.

196—Casey trip to Manila to pressure Marcos for gold bullion. We were told about this by

Doctor Peso, our source in the Marcos family, and have it on videotape. Doctor Peso was in the adjoining room at the Manila Hotel during this meeting.

197—We are not sure what happened to gold bullion stored in the underground vaults behind the summer palace in Mariveles in Bataan, designed by Robert Curtis and Wes Chapman; it may have been loaded aboard barges and taken to Subic. Or it may be the gold bullion currently stored in Marcos family vaults at Mt. Apo, and in Ilocos Norte, which is ruled by Governor Bong-Bong Marcos. This was the testimony of one of the witnesses in the *Roxas Court Case*, who visited Mt. Apo with Bong-Bong.

198—U.S. Treasury informed Ernesto Maceda that a gold certificate Marcos had with him in Hawaii was 'fake'. Zobel details are from the *Philippine Inquirer* in 1999. inquirer.net/issues/apr99/apr12/features/fea_main.htm That the gold certificate Zobel showed the Philippine Senate was pronounced 'fake' by the U.S. Treasury. Senator Pimentel's website. "Pimentel Asks PCGG to Verify Alleged $4-billion Marcos Money".

198—Casey resigned on February 2, 1987, Treasury Secretary Donald Regan resigned a week later.

CHAPTER FOURTEEN

The two failed recovery attempts at Corregidor provide readers with a useful contrast. The Curtis attempt on Crockett Battery required burning through thick concrete, and all seemed lost when the enhanced thermite went overboard. Yet new enhanced thermite could have been provided easily through diplomatic channels. A recovery effort involving a modern submarine should not be allowed to collapse because of inadequate supplies of thermite. But Curtis was so shocked and discouraged by the incompetence of his men in the field that he abandoned the effort when he could have persevered. The failure of the recovery attempt by Nippon Star was the result of inadequate preparation, and misguided expectations on the part of two generals – something crucial to any military operation. In the Philippines, rival military forces and rival police forces make any arrangement problematical. To avoid interference, Singlaub said he paid off everybody in advance, even including the New Peoples Army (NPA), yet he relied on a permit issued by a person who was not empowered to grant it. This cost Singlaub's group many millions of dollars in gold bars that were right under their feet. General Schweitzer stated that President Reagan, President Aquino, U.S. Ambassador Bosworth, and the commanders of both Clark and Subic were all thoroughly briefed and fully involved. So why did they not have the correct permit? If what Schweitzer said was true, they could have had a permit signed by President Aquino herself, with representatives of President Aquino present while the colonels dug. When generals make assumptions that are wrong, nobody is in a position to correct them. This is like putting the Pentagon, State Department, and White House in the hands of the Keystone Kops. Curtis taped all the meetings and phone calls associated with these recovery efforts, and we have full copies of all those audiotapes, which we have reviewed several times. Much of what Curtis said about these events was independently verified by *The Las Vegas Sun*'s Gary Thompson, and also by Arlene Friedman when she was working on the Roxas Buddha case for Daniel Cathcart. *The Las Vegas Sun* ran a 24-part series on this story in 1993.

200—"I was mad": Curtis to authors July 3, 2000.

200—Corregidor had a number of treasure vaults. Marcos had already opened up Golden Lily's "hospital site" in the Malinta Tunnels, but failed to find the gold hidden there. According to the maps in his possession, Curtis knew this was a 555 site. Curtis to authors March 31, 2001. Curtis decided against targeting this site, because two men could never do justice to a 555 site. So he chose the Crockett Battery site.

200—Valmores visited all these sites with Prince Takeda. "Ben is the one who knows all about the Corregidor sites," Curtis told us.

202—Ten years later, the same government sent its own commandos back to Corregidor, without involving Curtis, to open three sites including the Crockett Battery. This was during the same period when Singlaub's group tried to retrieve the gold at the Movie Theater site. Although many millions of dollars were at stake, both groups came away empty-handed because of bungling.

202—Toshi's story and photographs were given to us by a confidential source on the basis of anonymity.

202—Johnson-Mathey Bank became so reckless in its dealings with Marcos gold that a scandal broke in the press and there were rude questions in Parliament. To keep the scandal from spreading and forfeiting British domination of the world gold trade to Zurich, the Bank of England and the four remaining members of the gold cartel intervened. JMB was taken over by the Bank of England, and its executives sent packing. Prime Minister Thatcher blocked all inquiries, but there were reports that large quantities of black gold had been smuggled into Britain through JMB. The bullion division of JMB later was sold to the Australian banking and gold-mining syndicate, Mase-Westpac, also rumored to have been part of the Marcos gold-laundering web.

202—Konsehala V. Santiago, Marcos gold lady: One of the agents for the deal was Daniel K. Swihart, so this came to be called the Luxembourg deal or the Swihart deal. See Seagrave, *Marcos Dynasty*, pp. 348-351. Documents from the gold deal including those signed by the U.S. Consul in Luxembourg, are reproduced on our CDs. Dacus said when word leaked out, President Marcos had two of his gold brokers, Pedro Palafox Laurel and Domingo Clemente, murdered. Dacus was authoritative as a source because he was married to the daughter of a man who was employed by Marcos in the Black Room at Malacanang Palace where tortures and murders took place. Despite this indiscretion and murder, members of the Laurel family continued to be involved in gold deals. See Seagrave, *Marcos Dynasty*, p. 349. See also *Roxas Court Case*.

202—Dacus's story also appeared in the press. See William Rashbaum, "Marcos Gold", Hearst News Service, 28 July 1986, and Kathleen Ellison, "Treasure Hunters Seek Marcos' alleged troves", *San Jose Mercury News*, 23 November 1986.

203—One take on the *Awa Maru* recovery is Dingman, *Ghost of War*. However, Dingman supports the absurd position of the governments of the United States and Japan that no gold or treasure was aboard the ship when it was sunk. Technically, the *Awa Maru* was a "cartel" ship sailing under Red Cross rules, authorized to carry patients, food, and medical supplies destined for POWs, and was painted olive drab rather than white with a green cross (as were other Japanese hospital ships, real and fake). But she was sailing in violation by using this cover to carry weapons, ammunition, aircraft, war-loot and VIP families.

204—*Op ten Noort* recovery. The *Torrens Tide* has since had her name changed to *Star Tide II*. Information provided to the authors by Albert Kelder. Fifty-three color photographs of the Japanese-Australian recovery teams at work (from a confidential source) are reproduced on our CDs. We have not been able to confirm the Australians' escape with the gold, but the same source maintains that the Australian participants moved the gold into the market too hastily, causing angry repercussions.

204—The Enterprise was taken to court by The Christic Institute in May 1986, six months before the Iran-Contra Scandal broke. The 29 defendants included retired major generals

Richard Secord and John Singlaub; former CIA officers Ted Shackley and Thomas Clines, and Contra leader Adolfo Calero. The lawsuit charged that they constituted a criminal racketeering enterprise that had engaged in gun-running, drug-smuggling, money-laundering and political assassination, not only in the Contra war in Nicaragua, but during covert wars stretching back to the early 1960s. See Avirgan v. Hull, 86-1146-CIV-KING and Avirgan v. Vidal 87-1545-CIV-KING. U.S. District Court Southern District of Florida. The Christic suit was published in book form as *Inside the Shadow Government*. The case was thrown out of court. Interestingly enough, Daniel Sheehan, General Counsel to The Christic Institute at that time, then became personally involved in searching for Golden Lily loot in the Philippines in 2000. He attempted to get Robert Curtis to turn over the treasure maps to a colleague. We have seen the Sheehan agreement prepared for Curtis's signature.

204–Singlaub describes his release of the Allied POWs on Hainan Island. See Singlaub, *Hazardous Duty*, pp. 83-101. At that time, he was working in the field with Paul Helliwell. William Casey was his OSS case officer.

204–Nippon Star, Phoenix Exploration, and Helmut Trading. Documents on our CDs identify these PMFs, their officers, and locations of incorporation. Alan Foringer was an officer of all three companies, making for an interesting interlocking directorship. The exact relationship of these companies to the CIA is impossible to define, and not particularly significant, because one of the purposes is to obscure those connections. In any case, there is overlap in some personnel.

204–Phoenix Associates. See Valentine, *Operation Phoenix*, p. 428.

204–Singlaub describes his involvement with Nippon Star in *Hazardous Duty*, pp. 498-503. He avoids any mention of Phoenix in these pages.

204–Marcos's fortune came from recovered Japanese war loot, from only a few sites. More than a hundred remain. Singlaub, *Hazardous Duty*, p. 499.

204–Singlaub's percentage of a recovery and the percentages to be shared among others are detailed in the organizational chart Alan Foringer included in his letter to Robert Curtis (George Armstrong). Schweitzer as president and CEO of Nippon Star was entitled to 1 percent and an additional 1 percent for his role as military advisory. Singlaub, Graham, Keagan and Vessey were all marked down for 1 percent. In addition, Singlaub and Schweitzer were to take another 4-6 percent of profits going to Fleetwood. What this boiled down to in terms of hard cash depended on how much was recovered. They were expecting to recover $100-billion worth of treasure. The organizational chart produced by Foringer is included on our CDs.

205–Documents related to The Enterprise, and Curtis's involvement, are reproduced on our CDs. See especially the Foringer file, which contains letters from Foringer to Curtis, Enterprise organizational charts, Enterprise contracts signed with Curtis, Enterprise work-agreements.

205–Curtis provided us with tape recordings of these meetings he had with Singlaub and the others at the Mandarin Hotel in Hong Kong. Some transcripts of these recordings are reproduced on our CDs.

207–Singlaub's earlier efforts at the Alfonso site and the Calatigan Bay site. In addition to materials we obtained from Curtis and others who were present, Singlaub gives his own version in *Hazardous Duty*, pp. 499-502.

208–Teddy Locsin. Curtis tapes and Singlaub's *Hazardous Duty*, p. 502.

208–"Cory doesn't do anything". Singlaub tapes, Curtis archives. According to three independent witnesses, Singlaub and Ray Cline were talking directly with Jose Cojuangco,

President Aquino's brother. The Cojuangco family (which is of Hokkien Chinese origin) are among the richest and most powerful landowners in the Philippines. Seagrave, *Marcos Dynasty* and *Lords of the Rim*. See Belluck, "General's Mystery Philippines Trip".

208—Singlaub brought in 37 Special Forces veterans for treasure hunting. They were Americans, Asians and other nationals who served with the U.S. Special Forces in Vietnam, which probably means that many had participated in Operation Phoenix and later in El Salvador operations. They came in in groups of two and three travelling under false names. Kathleen Barnes, "Controversial US General Joins Fight in Philippines", *Toronto Star*, Feb. 17, 1987. *Philadelphia Inquirer,* Feb. 15, 1987 C.S. Manegold "US General Said Behind Mercenaries". Pam Belluck, "General's Mystery Philippines Trip", *San Francisco Chronicle*, Feb. 18, 1987

208—Foringer's letter to George Armstrong. This was Robert Curtis's codename at Nippon Star. Reproduced on our CDs.

209—Philippine American Freedom Foundation. Such names have a certain unctuous quality, which makes them smell artificial from birth. Foringer letter to Curtis, and the Enterprise organizational charts reproduced on our CD.

209—Contracts of C & B Salvage, Nippon Star, Phoenix Exploration and Helmut Trading are reproduced in full on our CDs.

209—Phoenix Exploration. John Harrigan was a veteran of CIA covert operations in Iran, Nicaragua, and El Salvador. He and his wife Joan were activists from America's religious right. They ran Phoenix Exploration and Nippon Star. Curtis was told that Harrigan set up Nippon Star around the generals, only to conclude, "it was the biggest mistake of his life". The quote is from John Lemmon, on the Curtis Hong Kong tapes for July 26, 1987. The Harrigans later divorced and Joan Harrigan married John Singlaub.

209—Singlaub said, "We will fly at least a ton of the gold to Benguet." Curtis Hong Kong tapes. See the transcript reproduced on our CDs. It is interesting that Benguet comes into the picture once again, having been involved repeatedly in the story of laundering Philippine gold since the mid-1940s, later passing into Mafia hands. The Agency has done a lot of 'hot-bunking' with the Mafia.

210—Schweitzer, Singlaub and the Corregidor debacle. Curtis to authors, 27 June 2000, 16 & 17 December 2000. Since Curtis 'gave' the Movie Theater site to the generals, a gift worth billions, it is fitting that he should have the last word on it.

210—Curtis told us this was Daniel 'Rock' Myers, a legendary figure.

210—General Fidel Ramos, head of the Philippine Armed Forces and later president,. was a West Point graduate with close family ties to Marcos. His father, Narciso Ramos, was Ferdinand's uncle.

211—Singlaub's high profile and flair for attracting publicity. Foringer letter to Curtis (George Armstrong) on our CDs.

211—GeoMiliTech. Seagrave, *Marcos Dynasty*, pp. 360-376, 423-430. Singlaub was on the advisory board of GeoMiliTech and brought many of his buddies into the group, including General Daniel Graham. All were involved in Iran-Contra arms smuggling as Singlaub details in *Hazardous Duty*, pp. 471-476, 487-492.

212—Foringer's ill-health, his colleagues in Manila, last days and death. Authors' correspondence with John Foringer, Alan's brother. John supplied us with the medical records from the Manila clinic where Alan died. We withhold these documents from publication at his request.

212–Curtis took the precaution of insisting that McDougald sign a confidentiality agreement in which he promised not to publish anything growing out of their discussions until Curtis approved the content. This confidentiality agreement did not stop McDougald from publishing several books that vilified Curtis, making him a scapegoat for everything negative associated with the Fort Santiago recovery project. We have seen the confidentiality agreement signed by McDougald.

212–Noel Soriano did not personally involve President Aquino in the Bonafacio Bridge project, but he appears to have brought in her billionaire brother, Jose Cojuangco, one of the most influential ethnic Chinese tycoons in the Philippines. Curtis wrote to President Aquino. His letter is reproduced on our CDs.

212–Booby-traps and the tragedy at Ft. Santiago. Authentic Golden Lily treasure maps often show what type of booby-traps were used. Bombs are depicted by a turtle. Water traps are shown by wavy lines. Sand and rock falls are shown by angle marks, ////// for left, \\\\\\ for right. But the fatal sand trap at Fort Santiago was not shown on the map Curtis was using. Curtis tapes, 28 May 1992, interview with Gary Thompson of *The Las Vegas Sun*.

213–According to a written statement, 21 February 1989, Craig Nelson said he had joined Soriano, McDougald, and Filipino attorney Mario Ongkiko in a new corporation to pursue the Bonafacio Bridge and Fort Santiago projects, and Soriano "directed all activities and made all final decisions".

214 –Statement by Colonel Canson to Charles McCubbins, 23 February 1989.

215–Bonafacio Bridge gold: One of Curtis's associates in the late 1980s and early 1990s was Jerry D, a supplier of gold jewelry to K-Mart, Wal Mart and a number of other large department stores. Jerry received a call from Soriano and was invited to Manila International Airport to see the gold. It was in odd-sized bars and not London Standard. Jerry made an offer for the gold, but Soriano would not accept the price. What happened to the gold after Jerry saw it is not known. Curtis videotaped discussions with Jerry about all of this, and provided us with a copy of the videotape. Curtis to authors, March 31, 2000. Videotape of Jerry D's meetings with Curtis, authors archives.

215–We have read the entire Grand Jury testimonies of Charles McDougald and George Wortinger. These were provided to us by a confidential source, and by law cannot be circulated or released on our CDs.

CHAPTER FIFTEEN

216–The Gold Buddha court award. The verdict of the jury was $22-billion. Plaintiffs were entitled to pre-judgment interest from the time the gold was stolen at 10 percent simple. After the verdict was received, plaintiffs made a motion before Judge Milks to add the interest due. She did. With interest, the judgment rose to $43-billion and change. The judgment entered against the estate of Marcos was $43-billion and change for the Golden Budha [sic] Corporation and $6-million in favor of the estate of Roger Roxas. Daniel Cathcart to the authors August 2, 2002. Except as noted, the narrative about the court case is taken from the public court records.

217–"We dismissed that story." Marcos reaction to Roxas lawsuit. Louis Trager, "Finder of Gold Buddha Says Marcos Stole It", *San Francisco Examiner*, November 17, 1986.

217–"As long as it's legal." Friedman quote, see Michael P. Lucas, "Golden Opportunity", in *Los Angeles Times*, December 3, 1996. elibrary.com.

217–Cathcart got Roxas on the television series "Unsolved Mysteries". Roxas spent a lot of time with Cathcart in Los Angeles, while he was participating in the television show.

218–"Eureka", Friedman. Al Martinez, "Drool-Drool", in the *Los Angeles Times*, January 10, 1997.

218–Some of Cheatham's story is taken from Bill Ibelle, "Jury Orders Marcos to Pay $22 Billion", from *Lawyers Weekly USA*, January 13, 1997. Cheatham also told Ibelle about the CIA threat. *Roxas Court Case* (reproduced on our CD).

218–We obtained the photos of Cheatham, Roxas and the Buddha from Gene Ballinger. Several of these are reproduced on our CDs.

218–Luis Mendoza testimony about his assay of the Buddha. See *Roxas Court* Case and Ibelle.

219–Dacus was a participant in the Marcos Swihart Luxembourg gold deal mentioned in earlier chapters. See Seagrave, *Marcos Dynasty*, pp. 348-51. Arlene Friedman's interview with Dacus was reported by Katherine Ellison in the *San Jose Mercury News*, "Treasure Hunters Seek Marcos' alleged troves", November 23, 1986. Friedman is identified under the pseudonym of Sally Denton Samuel.

219–Friedman mugged, Cathcart's law offices bugged and raided and spied on. See "Golden Opportunity", *Los Angeles Times*, December 3, 1996, and *Filipino Reporter*, January 30, 1997, at elibrary.com.

220–Roxas' death by poison. Details provided to us by Daniel Cathcart. See also *Filipino Reporter*, January 30, 1997, at Ethnic News Watch.

220–Roxas's brother Danilo was beaten by Ver and his thugs when the Gold Buddha was stolen in 1971. When the Roxas Case came to trial in Hawaii, another brother named Jose was bribed by Imelda Marcos to state that the fake brass Buddha, still on display in Baguio City Courthouse, was the one found by Roger Roxas. See *Roxas Court Case*. Before Jose changed his story, he had tattooed on his back: BRO OF FOUNDER OF THE GOLD-EN BUDDHA. Cathcart told us that both Jose and the two sons of Roger Roxas (one an infant at the time the Gold Buddha was stolen, the other not yet born) eventually came under so much pressure from the Marcos family that they sold out to Imelda. Correspondence between authors and Daniel Cathcart. Unscrupulous journalists and sleazy television producers seeking to make money by claiming that the Gold Buddha was only made of brass tend to use Jose as 'the true source' to 'prove' that the Roxas Buddha was never gold. Honolulu court records show that members of Jose's family testified that they accompanied him on several visits to Imelda Marcos and her attorney, and testified that Jose shared the Marcos bribe money with them. The Roxas family was extremely poor, and vulnerable, in part because they were robbed by the Marcoses of a great fortune. They still have not recovered anything from the Marcos estate because of stonewalling.

221–Filipino soldiers' lawsuit: They stated that President Fidel Ramos received a $1-million bribe from Marcos in the form of gold bars to keep his mouth shut about the gold recoveries. Don Enrique Zobel testified to the Philippine Senate on this point. See Donna S. Cueto, "Marcos Gave F[idel] R[amos] Gold Bars – Zobel", from *The Philippine Daily Inquirer*, October 28, 1999, at the *Inquirer*'s website.

221–Bob Curtis also sued the Marcoses. His suit in the U.S. District Court in Nevada in 1992 charges fraud and misrepresentation, breach of contract, outrageous conduct, and conversion of Curtis's property. In his suit, Curtis asserted that Marcos had recovered in excess of $1-trillion worth of gold, a figure supported by the *Roxas Court Case* evidence of three Australian brokers who gave the figure $1.63-trillion. It is estimated there is now over $23-trillion held privately around the world by what *The Economist* calls "high net worth individuals" or "the filthy rich". Curtis was awarded a default judgment of $78-billion. The lawsuit is reproduced on our CDs.

221–In addition to the concrete vaults, the soldiers also uncovered "Several steel cylindrical drums measuring approximately three feet long by 1.5 feet in diameter, and an undetermined number of rectangular copper boxes (3 feet x 1 foot x 2 feet)".

221–Tamaraw Security Services. See Cueto cited above.

222–A fourth potential claimant, Santy's second wife Julieta Huerto Santa Romana, and her daughter, have not been heard from since the early 1970s. Our efforts to locate them have failed. One source says they are living in poverty on their home island of Mindoro, having been used by President Marcos to make himself executor of Santy's Malacanang Palace will, and then discarded. Jim Brown asserts, on the other hand, that Julieta died long ago and Marcos recruited her sister as a stand-in. Brown to the authors, 30 March 2001.

222–Attorney Eleanor Piel cut her legal teeth in Tokyo during the Occupation, first working for the War Crimes prosecution team and then being transferred to Marquat's Scientific and Economic section. Piel told us that she believed, as did most others, that Hirohito should have been tried and that she was disappointed that democratic reforms in Japan were abandoned. Luz Rambano first began to work with Eleanor Piel in 1974. Piel to the authors, September 25, 2000.

222–Robert A. Ackerman describes himself as a Cold Warrior. Ackerman still practices law in Washington DC and Depontis continues his political lobbying efforts in the Caribbean, working out of Miami. See Ackerman's letter reproduced on our CDs. Ackerman's address is listed in the Washington phone book and Depontis is to be found on the internet.

222–Four exceptions when banks did not stonewall: When a Hong Kong bank admitted to Flordeliza Tan that the accounts existed but had not yet matured; when Luz was told by UBS Geneva that the Master Gold Account existed, but she should not try to remove the asset base; when Luz went to a different Swiss bank and was paid the accrued interest; and when Santy's daughter Diana by his second wife, Julieta Huerto, went to a bank in Zurich and was recognized by a bank official who recalled her coming in with her father many years earlier, and she was given access to the accrued interest.

222–Like the giant account at Union Banque Suisse, the Sellers Transaction Code for the Santy accounts at Citibank was "LANDSDALE" [sic]. The deliberate misspelling is a type of code commonly used in bank documents.

223–The Ramos document is reproduced on our CD.

224–Before anything could be done in New York State, it was necessary to have Luz recognized by New York courts as the Administrator of Santy's property. The problem for Luz as an heir was that in the Catholic Philippines, divorce was not legal. Santy's first marriage to Evangeline Campton ended only when she died in the late 1930s or early 1940s. Santy's second marriage was to Julieta Huerto. Luz was married to Angel Joson and they could not be divorced. Although Luz had a marriage certificate asserting that she and Santy had gone through a wedding ceremony before he died, it was easy to challenge its legality under Philippine law. Nevertheless, she was declared one of Santy's three legal heirs by a Philippine court, on the basis of Santy's holographic will. We were unable to locate Roy and Peter Diaz, Santy's two sons by his first wife, Evangeline Campton. In his will, Santy refers to them as Rolando and Pedro. We were told that Pedro Diaz owned a plantation in Hawaii. Their sister, Maryann Diaz, married after the war and could not be traced.

224–In Manila in 1974, Luz and her attorneys, accompanied by a member of the court, went to Citibank and found that the eight safe-deposit boxes there were empty. According to Clarence 'Jim' Brown, all Luz found in the first box, to which she had a key and which contained the keys to the other boxes, was a current dated newspaper, suggesting that the boxes were emptied just before they reached the bank that day. Brown said President Marcos later admitted to Luz that he, "in conjunction with certain bank officials", had emptied the boxes. Gone, Brown said, were "loads of bearer certificates of precious metal, and cash, in addition to real estate titles, personal jewellery and other items". Brown said Marcos also had Citibank block Luz's personal account, which contained more than $3-million that Santy had given her over several years. This is also discussed in Tarciana Rodriguez's sworn statement reproduced on our CDs.

224–Luz threatened by UBS officials. From Clarence 'Jim' Brown, correspondence with authors, and his website: www.sightings.com/political/pressrel.htm. We had extensive written and telephone contact with Brown. We know of him also through our correspondence with Piel and Arlene Friedman, who had frequent contact with Brown in the course of investigations for the Roxas court case. Luz Rambano's confrontation with Union Banque Suisse was related by Brown, who had worked with Luz, Eleanor Piel and Mel Belli. Piel to authors, November 2001. We only have been able to confirm independently some of the information Brown has given us.

224–The story of Christophe Meili and his treatment by UBS officials, Swiss government officials and assorted thugs, and how Senator D'Amato brought him to testify before the U.S. Congress about Swiss authorities' obfuscation on the issues of Nazi war loot hidden in Swiss banks: see Bower, *Blood Money*. See also *Hearing before House of Representatives, June 25, 1997 Eizenstat Report*, available online. CNN Interactive, "Guard Who Turned Over Swiss Banking Files Seeks Protection", May 7, 1997. Eric Wollman, *Nazi Gold and Other Assets*, Office of Alan G. Hevesi, Comptroller of the City of New York. The shredding was "unfortunate" was the way UBS officials described the incident to *The Economist*. The reader is also reminded of the experiences of Swiss professor and parliamentarian Jean Ziegler, who was indicted for treason by the Swiss government for his role in exposing Swiss banking corruption with regard to the hiding of Nazi assets.

225–The Aquino government's attempts to recover Santa Romana assets. Peter Nelson's meeting with representatives of the Aquino government concerning Santy's estate is taken from his book *Anatomy of a Bank Job*, pp. 232-236. After reading his account, published in 1995, we corresponded with Nelson to see what had happened in the case. Nelson came on the Santa Romana case cold. His involvement was accidental, like that of Meili.

225–Citibank's involvement in private banking. Private banks are "a highly confidential bank within the bank that provides white-glove service to clients with … $1-million." S.C. Gwynne, "Just Hide Me the Money", in *Time*, December 14, 1998.

225–Private Bank assets of UBS, Credit Suisse, Citibank, Chase and Merrill Lynch. See Gwynne.

225–By 1998, Citibank had 40,000 offshore private bank accounts. Edward Montero's testimony to the U.S. Congress. As quoted by Martin Mann, "Wall Street's Corruption Scandal", in *The Spotlight*.

225–Using private bank offshore accounts to shelter money from litigation. See Gwynne.

226–Santa Romana accounts. We reproduce a copy of the original New York State Tax Office record, complete with signatures of the New York authorities, on our CDs. The document has now disappeared from the New York State Tax Office.

226–Citibank wanted a waiver from Imelda. Tarciana said Citibank told her that the bank already had Imelda's permission to move the gold to the Bahamas, and that a signed agreement with the current head of The Umbrella (Bong-Bong Marcos) was being hand-carried to Citibank.

227–The necessity of brokering an agreement between Tarciana and the United States Government is from the Ackerman letter reproduced on our CDs.

227–Ray Cline's involvement with the Citibank transfer of Santy's assets to the Bahamas. See the Ackerman letter. Cline had been involved in Singlaub's treasure-hunting efforts in the Philippines in the late 1980s and was reported to have met with Enrile, Ramos and President Aquino's brother Jose Cojuangco. Cline testified before the Congressional committee during the Iran-Contra investigations about his knowledge of Singlaub's gold-hunts. We reproduce the censored pages of his testimony on our CDs.

227–The situation in the Bahamas was ripe for meddling by the U.S. Government and its many "private" associates. In July 1992, Prime Minister Lynden Pindling was in a crucial political struggle for control of the country against challenger Hubert Ingraham. Sir Leonard Knowles favored Ingraham. Depontis was a registered agent for Ingraham's Free National Movement, a center-right conservative party. Ingraham defeated Pindling and became Prime Minister in August 1992. Prime Minister Ingraham said that only legitimate business fueled Bahama's *declared* record $450-million in foreign reserves. AP Online, "OECD Publishes Tax Havens List", June 26, 2000; U.S. Department of State, *Background Notes: The Bahamas*, November 1994; Peter Newman, "A Sunny Welcome for Canadian Funds", *Maclean's*, March 28, 1994; Kenneth Bain, "Obituary: Sir Lynden Pindling", *Independent*, August 29, 2000; Scott West, "The Bahamas Politics", *Inter Press Service English News Wire*, May 25, 2000. Knowles died in 1999 in Macon, Georgia, embittered and impoverished. The role of the Bahama's in laundering loot for the CIA and The Umbrella – See Chapter 10.

227–Close business associates of Depontis told us he has old ties to the CIA, and was also well-connected in the Bahamas. They said that in 1990, Depontis was busy helping to replace the Bahamian government of Prime Minister Lynden Pindling, to install a new administration more cooperative toward the CIA.

227–Cline explained. The background quoted here on Santa Romana and his bank accounts is from the Ackerman Letter reproduced on our CDs. Cline and Lansdale's relations dated back to World War II.

227–Information about Ray Cline comes from a variety of sources. Ray Cline died on May 15, 1996. Wisner got Cline his job in Taiwan. Cline wrote: "One of my biggest headaches in Taiwan was keeping a weather eye on the main component of CIA's first established proprietary companies – the headquarters of the interlocking set of aviation enterprises that included Air America, Civil Air Transport (CAT), and Air Asia. ...The fleet was ... taken over financially by CIA to keep the pilots and aircraft available for clandestine or covert missions." Cline, *Secrets, Spies and Scholars*, pp. 173, 178. Cline's work with the Political Warfare Cadres Academy, quotes and information about the Anti-Communist League: Seagrave, *Marcos Dynasty*, p. 207. Cline in Taiwan, CIA and State Department: Seagrave, *Marcos Dynasty*, p. 196. Cline in Bonn. Cline, *Secrets, Spies and Scholars*, pp. 215-16. Cline's speciality: "international economic intelligence analysis": Cline, *Secrets, Spies and Scholars*, p. 218. Cline despised Nixon for his blunders, sneering at Nixon's "little band of ambitious opportunists who were his immediate advisors ... the gravest threat to...government and open society that the United States has experienced". Cline, *Secrets, Spies and Scholars*, p. 223.

227–Cline became a special advisor to Ronald Reagan and an official member of Reagan's presidential campaign team. During that campaign, there was an embarrassing moment when Richard Allen, George Bush and James Lilley were on a special mission to Beijing to meet with Premier Deng. At the time. Cline was noisily proclaiming a return to a "two-China policy" in which America would have recognized Taiwan as a separate state. During their meeting, a Chinese aide came into the room and delivered a piece of paper to Deng. "Who is Ke-Lai-Ne?", Deng asked, transliterating Cline's name. Bush, Allen, and Lilley had to do some fast back-pedalling to distance themselves from Ray Cline. This anecdote comes from Patrick Tyler, *A Great Wall*, p. 293.

228–Ray Cline's Iran-Contra testimony about Singlaub's gold hunts. Reproduced on our CDs. Like Singlaub, Cline would have been able to come and go from the Philippines through Clark Air Base without any formal entry into the country. Cline was reported in the American press as being with Singlaub in Manila, meeting with Enrile, Ramos and Jose Cojuangco. See Belluck, "General's Mystery Philippines Trip"; Manegold, "U.S. General Said behind Mercenaries", Neumann, "Ex-general Tied to Arms Deals in Philippines".

229–Depontis expected a commission of over $7-billion. Since Depontis stated on the tape-recorded telephone conversation that he had to share this out to various people, it would be interesting to know who they were. These statements by Depontis are from audio tapes made by Bob Curtis, and are reinforced by videotapes of Tarciana and others, record-ed during June and July 1992. Transcript of the Depontis Curtis phone conversation is reproduced on our CDs.

229–This information on Depontis offering Tarciana an 'unacceptable' payoff of $25-mil-lion, came from Jim Brown and is disputed by others.

229–When Santy's long-time business partner Jose T. Velasquez died on May 16, 1992, Tarciana gained priority as sole alternate and principal signatory of all the trust certificates of gold accounts, cash accounts, real-estate accounts and corporate accounts under the name of Severino Garcia Santa Romana.

229–The price for the Citibank gold assets was set at $305 an ounce, which was to be the net proceeds credited to the Santa Romana estate and his heirs, minus "Transaction Fees, handling charges, past due storage charges". At the time, gold was selling for just over $353 an ounce. The $50 difference represented the hefty commission that Citibank would be entitled to under this deal. The proposed agreement is reproduced on our CDs.

229–It is significant that the July 1992 agreement specifically includes a clause concerning the sanctifying of the Santa Romana gold bullion at Citibank – "re-smelting, re-hallmark-ing, and or re-certificating to enable the Sale and Delivery to be on a G.L.D." (Good London Delivery). This tends to confirm that Santy's assets sleeping in Citibank for all those decades were war loot not in Good London Delivery. (Marcos had brought in Robert Curtis and – later – Johnson-Mathey, to solve the same problem.) So no detail regarding the sale of this gold was being overlooked. The July 1992 agreement ends with the statement that Citibank will be given "Hold Harmless Agreements" by various parties, stipulating that the signatories agree "to hold Citibank harmless from any past, present or future claim" from the signatories and from "all claims of Third Parties" including "liabil-ity for any local, State, Federal of Foreign taxes or fees which might be due as a result of said transaction". The Hold Harmless Agreements were to be signed by Tarciana, Luz, Eleanor Piel, Depontis, retired Bahamian Chief Justice Sir Leonard Knowles, and others. The agreement is reproduced on our CDs.

229–In an effort to pin down Santy's assets at Citibank, in April 1993 Eleanor Piel took the deposition of James Collins, the officer at Citibank Manila back in 1971 when Luz said Santy had opened an account with $43-million in small-denominated U.S. bills. In his deposition, Collins denied all knowledge of this, and only remembered Santy asking him about borrowing some money. Piel correspondence with authors.

229–Belli's letter to Greenspun, October 15, 1993 and the lawsuit filed with the Superior Court in California, County of San Francisco, is No. 955366, reproduced on our CDs. The Belli lawsuit is fascinating for the light it shed on the network of Santa Romana accounts around the world. Looking closely, one finds itemized references to Santy's accounts in American banks that have the same numbers, codes and names as other Santy accounts at Union Bank Suisse and banks in other parts of the world. For example, Belli cites Citibank Master Account 787632. This number appears on other documents we acquired over twenty years, each of which reveals different details. Citibank Master Account 787632 definitely existed because it appears in the New York State tax document obtained by Tarciana in Albany (reproduced on our CD). It is the same account that is the target of the Bahamas suit by Depontis and Knowles. It is the same account that was moved mysteriously from Citibank Manila to Citibank New York in 1974. Its sellers transaction code is 'Landsdale' [sic] and the Tax Account Number is 429-3284-5. Both this number and the deliberately misspelled name 'Landsdale' appear again in a letter of instruction written to UBS in 1998 by Alfredo P. Ramos, an executive of Santy's Diaz and Poirrotte Enterprises. UBS documents show the original title-holder of that 20,000-metric-ton account was Crown Commodity Holdings, a subsidiary of Santy's Crown Enterprises. A letter from Virgilio Marcelo to UBS also refers to Santy's accounts at UBS in the name of Major Gen. Edward Lansdale. A 1994 letter to Australian gold broker Peter Johnston also refered to Citibank Master Account 787632. In many of these documents (all reproduced on our CDs), one code that is listed is 'Bergot Harbour King', referring to another of Santy's shell companies. From all these convergences, it is obvious that these big gold bullion accounts in major banks all over the world are linked – and by more than just coincidence. Other documents include a gold information sheet for Po Sang Bank in Beijing that gives the account name of J.G. [Jose Garcia] Santa Romana and code-names as Jose Antonio Severino Garcia Diaz. There are references to ten gold bullion certificates with group numbers 11833-1 through 11833-10, each valued at 1,000 metric tons, or 10,000 metric tons in all. Another document from the Australian firm Waratah Group, indicates that these ten Po Sang Bank gold certificates were moved from Beijing to Hong Kong branches of HSBC, Standard Chartered, Hang Lung Bank, Wing Lung Bank, and Po Sang Bank. Another document shows that one of Santy's accounts at Po Sang in Hong Kong was valued at US$466-million, another at US$5.3-billion, and another at over US$16-billion. Lastly, there are three Santy cash accounts mentioned at Hong Kong's Bank of East Asia, two valued at US$4-billion, a third at US$3-billion. All these convergences support the conclusions that there are interconnecting links, probably related to the global Black Eagle Trust. The interested reader can review all of these documents on our CDs.

230–The GAO report on Citibank and moneylaundering as revealed by the U.S. Congressional probe. See Gwynne; Kathleen Day, "Citigroup Called Lax on Money Laundering", in *The Washington Post*, November 30, 2000; Thom Masland, "The Lost Billions", *Newsweek*, March 13, 2000. Congressional testimonies of Shaukat Aziz, John Reed, Albert Misan, Edward Montero, and Amy Elliot of Citibank, available from elibrary.com. The official GAO report, "Private Banking: Raul Salinas, Citibank, and Alleged Money Laundering, November 9, 1999", and another GAO document, "Laundering: Observations on Private Banking and Related Oversight of Selected Offshore Jurisdictions, November 9, 1999", to be found online at www.access.gao.gov.

231–An account of the Russian money-laundering is in "Money-Laundering Probe Targets Citigroup", from *The Washington Times*, November 30, 2000, elibrary.com.

231–Citicorp and the $800-million in Russian money. See Kathleen Day.

231–Citibank's involvement with General Abacha and his sons. Tom Masland.

231–"Instead of monitoring formal compliance [with U.S. regulations] U.S. banking regulators try to identify what efforts the branches are making to combat money laundering and to determine whether the bank's corporate 'Know Your Client' policies are being applied to…private banking. Although examiners are able to review the written policies and procedures being used in these branches, they must rely primarily on the banks' internal audit functions to verify that the procedures are actually being implemented in offshore branches where U.S. regulators may be precluded from conducting on-site examinations." See the GAO report, "Money Laundering. The problem of money-laundering": "The Treasury has spearheaded a much-publicized effort to crack down on money laundering… but officials there repeatedly have declined to comment on why no top bank official or major bank has ever been seriously sanctioned for money laundering." See Day.

231–In this book, we have not discussed Golden Lily treasure vaults in Indonesia, which are another story entirely. Suffice it to say that Sukarno was not a rich man before World War II, but was immensely rich afterward. After the war, Japan wanted access to the Dutch Shell oilfields in Sumatra, which had been seized from the Dutch by Sukarno's independence movement. Sukarno was approached by Sasakawa, accompanied by Japan's top wartime military intelligence officer in the islands, and one of Japan's top bankers, one of the Four Heavenly Kings. See Nishihara, *The Japanese and Sukarno's Indonesia: Tokyo-Jakarta Relations 1951-1966*. They offered Sukarno treasure vaults containing large quantities of gold and platinum, in return for full access to petroleum from Sumatra. Sasakawa was also granted exclusive rights to negotiate all trade deals between Japan and Indonesia. Large quantities of gold and platinum were moved by Sukarno to Switzerland in 1947, copies of the documents being in our hands. But this is only part of the batik. The rest concerns Santa Romana, the Black Eagle Trust, and a network of 100 senior military officers and politicians such as Sukarno in many Asian countries, who were given mandates to share the proceeds of a black gold pool – so long as they remained cooperative toward Washington, and did not rock the boat. When Sukarno rocked the boat by becoming a leader of the nonaligned movement, he became a target of the Eisenhower Administration. We have discussed these covert operations against Sukarno with General Aderholt and others who participated. See Seagrave, *Marcos Dynasty*, Chapter 18, and Seagrave, *Lords of the Rim*, Chapter 14.

231–A fax to Peter Johnston discussing 'various gold metal offers', from Conrado A. Rubio Jr. in Manila, who appears to have been helping Johnston in a gold deal. Reproduced on our CDs.

232–Prosecution turned on the notion that Johnston *might* try to negotiate the certificate, and when he did the fact that it had been held briefly for safe-keeping by Westpac might enable him to claim that in doing so Westpac had authenticated the certificate. (In fact, the bank had noted on the receipt given to Johnston that by holding the certificate for safe-keeping the bank did so "without involvement of value".)

232–"to disguise the truth" Galbraith on money and the disguising of truth. Lawrence Parks, "Near Death and Resurrection of the Gold Mining Industry", *World Gold Council*, July 17, 2000. At the World Gold Council website.

233–Three men: Jones was told their names were Tom Atkinson, David Lock and Scott Alswang. Jones's story is reconstructed from his correspondence files with Senator Gramm, U.S. Department of Justice, etc., and from telephone conversations with the authors. His file is reproduced on our CDs.

234–"Back off or face martial law." See Valentine, *Operation Phoenix*, p. 428.

234–"SWAT teams into journalists' homes." CIA's James Bruce, chairman of Foreign Denial and Deception Committee. *Village Voice* July 31-6 August 2002, available online.

CHAPTER SIXTEEN

235–In January 2003, *The Economist* reported that President Arroyo was involved in treasure hunting in the Philippines. She had announced her decision previously not to seek a second term.

235–We were surprised to hear the name Will Farish bandied about in Manila. Most Filipinos would draw a total blank on Farish. Even the polo-playing set would be hard-pressed to identify him. So when his name became part of the buzz in Manila treasure-hunting circles, we concluded that there might be something to it. Everybody in Texas and Kentucky knows the name. Will Farish's father was a founder of Humble Oil, now part of Exxon. Information about Will Farish himself comes from a number of sources. See "Bush Donors Line Up for Embassies", *International Herald Tribune,* March 19, 2001. "$150,000 William Stamps Farish Fund", see *University of Kentucky News* at the university website. Pete Slover, "Bush Hopes to Unveil more Cabinet Picks", at dallas.new.com December 28, 2000. "Farish, William Stamp", *Handbook of Texas Online.* "Farish Nominated as Ambassador to Britain" on *Washington Watch,* March 6, 2001 (available online). University of Kentucky "Famous University Alumni" at the university website. We do not know if Farish ever was interested in Yamashita's Gold, and our source at the U.S. Embassy in Manila was evasive on this.

236–The full text of the San Francisco Peace Treaty 1951 can be found online at www.taiwan.virtualave.net/sanfrancisco01.htm.

237–Gold Anti-Trust Action Committee. GATA's assertion of mysterious quantities of gold bullion controlled by the U.S. Government raises the question – where has all this bullion come from? Santa Romana's accounts seem a likely source. The fact that both Citibank and Chase, long associated with Santa Romana's gold bullion accounts as we have demonstrated and documented, are the two banks targeted by GATA. See *The Economist*, September 15, 2001, "Fingered", p. 67.

237–"I try to think." E.L. Doctorow, "The Talk of the Town", *The New Yorker*.

237–"monopolized and abused" is from Price, "A Just Peace? The 1951 San Francisco Peace Treaty in Historical Perspective".

237–"Romulo demolished." Price, "A Just Peace?"

237–Japan's economic status in 1951, Romulo's role, conversations of Finance Minister Ikeda, the 100-billion yen budget surplus and the $200-million in gold in the Bank of Japan: Price, "A Just Peace?"

237–Dutch government deal. "What an outrage". Senator Smith's remarks are included in the Congressional Record, September 10, 2001 pp. S9209-S9246. This contains the text of the Senate debate on the issue and is available online from the U.S. Congress website.

237–The signatories to the Treaty waived all reparations claims, but recently declassified documents show that Dulles "in negotiating this clause, also negotiated a way out of it". Because of the reparations clause, Korea, China and the Soviet Union refused to sign the agreement and for a time it looked like the Netherlands was also going to refuse. Dulles worried that refusal by the Netherlands might encourage the United Kingdom, Australia and New Zealand to follow suit. Just hours before the Treaty was signed, Dulles arranged a confidential exchange of letters between Dutch foreign minister Dirk Stikker and Prime Minister Yoshida of Japan. In these letters, the government of Japan stated that it "did not consider that the Government of the Netherlands by signing the Treaty has itself expropriated the private claims of its nationals so that, as a consequence thereof, after the Treaty comes into force these claims would be non-existent." The revelations about Dulles providing for a secret clause to allow for reparations agreements: see Steven C. Clemons, "Recovering Japan's Wartime Past and Ours", *The New York Times*, 10 September 2001. The article is also available at www.asiamedia.ucla.edu. It is also the source for the quote from the Stikker Yoshida letters.

237–The deal finally worked out by Stikker for reparation payments had another secret clause in which the Dutch government caved into the demands of John Foster Dulles for clemency and early release of all Japanese war criminals. The details of these negotiations are revealed in declassified records of the Canadian Foreign Ministry, available online.

238–"As much as $100-billion" is from the U.S. Senate Committee on Foreign Relations, report of February 14, 1951 as quoted in Uldis Kruze, *San Francisco and the 1951 US-Japan Treaty Conference*, San Francisco: University of San Francisco, 2001. The pamphlet prepared for the 50th anniversary celebration was regarded by many people as another statement by apologists for Japan's actions during World War II. Ironically, Mr. Kruze includes many quotes from contemporary sources of Japan's looting of Asia. He even says the "peace treaty was kind to Japan". The pamphlet also includes a photograph of Dulles at the Asian Art Museum in San Francisco, where an exhibit of art treasures had been assembled for the peace treaty signing. The exhibit was prepared by Dr. Jiro Harada, head of the former Imperial Household Museum. Dr. Harada had presided over the imperial collections since the 1920s. In 1937, only a few months before the Rape of Nanking, the Imperial Household Museum was inaugurated. Here, the priceless manuscripts, art and religious treasure of Asia, looted by the Japanese, were stored and exhibited as part of the imperial treasures. At the end of the war, the Occupation authorities hastily renamed it the National Museum, but Dr. Harada continued as its chief. Today, Korea and many other Asian countries continue to petition the government of Japan for the return of artworks looted from their citizens, religious organizations and private collections.

238–The number of U.S. Government intelligence records that have been 'lost' is enormous. Consider the CIA's 1953 coup in Iran. At one time, according to a CIA historian, the Agency held 2-linear feet of records on the subject. Today, less than 25 percent of these documents are still in existence, the rest having been destroyed. See *Secrecy and Government Bulletin*, Issue Number 77, March 1999 at the Federation of American Scientists website. When the State Department released the volume of the *Foreign Relations of the United States*, concerning Iran in the 1950s there was not a single word about the CIA's role in the coup that ousted Prime Minister Mossadegh in 1953. These are manifestations of official amnesia.

238–*Japanese Imperial Army Disclosure Act* and the July 2002 report of the task force are both available online from the National Archives and Records Service. We reproduce both in full on our CDs.

238–The number of Japanese documents that have already vanished and the strange circumstances of their disposal is discussed in the task force report on the *Japanese Imperial Army Disclosure Act.*

238–Our experience with FOIPA requests and the vanishing Yamashita Gold documents. See Seagrave, *Marcos Dynasty*, p. 446, Fawcett edition, 1988. "The U.S. Government has taken pains to obscure many of its dealings with Marcos, so there is a limit to how much we are able to uncover, even under the FOIPA. When investigative reporter Don Goldberg repeatedly asked the Department of State to release its files on Yamashita's Gold, the Department told him he had no justification for asking. State then *reclassified* the entire

Yamashita Gold file to block further Freedom of Information attempts."

239—That in the mid-1990s the U.S. Government found nothing in its files about Japan, slush funds, Yamashita's gold: see the Norbert Schlei documents on our CDs, in particular the appeals court ruling of September 1997, which is also available online.

239—Federal Judge Vaughn Walker, supporting the State Department against U.S. citizens, overturned the lawsuits. See Charles Burress, "Bill Would Open WWII Treaty for POW Suits/Slave-labor victims", *San Francisco Chronicle*, March 22, 2001.

240—Johnson "abysmal moments of denial". See Price, "A Just Peace?"

240—San Francisco Peace Treaty Article 26. Burress, "Bill Would Open WWII Treaty for POW Suits/Slave-labor victims".

240—Settlements made to the Swiss government. The fact that the Swiss government and banks did many questionable favors for Japan (and Nazi Germany) during the war, such as using money sent to feed Allied POWS to repatriate Swiss funds from Tokyo, doubtless contributed to the generous postwar Swiss settlement from Japan. The Swiss banks kicked back about 30 per cent of this money to secret bank accounts, which many people believe were actually those of Hirohito. The emperor's foreign assets and secret wealth in Switzerland, see Manning, *Hirohito: The War Years*.

240—John Dower recently tumbled to a secret memorandum reporting discussions between General MacArthur and Emperor Hirohito concerning the nature and extent of reparations. In the same series of discussions, Hirohito registered his deep distress over the fact some of his wartime cabinet members were purged and were *being denied their retirement pensions*. Hirohito told MacArthur this was causing "such deprivations [that]...created anti-American feelings, which were not in the interests of the Occupation or of Japan itself". Among those being 'deprived' of their pensions was Kishi Nobosuke, then in Sugamo Prison. This memo was found among the papers of General Courtney Whitney at the MacArthur Memorial Library. See Dower, "The Showa Emperor and Japan's Postwar Imperial Democracy". *JPRI Working Paper*, No. 61, October 1999.

241—Japan's economic predicament. David Asher and Robert Dugger, "Could Japan's Financial Mt. Fuji Blow Its Top?" MIT JAPAN Program, May 2000. The article is available from the Massachusetts Institute of Technology website.

241—$1-trillion in bad loans on the books of Japan's banks. *The Economist*, June 27, 1998, p. 85.

242—Prime Minister Miyazawa's plan for the public fund to buy up stocks. See "Japan's Financial Markets, Crunch Time", *The Economist*, March 17, 2001.

242—Miyazawa's plan would take over $365-billion in bad bank portfolios. See "Japan's Economy: Another False Dawn?" *The Economist*, March 24, 2001.

242—Miyazawa was the top administrator in the Ministry of Finance. Details from "U.S.-Japan 21st Century Committee" at www.csis.org/usj21/3bios-jp. html Miyazawa was accompanied by then Minister of Finance Ikeda Hayato (who became Prime Minister just after the M-Fund was turned over to the LDP by Nixon) and another Ministry official Shirasu Jiro. See Schaller, *Altered States*. See also "Ikeda-Robertson Talks", *Kodansha Encyclopedia of Japan*, Volume 3, p. 266.

242—Miyazawa's resignation over the Recruit Scandal, see Hane, *Eastern Phoenix*, p. 57. That the Recruit Scandal involved moneys from the M-Fund. See Schlei, "M-Fund Memorandum", JPRI.

242—Miyazawa's deals with Kanemaru and Gotoda. See Schlesinger, *Shadow Shoguns*, pp.

213-214.

242–Miyazawa's pledge of loyalty to Kanemaru. See Schlesinger, *Shadow Shoguns*, pp. 213-214.

242–Christopher Lafleur and the FS-X negotiations, his marriage to Miyazawa's daughter. See Chalmers Johnson, "The Chrysanthemum Club", *JPRI Critique* Volume IV, Number 9, November 1997, at the JPRI website. Eamonn Fingleton, "The Anomalous Position of Christopher LaFleur", *Unsustainable*, May 15, 2001 on the web. Although Foley has left the State Department and Lafleur has been recalled to Washington after a storm of protest over his personal relations to Miyazawa, the Chrysanthemum Club is alive and well. For many years after World War II, Fingleton points out that American diplomats were automatically disqualified from serving in Tokyo if they were married to Japanese nationals. This rule applied even to officials of low rank, and in the case of marriages to Japanese nationals who had no connection to the Tokyo establishment.

242–Lafleur was the "defacto boss of the embassy": Johnson, "The Chrysanthemum Club". Johnson was one of the first to leak the information about Lafleur's marriage. Some journalists speculated that Lafleur also was the CIA station chief in Tokyo.

242–Foley's paid position with Mitsubishi: see *The Hill*, November 11, 2001. Available online.

243–Lafleur as a member of Japan's dream-team. See *Japan Economic Institute Report* No. 35, September 19, 1997.

243–The U.S. State Department's official position that "The peace treaty put aside" reparations: Ambassador Foley's remarks were widely reported in the international press. Kinue Tokudome, "POW Forced Labor Lawsuits Against Japanese Companies", *JPRI Working Paper*, No. 82, November 2001, available on the JPRI website. Since leaving government, Foley has now become a paid advisor to Mitsubishi, one of the *zaibatsu* being targeted by former slave-laborers. Foley and his wife, who is a paid consultant of Sumitomo, another *zaibatsu* involved in these lawsuits, see no "conflict of interest" in their employment by Japanese industry. State Department officially supported the Foleys' 'rights'.

243–The attack on the POWs made by three former U.S. ambassadors – Thomas Foley, Walter Mondale and Michael Armacost – who denounced the American POWs in the wake of the World Trade Center bombings, likening them to terrorists, was in an Op Ed piece that appeared in *The Washington Post*, September 25, 2001. They defended the rejection of POW demands for compensation, saying this "would undermine our relations with Japan, a key ally. It would have serious, and negative, effects on our national security". They accused Congress and the POWs of endangering the White House efforts "to forge a coalition to combat terrorism". The story was widely reported. See *San Francisco Chronicle* October 1, 2001. Their stance has been widely denounced by many, including John Dower. See Kinue Tokudome, "POW Forced Labor Lawsuits Against Japanese Companies", *JPRI Working Paper*, No. 82, November 2001, available on the JPRI website and also at www.expows.com/position1.htm.

243–"different issues." The Japanese government spokesman drew a clear distinction between POW and terrorist issues. See *San Francisco Chronicle,* October 1, 2001 "3 Former U.S. Envoys Blast Bill on POW Reparations".

243–"Two embassies": quoted in Johnson, "The Chrysanthemum Club".

CHAPTER SEVENTEEN

244–According to Ben's daughter, who gave us the photo, the prince ordered Ben to wear Japanese army uniform during their flight to Manchuria to avoid attracting attention and raising questions. The prince knew that if Filipinos saw Ben in Japanese uniform, they would consider him a traitor, putting him and his family in danger.

245–Although the U.S. Embassy in Manila continues to this day to deny any recoveries were ever made at Clark, the truth is that in 1959 Alberto Cacpal received permission from President Macapagal to attempt recoveries at Clark. The U.S. Embassy eventually gave its permission in a memo dated January 20, 1967. The permission granted by Clark base commander Colonel William Truesdell was reconfirmed by the embassy in a memo dated June 20, 1972 from Second Secretary John D. Forbes, who is today president of the Eastern Voyager Corporation and chairman of the American Chamber of Commerce in Manila. These recoveries involved over 100 Filipinos and Americans including active U.S. military. The list includes licenses issued to Santa Romana, under the pseudonym R.S. Diaz, in December 1973. U.S. military sources at Clark stated that "numerous recoveries were made". Cacpal was so successful that in 1987, President Marcos officially certified that Cacpal had turned over to the palace large quantities of precious gems, and 280,000 metric tons of gold. In the same document, Marcos identified General Lansdale as one of the trustees of Cacpal's vast fortune deposited at various major banks including Citibank. All documents supporting this brief summary are reproduced on our CDs.

246–The Pope. See above, Chapter 4.

246–This is supported by members of his family in Filipino court documents dated May 5, 1994, on our CDs.

246–For the Chinese in the Philippines see Seagrave, *Lords of the Rim*, *The Marcos Dynasty*, and *The Soong Dynasty*.

247–Judge Chua's relationship with Ferdinand Marcos is discussed in detail in Seagrave, *The Marcos Dynasty*.

247–Much more information on the Halksworth case is available online.

248–Marrs, *Rule by Secrecy*, p. 67

248–Marrs, *Rule by Secrecy*, p. 66

248–By 1815, the Rothschilds were the principal financiers to the British government and the Bank of England. They held that same position with the German Hapsburg monarchy.

249–Marrs, *Rule by Secrecy*, p. 64.

249–Marrs, *Rule by Secrecy*, p. 55

250–Blum, *The Morganthau Diaries 1928-1938*, pp. 324-326.

250–Larsen, "The Historical Fight for Honest Money". Arizona Breakfast Club address, reproduced in the Vila Marques files on our CDs.

250–Olsen and Wool, "Executive Orders and National Emergencies," in *Policy Analysis*, No. 358, October 28, 1999. Available online.

250–Many books recount how this was arranged, including Kevin Phillips' *Wealth and Democracy*, but the simplest and clearest summary is in Jim Marrs' *Rule by Secrecy*.

250–The Trading with the Enemy Act, Public Law 65091, Chapter 106, Section 5B.

250–Blum, *The Morganthau Diaries, 1928-1938*, pp. 452, 132 & 363.

250–Few people realize that the state of emergency concerning the possession of gold established by President Franklin Roosevelt was renewed by executive orders under Presidents Truman, Eisenhower and Kennedy. See Executive Proclamation 2914, Executive

Order 10896, Executive Order 10905, Executive Order 11037. These Executive Orders, which are not easy to find, are reproduced on our CDs.

250–Hamburg-Groppe, Dorothy, "Key to the Gold Vault." Available online.

250–Crown jewels in New York. See Hamburg-Groppe, Dorothy. "Key to the Gold Vault". Available online.

251–See Diebold, Inc., "Security Products and Services." Available online.

251–Hamburg-Groppe, Dorothy, "Key to the Gold Vault." Available online.

251–At the time, the Benguet mines in the Philippines were the second biggest gold producer in all U.S. territory, and one of its biggest and most prominent shareholders was Douglas MacArthur. For a history of the Benguet Mines and MacArthur's shareholding, see Seagrave, *The Marcos Dynasty*.

252–*The Marcos Dynasty*, p. 129

252–An excellent account of the working relationship between the Mafia and the CIA can be found in Douglas Valentine's book, *The Strength of the Wolf*.

252–See Valentine, *The Strength of the Wolf*.

252–See the photograph of Santy seated in an armchair, reproduced on our CDs, which was taken during this period.

253–Marcos's political campaign and victory in 1965 is discussed in Seagrave, *The Marcos Dynasty*, pp. 179–181.

253–The deaths of Laurel and Clemente are discussed in Seagrave, *The Marcos Dynasty*.

254–In 1950, the CIA bought CAT outright, through a holding company called Pacific Corporation. The deal was arranged by former OSS chief General "Wild Bill" Donovan, using money from the fanatical right-wing Texas billionaire, H.L. Hunt. (See also Chapter 16 of this book.)

254–Aldrich testimony: *The Scotsman*, 2003, www.thescotsman.co.uk/index.cfm?id=1040642003

255–Aldrich testimony: *The Scotsman*, 2003, www.thescotsman.co.uk/index.cfm?id=1040642003

255–See Seagrave, *Soldiers of Fortune*, p. 149.

256–Our source on the "Tricky Dicky Notes" prefers to be anonymous, for reasons of personal safety. An image of a "Tricky Dicky" Note appears on our CDs, and is different from other FRNs primarily in the type of paper used.

257–The resmelting of Federal Reserve gold bars. See Hamburg-Froppe, Dorothy, "Key to the Gold Vault." Available online.

258–This letter is reproduced in the Vila Marques files on our CDs.

258–The Taylor and Curtin letters are reproduced in the Vila Marques files on our CDs.

259–The public record of the case, and all available supporting exhibits and evidence, are on volume three of our CDs.

259–Abundant information on Leinenweber and his wife come from reliable sources on the Internet.

260–Posner's judgment in full is on our CDs.

261–Larsen, "The Historical Fight for Honest Money". Arizona Breakfast Club, April 1979.

261–Patman quoted by Larsen, op cit.

262–Lewis vs. United States, 680 F.2d 1239 1982, #80-5905 U.S. Court of Appeals 9th Circuit, reproduced in the Vila Marques files on our CDs.

263–The Diligizer Archive #23, online.

263–Documents of the Superior Court in Berlin are in the Vila Marques files on our CDs.

263–Concerning the possible destruction of the Laurel bonds in London, we quote from the letter of Paul Wheatley, Economic Crime Department, Police Headquarters, 37 Wood Street, London, September 14, 2004.

263–The Diligizer Archive #23, online.

EPILOGUE

265–Briody, *The Iron Triangle*. Among top men in The Carlyle Group are former president George H.W. Bush, former British Prime Minister John Major, former Philippine President Fidel Ramos, former Defense Secretary Frank Carlucci, former Treasury Secretary James Baker III, former Attorney General William Barr, and Defense Secretary Donald Rumsfeld (as an associate).

265–Marrs, *Rule by Secrecy*, pp. 13–14.

265–Marrs, *Rule by Secrecy*, pp. 13–14.

266–One of the clients of Sullivan & Cromwell, the Dulles brothers' law firm, was Franco.

266–In its 2002 annual report, The Manila Mining Corporation said, "In 1999, 66 percent of the company's revenues were generated by sales of gold to Johnson Mathey…".

267–FBI, Memo for Mr. Nichols, from Mr. Jones, 3-28-49, available on line as William Donovan and the OSS.

268–Valentine, *Strength of the Wolf*, p. 26.

268–Seagrave interviews with General Ray Peers. Detachment 101 used opium to pay agents. Ray Peers: "If opium could be useful in achieving victory, the pattern was clear. We would use opium." (Valentine, p. 47).

268–Mark Fritz, "The Secret Insurance Agent Men," *Los Angeles Times*, 22 September 2000.

269–Valentine, *Strength of the Wolf*, p. 75.

269–Valentine, *Strength of the Wolf*, p. 76.

269–Remnants of OSS personnel in France worked for Donovan and Britain's MI-6 under cover of a company called Electronatom Corporation. FBI, bureau memo, 4 March 1954.

270–Valentine, *Strength of the Wolf*, p. 76, and interviews with Pawley by Sterling Seagrave in 1960.

270–See Seagrave & Seagrave, *Lords of the Rim*.

270–One of the investors provided us with a transcript of the Cocke deposition and a copy of their lawsuit, which was awaiting trial before TK District Court in Virginia. [CK] These documents are reproduced for interested readers on the new Volume 3 of our CDROM set.

271–Roberts, *The Blood Bankers*, p. 77.

271–Vila Marques' cable is reproduced on our CDs.

271–The Laurel UBS files are reproduced on our CDs.

272–Ford's quote is found in Jim Marrs, *Rule by Secrecy*, p. 76.

INDEX